GODS OF THE BLOOD

D1617049

MATTIAS GARDELL

Gods of the Blood

The Pagan Revival and White Separatism

Duke University Press   Durham and London 2003

© 2003 Duke University Press
All rights reserved
Printed in the United States
of America on acid-free paper ∞
Designed by Rebecca M. Giménez
Typeset in Quadraat by Tseng
Information Systems, Inc.
Library of Congress Cataloging-
in-Publication Data appear on the
last printed page of this book.

CONTENTS

ACKNOWLEDGMENTS

This study has been long in the making. It all began with a postdoctoral academic year as a visiting scholar at the department of political science at Syracuse University in central New York, 1996–97. During that year, I made my first field journeys into the world of militant white racists, collecting material for a comparative study of black and white separatism that was published in 1998. I had expected to meet with the Ku Klux Klan, militia patriots, skinheads, and national socialists and was surprised to learn of a world beyond the fiery cross of the Hooded Order, populated by Aryan radicals who hailed the ancient Norse gods and goddesses of my native Scandinavia. Intrigued, I decided to focus on this vibrant but understudied milieu in a new project, the result of which is *Gods of the Blood*.

As a historian of religion by profession, I use anthropological methods with fieldwork, interviews, and participant observation. My first gratitude must therefore go to all hospitable folkish pagans who opened their homes for a traveling student of religion and guided me further through the multifaceted landscape of heathens in the United States. I am also very grateful to all other heathen ideologues and activists who agreed to share their worldview and practice with me during long hours of taped interviews or informal discussions. Some prefer to remain anonymous and may thus only receive my token of appreciation collectively. Others are possible to thank in person, and I sincerely extend my gratitude to David Lane, Ron McVan, Katja Lane, Michael Moynihan, Annabel Lee, Edred Thorsson, Robert N. Taylor, Valgard Murray, Stephen and Sheila McNallen, Robert Ward, Reinhold and Cathy Clinton, Richard Kemp, Frank Silva, Thórsteinn Thórarinsson, Wyatt Kaldenberg, Nathan Zorn Pett, Christina Robertson, Håkan and Brian Södergren, Michael Lujan, Max Hyatt, Elton Hall, and Else Christensen. Without you, the present study would not have been possible.

I am also greatly indebted to the multitude of nonpagan Aryan activists who accommodated me and/or granted me interviews, including John Baumgardner, Don Black, Richard G. Butler, Louis Beam, Willis Carto, David Duke, Randy Duey, Gerald Gruidl, Matt Hale, George Hawthorne, Michael Hoffman II, Kirk Lyons, Debbie Mathews, Tom Metzger, Jack Mohr, Troy Murphy, Neal Payne, William Pierce, Derek Stenzel, David Tate, Chuck Tate, John Trochman, Ted R. Weiland, Gay Yarbrough, and Ernst Zündel.

A disparate group of people—who are for various reasons outside the milieus of American pagans or racial activists, yet are related to the scene as heathens, observers, black separatists, or occultists—provided me with insights and information. My extended thanks also goes to Don Webb, Osiris Akkebala, Silis X. Muhammad, Laird Wilcox, Carl Abrahamsson, Benedikte Lindström, Mikael Hedlund, Troy Friscella, Adam Parfrey, Kevin Coogan, Magnus Söderman, and Hendrik Möbus.

Also crucial to my research was the generous aid offered by the staff at the department of political science at Syracuse University and the Spencer librarians at the University of Kansas at Lawrence where the Wilcox Collection of Contemporary Political Movements, the foremost collection of radical Aryan material, is located. Significant in that it provided an inspiring scholarly milieu was the Center for Research in International Migration and Ethnic Relations, Stockholm University.

Among my most valued colleagues whose encyclopedic knowledge in many ways has enriched my understanding of the scene, I am especially grateful to Professors Michael Barkun and David Bennet at Syracuse University; Jeffrey Kaplan at the University of Wisconsin at Oshkosh; Bron Taylor at the University of Wisconsin at Oshkosh; Nicholas Goodrick-Clarke at the University of Oxford; Stefan Arvidsson at Lund University; and Heléne Lööw, Erik af Edholm, and Charles Westin at Stockholm University. Barkun, Kaplan, Westin, Moynihan, and Goodrick-Clarke also provided constructive criticism after having read parts of the manuscript, thereby contributing greatly to whatever merit the present study may have. Also important in this respect were Reynolds Smith, Sharon Parks Torian, Leigh Anne Couch, and their co-workers at Duke University Press. Any faults, however, are all mine. Without the wonderful hospitality and friendship lavishly shown by Americans across the country, my years in the United States would not have been the great experience it proved to be, and I especially want to send my appreciation to Sherry, Melissa, and Orion Begnell; Jeff Ditz; Ingrid Kock; and Mark, Carol, and Emma Kaufman.

I also wish to gratefully acknowledge the financial support provided by the Humanistisk-Samhällsvetenskapliga Forskningsrådet and Forskningsråds-nämnden in Sweden, and the Harry Frank Guggenheim Foundation in the United States, support that made possible my research and helped put milk on my children's breakfast table.

Without support from my extended family of brothers and sisters back in sub-arctic Sweden, who always were there for me, providing insights, ideas, friendship, and laughs, I would not have seen this through. Among others I really need to thank are Anna-Klara Bratt, Thomas Hvitfeldt, Maria Hedman, Dirk Grosjean, Saman Ali, Börje Bergfeldt, Sanna Hedenborg, Jonas Lundborg, Thomas Persson, Bella Frank, Magnus Hörnkvist, Alexa Wolf, Rasmus Fleis-cher, Ulf B. Anderson, Adrienne Sörbom, and Anna Lindner. In additon to their friendship, Hvitfeldt and Sörbom contributed constructive criticism for which I am especially grateful. Initiates of the cultic, Ekens Gäll and Bajen Fans have in other respects supplied electrifying experiences during the years. However, most of all, my innermost feelings of appreciation and affection go to my im-mediate family: my children, Linus, Emma, Moa, Ida, Sofia, Stefan, Kim, and Amanda; and my beautiful wife, Anna-Karin. Your love and support has been an abundant source of comfort and joy. Kim and Amanda, who came to life during the course of the research, and Emma, who at times accompanied me during my journeys across the North American continent, have been very special parts of making this study.

Note on Sources

Primary sources for this study fall into two main categories: information gathered during fieldwork and material produced by white racist and pagan ideologues. As an anthropologist of religion, I have conducted extensive field research in the subcultures of white power activism, Aryan heathendom, and euro-tribal paganism. Staying with leading activists and their families, conduct-ing taped interviews with key persons, participating in day-to-day business, ob-serving ceremonial practice and political activities, and engaging in formal and informal discussions with leaders and adherents, I was always open about my identity as a researcher and about the aims of the study I was undertaking. Obvi-ously, this put certain limitations on knowledge production. All activists cited in this study were aware that what they said or did might be publicized. For every informant who wanted it, anonymity was granted herein.

Although a wealth of information was gathered during informal conversa-tions, I have primarily used quotations from taped interviews rather than field notes; references to taped interviews in the main text are cited in parentheses with the person and year in italics. Many secondary sources are also cited parenthetically. References to field notes and statements by anonymous informants, as well as references to Internet sources and written correspondence, are found in the endnotes.

As for the second category of primary sources, materials produced by white power and pagan individuals and groups are quite heterogeneous and include books, booklets, pamphlets, magazines, tabloids, leaflets, letters, speeches, poetry, artwork, and music. Much of this material will be hard to find in an ordinary bookstore, library, or record shop, and some are hard to get even through underground channels of distribution, with circulation restricted to initiated members only. Moreover, white power publications do not always conform to the standards of a university publisher. Many of the publications cited here appear irregularly, do not state annual volume numbers, and might be undated and unpaged. Articles, pamphlets, and folders do not always state the name of the author(s) and authors occasionally use various pseudonyms. To account for this, I have used n.d.a, n.d.b, n.d.c, etc., for multiple undated sources by one author.

Globalization, Nationalism, and the Pagan Revival

D uring the 1990s racist paganism emerged as one of the most dynamic trends of the increasingly radicalized but highly fragmented and schismatic radical-racist milieu in the United States. Currently surpassing traditional racist vehicles, such as national socialist parties and the Ku Klux Klan(s), in terms of numbers and influence, racist paganism has caught the attention of a new generation of racial activists and is well on its way to reducing earlier racist creeds, such as Christian Identity, to the status of an "old man's religion." The most cursory glimpse at white-racist publications, Web pages, and white-power lyrics reveals muscular heathens, pagan gods and goddesses, runes and symbols, magic, and esoteric themes in abundance.

Despite the rising tide of paganism in white-racist culture, the field is remarkably understudied. Although this trend has been acknowledged briefly in works on occult national socialism, radical religion, or Eurocentric paganism, no systematic investigation of this forceful but enigmatic phenomenon has previously emerged.[1] Drawing on years of extensive field research that involved observation of pagan ceremonies and gatherings, daily heathen routines and activities, as well as taped interviews and informal discussions with heathen ideologues and activists, *Gods of the Blood* offers a unique introduction to the world of racist paganism. While looking at a wide spectrum of "Aryan" pre-Christian pagan traditions, this book focuses on the scene's most vibrant elements: reconstructed Norse paganism—Asatrú or Odinism—and the dim underworld where heathendom meets racist Satanism and occult national socialism.

In addition to introducing the thoughts, practices, and goals of racial pagans, this study aims at reconstructing the mental universes of the racist activists involved and gives an account of the social processes of which they are a product. In accentuating the revolutionary position increasingly adopted by white underground activists since the early 1980s, racist paganism represents a further radicalization of the white-racist milieu. Denouncing Christianity as unnatural and anti-white, racist pagans distance themselves further from the American mainstream, forcibly rejecting even the far-right "Christian Patriot" as part of the problem. Racist paganism is, however, not unique to the United States but part of a global phenomenon. American reconstructions of Norse paganism have been successfully appropriated by "Aryan" revolutionaries in more than forty countries; these revolutionaries communicate electronically on a daily basis and construct their worldviews with material gained from the global flow of ideas.

Despite the pagans' common claim that they represent the resurfacing of ancient traditions, kept intact throughout the centuries by an unbroken succession of underground guardians, they may, from a scholarly perspective, be classified as a tendency within the broader category of new religious movements. During the past few decades tens of thousands of new religious movements have emerged worldwide, many of which are inspired by premodern traditions, suggesting that a global perspective may offer insight to our understanding of racist paganism in the United States.

Globalization and Neonationalism

An increasingly global social reality has gradually become the greater context for all cultures and religions of the world. Most economies are now part of the world capitalist system. The nation-state model has been adopted all over the world, with most countries participating in an international political system based on nation-states. Media, entertainment, military industry, tourism, migration, science, medicine, sport, music, and art know few borders and contribute to the advance of globalization. And communication technology now makes it possible to connect any two locations on Earth. In short, the world is gradually becoming "a single place," the term *global village* emerging to emphasize that the planet has become a small place where we know much about each other and where life differs greatly depending on whether you live in the nicer villas or in the huts among the village outcasts (Roland Robertson 1987, 43). At the same time, so-called fundamentalist interpretations are forcibly gaining ground in all major world religions—Christianity, Islam, Judaism, Hinduism, Buddhism, and Sikhism—and in societies with different histories and various economic realities and political systems. Fundamentalism is a global phenomenon and to paraphrase Durkheim, global facts need to be understood in the light of other global facts.

The gradual construction of a global culture implies the relativization of all other cultures, despite how universal the values and norms of each culture may once have appeared to those within it. For religious ideologues who have been accustomed to dealing in "universal truths," this realization might be especially painful. The Abrahamitic God of Judaism, Christianity, and Islam might be a jealous God, but in the global arena He must get used to having other gods beside Him. The global flow of ideas will undermine even the most ambitious monopolizing effort, and it will be increasingly difficult to demonize followers of other religions as wholly Other. However, while the grand narrative of globalization optimistically asserts that as cultures and religions come into closer contact, they will inform and become more tolerant of each other in a process that will culminate in a single humanity cooperating for the future survival of the planet and mankind—and while this trend most certainly is discernible—an opposing reaction in terms of ethnic, racial, and religious fragmentation is simultaneously identifiable, as evidenced by the rise of religious fundamentalism. The process of globalization accordingly involves a tension between centripetal and centrifugal forces.

That numerous neonationalist projects have been spawned in the wake of globalization might seem paradoxical, since globalization undermines the significance of the nation-state through an increasingly transnational, even postnational, social reality.[2] After all, the strongest economies in the world today are multinational corporations, not nation-states, and political efforts to adjust to changing realities by establishing regional trade blocs such as the European Union (EU) or the North American Free Trade Agreement (NAFTA) seem dated at launching. Corporate power is further underscored by the free trade zones on territory set aside and exempted not only from regular taxation but also from the jurisdiction a state would otherwise exert over its territory. Yet, the world map is being constantly revised as the number of nation-states continues to increase: in 1945 the United Nations counted fifty membership states; in the 1950s it had expanded by more than thirty new nation-states; the 1960s saw the formation of more than forty nation-states; the 1970s ushered in twenty-five more; and after a slow 1980s with a mere seven new nation-states, the twentieth century closed with a record of close to 200 nation-states, of which thirty-two were established in the 1990s.[3] Add to the list a number of unrecognized nation-states and the "national liberation movements" fighting to achieve independence—such as the Kurdish, Basque, Moro, Palestinian, or Tibetan movements—and a pattern of fervent nationalist activity becomes apparent.

At least three distinct types of neonationalist projects can be identified: *ethno-*

nationalism, which claims that ethnicity should be the foundation for an independent nation-state, as manifest in the nationalism that forced itself on the agenda in the civil wars of Rwanda and former Yugoslavia; *racial nationalism*, which asserts that all members of a given race properly constitute a nation entitled to self-determination in a state of their own, a position held by the Nation of Islam and other black separatist movements in the United States, as well as by the Aryan nationalists who aim at establishing a pan-Aryan "white homeland" that transcends the current nation-state borders of Europe, Australia, and America; and, finally, *religious nationalism*, which holds that adherents of a given religion "by nature" (and the will of God) properly belong to the same nation, a conviction that caused, for example, Muslims to secede from the Federation of India to form Pakistan as the "Land of the Pure" and that is voiced by Hindu nationalists in India and by Islamist revolutionaries such as Hamas or Ikhwan al-Muslimun (the Muslim Brotherhood). These neonationalist categories are hardly static and, not being mutually exclusive, often interweave with each other such that, for instance, religious identity turns into a national marker in an ethnonationalist project, as illustrated by Serbian and Croatian nationalism.

To some readers, the prefix *neo-* might seem curious, as many nationalist ideologies assert the cultural homogeneity of the nation and trace its origin to a specific ethnic or religious group of which the nation is held to be an "organic" outgrowth. What nationalists say, however, should not necessarily be accepted at face value. An overwhelming majority of the de facto existing nation-states (including, of course, the United States) have historically been, and still are, multiethnic, multilingual, and multireligious in composition. What is new in neonationalism, then, is the refutation of the state-sanctioned nationalist ideology in favor of an alternative nationalism that is aimed either at purging an existing nation-state of everyone held to be extranational or at establishing a new, secessionist nation-state composed exclusively of and by those deemed to qualify. But the nationalist conception of nation as "organic," as something given by nature—as though mankind had always been organized in different nations, or as though the nation were merely a modern appendage to the evolution of family-clan-tribe—lands far from the mark: a nation is not a product of blood but of ideology and social processes. Conflicting ideas of the nation's make-up may thus be present at the same time and place, and the dominant definition of a given nation may change over time.

The word *nation* is derived from the Latin *nascor* (I am born) and long signified only a lineage group or clan. "Insofar as it was attached to a territory," Eric Hobsbawn notes, "it was only fortuitously a political unit, and never a very large one" (1990, 15). The meaning of the concept began to change during the eighteenth century when it was applied to produce sentiments of solidarity between the inhabitants of a given territory and the state apparatus as a form of political administration. The now popular equation between "nation," "state," "people," and "homeland" made its breakthrough toward the end of the nineteenth century (Hettne, Sörlin, and Östergård 1998; Hobsbawn 1990). Although nationalist ideologies may still biologize the conception of nation, the original connotation of "kin related by blood" has thus in practice been detached from nation—not even citizens of microstates such as Andorra are all related to each other.

As convincingly argued by Benedict Anderson (1991), then, a "nation" may be defined as an "imagined community," involving feelings of solidarity and belonging between people traversing time and space. Members of a nation feel that they share something of importance with everyone else of the same nation, despite the fact that they will never meet more than a tiny fraction of these conationals and despite the fact that they often don't have that much in common with those they actually do meet. That people actually identify with anonymous strangers, strangers who might live in places they have never heard of, who are deceased or yet unborn, that people feel deeply connected to such unknown others as long as they "belong" to the same "nation" indicates that "imagined" cannot be equated with "unreal." Although a product of nationalist ideology, the nation imagined is a *social fact* of importance, politically and culturally, as evidenced in recent history.

Nationalists generally produce an imagined community by projecting the idea of a corporative nation back into legendary or mythological time, often presented as a "golden age," a time untainted by the ills of the modern world and liberated from whomever is designated the national enemy. Frequently, the nationalist intends to revert to the ideals of the glorious high culture, albeit adopted to suit current conditions. Thus the importance of pre-Christian Norse culture to Aryan pagans, Atlantis or Hyperborean culture to occult national socialists, the divine high civilization of the original man to the Nation of Islam, and Islamic society during the time of Prophet Muhammad ibn Abdullah to Islamic fundamentalists. The nationalist cause is often strengthened by inserting a (historical or mythological) "national trauma," that is, a time when the nation was subjugated, occupied, or severely threatened by national enemies. Slavery, for instance, is the trauma informing black nationalism, the Holocaust the trauma informing Jewish nationalism, the Civil War the trauma informing Southern nationalism, and the Battle at the Field of Thrushes in 1389 the trauma informing Serbian nationalism. The national trauma is often reenacted on memorial days, in commemorative ceremonies, and with theater productions, thus enabling members of the nation to identify with the co-nationals of the traumatic past.

Furthermore, endowed with a notion of eternity, the national trauma serves as a frame of reference with which to interpret current conflicts. In Serbian nationalist propaganda, Albanians turned into Ottoman Turks. Jewish nationalists may view Palestinian activists as Nazis, styling Arafat a Hitler. Spokespersons of the Palestinian Hamas typically interpret Israel as a crusader state. Black nationalists may talk about nonseparatist blacks as slaves and see slaveholders in contemporary white politicians. Using the metaphor of the individual organism when discussing the "features" and history of the nation in question reinforces the notion of national solidarity. Born during the golden age, the individual nation is endowed with certain inherent qualities, a personal history, and a destiny to be fulfilled in a glorious future. Nationalists accordingly bestow on the imagined nation a notion of eternal belonging, enabling contemporary nationals to identify also with future generations when "we" will secure national independence and fulfill the destined greatness.

A corporative dimension is typically attached to the notion of nation. Nationalists may contend, for instance, that a worker of a given nation has more in common with an employer of the same nation than with a worker of another nation or that a woman of a given nation "belongs" to the men of the same nation and not with a man or woman of another nation. This corporative character easily (but not necessarily) lends itself to xenophobic sentiments, fascist elements, authoritarian collectivism, and politics of purity.

The centrifugal movement toward ethnic, racial, and religious fragmentation seems linked to the centripetal movement of globalization. Urbanization, modernization, and market fundamentalism have scattered traditional communities. Facing an increasingly interlaced and condensed global reality, many take refuge in affiliations that espouse particular identities. Along those lines, many neonationalist movements are animated by the alarmist assumption that globalization is a leveling process of cultural homogenization. The emerging global culture is interpreted in monolithic terms as an exacting force that replaces all previous cultures so that everyone will soon live in one identical global culture, speak the same language, believe in one universal God, wear uniform clothing, eat the same food in identical restaurants, and share the same morals, worldviews, and values. From this perspective, then, individual cultures and religions stand at the brink of extermination and will, unless something is done to reverse the process, be present in the lives of our grandchildren only to the extent that they visit museums of ancient history.

Although this is a widespread notion that ideologues have frequently seized on to mobilize popular support for the nationalist cause, there is scant evidence to support such an alarmist interpretation. As noted by Ulf Hannerz, global culture can hardly be characterized as the homogenization of systems of meaning and expression: "it is marked by an organization of diversity rather than by a replication of uniformity" (1990, 237). This does not mean that the global culture can be perceived as the sum of its parts or as a cultural mosaic of separate, well-defined pieces. The different cultures of the world are instead becoming subcultures within the global culture, with all that this suggests in terms of intersecting, flowing, and ambiguous boundaries (Hannerz 1992, 218). Arjun Appadurai argues that the "new global cultural economy has to be understood as a complex, overlapping, *disjunctive order*" (1990, 296; emphasis added).

To explore such disjunctures, Appadurai suggests looking at the relationships between various dimensions of global flow, which he likens to "landscapes" to emphasize that they are not objectively given relations that look the same from every angle but are instead the perspectival constructs of different sorts of actors (multinational corporations, nations-states, diasporic groups, religious movements, political undergrounds). Appadurai categorizes five dimensions of global flow: *ethnoscapes*, the shifting flow of people in terms of tourists, guest workers, refugees, exiles, immigrants, students, and the like; *technoscapes*, the flow of technology; *financescapes*, the rapid and fluctuating flow of capital; *mediascapes*, the unevenly distributed capabilities of producing and distributing information and images; and *ideoscapes*, the flow of ideological and political ideas such as progress, human rights, development, freedom, and democracy. These rapid global flows currently follow nonisomorphic paths and contribute to shifting constellations of conflicts, raptures, and contradictions locally, regionally, and globally.

Although asymmetrical relations of power still structure these global flows, colonial centers no longer control the directions, and global networks can no longer be understood in terms of center-periphery models (Appadurai 1996, 33). There is no longer a center, no one is in control, and no civilization is in a position to monopolize or determine the processes of globalization. Yet, everywhere except in the West, globalization is frequently perceived as an attempt, led by the United States, to subdue the world to the hegemony of Western civilization. Besides the obvious ambition of the United States to shoulder the role of upholder of global law and order by policing the world community with the authority of its military might, this conclusion is understandable for two primary reasons.

First, certain commodities of American origin, such as Coca-Cola, Pizza Hut, Levis, Nike, Tommy Hilfiger, Juicyfruit Gum, and McDonald's, are found all over the world. Associated with a lifestyle seemingly at odds with the values of "traditional culture," the global flow of these products is frequently interpreted in terms of an aggressive American cultural imperialism. However, these multinational corporations are not carriers of American culture, but of globalized commercial culture. Americans may feel equally distressed as any Frenchman at the cultural impact of McDonald's, or may abhor the fact that Ronald McDonald has higher name recognition among the young than say Thomas Jefferson or other icons of Americanism.[4] Despite its American origin, McDonald's is a global corporation that serves kosher burgers in Tel Aviv, Halal Big Mac in Mecca, rice and chicken for breakfast in Manila. It is poor-man's food in Stockholm and luxury fare in Beijing, which points to the need to study the processes of *glocalization*, by which the global is localized and given meaning acccording to context. Instead of an American cultural imperialsm, it would be more accurate to discuss the global flow of branded commodities in terms of a *coca-colonization* of the world, led by a few global corporations that have invaded public space to such an extent that their brand names permeate the minds of a great portion of the world population.[5] Yet, this material and mental colonization is in many quarters still mainly conceived of as an American cultural imperialism, which facilitates the translation of social and economic conflicts into the cultural and moral arenas and thus may constitute a basis for anti-American populist mobilization against the symbols of what Ayatollah Khomeini denounced as *Westoxification.*

Second, and more important, globalization is considered inherently Western because everywhere, except in the West, globalization began as an exogenous process, as convincingly argued by Peter Beyer (1994). Combining the theories of Immanuel Wallerstein, Roland Robertson, and Niklas Luhmann, Beyer analyzes the process of globalization in terms of the dynamics of a social reality based on functional differentiation. The condensed time and space of global life and its rapid nonisomorphic flows represent only the current phase of a development that began at least as early as the sixteenth century. Beyer traces globalization's roots to the gradual shift in early modern Western society from a society based on social stratification to a society based on functional differentiation. In the former system, politics, economy, science, medicine, and art were subordinate to the interests of the religious-political elite, as illustrated in that science was confined to limits defined by established religious truths. With the shift to functional priorities, politics, economy, science, medicine, education, and art began to evade centralized control and in time emerged reconstituted as functionally differentiated instrumental systems, rationally structured to achieve specific results. With this shift, each field's potential to upgrade, innovate, develop, and expand was changed radically. The ability of the functionally differentiated subsystems to develop independently and yet interdependently became instrumental in their global expansion.

Although the scientific revolution and technological innovations had no territorial references, they facilitated imperialist conquests. The capitalist market economy extended to areas outside the control of the colonial centers, but the enterprises would have failed without active colonial support. The missionaries had their own motives, which not infrequently conflicted with the interests of trading houses and colonial administrators, but imperialism was critical for their success as well. As capitalist economy, secular education, secular science, technology, and secular medicine expanded globally, they were spread by people who were culturally Westerners. Globalization and modernization thus became identified as carriers of Western culture, both by colonizers who presented imperialism as a project of civilizing the world and by the colonized people subject to their rule.

Hindsight reveals that assumption to be erroneous. What globalized was not Western culture but instrumental techniques to reach specific ends such as profit (capitalist economy), truth (science), or healing (medicine). Functional orientation emphasizes rationality, efficiency, and adaptive upgrading, not cultural or religious identity. What is at issue is not *who* someone is but *what* someone does. Colonial efforts to establish a premodern system based on social stratification rather than on function—racist systems collectively known as white world supremacy—were in the long run undermined by demands for efficiency and rationality that arose from the functionally differentiated subsystems. Capitalist economy, for instance, is oriented toward profit and will in time find the skin color of a consumer or producer functionally irrelevant. Capital, not race or religion, qualifies a person for inclusion in the capitalist economy. Rational actors involved in science, medicine, education, sports, or music would similarly come to consider race secondary to producing the results desired. Thus, as functionally irrelevant rules of exclusion were removed, non-Westerners were gradually included in various fields; Chinese, Korean, and Japanese people, for instance, appropriated with great skill the techniques at hand and soon became better capitalists, engineers, and scientists than many Westerners without becoming Western culturally. Since anyone could learn the techniques of function-based systems, then, racism was not being refuted on moral grounds but as an obstacle to progress.

Modernity was, after all, not inherently Western but proved adaptable in many different ways in many different cultures. The nation-state model was appropriated by national liberation movements and turned against colonizers all over the world. The global expansion of functionally differentiated instrumental techniques can thus be seen as having propelled not only the global rise of Western culture but also its subsequent "fall," the latter process yet unfolding. Thus, despite the fact that globalization began in early modern Western society, it has inevitably led toward the construction of a global culture that is not Western. As this realization begins to sink in, many Westerners react with confusion and even panic.

The colonial era spawned an ideological discourse that identified Western civilization as the most advanced and the white race as the crown of creation. World dominion made objectification of Western ethnocentrism possible, and the norms and values of Western culture were presented as if they were universal. To this day, when these notions are challenged, many Westerners react with disbelief, as did the heads of European governments when Malaysian prime minister Mohammad Mahathir in 1996 declared, "European values are European. Asian values are Universal" ("Asia and Europe" 1996). But neither Mahathir nor his European detractors are correct. In the context of the emerging global culture, *every* other culture is relative, including the Western and Asian.

This is clearly a painful realization for many Westerners, as evidenced by American responses ranging from Pat Buchanan's reactionary extremism to the militia movement to the emergence of the Aryan revolutionary underground. Buchanan is fond of boasting that should he become president, "all surrenders of American sovereignty to any and all institutions of the New World Order come to an end," as will the "looting of the American nation by global socialists of the IMF [International Monetary Fund] and the Word Bank."[6] Loyalty to global society is disloyalty to America, Buchanan declares, which might be confusing to neonationalist activists of Asia, Africa, or America to whom globalization equals an American attempt at world dominion. To Buchanan, it is either "America First or World Government." "We don't want to be citizens of the world, because we have been granted a higher honor—we are citizens of the United States," he claims, going on to say that he "struggle of nationalism against globalism" is "the millennial struggle that succeeds the Cold War."[7]

As for American "patriots," fear of a global world alerted them to prepare for a final showdown, and during the early 1990s populist militias mushroomed in the United States, organizing to defend America's liberties against what was perceived to be a global conspiracy.

A yet more radical reaction to the process of globalization emerged in the racist nationalist projects launched by Aryan revolutionaries in America, as well as in Europe and Australia. Interpreting globalization as a process of homogenization engineered by a secret conspiratorial center known as the Zionist Occupation Government (ZOG), racist nationalists explain the relativization of Western culture and the gradual fall of white world supremacy with the theory that racial enemies have gained control over all "the once white countries." Corporate relocation of production to non-Western countries and Western localization of global flows of non-Western migrants, commodities, ideas, art, music, and religions are interpreted in terms of an antiwhite conspiracy that ultimately aims at exterminating the Aryan race.

The imagined community of Aryan revolutionaries transcends existing national borders in a vision of a pan-Aryan transatlantic homeland. Marginalized in their respective local settings, Aryan revolutionaries communicate electronically in cyberspace. Global flows of racist news information, music, histories, conspiracy theories, military tactics, religions, mythologies, dating services, and stories of heroic martyrs give even the loneliest Aryan a sense of belonging. He becomes part of a grand narrative that tells of a once-glorious race sinking into a corrupting morass of decay and filth, surrounded by enemy forces. With imagery drawn from pagan mythologies and fantasy novels, the few remaining warriors are urged to lift their swords in defense of race and honor and fight to protect the beauty of the white woman. Braving the apocalypse, few will survive to see the Aryan race rise again out of the ashes, but the slain will be immortalized in the annals of racial heroes. Such warrior dreams summon Aryans from all over the world and provide a sense of unity of purpose and identity, but have so far only occasionally erupted into seriously violent activities. When such violence does occur, information instantly reaches the whole network of Aryan revolutionaries through cyberspace, thus confirming the grand narrative as at least a virtual reality.

Conspiracy theory suggests, of course, that there is a conscious agent directing the course of events, a horror story that nonetheless provides a greater sense of security than recognizing that there is no one in control. A primary feature of globalizing modernity with its functionally differentiated social subsystems is the *absence* of orchestrated control. As science, for example, was gradually unfettered from the normative control previously exercised by religious authority, the scientific search for truth vigorously expanded in a multitude of directions. Discoveries and innovations propelled increasing divisions into ever more specialized fields of knowledge. Not even the most encyclopedic scholar of today can keep up with the knowledge produced by frontline research in more than a tiny fraction of the many differentiated disciplines of science.

Indeed, the state of globalized science illustrates well the conditions under which the global society is constructed. Globalization is moving at breakneck speed in conflicting directions, yet nobody knows where we are going and no cooperative body of orchestrated human control exists. While each globalized subsystem is totalizing in the sense that everything might temporarily be incorporated into any one system—for example, as soon as anything is assigned monetary value, it is included in the economic system—no subsystem is all-encompassing. "Everything has its price but not everything is commodified," notes Beyer (1994, 56). "Precisely because the differentiated functional systems concentrate on specialized means of communication and not, for instance, on the total lives of the people who carry them, they leave a great deal of social communication undetermined, if not unaffected" (ibid.). No specialized system articulates anything encompassing about life or the global system as a whole.

Functionally oriented and professionally specialized, the various globalized subsystems typically neglect problems generated by their activities as long as they do not turn into obstacles for their own activity. No specialized system articulates a sense of higher values and in no field of activity is God or morality functionally relevant. Such a system is thus in conflict with life itself as it appears from the perspective of the living, feeling, acting, individual man. People partake at different times in varying degrees and in various roles in the differentiated subsystems, yet maintain a holistic perspective on existence in a system that does not articulate holistic concerns. But neonationalist and religious fundamentalist ideologies do articulate these concerns. Proceeding from holistic articulations of meaning, neonationalists aim at seizing control in order to subordinate the differentiated subsystems to some form of higher values, such as the advancement of the race or the will of God.

Globalization and Religion

Religion is a mode of social communication that traffics in holistic issues (such as the meaning of life), which explains in part the fervent religious revival that is happening worldwide. Paradoxical as it might seem, globalization simultaneously pushes secularization and stimulates religious revivalism. Secularization questions not to what extent man believes in God, but to what extent religion exerts public influence in society. The shift toward functional differentiation gradually diminished the field of competence of God and the religious elite in favor of other experts, such as secular physicians, scientists, politicians, teachers, and attorneys. With the global expansion of instrumental techniques, *every* society, irrespective of how religious its citizens, has in some measure been secularized. From giant corporations down to the local car mechanic, the overwhelming majority of companies in the world are governed by corporate, not religious, concerns. Religious schools in most societies have lost ground to secular education, and where religious jurisdiction is still found, it has gradually been restricted to family law. It is precisely this secularized reality that religious fundamentalists single out as the chief cause of the perceived ills they organize to overcome. Why otherwise struggle to re-Islamicize Muslim countries?

Globalization means that religions and civilizations have been brought in acute contact with each other and eagerly seek to project their respective ideals and values onto the global culture in formation. Combined with the religious mobilization against secularization, the breathtaking speed and uncertain outcome of globalization provoke teleological concerns. Global flows of information about environmental destruction, AIDS, ethnic cleansing, racial strife, epidemic famines, widening gaps between the planet's rich and poor, terrorism, wars, drugs, crime, and natural catastrophes feed the unease. Are we really going in the right direction? Is humanity on the road toward salvation or doom? Globalization seems to spur three different religious responses: fundamentalism, interreligious cooperation, and new religious movements.

Fundamentalism reacts to relativization by forceful denial: there is but one truth, there is but one way. Organized as social movements, fundamentalism often mobilizes around residual problems generated but not solved by the process of globalization. Proceeding from conflict between globalized expectations of freedom, human rights, wealth, and progress and those consequences of globalization that prevent such expectations from being realized, fundamentalist movements often assume responsibilities that the state neglects or is incompetent to handle. Establishing programs for community improvement such as schools, rehabilitation, and shelters lends an aura of credibility to the fundamentalist message that it is time to try the way of God. Demonizing secular politicians, followers of other religions, and aliens as incarnations of evil is often inherent to the fundamentalist politics of purity and serves as an effective tool of populist mobilization. Articulating global ambitions rhetorically, fundamentalists in practice often adopt the isolationist themes of nationalistic policies and frequently organize under the rubric of religious neonationalist projects. Though effective as an oppositional position, fundamentalism in power still partakes of the global culture. The Islamic revolution in Iran, for instance, has not been able to shut out globalization or products of Western culture: young Iranians dress in green U.S. Army jackets, headbang to Metallica, and enjoy *Beverly Hills 90210* by satellite when they're not studying in rationally organized secular institutions of higher learning; Iranian leaders regularly sit down to negotiate with delegates working for the Great Satan; and the Iranian economy is undeniably part of the capitalist world system. Empowered locally, fundamentalist truth is as relative as before in the global context and is likely to find its program undermined by globalizing realities.

The ecumenical response of interreligious cooperation asserts that people of different faiths must come together in a joint effort to combat the residual problems of the process of globalization. As do fundamentalist movements, liberal theologies also often establish programs of social improvement but have far less simple long-term remedies. Respect and curiosity for other religions and cultures frequently result in the establishment of antiracist, multicultural, and interfaith forums to foster tolerance and knowledge of each other and to pave the way for programs of practical cooperation. In their refusal to scapegoat specific targets such as aliens, homosexuals, Jews, or Muslims as demonized Others, such programs are at a pedagogical disadvantage when compared with fundamentalist approaches. It is easier, after all, to mobilize against a personified evil using simple solutions of purification (extermination, repatriation, legal bans) than it is to address a depersonified evil in terms of structural injustices and social processes. Like a computer, the human mind seems to communicate meaning most easily in terms of binary oppositions. Without night there is no day, without sorrow there is no joy, and without "them" there is no "us." (Perhaps we need to find intelligent extraterrestrials against which to define ourselves if we are to establish one humanity.)

Newly created religious movements constitute the third empirically identifiable theological response to globalization. Such movements interpret the relativization of previously established religious truths as a sign of their invalidity. Globalizing modernity has led to what Giddens (1990) termed the "disembedding" of individuals from their traditional cultural and social contexts, and new religious movements provide an avenue for "reembedding" individuals and groups in a new context. Global flows of religious and philosophical ideas provide ample material from which creative entrepreneurs can assemble alternative religious bricolages, recontextualizing the elements. The new religious actors often have a distinctly global approach, interpreting globalization in terms of, say, a growing "planetary consciousness" or perhaps as the sign of an approaching apocalypse. Since the end of the Second World War, tens of thousands of new religious movements have been established worldwide, although far from all have endured. Conservative estimates suggest that there are between one and two thousand new religious movements in the United States, one thousand in Europe, some three thousand in Japan, and more than ten thousand in Africa, with no reliable statistics for Asia or Latin America (Melton 1992; Barker 1989, 148). (These numbers serve only as general indicators of the levels of new religious activity, rather than as specific empirical data. New religious groups arise and wane with amazing speed, with many operating on more than one continent, and reporters differ greatly in their definitions of "new" and as to whether New Age and other vaguely defined and less-organized religious milieus should be included.)

Broadly speaking, there are three types of new religious categories, each differing in its orientation and mode of organization: (1) the New Age scene, which is open and constantly transforming, populated by individual seekers who freely choose from a multitude of spiritual techniques and ideas offered by religious entrepreneurs; (2) new religious movements ("sects" or "cults"), which possess hierarchical organizational structures, systematic doctrines, and high missionary ambitions; and (3) pagan groups, which are autonomous or federated local communities with low missionary ambition, revolving around reconstructions of premodern pagan traditions. The typology should not be seen as if the borders were absolute and nontranscendable. A group may coalesce within the New Age community and develop a well-defined organizational structure to become a sect, and sects may disintegrate and members dissolve into the New Age milieu. Pagan groups may advertise in New Age bookstores, appropriate New Age elements, and turn into tight, sectlike organizations. Still, these categories are useful for analysis, as their general orientations differ significantly and adherents of groups in one category often take exception to the other two.

Within the New Age community, emphasis is commonly placed on individual healing and spiritual growth that aims at harmonizing with a world conceived as fundamentally good. The outer, material, objective conditions of life are generally seen as reflections of inner, mental, subjective conditions. Typically, each person is thought to have chosen his parents and designed his life in order to meet certain tests and acquire certain experiences necessary to promote his spiritual growth in this and coming reincarnations. Accordingly, the battered woman, the child laborer, the homeless, and the affluent have themselves chosen their own respective realities; global inequalities between countries reflect different "national karmas." New Age philosophies also tend to suggest that all knowledge is located hidden within oneself and that if one manages to connect with and evolve one's higher self, outer reality will change in accordance. In searching for spiritual keys to open up the inner world and log into eternal truth, individuals are left to explore the products offered at the global marketplace of New Age practices and to concoct their own truth according to taste, trial, and error—in other words, (spiritual) life is defined as a personal project. This egocentric focus is frequently combined with a global perspective linked to a palingenetic utopian vision: the world is at the brink of a spiritual revolution that will usher in a "new age" of planetary consciousness and a new, purified, spiritually advanced man.

While similar philosophical elements may be found in the new religious movements, which often cater in the Gnostic message "Thou art God," the orientation of the sect is on salvation by following a well-defined path. Being not infrequently extremely authoritarian, new religious movements may form global microcultures, with distinct dress codes, symbolism, routines, diet, and terminology identical for members worldwide. However, as the global is localized in Moscow, Berlin, Accra, Montevideo, or Sidney, and so on, the meanings ascribed to these elements differ according to context. Within this category, too, appear elements of fundamentalism, liberal ecumenism, and/or neonationalist mobilization, the process of globalization being variously interpreted in missions of world salvation. Take, for instance, the Nation of Islam (NOI) and the Baha'i. Like more established religions, the Nation and Baha'i both engage in community improvement programs to address social problems generated by the process of globalization, but each reaches a very different conclusion about today's world. Whereas the NOI identifies global culture as the evil product of white devils who will soon be consumed in flames by the wrath of the black god(s), Baha'i sees truth in all religions and believes that establishing a world government composed by and of men of all races and cultures is a viable project.

Reconstructions of pagan, premodern, and preglobal traditions constitute the third category of emergent religious response stimulated by the process of globalization. The rise of paganism has much to do with roots, identity, and urban man's romanticized notion of nature and "natural life." An Earth-based spirituality that holds nature to be sacred, paganism is generally dissatisfied with modernity's technological rationality and its objectification of nature and demystification of life. In addition to repopulating the cosmos with intelligent, nonhuman beings—guardians of nature, elves, trolls, ancestors, pagan gods and goddesses—pagans also bestow mountains, lakes, rivers, trees, and animals with souls and communicative power. While the resacralization of nature may also emerge now and then in the former two categories, paganism can be distinguished by its emphasis on traditions of the past, local communities, and tribalism. Pagans as a rule are less tightly organized than most religious groups. They rarely offer salvation or develop demands for orthodox uniformity of belief and practice. A local emphasis is frequently combined with a global perspective. Local pagan communities may base their spirituality on recontextualized traditions originally developed on a continent other than their own, as in, for example, the Swedish tribes that are animated by Native American spirituality or the American tribes of Norse heathens. Local pagan communities often form "global tribes" or small imaginary pagan communities that transcend national borders.

In envisioning the future in terms of the past, the pagan effort to revive or reconstruct premodern religious traditions not infrequently runs into ethnocentric considerations probably unknown to premodern man. Are techniques developed in Sioux spirituality open for everyone to explore or should this be considered "religious theft"? May a modern Asatrúer look to Wicca or ancient Egypt for inspiration or should he or she uphold a symbolic purity of tradition? Should revived Celtic spirituality be tied to Celtic ancestry or may an African be a Celtic pagan? Such issues have not found universally accepted answers but are at the heart of perennial debate and conflict in the pagan worlds. While many pagans consider any ancient tradition to be open to anyone irrespective of race or ethnicity, many heathens (who form the subject of this book) claim tradition on the basis of ethnicity or race.

Racist pagans tend to biologize spirituality. Somehow, gods and goddesses are encoded in the DNA of the descendants of the ancients. Blood is thought to carry memories of the ancient past, and divinities are believed to be genetically engraved upon or to reverberate from deep down within the abyss of the collective subconscious or "folk soul" of a given ethnic or racial group. Consciously or unconsciously informed by centuries of racist discourse, adherents of this philosophy often find mixed ancestry problematic, of course, as all systems of classification find problematic whatever blurs or negates the categories of classification. Mixed blood purportedly mixes up the memories of the ancient past and the engraved divinities of different heathen traditions, resulting in spiritual confusion. Accordingly, each individual needs to find *one* spiritual home. Pagans of this conviction tend to dismiss as New Age all pagan belief systems based on more than one heathen tradition. Despite racial pagans' claims of clear ethnic and/or racial foundations for their traditions, there are in fact more *inventions* of traditions, ethnicities, and races than most racial pagan activists acknowledge. Such inventions often become integral to the articulation of identity in the cultural economy of globalized reality and/or get inserted into the context of a neonationalist project aiming at political self-determination for the racial or ethnic community imagined.

Among pagans who link ethnicity with spirituality, the implicit racist logic is not necessarily acknowledged and may even be denied. Many activists publicly denounce the fascist and racist elements of the pagan milieu and declare solidarity with Native Americans and pagans of every other ethnicity who seek to preserve their traditions in the face of globalization and "imperialist" Christianity. However, a substantial number of racial pagans are explicitly racist in orientation and believe paganism to be at the heart of a long sought for racial revolution. Returning to the traditions evolved during an imaginary golden age of the "folk," they feel, is key to racial rebirth and empowerment. "Aryan" paganism, in particular, stands as the spiritual dimension of fascism, often fleshed out along Ariosophic lines; that is, it reflects a racial mysticism that considers the Aryan race divine. This racial mysticism connects the current revival of racist paganism to the occult roots of national socialism in the late nineteenth and early twentieth centuries, with many of the influential heathens of today specifically representing their projects as extensions of the effort made by philosophers and mystics of that era.

Indeed, observed from the perspective of globalization, the racist heathen milieu of the late twentieth and early twenty-first centuries in many ways parallels the pagan revival that emerged a century earlier in Europe, during what Roland Robertson terms the "take-off" phase of globalization, from 1880 to 1924. In the wake of industrialization, modernization, urbanization, rationality, positivism, secularization, and imperialism arose a nostalgic idealization of the agrarian past, ancient traditions, magic, occultism, secret societies, lost worlds, paganism, vegetarianism, Theosophy, anthroposophy, and primitivism. This was the time of Wagner, Nietzsche, Evola, Blavatsky, Crowley, Jung, von List, and Spengler—all philosophers and artists who also exert a powerful influence in the current pagan revival. Out of that earlier environment, the fascist and national socialist projects were eventually constructed, suggesting that the trajectory of the new pagan revival should be taken quite seriously.

Occultism, Paganism, and National Socialism

National socialism revolves around a palingenetic myth of racial rebirth and renewal. The German national socialist revolution aimed to rid society of parliamentary democracy, liberal humanism, capitalist economy, and communist class struggle, all of which were considered antithetical to the interest of the "organic race." Purified by a baptism of fire, the German Eagle would emerge from the smoldering ruins to usher in a millenarian New Order and a New Man. Attracted to this myth were different ideologues and groups with divergent views concerning what exactly this dream was supposed to mean and how it translated into political practice. Involved in its heated intrigues were scientists and mystics, Norse pagans and nationalist Christians, National Bolsheviks and reactionary aristocrats, rural romantics and urban industrialists, modernists and antimodernists. The efficient "total-state" machine envisioned was far from national socialist German realities. A significant constituency understood national socialism as essentially a spiritual project, a perspective represented in the national socialist leadership by Heinrich Himmler, Rudolf Hess, and Alfred Rosenberg. While Hitler accepted the support of esoteric societies in his bid for power, he remained largely indifferent to the project of Aryan self-theomorphosis, finding the loyal soldier more useful than the wandering mystic.

The study of occult national socialism has been approached from different perspectives. One school of thought seeks to explain the Third Reich in terms of metaphysical evil, analyzing the "occult machinations" behind its rise to power. Hitler is cast as a master magician who tapped occult forces to spellbind an unwitting German population. Speculations produced by this line of reasoning have inspired racist Satanists to see Hitler the devil as an exemplar, thereby contributing to the fear that clandestine cults are practicing black Nazi magic and lending a resemblance of factuality to that fantasy. American heathens tend to find important predecessors in the pan-German *völkisch* movement. Asatrú magazines and Web sites frequently carry articles about völkisch philosophy, secret societies, and pagan revivalism. Asatrú veteran and rune magus Edred Thorsson has popularized völkisch thought by translating Ariosophic classics and by publishing studies of Germanic magic and rune lore. The body of scholarly literature is more modest, the seminal work being Nicholas Goodrick-Clarke's 1992 *The Occult Roots of Nazism*, a detailed and balanced account of the Ariosophic undercurrent of national socialist ideology.

The subterranean maelstrom that animated the diverse milieu of occult national socialism was fed by a number of tributaries. Theosophy and the importation of other alternative religions met with revived Western esoteric traditions, paganism, magic, and monist pantheism, all cast in the context of a vibrant national romantic völkisch culture. The meaning of the German word *Volk* transcended the literal sense of "people" or "folk" to connote the spiritual qualities of the imagined nation, the unique personality of the German "folk soul." Searching for the soul of the German nation, völkisch ideologues turned to folklore and mythology, traveling the countryside to record old tales, folk music, and traditions. The völkisch movement was integral to the construction of a pan-German nationalism aimed at "reunification" of all German settlements at the territorial expense of other European states, a philosophy that later propelled the German war effort.

A romantic revolt against the "ills" of modern society, industrialization, urbanization, materialism, and rationalism, völkisch culture yearned for mysteries, irrationality, nature, and heroic legends. Constructing a counterorder by idealizing rural life and inventing traditions of the past, völkisch ideologues rejected democracy and egalitarianism, upholding instead the values of hierarchy, nobility, and spirituality. Fragmented according to orientation, völkisch activists engaged in sun worship, rune magic, nudism, pagan traditions, race mysticism, vegetarianism, herbal medicine, biodynamic gardening, and excursions into nature or sites of ancient "German" presence. Untainted German blood symbolized the spiritual link with the heathen forefathers and was envisioned as a carrier of ancestral memories harking back to the mythical golden age of national greatness.

Völkisch magus Richard Wagner celebrated the mysteries of blood and race in his grandiose operas; staged at the Bayreuth temple theatre, Wagnerian dramas assumed the qualities of transformative völkisch ceremonies, stirring the audience to the call of the racial soul. Wagner belonged to the völkisch category that sought to Germanize Christianity. The quest for the Holy Grail in *Parsifal* symbolized the völkisch longing for an Aryan Christ, a mystery cult centered on the redeeming force of pure German blood (Hollinrake 1982; Noll 1997a). "Whoever makes the assertion that Christ was a Jew is either ignorant or insincere," influential racist historian Houston Stewart Chamberlain concluded (quoted in Noll 1997a, 144).[8] "He had not a drop of genuinely Jewish blood in his veins" (ibid.). An Aryan Christ was central to Alfred Rosenberg's attempt to make Christianity a religion of Nordic supremacy. Eventually, the notion of an Aryan Christ crossed the Atlantic to emerge in the racist mission of Christian Identity. The effort to Germanize Christianity coexisted with other alternative constructs of Aryan religiosity. Among the ariocentric new religious movements, Theosophy was of special importance, exacting an influence far beyond its membership.

With its emphasis on elitism, racism and esoteric knowledge, Theosophy was well suited to the völkisch milieu.⁹ Drawing on Hinduism, Buddhism, Gnosticism, Masonry, and the latest developments of then modern scientific racism, Theosophy founder Helena Petrovna Blavatsky (1972 [1877]; 1888) elaborated an alternative view on man and world. According to theosophical precepts, the universe is a regulated, interconnected septennial hierarchy of septennial hierarchies, combined in an ever-transforming totality moving in cycles of birth, death, and rebirth. Man is a microcosmic reflection of the comprehensive whole, moving through time in a series of reincarnations regulated by karmic law. The cosmic whole strives toward perfection through a progressive spiral motion, with each round of birth, degeneracy, and renewal completed one step higher than at the point of departure. The history of mankind was similarly described as an evolutionary spiral motion of revolving cycles of degeneration and ascendancy.

Of special significance is a sequence of seven distinct "root races," each populating a different continent.¹⁰ The first human race was the last divine race and lived on an "imperishable" astral continent overlooked by the North Star. The three root races that followed were more material and populated now sunken continents: the hyperborean continent between the North Pole and America; Lemuria, between Africa and Australia; and Atlantis, located in the Atlantic ocean. The Aryan race is the fifth root race and is assigned the task of leading mankind's return into divinity, completing the sevenfold round at a stage higher than the divine point of departure.

During the era of gradual deterioration, Theosophy holds, divine knowledge fragmented into the different religions and mythologies of the world. Only an elite of enlightened Aryan sages fully preserved the original divine consciousness. Guarding the keys that could unlock the mysteries, the Aryan sages left the sinking Atlantis and relocated to the mythical subterranean cities Agartha and Shamballah, in the Himalayas and the Gobi Desert respectively. At a hidden Himalayan monastery, the white masters invited Blavatsky to read a sacred text that she translated and published with commentaries as *The Secret Doctrine* (1888). Divine truth, she claimed, will initially remain concealed to all but the spiritually most advanced. Eventually, though, voiced by the Aryan elite, theosophical truth will shatter the distortions of Semitic thought to implement the next evolutionary leap, leaving to karmic justice the leaders of the old order.

The theosophical themes of racial redemption, secret knowledge, subterranean cities, hidden masters, lost worlds, and exalted Aryan origins in the hyperborean motherland fit perfectly with völkisch imagination. The meeting between Theosophy and völkisch culture would birth Ariosophy, a peculiar brand of esoteric racism asserting the inherent divinity of Aryan man. Coined by self-anointed Austrian aristocrat Jörg Lanz von Liebenfels (1874–1954), Ariosophy was less a uniform school of esoteric thought than the direction in which several different race mystics headed when exploring the occult underground. With headquarters at a medieval castle ruin, Lanz in 1907 established an initiatory order of esoteric knights, Ordo Novi Templi (ONT), to serve the Ariosophic end envisioned.

Merging Theosophy and Gnosticism with anthropology and zoology, Lanz formulated the "theozoological" theory as the "scientific" basis of a dualist religion in which Aryans and non-Aryans were identified as carnal representations of the metaphysical principles of good and evil locked in a battle for world dominion. Lanz believed that the blond, blue-eyed Aryan was descended from an omniscient divine race that originally populated Arktogäa, a mythic Aryan motherland in the North Pole region. When Aryan women engaged in sexual relations with "daemon" races, the original race lost its superhuman powers. Aryan Christ came to redeem his race. His racist gospel was distorted by mainstream theology and forced underground, preserved throughout history by the Knights Templars and other initiatory orders. Centuries of uncontrolled procreation had increased the non-Aryan population, which gradually corrupted the German folk soul to the low point of modern society.

Surfacing with the rising tide of völkisch desire, the Aryan Christ summoned the race for the final battle. To restore Aryan supremacy, Lanz developed a program with striking similarities to the national socialist policies that were to come: an Aryan revolution was necessary to clear society of degeneracy; inferior races were to be exterminated, deported, or enslaved; enforced eugenics would improve the race, castrating the inferior element and actively supporting the reproduction of the superior; Aryan females were to be assigned to breeding convents and matched to an elite of Aryan studs; racial rejuvenation would then empower the Aryan god-men to launch a world war to exterminate the racial enemy; securing the Aryan birthright to sufficient lebensraum would lay the foundation of a millenarian reich of Aryan supremacy.

In terms of membership, the ONT remained small, with an estimated total of less than three hundred initiated knights distributed at a handful of local fraternities. Each secret center was subdivided into a hierarchy of seven orders that reflected degrees of racial purity and mastery of the Ariosophic mysteries. Lanz developed a New Templar liturgy and ceremonies and composed psalms to fit the "restored" gospel. A prolific writer, Lanz edited *Ostara*, a widely circulated journal dedicated to racial economics and anthropology that counted Hitler among its regular readers during his Vienna years. After World War I, Lanz moved to Hungary where he joined the right-wing counterrevolution of 1920, eventually serving at a Christian nationalist press agency linked with the foreign office. By then, Lanz had amended his Ariosophy with virulent anti-Semitism. ONT was supportive of the emerging national socialist movement and cultivated ties with a cross section of European fascists. In 1932, Lanz proudly proclaimed that Hitler was one of his pupils. However, this did not save the ONT when the Nationalsozialistische Deutsche Arbeiterpartei (NSDAP) regime turned increasingly hostile to secret organizations outside their control. In 1942, ONT was banned in Austria and Germany, which left the one chapter in Hungary. Lanz spent the war years in Swiss exile and made no recorded attempt to revive ONT in postwar Germany.

Among the celebrities associated with ONT was Guido von List (1848–1919), the revered guru of Ariosophic paganism. Dedicated to restoring national greatness by reverting to the wisdom of the ancients, von List made a völkisch career as a journalist, novelist, playwriter, folklorist, astrologist, poet, heathen, rune master, and magician. An acclaimed part of the völkisch literary establishment, von List in 1902 had a mystical revelation that would reorient his intellectual effort. While spending almost a full year in virtual blindness recovering from an eye operation, the secrets of the runes and the occult laws regulating the evolution of the Aryan folk soul came to him. He would spend the remainder of his life researching and resurrecting the hidden traditions of his ancestors.

His interpretation of Norse paganism was clearly influenced by Theosophy and Gnostic racism, the latter borrowed from the younger Lanz and other Ariosophists in the völkisch milieu. Von List claimed that the *Edda* (a collection of Norse myths and sagas) confirmed theosophical historiography. The different realms of Musspelheim (world of giants), Asgård (home of Aesir), Vanaheim (realm of Vanir), and Midgård (man's world) found in Norse cosmology corresponded to Blavatsky's cosmogony with its sub-sequence of manifest elements (fire, air, water, earth). The three subsequent Logoi (from Greek *Logos*) of theosophical speculation were identified as Allfather Wotan (Odin) and his two sons, Vile and Ve. Blavatsky's first four root races corresponded with the offspring of four giants (Ymir, Orgelmir, Thrudgelmir, Bergelmir) that in Norse mythology preceded the creation of man. Following Lanz, von List believed that the fifth,

Aryan, race originated at the vanished polar continent, Arktogäa, then built a new homeland on present-day Austria from which they expanded throughout the ancient world. Aryan man was to von List a reflection of the ancient Norse god/desses and a glimpse of future glory when man's innate divinity would be fully manifest. Cosmology corresponded with the microcosm of Aryan man, and von List introduced practices like rune yoga, rune meditation, and rune magic to serve the end of working with innate divine energies, techniques that would be adopted in the practice of Ariosophic pagans in America a century later. In accordance with Theosophy, von List believed that the immortal Aryan ego journeyed through time in cycles of reincarnations patterned like a continuous spiral staircase "in order to approach the final aim of the highest perfection, of a similitude to God, and ultimately to full union with God in this spiral form" (1988 [1908], 88).

The aboriginal religion of Aryan man was preserved in its most authentic form in the heathen world of the Teuton. Whereas Aryan Buddhism focused solely on the spiritual and Greco-Roman Aryanism stressed the material, Norse paganism cultivated the physical as coequal to the spiritual. To fully appreciate heathen religion, von List held it essential to distinguish between the exoteric and esoteric religious approaches on which the "national freedom" of antiquity supposedly had been based. The former was a religion of nature, known as Wotanism, adapted to the needs and level of sophistication of the heathen commoner. The latter was an initiatory mystical religion, termed Armanism, exclusive to the Armanenschaft, the elite class of Wotanist priest-king-scientists educated in occult and secular sciences at various Armanen lodge centers established throughout the heathen world.

With the advent of Christianity, the Armanenschaft initially sought to preserve paganism by blending the two religions and encoding its principles in the folklore of simple people. When Christian rulers initiated campaigns of violent aggression against any diversion from orthodoxy, the Armanenschaft went underground. To preserve Aryan faith and law, the Armanen encrypted its message in words, poetry, law, art, architecture, heraldry, and symbols, using a threefold code of interpretation to prevent noninitiates from detecting the secrets. Any given text or artifact would accordingly have three meanings — one exoteric and two esoteric. The latter two were divided into a low and high level to communicate messages of different magnitude to Armanen adepts and masters. A system developed already in ancient rune magic, whereby each rune communicated a meaning on three different levels, was now carried on in the secret cryptic language, *kala*. However, as Christian oppression continued with witch trials, inquisition, and reformation, the concealed meaning got lost or survived only as disparate remnants or misunderstood corruptions, like Free-masonry. Only the indigenous heraldry of German coats-of-arms still conveys uncorrupted esoteric wisdom for the initiates to read. Von List came to believe that he was a reincarnated Armanist priest-king, added the aristocratic "von" to his name, and developed an occult key with which to restore the hidden meaning embedded in artifacts and lore throughout the German landscape (von List 1988 [1908]; Flowers 1988).

The tribulations of modernity were to von List signs of the messianic woes of Aryan rebirth. The ambitions of the German nation were frustrated by an evil cabal of racial enemies organized in the "Great International Party" of von List's imagination, bearing the traits of then rampant anti-Semitic sentiments in völkisch thought. Von List argued for an Aryan war of aggression to exterminate the racial enemies and restore an Armanist empire. In accordance with his millenarian vision, von List initially was enthusiastic about the First World War effort. His apocalyptic dreams frustrated by the outcome, von List prophesied that an army of reincarnated Aryan soldiers slain at the battlefield would return under the leadership of the "Strong One from Above" to inaugurate an Aryan thousand-year reich. Based on theosophical and astrological calculations, von List set the year at 1932, one year before the ascendancy of Hitler.

Von List was a legend in his lifetime, with numerous groups formed to carry his ideas to fruition. In 1908, the Guido von List Society was founded as an exoteric outlet to support the works of the völkisch master. At a midsummer ceremonial working in 1911, von List founded the esoteric Hoher Armanen-Orden (High Armanic Order), the activities of which are less known. In Germany arose numerous Ariosophic societies, including the Germanenorden, an armed Armanen underground founded in 1910 to restore the ancient order. Its principal aims were to monitor Jewish and revolutionary anarchist and socialist activity, including in its clandestine operations assassination of targeted enemies. Germanenorden ceremonies were based on elements borrowed from von List, Norse mythology, Masonry, and Wagner.

In 1916, the Germanenorden adopted the swastika as its official emblem. Although widely used in theosophical and völkisch circles, it was from the Germanenorden and its successor group, the Thule Society, that the swastika found its way to the NSDAP. Instrumental in this story were the activities of self-proclaimed nobleman Rudolf von Sebottendorff, who organized the Germanenorden in Munich. When Soviet-inspired activism increased, the Germanenorden metamorphosed into the Thule Society to avert unwanted leftist attention. During the short-lived Communist Republic of Munich of 1919, the Thule Society kept the dual agenda of Ariosophic mysticism and terrorist activism. Thule members infiltrated communist cells, stockpiled weapons, and engaged in violent assaults against leftists, thus contributing to the defeat of the republic. Aside from participating in ceremonies and terrorism, von Sebottendorff organized völkisch lectures and political discussions, including among its invited guest speakers Alfred Rosenberg and Rudolf Hess.

The Thule Society had an upper-class orientation. To attract the working class for the Aryan cause, Thulean initiates in 1918 launched the Deutsche Arbeiterpartei (German Worker's Party), of which Adolf Hitler became a member. Impatient with its conspiratorial secrecy and lodge elitism, Hitler assumed control and reorganized the party into the NSDAP in 1920, aiming to create mass appeal.

If Hitler mainly had priorities other than those of the occult völkisch mystic, Rudolf Hess, Alfred Rosenberg, and Heinrich Himmler were more enthusiastic about the Ariosophic project. Born and raised in Egypt, Hess moved to Germany during World War I and caught the völkisch fever. A vegetarian who kept to a biodynamic diet, Hess was intrigued by anthroposophy, herbal medicine, astrology, magic, and Aryan race mysticism. Active in occult circles and a veteran member of the NSDAP who participated in the Beer Hall Putsch and took dictation for Hitler's *Mein Kampf*, Hess was eventually outmaneuvered in the constant intrigues of the national socialist inner circle. Hess's solitary surprise flight to Scotland in 1941 — intended, he said, to negotiate for peace — has variously been interpreted as insanity, a failed effort to impress Hitler, and a desperate last attempt by the Thule Society to correct an Ariosophic revolution gone astray.

Alfred Rosenberg, the NSDAP minister of culture asserted, "Race is the image of soul. . . . Racial history is therefore simultaneously natural history and soul mystique" (1930, 4). Tracing the "history of the religion of the blood" (4), Rosenberg believed that all high cultures of human history were the creations of a superior Aryan master race that had swarmed out from their northern motherland Atlantis. Racial memories of a prehistoric Nordic tradition were present in mythologies of southern Europe, North Africa, western Asia, Persia, India, and China. However, through desecration of the blood, all had perished. The German defeat in World War I was the outward effect of inward collapse, the cataclysmic outcome of Jewish corruption of true Aryan Christianity. However, the blood that had died had begun to live anew, and "in its mystical sign the cells of the German folkish soul renew[ed] themselves" (5), thus effectuating an Aryan resurrection. Rosenberg's comprehensive history of the racial soul, *Der Mythus der 20. Jahrhunderts* (The Myth of the Twentieth Century), sold more than a million copies, becoming a nonfiction bestseller, second only to Hitler's *Mein Kampf* (Rosenberg 1930; Whisker 1990; Godwin 1996, 58). To document the spiritual history of the Aryan race, Rosenberg also established research departments involving scholars of the history of religions, ethnology, Orientalism, linguistics, and anthropology.

A prominent patron of Ariosophy in the NSDAP leadership was Heinrich Himmler, Reichsführer of the Schutzstaffel (ss) and head competitor with Rosenberg for the leadership of the national socialist ideological apparatus. Recalling the ideals of Lanz, the black-uniformed ss troops would be a spiritual and physical elite, serving as progenitors of the future race of supermen. To direct Aryan destiny, of course, it was essental to control its history, and Himmler rivaled Rosenberg in recruiting scholars and funding research centers to that end.[11] In 1935, Himmler incorporated the Ahnenerbe Research Institute of Indo-German Prehistory and Archeology as an ss department and made its scholars uniformed ss officers.[12] The main objective of Ahnenerbe was to explore the geographical distribution of Aryan man and account for his material and spiritual accomplishments throughout history. Scholars engaged in a wide range of projects, including archeological excavations, comparative Indo-European mythology, medieval church art, and herbal medicine. Himmler was, however, attracted to subjects and knowledge extending beyond the limits of the mainstream academic world. Recruiting astrologers, magicians, and völkisch mystics, Himmler aimed to research the mysteries of the occult. Among the occultists enrolled in the ss was Austrian Karl Maria Wiligut (1866–1946) in whose esoteric expertise Himmler became especially confident.

Wiligut claimed to be the direct descendant of a royal family line of god-kings that ruled the ancient German nation. By tapping into the bank of ancestral memories, Wiligut could detail the marvels of racial prehistory, from its astral origins through its subsequent manifestations in worlds long vanished (Wiligut 2001). Outlining the hidden history of the present, or fifth, epoch, Wiligut revised von List's distinction between Armanism and Wotanism, casting them as two separate religions locked in perennial conflict. The Wiligut family had allegedly been champions of "Irmanist" monotheism, introduced by the German King Krist, a theology which had eventually been suppressed by Wotanist aggression. The Wiligut family secretly cultivated the Ariosophic legacy, but at the brink of national rebirth, an evil conspiracy of Jews and Freemasons sought to annihilate esoteric truth as evidenced by the outcome of the Great War. Wiligut grew concerned that the cabal was out to destroy him. Declared insane, he spent two years in an asylum, corresponding with New Templars and other völkisch mystics. Moving to Germany in 1932, he engaged with the Edda Society. In 1933 he was introduced to Himmler.

Finding Wiligut's ancestral memory to be a unique source of information about Aryan prehistory, Himmler designated him head of the department for pre- and early history. Joining the ss under the pseudonym Karl Maria Weisthor, Wiligut was ordered to document on paper his wealth of ancestral memories. Himmler evidently enjoyed listening to Wiligut's tales of prehistoric Aryan glory. Wiligut was also entrusted with reviewing the teachings of Italian radical conservative traditionalist Julius Evola. The perennial philosophy of Evola, with its romanticized notions of the spiritual nobility and hermetic traditions of the pagan past, had proved not wholly acceptable to fascist Italy. Finding fascism too compromising, Evola sought recognition by the ss and began lecturing in Germany from 1934 onward. Wiligut, however, discouraged further cooperation with Evola, finding him too reactionary and ignorant of Aryan prehistory (Goodrick-Clarke 2002).

The most "spectacular contribution" Wiligut made to national socialist Germany was the development of the Wewelsburg as the castle and ceremonial center of ss order. Acquired by the ss in 1934, Wiligut conceptualized the castle as the "center of the world," an Ariosophic "Vatican" and occult academy. The ceremonial center for the Ariosophic knights of the ss was the northern tower with its vault, Walhalla, Hall of the Slain, the floor of which was decorated with the Black Sun, the occult source of energy that invigorates Aryan theomorphosis. At Wewelsburg were held seasonal pagan festivals to celebrate the wheel of nature and name-giving rites for the progeny of ss officers. Wiligut also designed ritual objects, notably the striking ss *Totenkopfring* with its death's-skull and cross-bones, a swastika, a hagal rune, double sig runes, and an Ariosophic rune group.[13] In 1938, Himmler declared that the rings of dead ss men should be returned for ritual storage at Wewelsburg to express the notion of a chivalric order transcending death.

In the end, the thousand-year reich collapsed after twelve years, the millenarian dreams thwarted by the Allied war effort. The political collapse of national socialism did not, however, end the Ariosophic quest. Although völkisch activity fell sharply into disrepute in popular culture, a flickering occult subculture remained during the subsequent decades, and at the brink of the millennium, Ariosophic concerns suddenly resurfaced among a new generation heathens across the Atlantic. Völkisch pre–national socialist pagans are now commemorated in contemporary heathen ceremonies, lyrics, and art. The Wotansvolk project is cast as a continuation of the Ariosophic effort. Pagans often focus on Ariosophic themes such as blood mysteries, lost worlds, immortal Aryan sages, or the Ultima Thule mythos of Aryan origins. To some American pagans, this fascination is bereft of any political ambition. To others, Ariosophic paganism is part of a neonationalist project aimed at establishing a transatlantic white homeland.

A Few Words on Terminology

Racist paganism is linked with the political history of race in American society, so the terminology used herein might need some clarification. Some of the heathens categorized as "racist" in this study would probably object to the label due to the negative connotations associated with the concept in contemporary mainstream discourse. Many Americans consider racists to be uneducated rednecks at best, prejudiced oppressors at worst. However, racists have not always been considered public villains. Racism was long considered a divinely mandated order of nature and an important pillar of American society, protected by constitutional law

In this book, then, the term *racist* is detached from any moral assumptions and simply signifies a person who believes that mankind may be classified into any given number of "races" that "by nature" differ from each other not only in physical but also in mental and moral qualities; from this perspective, the races of mankind are often metaphorically thought of as "organisms" with different "personalities." A racist asserts that every individual member of a certain race shares fundamental mental predispositions unique to that race. To a racist, the importance of race goes beyond race as a social fact or construct generated by an essentialist reading of racial classification — for a racist, race determines how people *are*. Race is thought to provide man with his inner essence of which physical traits may be indicators. Accordingly, the color of the skin does not determine how people are; rather, innate mental qualities are believed to determine the physical characteristics. This does not necessitate a hierarchical ordering of distinct races in terms of "superior" or "inferior," even though this often has been the case. Not every racist arrives at the same conclusion when reflecting on the political and social implications of his or her racist worldview. A few of the racists introduced herein, for instance, would fully accept "integration" as long as racial "differences" were acknowledged and protected by policies preventing assimilation and miscegenation. Others would assert that multiracial or multicultural societies "don't work," claiming that social harmony is best served by implementing some degree of racial separation. While some talk about redefining American federalism in terms of a confederacy of monoracial "tribal" societies, others envision a division of the American continent into separate monoracial states, and yet another category talks in terms of global cleansing and the establishment of a worldwide white empire. What they all have in common is a desire to preserve a perceived "natural order" by instituting policies of purity to prevent the blurring of the units of classification.

A *religious racist* takes the racist mode of classification a step further by stipulating that the Divine, however defined, created the various races of man that differ not only mentally but also spiritually. This, in effect, makes "God" a racist, and preserving the purity of the different races of man may therefore be interpreted as respecting divine will. The organic notion of race is commonly strengthened by asserting that each race is endowed with a racial soul commonly thought of as its core essence. Each race has therefore "by nature" a relationship with the divine, a religion distinctively their own. In its mildest version this view might be expressed by rejecting the missionary efforts of agents who propound a universal interpretation of religion. In its more extreme versions, it might be worked into theories asserting that different races reflect in their beings metaphysical good or evil. World history may then be cast in apocalyptic terms as an ongoing conflict between races divine and diabolic that is now reaching its predestined end.

The racist pagans of this volume all believe that there is an organic link between biology and spirituality. Somehow the pagan god/desses of the ancestors are encoded in the genes of their progeny and might therefore reassert their presence to replace the "alien" religion of Christianity when conditions allow. In some, but not all, versions, this is elaborated to mean that the race, or ethnic tribe, "by nature" is divine. The divine energies represented within man by his pagan god/desses may be called on in ceremonies intending to raise their presence and recharge innate divinity in a project of self-theomorphosis set in a context of resurrecting the racial soul. The racist pagan worldview might occasionally extend to the thought that every "folk" is a creation of its god/desses. Here, the God of Christianity is defined as the tribal god of Jewry, who in trying to pose as the universal god of mankind reveals the megalomaniac traits of a demiurge who brings destruction to every nation that he possesses.

The words *pagan* and *heathen* did not originally signify a specific religious tradition. Practitioners of pre-Christian spirituality had no word for religion and no label with which to distinguish their orientation from those of other people.

Both concepts originated as pejoratives used by "enlightened" European Christians to signify the backward beliefs and customs of rural commoners. *Pagan* derives from the Latin word *paganus* meaning "country dweller" and already in Roman times connoted something similar to what modern urban Americans generally mean by *hick* or *hillbilly*. Similarly, *heathen* literally means "people of the heaths" and was used to refer to unsophisticated rural people who stuck to traditions of the past rather than converting to Christianity.

In time, *pagan* and *heathen* assumed the additional meanings of "unbelievers," "idolaters," "devil-worshippers," and even "atheists." When people attracted to ancient pre-Christian traditions began to use *pagan* and *heathen* to define themselves, they adopted a strategy akin to northern Americans calling themselves Yankees. The meaning of *Yankee* has, much like the word *bad*, thereby been redefined in the face of those who originally used it as a dismissive term. *Pagan* is herein used in the same spirit as when it used by modern pagans themselves, that is, as a generic term for pre-Christian traditions such as Norse, Celtic, Greek, Egyptian, or Yoruban, as well as more modern reconstructions of those traditions such as Asatrú, Wicca, voudou, or Santeria. *Heathen* is used specifically to signify pagans oriented toward Norse paganism, a common usage among Norse pagans themselves, who wish to differentiate themselves from generic pagans, pagans of other traditions, and to distance themselves from what might be considered the "New Age confusion" of what Norse paganism "properly" means. All heathens are therefore pagans, but not all pagans are heathens.

CHAPTER ONE

The Transforming Landscapes of American Racism

D
uring the past few decades, the phenomenon of racism has undergone dramatic transformations in public perception, from state-
sanctioned ideology with a significant presence in American society to its current standing as an unjust worldview cast on the dump
heap of obsolete ideas—a change that has left its subscribers in a state of desperation and confusion. How did white supremacy, long considered to reflect
scientific truth, manifest destiny, and the will of God, suddenly lose its grip not
only on American society but throughout most of the now decolonized world
as well?

The Alchemy of Race and Nation

Racism is a mode of social classification that determines who is who, who deserves what, who properly belongs where and does what; as such, it is inalienably
linked to power. From its inception, the United States of America classified the
inhabitants populating its territory of jurisdiction on the basis of race. At the
time of the American Revolution, persons of European, African, and American
Indian ancestry populated the colonies, but when Congress in 1790 restricted
U.S. citizenship to "free white persons," they effectively defined the new American "nation" as "white." Inhabitants of African ancestry, who accounted for
almost 20 percent of the population at the time of the Revolution, were excluded from the freedoms awarded white Americans, as were American Indians,
who, the argument ran, had no lawful claim to their native land. A full half of
the territory recognized as the United States in the Treaty of Paris, 1783, consisted of Native American land, the expropriation of which was sanctioned by
biblical and natural law. Judicial theoretician Emerich de Vattel formulated the
standard notion of *vacuum domicilium*. Linking possession with productivity, de

Vattel claimed that only those who met the obligation to cultivate the earth were entitled to own land (Stephanson 1995, 25). Where reality offered settled agricultural Native American cultures like the Iroquois or the literate Cherokee, the spread of civilization found other means of removing the annoyance.[1] "Treaties with Indians," the governor of Georgia stated, "were expedients by which ignorant, intractable, and savage people were induced without bloodshed to yield up what civilized people had the right to possess" (ibid., 26). In 1830 President Andrew Jackson secured the Indian Removal Act, granting the President authority to remove "civilized" Native Americans such as the Cherokee of Georgia and the Creek of Alabama by force.

If Native Americans were classified as savages associated with wild nature, Africans were associated with domesticated nature as beasts of the field. They were "property not persons," defined according to the original Constitution as "three-fifths of a man."[2] Slavery constituted, in effect, the first melting pot in U.S. history, unifying as it did Africans of different languages and cultures into a single, "inferior" race. In the late seventeenth century emerged the first systematic efforts to link black physical features with inferior mental qualities, beginning as a theological reflection designed to harmonize the facts of divine justice with the practice of slavery. "Blackness" was associated with the realm of evil, and black skin was interpreted as a divine curse that marked the descendants of original sinners Cain and/or Ham and Canaan.[3] So pervasive was the merging of moral quality with complexion that a good black man was said to have a white soul.

As time went on, various biological and anthropological theories contributed to the "scientific" construction of racism that became an integral part of U.S. society. Americans of African ancestry came to be considered "by nature" lazier, more prone to play and amoral sexuality, and less intelligent, less civilized, and less fit for self-government than white men. Defenders of slavery such as Secretary of State John C. Calhoun seized on scientific reports in rebutting the prospects of abolition as "neither human [n]or wise" (quoted in Stanton 1960, 61). Deprived of the "guardian care of his owner," the logic went, a black man would inevitably sink back into the state of idiocy that follows from his "inferior condition," while blacks in bondage "improved" in "comfort, intelligence, and morals" (ibid.). Emancipation would also, Calhoun reasoned, unleash a devastating race war on the new continent, as the two races could not coexist harmoniously in the land of the free. The latter argument was also voiced by a majority of the abolitionists, whose plans to end slavery were generally accompanied by schemes to remove emancipated blacks from the free white republic, either by repatriation, exportation, or systematic curtailment of their rights. With free blacks believed to pose a greater danger than blacks in bondage, racism grew in intensity following the emancipation.

According to the first U.S. system of demographic classification, the inhabitants of the U.S. territory constituted three distinct categories: Americans were white, free, and belonged to civilized world; Africans were black, bonded, and belonged at the plantation; Amerindians were red, wild, and belonged in nature. When Congress passed the first Immigration and Naturalization Act, only free white persons were considered fit for self-government. But who was to qualify as "white"? To the modern reader, the question might seem odd and the answer given, at least in approximate popular usage of the term. But, far from being given by nature, "whiteness" is a result of context and negotiation. Throughout U.S. history, whiteness has determined status and power in society and has been linked to the fundamental question of what it means to be an American. The contest over whiteness—who is white and who is not—has therefore always been a salient feature of U.S. history. The Founding Fathers appear to have equated "white" with "Anglo-Saxon," not foreseeing that, in the nineteenth century, millions of non–Anglo-Saxon Protestants would seek entry into the American nation by referring to their whiteness.

Benjamin Franklin argued that "Spaniards, Italians, French, Russians, [Germans], and Swedes are generally of what we call a swarthy complexion," and he wished for an increase of the "purely white" population, the "Saxon" and the "English" (quoted in Jacobson 1998, 40). Thomas Jefferson shared a then popular notion that Anglo-Saxon England had been a land of free and heroic yeoman farmers whose social and political system had been destroyed in the Norman Conquest of 1066. By separating from Britain, the American revolutionaries cleared society of Norman corruptions, such as monarchy, nobility, the state church, and feudalism, and emulated the system of their freedom-loving tribal ancestors (Horsman 1981, 18–23). Jefferson's ideal vision of micro-republics of about six square miles, each with its own direct democracy, school, militia, local police force, and responsibility for the welfare of the poor, old, and disabled, was modeled on his perception of the Anglo-Saxon "natural constitution" and is echoed among modern Norse pagans in their call for reverting society to the "tribal socialism" of their pagan ancestors. Although Jefferson's radical decentralism never materialized, Anglo-Saxon romanticism prevailed, strengthened by novelists such as Ivanhoe author Sir Walter Scott, and was soon to become racialized in the conflict with waves of immigrants from Catholic Europe.

Immigration increased dramatically between the 1820s and 1850s, from a low of between 6,000 and 10,000 per year in the early 1820s to 60,000 in 1832 to 380,000 in 1851. Many of the new immigrants were Catholics from Germany and Ireland. The Irish alone accounted for one-third of all immigrants in the 1830s. Following the Irish potato famine of 1845–51, close to two million people fled Ireland, many of whom headed to the United States. In 1851 alone a quarter million Irishmen arrived in the United States, seeking naturalization as "free white persons" to the consternation of Anglo-Americans. The anti-Catholic sentiment prevalent in Protestant America forcibly came to the fore, both spontaneously and in organized nativist movements. Anti-Catholic newspapers such as the *American Protestant Vindicator* mushroomed in major eastern cities. Alarmist conspiracy theories told of a secret Catholic plan to subvert the new nation's freedom and deliver the continent to the Vatican.

At the same time, a series of "confession" books by "former nuns" told of sadomasochistic rituals behind the convent walls in which decent young Protestant females were brutalized by Catholic priests, nuns, and monks. *The Awful Disclosure of Maria Monk* (1836) used such graphic language that versions of it appeared in adult bookstores a century later.[4] It became the best-selling book in American history until the publication of *Uncle Tom's Cabin* (Bennet 1995, 42). Conspiracy theories spiced with tales of ritualized sexual assault are still popular in American culture although the perpetrators of today are not necessarily Catholics but Illuminati, Satanists, globalists, or aliens. Analyzing the genre's popularity in the eighteenth century, David Bennet argues, "Women's role as moral authority was accentuated in an age of socioeconomic upheaval, when national values were under pressure and traditional relationships threatened. . . . Women, invested with moral authority, were pictured as abused, degraded, and shamefully cast away by the enemy. What a heroic setting for a true patriot. How better to defend the American way. If the symbolic woman is threatened by 'them,' certainly she must be saved by 'us' in a crusade against the lustful monsters of conspiracy" (ibid., 45). Acting on circulating conspiracy theories, "Americans" assaulted Catholic priests and neighborhoods. Catholic churches were set on fire in New York, Maine, Massachusetts, and Ohio, and angered Americans attacked convents in New Orleans, Galveston, Providence, and Chicago.[5]

The notion of the "free white nation" as Anglo-Saxon in character was racialized in the 1840s, using arguments developed in the new scientific racism of anthropology and phrenology. "Americans" began to explain their unprecedented achievements in terms of their superior blood. This reasoning was fueled by developments in continental European philology that showed that Germanic languages belonged to a common Indo-European family. Assuming that language affinity meant racial affinity, researchers began to search for a common Indo-European or, as it would come to be called in the late nineteenth century, *Aryan* homeland.

A popularized image of Indo-Europeans as a uniquely gifted people spilling "out from the mountains of Central Asia to press westwards following the sun, bringing civilization, heroism and the principles of freedom to a succession of empires" fit perfectly into American imagination. Soon, the westernmost outpost of these Caucasians, the Nordic and Anglo-Saxon, was seen as the elite for whom the concept "Aryan" was reserved. In line with the alleged Aryan imperative of following the sun, the superior Nordic-Anglo-Saxon civilizer then crossed the Atlantic and continued westward conquering the new land (Horsman 1981, 33, 83). At the brink of the war against Mexico that eventually added all the land north of Rio Grande to the United States, the notion of the westward march of the supreme Anglo-Saxon race merged with the Puritan concept of the divine mandate, leading to the peculiar American interpretation that the conquest of North America was their manifest destiny. Democrat ideologue John O'Sullivan proclaimed in 1845 "the right of our manifest destiny to overspread and possess the whole continent which providence has given us for the development of the great experiment of liberty and federated self government" (quoted in Stephanson 1995, 42).

The enthusiasm for the civilizing efforts of the superior Anglo-Saxon race was heightened by the unease caused by increasing non–Anglo-Saxon immigration. Racialized arguments held that immigrants from Catholic Europe would hardly qualify as "white." Irish people were described as an uncivilized, blackish, primitive, and savage "race"; like blacks, they were depicted with monkey features in newspaper cartoons. Germans were accused of swamping the nation, driving "white people" out of the labor market. Italians, Ashkenazi Jews, Slavs, and Iberians shared their fate and became less and less perceived as "white" during the late nineteenth century. The new science of anthropology told of a multitude of European "races," often defined as Nordic, Anglo-Saxon, Teutonic, Alpine, Slav, and Mediterranean. Although thought of as a given by nature, whiteness is not an inherent quality but a social contruct; its parameters subject to context, as Matthew Frye Jacobson demonstrates in *Whiteness of a Different Color*. Relative to Anglo-Saxon Americans, the other European races were felt to be less white, but relative to non-European people seeking naturalization, they were considered more white—provided that they "acted white" and were not associated with blacks or other non-Europeans.[6] To serve in the Mexican War or to confront free blacks in the South or Native Americans in the West, an Irishman would have been enlisted as white, although he would have been considered nonwhite in the Eastern cities. To some, a Japanese, relative to an African, was as good a white as a southern European or a Jew, while others argued that the latter had as poor a claim to whiteness as a Japanese (Jacobson 1998, 77).

Different pressures fed the conflicting views of Anglo-Saxon supremacy and an inclusive whiteness. Informed by the new science of racial hygiene, eugenics, and by the alarmist writings of racist intellectuals such as Lothrop Stoddard and Madison Grant, American greatness was generally interpreted in terms of the supreme qualities of the Nordic (white) race, which ostensibly faced threats from both the inside and outside. According to this perspective, the inside threats arose from the processes of industrialization and urbanization, which seemed to favor an increase of the inferior elements of the racial stock — the criminals, idiots, disabled, alcoholics, and lowlifes — at the expense of those considered "hereditary worthy." Through legislation, education, and sterilization programs, the applied eugenics movement aimed to improve racial stock by promoting the procreation of the superior elements and reducing the reproduction of the inferior elements. In 1907, Indiana passed the first sterilization act in the United States; others were soon enacted by several states in the North and West.[7] Marriage restrictions were applied to the "feebleminded" in a majority of states, and thirty-two states prohibited biracial marriage and sexual intercourse. The achievements of the American eugenics programs came to serve as a model for their European counterparts, including in national socialist Germany. In fact, the American Rockefeller Foundation funded German eugenic research even after the national socialists gained control of German science (Kühl 1994, 13–21).

The perceived outer threats to the supreme Nordic race were immigration and racial interbreeding. Racially mixed children were thought at best to "inherit two souls, two temperaments, two sets of opinions, with the result . . . that they are unable to think or act strongly and consistently in any direction," as articulated by Prescott F. Hall in 1919 (quoted in Stoddard 1920, 259). At worst, the offspring inherited the inferior identity. Wrote Grant, "The result of the mixture of two races . . . gives us a race reverting to the . . . lower type. The cross between a white man and an Indian is an Indian. The cross between a white man and a negro is a negro; the cross between a white man and a Hindu is a Hindu; and the cross between any of the three European races and a Jew is a Jew" (Grant 1916, 15). If inferior races were allowed entry in territory occupied by a superior race, the former tended, it was argued, to supplant the latter. Accordingly, immigration restriction was, in the words of Hall, a necessary instrument of "world eugenics . . . by which inferior stocks could be prevented from both diluting and supplanting good stocks" (quoted in Stoddard 1920, 261). Stoddard not only emphatically argued for restricting nonwhite immigration but was also opposed to the naturalization of inferior southern and eastern European races. Composed by the "very pick of the Nordics," he wrote, the "colonial stock was perhaps the finest that nature had evolved since the classic Greeks," with "magnificent . . . eugenic results" as manifested in the first thirteen colonies. However, with the "deluge" of "the truly alien hordes of the European east and south," devastating racial degeneration had set in. The "tide of immigration" had to be "stopped at all cost" lest nature's finest will be extinct forever. "If America is not true to her own race-soul, she will inevitably lose it, and the brightest star that has appeared since Hellas will fall like a meteor from the human sky, its brilliant radiance fading into the night" (Stoddard 1920, 266, 251–67, 308).

Alarmed, Congress passed the "Great Restriction" Quota Act of 1921 and the Immigration Act of 1924 to sharply reduce immigration and, through a system of national-origin quotas, to ensure that immigration reflected the "racial" heritage of the United States by favoring western and northern European immigrants over those from southern and eastern Europe.[8] At its moment of legislative triumph, however, the eugenic idea of a hierarchy of distinct white races had already begun to be undermined by an opposing process that would culminate in the construction of a single, unified white race. In a way, the quota act itself was instrumental to this end as it restricted entry of "inferior" white "races," which allowed the United States to focus on race as color. Although still holding sway in the West due to the Mexican War and ongoing struggles with Native Americans, the differences within the white race gradually lost their significance with the post-emancipation migration of free blacks to the eastern and northern industrial centers and with the civil rights movement's fight to desegregate the South.

During Reconstruction—the restoration of the former Confederate states to the Union—the possibility of including blacks as equal citizens of the American nation never really materialized. Radical laws were passed but either remained dormant or were soon suspended or declared unconstitutional. The Civil Rights Act of 1866, for instance, was left unenforced until 1968, and the Supreme Court declared the Civil Rights Act of 1875, which provided for equal public accommodations, unconstitutional after eight years. Nonetheless, in 1867, temporary military rule over the South forced the southern states to enfranchise blacks in order to reenter the Union. These Reconstruction governments were unique in including black former slaves in the government and the democratic process. South Carolina had a black majority, and in Louisiana half of the delegates were blacks. When power shifted to the new state governments, many ex-Confederates were prohibited from voting and a large black vote ensured landslide Republican victories. The new administrations initiated ambitious public-works programs. Railroads, roads, and bridges were built, and institutions to care for orphans, the disabled, and the mentally ill were established along with a public-school system. A disproportionate number of blacks enrolled in the state militias and many thousands of blacks served in the federal army.

Although a short-lived experiment, Reconstruction-era "black rule" still stands as an important symbol to southern racial activists. The defeat of the South in the Civil War and the subsequent military occupation serve as a "national trauma" among southern racist separatists. In the words of far-right attorney Kirk Lyons, "We southerners live in an occupied country. We're part of a country that was militarily attacked and destroyed by the United States' government. The best of our people, our men, were killed. Millions of dollars worth of property were turned loose, you know, the freed slaves, and then put over us as overlords. To me, this country stabbed itself in the heart in 1861, and it has been bleeding to death ever since" (Lyons 1997).[9]

Reconstruction also ushered in another phenomenon with lasting symbolic value: the Ku Klux Klan. In concert with other secret societies such as the Knights of the White Camellia, the Klan launched an armed underground resistance intended to restore white supremacy. Violence against "black criminals" and white "race traitors" proved instrumental in elections throughout the Deep South where blacks constituted about half of the electorate. In southern states where whites formed a safe majority, it was enough for the Democratic Party to appeal to white unity against Yankee rule and the empowerment of emancipated blacks. The Democratic Party won in North Carolina, Virginia, and Georgia in 1871; in Texas, Arkansas, and Alabama in 1874; in Mississippi and South Carolina in 1876; and in Florida and Louisiana in 1877. The Reconstruction experiment with racial equality was over.

A surge of vindictive violence swept through the South, targeting among others black teachers, professionals, business leaders, and politicians. Becoming a genre of popular family entertainment, lynching parties were advertised in local papers, and organizers would arrange transportations, seating, and refreshments. The new Democratic administrations institutionalized racism to a degree that would later inspire the South African apartheid regime. Laws restricting black voting were enacted. "Jim Crow" legislation separated blacks from whites in segregated public space, transportation, schools, parks, cemeteries, theaters, telephone booths, and living quarters. Segregation ensured that blacks were given few opportunities to earn their way outside the cotton fields in the sharecropping system that began after emancipation. By 1880, sharecropping had become the dominant economic system of the agrarian South. Merchants and plantation owners supplied sharecroppers on credit, securing their high-interest loan with a claim on each farmer's next crop, a system that forced many tenants into cycles of indebtedness.

Industrialization of the urban North provided a means of escaping institutionalized southern racism and perpetual poverty. Between 1910 and 1970, six-and-a-half million blacks moved to the North in what is known as the Great Migration. In 1870, 80 percent of the black population lived as sharecroppers in the rural South. By 1970, 80 percent lived in urban areas, nearly half located outside the South. The outbreak of World War I increased demand for unskilled industrial labor, and with the invention of the mechanical cotton picker, the migration turned into a flood. Between 1910 and 1920, more than half a million blacks moved north. The 1920s saw an outflow of close to 900,000, and five million moved after the mechanization of cotton farming in the 1940s.

The tide of black migration was accompanied by an upsurge of racial violence. A series of riots exploded in northern cities between 1900 and 1920, among the more notorious being those in New York in 1900; Evansville, Indiana, in 1903; Springfield, Illinois, in 1908; East St. Louis, Illinois, in 1917; and Chicago in 1919. In Chicago, fifty-eight black homes were bombed between 1917 and 1921, that is, one every twenty days. Racial tension increased further when northern industrialists began utilizing blacks as strikebreakers, often transporting them directly to the factories from recruitment bases in the South. A revived Ku Klux Klan moved north, and Stoddard (1927, 256) argued for pan-white solidarity and "bi-racialism," that is, an extension of southern-style black-white segregation as the "key to social peace." Subsequently, a system of northern segregation came into effect in employment, education, and housing. The black ghettos that in time would become home to a majority of urban African Americans were constructed by a series of institutionalized practices, public policies, legal means, and illegal actions by which whites aimed to keep blacks spatially contained. By the time of World War II, the foundations for the black ghetto had been laid in most northern cities.[10]

The massive black migration to the cities outside the South gradually undermined the preoccupation with distinctions between the various white races that previously had dominated the alchemy of race in the industrial North. With the subsequent African American civil rights struggle to end segregation, whiteness was solidified as a "monolith of privilege," as noted by Jacobson (1998, 95). Irish and other white Catholic "ethnics" had now unquestionably become "Americans" as symbolized by the election in 1960 of the United States's first Catholic president. "Race relations" was now primarily an issue of white-black relations, such that Martin Luther King Jr. could formulate the dream of an expanded American nation to include as equal races of all colors. Racism, long believed to be a reflection of nature and divine order, now came under serious questioning among larger segments of the American population. In the mid-twentieth century there was no contradiction between being a good citizen and being a racist. By the end of the century, however, being "good" and "racist" had become a contradiction in terms. Something had happened in American society, and happened fast. Following the end of World War II, the sanctified status of racism as a judicial principle and principle of social organization was undermined by a series of reforms.

Breaking ground for this postwar development was a series of events during the first half of the century. The first blow against white supremacy came with Japan's victory against Russia in the war of 1905–6, which proved to the colonized world that a white military power could be defeated. World War I provided the next major blow. Interpreted by both white and black racialist thinkers as a "white civil war," it cast doubt on the ideological claims that white culture was the highest possible form of civilization. Could a people who legitimated their world hegemony in terms of their superior racial qualities and Christian ethic but who then engaged in such a vicious war really be that advanced and refined?[11] Imperialist competition was an important factor in the war, and the European states enrolled large contingents of nonwhite soldiers in their clashing armies. An article in American pan-African ideologue W. E. B. Du Bois's paper The Crisis described the war in Congo under the headline: "Black soldiers fighting to protect European civilization from itself." Furthermore, when the United States entered the war in 1917, 370,000 black Americans were called to service. Returning black survivors expressed dissatisfaction with reverting to an inferior status at home after the victory in the "war for the emancipation of mankind." Black Americans had learned how to use arms, how to battle, and how to win, experiences that contributed to a revived black radicalism (Gardell 1996, 25). In addition, the period between the world wars saw a gradual retreat of scientific racism (Barkan 1996). Boasian anthropology, which stressed the basic equality of mental capacities between the races and explained man's differences in terms of environment and culture rather than biology, began gaining ground.[12] By midcentury, American society was ripe for change. Four primary factors influenced the sweeping reforms by which the status of racism was turned on its head in mainstream public America: (1) the Allied victory over the Axis in World War II; (2) the civil rights movement; (3) Cold War politics; and (4) progressing modernity.

U.S. intervention in World War II paved the way for the subsequent dismantling of American racism. The United States always goes to war with high moral overtones, so the Allied victory over the authoritarian, race-centered Axis regimes undermined possibilities for upholding domestic policies that might have resembled the practices of what had been defeated as evil incarnate in continental Europe. When the atrocities perpetrated by the German national socialist regime in the name of racial hygiene became public knowledge, scientific racism fell sharply into disrepute. In the aftermath of the Holocaust, anti-Semitic regulations that had excluded Jewish Americans from better universities, housing areas, and employment opportunities were expediently removed. The restrictions against Asian Americans acquiring U.S. citizenship were erased in the late 1940s, and a limited Asian immigration began.

These developments encouraged the civil rights movement, which led in 1954 to *Brown v. Board of Education*, in which the Supreme Court declared that segregated schools violated the Constitution. The next year, the Supreme Court ordered all schools to speed up their plans for desegregation (Marable 1984, 42). A milestone was passed when in 1956 federal troops were used for the first time in history to enforce a federal court order in favor of blacks, as U.S. paratroopers and soldiers from a federalized National Guard intervened to implement desegregation of a high school in Little Rock, Arkansas (Berry 1994, 140). In 1955, Mrs. Rosa Parks had been arrested for sitting in the whites-only section of a bus in Montgomery, Alabama, an event that spurred a successful boycott to press for desegregation of public transportation, a boycott headed by the young Martin Luther King Jr. The early 1960s saw thousands of desegregation civil disobedience protests in more than a hundred cities, with sit-ins, jail-ins, boycotts, marches, and freedom rides. The Civil Rights Act of 1964 outlawed Jim Crow in public accommodations of every kind in every state. The Voting Rights Act of 1965 removed restrictions for black voting, and Americans of all races were free to participate as voters in the democratic process. In 1968, the Supreme Court reinforced the Civil Rights Act of 1868, which banned public and private discrimination in the sale or rental of residential property. The same year saw the Fair Housing Act, which committed the federal government to implement nonracist housing. By 1968, most labor unions in the AFL-CIO had abandoned their discrimination against black membership, and some radical unions had even declared their commitment to antiracism and desegregation.

The civil rights movement's fight to end segregation was facilitated by Cold War politics (Dudziak 2000). Domestic racism seriously undermined U.S. credibility as the champion of the "free world" in the eyes of the world community. Soviet propaganda easily benefited from each lynching and racist policy, using these as recurrent themes in its presentation of communism as the true force of liberation. Harming foreign relations and thwarting Cold War goals in Africa, Asia, and Latin America made U.S. administrations from Truman to Johnson eager to polish their international image by making concessions to the civil rights movement's demands.

At the same time, the forces of modernity were advancing in American society. Originating as it had in premodern society, racism as a principle for exclusion and inclusion became increasingly irrelevant to the demands of modern society with its emphasis on rationality and instrumentality. A modern rational capitalist would, for example, find the racial identity of the producers and consumers completely irrelevant, for what matters to a rational capitalist is profit, not race or creed. Similarly, what matters in science is empirical knowledge, not the race of the scientist. As modernity developed, racism increasingly became an obstacle. The U.S. military was the first federal institution to integrate, as racial segregation proved functionally inefficient in combat. Morality was hardly an issue; rather, systemic demands pressed for reform. Accordingly, Jews, Asians, and blacks were gradually included in the functionally differentiated subsystems of economy, politics, science, and education as functionally irrelevant rules of exclusion were removed.

The fight against racial discrimination was extended also to immigration policy. The Immigration and Naturalization Act of 1965 abolished the eugenic national-origin quota principle in favor of a system that treats equally every country of origin. Together with later amendments and refugee laws, this marked a shift whereby nonwhite immigration increased dramatically. In the 1960 census, the population was 88.6 percent white. In the 2000 census, the number had dropped to 75.1 percent. If current trends in immigration and nativity remain, white Americans are estimated to lose their majority status somewhere between the year 2050 and 2060.[13] The population of the United States will then be truly multicultural, as no ethnic or racial group will constitute a majority. Reflecting on this fact, President Bill Clinton (2000) said in his State of the Union Address: "In a little more than 50 years, there will be no majority race in America. In a more interconnected world, this diversity can be our greatest strength. . . . We have members in this Congress from virtually every racial, ethnic, and religious background. And I think you would agree that America is stronger because of it." Not all white Americans agreed with Clinton.

Over the course of a few decades, constitutional racism vanished and public society made a decisive shift toward a multicultural America. That that did not end racism in American society should come as no surprise. An ideology that took hundreds of years to construct and long was legitimized as a reflection of the natural order can hardly be erased from society or popular mind by presidential decree. That an Indian Muslim may be a naturalized citizen does not mean that he is accepted as such by other "Americans." Muslims from India and Pakistan have, for instance, found a career niche in the low-budget motel circuit, provoking Anglo-Americans to compete with motel signs reading "American owned and operated." Neither has racial equality been implemented, as evidenced by the gap separating black and white America in terms of economic assets, social status, employment opportunities, education, and life-expectancy rates.[14] Americans have yet to see a reality in which their society provides "liberty and justice for all" irrespective of race, ethnicity, sex, or class. Nonetheless, at the very least, racism is no longer a respected pillar of American society, enforced by the Constitution, mainstream politicians, religious preachers, and the scientific community. Racism is no longer (at least officially) believed to be mandated by God or to be a reflection of natural order. No longer the epitome of a "good American," a racist today is considered a villain.

Explicit racism has been dethroned and is today an ideology of opposition, rather than a federal- and state-sanctioned ideology of dominion. Racist ideologues have been stumped, of course. Did the world go mad or was the course of events planned by some vicious cabal secretly maneuvering from behind the scenes?

A Divided White-Racist Opposition

Resistance against society's shift toward multiculturalism was never uniform and rapidly disintegrated as racism kept losing ground. A major division dates back to the mid-1950s when organized racist opposition to desegregation split into what can be termed "housebroken" and "noncivilized" camps. An example of the former, the first White Citizen's Council was formed in Indianola, Mississippi, in 1954. Organizing the "better element" of "decent" and "solid" southern racists, the movement spread rapidly, claiming a membership of 250,000 to 300,000 by 1957. Supported by a majority of southern whites, the councils aimed at overturning the Brown decision and defending the southern "way of life," that is, racial segregation. Attracting affluent and influential southerners, the councils stressed legal resistance and distanced themselves from the activities of "the lunatics" populating the then revived Ku Klux Klan(s). Klan members' purported insanity was not due to their racist ideology, as the councils considered racism sane, antiracism absurd. The disassociation was primarily an issue of tactics and public relations, not of worldview or aims. In any case, the councils held Klan members in contempt as irrational, violence prone, and lowbrow.

"Council members succeeded in convincing themselves and often their opponents that there were such a thing as 'good' racists and 'bad' racists," Klan historian Evelyn Rich (1988) notes. "The Councils had succeeded in convincing themselves and nearly everyone else, that a gas station attendant who went out and beat up a 'nigger' for belonging to the NAACP [National Association for the Advancement of Colored People] had nothing whatsoever in common with a factory owner who fired a 'colored' worker for the same crime" (1988, 28). While evidence of overlapping membership between the councils and the Klan indicates that at least some racial activists saw the distinction as complementary rather than contradictory, this does not obliterate the fact that a significant split among white racists did originate with the emergence of these two separate organizations.

Anxious to stay within the borders of acceptable public discourse, the housebroken segment of white racism began a process of semantic cryptification. Replacing the word race with culture, ideologues of this variety not infrequently found themselves elected to office, and some still have a discernible influence, although they have been unable to reverse American society to what it once was. Rephrased racism was part of the electoral campaigns of Presidents Reagan and Bush and has kept a foot firmly placed in scientific discourse as evidenced in The Bell Curve (1996), by Richard J. Herrnstein and Charles Murray, as well as in Harvard political scientist Samuel P. Huntington's dystopian arguments against a "multi-civilizational" United States in his Clash of Civilizations (1996).[15] While encoded racism evolved, explicitly racist elements of the culture fell into further fragmentation and radicalization as desperation grew after each defeat.

Trying to capitalize on white-racist resistance to desegregation was navy veteran and commercial artist George Lincoln Rockwell, who in 1959 founded the American Nazi Party (ANP). National socialism had never really appealed to Americans. Prior to World War II, it was primarily a product of state-sponsored programs for ideological export, programs created by the regimes of Mussolini and Hitler and targeted, with relatively poor results, at Italian and German immigrant communities.[16] In the 1930s, there were some 120 fascist/national socialist groups operating in the country, but most remained small and insignificant. Among the more notorious was William Dudley Pelley's Silver Shirts, which peaked with some 15,000 members.[17] Although Rockwell never got nearly that much support, he served as a forerunner whose legacy came to influence successive generations of Aryan activists.

Son of a famous vaudeville comedian, Rockwell was fond of staging theatrical media stunts. With swastika-adorned headquarters at "Hatemonger Hill," a Victorian mansion in Arlington, Virginia, across the river from Washington, D.C., Rockwell would parade his uniformed stormtroopers through the district to Capitol Mall. Surfing on a tide of white resistance to desegregation, Rockwell in 1961 sent a "Hate Bus" on tour through the Deep South, organized a national socialist counterdemonstration at the 1963 March on Washington, and matched King's 1966 open-housing march in Chicago with a white power march through the city's black section (Schmaltz 1999; Simonelli 1999).

Media coverage and popular outrage made the ANP look far more powerful than it ever was in reality.[18] Nationwide membership never exceeded 200, although an additional 2,000 to 3,000 names appeared on its mailing list (Simonelli 1999, 34–37). Running for governor of Virginia in 1965, Rockwell gained 5,730 votes, less than one percent of the total (Schmaltz 1999, 264). As noted by Frederick Simonelli (1999, 2), Rockwell's significance is instead found in the strategic legacy he bequeathed the white-racist counterculture. Rockwell in 1966 coined the battle cry "White Power" (Schmaltz 1999, 271), and ANP propaganda chief John Patler coined another classic: "The color of your skin is your uniform" (Rockwell 1967).[19] As indicated by these slogans, Rockwell initiated a national socialist shift away from the narrow Aryan/Germanic ultranationalist position of Hitler toward the pan–white race nationalist perspective that informs much of the current counterculture. At the time, Rockwell's willingness to include non-Nordic people such as the Polish, Russians, Greeks, Turks, and Italians as white provoked ideological resistance by Hitlerite Nordic purists

(Simonelli 1999, 101). However, given the era's construction of a monolithic white race in American race thinking, Rockwell was in line with the times, and his position would eventually secure the largest following.

In 1962, Rockwell cofounded the nationalist international World Union of National Socialists (WUNS) at a secret meeting in Cotswold Hills, England. Within months, Rockwell deposed its nominal leader, English national socialist veteran Colin Jordan, and embarked on an international career as WUNS commander (Schmaltz 1999, 131–65; Simonelli 1999, 81–95). By 1965, WUNS had grown to encompass chapters in nineteen countries, including two "nonwhite" nations, Lebanon and Japan (prefiguring the current trend of transracial racist networking).[20] Rockwell was, moreover, among the first Americans to seize on Holocaust denial as a national socialist comeback strategy. Already in 1959, Rockwell wrote a bogus story by a fabricated SS corporal relating how Jewish concentration camp inmates were used for vivisection experiments. He sold the story to the men's magazine Sir! and would thereafter cite publication of the article as proof that the Holocaust was a Jewish-/media-fabricated hoax (Schmaltz 1999, 49). In the years to come, Rockwell would establish himself as a vocal Holocaust denier, cooperating with other prominent "revisionists" such as Institute of Historical Review (IHR) founder Willis Carto. Despite his public Holocaust denial, Rockwell frequently alluded to it: in a letter to his supporters and sponsors, he urged them to focus on gaining power because "then, and only then can we exterminate the swarms of Jewish traitors in our gas chambers" (quoted in Simonelli 1999, 55); he designed propaganda items like soap wrappers marked *Judenschlaffe* (Schmaltz 1999, 80); and he had followers picketing the Israeli consulate in Los Angeles with signs reading, "What's Wrong with Gas Chambers for Traitors?" (ibid., 115).

Racial nationalism, transracial cooperation, and Holocaust denial later became standard tactics among revolutionary white racists. At the time, however, neither Rockwell nor the racist milieu had made the transition toward a revolutionary standpoint. Although calling himself a revolutionary, Rockwell insisted on loyalty to the Constitution and the laws of the United States and believed that the Jewish conspiracy for dominion could be stopped, as it was far from completion (Rockwell 1967). Yet, most racist organizations considered Rockwell's national socialism un-American and turned down any pleas for cooperation. The milieu was not yet ready. Rockwell decided to Americanize his party, which he symbolized by changing its name to the National Socialist White People's Party (NSWPP) and substituting the swastika with an American eagle. Rockwell designed an ambitious plan that would carry him to power by 1972. He would not live that long. In August 1967, Rockwell was shot to death at a strip mall parking lot in Arlington, Virginia, and his former propaganda chief John Patler was convicted for the assassination.[21] Among Rockwell's young admirers was David Duke whose failed efforts to revive the Ku Klux Klan would nonetheless contribute to the radicalization of white racism.

Konflicting Klan Koncepts

The world of Klandom had experienced both an influx of new members and an effort at Klan unity during the fight against the threat of desegregation. As the 1950s gave way to the 1960s, desegregation became more a reality than a threat, and the Klan had to face its complete failure to reverse the development. Overt racism was no longer in vogue, and young Americans seemed more attracted to the leftist counterculture of flower power than to an anachronistic hooded order that was clearly not in flow with the times. Prefiguring later developments, the almost-united Klan split into myriad competing dysfunctional factions, and combined membership dropped to an all-time low in the beginning of the 1970s. Reflecting on their dire prospects, new Klan leaders emerged with two opposing, publicity-oriented comeback strategies. David Duke (1997) aimed to present a "modern, intelligent and acceptable" image of the Klan, while his archenemy Bill Wilkinson cultivated the stereotypical image of an upfront racist order of terror.

As "national director" (Imperial Wizard) of the Knights of the Ku Klux Klan, Duke never wore a hood and often appeared in a tailored business suit rather than a Klan robe.[22] The Klan's racist message was carefully sanitized, with overtly vulgar, hateful, or condescending expressions excised in an effort to project a benign and polished image of both Duke and the Klan. To appeal to young Americans, Duke advertised on radio and television, opened the Klan to college students, and hired rock bands to perform at rallies. He began touring university campuses and appeared on hundreds of radio and TV talk shows, always careful to maintain the smooth veneer of a professional politician. Duke's analysis held that the rights of the Euro-American majority had gradually been eroded due to a willful "anti-white policy" and the "scientifically false" doctrine of racial equality (Duke 1997). White Americans were the "dispossessed majority," Duke concluded after a reading of Wilmot Robertson's book by that name (1981 [1972]).[23]

Capitalizing on white American xenophobic fear of losing their birthrights, Duke in 1977 staged a publicity stunt to present the Klan as an effective remedy for illegal immigration. Duke told the press that a thousand Klansmen were going to form a Klan border watch to assist the undermanned U.S. Border Patrol in apprehending illegal aliens crossing the Mexican border, from California to Texas. Although only eight Klansmen actually showed up, in three old sedans with hand-painted signs taped on the doors, the stunt was successful in producing widespread media coverage (Rich 1988, 228).[24] The first night, Duke told reporters that hundreds of Klansmen had assisted in arresting thousands of illegal aliens, while border patrol officials in fact reported a normal night with 400 arrested, slightly fewer than the night before (Bridges 1994, 67). Duke still continues to declare the Klan border watch a success, claiming that the flow of illegal aliens dropped dramatically for a few months as sensationalist media portraits of the dreaded hooded order scared off potential immigrants.[25] "I became well versed," Duke boasted, "in using the vast power of the media against itself in a form of political jujitsu pioneered by George Lincoln Rockwell" (1998, 591).

Duke's political ambitions led him to run for office, receiving 33 percent of the vote for the Louisiana state senate in 1975 and 26 percent in 1979, and he did eventually gain a seat after having undergone a public-relations cosmetic change (Rich 1988). In 1980, Duke came to the conclusion that the Klan was more a burden than an asset to his aspirations for personal power and his long-sought-after status as a "leader in the cause for our racial survival" (1997; 1998, 493). Duke left the leadership of the Knights of the Ku Klux Klan to his then second-in-command, Don Black (who is married to Duke's first wife, Chloê Hardin). In a letter of resignation sent to his Knights, Duke explained that the Klan had proved to be a dead end. "The bottom line is that we simply haven't grown fast enough and have not reached enough of the quality people we need," Duke complained. Many Klansmen, Duke lamented, had proved to be mere "weirdoes or nuts looking for publicity or violence."[26] Decisively, Duke decided to elect himself a new people. He invited those of "high caliber" among his old members to join his newly launched National Association for the Advancement of White People (NAAWP), a legal-political "white civil rights" organization to defend the rights of the country's Euro-American "silent majority" (Duke 1998, 607; Rich 1988, 282).

Among those who welcomed Duke's decision to step down was Bill Wilkinson, longtime antagonist and contender for the position of leading Klansman in America. Wilkinson broke off from Duke's Klan in 1975 to form his rival Invisible Empire of the Ku Klux Klan, and the two adversaries were locked up in a duel for the rest of the decade. If Duke represents an ideological radicalization of Klandom in his conclusion that whites already had lost their birthright privileges, Wilkinson's approach was more in the spirit of a traditional Klan defense of "good old America." Whereas Duke could spend hours detailing alleged Jewish-led conspiracies for the takeover of the United States and the world, Wilkinson speeches portrayed pre-*Brown* America as the good old days of harmonious race relations, leaving Jews completely out of the picture. If Duke dressed his radical critique in sophisticated terms, Wilkinson was content with being a redneck demonstrating his Knights's readiness for violent action. Despite their differences, the rivals sometimes adopted similar strategies such as allowing women full membership status and launching the Youth Klan Corps in response to black student unions in desegregated schools. Such mirror contests sometimes bordered on the comical, such as when both leaders simultaneously decided to establish Klan chapters in England, with both claiming to have arrived there first, gained the most publicity, and been most in trouble with the authorities. Like Duke, Wilkinson was fond of media stunts, and his display of weaponry and inflammatory rhetoric built his reputation while simultaneously undermining his rival's effort to construct an image of a polished Klan world.

During the latter part of the 1970s, Wilkinson's Invisible Empire engaged in a series of violent attacks against antiracist demonstrations in Mississippi, Alabama, and North Carolina. The most notorious was the lethal assault on a Communist Workers Party (CWP) anti-Klan march in Greensboro, North Carolina, on 3 November 1979. The event was the culmination of a series of confrontations between local national socialist and Klan activists and their communist and unionist opponents. After an incident in which two Confederate flags taken from outnumbered Klansmen were burned, a vengeance-obsessed United Racist Front coalesced, consisting of the Invisible Empire of the Ku Klux Klan, the American Nazi Party, and the Federated Knights of the Ku Klux Klan. When the CWP announced a "Death to the Klan" march, the united racists had found their opportunity to get even, and a national socialist–Klan caravan hit the demonstration. As videorecorded by a TV crew, Klansmen at the rear of the caravan calmly unloaded automatic shotguns from the trunk of a car and the shoot-out began, leaving five demonstrators dead and ten people, eight communists, one Klansman, and one reporter, wounded.[27] An all-white jury acquitted all the Klan and national socialist defendants in a verdict interpreted by Klansman Richard Savina as reflecting community support for the Knights fighting for "one-hundred percent Americanism" to "save this country from the Communists, niggers, and Jews" (quoted in Rich 1988, 250).[28] When another all-white jury reached the same conclusion in a second trial in which nine Klansmen were charged with civil rights violations, the world of Klandom was ecstatic.[29]

Referring to the event as "a glorious day," defendant Glenn Miller's only regret was "that we didn't kill more Communists" (quoted in Rich 1988, 251).

Known as "88 seconds in Greensboro," the attack video is today part of underground radical right memorabilia with the footage run again and again for new generations of activists. "H" is the eighth letter of the alphabet, so "88" signifies "Heil Hitler" in the cipher talk popular in the radical right milieu. The Klan's adoption of national socialist symbolism is a clear indication of the radicalization of parts of the hooded order. Compared with the Invisible Empire, Duke's Knights were much less involved with violent direct action, and Duke held Wilkinson in contempt as an unsophisticated thug, the epitome of what a Klansman should *not* be to ensure success. Wilkinson held Duke in matching low regard as a blank-bullet armchair patriot, whose writing for the intelligentsia and appearances on tea-and-crumpet talk shows were deemed fruitless vanity, while the racial cause only could be furthered by hard-hitting action. Obviously, racist activists were more attracted to Wilkinson's call for action, and despite Duke's claim that his Klan "grew dramatically" in numbers (1998, 605), he lost the tug-of-war with Wilkinson's Invisible Empire. Wilkinson doubled his membership base to an estimated 2,500, as compared to the estimated 1,500 members of Duke's "intelligent" order, and thus passed the Confederate Knights as the second largest Klan, becoming second only to Shelton's United Klans of America (UKA) (Rich 1988, 257).[30] Overall, though, as indicated by such insignificant numbers, the hooded order had lost dramatically its appeal. The combined world of Klandom was in 1979 populated by an estimated 9,000 to 10,500 members nationwide.

Illustrating the fractious realities of contemporary Klandom, the Duke-Wilkinson race ended in double collapse. Wilkinson crowned his eclipse over Duke with yet another publicity stunt, effectively portraying his arch-rival as a greedy traitor of his oath-bonded knights. According to Wilkinson, Duke had called him in January 1980, offering to sell him Duke's classified Knights of the Ku Klux Klan (KKKK) membership list for $35,000. Wilkinson agreed and arranged to meet with Duke to close the deal. Cunningly, Wilkinson also informed the media, installing reporters with hidden recorders at the place of the secret meeting (Bridges 1994, 84).[31] Wilkinson's day of triumph proved brief, however. Less than a year later, journalist Jerry Thompson published documents obtained through the Freedom of Information Act that detailed Wilkinson as a longtime FBI informant. According to Thompson, Wilkinson had worked as an FBI informant even when a member of Duke's Knights and had continued in this role while acting as Imperial Wizard of the violence-prone Invisible Empire

(Rich 1988, 283). The story was recycled with malicious pleasure in the press of his Klan rivals. With shortsighted satisfaction, Duke revealed to Klan researcher Evelyn Rich that he had long suspected Wilkinson to be an informant, a claim that backfired in raising the question of how Duke could leave his KKKK membership list to a suspected FBI informant (ibid., 284).[32]

FBI involvement with internal Klandom intrigues dates back to the 1960s. FBI documents and congressional testimony revealed that in 1965 no less than one-fifth of the sum total of Klan members nationwide in fact were FBI informants. During this time, FBI informants held top leadership positions in seven of the then fourteen nationwide Klan organizations and headed at least one state organization. Setting Klan leaders at each other's throats, the FBI was fond of "bad-jacketing" noninformant Klan leaders by circulating rumors that they were federal infiltrators (Sims 1996, 106–9).[33] The FBI had in addition orchestrated the creation of rival Klan organizations, such as Reverend George F. Dorsett's federally funded Confederate Knights of the Ku Klux Klan, and had launched at least one fictitious Klan organization to sow dissention and disrupt the world of Klandom.[34] The FBI counterintelligence activities contributed to the construction of a culture of paranoia, which is still a dominant feature within the radical racist underground scene.

Radicalization Continued

During the 1980s, Wilkinson's militant approach merged with Duke's theoretical analysis in the formation of a Klan ideology that was self-consciously revolutionary for the first time in its post-Reconstruction history. Many Klan members began to realize that the "good old America" they were defending did not exist and would never become reality without a violent overthrow of the administration in Washington, D.C., which they perceived to be run by enemies of the white race. Klan thinking thus opened itself up for merger with national socialism, holocaust denial, and the racist recasting of Christianity known as Christian Identity, a development that was "limited to certain Klan factions and [was] not applicable to the entire Klan movement, which for the first time became truly ideologically as well as physically fragmented" (Rich 1988, 290, 334). Although seeds and elements of these tendencies toward national socialism and Christian Identity had long been present within Klandom, they now emerged not as flickering undercurrents but as integral, driving forces behind Klan thinking, a process that deeply divided the hooded order into reactionary and revolutionary conglomerates.

The new revolutionary perspective elevated Jews to a key position in a presumed global conspiracy against the white race. The previously free white American people had allegedly been subjugated to their racial enemies in the Zionist Occupation Government (ZOG), a secret power center exercising control through marionettes in federal and corporate America. ZOG discourse had practical consequences on strategies developed within those parts of Klandom that embraced it. In two separate 1983 texts Klan ideologues Robert Miles and Louis Beam concluded that an effective and victorious model of resistance against an occupying government had been created by the original Klan, whose underground activities helped defeat military Yankee rule in the occupied South during the Reconstruction era. Both Miles and Beam saw the Klan as a serious revolutionary force, a means to the end of implementing the palingenetic mythos of a spiritual rebirth of the Aryan Race. This was a far cry from Klan traditionalists like UKA Imperial Wizard Robert Shelton, to whom the Klan was more an end in itself, a social and ritualistic fraternity of Americanism. Miles, a UKA Grand Dragon and Imperial Kludd (National Chaplain), argued that the Klan needed to revert to its origin as a military underground operating in "enemy controlled territory." [35] No longer could the Klan be content with being "merely television oriented," nor could it "return to its role supporting local police, because the local police, now totally federalized, no longer support[ed] its goals" (1983, 4). All references of loyalty to the U.S. Constitution, to the government of the United States of America, and to the officers of the law must unconditionally be dropped from the new Klan oath, he argued. "One cannot be loyal to a government which is not loyal to its own people," Miles stated. "When the Racial Nation exists, then such references merit consideration. As it stands today, such references only serve the foe in courts controlled by the foe" (ibid., 28).

Grand Dragon emeritus Beam argued along similar lines in his *Essays of a Klansman*.[36] America, he holds, is "moving irresistibly toward internal armed conflict between those who fight for their heritage and those who seek to destroy it. The enemy has managed to capture the government. So, for the third time in this nation's history, the government has become the enemy of the people." Beam modeled his envisioned military resistance on the minutemen of the American Revolution and on the first Reconstruction-era Klan, both of which he characterizes as decentralized cadres of covert guerilla bands that fought for independence from oppressive governments. "The American Revolution was anything but a broad based popular uprising of a dissatisfied people," Beam notes. "Rather, it was a very unpopular rebellion of a politically radical minority" (78). As in the days of the American Revolution, the masses of today cannot "read the footprints of tyranny or where they lead" (84). Undoubtedly, Beam concludes, the "vast majority of the White Race will continue to oppose the Klan and any other racial movement" (17). Instead of waiting in vain for the fantasy of a broad-based racial movement to materialize, the illuminated few must form independent underground cells and utilize the means of widespread violent terror and intimidation if the racial enemies in the federal government are ever to be defeated. The sole aim, he ventures, must be to establish a "homeland for the White Aryan Race" (viii) and purge North America from every "non-White person, idea and influence. . . . This continent will be white or it will not be at all" (50).

Two other events in the early 1980s would contribute greatly to the process of Klan radicalization: the Gordon Kahl incident and the activity of the Brüders Schweigen group. Gordon Kahl was an Identity Christian tax resister who in 1983 killed two police officers in a shoot-out, then managed to evade the police during a four-month long, widely publicized manhunt before he was tracked down and killed. The same year saw the formation of the Brüders Schweigen (Silent Brotherhood), popularly known as the Order, a name taken from the race-war novel *Turner Diaries* by National Alliance leader William Pierce. Founded by Odinist Robert J. Mathews, the Brüders was an Aryan guerilla group whose short but intense activities would serve as a model of underground militancy and provide the milieu with one of its most important martyrs following the 1984 death of its founder. Imprisoned members of the Order have achieved legendary status among Aryan revolutionaries globally. Many of these "prisoners of war," including influential Odinist ideologue David Lane, now adhere to Odinist tenets.

Radicalization accelerated following the 1989 fall of the Berlin Wall and the subsequent disintegration of the Soviet Union. With the removal of communism as a "distracting foe," the federal administration of the United States emerged as the primary locus of evil for an increasing number of radical racist activists in the 1990s. Negative opinion of federal authority was facilitated by two lethal sieges, each believed to confirm the autocratic ways of federal tyranny: Ruby Ridge and Waco.

Signs of Federal Monstrosity, Part One: Ruby Ridge

Former Green Beret Randy Weaver in 1983 moved his family from their native Iowa to the mountainous woodlands of Ruby Ridge in northern Idaho. Being Identity Christians, the Weavers occasionally visited Aryan Nations in nearby

Hayden Lake, although they never joined Butler's Church of Jesus Christ, Christian. In 1988, Randy Weaver ran for sheriff of Boundary County, promising to restore power to the local people whom he would protect from the federal government. He received only 10 percent of the vote. At the 1989 Aryan World Congress at Aryan Nations, undercover federal informant and biker Kenneth Fadeley (alias Gus Magisono) talked Weaver into selling two sawed-off shotguns.[37] The following year, Weaver was approached by ATF agents who told him that they had the gun deal on tape and offered to drop the charges if he would agree to spy on Aryan Nations. When Weaver refused to collaborate, he was indicted on federal firearms charges. His court appearance was set for 20 February 1991, although the note Weaver received from his probation officer incorrectly stated the date as 20 March. Although the officer confessed his mistake, Weaver was on 14 March declared a federal fugitive, and a warrant was issued for his arrest.

Most likely, Weaver would not have appeared in court even had he been given the proper date. In a letter to law enforcement authorities dated 5 January, the Weavers declared that the righteous "Messiah of Saxon Israel" had told them to "stay separated on the mountain and not leave." "You are servants of lawlessness," the letter continued, "on the side of the 'One World Beastly Government'" and should "repent, for the Kingdom of Yahweh is near at hand" (quoted in Bock 1996, 54). In another letter, sent to Maurice Ellsworth, the U.S. attorney for Idaho, the Weavers reiterated that they would never "bow down to your evil commandments" and, quoting Order founder Bob Mathews, warned in closing, "War is upon the land. The tyrant's blood will flow" (quoted in Dobratz and Shanks-Meile 1997, 201). While Weaver was warranted only for a misdemeanor, the tone of the letters might have provoked the authorities to step up the action.

Enlisting the help of a neighboring family and renting a ski resort as headquarters, the ATF began an eighteen-month surveillance operation. The Weaver family meantime kept their vow of separation, staying on the land, gardening, hunting, and birthing yet another child, Elisheba. On 21 August 1992, a team of six marshals from the SWAT-like Special Operations Group ventured onto the Weaver property. Armed with submachine guns and dressed in camouflage with black ski masks and body armor, they divided into two groups. Spotting Randy Weaver, his thirteen-year-old son, Samuel, and Kevin Harris, a resident friend of the family, in the garden, the forward team of marshals threw some pebbles from their hideout to see if they could get the attention of Striker, Sam's golden Labrador. Striker barked and began chasing the marshals, who retreated to a thick stand of woods. Thinking the disturbance might be a deer, Weaver ran down the trail while Sammy and Harris followed Striker along the logging road, which led them right into the arms of the marshals.

What happened next is controversial. Deputies Larry Cooper and Art Roderick testified that their colleague William Degan identified himself as a U.S. marshal and was shot by Harris. Cooper returned fire at Harris while Roderick shot the dog. Neither admitted shooting at Samuel. According to Harris, he and Samuel ran into camouflaged men who did not identify themselves. After one of them shot the dog, Samuel returned fire and was in turn shot in his right arm. Harris then shot to defend Samuel, possibly killing Degan, and yelled at Samuel to run back home. Meanwhile, Weaver, who in his own words realized that they had run into a "ZOG/New World Order ambush," fired in the air, shouting to Samuel to return home. As the boy tried to escape, he was shot in the back. Weaver and his wife, Vicki, retrieved Samuel's body, placing it a guest shed close to the cabin, and returned inside.

Federal officials then evacuated the residents of a five-mile area surrounding the Weaver cabin. The FBI mobilized its Hostage Rescue Team while the Idaho governor declared a state of emergency and called in the National Guard. Soon, hundreds of specially trained agents descended on the scene, bringing in military equipment, including armored vehicles, Humvees, and helicopters of Desert Storm fame, and the siege had begun. At 6 A.M. the next morning, Harris, Weaver, and daughter Sara ventured out of the cabin to see Sam's body in the shed. Without warning, FBI sniper Lon Horiuchi fired at Randy, hitting his arm. Hearing the shot, Vicki, carrying baby Elisheba, opened the kitchen door, yelling at her family to return inside. Horiuchi fired a bullet that went into her temple, through her mouth, tongue, and jawbones, severed her carotid artery, then hit Harris in the chest. Vicki fell bleeding on her knees and died within minutes, still holding her baby in her arms.

The standoff lasted for nine more days. Harris and Weaver were badly injured. Sixteen-year-old Sara and her ten-year-old sister, Rachel, nurtured ten-month-old Elisheba while their mother lay dead with half her face blown away. The federal camp grew to some four hundred agents. Local residents and friends of the Weavers assembled at the roadblock to protest the federal "baby killers." "Patriots," national socialist skinheads, Identity Christians, and Aryan revolutionaries from Oregon, Washington, Utah, Montana, and Nevada joined their ranks. The Red Cross set up a disaster action unit camp. Reporters and TV crews crammed onto the scene. Populist patriot James "Bo" Gritz came together with Pastor Dave Barley of the Identity Christian America's Promise Ministries of Sandpoint, Idaho, former Arizona state senator Jerry Gillespie, and retired police officer and conspiracy peddler Jack McLamb.

At the time, former Green Beret colonel and far-right Christian populist Gritz was running for president on the Populist Party ticket, and his slogan "God, Guns, and Gritz" was posted throughout the rural Northwest. (Gritz currently seeks to head a second American revolution. With a following mainly based in the patriot and militia milieus, Gritz is generally rejected as a federal agent or a self-boosting clown among radical racists.) He argued that as a former Green Beret commander and known Christian patriot he was uniquely suited to negotiate with Weaver. Finding the federal authorities reluctant to let him try, Gritz issued a "citizen arrest" of the commanding officers, FBI director William Sessions and Governor Cecil Andrus of Idaho. Gritz's note was brought to the attention of former Green Beret Jack Cluff, one of the U.S. marshals in charge of the Weaver case, who had served under Gritz's command in Vietnam. Ironically, then, the standoff at Ruby Ridge involved a triangulated drama between three Green Beret veterans, each of whom had adopted fundamentally different perceptions of evil when they brought their warrior ethic home.[38]

Together with Jacky Brown, Vicki's best friend, Gritz in four days managed to talk Harris and the Weavers into coming out, promising Randy that famous defense attorney Gerry Spence would represent him in court. Spence had not lost a criminal case since 1969 and would not lose this one either. In July 1993 Randy Weaver was acquitted on all charges except failure to show up in court. Kevin Harris was not convicted of anything. In August 1995, the U.S. Justice Department settled a civil suit out of court with the Weaver family, awarding them $3.1 million. In October of the same year, Louis J. Freeh, then the new director of the FBI, admitted that "law enforcement overreacted at Ruby Ridge." The employed "rules of engagement" stating that any armed adult observed in the compound "can and should" be subject to "deadly force" even "prior to a surrender announcement" was found to be "contrary to law and FBI policy."[39] Among revolutionary racists, the tragedy at Ruby Ridge is frequently recounted to illustrate the monstrosity of a federal government that has turned into an enemy of the people.

Ruby Ridge became a rallying point for "concerned citizens" and, together with the subsequent disaster in Waco, Texas, sparked the militia movement. In October 1992, some 250 people met in Naples, Idaho, to form the United Citizens for Justice. Among those represented were conspiracy-believing Eva Vail of the Concerned Citizens of Idaho and Randy Trochman, cofounder of the Militia of Montana. The atrocity at Ruby Ridge showed, it was argued, that the federal administration had transmogrified into a bloodthirsty, power-drunk monster that would stop at nothing to realize its aim of establishing a "One World Satanic dictatorship" (Vail 1996). Concerned citizens, it followed, must therefore join together in defense of American values and prevent anything like Ruby Ridge from ever happening again.[40]

Identity Christian minister Pete Peters of Scriptures for America organized another gathering, at Estes Park, Colorado, 23–25 October 1992, drawing some 160 spokespersons from the patriot and revolutionary racist milieus.[41] Galvanized by Ruby Ridge, the meeting managed to tacitly unite disparate and otherwise infighting factions in a common front against the federal government and the New World Order. "We will not yield this country to the forces of darkness, oppression and tyranny," vowed Beam, whose "leaderless resistance" strategy was unanimously endorsed (quoted in Dees and Corcoran 1996, 2, 207). To avoid infiltration, resistance was to be tactically divided into an overt propaganda arm consisting of already known revolutionaries who would stay within the confines of the law, and a military underground of autonomous "phantom cells" consisting of small groups or lone wolfs without any links to a central command. This strategy, according to the FBI (1999, 4), has been adopted by an "overwhelming majority of extremist groups." Somewhat prematurely termed a "watershed for the racist right" by antiracist attorney and activist Morris Dees (1996) of the Southern Poverty Law Center, the "Rocky Mountain Rendezvous" was an important impetus in the subsequent formation of various militias around the country. If the Estes Park conference ignited the rise of the militias, the spark that was Ruby Ridge was fanned into flames by the federal onslaught at Mt. Carmel, a sectarian Christian communal settlement outside of Waco, Texas, just a few months later.

Signs of Federal Monstrosity, Part Two: Waco

Mount Carmel was headquarters for David Koresh (born Vernon Howell, 1959) and his Students of the Seven Seals, a sectarian offshoot of the Branch Davidian Seventh-Day Adventist Association, itself a sectarian offshoot of a sectarian offshoot of Seventh-Day Adventism (SDA).[42] Koresh taught that the fall of Adam marked the beginning of a process of degeneration, separating man more and more from his original divine nature as an angelic being. Koresh saw himself as the Christ of our age, sent here to select a small, elite worthy of angelomorphosis and inaugurate the destruction of Babylon. To support him, the twenty-four elders of the Revelations had chosen to descend to Earth, embodied in the children of Koresh who, according to follower Livingstone Fagan, like Koresh, were born with God's DNA.[43] In 1989, Koresh began to instruct his male followers to observe celibacy while he fulfilled his mission by scattering his seed. All together, Koresh fathered seventeen children (with a selection of female followers, some of whom were already wed) to assist him in judging the nations. Despite their apocalyptic expectations, the reclusive commune of religious dissidents reportedly lived a quiet life with Bible studies, a warm atmosphere, harmonious children, and a quite relaxed Messiah who preferred singing the gospel, took an occasional beer, reintroduced meat on the menu, and took up the habit of smoking.

The federal tornado that was to consume the settlement on the Texas plains grew out of accusations from a disgruntled former associate and (unfounded) reports that the group was stockpiling illegal weapons and producing amphetamines.[44] The ATF directorate appears to have seized the opportunity to remove the taint Ruby Ridge had left on the bureau's image, as well as to further its prospects in the then upcoming congressional budget hearings. The ATF hired public information officers to promote the agency in good light, and it was decided that the raid (nicknamed "ShowTime") and its training sessions were to be filmed in the hopes of producing "a dynamic entry" at the congressional hearings.

On D-Day, forward observers had already taken up sniper positions around Mt. Carmel as the mile-long, eighty-vehicle-strong convoy headed north on I-35. The raid was to be a concerted operation, taking the "cultists" by surprise. While a contingent of fifty men was to burst out of cattle trailers in a run at the front door, two other groups were to scale the roof from the east, going for the second floor to secure a presumed armory and to hit Koresh's sleeping quarters. When plans met reality, the result was catastrophic. In retrospect, many wondered why the ATF did not try a less dramatic plan first, like having agents knock at the door and ask Koresh to come with them, or perhaps to arrest him when he came to his favorite restaurant in town. Many also wondered why the planners did not listen to advisors who suggested that there might be a better chance of taking the compound by surprise by starting the operation at night or at dawn instead of at 10 A.M.

Far worse, though, was that no one at the command center ordered the operation aborted, even after they had learned that Koresh knew about the coming assault.[45] Without the element of surprise, the plan was bound to fail. The ATF front men came under return fire from Mt. Carmel almost as soon as they had exited the trailers and started shooting. The two roof units fared badly. The first group came under fire as soon as they broke the glass of the window, and three agents were hit in the ensuing exchange of fire. The second commando unit cleared the window, threw in a flash-bang, and entered the room, only to be caught in crossfire with bullets coming through a wall, the floor, and the hallway.

Operation ShowTime thus turned into chaos, and intense rounds of gunfire exchange ended up lasting for an hour, largely due to the fact that the raiders lacked means of communicating with the raided. ATF commanders were later criticized for having failed to bring cellular telephones or even Mt. Carmel's number with them. Within minutes after the shoot-out had started, a Mt. Carmel resident dialed 911, yelling that they were under attack from seventy-five men circling their house shooting at them and that they had women and children inside. Lieutenant Larry Lynch, who took the emergency call, had to go through a policeman who then contacted the ATF, instructing them to call him to establish at least an indirect line of communication between the parties in conflict. After a couple of hours, ShowTime ended in a cease-fire. Four agents and six Mt. Carmel residents were dead, and a fifty-day siege that would last until 19 April had commenced.

The FBI was called in and assumed command on 1 March. As its hostage rescue team had come away from Ruby Ridge looking like trigger-happy gunslingers, the bureau decided to try, at least initially, a different approach. Koresh was allowed to explain his creed to the negotiators, who unfortunately did not pay much attention to the apocalyptic mindset of the modern Christ and did not call in theologians or sociologists of religion to assist them. During the initial five days of negotiations and theological expositions, seventeen children and two adults left Mt. Carmel. However, when a mass exit, arranged to occur after Koresh had been allowed an hour on national radio, was aborted by God's counter-order, the agents in charge sourly concluded that Koresh was a dangerous fanatic who held his flock hostage. Electricity, water supplies, and telephone lines were cut off to isolate the besieged. Banks of stadium lights were erected around Mt. Carmel and turned on twenty-four hours a day. A loudspeaker sound system was installed and for six weeks blared noise and music "specifically selected," the FBI spokesman told the press, "for its irritation ability" (Reavis 1995, 250). Thus blasted were the sounds of dying rabbits, dental drills, seagulls, bagpipes, an off-the-hook telephone, chanting Tibetan Buddhist monks, and music by Nancy Sinatra. Not only did such sound terror mentally exhaust the Mt. Carmel residents but it also sent the cattle of a nearby farmer into a frenzied stampede, running down fences trying to escape.

The level of irritation increased on both sides and might explain in part why the agents ignored Koresh when he said that God had allowed him to come out after he had composed a document detailing the message of the Seven Seals. Disregarding the offer as yet another stalling technique, the agents in command decided that it was time for action, clearing plans for a tear-gas assault with U.S. attorney general Janet Reno. At 6 A.M. on Monday, 19 April, tanks began punching holes in Mt. Carmel to inject CS gas into the building, a highly effective tear gas that was banned for use against foreign enemies by a Geneva Convention agreement in 1969. When residents opened fire at the tanks, a fleet of four military combat tanks took over, tearing down walls and pumping in rounds of football-sized canisters of CS suspended in methylene chloride, a petroleum derivative that in larger volumes form flammable vapor-air mixtures. In the meantime, the loudspeakers exclaimed messages such as "Vernon is finished. He's no longer the Messiah," which were mixed with the Orwellian message "This is not an assault. This is not an assault." Ramming into Mt. Carmel, the tanks demolished stairways and blocked underground passages, entrapping groups of residents who tried to get out as the building went ablaze after more than five hours of intensive gassing.[46] Mt. Carmel was reduced to ashes in half an hour, and an enthused agent hoisted the ATF flag over the ruins. Seventy-four members of the Branch Davidian died in the flames, including David Koresh and seventeen children. Eight survivors received a total of 240 years in prison for carrying firearms and aiding in the manslaughter of the four agents killed, and were in addition sentenced to pay $1.2 million in restitution to the ATF and FBI.[47]

The outcome caused an outrage in many quarters, the Aryan underground included, however strange it might seem that racist activists would throw their support behind Koresh. The Branch Davidian Students of the Seven Seals was largely an apolitical, prophecy-believing, Christian fundamentalist, pre-millenarian sect that included people of all races and many nations among its devoted members. During the siege, the commune flew banners declaring their solidarity with Rodney King, and like most evangelical Americans, Koresh and his flock supported Israel, something an Aryan radical would never do. Koresh's involvement with the gun-show trade, though, had introduced him to the worldviews of the revolutionary racist milieu. He subscribed to the populist weekly *Spotlight* and had adopted a belief in a Masonic-Satanic globalist cabal working for the Antichrist through front organizations such as the government of the United States and the Tri-Lateral Commission. Thus, when activists of the radical right began expressing their solidarity with the besieged, a sort of common ground was discovered, even beyond the enemy-of-my-enemy logic that propelled much of the sympathy.[48] The televised military action against the reclusive commune on the Texas prairie was interpreted as yet another demonstration of the totalitarian ambitions of the New World Order, aimed at leveling all opposition.

Waco rapidly became a rallying cry across a spectrum of radical underground movements, from the emergent militia milieu to the more radical scene of Aryan revolutionaries. Indianapolis attorney Linda Thompson, self-proclaimed adjutant general of the Unorganized Militia of the U.S.A., produced the video documentary *Waco: The Big Lie*, which reached an estimated audience of several hundred thousand viewers nationwide. The documentary's relatively large circulation provoked the FBI to rebut her charges in detail, which paved the way for the sequel *Waco: The Big Lie, Part II*. In another successful publicity stunt, Thompson also called for an armed march on Washington on 19 September 1994 (later aborted), the purpose of the march being to arrest on charge of treason every congressman if Congress did not, among other things, convene a full inquiry into the events at Waco.

Cyber museums and homepages, featuring photos of the siege and relevant articles, have kept the public updated on Waco, in an effort to prevent people from forgetting. Among the more professional sites are the Virginia-based *Waco Holocaust Electronic Museum*, founded on 19 April 1996 by Carol A. Valentine, and *Waco Never Again*, managed by Mark Swett.[49] Patriot singer Carl Klang's "It's Dangerous (To Be Right When the Government Is Wrong)" and "17 Little Children" quickly became classics, causing teary eyes for many a militia activist at survivalist gatherings and gun shows. Bumper stickers like "Is Your Church ATF Approved?" and "Remember Waco: You Are Next" mixed in with standard militia appeals to defend the right to bear arms: "Fear the Government that Fear Your Guns" and "Ban Guns. Make the Streets Safe for a Government Takeover." Pictures of tanks, military helicopters, armed federal snipers, smiling children now dead, the burning church, death scenes, incinerated skeletons, and the ATF banner flying triumphantly over the smoking ruins were widely circulated lest "concerned citizens" should forget who the enemy was. In short, the Waco tragedy was used as evidence to support the thesis that traitors had gained control of the administration and would stop at nothing to subjugate completely the once-free Americans. The so-called Waco Holocaust continues to be commemorated at yearly gatherings and concerts and, among militant racists, is often attached to the yearly celebrations of Hitler's birthday on 20 April.

Among radical Aryans, 19 April is also remembered as the day when Identity Christian and "prisoner of war" Richard Snell was executed for killing a pawnshop owner he erroneously thought was Jewish and a black Arkansas state trooper during a routine stop. Linked with Identity communes such as James Ellison's (now-defunct) Zarephath-Horeb and Robert Millar's Elohim City, Snell believed himself acting on a mission of the Aryan Christ, and his final words delivered a stark warning to the authorities of God's coming retribution. Snell was executed on 19 April 1995. On that same day, a huge homemade bomb devastated the Alfred P. Murrah Federal Building in Oklahoma City. With a death toll of 168, the Oklahoma City bomb was, at the time, the worst paramilitary terror attack ever to have occurred in the United States. Convicted perpetrators Timothy McVeigh and Terry Nichols were loosely tied to the Michigan Militia and to Elohim City.

Although many racist activists believe that McVeigh and/or Nichols were innocent or mind-controlled instruments used by a federal government to blow up the federal building to demonize the righteous militias, evidence suggests that they were instead products of the frustrated subcultures of armed patriots and radical racists. The act itself reveals the sense of urgency and desperation that still pervades the scene, and the date was as significant as the choice of target. The building houses an agency headquarters and has long occupied a key role in various conspiracy theories circulating in the cultural underground. Oklahoma City is thought to be the site of concentration camps and/or of transfer terminals for imprisoned patriots and/or of four giant crematoria with the capacity to incinerate 3,000 freedom-loving white Americans a day, all these institutions allegedly masterminded from the targeted federal building.[50] Paradoxically, while the ashes of Waco propelled further radicalization of the scene, it might also have helped to mainstream some of its primary beliefs and actors. Post-Waco surveys showed that the public's trust in the federal administration had reached an all-time low. According to a 1995 USA Today/CNN Gallup poll, 39 percent of the respondents agreed with the statement "the federal government has become so large and powerful [that] it poses an immediate threat to the rights and freedoms of ordinary citizens." Another survey revealed that a mere 6 percent of the respondents "trust[ed] the federal government a lot."[51] To radical racist attorneys Kirk Lyons and Neil H. Payne, Waco offered an unexpected opportunity for moving into mainstream circles.

Born 1956 to an air force officer, Lyons styles himself a Victorian, "unreconstructed" Confederate, sporting red suspenders and other retro accessories from pre-*Brown* America. Lyons (1997) and Payne (1997) define themselves as "staunch Anglicans," but underscore that "the Anglican Church is and always has been an Identity Church." Their belief in whites as the Adamic race and the people of the covenant was demonstrated in a ceremony at the Aryan Nations in 1990. Walking through rows of uniformed men with arms raised in national socialist salute, Lyons and Neil married two sisters of imprisoned Order member David Tate. Pastor Butler of the Church of Jesus Christ, Christian, performed the service that Payne calls the "most famous wedding the FBI ever has recorded." Having started out as a "conservative patriot," Lyons now calls himself a "revolutionary," identifying "the government [as] the great evil. It's Babylon and it needs to go away." Lyons claims to be unable to "see a nickel worth of difference between this government and the Soviet Union," characterizing the United States as "a socialistic police state." Alleging that "advocacy for white survival [is considered] a greater crime than child molesting, rape and murder," Lyons says he realized that "Beam and Butler and people like that needed an advocate and needed one bad," unless they wanted to end up in the "federal gulags" (1997).

Acting as defense attorney for Louis Beam at the 1987 Forth Smith sedition trial, Lyons established the Patriot's Defense Foundation, which evolved into the CAUSE Foundation in January 1992. "CAUSE Foundation has a global, international perspective as opposed to a regional or national perspective," Lyons (1997) clarifies. "Everywhere where Western legal traditions prevail, people are losing rights . . . the governments are becoming more repressive and less free . . . and so to me, it needs an approach from an international perspective. And that's why we chose the CAUSE Foundation: Canada, Australia, United States, South Africa, and Europe, to give it an international perspective. Still the focus is on the United States as the CAUSE Foundation believes that the United States government is the greatest threat to civil liberties in the world today."

With headquarters in the idyllic Black Mountains of the North Carolina Appalachians, CAUSE aims to be something of a radical-right counterforce to the Southern Poverty Law Center (SPLC), "telling the truth about the same groups and people that the SPLC lies about." Organized as a legal network of about a hundred like-minded lawyers in the United States and an additional twenty in Europe and Australia, as of 1997, CAUSE claims to be a "civil rights organization." Its purpose is to defend activists who dare to "defend their people" and are "demonized" by the "professional haters" who are "afflicted by this mental disease of liberalism" (*Lyons* 1997).[52] In addition to defending Louis Beam,

Lyons represented Identity Christian militant James Wickstrom; White Patriot Party member Douglas Sheets, who was charged with murdering five homosexuals in a porn bookstore in Sheridan, North Carolina; Fred A. Leuchter, a self-styled "execution engineer" who with phony credentials was brought in by Ernst Zündel as an expert witness in a much-publicized trial staged to prove that the Holocaust never happened; and Andreas Carl Strassmeir, an illegal alien from Germany serving as chief of security at Elohim City when he surfaced during the Oklahoma City bombing investigation. Lyons also appeared as "expert witness" for the defense in a trial against White Aryan Resistance leader Tom Metzger.

With the advent of Waco, CAUSE's role as a marginalized law firm defending radical Aryan activists changed dramatically, at least in the short run. Lyons helped provide David Koresh with top attorney Dick DeGuerin and filed suit against the "perpetrators of the heinous Waco tragedy" on behalf of twenty-three incinerated Students of the Seven Seals, five dead children, and three survivors ("Special Report on Waco" n.d.). Suddenly, Lyons was welcome everywhere, he says, beaming with contentment. "I can walk into the National Organization of Women, I can walk into the Democratic Party, I can just about walk in anywhere." Waco demonstrated that "the government now [is] willing to blow nursing mothers away and incinerate people in church buildings," which, finally, "did strike a chord" among the people, "and that," Lyons mused, "is what pretty much propelled us into the mainstream. Four, five years ago, I would probably have admitted with you that probably I'm outside the mainstream. Right now, we are very mainstream. Because it's very easy: are you in favor of your government surrounding people and killing them? If you're in favor of that, then I am not on your side. If you're not in favor of that, then I am with you" (Lyons 1997).

CHAPTER TWO

The Smorgasbord of the Revolutionary

White-Racist Counterculture

Originating as a conservative opposition to desegregation and the multicultural redefinition of the American nation in the 1950s and 1960s, organized white racism passed through a transitory reactionary phase to adopt an increasingly revolutionary position during the 1980s and 1990s. Rarely in agreement on much else, revolutionary ideologues typically denounce the conservative right wing as part of the problem, blinded by their patriotism to the "fact" that the administration of the United States is a primary enemy of the white race. While admitting that "many of the rank and file" patriots are "good-hearted people," Odinist ideologue David Lane (1996) emphasizes that white Americans "can no longer play the game of half-measures" and calls for "a paradigm shift" in terms of a total revolutionary perspective. In the white-power music fanzine *Resistance* Jim Christensen (1995) complains that many white Americans don't yet see that "their loyalty to America is helping to destroy their own race" as "more crimes have been committed against the White Race by the United States government than any other single source." To Lane, any white-racist group that still flies the star-spangled banner is "beyond irrational." "What flag flies in the courtrooms of the Federal judges who order the mixing and extermination of our race," he asks rhetorically. "What flag did the Union fly when they destroyed Dixie? What flag did the 101st Airborne fly when they used bayonets to integrate the schools of the South? What flag did the destroyers of our ancient European homeland fly?" (David Lane 1995d).

The rise of racist paganism is part of the process of radicalization. By denouncing even Christianity, racist radicals distance themselves further from the American mainstream, burning yet another bridge to the society they want consumed by the cleansing flames of an Aryan revolution. Anti-Americanism is, in fact, a contributing factor to the globalization of racial nationalist white power culture and essential for connecting with the traditionally anti-American fascist scene in Europe. In the racist radical paradigm, the federal administration is seen as a vehicle for a globalist conspiracy aiming at transforming the planet into one giant plantation, populated by one mongrel race of underlings. To realize their scheme, the story continues, the One-Worlders must exterminate the freedom-loving Aryan man lest he regain his true warrior instincts and rise up to crush the cabal. Accordingly, slavery was not a mistake but part of the plan for browning the world through miscegenation, a scheme now stepped up through immigration, multicultural policies, civil and military U.N. operations, transnational cultural exchange, and multinational corporations. The process of globalization is thus interpreted as a process of homogenization, by means of which the New World Order will destroy all the world's distinct races and cultures. This fear is shared by racial and religious nationalists worldwide and has led to an amazing array of cooperative efforts across racial, religious, and national borders.

The secret cabal is often, though not exclusively, referred to as the Zionist Occupation Government (ZOG). Cunningly operating from behind the scenes, ZOG seems innately elusive in character, and most Aryan ideologues typically turn vague and often all-inclusive if asked to specify exactly what ZOG is and what its components are. Commonly, ZOG is thought of as an omnipresent and omnipotent cabal involving at its heart varying constellations of Jews, Illuminati, Freemasons, plutocrats, and multinational corporations. It operates through many social "front" institutions, from the United Nations to Parent-Teacher Associations. Being omnipotent and omnipresent, ZOG can be used as a metaphor for just about everything that is wrong in the world. Held accountable for systematic discrimination against white Americans, ZOG can even be blamed for personal failures. Accordingly, ZOG can be used to explain not only the existence of affirmative action, environmental pollution, and pornography but also why a certain individual made poor grades in school, lost his job, or seems unable to find a partner. Promoting sick values to contaminate the pure Aryan mind, ZOG controls television, media, music, art, fashion, religion, science, and education. It constructs corrupting "isms" such as humanism, egalitarianism, communism, and feminism to feed the minds of the gullible masses and make them easier to manipulate. ZOG makes white men ashamed of their maleness, race, history, and cultural greatness. To divide and conquer, ZOG frequently promotes white infighting: it was behind the two fratricidal World Wars; it masterminded the conflict in Northern Ireland and the Balkans; it constantly distorts the racist scene to prevent Aryan unity. To deprive the white world of its resources, ZOG relocates once-white corporations to nonwhite countries, whose population is then "exported" to the white world to further race-mixing and moral depravation. ZOG is about to complete its evil scheme. In his writings, Lane informs the radical racist scene that whites constitute a mere 8 percent of the world's population, with white women in their fertile years representing only 2 percent. The vicious ZOG cabal targets the minds of these women, convincing them to become feminists, focus on their careers, and have abortions. Fertile white women are furthermore taught to hate males of their own race and to seek partners among their own sex or among males of other races — all of this brainwashing being intended to curtail women's power to bring new Aryans to the world. Aryan man, once the pinnacle of civilization, is thus at the brink of total extermination.

Aryan activists see themselves as the last resort of a righteous resistance. The brave heroes who dare to resist ZOG rule risk being assassinated or unjustly thrown away in the "federal dungeons." With a logic that might seem bizarre from the perspective of an African American or a Hispanic, white-racists accordingly adopt an underdog position. In the mental universe of Aryan revolutionaries, whites are the bottom rung of society. Whereas mainstream social critics point to persistent vestiges of institutionalized racism that place non-whites at systemic disadvantage, Aryan activists claim to belong to an oppressed minority, systematically reduced to second-rate citizens. The appropriation of the role of the underdog is a key factor in the processes of identity construction in the radical racist culture. The underdog has long been an all-American folk hero, the righteous individual who, with trust in himself, his God, and his gun, fights against all odds for what is right and decent, emerging victorious at the end. Identifying with the trope of the underdog lends the Aryan activist moral superiority and heroic qualities as a modern-day David fighting ZOG.

The romanticized warrior figure is also influential in the construction of an Aryan male identity. Knightly values such as courage, strength, honesty, honor, glory, fearlessness, and valiance are hailed as primary Aryan virtues. Robin Hood and Ivanhoe are in many respects more important role models for the Aryan activist than Adolf Hitler or Benito Mussolini. The white woman is presented as an endangered species, a shining jewel of pristine cleanliness surrounded by dribbling perverts at a sinking island in an ocean of filth, which sets the stage for the noble Aryan warrior to come to her rescue. "A true White man fights," David Lane (1996) emphasizes, "because the beauty of the White Aryan woman must not perish from the earth." Frequently illustrated with medieval knights and raging Vikings, Aryan revolutionary papers, Web pages, and white power

CDs feature bombastic language more suited to heroic legends of the past than to contemporary politics. Aryan activism provides its adherents with an opportunity to be part of a grand narrative through which they can rise above the shabby trifles of the everyday commoner and emerge in shining armor at the battleground for the final conflict, lifting their swords for race, nation, blood, and honor.

Accompanying the radicalization of Aryan racist nationalism were the related factors of a generational shift, the rise of the white-power music industry, and the revolution in communications technology. The past two decades have witnessed the influx of a new generation of racist activists into a scene that had begun to look like a home for retired people. Bringing in their music, the new generation offered a prime recruitment tool that also proved financially profitable. The Internet, too, has become one of the main avenues for disseminating the revolutionary racist message. Transcending national borders, music and electronic communication have facilitated a global flow of ideas, engaging racist radicals across the world in the vision of a future in which race will define nation in a transatlantic white homeland. However, the new generation of racist activists, white-power music, and the World Wide Web have not enabled the scene to coalesce into a full-blown racist movement. If anything, the effect has been the opposite, as new men and new means have led to further fragmentation.

Aryan resistance to ZOG is far from united, being scattered in literally hundreds of mostly dysfunctional organizations and divided into a multiplicity of ideological persuasions engaged in almost constant infighting. The revolutionary racist scene is far more fragmented than the Trotskyite scene of the 1970s ever was, with racist organizations and leaders emerging and fading with amazing speed, such that any effort to create an "organizational catalog" is already obsolete when it leaves the researcher's desk for the print shop. Few Aryan revolutionary organizations gather more than a hundred members, and most groups could probably fit their nationwide membership into a telephone booth. Some parties exist on paper or in cyberspace only, and there seems to be an inverse correlation between how united an Aryan front claims to be and how many members it actually has. Generally, it is men with high self-esteem and personal ambition for absolute power who head most of these organizations, and such men invest more energy in personal vendettas against other wanna-be leaders than in implementing their futuristic dreams of an Aryan takeover. Paradoxically, then, cantankerous individualists who are hardly capable of cooperation, much less of taking orders, populate a milieu that stresses an organic view of race and holds as ideal an authoritarian collectivism.

I have never been exposed to more gossip than during my fieldwork among those preaching "racial solidarity." Almost every Aryan wanna-be leader accuses almost every other Aryan wanna-be leader of being a secret Jew, a secret homosexual, and/or a secret police informant. Oddly enough, all three accusations have not infrequently proved to be correct. Although their actual number obviously is far less substantial than rumor would have it, individuals with Jewish ancestry have occasionally been found in influential positions in anti-Semitic organizations; these are not Jewish infiltrators working for the authorities or for civil-rights organizations but committed fascists whose personal lives have been ruined when their ancestry has been revealed. Frank Collin, founder of the National Socialist Party of America had a Jewish father. Leonard Holstein, California organizer of the ANP, was Jewish. ANP national secretary, author of *Stormtroopers Manual*, and organizer of United Klans of America, New York, Dan Burros shot himself to death after his Jewish heritage was exposed (Schmaltz 1999, 80, 82, 99, 262). Andy Greenbaum changed his name to Davis Wolfgang Hawke before founding his national socialist Knights of Freedom but was exposed by the SPLC in 1999 (SPLC 1999b, 1999c).

Given the homoerotic iconography of muscular, half-naked men with leather stripes and guns roaming the pages of the Aryan press, it is maybe not that surprising that gay men have been attracted to the scene. A few scandals in which national socialist leaders recruited young stormtroopers for other ends than implementing the Aryan revolution have blasted this otherwise extremely homophobic scene and contributed to the culture of paranoia.[1] And finally, the Aryan revolutionary scene remains thoroughly infiltrated by informants in service of the local, state, and federal police authorities or civil-rights and antiracist organizations, and to such an extent that most groups seem almost transparent. Moreover, many an activist has proven capable of making deals with the authorities when taken into custody, selling their brethren-in-arms for a reduced sentence or escaping into the witness-protection programs.

In sum, the level of discord, mutual enmity, organizational fragmentation, and ideological division characterizing the world of white racism is far too high to be able speak of a white-racist movement in any meaningful way—depending, of course, on how the category "movement" is defined. In popular usage, "movement" implies a unified ideological body going somewhere, which is *far* from true for radical racism. Adherents are not in agreement on even the fundamentals: who they are, what they are doing, where they are going, or how they possibly are going to get there. In the social sciences, "movement" is often distinguished from other political action—such as popular protest and conventional political participation—as a mode of organized nonparliamentary political action intended to further a specific cause. Its applicability to the white-racist milieu is not entirely unproblematic, as is often realized by researchers using the analytical framework of the social sciences. Operating with Marx's and Mac-Adam's definition of social movement "as organized efforts to promote or resist change in society, that rely, at least in part, on non-institutionalized forms of political action" to analyze what they term the "white separatist movement," Betty A. Dobratz and Stephanie L. Shanks-Meile admit that "analyzing white separatists as participants in *one* movement is not without pitfalls" (1997, 13). Not only did they find that different groups had "different beliefs and strategies, which makes it difficult for them to exhibit solidarity" (ibid.), but also that a large segment of the scene remains disorganized.

In their study of the emerging transatlantic radical right, Jeffrey Kaplan and Leonard Weinberg seek a definition of "movement" that takes into account the level of organizational disunity characterizing the scene, arguing that a movement is not necessarily "a single cohesive organization" but that "movements may be fragmented." Following Sidney Tarrow, they argue, "movements are sustained interactions between aggrieved social actors and allies, and opponents and public authorities." Representing a "form of collective action," movements "coalesce" when there is a "common purpose," a "sense of solidarity," and a realization that participants "share a common concern" (Kaplan and Weinberg 1998, 13, 77). Although the advantage of this definition is obvious, it is still difficult to apply to a scene that for all practical purposes could instead be characterized by a basic lack of solidarity, common purpose, and collective action. Adherents of the various ideological strains that abound on the racist scene are far more likely to be at each other's throats than to be found coalescing into a movement any time soon. While they may engage in "sustained interaction" in terms of keeping track of each other, they do not necessarily like each other, agree with each other, or ever want to do anything with each other except, possibly, tear each other apart.

In theory, many activists articulate their dedication to the cause of white survival, racial solidarity, an Aryan revolution, or a white homeland, but few would agree with each other if asked to specify exactly what they mean. The isolated voices that *in practice* manage to rise—and stay—above the intrigues and imploding realities of the radical racist milieu are few and far between, and have yet to inspire any notable collective action. While the category "movement" seems useful for analyzing certain defined parts of the scene—such as hardcore Odinism, Klandom, or the militias—it is harder to apply to the scene as a whole.

Yet, if there is not a "movement," there is still a "something" that all or most of the different networks, channels of communication, organizations, activists, and tendencies may be seen as parts of. Inspired by the approach developed by Michael Barkun and Jeffrey Kaplan in analyzing the scene in terms of a "cultic milieu," I suggest that this "something" may be understood as a white-racist "counterculture." British sociologist Colin Campbell advanced the concept "cultic milieu" as an analytical tool to make sense of the emerging New Age scene in Britain in the early 1970s. If "cults" are substituted with "racist groups," his description of the New Age scene aptly corresponds to the cultural underground of militant racism in the contemporary United States. Writes Campbell, "Given that cultic groups have a tendency to be ephemeral and highly unstable, it is a fact that new ones are being born just as fast as the old ones die. There is a continual process of cult formation and collapse, which parallels the high turnover of membership at the individual level. Clearly, therefore, cults must exist within a milieu, which, if not conducive to the maintenance of individual cults, is highly conducive to the spawning of cults in general. Such a generally supportive milieu is continually giving birth to new cults, absorbing the debris of the dead ones and creating new generations of cult-prone individuals" (1972, 121–22).

Whereas most individual cults are a "transitory phenomenon, the cultic milieu is, by contrast, a constant feature of society. It could therefore prove more viable and illuminating to take the cultic milieu and not the individual cult as the focus of sociological concern" (1972, 122). Regarding the cultic milieu as a cultural underground of society, Campbell notes that it includes "deviant belief-systems" and institutions associated with the articulation of these beliefs, and is "kept alive by the magazines, periodicals, books, pamphlets, lectures, demonstrations and informal meetings through which its beliefs and practices are discussed and disseminated" (1972, 123). The cultic milieu implies a "forbidden vision of the world," notes Barkun (1997, 247). Discussing the milieu's acceptance of "truths" unaccepted as such by society's authoritative institutions for knowledge production, such as universities, the media, and conventional religion, in terms of "rejected" or "stigmatized" knowledge, Barkun applies Campbell to make sense of the radical right and the cross-fertilization of ideas that takes place between the worlds of conspiracy believers, New Age seekers, and militant racism (Barkun 1995). Building on Campbell's observation that a notion of "seekership prevails throughout the cultic milieu" (Campbell 1972, 122), Kaplan describes a segment of radical-right activists as a "community of seekers" to explain the high membership turnover and the seemingly incompatible mixture of unorthodox ideas that characterize many groups of the scene (Kaplan 1997; Kaplan and Weinberg 1998). Combined, the theoretical perspectives of Campbell, Barkun, and Kaplan suggest an analytical approach with which to comprehend the cultic milieu of what herein will be termed the revolutionary white-racist counterculture.

The usage of the concept "counterculture" here does not refer to the leftist counterculture of the hippie era of the 1960s and 1970s. While a mainstream cultural orientation can be identified in any given society, it is not a monolithic entity but rather a complex and multifaceted constellation, involving the dominant perceptions of reality, history, ethics, religion, society, nature, and man as articulated in that culture. Although dominant, the hegemony of the mainstream will never, at least not in any modern society, be total, no matter how totalizing its ambition. Alternative perceptions of reality, society, morality, gender, and so on will always exist to constitute a more or less repressed, ignored, or ridiculed cultural underground. Because it is, in the end, part of the same culture, the underground may coincide in significant ways with the mainstream, although neither element of the culture will necessarily acknowledge such similarities. Rather, the underground's conception of reality appears as a *mirror image* of what is articulated by the cultural mainstream, accepting as truth much of what orthodoxy rejects as false. To the extent that adherents of deviant cultural perceptions understand their alternatives to be contrary and superior to the orientation articulated by the mainstream, countercultures may form, provided that enough numbers participate in their formulation.

While there is only one mainstream at any given time in any given culture, several countercultures of different orientations may exist simultaneously. It would, perhaps, be possible to argue that a plurality of countercultures is present in the contemporary United States, as evidenced by the factious worlds of black nationalism, New Age spiritualism, revolutionary white racism, and green anarchism/radical environmentalism. Despite the fact that adherents of these various countercultures often take exception to each other, cross-fertilization is certainly possible, given that knowledge rejected by the mainstream tends to circulate throughout the broader underground and its constellation of countercultures. Those who cherish one form of rejected knowledge seem to be more willing to accept other forms of rejected knowledge, reasoning that the fact that it has been rejected by the mainstream probably means that there is something to it. This may in part explain why modern-day fascists so readily embrace theories about UFO abductions, sunken cities, hollow-earth civilizations, and alternative medicine.

At certain times a single counterculture gains enough momentum to really make an imprint on history, to become *the* counterculture. During the 1960s and 1970s, when the left-leaning culture of flower power peaked and attracted musicians, philosophers, artists, and the younger generation to invest energy, belief, and activism in its alternative visions, it was forceful enough to pose as the counterculture. A similar situation occurred at the end of the nineteenth century in the völkisch counterculture of continental Europe. Whereas the mainstream at that time was oriented toward the ideas of eternal progress, scientific rationality, industrialization, and modernization, the völkisch counterculture expressed alternative ideals in terms of mysticism, national romanticism, nature worship, invented pasts, and antimodernism. Accordingly, countercultures are not inherently left or right, progressive or reactionary, but are determined by what exactly they oppose in the mainstream's conception of reality. Again, a counterculture is part of the same general culture as the mainstream, meaning that both, as prisoners of their time, will possess common features. However, both mainstream and counterculture tend to ignore these commonalities, as *mutual rejection* defines their relationship. For instance, although flower-power hippies and mainstream, white, middle-class Americans abhorred and ridiculed each others' lifestyles and belief systems, they in fact had much more in common than they ever acknowledged. This is also true of the relationship between revolutionary white-racist counterculture and contemporary American mainstream culture. Although neither acknowledges any common ground, both are products of American society and therefore do reflect common sentiments and conceptions.

Although the white-racist counterculture defines itself in opposition to the multicultural orientation of the public institutions of what is now the dominant culture, it nurtures many values, norms, and conceptions of reality that in the past defined American mainstream culture but that have since been rejected as offensive and erroneous. Convinced that the racial enemies in power have repressed these "truths," racist adherents tend to easily accept other stigmatized knowledge, produced in the milieus of conspiracy believers, alternative science, and religion. Accordingly, those in the counterculture consciously try to minimize their dependency on mainstream institutions. Many home-school their children rather than sending them to private or public schools. They believe that babies should be delivered at home rather than in hospitals. They strongly recommend alternative medicine and nonprocessed food. Instead of reading "ZOG-controlled" newspapers or watching TV, most rely on counterculture channels of information. The counterculture has its own artists, musicians, authors, and ideology producers who through magazines, publishing houses, bookstores, Web pages, and meeting forums express cultural values and render an amount of institutional stability to a counterculture in which organizational modes of expression are otherwise anything but stable.

The revolution in information technology has greatly facilitated the development of an alternative news service, networks of communication, and means of disseminating dissident views. Aryan revolutionaries quickly realized the new potentials of electronic communication through e-mail, USENET, and the World Wide Web. Pioneering white revolutionary cyber activities were former Klan leaders Louis Beam and Don Black. By 1984, Beam had organized the Aryan Nations Liberty Net, which linked together about a dozen computerized radical-right information bases to facilitate communication exchange. During a lunch meeting in 1996, Beam emphasized the importance of "cyber warfare." The Internet, he claimed, severely undermines the "Jewish media monopoly." Convinced that the Clinton administration and "pressure groups" would do anything to curtail this "vestige" of "free information exchange" and "free speech," Beam urged Aryan revolutionaries to focus on cyber activity before "an electronic Iron Curtain" might be erected to censor "informed opinion." [2]

Don Black (1996) believed that it would be impossible to control electronic information exchange and emphasized that he was able to do far more for the Aryan revolution as a cyber warrior than he ever did as Imperial Wizard. Established in March 1995 as the first white-racist site on the Web, Black's *Stormfront* is still one of the more professional Web sites. With an estimate of more than a thousand daily visitors, *Stormfront* has mirror sites in Spanish, Russian, and German, and visitors are guided through a wealth of information through a search engine. It features text and graphic libraries, chat/discussion forums, press coverage, a news service that lists upcoming events, audio and video libraries, a dating service, kids pages, women's pages, mailing lists, ads for counterculture artifacts and "forbidden books," and links to numerous white-racist organizations of many different persuasions all over the world.

In addition to hundreds of home pages with counterculture content, there are cyber-only organizations and newspapers, such as *Western Imperative Network* and *Wake Up or Die*, and electronic news agencies, such as *Nationalist News Agency*, *Stormfront News Bulletin*, *Klan E-Mail News*, *Nationalist Observer*, *Vinland News*, *American Dissident Voices*, and *Wolfreign Update*. Many groups offer e-mail subscriptions for less regular newsletters, such as the *Allgermanische Heidnische Front Newsletter*, and provide chat forums for members only, such as *Wotansvolk*. However, the world of cyber activism is as unstable and transformable as the white-racist counterculture at large; although a Web site or an electronic news service does not demand a large budget, it does require time and energy to manage. *Aryan News Agency*, one of the more active disseminators of "racially relevant" information in 1997, was gone by 1999, and Alex Curtis's *Nationalist Observer* and *Weekly Racist Message* disappeared in 2001 due to the arrest of its editor.

Another aspect of cyber warfare is the ease with which enemies can enter a racist Web site and alter its contents. Many cyber guerillas dedicate much of their time at the computer to E-bombing, hacking, spreading disinformation, creating phony sites, launching nonexistent groups, and going undercover to enter chat forums. Furthermore, electronic information exchange through the Internet, discussion groups, and e-mail correspondence is extremely easy for intelligence agencies to tap, although the extent to which this is done is unclear. Computerized surveillance of electronic communication has one major disadvantage, however: the overwhelming quantity of electronic information flow. The fact that intelligence agencies operate global, satellite-based surveillance systems to supervise cyberspace has moreover caused many Aryan activists to use cipher programs when discussing "forbidden" topics and illegal activities.

Out of the revolutionary white-racist counterculture, numerous organizations, subcultures, and ideologues arise, each attempting to unify and electrify its adherents into a movement, so far without any significant measure of success. Some of these ideologues might become temporary stars, enjoying brief moments of fame and publicity, only to fade away in downfalls caused by anything from internal fights to incarceration. The membership of the dissolved groups will generally be absorbed back into the counterculture, either disillusioned or ready to find or establish another bandwagon of organized expression. Almost everyone I encountered in the counterculture—the leaders included—had begun to realize that none of the present wanna-be leaders is the leader, but there is a widespread belief that he—it is always a he—is bound to come. Another realization that had begun to dawn on racist activists was that there was no possibility of gaining the support of a majority of white Americans. (Most white Americans seem to have plenty of other things to do than joining the ranks of the Aryan revolution.) The idea of leaderless resistance can thus be understood as a rationalization of the fact that none of the mainly dysfunctional racist organizations attract wide enough support to organize a more conventional resistance. Combined with the warrior ideal and the almost religious conviction that Aryan man is at the brink of extermination, recognition of how unlikely it is that an Aryan ideology will prevail can lead racists to desperate acts of panic, such as the Oklahoma City bombing.

The lack of effective remedies for reverting social reality has led to increasing ideological fragmentation as activists and wanna-be leaders search for the keys to a viable solution. Aryan movements and organizations populating the counterculture are as disparate as the belief systems and conceptions of reality are divergent from each other. Involved in uneasy coexistence are Identity Christians and militant pagans, sectarian Mormons and racist Satanists, national socialists and Third Positionist/National Bolsheviks, party bureaucrats and rampaging skinheads, white supremacists and separatists. Adherents to the Aryan counterculture may explore deep ecology, practice runic yoga, be vegetarians, circumcise their sons, headbang to "hate core" or black metal, engage in survivalist practice, stockpile food and guns, and spend hours studying encrypted messages in the Bible, the stars, or TV soaps. They may be technology freaks or critics, radical localists or urbanites, modernists or antimodernists. They may cooperate with or fight separatists of other races. While the counterculture does spawn new generations of Aryan revolutionaries, the overwhelming majority seems to consume the ideas and artifacts produced without actually getting involved in an organization, at least not for any extended periods of serious activist time. They might subscribe to one or a number of racist periodicals, listen to white-power music, appear at a 20 April concert to get drunk on Hitler's birthday, browse the white-racist home pages, check out a pagan blot ceremony, participate in a nocturnal cross lighting, hang out with the local skinhead crowd, recycle the legends of Bob Mathews, sport a counterculture tattoo, and keep informed through mailing lists and counterculture gossip. Also circulating in the counterculture is what Kaplan terms a "community of seekers," searching for the "truth that has to be out there" by investigating the ideologies and practices presented by the individual organizations of counterculture orientation. If what they find seems interesting enough, they might become active members of a group for some period of time, only to move on when their expectations are frustrated for any reason, be it the leader's autocratic ways, internal intrigues, an accumulation of doubt, or the meeting with a proponent of some other racist creed that seems more attractive for the moment.

Much like New Age spiritualism, the white-racist counterculture offers a smorgasbord of dishes from which individuals rather freely compose their own plates. While this does not exclude the existence of numerous authoritarian organizations whose leaders might condemn any and all deviations from the specific path of Aryan liberation they advocate, it is a fact that no organization or leader so far has been able to set the menu of the smorgasbord. It is instructive to observe the main dishes served on the white-racist smorgasbord. Every counterculture adherent does not choose from every dish, nor does every Aryan activist who tries a dish find it tasty, but everybody involved knows that the following are standard "dishes" of the smorgasbord: (1) Klandom; (2) national socialism; (3) white-power music/skinhead culture; (4) warrior ideals; (5) conspiracy theories; (6) anti-Semitism; (7) populism; (8) separatism; (9) Christian Identity; (10) race as religion; and (11) Asatrú/Odinism.

Some of these dishes are easily combined to create favorite counterculture treats: the populist Texas separatist and Identity Christian Klan member who believes in a Jewish conspiracy and listens to racist country and western, or the anti-Semitic national socialist skinhead who hails the warrior aspect of Odin in his white-power music lyrics. Other dishes do not go that well together. Few will try out the race-as-religion creed of Creativity or Norse paganism together with prayers to the Aryan Christ, but may well taste them one at a time. Some dishes (national socialism, Identity, skinheads) are extremely distasteful to white Americans outside the counterculture, while others (conspiracy theories, warrior ideals) may be as American as apple pie.

Klandom

The hooded order of the Ku Klux Klan ranks as one of the most renowned symbols of white American racism globally. Its current counterculture value is derived primarily from its symbolic potency. The name sells well enough to be appropriated in strategies for gaining media attention, and the flaming cross may produce fear among those who are uninformed about present Klan realities. Founded in 1865 by former Confederate officers in Pulaski, Tennessee, the white-racist brotherhood of the first Ku Klux Klan spread throughout the South in 1867 as an underground resistance to the "radical" Reconstruction governments, growing to an estimated half a million members before its dissolution in 1871–72.[3] However, the idea of the Klan as a mysterious nocturnal knightly order on guard against all enemies of Christ, chastity, and white Americanism remained. Periodically reignited, the idea of the Klan has recurred in American history, although its manifestations have varied considerably.

Following Klan ideologue Bob Miles (1983), many Klan researchers divide Klan history into five different eras. In 1915, former Methodist minister and fraternity organizer William J. Simmons launched the second-era Klan in Atlanta,

Georgia.[4] Its inauguration coincided wisely with the premiere of *Birth of a Nation*, a silent movie based on *The Clansman*, Thomas Dixon's "historical romance" about the first Klan. Produced at a time when movies were usually short slapsticks, the almost-three-hour-long epic, which portrayed the white knights as the heroic redeemers of the South during Reconstruction lawlessness, became a classic seen by tens of millions Americans.[5] "It is like writing history with lightning," a moved President Woodrow Wilson said after a White House showing, characterizing its content as "terribly true" (quoted in Chalmers 1987, 26). Inspired by Masonry, Simmons wrote the Klan *Kloran* (book of Klan rituals, or "Klankraft"), including its four-degree system, oaths of secrecy, initiation ceremonies, "klannish" practice, and its "kreed" of "pure Americanism."[6]

In the early 1920s the second-era Klan became a populist mass movement with an estimated four to six million members. In addition to its significant following in the South, the Klan prospered in Northeast, particularly in Pennsylvania, New Jersey, and New York, and built influential organizations west of Mississippi, in Texas, Oklahoma, Arkansas, Kansas, Colorado, Montana, California, and Oregon. But its strongest followings were found in the Midwest, in Ohio, Illinois, Michigan, and Indiana. During the 1920s between one-quarter and one-third of all native-born white men in Indiana were initiated into the secret order, which ranked as the "largest organization of any kind in the state" (Moore 1991, 7). At the time, the Klan published 150 magazines, organized state fairs, and dominated local politics in many areas. Klan-supported candidates won Congressional, Senate, and gubernatorial elections in Alabama, Colorado, Georgia, Indiana, and Oklahoma (ibid., 2).[7] Hardly a marginalized organization, the Klan represented a cross-section of Protestant white Americans. In addition to its antiblack, anti-Semitic, anti-Catholic, anticommunist, and antifeminist agenda, the Klan was concerned with corruption, crime, and immigration, and sought to enforce prohibition, civic unity, and traditional values. However, internal intrigues, corruption, and the much-publicized conviction of Indiana Grand Dragon David C. Stephenson for the rape and mutilation of a white woman contributed to a rapid fall in Ku Klux Klan membership in the late 1920s and early 1930s.

The hooded order disintegrated into competing factions and would never regain its unity or popularity. Even when recruitment increased during the Klan's fight against desegregation, the combined membership of the third-era Klan did not exceed 55,000 (Rich 1988, 54). Whereas the Klan of the 1920s in many areas had managed to elect or had even themselves been legal authorities, the Klan of the 1950s and 1960s remained an unofficial, covert arm of the local police. During the fourth, or "television," era of the Klan, as espoused by Duke and Wilkinson, Klan support dwindled further, leaving the organization bereft of any real power, although individual officers of the law might still have belonged to a Klan or supported its aims. With the shift toward a revolutionary perspective in the early 1980s, all state and federal authorities became the declared enemies of the fifth-era Klans. Klandom became at that point deeply fragmented ideologically as well as organizationally.

While some current Klan groups, such as Thomas Robb's faction of the Knights of the Ku Klux Klan take exception to national socialists and skinheads, other Klans seek to appeal to any Aryan revolutionary group, save, perhaps, racist heathens. Robb, who emulates Duke's (failed) efforts to present a nonviolent, "white civil rights," and media-oriented Klan, is in the world of revolutionary Klandom known as the "Grand Lizard." In Miles's categorization, he would be classified as a fourth-era remnant, the fifth-era tag being reserved for revolutionaries operating strictly underground. In *33/5* (three times the eleventh letter of the alphabet slash five, reads KKK/5th era), Miles argued that the Klan had to regain its mystical appeal as a truly invisible empire, vanishing in the mist as a secret army of the Folk, untouched by its enemies and breeding on the fear of the unknown (1983, 5). Designing a Klankraft based on Ariosophic Christianity, Thulean mysteries, and theories of an extraterrestrial North Star origin of the divine white race, Miles combined an emphasis on ritual with a revolutionary call for guerilla warfare. Although not as decentralized as Beam's leaderless resistance strategy, Miles's vision of the Klan as an invisible army organized as a web of autonomous tribal chieftainships was predicated on avoiding infiltration, but the number of non-infiltrated revolutionary Klan units is probably quite limited. "Given the success of federal agencies at infiltrating Klan ranks and inducing Klan leaders to cooperate in federal investigations," Kaplan suggests that it would be "tantamount to organizational suicide" for a Klan group to undertake or even seriously contemplate violent action" (2000a, 164). Moreover, the "successful use of civil litigation" initiated by Morris Dees of the SPLC "on behalf of victims of Klan violence has the intended effect of putting those Klan organizations whose members do perpetrate acts of violence out of business" (ibid.).

In 1979, Dees and the SPLC established the Klanwatch project to monitor the radical right. Since then, a number of Klan organizations have gone bankrupt after having been defeated in widely publicized trials, including the United Klans of America for the lynching death of a black student in Mobile, Alabama; Beam's Texas Emergency Reserve (ruled to be the military arm of the Knights of the Ku Klux Klan) for using violence to force Vietnamese fishermen out of Galveston Bay, Texas; and the Invisible Empire of the Ku Klux Klan for assaulting civil-rights marchers in Forsyth County, Georgia.[8] Dubbed "the Sleaze" by Aryan activists, Dees stands forth as ZOG personified in the demonology of the radical Aryans. Portrayed as a super-rich, homosexual, amoral Jew who will "stop at nothing to discredit, harass, and imprison white activists who fight for the survival of their race" ("All You Ever Wanted to Know" n.d.), Dees has metamorphosed into something of an evil vampire feeding on the blood of innocent and righteous Aryans.[9] To describe a counterculture rival as a Morris Dees "informer" has become a favorite piece of defamation, and stories to this end circulate widely throughout the milieu.[10]

Thoroughly infiltrated and monitored, Klandom is moreover deeply engaged in internal intrigues that have propelled further fragmentation. As of 1999, Klandom consisted of more than thirty bitterly competing "nationwide" Klans, all claiming to be the true heir of the legendary Klan headed by General Nathan Bedford Forrest during the Reconstruction.[11] In the year 2000, thirty-six nationwide Klans competed for recognition (SPLC 2000a). With an estimated combined membership of only 6,000 to 8,000, Klandom is a far cry from what it once was. The fifth-era Klan is more a revolutionary fantasy than a reality.

National Socialism

There are currently more than thirty national socialist organizations active in the United States.[12] With some notable exceptions, most of these experience a high membership turnover, few have any activities to speak of, and most rarely manage to handle whatever press they may run. The National Socialist Vanguard (NSV), led by director Ricky E. Cooper from The Dalles, Oregon, is a good example. The quarterly *NSV Report* began its January/March 1997 issue, "This NSV Report is currently 1 year late but the information contained herein is considered too urgent to be delayed for publishing" (Cooper 1997).[13] A notable exception to the rule is the National Alliance (NA), founded by William Pierce, with headquarters in Hillsboro, West Virginia. With more than forty local chapters, NA also offers regular radio broadcasts, E-zine newsletters, and *National Vanguard* magazine, and has during the past few years acquired some of the more important white-power music labels.

Together with fellow NSWPP officers Joseph Tommasi and James Mason, Pierce was prominent in the transition toward a post-Rockwell, national socialist revolutionary position. Pierce, who fought Koehl over the direction of the

NSWPP, encouraged the militancy of Tommasi and his National Socialist Liberation Front (NSLF). When Koehl in 1973 purged Tommasi for smoking marijuana at headquarters and leading unauthorized armed paramilitary maneuvers (Jenkins 1992, xviii; Kaplan and Weinberg 1998, 132), the NSLF was set free to develop a revolutionary strategy. Dismissing as unrealistic the "conservative" national socialist hopes of reaching the masses, Tommasi conceived terrorism to be the only viable option. Borrowing from Mao, Tommasi declared, "Political Power Stems from the Barrel of a Gun." "NSLF believes that it is necessary to begin the development of an armed struggle immediately," Tommasi wrote. "Instead of trying to educate and organize people who don't see it our way, we write them off as enemies and neutralizers of the National Socialist Revolution" (n.d.a). Prefiguring the leaderless resistance concept of Beam and Lane, Tommasi (n.d.b) envisioned an underground of small autonomous guerilla cells. "Do not wish for law and order," Tommasi declared, "for law and order means the continued existence of the rotten rip-off Capitalist Jew System. We wish for anarchy and chaos which will enable us . . . to intensify our assault that we could very well plunge the entire System to its death." [14] In 1975, a NSWPP member assassinated Tommasi, and most NSLF members were either imprisoned or drifted apart (Kaplan and Weinberg 1998, 134; Jenkins 1992, xviii).

Setting out to "smash the system," James Mason in 1980 revived the NSLF and its monthly *Siege*, declaring "war against the establishment" (Mason 1992, 11). Mason was convinced that ZOG already had won. Parliamentary measures could no longer revert society—what was needed was "total change." "It's no longer a contest in the United States, it's a matter of REVOLUTION, a struggle to overthrow the Enemy and for survival as a race" (ibid., 16, 21, 31). In 1980 Mason contacted Charles Manson, who is serving a life sentence for masterminding a series of grisly murders in Los Angeles in 1969, including that of Sharon Tate Polanski. Manson's practice of "tribal socialism," his belief that racial tension would cause an imminent breakdown (helter skelter), his ecological ATWA (air, trees, water, animals) philosophy, and his insistence on living the revolution *now* all greatly impressed Mason as a logical extension of revolutionary national socialism. While most of the radical right dreamed of revolution while "simultaneously working their System jobs and living their Establishment lives," Manson and his followers "LIVE IT, by dropping out of the System and by attacking the System" (ibid., 332, 428). Convinced that Manson was the new leader, the only worthy successor of Hitler and Rockwell, Mason in 1982 dropped the NSLF to launch the Universal Order.[15] Although white-power music fanzine *Resistance* in 1995 acknowledged a "growing body of Manson supporters" in the counterculture (editor's introduction to "The Manson Debate" 1995), Mason's push for Manson met with strong resentment. Mason "shamelessly compares this madman with Adolf Hitler," an angry rebuttal read. "Is the road to Aryan victory to be found in grotesque murders of Jewish Pawns and in the lyrics of old Beatles songs? Should we all carve backward swastikas in our foreheads and do anything possible to enable ourselves to rot away uselessly in mental hospitals?" ("James Mason" 1995).

What limited support for Manson as an avatar of Hitler does exist is mainly found in the underworld of occult national socialism and racial Satanism. Mason would later try Christian Identity as well as Norse paganism, for a while heading the Vinland faction of the Allgermanische Heidnische Front. Casting national socialism as a religious project is typical among its American ideologues. Interpreting national socialism from the perspective of Theosophy and the occult was James H. Madole, eccentric leader of the National Renaissance Party. Insisting that America was the new Atlantis and the "cradle of a new Godlike race," Madole developed contacts with Satanists, warlocks, witches, and esoterics. Much like Rockwell, Madole was fond of marching uniformed national socialist stormtroopers through the streets of northeastern cities but, despite much publicity, never gained more than a tiny following before his death in 1978 (Madole 1974–1977; see also Kaplan and Weinberg 1998, 106–15). A religious dimension was present already with Rockwell, who claimed to have received a calling from Adolf Hitler and kept a Hitler shrine at ANP headquarters.[16] Among his associates was Savitri Devi, whose esoteric Hindu Aryan national socialism enjoys a growing appeal among contemporary racist heathens.

Rejecting the "paramilitary adventures" of Tommasi and Mason as "silly and ludicrous," Rockwell's successor Matt Koehl stressed "all the problems we face here in North America today are fundamentally spiritual in origin" (Koehl n.d.a; Koehl 1986). Shortly before his death, Koehl claims, Hitler declared that national socialism as a political phenomenon was over but thought it could "be resurrected as a religious Movement" (1985d). Koehl then realized why NSWPP had completely failed in reaching the masses: "A movement which bore an essentially religious mission could not successfully pursue a political program" (1985d). In 1983 Koehl replaced the NSWPP with the "holy" New Order, conceived of as a "community of faith" and a "spiritual SS."[17] Hitler "came to offer hope and salvation for an entire race," Koehl claims (1985b). "Adolf Hitler was a gift of Almighty Providence. And in rejecting him, we rejected God himself," Koehl stated, pushing a Hitler–Jesus analogy. "Adolf Hitler came into the world in human form. He was born, and he died. He gave his very life in a supreme act of devotion of sacrifice"(1985c). Rejecting the popular counterculture legend that tells of Hitler's escape, his post-1945, adventures and present whereabouts, Koehl insisted that Hitler did die on 8 May 1945, the "Good Friday" of religious national socialism. "And we all know what comes after Good Friday" (ibid.). "Just before His immolation," Koehl jubilantly declares, "the Leader uttered these fateful words: 'It is necessary that I should die for my people; but my Spirit will rise from the grave, and the world will know that I was right' The cycle of life and death was to be perfected through His reappearance on Earth—not in flesh and blood, but in spirit: His immortal spirit." Yes, "our immortal Leader," Adolf Hitler, "has risen from the grave. He lives! We sense it; we recognize it. . . . This is the spiritual dynamic of our time. This is the good news of the age" (1985a).

White Noise and Skinhead Culture

The industry of "white noise" music is a global phenomenon with several hundred contributing acts from all continents. Defined by white-power lyrics, white noise covers a wide range of genres, including ska, oi, noise, hatecore, metal, and folk. Transnational since its inception, white noise has been instrumental in constructing a global white-power culture and is a main route by which the new generation of Aryan activists joined the scene. With important predecessors in the "rebel music" genre of country and western that accompanied the failed Klan effort to defend segregation during the 1960s, white-power music proper began with English skinhead Ian Stuart Donaldson's Skrewdriver in the late 1970s. A member of the National Front, Donaldson launched Rock Against Communism (RAC) to counter the anarchist/leftist punk scene and its Rock Against Racism gigs. Organizing RAC concerts during the early 1980s, Donaldson was involved with the first white-racist record label, White Noise Records, and early fanzines such as *Bulldog* and *Blood & Honor*. Touring Europe, Australia, and North and South America, Skrewdriver set the tone picked up by racist youths all over the "once white world." During the 1980s, there were only a few record labels, notably Rebelles Européens (France) and Rock-O-Rama (Germany), producing white noise. During the 1990s the scene exploded. Today, white noise is a lucrative business with countless record labels and distributors competing, sometimes violently, for profit and market control.

Pivotal to the rapid development of the white-noise industry was George Burdi Hawthorne, vocalist of Rahowa (Racial Holy War), who "assumed the role of Donaldson" on the American scene (Lööw 2000, 341). Born in 1970 to an upper-middle-class family in Toronto, Hawthorne went to private Catholic schools and found fascism during a literary journey through nineteenth-century Western philosophy. In his late teens, Hawthorne was ordained a reverend in the militantly racist Church of the Creator. He spent the following years as a street activist, teaming up with Ernst Zündel (a famous national socialist activist and Holocaust denier living in Toronto), fighting antiracists and recruiting for the cause. Finding that he never really accomplished anything, Hawthorne came to see as obsolete conventional methods of political mobilization. Searching for a "more intelligent approach" for promoting white power, he found his answer in music. Whereas he had to drag people to attend political meetings, he had only to announce an upcoming concert to a handful of people to find an enthusiastic crowd jamming the hall. Music proved superior to all other methods of conveying radical racism. "If you put out a piece of literature, the young person you give it to is not going to go to the photocopier and start photocopying it to people. But if you give him a CD, he'd copy it for his friends, and they bring it to parties and put it on when they're driving their cars. Suddenly, these people are hearing [Rahowa] everywhere they go" (*Hawthorne* 1996). Through music, Hawthorne says he basically sought to "instill a sense of racial pride" in the minds of "guilt ridden" Aryan youth.

> We, the white people of this world are only 8 percent of the world's population. Yet, we represent 75 percent of the world's accomplishments in science, in medicine, in philosophy. We have forwarded this world so much, this planet owes us thanks. And yes, we have not always treated other people well, but this was always the price for our expansion, the price of our advances. Every species on this planet will push other species out if needed to survive and prosper. We are the strongest, we are the smartest; we are the bravest and the boldest. This is what our ancestors were, and just like the wolf should not be embarrassed or should not be guilty or ashamed for having to kill the deer, so should we not be embarrassed for being strong. We should be proud of being mighty! (ibid.)

In early 1994, Hawthorne brought the industry of white noise to a new level by incorporating Resistance Records and *Resistance* magazine.[18] A glossy publication with color print on expensive paper, *Resistance* surprised activists accustomed to the barely readable, photocopied, cut-and-paste zines usual to the scene. Blending interviews and reviews of white-noise bands with informed essays on topics of counterculture concern, the magazine also generated profit by offering mail-order sales of compact discs, clothes, and counterculture merchandise. Resistance Records formed at a time when American white-noise bands had to sign with European labels. In 1993 Rebelles Européens paid Rahowa to record its first album but then went out of business. To release their album, Rahowa decided to start its own label. Word spread and a stream of other American musicians looking for an American producer contacted Hawthorne. Resistance Records was an instant success, boasting a dozen leading bands, including Bound for Glory, Nordic Thunder, No Remorse, Berserkr, and Aryan. Distributing an additional fifty titles and setting up an electronic mail-order site on the Internet, Resistance saw its yearly sales of CDs and cassettes reach tens of thousands, securing a substantial profit, which was then reinvested in the magazine, initially distributed free of charge to some 15,000 subscribers. In Sweden white-noise activists successfully introduced the Resistance concept with the Nordland records and magazine conglomerate. Transatlantic cooperation secured entry in their respective markets, and the Resistance–Nordland axis emerged as a world-leading distributor of white noise, provoking its share of envy and throne pretenders.[19]

White noise attracted a new generation to the racist cause. Interestingly, this rarely led to a substantial membership increase for preexisting counterculture organizations. The new generation generally remained disorganized or formed their own groups with their own leadership. As typified by the skinhead scene, many of these groups were loosely structured "tribes" rather than conventional party bureaucracies. White-power music was integral to the emerging American skinhead scene, which had begun as a British import in the mid-1970s.[20] White noise is not confined to skinhead culture, of course, nor are all skinheads white racists. Skins may be of any ethnicity and political persuasion, and there are anti-racist, anarchist, and apolitical tribes. However, a sizeable number of American skinheads are animated by the ideology of white power. The first explicitly racist street gang of skinhead warriors was Chicago's Romantic Violence of the early 1980s, reflecting in their name a *Clockwork Orange* attitude to life. By 1990, there were some 3,000 to 4,000 racist skins nationwide, a number that would increase significantly with the booming white-noise industry. While most tribes of racist skinheads retain a local presence only, there were a few larger federations of skinhead "nations," notably Hammerskin Nation and Underground Skinhead Action with affiliates in the United States and abroad.

In their own eyes, white-pride skins expressed the superior quality of the white worker: they were upright men of honor and courage, loyal to blood and tribal brothers. Yet, they often came across as an unruly crowd of nihilistic berserkers, useful, perhaps, as street fighters but otherwise barely tolerated and in dire need of direction. A few old-generation racist leaders, notably Tom Metzger, wholeheartedly embraced the skinhead scene. Trying to hang on, others would perhaps throw a concert but never really knew what to do with those who showed up. Still others saw skinheads as unrefined thugs and sought to keep them at arms length by stressing party rules of conduct and clothing. As for the skinheads, many would perhaps respect a certain veteran, but their attitudes toward the leaders of the old generation was generally dismissive: "You don't ask a blind for directions."

To the young, the Aryan message was much more powerful in white-noise culture than in the old politics of national socialism. Concerts organized for 20 April (Hitler's birthday), 17 August (death of Rudolf Hess), 8 December (Day of Martyrs), or other holy dates came to function as revivalist white-power meetings, with the musicians acting as high priests inviting born-again Aryans to accept the transformative Truth of white power, the frenzied crowd responding in chorus *Sieg Heil! Sieg Heil! Sieg Heil!* Concerts instilled in American participants a sense of being part of something larger than ordinary life, a conviction reinforced by reports of similar emotions evoked in youth all over world. The new generation felt that, as the world awakened to the primal force of the blood, the mighty roar of white power would rise to consume the planet. Hawthorne wrote in a *Resistance* editorial, "Once we have 300,000–400,000 skinheads around the world, plus a massive support base of 30,000–40,000 non-Skinhead Racialists, coupled with the support from the general White populace, we will be able to seize power around the globe" (1995a, 4).

In 1997 Canadian and American tax authorities in concert raided the Hawthorne residence in Windsor and the Resistance headquarters in Detroit, confiscating company records and computers along with 200,000 compact discs. Shortly thereafter, Hawthorne served a one-year prison term for battery and assault for his part in a violent street clash between racists and antiracists on the night of an aborted Rahowa concert. Hawthorne never reassumed his role on the scene. Instead, in 2000 Hawthorne sent a shockwave through the global white-noise community by launching Novacosm, a multiethnic rave/industrial band with a Hindu/New Age bent celebrating love as the unifying force of life. Racist activism was "ignorant" and "misdirected," Hawthorne now claimed.

> Where the racialist views the world's problems as genetic/biological, I [came to] see them as spiritual and cultural. To continue to idealize my own kind as superior to others as I have become increasingly conscious of both the shortcomings of my own people and the commonality I share with all men of tradition and spiritual perspective would be false. The battle is not

against races. The battle is not the Jews vs. the world. The battle is between the men of tradition and the modern lie of progress. The white Western man has embraced science in the name of progress, but this notion of progress is illusory and dangerous. Severed from the wisdom of the ancients, the greatest hope of Western man is to be found in returning to the faith of tradition, which requires him to learn to appreciate the teachings of other cultures that have successfully preserved the wisdom of antiquity.[21]

Well before Hawthorne's public defection, shadowy counterculture powers schemed to take over the flagship of the lucrative white-noise industry. Initially contemptuous of lowbrow skinheads and "unrefined" white-noise music, Willis Carto and William Pierce, archrivals of the old-generation racists, wrestled to gain controlling power over Resistance after the tax bust.[22] By the end of 1999, Pierce emerged victorious and ventured further into white-noise territory by buying Nordland and securing shares in Cymophane, a label producing racist heathen black metal. "Music can be a very effective medium," Pierce said in 2000. "Resistance music . . . expresses anger against the government. It expresses resentment against the Jewish planners behind the government's multicultural programs. It expresses hostility against non-Whites and against everyone who is allied to the non-Whites. It is fighting music."[23] Later that year, Pierce stated, "The young people who listen to resistance music will be the vanguard of our army of liberation. Woe to those who try to stand in their way."[24]

Warrior Ideals

America has always had a war culture. Warrior ideals are accordingly not unique to the counterculture but in fact one of several "bridges" to the mainstream. American war culture celebrates two different warrior ideals: the individual gunman who acts alone (or with a loosely structured tribe of warriors) and the valiant soldier who belongs to a military or police unit. The Wild West, for instance, gave rise to romanticized legends of the armed individual who, with trust in God and his gun, mediated between untamed nature populated by savage (red) man and culture populated by civilized (white) man. Significantly, outlaws like Jesse James or Billy the Kid are celebrated on a par with armed frontiersman and legendary sheriffs. After the West was "won," there was no more wilderness or savages to fight, so the good soldier became the dominant warrior ideal instead.[25] The heroic saga of the valiant soldier was constructed in an unbroken series of military victories, against Mexico (1845–47 and 1916–17); against

Spain (1898); in the two World Wars; in the invasions of Haiti (1915–34), the Republic of Dominica in (1915–24), and Nicaragua in (1912–33); and in the Korean War (1950–53). With the defeat in Vietnam, the warrior ideal changed again to be the individual gunman. To explain how the invincible American military could be beaten by a poorly equipped, nonwhite nation, conservative columnists argued that media, antiwar activists, and liberals made the Pentagon adopt a policy of self-imposed restraints, thereby preventing military efforts that would have secured American victory. By the late 1970s, this explanation was widely accepted. Later, merging with post-Watergate distrust of the administration and with the tradition of conspiracy thinking, it would contribute to the creation of the New Warrior recycled in an endless series of Hollywood productions.

As James Gibson (1994) notes in his study of war fantasies, manhood, and violence in post-Vietnam America, the warrior-hero is a man set apart. If there is a family, the hero's girlfriend, wife, or children are typically killed (*Mad Max, Lethal Weapon*) or nearly killed (*Patriot Games*). The Hero acts alone, with a partner, or with a tribe of male warriors. If he belongs to an organization, he will not abide by their regulations but creates his own rules of engagement to serve a Higher Justice (*Dirty Harry, Death Wish*). The Hero always fights for righteous American values but is typically frustrated or betrayed by representatives of the System (*Rambo III, Clear and Present Danger, Black Berets*). War and paramilitary adventure are best-selling male fantasies in American culture, as shown in the profitable markets of action movies, arcade and PC games, novels, comics, gun shows, and *Soldiers of Fortune*–style magazines. In the 1980s and 1990s, paramilitary warrior dreams influenced the construction of a "neo-male" identity, with a whole industry arising to provide services and artifacts to the new male. Expensive weekend classes took urban professionals out in the wilderness to reconnect with their "true," barbarian, untamed male nature. Survivalism, paintball, paramilitary classes, and warrior theme parks began attracting millions of predominantly white American males.[26]

In the 1980s warrior fantasies began manifesting in multiple murders.[27] The fact that perpetrators typically dressed up in paramilitary uniform and used semiautomatic rifles of military design suggest a cultural pattern, reinforced by the extensive media coverage of each mass killing. Detailed reportage fed the new warrior dreamer with material of what was possible to do and how to go about it, and he could easily imagine the nationwide fame he would gain if he did it. During the late 1990s, the series of paramilitary-style mass murders escalated, the perpetrators often being children who slayed other children at middle schools and high schools. On 1 October 1997, a sixteen-year-old boy in Pearl,

Mississippi, killed his mother, then shot two students to death and wounded seven more. On 1 December 1997, a fourteen-year-old student at Heath High School in West Paducah, Kentucky, killed three and wounded five other teen-agers. On 24 March 1998, two boys, aged eleven and thirteen, killed five and wounded ten persons attending their middle school in Jonesboro, Arkansas. On 21 May 1998, a fifteen-year-old boy first killed his parents, then opened fire in his high school in Springfield, Oregon, killing two and wounding twenty. On 20 April 1999, two students at Columbine High School in Littleton, Colorado, brought shotguns, a rifle, a semiautomatic TEC-DC9, and homemade bombs to school, killing thirteen students before shooting themselves.[28]

In the aftermath of the Littleton killings, the Clinton administration began pressing for gun control and for measures to prevent children from being ex-posed to guns and violence on TV, the Internet, and in video games. "America's culture of violence is having a profound effect on our children," Hillary Clinton stated during her introduction to her husband's speech on the matter, "and we must resolve what we can do to change that culture."[29] President Clinton was then four weeks into the massive air war campaign in Serbia, seeking to bomb Serbian president Slobodan Milosevic into submission. Reports of technowar with laser-guided bombs mixed in with stories of civilian Serbian casualties and the Littleton massacre.[30]

Warrior ideals are ever-present in the revolutionary Aryan counterculture. Paramilitary modes of organization and war fantasies manifest in leaderless re-sistance, the Order and its copycats, lone-wolf assassins, skinhead gangs, para-military training camps, Asatrú/Odinist warrior guilds, hatecore music, and race-war novels such as best-sellers *Turner Diaries* and *Hunter*, both by William Pierce (pseud. Andrew Macdonald), or the Odinist *Hear the Cradle Song*.[31] Racist organizations and völkish pagans frequently advertise in New Warrior magazine *Soldiers of Fortune*; National Alliance leader William Pierce once bought its mailing list in search of a receptive audience, offering among other things a new edi-tion of his race-war novel *Turner Diaries*. Aryan revolutionaries engaged as mer-cenaries in Africa, Latin America, Asia, and post-Yugoslavia. Among the more noteworthy paramilitary mercenary operations was the 1981 national socialist–Klan attempt to overthrow the government of Dominica, a plan thwarted by an FBI informant.[32]

In the aftermath of Ruby Ridge and Waco, American war ideology came together with populist and conspiracy notions that were circulating in the cul-tural underground during the rise of the militia movement. Positioned in the gray area between the counterculture, right-wing American patriots, and radical localists, who reject as unconstitutional federal authority in favor of county supremacy and common law courts, the militia movement spread rapidly through talk-show radio and other small-town and rural means of grassroots communication. In February 1994, the Trochman brothers, John and David, launched the Militia of Montana with headquarters in Noxon, a quiet town in the western part of the state. "The Militia of Montana was started because of that government shooting [at Ruby Ridge] a mother in the face and her son in the back," John Trochman explained, "and because we believe the government burned those folks at Waco deliberately; because of the Brady [gun control] Bill and the other things that the government has done against the oath they swore" (1996). Trochman was convinced that the administration was in service of a cabal that sought to establish a totalitarian "global dictatorship." Operating through front organizations such as the United Nations and the World Bank, the cabal used the U.S. military as a "mercenary peace keeping force" abroad and intended to bring in a 100 million foreign soldiers by air, ships, and tunnels between Siberia and Alaska to "put us under UN domination." "There's a plan to reduce two-thirds of the world's population," Trochman gravely insisted. The cabal "created the HIV virus," which was "administrated by the World Health Organization," and had already caused "man-made famines."[33] Facing tyranny, Americans must take on their responsibilities as militiamen. "Nobody can form a militia," Trochman argues, "because the militia already exists" ("Who Is MOM?" 1994). Pointing to the second amendment, Trochman cites as an example the Montana constitution, which defines "militia forces" as consisting of "all able-bodied citizens." Accordingly, "the militia is the American people. There's nothing to join, nothing to sign up. If you're an American citizen, you're already in the militia. It's your responsibility" (Trochman 1996).

Between 1994 and 1996, militias sprang up in every state, although the SPLC estimate of 441 militia units and 368 allied patriot groups may have been inflated (Dees 1996, 199).[34] Initially, quite a few militias were eager to demonstrate their paramilitary New Warrior ethics to the press, a strategy Trochman dismissed as "counterproductive" as it "gives the wrong impression of what the militia is all about." "Most of the militias now understand that the primary thing to do now is to educate the people. It's probably only three or so [militias] that do any training at all with the public watching, wearing their stupid camouflage clothes." Yet Trochman's worldview was loaded with New Warrior themes. Not only did he cast the system in terms familiar from Terminator or X Files, but he presented himself in terms worthy of a Clint Eastwood character: "I'm just a plain old cowboy who wants to go fishing when his country is back together" (1996).

Although Trochman was known to have addressed meetings at Aryan Nations and did favor racial separation, he rejected revolutionary racism as immoral and un-American, and was, in return, frequently charged with being an FBI informant by Aryan activists.[35] This reflected a generally deep-seated mutual distrust between the militia movement and the white-racist counterculture. Aryan revolutionaries might consider the militias to be a healthy sign and a recruitment ground but tend to dismiss most militias as misguided American patriots. Although a majority of militias consist primarily of white American males, there are militiamen of all races, and most militias would probably denounce Aryan activists as un-American. While this does not mean that no militias harbor radical white racists among their rank-and-file, the militia movement as such does not really belong to the Aryan revolutionary counterculture. Outside the militia movement proper are white-racist militias, such as the Oklahoma White Militia, but these seem more an exception than a rule.

Realizing that "the majority of militia members engage in and support law abiding activities," the FBI set up a "program of reaching out to the militias" and established "open lines of communication." The same FBI statement read, "contact with militia members has proven effective in that more mainstream militia groups have been helpful in identifying the more extremist elements of the militia."[36] In 1999 alarmist theories of an approaching breakdown caused by a Y2K computer failure reached hysterical proportions. Fearing that racist groups would use the anticipated chaos, some militia leaders openly cooperated with the FBI to "prevent renegade hate groups from launching a race war" (Rhodes 1999). Lynn VanHuizen, "general" of the 15,000-strong Michigan Militia Corps Wolverines, told a reporter that he had "no qualms in working with the government" against Aryan revolutionaries: "I think we will be forced to take these groups out—to kill them if necessary" (ibid.). Not surprisingly, cyberspace exploded with Aryan calls for retribution, insisting that VanHuizen be "charged with Treason and executed."[37] Peaking in 1996, the militia movement then sharply declined. In 1997 the SPLC identified 523 militias and allied patriot groups. By 1998 the number of groups was down to 435; 1999 saw a dramatic drop to 217 groups (SPLC 1999d; SPLC 1999a); and by the year 2000 the number had decreased to 194, out of which 72 were militias (SPLC 2001).

In its counterculture setting, the paramilitary new war hero of American war culture has occasionally manifested as racist serial killers acting out their fantasies. *Hunter* is dedicated to racist serial killer Joseph Paul Franklin, "the Lone Hunter, who saw his duty as a White man and did what a responsible son of his race must do." Targeting mixed-race couples, Jews, and black teenagers,

Franklin traveled across the country between 1977 and 1980, assassinating eighteen people, bombing a synagogue, and is currently on death row in Missouri.[38] By the late 1990s, lone-wolfism was frequently hailed as ideal by counterculture ideologues. Two cases in particular from the end of that decade illustrate this well. In July 1999 former World Church of the Creator member Benjamin Nathaniel Smith committed suicide after having shot to death two and wounded nine Asians, blacks, and Jews during a three-day shooting spree in Indiana and Illinois. The following month, former Aryan Nations member Buford O. Furrow walked into a Jewish community center, spraying the lobby with his Uzi, wounding five, including three children, and killing a Filipino postal worker. On turning himself in to the FBI, Furrow reportedly told agents that his deed was a "wake-up call to America to kill Jews" (Heinze 1999).[39]

The counterculture was, unsurprisingly, divided in its assessment of the lone-wolf assassins. While some condemned Smith's shooting spree as "stupid and very damaging," as it drew "negative attention to our movement from other whites who might otherwise join our cause," others hailed him as a valiant "kamikaze" and as a "hero and great warrior for our race."[40] Others had more trouble with the fact that Smith had not killed all his targets — "shoot to wound is never good operating procedure" — and they believed suicide to be an act of "cowardice."[41] Boasting a membership increase of 10 to 15 percent because of the attention the serial killings had given Creativity, Reverend Max Hale of the World Church of the Creator said that although he did not "agree with [Ben's] actions," he "could not say anything bad about" such a "loyal friend" (1999). Pastor Butler of the Aryan Nations defended Furrow as "a good soldier," saying, "Your president is killing babies in Yugoslavia. If it's alright to do that, it's alright to do this."[42] One racist thought that Furrow's gunning down of Jewish children was "the worst thing that could have happened," as the "only thing to come out of this was a lot of sympathy for the Jewish people. . . . Even militaries invading countries do not target women and children."[43] Another dismissed Furrow as a "fucking idiot and coward. If he had any balls and brains he would have gone down to Hollywood . . . and took out some of those Jews instead of killing innocent children."[44] Alex Curtis responded by hailing Furrow as "Aryan of the Month."[45] "Whoever has sympathy for kikes getting killed or shot is already our enemy,"[46] he wrote. "If the children were Jewish, then they were not innocent. What kind of fucking anti-Semite are you to ever say any Jew is innocent?"[47]

Conspiracy Theories

Conspiracy theory has a long American history and is a tremendously popular movie genre, as evidenced by The X Files, Conspiracy Theory, Men in Black, and The Matrix. Accordingly, its counterculture prominence simply reflects the currents of mainstream culture. John Adams, the second president of the United States, was one of the first great conspiracy theorists. He believed in a giant conspiracy that he called the "infernal confederacy," composed of corrupt preachers, politicians, and aristocrats who aimed to deprive the young nation of its newly gained liberties (Herman 1997, 150). In effect, Adams established what Richard Hofstadter termed the "paranoid style in American politics" (1996, 7). The paranoid style considers gigantic and omnipotent conspiracies to be "the motive force in historical events. History is conspiracy, set in motion by demonic forces" evoking the powers of the Anti-Christ. Therefore, the "paranoid spokesman sees the fate of this conspiracy in apocalyptic terms—he traffics in the birth and death of whole worlds, whole political orders, whole systems of human values. He is always manning the barricades of civilization. He constantly lives at a turning point: it is now or never in organizing resistance to conspiracy" (ibid., 29–31).

Exactly who the conspirators are assumed to be has shifted in time and place. They were French Jacobins in the 1790s, the Illuminati in the early 1800s, Masons in the 1820s and 1840s, Catholics in different waves between 1840 and 1925, Jews between 1881 and World War II, "reds" in the late 1910s, Zionists after 1948, communists during the McCarthy era, and Satanists in the 1980s.[48] Following the fall of the Soviet empire, conspiracy theorists became preoccupied with an emerging "New World Order." Globalization and relativization of Western civilization was interpreted as the plan of an omnipotent cabal, working through the administration of the United States and through global institutions like the UN, WHO, or the World Bank, to terminate the American way of life. While any or all of the earlier evil conspirators might still figure to varying degrees, modern conspiracy theorists believed, the more prominent plotters would now be One Worlders, plutocrats, Satanists, aliens, ZOG, or the Illuminati, these being easily combined in various configuration, such as the popular thesis that satanic Illuminati aliens head the communist Jew world order.

Although references to a malicious cabal working to establish a New World Order (NWO) date back at least to the early 1980s (Barkun 1998b), it gained widespread popularity after President George Bush the elder used the term during the 1990–91 Gulf War to connote the emergence of a post–Cold War era of global security and cooperation.[49] Given their distrust of the U.S. administration, conspiracy believers readily interpreted Bush's use of the term as a blatant confirmation of their theories. Moreover, if "George Bush, President of U.S., CFR Director, Trilateralist, 'Lip-reader,' CIA Director," and a member of the "occult, elitist Skull & Bones Society" was bold enough to reveal his plans for a New World Order, then surely the "long planned and covertly implemented [plot to terminate the American way of life] is well on its way to fruition"(McLamb 1996, 5, 9).[50] For some reason, conspiracy believers tend to think that exposure somehow will thwart the efforts of the omnipotent cabal. "Like vampires," conspiracy theorist Jack McLamb states, "the New World Order globalists are secretly draining the vitality of our nation. Fortunately, like vampires, they can't stand the light of the day" (n.d.).

Accordingly, such theorists spend a lot of time collecting, interpreting, and disseminating information about the grand conspiracy. Hillary Clinton receiving healing from a Native American, barcodes on groceries, the ring symbol of the Olympic Games, the eternal flame on John F. Kennedy's grave, and Princess Diana's death are all signs to conspiracy researchers. Hillary Clinton's visit with the Native American exposes her, Tex Marrs argues, as an occult feminist communist who is the dark power behind her husband's presidency and reveals the diabolic quackery she wants to force on all Americans under the pretext of extending healthcare benefits (Marrs 1993). Barcodes on groceries represent a computerized system designed around the biblical numerical configuration "666" (the mark of the beast), Terry Cook (1996) explains. The technique now extends to national identification cards and bank cards, and will soon be perfected in microchips that will be implanted in the forehead or right hand of all people, in fulfillment of Revelations 13:16–18: "And [anti-Christ] causes all, both small and great, both rich and poor, both free and slave, to be marked on the right hand or the forehead, so that no one can buy or sell unless he has the mark, that is, the name of the beast or the number of its name . . . six hundred and sixty-six." The ring symbols of the Olympic Games are designed by the "bloodthirsty devil" behind the Illuminati and tie in with the yin-yang symbol, the "very epitome of the dialectic, alchemical process, combining the dark and the light, the masculine and the feminine, inside a circle with its satanic 'S' shooting through its diameter" (Marrs 1996, 219). The assassination of JFK and the death of Princess Diana were, David Icke reveals, sacrificial murders of the "King" and the "Queen," orchestrated by the Babylonian Brotherhood, an extraterrestrial reptilian race that in human disguise conspire to take over the world.[51] President Kennedy, a Catholic, was killed on the anniversary of the day the Catholic church banned the reptilian Knights Templars in 1307, whereafter the conspirators triumphantly placed the brotherhood signature—the eternal flame—on Kennedy's grave. Diana had at her birth been chosen by the reptilians as a symbol for the ancient moon goddess Diana, and they subsequently orchestrated her whole life, right up to the fatal day when she was placed in a car with a mind-controlled chauffeur who aimed at the thirteenth pillar (thirteen being a brotherhood number) in a Paris tunnel on 31 August ("13" in reverse), a brotherhood holy day (Icke 1999, 404–61).

One feature of conspiracy theory is thematic continuity. Recalling the disclosure-by-former-nun genre in nineteenth-century anti-Catholic conspiracy theories, a growing number of female NWO-conspiracy survivors have contributed to the scene with chilling inside information. The most influential work is Cathy O'Brien's autobiography TRANCE Formation of America (O'Brien and Phillips 1995b), which details the horrors of her life as a NWO sex slave between 1966 and 1988, before she was rescued by deprogrammer Mark Philips. "Through recovery, I remembered decades of details of New World Order plans—many of which were inadvertently revealed in my presence by those believing that I would never survive to remember, or merely considered me a robot. While they discussed the demise of humanity, as we know it, I photographically recorded every word" (O'Brien 1995). Born in 1957 to a "pedophile father" and "mind controlled mother," O'Brien claims to have been abused since she was a toddler. Forced to partake in satanic sadomasochistic child pornography movies produced for Gerald Ford, she was eventually sold to the CIA, which was looking for traumatized children for their mind-control program MKUltra Project Monarch. Tortured at programming centers—Catholic churches, Disneyland, NASA—O'Brien developed multiple-personality disorder by which her brain was completely compartmentalized, enabling programmers to use her as a sex slave and conspiracy dispatcher. U.S. presidents Ford, Reagan, Bush, and Clinton; Canadian prime ministers Pierre Trudeau and Brian Mulroney; Mexican president Miguel de la Madrid; Haitian dictator Baby Doc Duvalier; Panamanian president Manuel Noriega; and King Fahd of Saudi Arabia all sexually brutalized her. She recounts in graphic detail how the elder George Bush raped her three-year-old daughter and how she was forced to have oral sex with Illuminati witch Hillary Clinton. She tells of top politicians and industrialists who convene at Bohemian Grove in California to engage in satanic sex orgies, and she details George Bush and Bill Clinton playing the Most Dangerous Game (i.e., hunting mind-controlled men, women, and children). While being sodomized, whipped, bound, and raped, O'Brien overheard the globalist elite planning a military coup in the United States and conspiring to usher in the satanic New World Order (O'Brien and Phillips 1995b). Fortunately, O'Brien was rescued and deprogrammed by Mark Phillips, and they have since sought to expose the conspiracy. "By arming ourselves with knowledge and spreading their secrets can we disarm their world dominance" (O'Brien and Phillips 1995a).

As it is recycled in the revolutionary white-racist counterculture setting, the conspiracy aims at exterminating the freedom-loving Aryan race, the only viable force able to thwart the NWO plan of global dominion. In most white-racist conspiracy theories, Jews figure at the heart of the sinister cabal, as illustrated by the likes of Jack Mohr, Willis Carto, William Pierce, and Ernst Zündel. Anti-Semitism is prominent also in the worldview of Michael Hoffman II, one of the counterculture's more original conspiracy researchers. Born in 1957 to a Catholic family in Geneva in central New York, Hoffman was taught about the fate of William Morgan, a former Mason from nearby Batavia who had been writing a book exposing the secret society when he was abducted and presumably murdered by a group of Masons in 1826, an event that spurred the relatively successful Anti-Masonic Party (Hoffman 1998).[52] Informed by his maternal grandfather about secret Mob orchestration of U.S. elections, he arrived at the starting point of every conspiracy theorist: "Nothing is as it seems to be." The conclusion led Hoffman into a "life long vocation, researching the subterranean workings of the occult cryptocracy's orchestration of American history." "Itching to get to the forefront of the Cause and lead it, because it is my Destiny, I was born to it," Hoffman worked with the counterculture projects of Ernst Zündel, Willis Carto, the Institute of Historical Review, David Irving, Tom Metzger, and Veritas Press, but he came to favor an antimodernist vision modeled in part on the Amish communities of his native New York (Hoffman 1998).[53]

In 1996 Hoffman moved his wife and nine children to the "white bastion" of northern Idaho and launched his own projects, Independent History and Research, the Campaign for Radical Truth in History, and the online newsletter *HoffmanWire* (Hoffman 1998). Announcing these vehicles as the "most competent, dynamic and professional" alternatives with "huge potential to turn the System's agenda inside-out," Hoffman dreamed of establishing a revisionist center and a Holocaust museum that would detail the "real" holocausts in history, that is, the "Communist Holocaust," the "German Holocaust" (Dresden), and the "Japanese Holocaust" (Hiroshima and Nagasaki). Arguing that the "myth of the six million" affects everything, he is convinced that a revisionist center would be instrumental in bringing down the System, would move him to the White House, and would return America to its "natural constitution."[54] However, as with most counterculture projects, grandiose plans clashed with harsh realities, and Hoffman constantly complained about a lack of support and funding.[55]

His conspiracy theory revolving around the occult "cryptocracy," as laid out in *Secret Societies and Psychological Warfare* (1995b), is particularly original. Hoffman traces the origin of the cryptocratic mind-control back to prehistoric times, when man began to see himself as separate from and above nature. Under the cover of human progress, the cryptocracy gradually established an artificial replica of creation that in effect has turned man against nature. While agreeing with contemporary pagan critiques of nature-destroying modernity, Hoffman rejects the ecological concerns of Wiccans and Asatrúers as Orwellian newspeak, on par with the pagan pretense of having been persecuted. The cryptocracy's tyranny over humanity, he argues, has always advanced under cover of victimhood, the paramount example of which, obviously to Hoffman, would be the Jews. While presenting themselves as supreme friends of Mother Nature, pagan leaders have throughout history worked against her.[56] The cryptocracy has from the outset orchestrated American history. The famous Route 66, for instance, was laid out with the secret intention of sending masses of automobile riders into a self-processing occult trip between satanic centers. American citizens are thus unwitting targets of occult mass manipulation, projected not least through television and advertisements that carry encrypted subliminal messages.

A significant method of mass manipulation, Hoffman asserts, is the broadcast of the psychodramas of public ritual sacrifice and serial killers. The televised sacrifice of the "King of Camelot," JFK, at the thirty-third north parallel, close to the site of the first Masonic temple in Dallas, sent shock waves through the American mind, and society began to disintegrate. Popular music became faster and louder; drugs and occult religion became popular; beatniks, hippies, and race riots ripped the social fabric, causing people to beg for increased security, thus empowering the cryptocracy. Furthermore, Hoffman ventures that the Manson Family's killing of Sharon Tate, then pregnant by *Rosemary's Baby* director Roman Polanski, served as a ritual predecessor of the coming mass sacrifice of unborn children (the subsequent legalization of abortion). Modern American society then proceeded to give birth to a generation of Rosemary's babies (children of Satan) through systematic doubletalk (such as television news reports that condem a murderer but are followed by an action movie that idealizes violence) and disinformation in media and education. Important, Hoffman believes, to the alchemical processing of the mass mind is the cabal's "revealing of its method." The cryptocracy sends a serial murderer on a killing spree, or it murders a celebrity, covers up its tracks, catches a "lone nut" scapegoat, then intentionally reveals enough of the initial cover-up to mock and disorient the public, so no one gets prosecuted, thus increasing occult prestige and potency.

Magnified by the electronic power of the media, Hoffman continues, serial killers perpetuate large-scale human sacrifices to the goddess Ceres of antiquity. With "cereal" killers, such as the Unabomber or the Son of Sam, the alchemical processing of American collective unconsciousness is conducted in a prolonged Black Mass that may take years. Each new *cere*-monial killing triggers other catastrophic events (murders, suicides, black-outs, plane crashes, and so on) of ritual significance, which is evident if one watches the news in the days immediately after, for example, a Unabomber act. The cryptocracy has now advanced its Frankenstein object of producing an artificial, technological reproduction of life to the extent that man is almost completely distorted mentally (Hoffman 1995b). Currently in its final phase, the cabal has begun revealing the truth in movies such as *They Live*, *Videodrome*, and *The Matrix*, by means of which the system nudges humanity ever further into the tantalizing, counterfeit world of electronic virtual reality. We are living inside the movie *The Matrix*. The cryptocracy is in total control. Cunningly, the occult cabal openly "reveals its method" on the silver screen. By entertaining the entrapped with a movie portraying their entrapment, the system diverts attention from their entrapment. Embedded in *The Matrix* is also a subliminal message to the elite youth who want to get out of the sick system, encoded in the image of Keanu Reeves, dressed in a trench coat, who with blazing guns and duffel bags with bombs acts out an uncompromising defiance. *The Matrix* is a counterfeit model of counterfeit reality, a mirror image of a mirror image, and when the Trench Coat Mafia at Columbine High School in Littleton, Colorado, copied the copy of the copy to reenact Reeves's desperate attempt to escape the Matrix with blazing guns and duffel bags with bombs, the system was empowered to further increase its control, imposing gun control and extending the police state.[57]

A nonbeliever might feel bewildered by the complete recasting of reality presented by conspiracy researchers, exhausted by the multitude of details and the dramatic appeal to act in an ever-prolonged now. Conspiracy believers, however, tend to be unsatisfied with the large residue of events that commoners leave without explanation. There is no such thing as "fate," "bad luck," or "chance." Nothing happens by accident; every event is by design; everything has an intentional meaning. Conspiracy theory provides its believers with a comprehensive system that leaves nothing unanswered. Personified evil facilitates catharsis by directing dreams of revenge on visible targets. "Nothing happens by accident," one Aryan underground activist said. "If something occurs it is by design. If it is by design, then someone has designed it. If their identity and intent is concealed, then there is a conspiracy. If there is a conspiracy, it may be exposed. If it is exposed, it could be dealt with. We need only determine who to aim our guns at."[58] Living in a world where significant clues to world events are encoded on TV soaps, where your boss may be an alien, and nocturnal rites of necrophilia may take place in the basement of your parish church makes the ordinary extraordinary, your life and personal significance included.

Contributing to the popularity of conspiracy theory in the cultural underground is the number of actual conspiracies exposed. The American administration has long engaged in covert operations, as shown by Stephen Knott. "The United States has a rich history in clandestine operations—operations conducted in times of war and peace—that range from kidnapping to covert efforts to topple foreign governments" (Knott 1996, 4). Clandestine methods pose a dilemma between a democracy's ideal of transparency in the process of decision making, the idea of government by the people, and the praxis of executive government. An administration capable of orchestrating such a complex conspiracy as the Oliver North–Contra–Iran scandal could easily be suspected of every kind of conspiracy, nothing excluded. Thus, the exposure of one actual conspiracy renders, for the conspiracy theorist, an aura of probability to any other conspiracy theory "not yet exposed." This logic came to fore at a Preparedness Expo (a militia/conspiracy/survivalist conference) in Denver, November 1996. During the three-day event, housed at the giant coliseum, thousands of visitors listened to conspiracy theories by the likes of John Trochman, Terry Cook, Bo Gritz, and Jack McLamb on subjects ranging from space aliens in control of the government to computer chips soon to be implanted in every newborn American. Among the lecturers was also Gulf War veteran and nurse Joyce Riley, who talked about the Gulf War syndrome and the government cover-up.[59] During the final day of the conference, the Pentagon suddenly confessed that there was something like a Gulf War illness and that American soldiers possibly had been exposed to chemical and/or biological agents during the war. The news was readily interpreted by many conference participants as confirmation that made *all* theories presented at the forum seem likely, not just the Gulf War cover-up.

Anti-Semitism

Anti-Semitism came to the fore in American society in 1881 as Jewish immigration shifted from a few low-key, middle-class German families to some three million Yiddish-speaking, working-class Jews from Tsarist Russia and eastern Europe, arriving before the immigration restriction acts of 1921 and 1924.[60] The 1920s and 1930s saw a fervent anti-Semitism popularized by automobile tycoon Henry Ford and populist radio-priest Father Charles E. Coughlin. In the early 1920s, Ford's widely distributed Michigan weekly, *Dearborn Independent*, became the major mainstream outlet of anti-Semitic propaganda, including the *Protocols of the Elders of Zion*.[61] A compilation of articles from the *Dearborn Independent*, *The International Jew*, sold millions of copies, was translated into sixteen languages, and still appears at Aryan bookstores and on recommended reading lists.[62] Following a lawsuit, Ford in 1927 apologized to the Jewish community and closed down the paper.[63] In 1926, Roman Catholic priest Father Coughlin began preaching over the radio and quickly became a national celebrity with a weekly audience of millions.[64] During the Depression, Coughlin's sermons turned increasingly political, fiercely charging Wall Street "banksters" and the Hoover administration with ruining the life of ordinary Americans. In 1934, Coughlin founded the populist National Union for Social Justice, which soon boasted a following in the millions.[65] Initially supporting Franklin D. Roosevelt, Coughlin grew disenchanted with the New Deal. He launched the Union Party for the 1936 elections but received a mere 2 percent of the vote. Coughlin then made a radical turn to the right, praising the social justice of the Third Reich and preaching against the Jewish menace, eroding the ranks of his supporters to a coterie of fascists.

After the war, hostility toward Jews declined dramatically in American mainstream culture. Jewish civil-rights organization successfully rid discriminatory legislation and anti-Semitic opinions dropped to an all-time low. The American Jewish community in a few decades became the "largest, wealthiest, most influential and politically powerful that has ever existed in Diaspora history" (Wistrich 1991, 114). Despite Jewish empowerment and mainstream American disdain for anti-Semitism, a Jewish American self-image of vulnerability remained intact. The percentage of Jews who agree with the opinion that anti-Semitism is a "serious problem" in America doubled in the 1980s and scored a record 85 percent in 1990, a perception gap that can at least partly be explained by the virulent hostility against Jews formulated in the white-racist counterculture (Goldberg 1996, 6).[66]

Throughout the racist counterculture, Jews are typically portrayed as the archenemy of Aryan man. Bestowed with semi-divine powers, the Jew as imagined is construed as a metaphysical entity of evil. Two main strategies to alert mainstream American whites to the Jewish peril have developed. The first consists of exposing the alleged Jewish stranglehold on America and their efforts to secure world supremacy. This traditional method is obviously less effective in post–WWII society, as the Holocaust serves as a reminder of the horrific potentials inherent in anti-Semitic politics. The second strategy, probably designed to get around this obstacle, revolves around Holocaust denial. However, although most Aryan activists seem to believe in a vast Jewish conspiracy, the second strategy has not met with universal agreement, with some activists arguing that the Holocaust properly should be celebrated, not denied. Another factor is an accumulating Holocaust-denial fatigue.

Many organizations employ the first strategy, publishing detailed lists of Jewish-owned corporations and Jewish persons with top positions in the administration, the entertainment industry, and news media. Were Jews seen as individuals and not as cells of an organic body of metaphysical evil, there would be no point in producing all these name lists. The underlying assumption, of course, is that the thoughts and acts of every Jew everywhere by nature are synchronized to the end of exterminating the Aryan race to secure global supremacy. A Jew somehow carries such a transcendent power that his existence at one position in an organization contaminates the operations of other organizations even remotely linked with his own. The chief executive officer of Seagram Company, the National Alliance trumpets, is a Jew, Edgar Bronfman Jr. Among the many corporations owned by Seagram is MCA, a production conglomerate that among other companies owns Interscope Records that among other musical genres sells gangsta rap, which, the NA implies, makes gangsta rap a product of the Jewish conspiracy rather than of artists rooted in the African American experience and music history.[67]

Decorated war veteran Lieutenant Colonel Gordon "Jack" Mohr has toured the country on hundreds of anti-Semitic "crusades" since his retirement in 1964.[68] Ousted from the far-right conservative John Birch Society for his anti-Semitic opinions, Mohr has since cooperated with a wide range of counterculture Identity preachers and ministries (Mohr 1997).[69] He runs a prison-outreach ministry from his home in Little Rock, Arkansas, and has published numerous books exposing the Jewish conspiracy, including Christianities Ancient Enemy and America's Destiny: Christ or Anti-Christ?[70] Mohr argues that Judaism really is Babylonian Satanism practiced by a sinister people obsessed with a desire to destroy Christian America en route to world dominion, as laid out in the Protocols of the Learned Elders of Zion. Acknowledging that scholars dismiss Protocols as a counterfeit work, Mohr argues, "We must remember that before there can be a counterfeit there must first be an original, and one accomplished at forgery makes his copy as close to the original as possible" (1992, 41).[71] According to Mohr, the Jews masterminded the slave trade to import an alien race to contaminate the purity of Aryan race and culture (Mohr 1997).[72] In the early 1900s the Jewish Rothschild clan secured control of Europe, and the Jewish Rockefeller clan (who "hide their Jewishness under the façade of Protestantism") took over North America.[73] When Adolf Hitler defied Jewish world dominion, Jews masterminded a white civil war to get rid of him. The subsequent Cold War was a hoax diverting attention from Jewish consolidation of world supremacy, as evidenced by the fact that the Jews dismantled the Soviet Union once it had served its purpose. The world is now entering the final phase. Vast numbers of Jewish-controlled Russian and Chinese troops have arrived in Mexico and in Canada, preparing to invade by constructing highways into the United States (Mohr 1997). "Time is getting short. The forces of evil are gathering for a final assault against the Lord's anointed [Aryan man]. The assault against Zion [America] is already underway, led by the forces of Hell itself" (Mohr 1993a, 7).[74]

Holocaust deniers typically claim to be "revisionist historians," a reference to a school of respected historians who sought to revise official Allied historiography of World War I. Revisionists documented German peace pleadings ignored by the French and revealed that British war propaganda had falsified evidence about German atrocities against civilians, including their gassing of noncombatants, use of babies for target practice, and mutilation of Belgian women. Holocaust deniers cast their efforts in the revisionist tradition, portraying reports about the Holocaust as yet more false atrocity tales. Historian Harry Elmer Barnes is the only direct link between WWI revisionists and the new generation of Holocaust deniers. In the late 1940s, Barnes challenged the official historiography of WWII. He argued that the Allies had willfully misunderstood Hitler and accused Roosevelt of inciting Japan to attack Pearl Harbor. Turning his attention to Holocaust reports, Barnes called them exaggerations, although he stopped short of denying the existence of gas chambers (Lipstadt 1994, 31, 67–83).

In the 1970s a growing number of national socialists in America and Europe began denying that the Holocaust had ever happened. Initially venturing their arguments in publications of limited circulation, Holocaust deniers eventually made an effort to take their philosophy mainstream. Instrumental to this end was Willis Carto's Institute of Historical Review (IHR).[75] Carto, who founded Liberty Lobby and Populist Party, is editor of Spotlight, the largest radical-right weekly with an estimated circulation of 100,000, which aims to unite the conservative right wing with the counterculture. Dividing his time between his Washington, D.C., headquarters and his spacious villa in fashionable Escondido, California, Carto rarely gives interviews, preferring to work as the controlling power behind various front organizations. Through the IHR research center, publishing house, and *Journal of Historical Review*, Carto sought in the 1980s to take Holocaust denial beyond the confines of the counterculture. The annual IHR conventions attracted leading European and American deniers, such as Arthur R. Butz, David Irving, Robert Faurisson, Ernst Zündel, Mark Weber, Michael Hoffman II, Bradley Smith, and Ditleib Felderer.

IHR associates sought to present themselves as apolitical scholars concerned with an accumulating body of evidence indicating that the extermination of six million Jews simply was not technologically possible, and they targeted university campuses with proposals to "debate the issue." Not all revisionists, however, are scholars, and those who are often hold credentials that hardly seem relevant. Faurisson is a former professor of literature, Butz a professor of electrical and computer engineering. Weber holds only a master's degree in history. Hoffman II and David Irving are both autodidacts, and at least one, "execution specialist" Fred A. Leuchter, claims phony credentials as an engineer. Brought in as an "expert" defense witness in a 1988 Canadian trial against Ernst Zündel for distributing revisionist publications, Leuchter produced "an engineering report" based on "chemical analysis" and "on-site inspection and forensic examination" at Auschwitz, Birkenau, and Majdanek, concluding that there had been "no gas chambers at any of these locations" (Leuchter 1988).[76] The court dismissed his expertise, as he could only present a bachelor of arts (in history) and had no degree in engineering. Neither that ruling nor a later out-of-court settlement in which he signed a consent agreement admitting that he was not and never had been a professional engineer has, however, prevented his report from circulating the cultural underground as irrefutable scientific evidence (Lipstadt 1994, 166–73).

This was not the only revisionist legal setback. The IHR had in 1979 offered a reward of $50,000 to anyone who "could prove that the Nazis operated gas chambers to exterminate Jews during World War II." Auschwitz survivor Mel Mermelstein accepted the challenge and filed a lawsuit against the IHR that in 1985 landed him the reward plus an additional $40,000 for pain and suffering (Lipstadt 1994, 137–41). Then, in April 2000, David Irving lost a widely publicized libel suit against Deborah Lipstadt for ruining his reputation by describing him as "one of the most dangerous spokespersons for Holocaust denial" in her 1993 study *Denying the Holocaust* (Zacharia 2000; Reid 2000; "Hitler Historian Loses" 2000; Kelland 2000). By then, Carto had lost control of his revisionist empire in one of the perennial internal intrigues characterizing the Aryan counterculture. Following a palace coup in October 1993, the IHR leadership accused Carto for having diverted seven million dollars to his Liberty Lobby; he in turn charged them of being secretly controlled by a cabal of scientologists and Jews with the hidden purpose of closing down revisionism. Carto in 1994 launched the *Barnes Review,* and the IHR continued to organize revisionist conferences under the new directorate of Mark Weber and Greg Raven.[77] Looking back, Carto (1996) took pride in his accomplishments: "Whereas in the 1980s, the Holocaust was absolutely sacrosanct, the average person today is much more likely to realize that it is a controversial question. I think that the people who are trying to destroy the IHR is trying to block the door after the horse has run out, and its out there and running like hell, and there's no way they're gonna get it back. It's been just too much water running under the bridge. So, I am very proud over the work that I did with the IHR."

It is hard to determine to what extent Aryan revolutionaries actually believe in Holocaust denial and to what extent it is only a national socialist comeback strategy. Certainly, there are revisionists who are not national socialists or racists, and there are counterculture people who do seem to believe that the Holocaust never happened. But there are undoubtedly also those who disseminate revisionist material to clear the ground for a national socialist renaissance. Harold Covington (pseud. Winston Smith) of the National Socialist White People's Party illustrates this. While running staple Holocaust denial articles ("40 Questions" 1996, for example), his purpose is explicit: "The destruction of the Myth of the Six Million in the minds of Aryan peoples worldwide is one of the most important tasks the Movement faces. It may be said that when we have won the battle on the Holocaust, we will have made National Socialist revolution certain" (Smith 1995). "Without their precious Holocaust, what are the Jews?" Covington asks in his e-zine, "Just a grubby little bunch of international bandits and assassins and squatters who have perpetrated the most massive, cynical fraud in human history."[78] Should, however, Covington be presented with irrefutable evidence that the Holocaust had in fact occurred, then "it would probably cheer me up to think that at least some of those reptiles in human form who caused it all got theirs."[79]

Other Aryan activists find Holocaust denial bizarre. "Why deny one of our rare victories?" a national socialist pagan asked. "We should celebrate the Holocaust!" (*Anonymous* 1998). The majority, however, do not seem to care. "No sensible person would be excited about anything this dated," a *WAR* article read (Frenz 1994). Throughout the counterculture Holocaust-denial fatigue is accumulating. "Much of this stuff, excuse me, is rehashed, 'been there, done that, said that.' "[80] Many suspect that Holocaust deniers milk the counterculture for profit while staying away from the real struggle. Revisionism is dismissed as "a German thing," "irrelevant except for the people who earn their living from it" (Frenz 1994).

Populism

Populism has been a salient feature in the history of U.S. politics. As with many of the other elements of the counterculture, populism has hardly been the sole property of reactionaries, showing up as it has taken many different forms. Found among rural farmers, small town artisans, and urban industrial workers, among others, populism has emerged within milieus of both the left and the right, and has served as means to both democratic and autocratic ends.[81] With its many different faces, populism has been problematic to define.[82] Populists generally posit themselves as the organic voice of an idealized "people," the definition of which often excludes or scapegoats "aliens," "parasites," or "debasing elements." Hostile to "corrupt" politicians, populism tends to reject representative politics in favor of people's rule through radical localism, direct democracy, or vague ideas of a corporate or organic state. Idealizing the common sense of the common man, populism is generally anti-elitist and anti-intellectual, typically proposing simple solutions to complex problems. A dimension of Jeffersonian direct democracy, populism was a motif for the anti-elitist "Americanism" of Jackson and the anti-Catholic nativist movements, and was key to the People's (Populist) Party in the late nineteenth century. A progressive mass movement that grew out of radical agrarian resentment against the East Coast banking establishment, the People's Party aimed to restore government to the "plain people."[83] It called for federal intervention to check the power of the elite and support the ordinary toiling man.[84] Running as a third party alternative in 1882, the party's presidential candidate polled a million votes, and the party won a three gubernatorial races — ten seats in the House and five in the Senate — but dissolved after being unsuccessful in the following presidential race.

Also steeped in the populist tradition was the Share-Our-Wealth movement of folksy Huey Long, who built a mass following by railing against the Wall Street elite. Planning to redistribute the excessive wealth of the ultrarich, Long promised to provide every American with a basic income, an automobile, a home, and a pension. As governor and later senator of Louisiana, Long provided free schoolbooks, introduced night schools, and invested in roads and schools for the rural poor. Seeking the support of the Klan while trying not to offend Louisiana's Catholic community, Long manipulated themes of antiblack Americanism and opportunistically altered his message according to his audience. In time, flamboyant Long centralized power to the degree that he became known as the "dictator of Louisiana." Long might have been able to pose a challenge to Roosevelt in the 1936 presidential election, but he was assassinated the year before (Hair 1991; Bennet 1995; Taggart 2000, 37; Berlet and Lyons 2000, 125).[85]

Politicians such as George Wallace and, more recently, "folk billionaire" Ross Perot and nativist Pat Buchanan carried the populist tradition forward (Berlet and Lyons, 2000; Westlind 1996; Åsard 1994). In its counterculture setting, populism revolves around restoring power to the white people who "built this land." Among its more significant manifestations are the Posse Comitatus with successors, the "reincarnated" Populist Party, and the white workers' militancy of Tom Metzger's White Aryan Resistance effort. The radicalization of white racism during the 1980s coincided with a farm crisis in the American heartland. Thousands of indebted family farmers lost their land to corporate agribusiness. Predictions held that by the year 2000, fewer than 50,000 huge corporate farms would produce three-quarters of America's food, and more than a million small farmers would have been driven off the land. Blaming rural poverty on (Jewish) banksters and declaring interest rates and income tax unlawful, Posse Comitatus (Power to the County) emerged as a network of some 1,700 groups with an estimated 50–100,000 members.[86] Posse held "the county government as the highest authority" and the county sheriff "the only legal law enforcement officer." Responsible to the people, the sheriff should protect common man also from banksters and the federal administration, and Posse became notorious for issuing death warrants for sheriffs failing to meet this end.[87] Posse encouraged people to reclaim their sovereignty by refusing to pay taxes, returning their driver's licenses and birth certificates, driving cars without license plates, and staying on the land even if declared evicted by a bank.

Animated by the racist creed of Christian Identity, the militant wing of Posse Comitatus made headlines in the late 1970s and early 1980s with a series of illegal actions, including armed intervention to block auctions of farmer's land, assaulting IRS officers, and producing counterfeit money.[88] In 1983, two federal marshals were killed in a shootout with Posse organizer and Identity Christian Gordon Kahl, who then managed to stay on the run for several months in a widely publicized manhunt. Following a tip, the FBI surrounded Kahl's Ozark safe-house. In the subsequent shootout, the ammo depot exploded and Kahl became a counterculture martyr.[89] In the mid-1980s, the Posse fragmented into a multitude of groups, such as the Freemen, Farmers' Alliance, and Farmers' Liberation Army, espousing, variously, radical localism, constitutional fundamentalism, and agrarian populism. In the early 1990s, these sentiments contributed to the makeup of the militias and will most likely continue to feed cycles of fervent activism.

In 1984, Carto launched the Populist Party, presented as a "reincarnation" of the People's Party. Steeped in populist ideology, Carto cast himself as the interpreter of the people. "On virtually every core issue . . . the vast majority is on our side" (Carto 1996). The "people," he claimed, are against immigration, racial integration, bussing, affirmative action; don't like intervention in foreign affairs; fight the income tax; and celebrate the traditional values of common man. The "fact" that the people are "fundamentally opposed to the policy of the government" proves that the United States is not a democracy. "The laws are not passed by the people, the laws are passed by politicians, and the politicians are not controlled by the people, politicians are controlled by the plutocrats, the very rich, and by special interest pressure groups. . . . We have a judicial and legislative dictatorship in this country that couldn't care less about the American public." Carto suggested that there was a "cabal that are responsible for all the problems of this country." Since the beginning the "plutocracy has been the enemy of America" and is now under way to establish a New World Order that in effect means the end of national sovereignty and individual liberties. To secure the free-trade project globally, international banksters will press for a world government with enticing notions of world peace and multicultural harmony. "People are referring to the global village," Carto said indignantly. "It's a global plantation! You have the master up on the hill and the plutocrats and their servants are there and you have all of us down here as their niggers on the plantation, and that what's they want!" (ibid.).

To "reinstate" popular government, Carto hoped that a populist third party alternative could challenge the two establishment parties. The Populist Party did bring together regional populist groups but hardly had the success that its appropriated predecessor had had. The 1984 Populist Party presidential candidate, Olympic star Bob Richards, quit campaigning after learning of Carto's prominence in white-racist and anti-Semitic milieus. Internal squabbles in the Populist Party also affected the 1988 race. Presidential candidate David Duke and his running mate, Bo Gritz, parted ways, and Gritz was replaced with Floyd Parker. Duke received less than 50,000 votes, a mere 0.4 percent of the total. Gritz came close to doubling that result as the party's 1992 presidential candidate, receiving most votes from Utah (4 percent) and Idaho (3 percent). By then, Carto had withdrawn as the power behind, and the Populist Party had split in two: the Populist Party of the United States and the Populist Party of America.[90] Frustrated, Carto in a 1996 interview endorsed leaderless resistance as a "last ditch strategy" that "got to be used," as conventional methods have failed.

Carto's longtime adversary is Tom Metzger, founder of White Aryan Resistance (WAR), with headquarters in Fallbrook, north of San Diego. Born in 1938 in Warsaw, Illinois, Metzger enrolled in the army at age eighteen. Returning to work for Douglass Aircraft in Santa Monica, Metzger engaged in company-sponsored anticommunist training. Gravitating toward radical racism by way of the Barry Goldwater campaign, the John Birch Society, and the tax rebellion scene, he found Christian Identity. Converting in 1971, Metzger served as pastor in the California faction of Church of Jesus Christ, Christian until 1980, when he dropped the creed as historically unsubstantiated. Meeting Duke at an Identity gathering in 1975, Metzger joined the Knights of the Ku Klux Klan, eventually becoming its California Grand Dragon. Disenchanted with Duke's womanizing and his "cowardly" reaction whenever antiracist activists attacked Klan rallies, Metzger in 1978 founded the supposedly more combative California KKK. In 1980, Metzger won the Democratic primary in California (but lost in the general election) and in 1982 gathered some 75,000 Californian votes for the U.S. Senate on an openly racist "white workers' rights" platform. Two years later, Metzger renamed his political action committee White Aryan Resistance to provoke his enemies and signal a more revolutionary racist populism. Metzger currently runs the *Race and Reason* cable-TV show and the aggressively racist *WAR* zine, popular not least among racist skinheads. In 1988 two Portland skins of the East Side White Pride crew beat the brain out of Mulugeta Serew, an Ethiopian guest student, with a baseball bat. Morris Dees of the Southern Poverty Law Center filed suit against Metzger and WAR on behalf of the victim's family. Dees argued that the murderers were acting under influence of WAR propaganda and had received training by an agent of Metzger. Handling his own defense, Metzger lost the case. With damages assessed at $12.5 million, the WAR organization barely survived.

Inspired by Jack London and populist icons Huey Long and Father Coughlin, Metzger construed an Americanized version of the "third position," which advanced national socialism as an alternative to communism and capitalism, "neither left, nor right, but forward," as with the left-leaning, national socialist continuation of Strasserite national socialism and the leftist tendency of early

Italian fascism. While admiring Hitler, Metzger recognized as glaring errors the Night of the Long Knifes—the 1934 purge in the NSDAP of leftist and National-Bolshevik elements—and the overturn of the Molotov-Ribbentrop Pact—a non-aggression pact signed in 1939 between Germany and the Soviet Union and broken by Germany in 1941. Metzger believed that in suppressing the socialist wing of NSDAP, Hitler had "stuck the wrong pig" and moved toward an alliance with capitalism. Had Hitler not attacked Soviet Russia, Metzger believed, the war might have ended differently and Soviet Russia would have developed a National Bolshevist ideology. From Metzger's third-positionist point of view, revolutionary racism "can't move much further with the right-wing in our way," Metzger (1996) claimed. "Just as it was in our way in [national socialist] Germany, the right wing slows us down." The "main problem" of today is that "transnational corporations . . . now virtually runs the world," Metzger said. "All of the racial problems are a side issue that comes from economic problems caused by the multinational corporations."

Metzger differs from many other counterculture ideologues in not using global capitalism as an anti-Semitic euphemism. "I don't take the extreme position and say that the Jews run everything, because they don't. Take the 400 most important multinational corporations and you got your structure for the global government . . . and Jews are just a small faction of it." While finding race to be an agitating issue—and seeking to fan the flames by using vulgar racist rhetoric in WAR—Metzger foresees a revolution sprung from conflicts generated by the world capitalist system. "As the rich are getting richer and the poor are getting poorer, and the massive influx of people from other nations, mostly nonwhite, and the exporting of more and more jobs from this country, you know, the chemistry is there, it's like a bomb, waiting for someone to light the fuse." The violent cleansing deemed necessary will, Metzger reasoned, most likely be triggered by riots in depressed black and Hispanic inner cities, wreaking havoc, which white revolutionaries will capitalize on. The future Aryan homeland will guarantee "free education," "free medical and health care," ecologically sustainable production, and "economic justice." "Major white collar criminals would be publicly executed, so that poor people realize that justice is for everybody." Moving units of production overseas will be banned and military intervention in foreign affairs will cease. The border will be permanently sealed. Millions of non-Aryan immigrants will be deported by force, and negotiations with African Americans will set the terms for racial separation by "repatriation" or territorial division. Addressing the issue of how the Aryan republic would be governed, Metzger in one breath described both a system based on "direct vote of the people" and a dictatorship where "strong men with forward ideas maintain power," admitting, "I know, its very contradictory, it's a problem in my own mind" (1996).

Separatism

Dreams of racial separation and an Aryan homeland are not unique to Metzger but reflect a widespread trend in the counterculture. Inspired by the Declaration of Independence, many white racists argue that the history of the present administration is "a history of repeated injuries and usurpation" against the white people, "all having in direct object the establishment of absolute Tyranny." Therefore, Aryans have the right and duty to abolish the government and institute a government of their own. At its core, white separatism holds that different races cannot coexist harmoniously because "nature" dictates racial separation. "The people who cause the racial hatred and tension are the people in government who unnaturally force people of different races to live together," George Hawthorne (1996) said. "We are not meant to live together. We are meant to have our own nations, our own culture, our own way of life." Looking at world history from a social Darwinist perspective, some separatists now even question the doctrine of white supremacy. "We once controlled 85 percent of the surface of the world but now suffer under ZOG rule," an Aryan pagan said (under condition of anonymity). "I don't see anything supreme in that at all." When asked, most separatists invest superior qualities in the Aryan race but consider white supremacy disastrous as a political ideology. "Supremacy is a fallible doctrine, because to be supreme over someone else, is to have contact with them, whereas separation divides you off from them," imprisoned Order member David Tate (1997) explained. "I believe that I, as an Aryan, have a supreme intellect compared to other races but the doctrine of supremacy in a government will get you destroyed."

Separation is considered key to Aryan survival. In the early 1980s Robert Miles introduced the idea of territorial separation in his seminal *Birth of a Nation*. White Americans constituted a separate, racial nation, Miles argued, and urged white families to move out from multicultural regions to the Pacific Northwest where whites remained a majority. "Let us go in peace," Miles wrote. "Let us be considered a Racial Nation of Aryans" (2) Miles originally designated the states of Washington, Oregon, Idaho, Montana, and Wyoming, plus northern California, as an Aryan sanctuary. In a 1986 speech at Aryan Nations, Miles outlined how the Northwest Territorial Imperative would become reality "by White racialists moving to the area, buying land together or adjacent to each other and having families consisting of five and ten children. These children would be raised and educated in the tradition and fighting heritage of our own White people. We will win the Northwest by out-breeding our opponents and keeping our children away from the insane and destructive values of the Establishment."

The idea of separatism caught on within the counterculture, being to various extents endorsed by the likes of WAR, Wotansvolk, Aryan Nations, White Order of Thule, and Northwestern Imperative. "We do NOT want the tired, the poor, and the huddled masses," ss unit leader Ryker of Northwestern Imperative said in reference to the poetic claims of the Statue of Liberty (Ryker 1994, 2). "We want the hardy, the strong, the stout, the thinkers, the educated. . . . We want people like our forefathers, who fearlessly braved this unknown frontier and conquered it away from the savage Indians. We want individuals who will stand courageously, able and willing to enact an 'apartheid' against world politics" (ibid.). Derek Stenzel, a Portland skin and editor of *Northwestern Imperative*, emphasized that the Constitution of the State of Oregon, 1859, stated in clear terms that "no free negro, mulatto or Chinaman" could reside, vote, hold contract, or make business in the state. An exclusively Aryan Northwest would therefore be in line with "the high racist ideals" of the original settlers (Stenzel 1997).

At a gathering on 20 April 1996 (Hitler's birthday), Aryan Nations issued the Aryan Declaration of Independence, stating that the "Aryan People in America, are, and of right ought to be, a free and independent nation; that they are absolved from all allegiance to the United States of America" (Aryan Nations 1996a). In the platform ratified for the Aryan national state, Aryan Nations outlined a constitution for the "free white" republic: media, education, politics, and economics would be required by law to serve the "common interest" of racial greatness; every activity and opinion "not conductive to National Welfare" would be forbidden; promotion of Judaism and communism would be a capital offense; and "satanic, heathen beliefs will be outlawed" (Aryan Nations 1996b). Unsurprisingly, racial heathens merely shrugged at the thought of living under Identity Christian rule. "The concept of having an Aryan Nation in the Northwest is a good one, and it brought a lot of people up here," Ron McVan of Wotansvolk commented (1996). "But when people come up here and meet the Identity people, they're turned off. I mean, you won't have freedom of religion. People either follow their religion or die, and I don't wanna live under that structure. No one has the freedom to do what they want, and we'll never accept that."

Other Aryan activists reject as unrealistic the plan of a secessionist white state. "The government isn't going to allow that any more than they're going to allow a black separate nation, any more than they allowed the Confederate states to become a nation," John Baumgardner of the Florida-based Black Knights said (1996), citing as evidence the 1988 sedition trial in which the Justice Department (unsuccessfully) charged Robert Miles, Louis Beam, Richard Butler, David Lane, and ten other counterculture ideologues for planning to overthrow the government. "Besides, I don't wanna live in the Northwest. It's too cold. I would prefer, maybe, Costa Rica, you know."

The desire for an Aryan homeland has propelled white racists to forge links of cooperation with black nationalists such as the Black Panthers and the Nation of Islam and to invest much energy in producing plans for a division of U.S. territory into several monoracial states. Unlikely as it might seem, these cross-racial links go far back in history. Abolitionists, slave owners, and black freemen worked together in repatriation projects; populist black nationalist Marcus Garvey "believed in a pure black race, just how all self-respecting whites believe in a pure white race" (1986a, 37) and saw Klansmen as better friends of African Americans than white liberals (1986b, 71); Malcolm X of the Nation of Islam in a series of secret meetings with the Klan sought to develop a joint program for racial separation; and George Lincoln Rockwell was in 1962 invited to address an NOI convention.[91] These occasional contacts would expand with the emergence of the revolutionary white-racist perspective. The 1980s saw the formation of an underground network between racists of different color, involving Tom Metzger, David Duke, Willis Carto, Don Black, Louis Beam, Jack Mohr, John Baumgardner, and the British National Front on the white side, and the Nation of Islam, the Lost-Found Nation of Islam, and the Pan Afrikan International on the black side.[92]

The eagerness with which modern Aryan revolutionaries seek to cooperate with black nationalists points to a revaluation of black capabilities. During the fight against desegregation, white racists generally considered black power to be masterminded by Jews who manipulated gullible blacks to their own end. Today, whereas white-racist culture has been reduced to dysfunctional, ranting sects that accomplish few things of value, the black separatist Nation of Islam builds schools, opens supermarkets, patrols neighborhoods, and triumphantly headed the largest rally ever in U.S. history—the 1995 Million Man March. Almost every white-racist spokesperson of today emphasizes the need to emulate Louis Farrakhan. "First of all, we need to do what the Nation of Islam has done,"

George Hawthorne said. "When we can mobilize a million white men, like the Nation of Islam could do, when we have our own companies, our own businesses, our own lobby groups, we could lobby the government for change. Then, our million white men could meet in Washington, D.C., with the million black men of the Nation of Islam and we could shake hands. We could say, 'Together we will work to bring back sanity in this country. Together we will work for true racial separation' " (Hawthorne 1996).

In 1992 robed Klansmen and black nationalist PAIN (Pan-Afrikan International) activists organized a joint rally at the old slave market in St. Augustine, Florida. The first in a series of black–white-racist rallies led by John Baumgardner and Chief Osiris Akkebala, the provoking event was the public announcement of a black–white-racist alliance that would continue in the years to come. Born in Georgia in 1954, John Baumgardner is not the stereotypical Klansman. A former hippie with a past in Students for a Democratic Society who keeps Che Guevara on the wall and favors reggae music, he combined full-time activism with home-schooling of his two children. Joining the Invisible Empire of the Ku Klux Klan in 1984, Baumgardner eventually served as its Florida Grand Dragon, Imperial Klaliff, and *Klansman* editor.[93] After the demise of the Invisible Empire, the Florida klaverns (or local Klan unit) broke up into twenty-some independent Klans. Baumgardner today heads the underground Black Knights and is chief architect behind the Inter-Klan Kartel, a network of independent Florida Klans. A staunch Identity Christian, Baumgardner retains in part the class perspective of his leftist past and has a working relationship with Metzger.[94] Baumgardner has "constantly preached revolution" to a "traditionally reactionary Klan" and is pleased that the hooded order has finally come to realize that "the government is the enemy" (Baumgardner 1996; Baumgardner 1996).

Founding Elder of PAIN is former Baptist minister and CORE (Congress of Racial Equality) activist Chief Osiris Akkebala (b. Jack Mitchell) who teaches that the divine black man has an extraterrestrial origin. At the beginning of time, the black Man-God descended to Earth to establish its first civilization at Chemi (present-day Egypt). During what is known as the "Fall of Adam," man and God were separated, and the black man lost knowledge of his divine nature. Afrika was invaded by evil spirits in carnal hues who brought blacks in bondage to North America. By reconnecting with Amon-Ra and the ancient gods of Chemi, blacks will be mentally emancipated, which will set the stage for repatriation to Afrika. An esoteric link exists, the scenario continues, between the Holy Land and restoration of primordial Man-God; by returning the divine sparks to Afrika, the black man will re-ascend into divinity and establish a superior Pan-Afrikan nation (Akkebala 1996; Akkebala n.d.a; Akkebala n.d.b; "PAIN Organizational Structure" n.d.).

In 1987 Baumgardner was invited to Akkebala's talk-radio show following a Klan rally at all-black Eatonville; they learned that they were both racial separatists and have "been friends ever since." Baumgardner introduced Akkebala to David Duke, resulting in PAIN's endorsement of Duke for the 1988 presidential race on the Populist Party ticket. Akkebala introduced Baumgardner to Silis X Muhammad of the Lost-Found Nation of Islam (an NOI competitor that claims to be rightful heir to Elijah Muhammad and considers Farrakhan to be the "second beast of the revelations"), and Baumgardner has since helped their campaign promoting reparations and repatriation. Akkebala furthermore linked Baumgardner up with freelance black nationalist agitator Khallid Abdul Muhammad (a former lieutenant in the NOI and chairman of the New Black Panther Party, he died in 2001) and African socialist Black Uhuru.[95] Baumgardner then introduced Akkebala to Tom Metzger and helped negotiate a (later aborted) deal with John Trochman that the Militia of Montana would provide training for a PAIN black militia.[96] Baumgardner and Akkebala then launched the United Separatist Front as a nationalist international or multicultural racist network, claiming a mailing list of several hundred separatist groups globally. In 1997 the first annual Conference on Racial Separatism convened with Akkebala, Baumgardner, Willis Carto, Don Black, and Robert Block as featured speakers.

How do people react to robed Klansmen and black separatists in African outfits standing together? Past Klan activities like lynching, castration, and nightly terror have planted a negative image of the Klan in the minds of black people, Akkebala admits. But the fifth-era Klan comprises is a very different breed of Klansmen. The Klan of the 1920s and 1960s was part of the Southern white power structure, the unofficial arm of white justice. Today, with no member being part of the mainstream power structure, the Klan is as revolutionary and antisystem as their fellow black separatists (Akkebala 1996). Baumgardner (1996) acknowledged, "Traditionally, the Klan has been pretty ignorant in its public appearances." A truly underground Klan must focus on fighting the system and cannot afford to alienate potential allies, even allies who happen to be black. Baumgardner did admit, however, that strategy of black-white cooperation had met with opposition from "the reactionary remnants" within the Klan. Initially, resentment was greater, and Baumgardner named his group Black Knights partly because they "were the black sheep of the Klan." In the face of bewildered reactions from the public, he maintained that "all of us separatists goes along fine. It's the rest of these civilians who have a problem. We're beyond hate. We figured it out, you know. Be honest enough to abide by your feelings and don't seek to assimilate. We don't have a problem with each other. We get along fine."

Christian Identity: The Gospel of Aryan Israel

Christian Identity is a racist recasting of British-Israelism, a lay school of theology that identified the peoples of northern Europe with the lost tribes of Israel.[97] Introduced in the United States at the turn of the century, British-Israelism found resonance with the Puritan legacy that identified America as the New Israel to which Providence had brought the chosen through an exodus from European bondage. Substituting biology for analogy, British-Israelism carried the argument further by insisting on a genealogical identity with the chosen people. A creed of Anglo-Saxon–Nordic supremacy, American British-Israelism attracted laymen with anti-Semitic and pro–national socialist leanings and began transforming into Christian Identity in the 1930s, as detailed by Barkun (1997).[98] During the 1970s Identity contributed to the radicalization of white racism as key Identity preachers "came to occupy positions of leadership in Klan organizations" (Rich 1988, 294).

Far from a cohesive creed, Identity is highly fragmented theologically and organizationally. As of 2002 there are about forty "open" Identity ministries, the majority of which are "cassette ministries," spreading the gospel of the Aryan Christ primarily by mail-order sales of audio- and videocassettes, Bible study material, talk radio, and the Internet. Believers are not necessarily members of an Identity congregation but may form Bible-study groups that convene regularly in the readers' homes. Reflecting their Israeli identity, families may give their children names such as Seth, Elisheba, Levi, Rebekah, Melchizedek, and Sarai, and adopt Israeli surnames such as Weisman or Neuman. To distance themselves from corrupted Judeo-Christianity, believers prefer the ancient Israeli names for God—YHWH or Yahweh—and for Jesus—Yahshua or Yahweh-Yahshua. Many observe Sabbath, celebrate Passover and Purim, follow the dietary laws of Deuteronomy and Leviticus, and practice male circumcision to symbolize the Covenant. Given the anti-Semitic attitude typical to the counterculture, this may be a source of confusion. After all, not every Aryan warrior can appreciate the activities of a *Mission to Israel* (a Christian Identity outreach program) or an *Army of Israel* (a skinhead gang that uses violence to assert white power). Estimates of the combined membership of Christian Identity vary considerably, but the number is generally thought to be less than one hundred thousand, although Barkun suspects that could be reduced by half (Barkun 1997, viii). Peaking in the 1980s, Identity now seems on the decline. Although some white-power bands refer to Identity themes and Identity summer camps still attract hundreds of youth, Identity does have a ring of an old man's religion to it.

Christian Identity is best understood as an umbrella concept under which a wide variety of different theologies are found. Ministries and laymen differ considerably in matters of dogma and religious observance. During the 1980s and 1990s, a series of violent events brought Identity to public attention with chilling reports of fortified compounds, armed underground activities, and leaders paying homage to Jesus and Hitler. This contributed to the crystallization of two major Identity Christian "schools," here referred to as "hardcore" and "soft" Identity. Major differences involve conflicting notions of how to understand "Counterfeit Israel" (the Jews), Aryan Israel's relation to Gentile races, national socialism, and apocalyptic expectations. Hardcore Identity believes that Jews are literally the descendants of Satan. The gospel is for Aryans only. Christianity and national socialism are therefore two sides of the same coin. Soft Identity understands Satan's fathering of the Jewish people in terms of allegory rather than biology. Israel is a guide of mankind, and other people will benefit from accepting the rule of Aryan Christ. National socialism is dismissed as an unwanted secular diversion or as ungodly occultism.

Another widespread hardcore belief is that God calls his people to prepare for, or even trigger, an apocalypse in which Israel quite literally will be the Army of God. This is often accompanied by the belief that God calls an elite cadre (sometimes known as the Phineas Priesthood) to punish transgressors of divine law. It is from the hardcore scene that the most notorious outbursts of violence have come, and spokespersons of soft Identity complain that the whole world of Identity has been painted with the same brush, thereby transforming Identity into an icon of evil in public mind. While rarely pacifists, soft Identity rejects as misguided the hardcore theology of violence. Ministers have campaigned against the Phineas Priesthood concept of vigilantes executing offenders on behalf of God, claiming that, while preparedness for the Final Battle is advisable, believers should leave its start-button to God. In the 1990s, influential ministers of the soft school began to distance themselves from the hardcore by rejecting the Identity label in favor of nonstigmatized terms like "Kingdom Israel" or "Covenant People." Increasingly hostile to each other, ministers on both sides came to identify the other school as the one obstacle preventing the Second

Coming. While there still are areas of crossover between the schools, the process of polarization is likely to continue and may result in two separate religions of Aryan Israel. Among hardcore leaders are Richard G. Butler, Neuman Briton, Mark Thomas, James Wickstrom, Richard Kelley Hoskins, Robert A. Balaicius, the Eleventh Hour Ministry, and Kingdom Identity Ministries. The soft Identity school includes Pete Peters, Ted R. Weiland, Jack Mohr, Bob Hallstrom, Dan Gayman, Gospel Ministries, Paul Hall, and *Jubilee*, currently the most widely circulated Identity tabloid.[99]

At the core of Identity is the exclusive belief that only whites are of the Adamic race. Non-Jewish nonwhites are pre-Adamic, while the Jewish "race" is post-Adamic. In Genesis 2:5–7, God contemplates his creation. As there is no man to till the ground, God creates Adam out of dust, gives him the "breath of life; and man became a living soul." Correctly translated, *Adam* means "white man," according to Identity Christians, who cite as evidence *Adam*'s derivative meaning of "to show blood in the face" and who furthermore assume that only whites have the ability to blush. "The colored races, not having been endowed with God's Spirit, have no abstract sense of right or wrong," Identity minister Thomas O'Brien claimed, "and consequently are never embarrassed" (n.d., 7). Jack Mohr (1997) emphasized the innate "moral difference" between a "white Christian" and a "non-white Christian." God "placed His law in our heart," Mohr explained. "Even a [white] man who has never gone inside a Church or received any religious training at all" knows "by heart" what is right and what is wrong thanks to this "divine nature." God made Adam a "living soul" and "that thing in itself set him apart" from the rest of mankind.

This notion forms the basis of a racial gnosis in the Ariosophic undercurrent of Aryan Israel. Imprisoned Order member Gary Yarbrough (1997) asserted that there "is a spark of life, divine life, in the DNA" of Aryan Man. God is energy, a divine creative force animating the white race. Every individual white man is thus *of* God and *is* God. When Adam and Eve fell from the Garden of Eden, David Tate (1997) explained, "they fell from a state of perfection into a state of imperfection," thrown into the "hell-like battleground" of Earth. Tate believed that only a select elite would return into divinity.[100] To sift the wheat from the chaff, God surrounded Aryan man with enemy races. War was to Tate a baptism of fire, qualifying the superior element for the government of God. To Yarbrough, a united race equaled a unified God-force, which would serve as the Second Coming of Christ in the body of divine believers. Aryan man is accordingly holy, that is, "set apart" as the embodiment of God, his body being a container for the spark of divinity. As the "Temple of God," Aryan man must be separate from the contaminating influences of Babylon and the impure, non-white races. Above all else, the God Within must be protected from the bodily fluids of other races. The divine spark cannot be corrupted, Yarbrough (1997) explained: if a white "becoming-God" takes a nonwhite partner, the offspring will not be half-God, half-Beast; instead, the divine spark dies if it comes in contact with the impure genes of nonwhite "mud races," making biracial love the highest of capital crimes.

Non-divine races divide in two categories: the pre-Adamic "colored" races and the post-Adamic "serpent" race. The theory that humans existed on Earth prior to Adam and Eve is not novel to Identity but has been part of Christian speculation since at least the seventeenth century. If Genesis is to be believed, how else could one explain the wife Cain married when he dwelt in the land of Nod, east of Eden, where he founded a city?[101] At the bottom ladder of pre-Adamic races is the black "servant race."[102] "God put His people here to bring light to the world," Butler (1996) said. "We taught the blacks everything they know. We gave them clothes and shoes and some education. It didn't come out of them—it came from us. We trained that animal, and learned that animal to do certain things; it's like, you can take a monkey and train it to ride a bicycle, same thing with negroes. So, as for the black man, whatever he can do, a white man has taught him. Take football and basketball, they didn't invent it, they didn't think out the rules for it, whites did. They've been trained to play it to entertain us. We are the light of the Earth."[103]

Hardcore Identity Christians identify blacks with the beasts of Genesis 1:24–25, where God "made the beast of the earth after his kind, and the cattle after their kind," prior to making man in his image.[104] God then gives Adam "dominion" over all of the creation (Genesis 1:26). Thomas O'Brien (n.d.) comments, "The Adamic Race is to have dominion over every form of life previously created. This includes not only the four-legged beasts, but the two legged as well. The negro is merely an articulate member of this beast creation" (14). Backing his thesis with biblical exegesis, O'Brien refers to Jeremiah 21:6, where God says he "will smite the inhabitants of this city, both man and beast." "Would God refer to a four legged beast as an inhabitant of a city" (16)? O'Brien asks. In Zechariah 8:10, it says, "For before these days there was no hire for man, nor any hire for beasts." "Here we have beasts that can be hired," O'Brien notes. "If there are four legged beasts that can be hired, someone should alert Internal Revenue" (16). The black race, O'Brien concludes, is part of the animal kingdom. "Even though he has not been given the intelligence and Spiritual understanding of the White race, he can think and reason up to a point, therefore he is to have dominion over the other animals. Let us give credit where credit is due, the negro is King, KING OF THE BEASTS" (17).

Inferior by nature, pre-Adamic man can never challenge white world dominion. The formidable enemy of God entered the scene after Adam: the Jews. Hardcore Identity believes that Satan literally seduced Eve who fathered his evil son Cain, progenitor of the Jewish race. Earth was thenceforth populated by two ontologically distinct "seedlines," the divine Aryan race and the diabolical Jewish race. Soft Identity balks at such a literal interpretation. While believing Jews to be "of the Serpent," they claim this to be true only in a metaphorical sense.[105] The two-seedline theory was developed in different versions by first-generation Identity theologians Wesley Swift, Conrad Gaard, William Potter Gale, and Bertrand Comparet.[106] Representing the theory's mild version (and reminiscent of nineteenth-century racist theologian Charles Carroll), Gaard and Comparet suggest that a pre-Adamic man had seduced Eve. The Original Sin, therefore, was miscegenation, transgressing God's order of creation that every living thing should only be with its own kind. Eve bore the bastard Cain who, after slaying his half-brother, the racially pure Abel, continued the evil pattern of miscegenation by marrying a pre-Adamic wife. The original sin became part of the genetic makeup of all subsequent descendants, the mongrelized Jewish race, constantly defiling the purity of the original classificatory order. "By nature a mongrel can only do one thing and that's to mongrelize," Tate (1997) said, "and mongrelization is the enemy of any pure race."

In its stronger version, the seducer is the Devil himself. Both Gale and Swift introduced Gnostic visions of pre-existing good and evil beings, and made the earthly racial battle key to a larger intergalactic space war. As Swift was Gale's mentor, his version will suffice. Swift taught that the divine white race was of God's own household, "His Elohim, which is plural for God" (n.d., 29). Thus said the Lord, "Ye are gods; and all of you are children of the most High" (Psalms 82:6). Swift asserted that the "almost timeless" white race originally were "celestial beings" assisting God in his creation. When God was busy creating Earth and its solar system, a fleet of space ships piloted by Lucifer and his demons attacked. Returning fire, the Space Aryans won the battle, and surviving demons sought refuge on Earth. Lucifer, his "fallen angels," and demonic soldiers now roomed among the Earth's inhabitants. The "dark and curly-headed . . . race of warriors" that "we call Negroes today . . . came in with the warring ships and the fallen angels whom they served," Swift explained, and "started to mix races" (Swift n.d., 27, 35, 40). The second extraterrestrial race was the fallen Luciferian Angels who by race mixing produced a race of pure evil, the Jews. To combat the evil mongrels, God provided carnal hues to his divine warrior race. He commanded Adam and Eve not to eat from the "racial tree" of good and evil. "You can't touch that one," Swift explained. "You are not to mongrelize. You are to maintain a holy seed" (31). Satan then seduced Eve and fathered an evil son. Cain's murder of Abel was not fratricide but the first attempt of the devil's spawn to exterminate the children of God. World history has since been an escalating race war. Exiled from Eden, the divine seed was threatened by the ultimate Aryan nightmare: a race of Jewish giants. "They were Jews," Swift wrote, "but bigger than anyone had ever seen before. There were giants in the land of those days (Genesis 6:4) that were killing and maiming and destroying, capturing and seeking to absorb your race by extreme mongrelization" (ibid.).

With or without the prelude from outer space, Swift's view of Jews as the mongrelized offspring of Satan and Eve became standard to hardcore Identity. The influential American Institute of Theology (AIT) echoed Swift in regard to the fallen angels, Satan's world dominion, the racial tree, and the original sin of miscegenation. The seducer "was not a snake or any reptile," AIT explained in its Bible school correspondence course (1981a), "but Satan, in one of his many appearances." Serving his father, Cain then slew Abel and the evil seed has ever since sought to exterminate the righteous. When Jesus came to redeem Aryan man, he lambasted his Jewish adversaries, asserting that they were of their father, the devil. "In this," AIT (1981b) explained matter-of-factly, "he was simply stating a biological fact with scientific precision and identifying the persons with this ancestry." Aryan Israel disregarded the wisdom of Jesus, which left the House of God in peril. "He told us to arm ourselves (Luke 22:36) and utterly destroy that evil serpent race (Luke 19:27)," wrote Pastor Mark Thomas, then head of the Christian Posse Comitatus of Pennsylvania. "We failed to obey His commandment and we now serve the jews as their slaves."[107] The evil "space aliens" may temporarily rule the Earth, but Aryan Christ did not die in vain. "Christ, Who was God Incarnate was perfected along with the rest of the Adamic race by His crucifixion," Thomas explained. "God lives with us and our entire race is one living organism, the body of Almighty."[108] This balances the fact that "Satan became a man." We are "locked in mortal combat with his children who are incarnate among us. They are found among the jews as the progeny of Cain."[109] Hailed as the "greatest White man to stand on this earth since Jesus Christ," Adolf Hitler serves as role model, instilling a sense of duty in the Aryan warrior-gods.[110] "We are born to throw down this wicked murdering system of jew-inspired globalism," Thomas exclaimed. "Do not speak with me of building the Kingdom of God on any other foundation than the blood-soaked ashes of Babylon!"[111]

Linked with the Aryan Nations, the ministry of Mark Thomas was characterized by militant bravado with repeated call to arms. "White man, this is your final call; there is nowhere else to run or hide," Thomas exclaimed. "Either fight, die, or prepare to turn your daughters over to the mongrelized descendants of dusky two-legged beasts. The choice is yours."[112] Inspired by the inflammatory rhetoric of Thomas, Peter K. Langan and Richard Lee Guthrie Jr. in 1993 established the Aryan Revolutionary Army (ARA). Modeled on the Order, the ARA built a war chest through a series of twenty-two robberies in the Midwest. "Our basic goal," a hooded commander said in an ARA recruitment video, "is to set up an Aryan republic" (Cohen 1997; Weber 1996; Macko 1996). When police in 1996 made a deal with an ARA turncoat, the guerilla group was finally apprehended. In Babylonian custody, Mark Thomas lost his bravery. He turned against his Aryan brethren and disappeared into the Protected Witness Program.

Soft Identity rejects the seedline theory as "unbiblical" in favor of other theories concerning the true identity of "Counterfeit Israel." The two most prominent theories state that Jews cannot possibly be the covenant people as they in fact descend from Esau and/or the Khazars; these two theories are not mutually exclusive and are sometimes also adopted by seedline historiographers. "Satan seducing Eve originated as a Jewish fable," Ted R. Weiland (1999) nailed down. "It is not found in the Bible but in the Babylonian Talmud." Paul Hall (1996) of *Jubilee* sought to refute that Identity is anti-Semitic, claiming that whites, not Jews, are descendants of Shem, and how could Aryan Israel be "anti-ourselves"? From the perspective of the mainstream, however, soft Identity easily qualifies as anti-Semitic. Among its ranks, after all, are passionate anti-Semites like Jack Mohr, and fighting counterfeit Israel remains a top priority.

Soft Identity believers hold that "contemporary Jews are the descendants of Esau (Edom) and were *not* the offspring of 'Satan and Eve,'" as a fact box in a *Jubilee* rebuttal read ("Glossary of Lies" 1996). The Esau/Edom connection derives from the biblical story about the twin brothers Esau and Jacob (Israel), sons of Isaac and Rebekah. God informs Rebekah that she will birth two nations that will fight each other, adding that He will elevate the younger Jacob over Esau (Genesis 25, 27, 32, 33). Identity equates Esau's degradation with his desire for women of other races, which causes God to hate him and his mongrel offspring, called Edom. When God exalts Jacob to be Israel, Esau desires to kill his brother, an obsession inherited by his offspring. *Esau* means "red," which to the Identity mind links Edom with communism, Babylon, and the anti-Christ. At the

Day of the Lord, Identity holds, Edom will be punished for her violence against Israel by complete extermination, "and there shall not be any remaining of the house of Esau" (Obadiah 18). The resemblance of this to the "Final Solution" has not been lost on Identity believers. Weisman observes that the Bible "actually prophesies the genocide of Esau-Edom!" (1991, 115). To Weisman, this explains the Jewish concern with the Holocaust. "It is because in God's Script for the world, the Jews are scheduled to be exterminated, and that impending reality is why they are so paranoid about 'genocide' " (ibid., 117).

The Khazars once populated the steppes between the Black and Caspian Seas, north of the Caucasus Mountains. Squeezed between the Byzantine Empire and the Umayyad Caliphate in the mid-eighth century, the then Khazar ruler reportedly converted to Judaism. With the thirteenth-century Mongol invasion, the Khazar Empire declined, and the history of the Khazars was lost in obscurity. In the nineteenth century, scholars of philology and anthropology suggested that Ashkenazi Jewry were largely of Khazar ancestry, an idea seized on in British-Israelite circles. By the turn of the century, this theory was adopted by nativist Anglo-Americans calling for immigration restrictions. If eastern European Jewry in fact were of Asian origin, their entry as "free white" persons could be terminated. This theory also circulated among the ranks of the second-era Klan, was featured in the writings of Lothrop Stoddard and Wilmot Robertson, and was readily embraced by Identity activists (Barkun 1997, 136–42).

In 1976 Jewish novelist Arthur Koestler published *The Thirteenth Tribe*, a work received with enthusiasm by Identity Christians. Koestler argued that there was no Jewish race. Partly based on amateur anthropology, Koestler concluded that Jews are notably diverse in physical characteristics and that Jews are markedly similar to the various Gentile nations they have lived with, a finding he explained by pointing to a pattern of extensive interbreeding. A substantial percentage of Eastern Jewry Koestler finds to be Khazar-Turkish rather than Semite. "If so, this would mean that their ancestors came not from the Jordan but from the Volga, not from the Canaan but from the Caucasus . . . and that genetically they are more closely related to the Hun, Uigur and Magyar tribes than to the seed of Abraham, Isaac and Jacob" (17). Hoping to prevent the possibility that his work "may be maliciously interpreted as a denial of Israel's right to exist," Koestler argues that Israel's right to exist is "not based on the hypothetical origins of the Jewish people" nor "on the mythological covenant of Abraham with God" (223) but on international law, that is, on the United Nations decision of 1947. Such a secular argument was completely lost on Identity ideologues, who triumphantly declared that counterfeit Israel had been exposed by one of their own. "The Jews have never been part of Israel," Pastor Butler (1996) trumpeted. "The Jew Koestler [admits they] "are tribes from central Russia, the Khazar kingdom" who are "trying to say that they are the chosen people, but the Bible says we are the chosen."

Christian Identity preachers generally adopt an underdog perspective that would have been alien to their British-Israelite predecessors, who saw the British Empire as confirmation of their claim of being the chosen people. A century later, though, colonialism was gone and interpretation of global politics reversed. "It is important to understand that Satan has dominion over this world," an Identity Bible course informed its students (AIT 1981c). All the once-white nations suffer under the yoke of the Jew world order. The root of it all, Identity teaches, is spiritual corruption. With the advent of Aryan Christ, Satan realized that he was endangered. Taking control of the Roman Empire, Jews maneuvered to redirect Christianity by corrupting its racial teaching. "It was transformed by its jewish conquerors into a religious system that they used to conquer the Aryan world," Mark Thomas wrote. "This system is today commonly known as Judeo-Christianity and it has been the ruin of every civilization that has adopted it. That was the purpose of its inventors and its teachings have nothing to do with those of Jesus, rather, they are the direct opposite of them." [113]

Echoing Thomas, Jack Mohr (1997) was convinced that the "Jews are infiltrating Christianity. That's how the Spanish Inquisition came about. They infiltrated the Catholic Church, they became cardinals and popes; seven popes were Jews." To corrupt Protestantism, they infiltrated German seminaries and introduced "higher criticism," which "pervades the modern church now. Jews say that the Bible really isn't the word of God, it's just some sayings by man, and now they're trying to say, you know, that God is a he and a she, and that Jesus was an homosexual." Mohr believes that Jews command "most of all churches" in the United States, have the "National Council of Churches under strong control," and "dictate the teachings" in "almost every seminary" to "teach that the Jews are the chosen people." Judeo-Christianity or "Churchianity" is diametrically opposed to the gospel of Aryan Christ. It teaches that God loves all of humanity and hates discrimination, when God in fact is a racist and discrimination the bedrock of divine law. Churchianity preaches pacifism and turns the other cheek, while Christians are commanded to arm themselves and enforce an-eye-for-an-eye. Churchianity teaches equality and idealizes weakness instead of nature's eternal hierarchy and "might is right." "One of the greatest mistakes made by the Third Reich was the burning of only the synagogues," Pastor Thomas concluded. "How utterly tragic because this mistake cost Germany and all of our race the war. He should have . . . leveled every church in Germany."[114]

The global reign of anti-Christ is a sign of the end of time. Identity has no equivalent to the rapture doctrine of evangelical Christianity, which states that God will provide a heavenly refuge to spare the righteous from experiencing Armageddon. Patterned on the Old Testament, in which God descends to command his people in earthly warfare, Identity believers expect to partake in the global cleansing. John Baumgardner (1996) explained. "The ideal government of the world is God's government with Christ as the king. And so that's what we're looking for, and I think that God uses His people to accomplish that. He has historically used His people to overthrow governments. And so we're entering this so-called messianic age. We're not going to be pulled off into the sky and saved from a world of destruction. We're gonna see an apocalyptic change on this planet, the dawn of God's government." In Joshua, God intervenes to command the army of Israel in taking possession of the Holy Land, ransacking thirty-two cities and wiping out its inhabitants. Joshua "left none remaining, but utterly destroyed all that breathed, as the Lord God of Israel commanded" (Joshua 10:40). According to Baumgardner, this pattern was repeated in North America. "God said to Israel, 'Go in and kill every human being and then possess the land.' That's called divine conquest," Baumgardner (1996) explained. "We obtained this land by divine conquest. This land does not belong to the Indians. This land was given to us." In return, he continued, Israel was to remain pure of foreign influences or suffer the wrath of God. "The Bible teaches us that when we bring strangers and aliens into our land, people of other religions who worships other gods, we begin to take their gods as our own," he said. "We, who are part of Israel, are punished today for that very reason, the same reason that ancient Israel was punished! We haven't learned yet."

In 1990 hardcore Identity ideologue Richard Kelly Hoskins suggested that individual zealots could atone for Israel's transgressions by assassinating homosexuals, interracial couples, and prostitutes. Hoskins (1990) believed such zealots belonged to an underground tradition of racial purists, the Phineas Priesthood, and traced its history into antiquity. In Numbers 25 God finds Israeli men engaged in miscegenation with Moab women and is jealously about to consume them when Phineas dashes into the tent and throws his javelin through the transgressors' bodies. Pleased, God announces, "Phineas hath turned my wrath away from the children of Israel" and bestowed on Phineas and "his seed" a "covenant of an everlasting priesthood because he was zealous" (Numbers 25:

11, 13). During the 1990s, individual hardcore activists embraced Hoskins's fantasy as an Identity variation on leaderless resistance. Self-proclaimed Phineas Priest Walther E. Thody was sentenced to life and 125 years for twenty robberies he masterminded in 1990–91, intending to finance an a squad of Identity assassins; in 1993 Paul Hill wrote an article advocating Phineas-like actions and graduated by assassinating doctor John B. Britton outside his Florida abortion clinic; Charles Barbee, Robert Berry, and Jay Merrell were convicted for a 1996 Spokane bank robbery, during which they left a letter signed with the Phineas Priesthood symbol.

Horrified that racist vigilantes with "as much spiritual insight as the length of their bullets" would justify "unlawful deeds" by reference to the Holy Writ and by claiming to be called by the God of Christian Israel, Ted R. Weiland launched a campaign of correction. He argued that it would be impossible for anyone to prove a Phineas ancestry. There is no biblical sanction for the thought that a "Phineas act" qualifies a man for the priesthood, and nowhere does God authorize vigilantism. Anyone could claim to act on behalf of God but nowhere does the Word ordain any man to transgress divine law. "The Phineas priesthood," Weiland concluded, "essentially are 'Phineas hoods' because they themselves are in contradiction to the laws of Yahweh. They're looking for a quick fix, but there are no shortcuts, and there are no Phineas priests" (Weiland 1999; Weiland 1998). Divided over the Phineas Priesthood concept, hardcore and soft Identity Christians also part ways concerning what attitude God expects his chosen to take concerning the approaching apocalypse. "It's gonna be a total war, a revolutionary war, and [Israel] gonna have to fight!" Baumgardner (1996) stated emphatically. "We need people be preparing for guerilla war, we need terrorists, we need that, because a system that breeds violence, practice violence, only understands violence." While Weiland (1999) believes that "God's law require us to be armed [and condones] self-defense," he dismissed the notion that God commands Israel to launch guerilla warfare at this point in time. "I know that some people believe that that's the only thing left, an armed revolution, but right now it is naïve to believe that we can win this battle with arms. It's nowhere close to that."

Hardcore militancy has occasionally manifested in establishments of armed communal settlements. In 1976 Covenant, Sword, and Arm of the Lord (CSA) founder "King" James Ellison set up the paramilitary commune Zarephath-Horeb on a 224-acre tract in the Ozark wilderness in northern Arkansas ("Who We Are" 1982). Ellison believed that Aryan Israel literally was a divine race predestined to inherit the Earth ("The Coming Race of Gods" 1981). "As Sons of

God," a CSA article exclaimed, "we shall drive out those tenants who now occupy our possession and shall therefore rule our enemies under our footstool. Praise His Holy Name! With violence shall we enter" ("What Is Identity" 1982). Convinced that "Jesus is building an army which shall show forth the Arm of the Lord, bringing judgment against the enemies of God" ("Deep Calleth" 1982), Ellison organized paramilitary training and prepared to advance into enemy territory. "Warfare is in the genes of every true son of God," CSA declared, continuing, "NO compromise, NO quarter, NO mercy" with the "Seed of Satan" as "ALL racial Jews are the enemies of Christ and His people" ("Why Do We Hate" 1982). The CSA became a refuge for racist activists. Reciprocating for funding received by the Order, it provided shelter for the likes of wanted David Tate and Richard Snell but would not stand the test when challenged by federal authorities. Surrounded by the ATF in 1985, the CSA gave up without resistance. Ellison was sentenced to twenty years, but appeared as a government witness in the Fort Smith sedition trial in exchange for a sentence reduction.

Failure to show contributed to the fading image of Aryan Christ in counterculture eyes. Identity was in the 1980s by and large the religious dimension of revolutionary racism but was soon to be challenged by Creativity, Cosmotheism, and racist paganism. In the 1980s Richard G. Butler, pastor of the Church of Jesus Christ, Christian, could summon several hundred Aryan leaders and activists of different streams at his yearly Aryan World Congresses at the Aryan Nations Hayden Lake headquarters. In the mid-1990s Aryan Nations remained, perhaps, an important symbol of white power but was in practical respects a star of the past. By then, no armed guards regularly patrolled Aryan Nations property. Few would dare the hazardous climb up the crumbling watchtower. No electricity charged the fencing wire, the church badly needed repainting, and the "Whites Only" sign was slanting. Butler continued to hold Aryan World and Youth Congresses but fewer people showed up, since counterculture activists had come to see Aryan Nations meetings as an infiltrators' haven and believed the buildings to be jammed with bugs and hidden video cameras. By 1998 conditions had deteriorated to such a point that local youth found pleasure in embarrassing the Aryan world headquarters by sneaking onto the property to spray paint buildings or steal the Aryan Nations banner. Infuriated, Butler ordered heightened security, a move that contributed to his final downfall when his guards mistook a passing-by mother and son for intruders. After a two-mile car chase with blazing guns, the guards shot out a tire and forced the chased car into a ditch. Interrupted by approaching neighbors, the AN guards made a Hitler salute and took off. Represented by Morris Dees's Southern Poverty Law Center, the mother and son were awarded $6.3 million in damages by a civil-court jury in 2000.

Vincent Bertollini of the Eleventh Hour Ministry provided Butler with a new residence, but the Aryan Nations headquarters was gone. On 27 September 2001, Pastor Ray Redfeairn of Ohio was named Butler's successor and AN national director. Pastor August B. Kreis III, formerly of the Sheriff's Posse Comitatus was named new AN minister of information.[115] The future will see to what extent these two leaders will manage to revive Aryan Nations, which for all practical purposes had been long since dead when the SPLC closed down its Hayden Lake headquarters. While hardcore Identity is likely to live on, the counterculture was by the turn of the millenium largely animated by other religious creeds.

Our Race is Our Religion

During the radicalization process of the 1980s, many revolutionary Aryans came to see Christianity as key in the "ZOG effort to mind control the white race" (*Anonymous* 1999). Not all were content with Identity's endeavor to differentiate between "true" Aryan Christianity and "false" Judeo-Christianity, rejecting as historically unsubstantiated and basically nonsensical its thesis that white Americans were the lost tribes of Israel. Paving the way for the subsequent rise of racist paganism was an anti-Christian, nontheistic tendency to focus on the Aryan "race" with religious devotion. Metzger aptly summarizes this position in his declaration of WAR: "Our race is our religion. WAR condemns priest craft and all religions. WAR will not allow religious theories and unproven myths to interfere with Aryan survival and advancement. Whites must deal with reality and the world around them. We must demand evidence of those who attempt to control us with unsubstantiated stories from the Middle East" (n.d.b). This attitude was elaborated along the lines of either racist atheism or pantheism, here represented by their most successful vehicles Creativity and Cosmotheism.

Creativity was the brainchild of Ben Klassen, self-appointed Pontifex Maximus of the Church of the Creator (COTC), founded in 1973 and gaining counterculture momentum in the 1980s and early 1990s. Born in Ukraine in 1918 to Mennonite parents, Klassen was brought up in Canada and later moved to Florida where he worked as a realtor. He joined the John Birch Society (which he would later dismiss as "Kosher Konservative"), briefly served as Florida State Legislator in 1966 (on an antibussing Republican platform), and founded the dysfunctional White Nationalist Party before eventually abandoning secular politics in favor of a religious approach to securing a white-racist revolution. Though basically an atheist, Klassen observed that religion has been a constant feature of all known cultures of man and concluded that the only feasible choice was between "bad" and "good" religions, which could be defined according to their role in promoting racial loyalty and survival in a hostile world.[116] The white man, Klassen taught, needed to realize that "(a) We are embroiled in a racial war for survival on this Planet Earth; (b) All mud races are our enemies in this fight for survival; (c) The Jews are leading and orchestrating this war against us; and (d) The Christian Churches are their most ardent ally and most potent weapon" (1987, 12). Christianity was to Klassen a "Jewish creation," "designed to unhinge and derange White Gentile intellect and to cause him to abandon his real responsibilities" by promoting a "completely perverted attitude" toward life and nature (Klassen 1992 169). Based on superstitious beliefs in "spooks in the sky" and unsubstantiated theories about life beyond death, Christianity was to Klassen a compilation of suicidal advices to love your enemy, turn the other cheek, and have compassion for the weak; a theology of mass insanity that has brought down every society in which it had taken hold (1981, 311, 350). Terming his religion "creativity" and the members "creators" to capture the essence of the white soul, Klassen aimed to replace Christianity with a religion based on "Nature's Law" to "propagate, advance, and expand the White Race, the highest pinnacle reached in the handiwork of Nature" (1992, 1, 253). Following Gobineau, Klassen believed that the white race was the sole builder of civilizations, the founder of every high culture of antiquity—China, India, Egypt, Sumeria, Greece, Rome, the Aztecs and Incans—all of which were destroyed by miscegenation. Whereas other modern readers of Gobineau conclude that imperialism was a mistake and advocate white separatism instead of supremacy, Klassen regarded any such strategy as racial treason. Issuing the battle cry RaHoWa, Klassen held the "winning of the west" as "prototype for the winning of the world" (1987, 12) in the COTC program to "expand the White Race, shrink the colored races, until the White Race is the supreme inhabitant of the earth" (1992, 262).

Klassen outlined the basic creed of Creativity in three "holy books," *Nature's Eternal Religion* (1973), the *White Man's Bible* (1981) and *Salubrious Living* (1982), the latter co-authored by Arnold DeVries, and in a rich production of secondary writings. An early critic of the patriot scene, Klassen emphasized the primacy of race. A man's foremost duty was to further the survival and empowerment of his racial family, and he ought not be distracted by loyalties to country, flag, or constitution (Klassen 1992, 242). Reflecting deep-seated counterculture sentiments, Klassen spent much energy on "exposing" the Jewish stranglehold on

the white race and railing about the black menace. Equaling Metzger in his preference for lowbrow "straight talk," Klassen, for instance, found *nigger* an apt
term that accurately defined the COTC view of blacks, the word being, as Web-
ster's dictionary defines it, "a vulgar, offensive term of hostility and contempt
for the black man" (Klassen 1981, 166). The white American's failure to recognize the imperative to cleanse "his" territory of the nonwhite "mud races"
was due, as Klassen would have it, to the mind-muddling influence of religion,
particularly Christianity.

With iconoclastic fervor, Klassen ridiculed Christianity, highlighting biblical inconsistencies and scientifically unsubstantiated articles of faith. Anyone's
religious faith was to Klassen hardly a private matter but of central concern to
the death-and-life battle for the survival of the race (Klassen 1987, 129).[117] The
racist recasting of Christianity Identity was to Klassen of no avail as it retained
delusions of a heavenly superspook and wasted energy on irrelevant theories of
an imaginary ancient past. "There is not a shred of historical evidence that there
ever were any Ten Lost Tribes of Israel, and if they ever existed and got lost, all
I can say is GOOD RIDDANCE," Klassen wrote, wondering why "any sane, intelligent white man [wants] to break [his] neck to distort history [only to pose
as] a descendant of such trash?" (1987, 125). With the rise of racist paganism,
Klassen would also fiercely resist Odinism as a "silly hangover from our Stone
Age ancestors" (ibid., 190). Reviewing the history of religions, Klassen traced
the belief in God to primitive superstition. Rejecting any notion of gods, demons, spirits, and souls, he felt that "the creators" do not believe in heaven and
hell, immortality after death, or the hereafter, however imagined. "We have dis-
pensed with that nonsense," Klassen wrote, "and can better concentrate our
thoughts and energy on living in the here and now, the only life we will ever
experience" (1981, 360). The rational creator "does not worship anything, or
anybody," his sense of purpose and morals being based on racial loyalty and the
laws of nature (ibid., 436).

While acknowledging common ground with atheism, Klassen maintains
that only Creativity both seeks to destroy religious superstitions *and* offers
a comprehensive alternative philosophy that answers to all the fundamental
aspects of life, summarized in the "sixteen commandments" and the "four-
dimensional" COTC program: "A sound mind in a sound body in a sound society
in a sound environment" (Klassen 1987, 166, 179; Klassen 1981).[118] Freed from
the mental shackles of spook-oriented religion, the sound mind lives by the
COTC golden rule: "What is good for the White Race is the highest virtue, what
is bad for the White Race is the highest sin" (Klassen 1981, 11). In line with

the health fad of the 1980s, Klassen issued a "salubrious living" program for keeping the body fit and free from diseases. "Exposing" modern medicine as a Jewish multibillion-dollar racket, Klassen held all medicines to be harmful, intoxicating drugs that might remove symptoms but would never cure, since diseases were not caused by germs or bacteria—they only affected a weakened, enervated body. To secure a wholesome life free from cancer and other diseases, Klassen prescribed fasting, physical exercise, sufficient rest, and a fruitarian diet of organically grown uncooked and unprocessed fruits, vegetables, grains, and nuts (Klassen and DeVries 1982; Klassen 1981). Building a COTC elite of healthy racial loyalists, Klassen hoped to set the stage for a worldwide white revolution. According to the secular millenarianism of the COTC, a racial golden age would commence once the Earth was rid of the mud races and nature's finest were perfected by enforced eugenics and salubrious living. Inspired by romanticized notions of the Roman Empire and the statecraft of Hitler's Germany, Klassen envisioned the government of the future as "racial socialism" (Klassen 1990, 303), defined as an authoritarian collectivism based on the "leadership principle," an orchestrated team working for the welfare of the globally united race, communicating in revised Latin as its universal language (Klassen 1981, 420).

The realities of the Church of the Creator stand in sharp contrast to the grandiose visions of its Pontifex Maximus. Investing a substantial part of his personal fortune, Klassen in 1982 established a World Creativity Center in Otto, North Carolina, in the Blue Ridge Mountains, where he founded the *Racial Loyalty* tabloid and distributed his books (often free of charge). A mail-order seminar enabled members to become reverends for a small fee. Continuing education and military training in the paramilitary White Berets was offered at headquarters. By the late 1980s and early 1990s COTC began attracting the new-generation Aryan activists. Popularized by acts involved with the white-power music scene, its membership became increasingly dominated by youth, skinheads, and prisoners. Abroad, COTC missionary activities produced chapters in western Europe, Australia, New Zealand, and South Africa. Yet, COTC remained miniscule, with a worldwide membership of less than five thousand, out of which a couple hundred were ordained ministers. Organizationally, Creativity was hampered not least by financial difficulties and Klassen's stubborn reluctance to delegate power and responsibilities. By 1993 Klassen concluded that he had done his duty. The *White Man's Bible* recommends suicide as a dignified way to die, preferable, in fact, to prolonging a life that, for any number of reasons, no longer is worth living. Following the suicide of its founder, COTC split into several competing factions. In July 1996 a rebuilding process commenced with four out of five "Guardians of Faith" recognizing law student Matt Hale of the World Church of the Creator (WCOTC) as the new Pontifex Maximus (*McVan 1996*; conversation with McVan, St. Maries, Idaho, 1999).[119]

Born in 1971 in East Peoria, Illinois, as the youngest son of a police officer, Hale had operated the dysfunctional American White Supremacist Party and the equally unsuccessful White America National Socialist Party before stumbling on the *Racial Loyalty* tabloid in the early 1990s. Finding Creativity a perfect blend of national socialism and Nietzschean social Darwinism, Hale applied for membership in 1995 (*Hale 1999*). Despite being a late convert, Hale in a few years managed to reunite a majority of the competing Creativity factions in the United States, and a number of new youth-dominated local chapters were founded. In the year 2000 seventy local chapters distributed across twenty-eight states were affiliated with the WCOTC world headquarters.[120] Abroad, WCOTC claimed chapters in Canada, Norway, Sweden, Ireland, England, France, Spain, Switzerland, Germany, Austria, Poland, Russia, Australia, New Zealand, Argentina, Brazil, and South Africa (*Hale 1999*). By then, however, Creativity had been dwarfed by the rise of Odinism, and it remains to be seen to what extent Hale will be able to make WCOTC more than a distributor of Klassen classics. The one novel sphere of activity launched after Klassen's death was the effort to organize white women to the cause.

Noting that "most pro-White organizations today do not make a focused effort to recruit women" nor "encourage women to pursue leadership roles" in the racial struggle, WCOTC in 1998 launched the Women's Frontier, headed by Lisa Turner, WCOTC women's information coordinator.[121] A people's revolution would hardly benefit from engaging only half of its population, Turner argued.[122] White women needed to realize that they had been coopted by the racial enemy by defining women as minorities oppressed by the white male. Solidarity belonged to the racial nation and not to any universal womanhood.[123] With the exception of Pontifex Maximus, all WCOTC positions of authority were open for women.[124] This should not be confused with feminism, Turner pointed out. "We recognize, in accordance with Nature's eternal laws, that men and women are vastly different genetically and biologically and are in no way equal."[125] Although female participation in the white revolution includes "lone wolf" Kathy Ainsworth (bomber of synagogues and private Jewish residences), Eva Braun, and Katja Lane in the white women's hall of fame, it does not necessarily imply military service, and Turner stresses that a white woman's primary role is that of wife and mother.[126] By the year 2000 some ten chapters of the sisterhood of the WCOTC had been established locally and the Women's Frontier expanded not least in cyberspace with an E-zine, kids pages, and articles by and about female revolutionaries.

Prior to committing suicide, Klassen sold his property to William Pierce, leader of the National Alliance and the Cosmotheist Community Church, founded in 1974 and 1978 respectively. Having completed his doctorate in physics at the University of Colorado, Pierce was on the faculty at Oregon State University as an assistant professor during the early 1960s. Aghast at the "liberal" university atmosphere—students supporting civil rights, the anti-war movement emerging—Pierce gravitated towards racial politics. Finding the John Birch Society too passive, he eventually joined the American Nazi Party. Relocating to ANP headquarters, Pierce became its house intellectual, editing the theoretically oriented ANP quarterly, *National Socialist World*. Following Rockwell's assassination, Pierce stayed for three years with Matt Koehl, pursuing a dual recruitment strategy that would remain his earmark. By raising the intellectual standard of American national socialism, Pierce hoped to organize university students. An early proponent of total revolution, Pierce also brought in young militants like Joseph Tommasi, James Mason, and Joseph Franklin. Though Pierce was only modestly successful, it was enough to annoy Koehl, who in 1970 expelled his potential rival.

Pierce then teamed up with Willis Carto in the National Youth Alliance (NYA). Earning a reputation for committing violent assaults on antiwar activists and for rallying to "nuke Hanoi," the NYA soon split in two competing factions following a personal conflict between Carto and Pierce that continues to this day. Renaming his group the National Alliance, Pierce crowned himself American führer. In 1985 Pierce relocated to a 300-acre property near Hillsboro, a quiet hamlet in the remote Appalachian region of southeastern West Virginia. NA headquarters housed printing facilities, the *National Vanguard* magazine, the National Vanguard book publisher, a radio station that aired the monthly *American Dissident Voices*, a video studio, a Cosmotheist church, and guest sheds and private quarters for a handful of residents. Famed for his race-war novels *Turner Diaries* and *Hunter*, Pierce ranks as one of the more important counterculture ideologues. While the NA was the largest national socialist group on the scene, its overall membership remained insignificant. In 1997 the National Alliance consisted of the headquarters and a mere twelve local chapters, each with a minimum of five dues-paying members (Pierce 1997). Pierce began to realize that his dream of a perfected Aryan society in which "young men and women gather to revel with polka or waltzes, reels or jigs, or any other White dances, but never to undulate or jerk to negroid jazz or rock rhythms" was not really selling to the new generation Aryan activists (*National Alliance Membership Handbook* 1993, 29). Decisively, Pierce pushed his contempt aside and ventured into the burgeoning white-noise scene. Early in 1999 Pierce bought Resistance Records (under the nose of rival Carto), then acquired the Swedish Nordland and continued into the misty underworld of heathen national socialist black metal. Riding on the wave of white noise, National Alliance membership increased to some forty local chapters in twenty-four states by the close of 2000, with an estimated nationwide membership of 3,000.

Fundamental to Pierce's interpretation of national socialism was his creed of racist pantheism, termed "Cosmotheism" to connote the central thesis that cosmos is a manifestation of immanent divinity. Inspired by German romanticism, Darwinism, and the monist philosophy of Ernst Haeckel, Pierce (1997) cast Cosmotheism as a "scientific religion of nature" defined as an "evolutionary pantheism." While convinced that Cosmotheism "will be the dominant idea of tomorrow," he contends that it was far too sophisticated to be appreciated by average man. Therefore, Pierce generally prefers to leave his Ariosophic monism implicit in his works. Embracing Cosmotheism is not a requirement for National Alliance members, who are free to follow the religion of their choice. However, since Pierce sees Cosmotheism as the religion of nature, members are expected to live by Cosmotheist truth, as translated into the National Alliance rules of conduct and political platform. Cosmotheism is accordingly key to the National Alliance project.

Central to Cosmotheism is the belief in the oneness of all material and spiritual elements of the universe. "There is only one Reality, and that Reality is the Whole. It is the Creator, the Self-Created" (*The Path* 1997). Monism bridges the illusory separation between God and man, creator and creation, mind and matter suggested by the Judeo-Christian tradition. The self-created whole is constantly evolving along the path toward perfection, propelled by a pre-biological force that animates all things in the tangible universe. Man is part of nature and subject to nature's laws, principal of which is the law of inequality and survival of the fittest. Evolving through a succession of states, the purpose of man is to ascend into godhood. Reflecting different levels of development, the dynamic whole is a neatly structured cosmic hierarchy. Crowned by the superior white man, the different races of man are distributed on the ladder of evolution. History is a continuation of the broad evolutionary process and may be genuinely appreciated only from a racial standpoint. Whereas Africa had no history prior to the age of discovery, the history of civilized man is exclusively European, with Japan as the one exception to the rule. Just as the races differ according to degree of development, so do whites differ individually. Society should ideally reflect nature's eternal hierarchy by being governed by an elite of strong, capable, and intelligent men who fully realize the Cosmotheist truth. "We need a strong, centralized government spanning many continents to coordinate many important tasks the first few decades of a [postrevolutionary] White world: the racial cleansing of the land, the rooting out of racially destructive institutions, and . . . [the implementation of] a long termed eugenics program involving at least the entire populations of Europe and America."[127] Thus Pierce hopes to fulfill the frustrated vision of Hitler by producing a race of supermen that ultimately will evolve into self-perfected divinity. The National Alliance is to Pierce not so much a national socialist party as a holy order of religious zealots serving the sacred cause of racial redemption (Pierce 1997; "Cosmotheism" 1977; Pierce speech 1977).

Advocates of Creativity and Cosmotheism agree that substituting otherworldly Christianity with a this-worldly religion of nature is necessary to secure Aryan survival. Both are nontheistic religions that reject the notion of a transcendent divinity of a nature that is fundamentally Other than man. Aryan man needs to understand that he is part of nature and subject to the laws of nature, interpreted in terms of social Darwinism. And above all, man must realize that redemption will only come from himself. Confronting "Jewish" Christianity became standard to the emerging counterculture scene and helped pave the way for the rising tide of racist paganism. Not all of those influenced by the anti-Christian rhetoric find atheism and pantheist philosophy spiritually satisfying. Although paganism shares an anti-Christian attitude with Creativity and Cosmotheism, sometime rivaling Klassen in its iconoclastic fervor, it has the advantage of offering religious alternatives with ancient gods, mythologies, rituals, and mysteries, and is cast as the "original" religion of Aryan man. If Christianity is a Jewish conspiracy to mentally control Aryan man, pagans believe, then returning to pre-Christian pagan traditions is an act of spiritual emancipation—a prelude to racial rebirth and the restoration of Aryan independence.

CHAPTER THREE

The Pagan Revival

P aganism has during the past few decades transformed the religious landscape of the United States. It involves reconstructions or reinventions of pre-Christian religious traditions, typically perceived as a "return" or "revival" of some old-time religion of the premodern era. Pagans in general are dissatisfied with mainstream Christianity's transcendent conception of the divine as being of a nature fundamentally Other than man, believing instead that the divine is immanent in man and living nature. Looking for meaning beyond secular science and consumer society, propelled by a search for roots and identity, and entertaining romanticized urban notions of nature, pagans generally find the future in the past. The ideological return to tribal traditions and ancient esoteric knowledge often lends paganism a decidedly ethnocentric flavor. Thus one finds clusters of pagan practices geared toward Native American traditions (shamanism, drum journeys, sweat lodges, sun dances, Mayan calendars) or developed along Afrocentric or Eurocentric lines, as is evidenced by mushrooming numbers of "traditional African" Santeria, voudou, and Candomlé societies, as well as bands of Druids, Wiccans, and Asatrúers. The global flow of information encourages an element of eclecticism, and many pagan groups seem open to trans-traditional borrowing and experimental innovation. Herein pagan ideologies inspired by pre-Christian European traditions are of primary concern, as Asatrú belongs to this scene. Numerically, the strongest of these Euro-pagan reconstructions are Wicca, Druidry, goddess paganism, and Asatrú/Odinism.

Out of the Ashes Return the Witches

With an estimated few hundred thousand practitioners in the Western world, Wicca counts as the leading Eurocentric pagan tendency. Wicca is an Old English term for "witchcraft" that etymologically is thought to derive either from the root *wit*, meaning "wisdom," or the Indo-European root *weik*, meaning "to bend" or turn. From a Wiccan perspective, then, *witchcraft* means "the craft of the wise" or "the craft of bending, shaping, and changing reality" in conformity with one's will, and has little to nothing to do with the stereotypical evil witch of Christian-influenced narratives.[1] Interestingly, there is an emerging revaluation of "witches" in popular culture, as symbolized by the show *Sabrina*. To many Wiccans, though, the "teenage-witch industry" seems a mixed blessing, fearing that commercialization will distort the concept to a greater degree than the horror stories of Christian fundamentalists ever did.

Wiccans seek the return to or revival of a pan-European, pre-Christian religion frequently but not exclusively conceived of as Celtic. What is meant by "Celtic" is, as observed by Marion Bowman (1996, 243), rather fluid. Within the British Isles, where Wicca originated, Celtic identity is more and more broadly defined, often held to embrace all Scots, Irish, Welsh, Manx, and sometimes even southeastern Englishmen. Historically, the heterogeneous Celts were found across much of continental Europe, a fact often interpreted to mean that Celts were the first Europeans. While this pan-Celtic, pan-European notion is privileged by some Wiccans, others emphasize specific Celtic traditions (Welsh, Gaelic Highlander, Irish) while simultaneously embracing the homologies between various traditions widely thought to have derived from a common prehistoric origin. This is generally true also for Wiccans oriented toward extra-Celtic traditions (Norse, Greek, Sumerian, or Egyptian Wicca), as all hark back to the religion of the golden age envisioned. Combined with this nostalgic projection is the belief that the aboriginal "nature religion" in some way or another survived during the many centuries of oppressive Christian hegemony and now has begun to resurface. This view might be summarized in what Margot Adler (1986, 46) terms the "Myth of Wiccan revival": witchcraft is the old religion that dates back to Paleolithic times, to the worship of the earth goddess and her male consort, the horned god. This religion was pan-European, as supposedly confirmed by archeological findings of goddess figurines and cave paintings. The names changed according to culture and language, but the basic deities were the same. Religion in these nonpatriarchal and egalitarian societies was goddess centered, celebrated nature, and emphasized harmony, fertility, and life affirmation. When Christianity came to Europe, it was long a religion for the ruling classes, while rural folk, the "pagans" and "heathens," continued to practice the old religion. Turning pagan festivals into Christian holidays and building churches on pre-Christian sacred sites, Christianity slowly gained ground among the larger population. In time, this process of cooptation gave way to an intolerant policy of militant Christianity during "the Burning Times." The horned god was recast as the Christian devil, and his demonized followers were met with stern persecution, as evidenced by the Inquisition and the witch craze.

Forced underground, the old religion was cultivated in secret by individual families until legal sanctions against paganism were cleared and a more liberal attitude allowed its practitioners to come out in the open. The retired British civil servant Gerald B. Gardner (1884–1964) is considered to have been the first Wiccan to "surface."[2] Claiming to have been initiated in 1939 by "Old Dorothy" into an authentic witch coven that had kept the Craft tradition unbroken over hundreds of years, Gardner introduced Wicca in two books published in the 1950s: *Witchcraft Today* (1954) and *Meaning of Witchcraft* (1959). Although many Wiccans today doubt Gardner's story and suspect that Old Dorothy was a fictional character, most Wiccan groups embrace Gardner's basic components of the Craft.[3] Gardner saw witchcraft as a peaceful, life-affirming, and goddess-oriented mystery religion organized in covens, each led by a priestess. In nocturnal rites, witches met in the nude, raised energy through dance and meditation, and mastered the art of magic. In tune with nature, they celebrated eight ancient pagan festivals following the agricultural cycle and sought to harmonize with the "Great Triple Goddess" of birth, death, and rebirth. Mimicking Gardner, a series of "Act Up" witches soon came out of the closet, each claiming to have been initiated by an old female sage, typically a great-grandmother, and Wicca broke up in several different traditions named after the founder (Gardnerian, Alexandrian, or Georgian Wicca), a goddess or other deities (Dianic or Faerie Wicca), or ethnic focus (Norse, Welsh, or Greek Wicca).[4]

In time, the distinctions between these various traditions decreased in importance. "Most people who join the Craft," Adler observes, "join the 'tradition' that happens to be 'around,' that exists in their particular area" (1986, 115). Wiccans of different traditions interact at pagan festivals and in cyberspace, read the same Wiccan books, and participate in pagan networks transcending sectarian borders. Instrumental in generating this notion of pan-Wiccan solidarity is the construction of a Wiccan "community of memory," discussed by Helen A. Berger in her seminal sociological study of contemporary American witchcraft. Applying a concept developed by Robert N. Bellah, Berger argues that group cohesion is constructed by recounting stories of the glory of the old religion and the persecutions suffered during the witch craze.

Many Witches acknowledge that they are not the direct descendants of the victims, primarily women who were executed as Witches in the early modern period. Nonetheless, the witch trials remain symbolically important to help unify a diverse group of people from different ethnic and religious backgrounds. . . . Some Witches claim to be either direct descendants of those executed in the trials or to have themselves been victims of the witch craze in a previous life. Most Witches, however, see the link as symbolic—between themselves and people, who like them, participated in an ancient religion; were folk healers, magicians, or women of power; or who just practiced the "old ways." (Berger 1999, 71)

Gardner's student Raymond Buckland is credited with introducing Wicca in the United States during the counterculture era of the 1960s with its fusion of self-experienced spirituality, psychedelic experimentation, sexual liberation, and left-leaning politics. In the United States Wicca took on a "particular American flavor," Berger notes. "Mysticism, ecological concerns, women's rights, and anti-authoritarianism have all been incorporated into this new religion. Wicca in the United States is more eclectic than the religion in present-day Great Britain" (ibid., 12). Estimates of the number of practicing Wiccans in the United States vary considerably, but Berger sets a "conservative number" of 150,000 to 200,000, with the largest percentage of pagans living on the East and West Coasts (ibid., 9; see also Hutton 1999, 400). Wicca is predominantly a religion of well-educated, white, middle-class, female Americans living in metropolitan areas. In her "pagan census," Berger found that 90.4 percent of the respondents were white, 65.4 percent had at least a college degree, and 50.7 percent lived in an urban or suburban area (Berger 1999, 8). Almost two-thirds of active American Wiccans are female, with the number of male witches estimated to be between 52, 800 and 76,000 (ibid., 40).[5] An open-minded attitude to sexual preferences has drawn a comparatively high percentage (27.5) of homosexual and bisexual men and women to witchcraft. There are gender-exclusive witch covens, as well as covens for gay men or lesbians only, but the majority tend to be inclusive and open to all irrespective of gender or sexual orientation (ibid., 43).

While there is no centralized bureaucracy empowered to establish orthodoxy of religious dogma or orthopraxis of ceremonial patterns, most Wiccans share a (often combined) pantheistic and polytheistic worldview, celebrate life and nature, and perform rites according to a basic ceremonial structure. Essentially a homemade experimental creed based on sources ranging from archeology to fantasy novels, varieties in Wiccan thought and praxis are more rule than exception.[6] Therefore, although there are common denominators among the various American Wicca practices, different practitioners might elaborate these basics differently.

Witches generally engage in four different types of ritual: sabbats, esabats, rites of passage, and magic. Following the cycle of nature, eight yearly sabbats commemorate the beginning and height of each season in the "wheel of the year." Celebrating the beginning of each season are the Celtic fire festivals of Samhain (Halloween), Imbolc (February 1–2), Beltane (April 30–May 1), and Lughnasadh (or Lammas, August 1–2). The seasonal heights are represented by the winter and summer solstices and the fall and spring equinoxes. Harmonizing the individual with nature, the sabbats include elements of the macro-micro correspondence between the cycle of life in nature and the participants. Thus, Samhain focuses on death and renewal in nature and man (either an aspect of a person's life or the prospects of reincarnation), while Beltane focuses on the seeds of change, growth, and new life in nature as well as in the lives of participating witches.

Conducted in woods, parks, or indoors, a celebration typically starts with the creation of sacred space by rites of purification with the four elements of fire, water, earth, and air, and the casting of a circle with a ritual sword or dagger. Practitioners then call in the powers of east, south, west, and north, and invoke the gods and goddesses to participate in the ceremony. Although different gods and goddesses are addressed according to season and tradition, there is a tendency within Wicca to approach the specific deities as particular manifestations of One Goddess and One God. Since there is no universal theology developed, the goddess(es) and god(s) may be conceived of variously, as the archetypical forces innate in man or as living entities independent of man (although in the latter case, corresponding to forces embedded in man). In some covens, the goddess and god powers are ritually "drawn down" into the acting high priestess and high priest respectively, and they then embody the divinities during the ritual. During the fertility rites of Beltane, the incarnated divinities may in a few covens celebrate *Hieros gamos* (sacred marriage) in a ritual sexual union. Usually, the sabbats begin in the evening and last up to three days, including, in addition to the actual ceremonies, social functions such as potlucks. While sabbats follow the solar cycle, esabats are oriented toward the lunar cycle, the moon symbolizing the goddess in her three manifestations as maid (new moon), mother (full moon), and crone (the waning quarter moon). Each phase is considered to have special powers and to provide an appropriate atmosphere for specific magical workings.[7]

Many Wiccans claim that their magic is either directly or indirectly a continuation of ancient esoteric knowledge developed in the mystery religions of European or Asian cultures of antiquity. As has frequently been observed by non-Wiccan scholars, though, the actual heritage of Wiccan magic appears to be an outgrowth of nineteenth-century occultists and magical groups, particularly the legacy of Aleister Crowley (1875–1947) and the Hermetic Order of the Golden Dawn. Having spent a "boyhood in Hell" at a fundamentalist Christian boarding school, Crowley gravitated toward occultism and earned a reputation as an enfant terrible.[8] In 1896 he was initiated into the Golden Dawn, a magical order drawing on Theosophy, kabbalah, and the Western hermetic tradition. Geared toward mysteries and the occult, Crowley immersed himself in the esoteric traditions of India, Southeast Asia, Egypt, and Mexico during his globe-trotting year. During a magic experiment in Cairo, Crowley was visited by the entity "Aiwass," which dictated to him *The Book of the Law*. Crowley was now the herald of a new "Thelemic" era, in which "every man and woman" would be "a star" and "do what thou Wilt shall be the whole of the Law" (Aleister Crowley 1994 [1913], 305, 386).[9] Crowley was introduced to sexual magic by joining the quasi-Masonic magical order Ordo Templi Orientis (OTO) and became head of its English chapter. In 1920 Crowley established an Abbey of Thélème in Sicily but was eventually expelled by the fascists as a degenerate sectarian dandy. In 1925 he became international head of the OTO, which transformed into a Thelemic Order, thereafter inalienably associated with the legacy of Crowley. In his voluminous writings Crowley outlined his Thelemic philosophy within an esoteric context according to which the whole universe was interconnected and could be changed according to will by magically working on the correspondences. Drawing on Gnosticism, kabbalah, Eastern esotericism, and the hermetic tradition, Crowleyan magic, tarot, sexual workings, ceremonies, and libertine policies would inspire groups as different as the Wiccans and the Satanists. In the mid-1940s the aging Crowley was visited several times by Gerald Gardner. From surviving correspondence between the two, it seem as though Gardner was a °VI initiate in the OTO and for a while contemplated the prospect of reviving the declining OTO faction in Britain (Hutton 1999, 221).

The suggestion that the Wiccan tradition might derive from Crowley's magical mysticism is somewhat controversial among apologetic Wiccan milieus that uphold as truth the Paleolithic origin of Gardnerian traditions and rebut Crowley as an emissary of evil. Nonetheless, Gardnerian Wicca rituals and magical workings did borrow extensively from Crowley, OTO, and the Golden Dawn, as do many other Wiccan traditions. The almost universally acknowledged Wiccan golden rule—"If it harms none, Do what you Will"—is basically a clarification of Crowley's Thelemic motto "Do what thou Wilt shall be the whole of the Law," reflecting the Wiccan imperative of serving the life force. Adopting a Crowleyan understanding of magic as the art and science of causing change to occur in conformity with one's will, many Wiccans depend on a Jungian conception of an individuated Self (and/or a Nietzschean "true self") in specifying that magic properly deals with raising one's consciousness. Far from interpreting one's will as gratifying egoistic desires at the expense of other life forms, then, Wiccans commonly understand greater magic in the context of self-transformation, or as the progressive art of becoming god.[10] Not even in the myriad mundane tasks of lesser magic (which assists more practical efforts, such as getting a job or a lover or seeing into the future) is there any room for the stereotypical cunningly evil "black" magic of the medieval witch craze. Witchcraft practices are in fact utterly devoid of necrophilia, cannibalism, and pacts with the devil.

A quasi-Masonic and Crowleyan influence is noticeable also in the initiatory structure of Wiccan covens (local congregations). Not all Wiccans are necessarily members of a coven—the number of solitary and/or cyberwitches in fact seems to be increasing—and not all covens operate the same way.[11] According to influential witch and publicist Starhawk (née Miriam Simos), a coven is "a Witches' support group, consciousness-raising group, psychic support center, clergy training program, College of Mystery, surrogate clan and religious congregation all rolled into one" (Starhawk 1979, 35). Typically, a coven consists of a small circle of initiated witches and has no paid clergy or staff, no dues paying members, and no separate building to meet in. Its relative longevity depends primarily on how meaningful membership is felt to be, the amount of (unpaid) time and energy invested by coven elders and individual initiates, and whatever else might happen in their lives. The initiatory pattern generally follows a hierarchical structure of three degrees, intended to reflect levels of increasing consciousness and mastery of esoteric knowledge. A code of secrecy is frequently demanded, and most witches do not reveal to the uninitiated what has been learned in the inner working of a coven. To the consternation of some witches, however, the basics of the Craft have been published by active Wiccans, including various descriptions of the initiation ceremonies.

To illustrate with an account given by Alexandrian Priestess Vivianne Crowley: The first degree introduces the initiate to the world of the goddess. The initiate is brought into the circle *skyclad* (naked), blindfolded, and bound with ritual cords. "To be initiated, we have to be willing to cast aside our persona, the mask which we present to the world, and to enter the circle as we first entered the world—naked and vulnerable," Crowley explains. "The symbolic message is about acceptance—that what we are and may become once freed of our persona, our mask, is acceptable and welcomed" (1996b, 88). The second degree involves a heroic quest enacted dramatically in a mystery play called the "Legend of the Goddess," in which the hero or heroine descends into the underworld to meet the deity of the opposite sex. The ritual involves sexual mysticism, reversal of gender roles by bringing forth the opposite sex from within (anima or animus), and the symbolic death of the ego. Initiation into the third degree is designed to symbolize that the initiate is at the end of the initiatory journey. The false persona is gone, anima and animus reconciled, and the birth of the true self is symbolized by the sexual union (literally or symbolically) of the god and goddess, as reenacted by the couple to be initiated. Typically, a witch may change the magical name taken at the beginning of the journey to symbolize successive growth and mission accomplished.

Druidry and goddess paganism resemble Wicca but have developed along separate paths, putting emphasis on different aspects of the Craft. Druidry represents the longest tradition, with roots in the all-male esoteric Christian fraternities of the eighteenth century. Its first leaders rejected the pagan label, insisting, like the Masons, that they were guardians of ancient Christian mysteries tracing their roots to King Solomon and/or the lost tribes of Israel via the Knights Templars. With the pagan revival of the 1960s, many but not all Druid orders evolved toward Celtic paganism. In line with the former elitist self-conception, many Druids claim to be a continuation of the Celtic, pre-Christian, tripartite priestly class of bards (poets, storytellers, and singers), ovates (philosophers, prophetic seers), and Druids (priestly politicians/spiritual leaders). To British Druid Philip Shallcrass, the ancient Druids functioned like the Brahmin caste of India. They cultivated their own beliefs and rituals but acted also as priests for their local communities (Shallcrass 1996, 65). In modern Druidry the three roles of bard, ovate, and Druid are often considered to be progressive initiatory designations (Harvey 1997, 32). Druids practice esoteric wisdom and consciousness-raising through poetry and music and by reconnecting with land and heritage.

Druidry and Wicca are both mystery religions and celebrate the same eight Celtic festivals, although with differences in what they emphasize. Druids orient around the four midseason festivals, revere the sun, and perform their ceremonies in daylight, while Wiccans consider the fire festivals at the beginning of the seasons to be the greater four festivals, revere the moon, and celebrate nocturnal rites (Shallcrass 1996, 67). Rebutting charges that Druids are patriarchal, Shallcrass argues that modern Druidry "no longer [is] the exclusively male preserve some of the eighteenth century revival groups tried to make it." While that undoubtedly seems correct, echoes of patriarchal structures and ideology still appear in modern Druidry. Though most, but not all, Druid orders admit women members, a male chief leads a majority of Druid organizations, even if some leaders have an "equal female partner" (Harvey 1997, 33). Shallcrass (1996, 68) claims that although they privilege rationality, Druids no longer "neglect the feminine and the intuitive," a statement, of course, that implies that rationality is exclusively male.

If Druidry in part embodies the patriarchal tradition of Western culture, goddess paganism explores a supposedly more ancient, pan-European spirituality that predates the emergence of patriarchy. Developing an alternative "herstory" to answer traditional history, goddess-oriented pagans make frequent reference to evolutionist-school matriarchal theorists such as J. J. Bachofen and Friedrich Engels as well as to modern archeologists such as Marija Gimbutas.[12] Archeological findings of female figurines from Paleolithic times are interpreted by goddess pagans to mean that the primary religious experience was based on goddess worship. Based on respect for the female power of reproduction, the first societies were matriarchal and worshipped the feminine principle as divine. Generally, goddess pagans interpret ancient matriarchy as an egalitarian, matrifocal, women-respecting, and nature-venerating social organization based on cooperation (Harvey 1997, 73; Morgan 1996, 95). Following Gimbutas, herstorians assert that these peaceful aboriginal cultures were conquered by patriarchal, warring, nomadic hordes that imposed the dominion of men and their male sky-gods.[13] "In the mythologies of these cultures, the Goddesses of the Neolithic and Paleolithic eras are slain or made subordinate to the new Gods of patriarchal warriors," goddess pagan Carol Christ (1997, 62) claimed in a historicist reading of mythology. For many centuries the goddesses who survived could still be venerated, incorporated into prevailing European paganisms as wives and daughters to male gods, and later into Christianity in the image of Virgin Mary or as saints. With Protestant Christianity male dominion reached its apex in Western religion and culture, bringing about a cosmic imbalance as reflected in environmental destruction, sexism, wars, and acute social injustices that endanger the future of the planet.

Among its adherents, the "thealogy" of goddess paganism is considered a remedy to the imbalance of patriarchy, empowering women and goddesses to "reclaim" their lost position in society and religion. Informed by feminist discourse, goddess paganism evolved out of the counterculture of the 1960s and has branched out in several directions. Generally very similar to Wiccan theory and practice, goddess pagans differ mainly in their more exclusive emphasis on female spirituality and deities and the frequently all-women mode of organization. With the exception of the groups that are open to lesbians only, most women's separatist organizations thus exclude families from partaking in their spiritual celebrations (Christ 1997, 140).[14]

Primarily a white middle-class phenomenon, goddess paganism has generally been Eurocentric in orientation. During the 1990s this began to change, as many goddess pagans came under the influence of black and Native American womanist writers who insisted that feminism must also deal with racism and classism (Harvey 1997, 79, 83). This tendency is discernible also within Wiccan circles, although the picture is far from unambiguous. While there is a strong left-wing element—not least, the Green Anarchist variety, which combines environmental activism with a feminist anticapitalist, antiracist, and libertarian socialist position—there is also a large apolitical contingency, as well as a right-wing and racist minority ideological strain. Celticism, for instance, is regarded by some Wiccans as the bulwark of Western tradition against Middle Eastern Judaism/Christianity/Islam and Eastern spirituality, referring to the mystery of blood as the carrier of racial memories from the Celtic golden age and decrying non-Celtic influences and members. Some Wiccans even suggest a Celtic foundation for white racial unity. In 1994 Pamela Constantine argued that "it is the Celtic spirit which not only keeps company with the national folk-soul but, through it, with the folk-souls of other [white] nations, so maintaining a unity which is at the very soul of our race" (quoted in Bowman 1996, 243). Celtic Druid Ecole Druidique des Gaules echoes this reasoning. "The spirituality of the Celts is the only one which represents the collective Indo-European heritage common to all Europe"(ibid., 248). This biologization of spirituality is a dominant feature of racist and ethnically orientated Norse pagans but is contested by antiracist Asatrúers, Celtic Wiccans, and Druids. "Celtic ethnicity is not a prerequisite, as might be imagined," Caitlin Matthews nailed down. "We have entered a phase of maturity wherein spiritual lineage transcends blood lineage" (ibid., 246).

Norse Gods in Vinland

Much as in black America, where Afrocentric theories about possible pre-Columbian African and Muslim voyages to the New World play a pivotal role in the missionary efforts of black Islamic or reconstructed African traditions, modern Asatrúers frequently refer to information indicating a possible pre-Columbian Norse presence in North America (Gardell 1996). Icelandic sagas record a series of Norse attempts to colonize a land of plenty that was called Vinland (land of wine), following a pattern familiar from the colonization of Iceland and Greenland: chance sighting followed by planned exploration and intended settlement (Magnusson and Pålsson 1976, 23).[15] Sailing from Iceland to Greenland in 986, Bjarni Herjulfsson was blown off course and reached the shores of an unfamiliar wooden land that might have been North America. Refusing to land, Herjulfsson sailed along the coastline for five days, then managed to catch a wind taking them to Greenland, where his story spurred talks about discovering new countries.

Among those inspired were Leif Erikson, son of the famous, hot-tempered voyager Erik Röde (Erik the Red), founder of the Norse colony in Greenland. Leif bought Herjulfsson's ship and about the year 1000 made the first of several Norse voyages to the new land. Leif spent a winter in Vinland, described in the *Graenlendiga Saga* as a benign land of abundance, filled with grapes and vines, plenty of salmon in the river and good pastures (Magnusson and Pålsson 1976, 49–72). Subsequently, Leif's brother Thórvald headed another voyage to Vinland, staying two winters in Leif's houses. Exploring the land during summer expeditions, Thórvald and his men came upon a group of *scraelings* (native inhabitants). Following a fatal skirmish that left eight scraelings dead, a revenge squad came in "a great swarm of skin boats" and attacked the Norsemen. Killed by an arrow, Thórvald might have been the first Northern European to be buried in the New World, and his expedition subsequently returned to Greenland with grapes and wine as cargo.[16]

According to *Eirik's Saga* (in Magnusson and Pålsson 1976, 75–105), a relatively successful effort to colonize Vinland was made in the early eleventh century. With 160 men and women in three ships, Thórfinn Karlsefni reached a place he named Straumfjord, which became a base for further expeditions to the north and south. The settlers stayed for three prosperous years, establishing trading relations with the scraelings, until erupting hostilities forced them to return to Greenland. Icelandic annals tell of other voyages in the subsequent centuries. In 1121 Bishop Erik Gnupsson of Greenland reportedly went in search of Vinland but never returned. There are no trees on Greenland, and it seems that the Norse settlers regularly sailed west to get lumber. In 1347 a group of seventeen to eighteen Norsemen en route to Vinland almost lost their ship in a storm, then drifted eastward to the shores of Iceland where they could tell their story. By the end of the fifteenth century, the Norse colony on Greenland was abandoned due to an increasingly colder climate, and living knowledge of the sailing route between Greenland and America came to an end (Larsson 1999, 26).

According to some researchers, archaeological evidence and comparative art might indeed confirm the saga's claims. In 1930 archaeologists found an arrowhead from North America in a Norse burial site in Greenland (Larsson 1999, 36). Excavating a large Indian site at the mouth of Penobscot Bay, Maine, in 1957, two amateur archaeologists found a silver coin, later identified as Norwegian coinage stamped during the regime of King Olaf Kyrre (son of Harald Hårdråde), 1067–1093 (ibid., 37).[17] In 1962 the Norwegian scholars Helge and Anne-Stine Ingstad discovered remains of a Norse settlement of seven to eight houses and boat sheds at L'Anse aux Meadows, Newfoundland, which they dated at approximately A.D. 1000 (Ingstad 1985, 255–87). Among the finds excavated were a ring-headed bronze pin, iron rivets, nails, and a spindle whorl of Viking origin. Following philologist Sven Söderberg, the Ingstads argued that Vinland meant "land of meadows" (i.e., good pastures), which they deemed to be of greater importance than wine to cattle-keeping Norsemen, and they identified the site as the Vinland of the sagas despite the fact that it is north of where grapes grow.[18] To Magnusson and Pålsson, the absence of grapes automatically disqualified Newfoundland as Vinland, and they agreed with the scholarly majority that located Vinland somewhere further south, possibly in the New England region. The Norse settlement at L'Anse aux Meadows, then, is most likely the result of another expedition that is not recorded in the sagas (Magnusson and Pålsson 1976, 9, 58).[19]

Berry Fell speculates in yet more extensive Norse explorations in the New World. In Beardmore, Ontario, a Viking-style sword, battle-axe, and spearhead dating from A.D. 1025 was found in the early 1930s. Although doubts were later raised as to "the authenticity of the story of [the artifact's] alleged discovery," enthusiasts point to the possibility of a Norse expedition reaching Ontario through Hudson Bay.[20] In further support of the thesis, Fell (1980, 341, 346, 358) looks at similarities between Viking coins and Algonquian and Iroquois *runti* shell beads and engraved shell disks found in burial mounds in the eastern United States. Fell also speculates that there was one or possibly several southern voyages, which took the Norsemen around Florida, up the Mississippi River and its tributary the Arkansas into Oklahoma. When Cherokee and other eastern Indians straggled westward in the Trail of Tears of the 1830s, remarkable rock inscriptions with runes of the elder *futhark* (runic alphabet) were discovered in Shawnee, Haevener, and Poteau, Oklahoma. Together with the discovery in Colorado and New Mexico of petroglyphs resembling Norse warriors and battle shields, these finds, albeit disputed, are taken to indicate a possible presence of Vikings or their descendants in the area (Fell 1980, 341–70).

Adding information gained from myths and visionary experiences, some Asatrúers and Native Americans have developed theories suggesting a Norse origin of certain Native American traditions. Thus, the sweat lodge is believed to be an appropriation of the Norse sauna, and the Sun Dance is allegedly inspired by the Norse midsummer ceremony. In one story, retold by Native American Hyemeyohsts Storm, a fair-haired and blue-eyed race of nomadic warriors, variously known as the "Sweet Medicine People," the "Iron Shirts," or the "White Water Spirits," descended on the Southwestern Native American people in search of land.[21] Having been stranded on the eastern coast of North America, the Iron Shirts had fought their way westward, their reputation traveling ahead. When the Southwestern pueblo people heard that their land had been invaded by "white hordes from the North," they gathered their warriors. Following a series of negotiations and conflicts, the two peoples eventually merged into one and the early settlements and *kivas* (an underground ceremonial chamber used by Pueblo Indians) found throughout Utah, Arizona, Colorado, and New Mexico supposedly bear witness to this intermarried people. Among the traditions the nomadic white warriors shared with the Native Americans was the Norse summer solstice ceremony, which became the Earth Sun Dance and "became known to many of the peoples of North America" (Storm 1994, 320–27).[22]

The theory of a pre-Columbian European presence in the New World gained further ground in pagan revivalist circles in the summer of 1996 when a remarkable skeleton was found near Kennewick, Washington. The initial analysis of the skull by local forensic anthropologist Jim Chatters indicated that it had non-Amerindian, possibly Caucasoid features, so it was at first thought to be the remains of a nineteenth-century trapper. Radiocarbon tests then showed that the skeleton was 9,200 years old, making it one of the oldest skeletons found in the United States (Lee 2000; Lee 1997b; Lyke 1997). A complex, three-sided conflict soon centered on the skeleton, with scientists, Native Americans, and Asatrúers all claiming the rights to the remains. A group of eight internationally known archaeologists, including researchers at the Smithsonian, wanted the right to study the skeleton. They were opposed by two groups of American Indians, the Nez Perce and the Confederate Tribes of the Umatilla Reservation, who considered a study of the remains a desecration, claiming "their ancestor" should be properly reburied. "This is not a scientific issue to us," Native American spokesperson Debra Croswell stated. "It's a religious issue" (quoted in Lee 1997a). Citing the 1990 Native Graves Protection and Repatriation Act (NAGPRA), the

Native Americans demanded all scientific testing be stopped. Speaking for the third party involved in the conflict, Asatrú leader Stephen McNallen (1996) suspected another motive behind the Native American legal action. "They literally want to bury the evidence. I mean, this is a politically hot potato. The idea of Caucasians that might have walked across the Bering land bridge along with the Native Americans is awesome. It changes the whole question of who was here first! Who genocided who?"[23]

With the case pending, the skeleton was locked up in custody of the Army Corps of Engineers in Richland, Washington. When Alan Schneider, attorney for the scientists, got news that the corps three times had allowed the Indians to perform religious ceremonies with the bones, he strongly protested, saying, "no one should be allowed access until the lawsuit was resolved" (quoted in Lee 1997c). Upset, too, were the Norse heathens, whose attorney Michael (Reinhold) Clinton, himself an active Asatrúer, managed to give the pagans access to the bones for an Asatrú ceremony that was conducted in the vault in August 1997, under heavy protests from Native American spokespersons (Lee 1997d; Lee 1997e). The religious battle raging over the bones made the scientists despair. "If every time a skeleton shows up, we toss it back in the ground for fear of offending someone, we will never learn anything!" exclaimed forensic anthropologist Chatters, expressing his impatience with "racial politics"(quoted in Lyke 1997). DNA testing performed in 2000 proved inconclusive (Lee 1999; Lee 2000b; Lee 2000d; Lee 2000e; Lee 2000f), and based on geography and Native American oral history, the U.S. Interior Department ruled in September 2000 that the bones belonged to the American Indian tribes (Lee 2000f; Lee 2000g). The decision rests on the Interior Department's interpretation of the NAGPRA to mean that anyone on the continent "before the historically documented arrival of European explorers is legally 'Native American.' "[24] The interpretation means that if archaeologists find skeletons when excavating possible Norse settlements along the northeastern shores, these would be classified as Native American and removed from further studies. Paula Barran, lawyer for the scientists, said that using Columbus as the dividing line clearly is arbitrary: "Why Columbus? Why not Leif Erikson? Why not the Kennewick Man?" (quoted in Lee 2000a).[25] "It is the equivalent of discovering the body of Moses in the West Bank and handing the remains over to the Palestinian Arabs because they occupy that area and their histories tell them this was always the case," a Los Angeles Times editorial comment read (Michael Kelly, quoted in Lee 2000h).

The Kennewick Man conflict highlights the political dimensions of prehistoric archaeology. The remarkable skeleton was worked into the ethnonation-alist ideologies of both the Native American and Asatrú communities. To the former, the finding confirmed oral history and American Indian mythology, which informs them that they have lived on the land since times immemorial. To the latter, it was further evidence of a pre-Christian European legacy in North America. "Kennewick Man is our kin, forged by the same powers that made us," said McNallen in a prepared statement. "The Asatrú Folk Assembly will con-tinue to stand by this Ancient One and will not let our heritage be hidden by those who seek to obscure it" (quoted in Lee 1997b). The skeleton was thus used to strengthen the pagan claim that Asatrú is an "organic" religion that is natu-ral, not alien, to white Americans. "The religion of the first European settlers to inhabit North America, a full five hundred years before Columbus, was Asatrú," declared Valgard Murray (n.d.a) of the Asatrú Alliance. "Ours is an ancestral religion," the Asatrú Folk Assembly adds, "one passed down to us from our forebears of ancient times" ("Declaration of Purpose" n.d.).

Much like the mainstream American reverence for the Founding Fathers, Asatrúers pay respect to Leif Erikson as "the founder of Vinland" (i.e., America). On 9 October Leif Erikson Day is celebrated, and his father, Erik Röde, is com-memorated on 8 October ("Asatrú Calendar" 1996). This line of reasoning got a boost in 1999 and 2000, when Norway, Sweden, Iceland, Greenland, Canada, and the United States celebrated the one-thousandth year anniversary of Euro-American contact. President Clinton proclaimed 9 October Leif Erikson Day, announcing a year of festivities, with exhibitions, plays, study tours, restora-tions of Viking settlements, and inaugurations of Leif Erikson statues in Nor-way, Greenland, and Canada. On the Viking Days during the millennium New Year celebration, a replica of Leif Erikson's longboat, Skidbladner, was publicly displayed in Stockholm. Plans were made for a commemorative voyage from Sweden via Norway and the Faeroe Islands to Erik Röde's farm at Eirikstadir in Iceland and then to his farm at Brattahild (today's Qassiarsuk) in South Green-land. Greenland festivities included reenactments of Viking and Inuit teams, and Islendingur, another long boat, repeated Erikson's journey, sailing to L'Anse aux Meadows in Canada before continuing southbound along the coast to the United States (Hellberg 2000).[26] "This country has been far too focused on Columbus, and he wasn't even here," Tucson, Arizona, Asatrúer Thórsteinn Thórarinsson (1998) commented. "Norse pagans were here long before that. If any white men should be credited as founders of America it should be Viking heroes and not a Catholic who lost his way to India."

Living Asatrú

The late 1960s and early 1970s saw the first efforts to reconstruct pre-Christian Norse paganism. The first more important Norse heathen groups to appear on the scene were the Odinist Fellowship, founded by Else Christensen in 1969, and the Viking Brotherhood (later renamed the Asatrú Free Assembly [AFA]) founded in 1969–70 by Stephen McNallen. Both Christensen and McNallen are still involved with the scene, although the activities of eighty-eight-year-old veteran Christensen have slowed down considerably since she was deported to Canada from the United States after having served a five-year prison term for drug transportation. McNallen's AFA folded in 1987 and was reestablished in the mid-1990s as the Asatrú Folk Assembly to present a "folkish" alternative to the then vital "non-ethnic" Asatrú scene. Christensen and McNallen represent two separate tendencies within contemporary Norse paganism. Christensen offered a more political and racial interpretation with notable national socialist influences, while McNallen espoused a more religious and "ethnic" interpretation, although his vision about a future stateless American confederacy based on decentralized tribal units and ecologically sustainable production was not bereft of political implications. The differences between the two schools of thought are sometimes said to be of such a magnitude that Odinism and Asatrú are better described as two separate religious movements, with Odinism revolving around the primacy of race and Asatrú serving as its nonracist counterpart, positioned squarely in the wider milieu of neopaganism and the occult. In reality, however, there seems to be no such neat division, but a much more complex picture, with self-defined Asatrúers centered on race and active Odinists heavily involved in occult pagan practices.

The rising interest in pre-Christian heathen traditions is related to two distinct albeit not mutually exclusive trends. On the one hand, it is part of the surge of Eurocentric paganism. As such, Asatrú shares a substantial body of features with Celtic Wicca in both theory and practice. Both Wicca and Asatrú are homemade, self-experienced, and nondogmatic polytheist spiritual pathways celebrating a resacralization of nature and man's physical embodiment. On the other hand, the upsurge of Norse paganism in the Aryan counterculture is related also to the progressive radicalization of the white-racist milieu. As such, it is a continuation of the refutation of Christianity that took hold in the white-racist counterculture in the 1980s. Similar to the iconoclastic rhetoric of Creativity and Cosmotheism, many racist heathens single out Christianity as a chief cause of the perceived demise of white power and Western civilization.

Dissatisfied with the lack of deeper spiritual content in these racist creeds, Aryan heathens turned to history in search of an alternative, opting to replace Christianity with reconstructed ancient traditions as the white man's "true" religion. The existence of these two separate tributaries, paganism and white power, contributes to the apparently ambiguous image of Norse paganism, as it appears to some outside observers. Among Asatrúers are found anarchists, homosexuals, blacks, and environmental activists, as well as racist skinheads, national socialists, and Aryan revolutionaries. But a closer look reveals that these strange bedfellows in fact rarely share any bed.

Far from being a monolithic entity, the world of Norse paganism in the United States is extremely diverse, with many distinct ideological variations and organizations with profoundly different opinions concerning what Asatrú/ Odinism is all about. The key divisive issues are centered on race and for whom the Nordic path is intended. Here, three distinct positions of an Asatrú "triangle" can be identified: an *antiracist* position that welcomes any genuinely interested person irrespective of race or ethnicity; a *radical racist* position that defines Asatrú/Odinism as an expression of the Aryan race soul and sees it as an exclusively Aryan path; and an *ethnic* position that, not always successfully, tries to get beyond the issue by claiming that Asatrú is linked with north European ethnicity. The antiracist wing seems to be numerically strongest, although there are no reliable statistics available. Veteran Edred Thorsson (1997) estimates the ratio of racist versus nonracist Asatrúers to be 40:60. He also believes that those involved with the racist wing more likely have found their spiritual home and will stay there, whereas the nonracist wing tends to be more transient, composed of seekers who might be into Norse religion this week, Wicca the next week, and turn to an Eastern creed the week after that. Another veteran, Valgard Murray (1997) of the Asatrú Alliance, estimates the ratio at 50:50, and, like Thorsson, believes that the "racially aware" component is more devoted than the nonracist faction.

Momentarily leaving race out of the picture, the following section will briefly introduce the world of Norse paganism, the term *Asatrú* being used to refer also to Odinism. While there is a growing number of scholars exploring the contemporary pagan landscape in the United States and abroad, there are few studies of Asatrú communities. Margot Adler includes a brief of the subject in a revised edition of her classic study *Drawing Down the Moon* (1986, 279–82). Based almost entirely on an interview with Stephen McNallen, Adler's 1986 observations have since been recycled in many other studies. Jeffrey Kaplan made a more in-depth analysis of Asatrú in his comparative study *Radical Religion in America* (1997, 14–

32, 69–99). Other scholars who include discussions about Norse paganism are Graham Harvey, Michael York, and Goodrick-Clarke. Still, there has been no monograph-length study published.

Since there is no uniformity in Asatrú belief and practice, the descriptions of pagan ideas and activities that serve primarily as an introduction to the basics to which most Asatrúers generally subscribe, although they might differ in any number of details.

Gods and Goddesses

Asatrú is an earth-based polytheist "tribal" spiritual worldview more akin to Native American religions or Wicca/Druidry than Christianity. Opposing the global ambitions of Christianity as spiritual imperialism, Asatrú has no missionaries and is generally hostile to the notion of universal religious truth, emphasizing instead self-experienced spirituality. In Christianity an ontological gulf separates creator and creation: God is a transcendent omnipotent Lord, and man is set apart as created in his likeness and as the only creature bestowed with a soul. Asatrú is less anthropocentric. Man is not free to exploit an objectified nature, Asatrúers maintain, but shares a sacred environment with other soul-bestowed beings.

Generally, Asatrú combines a pantheistic notion of the divine as immanent in nature with a polytheist belief in the condensation of divine energies in a plurality of god/desses. Mother Earth is approached as a living entity. Trees, mountains, lakes, groves, and ponds may be seen each as locus of spirits as may individual mammals, reptiles, and birds. The world of man is but one of nine interrelated worlds, linked with the giant world tree, Yggdrasil. Our world, Midgård (midyard), is at the center of a tripartite structure of worlds above and below. These other worlds are populated by beings other than man—divinities, ancestors, giants, dwarves, and elves. North of Midgård is Niflheim, land of frost and cold, populated by ice giants. Mörkskogen (dark woods) in the south borders the land of fire and heat, Muspelheim, which is ruled by Surt, a primordial fire giant. Gods and goddesses inhabit two worlds, Asgård and Vanaheim. There are worlds of giants (Jotunheim), worlds of chthonic black elves (Svartalfheim), and worlds of the ancestors (including Hel, a shadowy underworld, and Valhall and Sessrúmnir in Asgård). While the worlds are distinct, there are no fundamental borders of separation. Traveling between the worlds is possible by those with appropriate knowledge. Our world, Midgård, is not only populated by man but by a multitude of other intelligent beings. There are guardians of nature, land spirits, dísir (a collective of female guardian spirits, sometimes identified with female ancestors), landvaettir (a collective of mainly male guardians of nature), norns (female guardians and givers of man's destiny), elves of various races, trolls, and giants.

The different realms of the Norse universe correspond to mental states, realms, ways of being, and mindsets among men. Yggdrasil is both an outer macrocosmic world tree and an inner microcosmic world tree within the mental universe of an individual man. Time is not linear but cyclical, with everything moving in cycles of birth, death, and rebirth. Often, a hidden plan is thought to govern the movements of individual man as well as the worlds of all things living. This notion is expressed through the metaphor of the "web of Urd," which connotes the combined working of the three norns—Urd (that which has become), Verdandi (that which is becoming), and Skuld (that which shall be)—who live by the Well of Urd at the foot of Yggdrasil. Everything present is thus rooted in the past and carries the transformative seeds of the future in an ongoing dialectical process of eternal becoming. From this perspective, nothing happens by chance or accident. Life and nature are full of signs for the wise to read, as everything in the cosmos is interconnected in a multilayered series of correspondences. Forming the underlying logic of rune divination, the web of Urd also influences the apocalyptic expectations of a return to the golden age following the approaching twilight of the gods, Ragnarök.

The gods and goddesses are organized in two major collectives, the Aesir and Vanir. The first category is a community of astral sky gods who reside in Asgård, an upper world connected with Midgård by Bifrost, a bridge traversed by gods, sejd-masters (shamans), and the souls of the dead. The Vanir are gods of earth and fertility who master the magic of rejuvenation and reside in Vanaheim. A considerable overlap in functions makes the colorful Norse gods and goddesses complex personalities, but a rough characterization of the more commonly addressed divinities might be made. The one-eyed Odin, with his two ravens, two wolves, and eight-legged horse Sleipnir, is generally thought of as the "all-father," though not in a Christian sense. As a giver of gnosis, Odin is often the patron deity of the acting goðar (ritual leaders), as well as the god of magic, ecstasy, wisdom, writing, culture, poetry, death, and victory (both spiritual and physical). The red-bearded robust Thór is often the favorite of warrior-oriented individuals. As raw and untamed strength personified, Thór is the reliable and fearless defender of the sacred and mundane order. Replicas of mjölnir, the mighty hammer of Thór, are a popular Asatrú piece of jewelry, used both for protection, in ceremonies and meditation, and as a symbol of Norse identity.

The one-armed Tyr is a god of war, rationality, reason, good judgment, law and order, overcoming obstacles, as well as of the knightly spirit of the individual self to serve the interest of the greater whole. The huge "White Aesir," Heimdall, born of nine sisters, is the divine warden who lives at the end of Bifrost. When he blows his *gjallarhorn*, the sound will carry throughout all the worlds and summon gods and worthy warriors to the battle of Ragnarök. An important female Aesir is Frigg, wife of Odin, goddess of motherhood, courage, dedication, sexuality, and female power. Her son with Odin, Baldr, abiding in one of the realms of the dead, is the righteous god of the world to come following the death of the god/desses in the next Ragnarök, when the present world cycle ends and a new cycle will commence. Loki, who was instrumental in the death of Baldr, is the Norse trickster, an unreliable, ambiguous, and amoral god, paradoxically both a strong friend and an enemy of gods and man. Among the Vanir, the three most popular deities are Njord, the wealthy god of sea and wind, and his more commonly addressed son and daughter Frey and Freya. These three are all gods of fertility, eroticism, sexuality, prosperity, wealth, pleasure, satisfaction, and inner peace, but also powerful masters of warfare and magic. Other important deities include Vidar and Vale (sons of Odin, gods of rebirth and revenge), Hönir (giver of spark of divinity, god of exalted inspiration), Brage (god of poetry), Idunn (goddess of eternal youth and eroticism), Gefjon (goddess of plowing and agriculture), Ludhkona (goddess of the growing seed), Forsete (god of negotiation and agreement), Ullr (god of winter and bow hunt), Saga (goddess of storytelling and transmitting knowledge), and Sjöfn (goddess of sexual lust).

Representing forces of nature, aspects of life, philosophical principles and abilities of various kinds, none of these gods and goddess is "good" or "evil" in the Christian sense, but could be either, both or neither depending on context and perspective. Together they are held to represent the plurality of a dynamic multiverse of birth, death, and renewal and present paths of connection between man and the divine according to a multitude of circumstances. An important difference between Wiccans and Norse pagans is that while the former tend to reduce the differences between the various gods and goddess to aspects of One God and One Goddess, Asatrúers tend to keep them separate in a more polytheist worldview.

Concerning the nature of the gods and goddesses, there is no unanimously accepted theology. Some Norse pagans hold that the god/desses have a separate existence independent of man, whereas other pagans, at the opposite end of the spectrum, feel that the pantheon should be understood as Jungian archetypes. Thus while Asatrúer Max Hyatt (1998), goði of Wodan's Kindred, claims to frequently be visited by anthropomorphic gods, even to have had Odin and Frigg stay for days as honored guests in his house, Else Christensen (1998), for example, impatiently dismisses every such tale, saying that she never will meet Odin in person this side of a mental institution.[27] More general agreement is found in the notion that the gods and goddesses also represent different forces within man that it is possible and useful to get in touch with. Connecting with the divine within is thought to be instrumental on several levels. It establishes interdependent links between man and nature; it facilitates personal development and self-growth; and, for some, it is a vital part of an esoteric journey on an ascending spiritual path toward divinity.

Tribal Organization and Ritual Leadership

Generally tribal in orientation, Asatrúers are organized into *kindreds* or *hearths* that either remain independent or federated with a network of autonomous tribes. Criteria of inclusion may or may not include race and ethnicity but will almost universally involve character. Most heathen kindreds expect their members to embody the "nine noble virtues" of Asatrú: courage, honor, truth, loyalty, discipline, hospitality (friendliness), industriousness, self-reliance (freedom), and self-perseverance. While in part compatible with the Protestant ethic of American mainstream culture, this set of virtues differs from its Christian counterpart in that it dismisses every notion of self-denying asceticism in favor of a life-affirming perspective, accepting pleasure and sexuality as good. For Asatrúers, reflecting in their lives this norm of conduct constitutes an important part of being "true to the Gods," which is the literal meaning of *Asatrú*. Some kindreds require potential members to have recommendations from a trusted sponsor; others require a period of prospective membership before allowing initiation as full member, still others have more lax rules of inclusion.

In theory, a kindred is a local community of heathens. In practice, this is not always possible. Some kindreds encompass members hundreds of miles apart. There are nationwide organizations without any kindreds, and kindreds existing in cyberspace or as mail ministries only. In addition, there is an unknown, but probably rather substantial, number of solitary practitioners.[28] Differences apart, kindred ideals are modeled on romanticized notions of "tribes" or "clans" united by blood, land, and/or values, worldviews, and aspirations in life. Much like a Wiccan coven, a kindred is a brother- and sisterhood of mutual support, spiritual development, ritual practice, pagan education, consciousness-raising, and fun, but may be less secretive than a coven (although several notable exceptions do exist).

The ritual leaders in Asatrú, the male *goði* and female *gyðia* (plural *goðar*), are not necessarily third-level initiates as in Wicca, nor are they priests in the Christian sense. There is no orthodoxy and no religious elite invested with authority to grant absolution. Instead, Asatrú is generally a path of spiritual self-experience, and although communal in orientation, it allows a wide spectrum of individual ideological variation. The goði or gyðia is seen as "first among equals" and exercises authority only in terms of his or her spiritual growth, acknowledged ritual competence, and religious knowledge. In theory then, to become a goði or gyðia is to have advanced on the heathen path to a level where a kindred recognizes one's wisdom and mastery of Norse lore and ceremony. In practice, however, there are quite a few examples of the opposite logic, where a self-appointed goði stands alone or tries to establish a kindred, thus reversing the ideal notion of power growing "organically" from the bottom up.[29] A "council of elders" commonly runs kindred administration, with appointed trustees for tasks such as treasury, education, internal affairs, and public relations. Some kindreds have in addition developed "guilds" to pursue special interests such as mead brewery, rune magic, hunting, or handicrafts. A kindred is always self-governed and independent but may belong to a network of autonomous kindreds. Governed by tribal democracy, kindreds negotiate decisions of a pantribal nature at the yearly Althing, where an Allsherjargoði (goði of goðar) may also be appointed to represent the network of independent kindreds.

Ceremonies

Methods of communication with the divine vary according to the perceived nature of the divine, and "contact" is usually made at communal ceremonies or individual rites, through meditation, rune magic, soul journeys, or other shamanistic techniques. The most important communal ceremony is called blot, held in honor of one or more gods eight times a year following the seasonal cycle of nature. Corresponding roughly (though not exactly) in time with Wiccan sabbats, the Asatrú wheel of the year begins with a Yule blot, 21–22 December, often held in honor of Thór and Frey.[30] February 1–2 marks the beginning of the agricultural season, some Asatrúers celebrating it as the "Charming of the Plow" and others as Barri, a blot celebrating the marriage between Frey and Mother Earth. Depending on tradition and where the kindred is located, a Thór blot is celebrated either 14–15 January or 14–15 February. The Festival of Ostara at the spring equinox marks the end of winter and the beginning of the season of rebirth, and is celebrated by a blot in honor of Frigg and Freya and/or to the disir, the collective of female fertility deities. Walpurgisnacht (Wiccan Beltane) is dedicated to the goddess Walburg (often seen as Freya's sinister side) and continues until May Day as a fertility celebration centered on the maypole as a phallic symbol. The midsummer blot (often associated with Baldr) is celebrated during the summer solstice, 21–22 June, and is commonly, though not always, held to be an appropriate time for an Althing gathering. Instead of the Wiccan Lammas (1–2 August), Asatrúers celebrate a Frey blot at the beginning of the harvest as Freyfaxi, 28 August. The fall equinox, 20–21 September, marks the end of the harvest season with a lavish feast. Winter Nights, celebrated somewhere between 11 and 17 October, is another blot that does not correspond to Wiccan traditions. Held at the beginning of winter in honor of Freya, the Vanir, and the disir, it celebrates the bounty of harvest. Some Asatrúers do celebrate Samhain (Halloween) as the day of death and rebirth, while others begin a prolonged Yule festival by honoring the slain and the ancestors on 13 December, the longest night of the year according to Norse tradition.

A blot is often organized as a three-day outdoor camp, filling an important social as well as religious function, providing a forum in which people can meet, share communal meals, and drink together. Some kindreds or kindred members have bought land where a more permanent place of worship has been established, either a *hörg* (a sanctified place of nature, such as a sacred grove or a stone circle) or a *hof* (a wooden temple).[31] At the place of worship is an altar, representing the cosmos, on which are placed sacred ritual items such as a drinking horn, a ceremonial hammer, a *gandar* (a rune staff), a sacred bowl, and a leafy twig used for sprinkling mead. Modern Asatrú substitutes blood sacrifice with mead, said to perform the same blessing function when offered to the gods or sprinkled on participants.

As in Wicca, a blot celebration generally begins with the goðar sanctifying ceremonial ground by casting a circle, inviting the forces of north, east, south, and west, and proclaiming peace in Norse, *Helga vé detta ok hindra all illska* (sanctify this space and hinder all negative forces). There are no Christianlike prayers to the gods and goddesses. Rather, the ritual leader invokes the divinities, inviting them to participate in the communal blot ceremony, which may continue with readings, reenacted drama, poetry, music, and offerings of seed, flowers, or mead. An integral part of each blot is a circular drinking ritual termed *sumbel*, which may also be performed at other occasions. A sumbel consists of at least three rounds of mead drinking, in which each participant raises his horn to hail in turn a god, a hero, an ancestor, or an absent friend, and sometimes involving declarations of a more personal, self-improving, or boasting nature.

Other important communal ceremonies include rites of passage, such as birth, marriage, initiation, death, and rites of scorn to ward off perceived enemies. Many Asatrúers perform individual rites on a daily or, depending on one's objectives, nightly basis. These rites vary from shorter daily routines to function-oriented magic to achieve specific goals. Of special significance for Norse magic are the runes, used in meditation, spells, incantations, divination, art, and communication with the divine. There are three different *futhark* (an anagram of the first six letters, meaning alphabet): the elder futhark (twenty-four runes), the younger futhark (sixteen runes), and the Anglo-Saxon or Frisian futhark (thirty-three runes), of which the first is considered to be the most magically potent. According to Norse myth, Odin obtained the secrets of the runes through an initiatory ordeal, in which he sacrificed himself to himself, hanging from the windswept world tree, Yggdrasil, for nine nights, thus passing through the nine worlds, before grasping the mysteries.[32] Each rune consists of three elements: the "song," or phonetic sound, corresponding to its exoteric meaning; the stave, or shape; and the hidden meaning or esoteric interpretation. The runes can be used individually, laid out according to Tarotlike systems of varying complexity, or be blended together in a bind-rune to combine their inherent forces. In some modern systems each rune also has a numerical value, an astrological correspondence, and an assigned color.

Several techniques of runic yoga have been developed. Runes might be used to provide a contemplative mental focus and identified with the chakra centers of energy positioned along the runic tree of man. Incorporated as instrumental devices in Norse magic, the runes are often seen as carriers of a subtle energy that animates the universe. Runes may thereby influence the course of events in the material world and provide links between the microcosm of man and the macrocosm of the universe. In gymnastic rune yoga, energies are channeled through the body according to the runic posture taken. Practitioners may perform runic dances, chant runic mantras, or work on the energies in runic sexual magic. More than any other element of the Nordic path, the runes have been popularized and embraced throughout much of the wider pagan, occult, and New Age scenes, a fact of great concern to Asatrú purists trying to guard the sacred runic traditions.[33] Less commonly practiced in living Asatrú is the art of *sejdr*, in which arduous shamanistic techniques of ecstasy are used to induce alternate mental states. A master of sejdr might travel in this world or beyond, in the past or future, to harm or to heal, to foresee the hidden or engage in spiritual battle. A more common practice is *útsittning* (sitting out), the heathen equivalent of the Native American vision quest. The practitioner walks out in the wild to find an appropriate place for isolated meditation by reading the signs of nature. Casting a circle by calling the powers of north, east, south and west, the practitioner then blends in with cosmos in an all-night meditative wake to communicate with ancestors and/or other beings. In some traditions, this is also considered to be an appropriate technique for acquiring or meeting with "power animals" or zoomorphic spiritual guides.

Heathen Anthropology

As there are nine worlds and a plurality of gods and goddesses, man is said to be a composite character of body, mind, and a number of souls. The notion of multiple souls varies in its elaborations but can be likened to leaves in a book or fingers in a hand—separate, yet bonded together. Of the four to five souls thought to govern different mental and bodily functions, two are said to survive beyond the body's physical death. One soul, the *hugh*, travels to one of the realms of the ancestors, the destination determined by the worth of one's earthly life. Warriors may go to Freya's hall Sessrúmnir in Fólkvangar or earn entrance into Odin's Valhall, the hall of the slain, hosted by the *einherjar* who will fight on the side of the Aesir at Ragnarök. A more general realm of the dead comprises the nine underworlds of Hel, daughter of Loki and a giantess. Few seem to believe that any ancestral world would be a final destination, preferring instead theories of new challenges to be met in the new existence, suggesting also that there is death beyond death. The other surviving soul, the *fetch*, departs to await its next reincarnation, the conditions of which might be determined by one's achievements in this life or combined with the sum of past life experiences.

Reincarnation is frequently thought to follow family lines, and the fetch abides in the realm of the dead until a clan member gives birth. The ancestral soul then reattaches itself to the newborn child during the first nine nights of its life. As is true of many other aspects of Norse paganism, widely different opinions about reincarnation coexist. Whereas Edred Thorsson (1992) claims a "true man and woman desires above all things rebirth in Midgård," Ron McVan of Wotansvolk says the opposite. Only the worthy gain entrance to the exalted domain of Valhall, McVan asserts, and a person is "destined to return to Midgård at a future time to repeat the process until he at last reached this highest level of completion."[34] In the doctrine of reincarnation in one's clan, one of several aspects of Asatrú opens for merger with racist speculation. While race as a concept was probably unknown to the pre-Christian Norse communities, its modern followers live in a society in which it can hardly be avoided.

Antiracist Paganism

Arguing that Asatrú is open for everyone who sincerely dedicates herself to the Norse way and its gods and goddesses, the antiracist camp is currently populated by more than a hundred independent kindreds that may or may not be federated into networks of independent tribes, such as the Ring of Troth, the Irminsul Aettir, or the American Vinland Association. The Massachusetts-based Raven Kindred was founded in 1991 by Janna Pereira, Lewis Stead, and Bill Dwinnells. Raven Kindred spokespersons assert "Asatrú is a tribalist faith (the Folk of Asgård) but that the Gods call those who they will to join our Folk [irrespective of] race, ethnicity, national origin, sex or sexual preference."[35] Condemning the "racist morons" who try "to exploit our faith for their unholy aims" as "traitors to our Gods," members of the Raven Kindred distance themselves from both the racist and the ethnic positions they believe will "remain small and marginal" due to their racist discourse.[36] Among the Raven Kindred, Asatrú is seen as a tribal-based earth religion, with gods and goddesses existing independent of man, and members envision a revived Norse heathen religion with pagan communities, schools, and public hofs in every major American city. As of 1999, the Raven Kindred had only two associated kindreds and published the *Asatrú Today* journal. Through founding member Bill Dwinnell, the Raven Kindred is loosely linked with the Ring of Troth and uses its Goði training program.[37]

Founded at Christmastime in 1987 out of the ashes of McNallen's Asatrú Free Assembly, the Ring of Troth is a network of independent kindreds established along the lines described in founding member Edred Thorsson's *A Book of Troth*. Thorsson, or Stephen E. Flowers, is one of several scholars involved in the current pagan revival in Vinland. He received his doctorate in Germanic studies with a dissertation about runes and magic, has studied Indo-European linguistics and Comparative Religion, is fluent in all past and present northern European languages of relevance, and has studied runology at the University of Göttingen, Germany. In addition, Thorsson has published several books on rune magic, Norse mythology, and Germanic mysticism, and translated a number of völkisch scholars, including Ariosophist Guido von List.[38] This dual field of activity has given him a key role within the evolving heathen scene at the expense of his academic career. Although he still occasionally teaches at University of Texas at Austin, he believes that his esoteric explorations of Teutonic lore will prevent him from ever gaining a full professorship (Thorsson 1999). Thorsson envisions Asatrú as a future mainstream American religion, "something a local mechanic could be comfortable with," a community-based nature religion honoring family values and libertarian ideals. He argues that heathens should build Asatrú seminars around American university programs, sending new generations Asatrú priests and priestesses to be educated in Norse history, culture, mythology, and languages, thereby giving the current revival a chance to ensure continuity (Thorsson 1997).

In its first phase between 1987 and 1992, the Ring of Troth involved a growing number of kindreds, established the Asatrú paper *Idunna*, and was generally oriented toward the wider pagan community in all its diversity. Beside Asatrú activities proper, many activists engaged in shamanic practices and/or experimental magic, held dual membership in Wiccan, Druid, or Esoteric Western groups, or incorporated elements from the multifaceted world of New Age. Politically, the Ring moved leftward, with members engaging in the environmentalist and Green Anarchist scene and developing a strictly antiracist and antisexist ideology. Of importance to this development was yet another scholar, KveldúlfR Gundarsson, who pointed out that "racial purity" had no meaning to the ancient Norsemen and that their god/desses were indifferent to race. Gundarsson argued that marrying "outsiders" was common and highly respected during the Viking era, a practice that also was reflected in Norse mythology. Odin, for example, was the son of the god Borr and the giantess Bestla, and thus a "half-breed." Njord married the giantess Skadi, and his son Frey married the giantess Gerd. With the giantess Jarnsaxa, Thór had two sons, Modi and Magni, who shall inherit his hall and hammer after Ragnarök. Discussing the Norse notion of a hereditary aspect of the soul and reincarnation within the clan, Gundarsson rebuts the conclusion that only those related by blood to ancient followers of the Aesir and Vanir are suited to revert to the old gods. Acknowledging that the ancient Norsemen emphasized the inherited might of the clan, Gundarsson points out that the Norsemen also had several rituals by which that might could be passed on to those who were not related by blood, including adoption, rituals of blood-brotherhood, and ceremonies by which an individual ancestral soul might be passed on to a new child of another clan line.[39] Advocating gender equality as a heathen practice, Gundarsson emphasized the leading role of strong, independent Norse women in history, as well as the role of the goddesses (Kaplan 1997, 77). To the abhorrence of spokespersons from the other two Norse pagan (ethnic and racist) perspectives, Ring-affiliated kindreds boasted Jewish, black, homosexual, and transsexual members, and had no problems with biracial marriages (*Thorsson* 1997; Kaplan 1997, 21).[40]

Controversy soon developed around Thorsson's dual membership in the Satanic Temple of Set and his exploration of sadomasochistic sex magic. The heated debate continued until Prudence Priest accepted the position as steerswoman in 1992 of the Ring, but the Ring refused to stabilize. Priest was in 1995 forced out of office following new intrigues, again involving the two competing scholars Thorsson and Gundarsson, and William Bainbridge took over as steersman.[41] Priest continues to be active as editor of *Yggdrasil* and cofounded in 1995 the San Francisco–based American Vinland Association, a heathen network that like the Ring of Troth promotes the pagan revival without discriminating "on the basis of race, gender, sexual orientation or any other irrelevant criteria." [42]

CHAPTER FOUR

Wolf-Age Pagans: The Odinist
Call of Aryan Revolutionary Paganism

U nderstanding Asatrú as a religion of the blood, eternally connected with Aryan man as his spiritual root of existence, racist Asatrú organizations and activists dismiss the antiracist position as the distorted product of politically correct, pagan, universalist, New Age confusion. Many, but not all, racially militant pagans in the United States prefer to call their warpath of revolutionary spiritual politics "Odinism" or the Germanic "Wotanism" rather than risk being lumped together with nonracial Norse pagans. Far from being a unified ideology, Odinism has many faces. Some, like Wyatt Kaldenberg, focus on Odin's warrior aspect and outline Odinism as a cult of violence. Others, like Jost (surname omitted by request), are more oriented toward Odin as a master of mysteries and have developed an Ariosophic Odinic philosophy aimed at racial and/or individual ascendance into divinity. Still others are more attracted to Odin's darker aspects and make him a locus for exploring the sinister side of the Aryan psyche. Beginning with presenting the lifework of Odinist veteran Else Christensen and her Odinist Fellowship, this chapter will then examine the first two Odinist pathways mentioned above. The following chapter will focus on Wotansvolk, currently one of the more prominent promoters of Odinism as the original religion of the Aryan race and key to a revolutionary project aiming at racial self-determination in a white transatlantic homeland. The emerging phenomena of darkside heathens combining occult Asatrú with ariosophic Satanism will be presented in chapter 7.

The Odinist Fellowship and the Grand Mother of Racial Paganism

Established in 1969, the Odinist Fellowship is the oldest organization on the Norse pagan scene. Primarily a ministry by mail, it was long based in founder Else Christensen's mobile home in Crystal River, Florida, but has relocated to her small trailer in Parksville on Vancouver Island, British Columbia. For the past thirty years, Christensen has dedicated her life to the revival of Norse paganism as a vehicle for racial unification and rejuvenation. As the "Grand Mother" of racial Odinism, Christensen introduced many concepts and fields of activities later adopted among Odinists and racially aware Asatrúers. Among these are a Jungian reading of Norse paganism as the racial soul of the Aryan folk, her Jungian view on the heathen gods and goddesses as race-specific and genetically engraved archetypes, her political and economical ideal of "tribal socialism," and her focus on recruitment through prison-outreach ministries. Through Christensen, many of the current Asatrú and Odinist ideologues first became acquainted with Norse traditions, although many of them would later embark on independent routes: some came to express impatience with her insistence on a low political profile; others explored more in depth the ritual and magical paths Christensen was less inclined to tread. Slowed down not least due to her age, Christensen, along with her Odinist Fellowship, has been bypassed by far more aggressive groups of racial pagans who nevertheless pay her homage as a gray sage and herald of the dawn of a new era.

Born Else Oscher in 1913 in Esbjerg on the west coast of Denmark, Christensen became a professional handweaver and moved in 1933 to Copenhagen, where she got involved in revolutionary unionism and radical politics.[1] Copenhagen had during the 1930s a lively underground scene of political activism, with frequent clashes between Trotskyites, Stalinists, anarcho-syndicalists, and national socialist revolutionaries. Starting out as a follower of the revolutionary anarcho-syndicalist ideologue Christian Christensen (not a relative), Christensen was then attracted to the left-leaning Strasserite wing of the emerging national socialist movement. Shortly thereafter, in 1937, she married woodcarver and unionist Aage Alex Christensen, who had briefly served as top lieutenant of Caj Lenbacke, führer of the miniscule Danish National Socialist Workers' Party. Alex belonged to the faction ousted when Fritz Clausen in 1933 staged a palace coup and gained control over a party that remained largely uninfluential throughout the war years, despite its wholesale cooperation with national socialist Germany.[2] Floating around in armed cells, most of the dissident Danish national bolshevist faction was rounded up when Germany occupied Denmark in 1943. While Else was released after three days' interrogation, Alex was convicted of illegal weapons possession and kept in a detention camp. After six months, Else managed to convince her father's cousin, who was minister of justice, that Alex did not really belonged to the resistance proper, thus securing his parole. Following the war, Else and Alex Christensen set sail for England, from where they in 1951 crossed the Atlantic and settled in Toronto, Canada, where Else worked at various hospitals until her retirement. Pursuing her interest in class-based racial radicalism, Christensen developed contacts across the border. Among her closer associates was the seminal populist anti-Semite Willis Carto. Through Carto, Christensen was put in contact with American Nazi Party organizer James K. Warner, who at that time resided in Kingston, New York. Warner—who would later become an influential Christian Identity minister of the New Christian Crusade Church and Louisiana Grand Dragon of David Duke's Knights of the Ku Klux Klan—had made an aborted attempt to launch Odinism as the religious dimension of revolutionary national socialism. Disappointed by the failure of his (Sons of Liberty) Odinist Religion, Warner gave Christensen all his leftover Norse material, among which she found a pamphlet by the Australian lawyer and Odinist Alexander Rud Mills, the *Call of Our Ancient Nordic Religion* (Christensen 1998).

Mills was a national socialist and firm believer in old-school Anglo-Saxon supremacy, who like Rudolf von Sebottendorf and the Germanenorden merged his racial mystical Odinism with Masonic and Rosicrucian elements. As did the Germanenorden, Mills concluded that the racial archenemy, the Jews, had construed a sinister spiritual plot to fool Aryan man in worshipping the Jews as the chosen people. The once-glorious Nordics, the builders of the noble civilizations of Sumeria, Egypt, Persia, Greece, and Rome, had weakened due to "foreign immigration and miscegenation" and succumbed to the Jewish-Platonic thought that man is separated from God (Mills 1957, 3). This had paved the way for effeminate (Jewish) Christianity and its claims that all men were created equal, "a stentorian conclusion too pathetic to laugh at" (ibid., 25). As a remedy, Mills founded the Anglecyn (later Anglican) Church of Odin, hoping to replace all British-Anglican-Christian institutions with those of an Anglo-Saxon racial religion that would reconnect Aryan man with the divine and thus with his true self. Reportedly, A. Rud Mills helped establish polygamist Odinist groups in Australia, the United Kingdom, South Africa, and North America during the 1920s and 1930s (Kaldenberg 1998a), although there is scant evidence that any of these pagan communes survived for any length of time. In the 1950s Mills launched the First Church of Odin, again without any apparent success. What legacy he left is found in his writings, much of which Christensen (1998) dismissed as too Masonic to be useful. Still, the few Odinist tracts that did find their way to Christensen appear to have had a profound influence on their expatriate Danish reader; some of these tracts were recently reprinted by Wodanesdag Press, run by Max Hyatt, acting Godi of the Vancouver, British Columbia–based Wodan's Kindred.

At the time when Warner pointed her to Mills, Christensen had been intrigued by her reading of *Imperium* (1962) by Francis Parker Yockey. A lawyer by profession, Yockey served as prosecuting attorney for Wayne County, Michigan, before being offered a position with the war-crimes tribunal after World War II. Assigned to Wiesbaden, Yockey's earlier noninterventionist and pro-national socialist leanings were reinforced by observing the miserable condition of defeated Germany. Suspecting that the war effort had been more than a mistake, Yockey came to believe that it was designed by the sinister "culture-distorter" (i.e., the Jewish people) to revert Europe into barbarism. Having concluded that, along with stories of "torture" and "fabricated evidence" designed to present the war's true heroes in bad light, the war-crime tribunal was part of the Jewish scheme, Yockey was forced to resign from his position in 1947.[3] Later that year he returned to Europe, spending six months in isolation at a quiet inn in Brittas Bay, Ireland, writing his two-volume magnum opus on the racial history of philosophy, guided, he believed, by the "Spirit of the Age." The conclusions he reached were therefore, according to him, "not arbitrary" but "absolutely compelling" (1991 [1962], xlvii). Convinced that only heroism could remedy the ailing racial spirit of Europe, Yockey in 1949 established the European Liberation Front (ELF). Opposing the Jewish-American effort to control Europe, Yockey sought to oppose NATO and advocated a tactical national socialist cooperation with Soviet Russia. Yockey also journeyed the Arab world and established contacts with exiled Nazis Johann von Leers and Otto Remer, who produced anti-Zionist material for the Egyptian ministry of propaganda urging German expatriates to assist in building a strong Arab military (Coogan 1999). While finding some support within the left wing of Italian postwar fascism and among the intellectual architects of an emerging radical conservatism, Yockey was ahead of his time. Finding his call to arms falling on deaf ears and ELF dysfunctional, Yockey eventually returned to the United States where he was arrested for passport fraud in 1960. Before Yockey committed suicide in prison, Willis Carto paid him a visit, securing the rights to *Imperium*. Re-edited into a single 600-page volume, *Imperium* became a widely read far-right classic. With the radicalization of the American racist milieu some three decades after his death, Yockeyan perspectives eventually found an audience in the United States.

Yockey conceived of culture as an organic Being bestowed with a soul from which its unique individuality was derived. As with any organism, a culture passed through succeeding phases of gestation, birth, growth, maturity, fulfillment, decline, and death. World history was the record of the lives and deaths of eight high cultures, defined as a "Life-form at the peak of the organic hierarchy of which plants, animals, and man are the lower beings" (Yockey 1991 [1962], 39). Yockey thus confronted the linear view of history, including the Hegelian notion of eternal progress culminating in Western civilization as the crown of creation. Civilization was not peculiar to the Western culture, Yockey contended, but a certain phase in the life of each high culture, which, as any life form, would eventually decline and die. As the high cultures thus belonged to the same genus, they had common features but differed according to the unique characteristics of their individual souls. The reaction of each "Culture-soul" to events, population streams, and ecological habitat was different. Most important, each "Culture-soul" developed its own organic religious expression that continued throughout the lifespan of the culture and determined its science, philosophy, morality, art forms, state structure, and civilization. Yockey considered the races to be material for cultural expression, differing in their degree of will-to-power, and to be biological-spiritual entities: "beneath is the strong, primitive beat of the cosmic rhythm in a particular stock; above is the molding, creating, driving Destiny of a High Culture"(ibid., 288). Far from being permanent entities, races were thus fluid constructions of culture and could transform in accordance with the evolving organic process. Thus, the nineteenth century's multitude of white races (Alpine, Nordic, Teutonic, Anglo-Saxon, Mediterranean, and so on) reflected the materialistic "Culture-crisis" of that age, while from the imperial success of Western high culture, which Yockey predicted, would emerge a vital pan-European race.

Decisive for this outcome would be the extent to which remedies might be found to cure the "illnesses" that seriously threatened Western culture. In his "cultural pathology" Yockey defined the interrelated sicknesses of "culture-parasitism," "culture-retardation," and "culture-distortion." A parasite is a life-form that lives in the body of another life-form at the expense of the latter, such as the black, Jewish, or Asian organisms in the West. The harm increases according to the extent to which the parasite spreads and takes active part in the life of the culture, thus distorting the culture's organic life-path and retarding its spiritual Idea. According to Yockey, the single most harmful parasite afflicting Western culture, including its American colony, is the Jew, to which there is but one natural remedy. "Anti-Semitism is precisely analogous in Culture-pathology to the formation of anti-bodies in the bloodstream in human bodies. In both cases, the organism is resisting the alien life. Both are *inevitable, organically necessary* expressions of Destiny" (ibid., 391). Engaged for millennia in organic warfare against the West, the Jew took advantage of the cultural maturity crisis, which he thought of as modern civilization, by promoting dangerous and distorting ideas such as democracy, equality, feminism, humanism, capitalism, and communism. America, being a colony of the Western high culture and bereft of any Idea (meaning the highest expression of personality, which makes a unique contribution to world history), found it difficult to resist the malign extracultural forces. Culturally weak but militarily powerful, America was taken over by the parasite, who used its mighty imperialistic impulse to divide Europe when the first wave of the "resurgence of authority" commenced with Hitler (ibid., 451–501). Yockey was, however, convinced that an inner organic force was accumulating. "A deep yearning is going through the Western world to be free from the dirt and uncleanness of party-politics, class-war, financial usury and complete absence of heroic spirit" (ibid., 365). The West would "return to the purity of its own soul for its last great inner task, the creation of the Culture-State-Nation-People-Race-Empire unity of the West as the basis for the fulfillment of the Inner Imperative of Absolute Imperialism" (ibid., 439). Heroism, religion, and stern racial socialism would characterize the authoritarian state, which was to launch "the greatest war the world has ever seen against the Barbarian," to realize a "new," "total," and "authoritarian Imperialism, which will plant the Western banner on the highest peaks and most remote peninsulas" (ibid., 365).

The works of Yockey and Mills greatly influenced Else Christensen's worldview, merging with Jungian philosophy into a peculiar synthesis. Following Yockey, Christensen (1998) concluded that the Aryan high culture had reached its "senility phase," pervaded by internationalist forces of degeneration, Christianity, capitalism, and communism. Zealously promoting the "unnatural" idea "that all people are equal" and should unite in a "universal brotherhood" at the expense of their racial and national identities, the Christian Church has been especially detrimental for Aryan man ("Neo Tribalism" 1979; "Universalism" 1982). Capitalism fosters materialism, favors individual enrichment over folk solidarity, and exploits nature for short-term profit. Sharing deleterious materialism with capitalism, communism also destroys the organic unity of a race with its call for class struggle and international solidarity. Seizing on Yockey's idea that "disease to a Culture could only be a spiritual phenomenon" (Yockey 1991 [1962], 373), Christensen rejected "Spengler's pessimistic view" (1998). An organic racial civilization "need not decay like a plant." The present decline of Aryan high culture is primarily a "spiritual malady" that can be remedied with a religious antidote ("Odinism—Religion of the New Age" 1985).

Following Mills, Christensen (1998) found the remedy for cultural demise in the revival of Norse paganism as a genuine, primordial expression of the Aryan folk soul. "The role of Odinism is clear—the pathogens must be destroyed, and healthy organisms raised to serve the purposes of Aryan spiritual liberation and all-around advancement" ("Odinism—Religion of Relevance" 1984). The seeds of the revived racial high culture are found "in the subconscious elements of Urd," understood in Jungian terms as a genetically transmitted collective unconscious, where the power of the Aryan gods are condensed in form of archetypes (*Christensen* 1998).[4] By searching deep into the racial unconscious, below the deceptive surface of induced Christianity, "you will find the wisdom of our pre-Christian forefathers which we today call Odinism, and which expresses the essence of our folk on the moral and religious plane."[5] Christensen thus stipulated an organic relationship between a race and its religion. The "primary source" of Odinism she thought to be "biological: its genesis is in our race, its principles encoded in our genes. As the instinctual religious impulse of our Folk, Odinism embodies age-old realities and paramount amongst these realities are the reality of inexorable change and the reality of multifaceted struggle [to defeat our enemies] and fulfill our Destiny" ("Odinism—Religion of Relevance" 1984).

Although she established the Odinist Fellowship in 1969, it was not until 1971, when her husband, Alex, died, that Else Christensen decided to really get active. That year the first issue of the *Odinist* newspaper appeared, and Christensen began touring the continent, discreetly trying to establish Odinism as a vehicle for racial rejuvenation. Convinced that any overtly militant racial agenda would attract unwanted attention from the authorities, Christensen (1998) pointed out the advantage of a pagan approach: "You have to go in the back door! You have to sway with the wind. . . . I don't think that anybody mistook my opinions from what we wrote in the *Odinist*, but nobody could put a finger on what we said, because we said it in such a way that it couldn't be clamped down at. We still have to do that." A carefully veiled racialist pagan message would, Christensen argued, prevail where others had failed: "Metzger thought he could twist the noses of the Jews, but you can't do that, so he collapsed. He just disintegrated. It was the same with Klassen. . . . You cannot repeat the mistake that Hitler made. . . . Everybody knows that the Jews rule the whole damned world, so you cannot fight their combined power. You need to watch your step."

Exactly how carefully veiled the message really was might be subjective. A couple of disgruntled ex-subscribers to the *Odinist* publicly accused the editors of "doing a disservice to paganism by promoting religious zealousness in the form of politics, especially 'Nazi politics' and [printing articles with] offensive racial overtones" (Letter 1985). In a rebuttal, the *Odinist* editor claimed that the "Nazi charge was the cheapest of all cheap shots that can be aimed against anyone who finds something positive to say about . . . National Socialism . . . or who merely desires some degree of objectivity in dealing with this grossly maligned movement." The editor, continuing, claimed that the paper examined a broad spectrum of political philosophies—from anarchism to national socialism—from a pagan perspective and left it to the readers to make up their own minds about the variety of ideas presented. Concerning the "offensive racial overtones," the editor lifted what remained of the veil, stating, "If any Odinist is ashamed of the 'racial overtones' of being Aryan, of standing up for Aryan rights, then we wonder why such a skittish a person ever want to be an Odinist." Because Odinism is a manifestation of the Aryan soul, one cannot have the former without the latter, the editor reasoned, declaring, "We, as Odinists, shall continue our struggle for Aryan religion, Aryan freedom, Aryan culture, Aryan consciousness and Aryan self-determination." ("Odinism and Racial Politics" 1985).

Christensen (1998) argued that the present power structure is bound to collapse, calling to racial pagans to be prepared for what is coming. No Aryan in touch with his true self can stand the present state of racial insanity and oppressive government, Christensen said, suggesting that a "revolutionary imperative" is a natural instinct evidenced throughout Aryan history, "from Jefferson to Hitler" ("Aryan Freedom" 1983). Wary that many youth would consider the racial conditions so critical that they would support an effort to establish a stern, authoritarian, völkisch state to ensure racial survival, Christensen argued that the history of fascism and national socialism contains warnings, rather than examples to be emulated. She saluted the early, left-oriented, ultranationalist ideology of Mussolini and his alliance with the national-syndicalist organization *Fasci*, but claimed that he later betrayed the cause by compromising his doctrine's integrity by "collaborating with the capitalist element" and erecting a centralized dictatorship. She regretted, along similar lines, that the "true potential" of national socialism never became realized, because Hitler purged the movement of the Strasserite national bolshevist element (*Christensen* 1998; "Communitarian Imperative" 1982).[6] Hitler, Christensen argued, should have kept to his "original, socialist and folkish agenda," but was "diverted" into a total war effort and aligned himself with the far right. In both historical examples of implemented fascism, she asserted, the "truly revolutionary ideals" could be "betrayed" only because of the centralized totalitarian power structure established by the leaders of the once-revolutionary movements.

In this argument the anarchist and anarcho-syndicalist leanings of Christensen's youth shine forth. Anarchism seeks the dissolution of authoritarian government, the decentralization of responsibility, and the replacement of states and similar monolithic forms of political administration with a radically decentralized federalist organization of citizens. In this way, the sovereignty of the individual and of the primary local units of society will be restored, based on voluntary cooperation, and government will proceed by direct democracy. Christensen then departs from mainstream anarchist philosophies by insisting on the primacy of race. Whereas the contemporary anarchist scene generally is staunchly antifascist and antiracist, Christensen describes anarchism as a fundamentally *Aryan* ideology of freedom. She believes that anarchism originated in the "nature" of Aryan man, and she therefore limits along racial lines the scope of her call for social revolution, arguing for a decentralized society based on voluntary cooperation of free *Aryan* individuals (*Christensen* 1998). Christensen upholds as ideal a decentralized folkish communalism, modeled on self-sufficient communes, like those of the Amish or the early national syndicalists in Spain, described as an effort "to unite Anarcho-Syndicalist ideals with the nationalist spirit" that was later suppressed by "reactionary Francoite authoritarianism" (*Christensen* 1998; "Aryan Freedom" 1983).

By projecting her ideals back into legendary times, Christensen claims that pre-Christian Norse society was governed by the Odinist principle of "tribal socialism," and she urges Aryan man to retribalize as a route to liberation ("Neo Tribalism" 1979; *Christensen* 1998). The anarchist ideas favored by the Odinist Fellowship are said to require "a tribal setting," and Christensen argues that a "certain form of [non-Marxist] socialism is inherent in tribalism" (ibid.). Christensen claims that tribal socialism allows "freedom of self-expression," private enterprise, and "encouragement for every member of the tribe to reach his fullest potential" (1998), while also addressing the socialist concerns of sharing resources, responsibilities, and caring for the young, the elderly, and the disabled of the tribe. "The concerns for the community as a whole and the welfare and the future of the tribe are of paramount importance, superseding those of the single member of the tribe" ("Anarchism" 1989).

Though repeatedly stating that a neotribal order would be based on voluntary cooperation, Christensen implies that no man would voluntarily choose to cooperate with persons of another race or ethnicity. "Man is a social animal, capable of self-realization only within a community of racial and ethnic kin" ("Neo Tribalism" 1979). Supposedly, there is an "ethno-biological foundation of collective human behavior" ("Neo Tribalism" 1979), and the tribes envisioned by Christensen must, she insists, be permeated by a "racial consciousness" ("Racial Consciousness" 1984), and guided by the principle that the "interest of the racial community must come before those of any individual or subsidiary group" ("Communitarian Imperative" 1982). As the primary interests of a racial community are racial purity and advancement, a ban on interracial marriage must be enforced. "Individuals will die [while] the Race has the potential for immortality" provided that "the members of the race guard themselves from racial mixing. Keeping the race pure should be, must be more important than climbing a social ladder in the name of material success" ("Racial Consciousness" 1984). Christensen (1998) argues that this has "nothing to do with fantasies of white supremacy." Odinism "harmonize[s] with the interacting forces of Cosmos and Mother Earth" and honors "the diversity of Nature, including the natural variations of human beings" ("What Is Odinism?" 1987). The much-repeated denunciation of white supremacy that runs through much of the racist-heathen scene does not necessarily mean that activists consider all races equal. Most racist pagans I have spoken with express feelings of Aryan supremacy on a personal level or in terms of intelligence, accomplishments, and honorable behavior to most or all other races. What their denunciation does imply is that white supremacy as a political ideology is thought to be dangerous. The doctrine of supremacy, the argument runs, leads invariably to imperial ambitions of world dominion and thus to unwanted racial coexistence, threatening mongrelization. Better, then, to keep the races apart to develop according to their unique racial souls in relation to their various ecological habitats.

Christensen connects the imperative of racial consciousness with the necessity of ecological awareness. Materialism, consumerism, and unabashed capitalist exploitation have brought on a global ecological crisis of such magnitude, she believes, that it could only be reversed by implementing a pagan back-to-earth program of retribalization and ecological sustainable production. Again, idealized pre-Christian Norse culture serves as her model of inspiration in her Yockeyan reading of cultural history in which "culture" is an organic life form of itself. Before the devastating impact of "culture-distorting" Judeo-Christianity, "the Nordic forefathers" are believed to have lived "fully integrated with Nature," which stands in sharp contrast with "our industrial culture" that has "decided to cannibalize Nature, believing that it has overcome Nature and no longer needs her" ("Ecology" 1984). This has led alienated modern man to proceed with his consumerist lifestyle, not realizing that he is "unwittingly standing watch by the death-bed of Nature" ("Exploiting the Earth" 1984). The solution is "a return to the one-with-Nature attitude of our forefathers," feasible only through an Odinist spiritual revolution ("Ecology" 1984). Through Christensen's philosophy runs a streak of preoccupation with purity peculiar to the national socialist version of environmental concern and ecological activism. In this worldview, a chain of idealized, pure entities links macro to microcosmos, reflecting the postulated interdependence of the purity of mind-body-race-environment. Thus, a pure individual nurtures a pure mind in a pure body and lives a wholesome life in purity with an equally pure partner in a pure— that is, heterosexual and monoracial—relationship. This pure family provides a wholesome environment for bringing up pure and healthy children and is the primary building block of a pure racial organism living in harmony with a pure, unpolluted ecological system.

In accordance with the all-American longing for the simple lifestyle of the free yeoman in the "good old days," Christensen envisions a future return to "small-town America" without monstrous cities and industrial pollution. Small-scale family farms would replace agribusiness, and one would again be free to pursue one's personal happiness through hard work and natural industriousness in voluntary cooperation with other free Americans in a Jeffersonian— though folkish pagan—utopia. Espousing her Odinist tribal socialism, Christensen envisions a long-term strategy in which small, cooperative intentional communities of pagans would be established. Striving for autonomy, they would avoid federal attention by keeping an extremely low political profile. Growing through the power of example, regional networks of independent, heathen folk communities could then serve as springboards to meaningful activism. Self-sufficient, ecologically sustainable, monoracial tribes would, Christensen suggests, be a practical method for redefining American federalism and for establishing an Odinist union of Aryan republics.

In the early 1980s, Christensen began a prison-outreach ministry. Within a few years, she managed to establish Odinism as an officially recognized, legitimate religion in the state of Florida, which enabled her to send literature and hold services. Leading regular seminars and serving at seven Florida prisons with Odinist kindreds ranging from five to fifty members, Christensen was a forerunner whose example has been emulated by other militantly racist pagan activists. In terms of ceremonial content, her prison ministry remained rather undeveloped, which seems true also for the fellowship as a whole. The Odinist Fellowship held few communal rites and had no goði/gyðia training seminaries. Aside from celebrating Hitler's birthday, it held only four seasonal meetings a year, generally restricting the ritual content to sumbel. Feeling awkward at pagan ceremonies at which people might dress up in Viking-inspired clothing, Christensen had a more theoretical than practical approach, studying Norse paganism through books rather than relying on self-experienced encounters with the divine or on experimental magic. It is from observing the Odinist Fellowship that many active Asatrúers incorrectly assume that Odinism, as a whole, is a political rather than a religious ideology.

Christensen's activities came temporarily to a halt in 1993, when she was sentenced to five years and four months for involvement in a drug-trafficking scheme. According to Christensen, she had agreed to drive a car from Texas to Florida to reciprocate favors she had received from a younger couple in her neighborhood, not knowing that the trunk was loaded with marijuana and synthetic heroin (Voyles 1993a; Voyles 1993b; Christensen 1998). Throughout much of the Asatrú/Odinist and radical-racist scene, her conviction was interpreted as a political frame-up. Valgard Murray of the Asatrú Alliance (AA) organized a "Free Else Christensen Committee," and Stephen McNallen of the Asatrú Folk Assembly initiated a defense fund with the support of the AA and independent kindreds in the United States and Canada. Christensen herself hesitated to call the conviction political, saying that those who caused her problems simply were drug dealers. Blaming her misfortune on her naïveté rather than the system, Christensen nonetheless expressed bitterness with American authorities for deporting her as a criminal alien following her release. Sent to Canada, Christensen accepted an invitation by Max Hyatt, goði of the Wodan's Kindred of the Asatrú Alliance, to live at his Vancouver Island residence. Minor friction of a religious and political nature soon developed, and Christensen now resides by herself in a tiny old trailer stuck between pine trees at a quiet R.V. park, from which she tries to reorganize the fellowship. Assisted by Hyatt, Christensen in 1998 began publishing the *Midgard Page*, both in paper and on-line, the cyber version being housed by Hyatt's Web site, *Wodanesdag Press* (Christensen 1998).

Age combined with stricter Canadian gun laws and less generous attitudes toward freedom of expression have caused Christensen to adopt an even more cautious tactic, thus distancing her further from much of the racial-pagan milieu she was part of establishing. She now argues that the main focus of the fellowship needs to be cultural, declaring that she aims to keep pagans inclined to "political excesses" out of the revived Odinist Fellowship. "I have been too receptive before and we had problems in some of the prisons because some who really did not know what Odinism was disgraced us by acting stupid and saying stupid things in the name of our ancestral faith" (*Christensen 1998*). Applicants need now to sign a statement affirming that they intend to live by an Odinist code of conduct, which includes staying "within the legal laws of the country" of residence (*ibid.*).[7] Refusing to speak publicly about Aryan empowerment, Christensen probably prefers to serve as a revered icon than to make a comeback at the forefront, allowing the banner of radical racial paganism to be carried further by more outspoken ideologues.[8] Among these are Wyatt Kaldenberg, editor of *Pagan Revival* and longtime associate of Metzger's WAR effort; Jost, founder of the National Socialist Kindred and the Volksberg commune; and David and Katja Lane and Ron McVan of Wotansvolk. These figures represent the three primary directions of the evolving Odinist scene. Kaldenberg cultivates a more political Odinism, characterized by lone-wolfism and calling for violence, while Jost has developed an esoteric synthesis of Norse mysticism and tantric Hinduism. Wotansvolk, which has emerged as the most influential vehicle for racial Odinism, will be the subject of the next chapter.

Wyatt Kaldenberg and the Odinist Cult of Violence

Born in 1957 to a family of racist Mormons living in a small, all-white, working-class town in the Californian Mojave Desert, Wyatt Kaldenberg in his early teens got involved with the Young Socialist Alliance, trying in vain to get his redneck neighbors to appreciate the prospects of a Trotskyist revolution. Enrolling in a Job Corps training program at Salt Lake City in the 1970s, Kaldenberg (1998) claims, made him wake up to racial realities due a series of fights with black fellow students, some of whom were Muslims. Learning about the black separatist creed of the Nation of Islam inspired him to search for a racial religion of his own, plowing through books about pre-Christian European mythology at the library. From an ad in the *Soldiers of Fortune*, Kaldenberg came in contact with the Odinist Fellowship and later the Asatrú Free Assembly, which he joined in the late 1970s. Socialism, racism, and Odinism would constitute the platform of Kaldenberg's worldview for decades, eventually merging with an evolving misanthropy.

Kaldenberg's brief involvement with the Asatrú Free Assembly coincided with its founder Stephen McNallen's decision to take a stand against the growing presence of national socialists at AFA gatherings. McNallen (1996) dismissed as unwanted the fascist ideal of a totalitarian centralized dictatorship, held to be incompatible with the pagan vision of a future free society. Announcing an end to tolerance with Nazi involvement in the Norse pagan scene (in Kaplan

1997, 19), McNallen in 1978 made an effort to weed out explicit national social-ist activists and other race-political extremists from the AFA. Among those who left were Jost and Wyatt Kaldenberg. Recalled Kaldenberg (1998), "McNallen was never racial, and we didn't have the same ideas. I wanted to make Odinism into a white Nation of Islam, and he didn't go there. He never used the word *Aryan* or *white*. He said *folkish* a little now and then, but when you said *race*, he'd turn pink." But you can't be folkish without being racist: "you're either racist or not racist," Kaldenberg insisted. "Either you are on the bus or you are not. There is nothing in between."

Disgusted with McNallen's "soft stand on race" and "middle of the road poli-tics," Kaldenberg along with Tom Paget and Sigi Hubard left the AFA and aligned instead with Else Christensen to launch the greater Los Angeles chapter of the Odinist Fellowship. For the next coming years, the Los Angeles chapter was one of the more active branches of the fellowship, organizing weekly meetings, radio and TV appearances, and yearly Folk Moots (or get together) for the nation-wide fellowship membership, until sharpening disagreements culminated in yet another split, again due to issues of race. Christensen's strategic insistence on a low political profile clashed with radical national socialist/Odinist state-ments by members going on air and with an invitation extended to Tom Metz-ger to speak at the Odinist Fellowship's Folk Moot. Metzger, who had recently won the Democratic Party nomination for a congressional seat on an openly racist, white working-class platform (he was defeated in the general election), continued to visit the Los Angeles chapter's weekly meetings despite the mis-givings of Else Christensen. When the media reported on Order founder Robert Mathews's Odinist beliefs following his death in the shoot-out with the FBI at Whidbey Island in December 1984, the heat propelled another partition between "overt" and "veiled" Aryan revolutionary Odinists. When Christensen urged her members to tone down, radical activists of the Los Angeles chapter left the fel-lowship to form separate groups, like the Thor's Hammer Kindred, or to team up with the National Socialist Kindred or with Metzger's newly established White Aryan Resistance (Kaldenberg 1998).

Attracted to Metzger's Third Positionist ideology and "in your face" ap-proach, Kaldenberg became managing editor of *WAR*, in which capacity he pro-moted raw racist paganism through articles and editorials. The style of Metz-ger's organization was from the outset to "use whatever means necessary to further a White revolution. And if it takes violence and pure hate to get what we want, that's what we gonna use" (Metzger 1996), a position suitable to Kalden-berg's berserk version of Odinist rage. In the early 1990s Kaldenberg began publishing the highly irregular *Pagan Revival*, ambitiously proclaimed as the "central voice of racial Odinism in America."[9] To counteract Christensen's "doomed-to-failure" strategy, *Pagan Revival* would "say things openly," Kaldenberg declared. "Else went out of her way to avoid being N.S., and they nailed her anyway, so what's the point? The people who are really antiracial, when they come in and figure out that you really use code words, they got turned off, and the people who are racial when they see that you are using code words, they're thinking that you are a pantywaist, so you can't win" (*Kaldenberg 1998*).

Kaldenberg outlined a pronounced Manichean paganism, his worldview being based on the continuous struggle between the Aryan children of the sun and the demonic followers of the demiurge Yahweh. "Aryan people are the spirit of life and creation. We are God. Everyone who threatens God is a demon." The monotheists are "the maggots at the bottom trash of heap of Cosmopolitanism" who seek to destroy the Aryan world, as they are "sickened by the Sun and can rule only in darkness." When Aryans practiced paganism and lived in harmony with nature, they lived in a glorious golden age. With the onslaught of Judeo-Christianity, the divine civilization abruptly fell into a dark age that has lasted for a thousand years and now rushes towards its dramatic ending. The Aryan race must now "regain his prehistoric soul," and return to the "religion of rebirth" (Asatrú), and raise again the shining banner of the swastika from which the "devils scatter like cockroaches from a kitchen light." Only thus will a new pagan golden age regenerate the race and save the planet. "We are spiritually connected with the growth and life of the Earth. The reason the Aryan race is dying is because the Earth is dying. The reason the Earth is dying is because the Aryan race is dying." The Aryan race is presented as "the light of the Earth and also the Earth itself," identified with "the blue sky, the flowers in the spring, the birds singing in the trees," whereas the "mud races are death," the "decay of winter," and "the maggots which feed on life." Nature is counting on the children of the sun to yet again take on her ancestral foe, darkness. "If we don't stop the decay and push the serpent back into Hel's pit, then within our life time all the forests will be gone" and winter will rule for cosmic eternity (Kaldenberg 1995a).

Having dehumanized his racial enemies as "cockroaches" and "maggots," Kaldenberg recommended pesticide as the only remedy against the vermin he saw as an acute threat to racial survival. His wording was designed to appeal to the warrior element among unschooled macho youth, not least prolific in the skinhead scene. Kaldenberg's style would have been abhorred by many of the more sophisticated ideologues in the spectrum of racist heathen philosophy presented herein. Still, the cult of violence had its place on the Odinist scene, and the unleashed hate Kaldenberg spewed forth in his verbal crescendos, including their somewhat histrionic dimensions, was representative thereof. The extent to which he himself would walk his talk was, however, a completely different subject. His joyful personality, whose impressive hue revealed an inclination toward sharing a good meal, lots of beer, and a good laugh rather than engaging in military discipline and exercise, left at least this author with the impression that Kaldenberg was not always altogether sincere in his rambling exhortations to unfettered violence. "What is wrong with hate? I hate anyone who threatens the white race and I want him dead. I love the White Race so much that I'll die for it and kill others," Kaldenberg (1996a) proclaimed. "There is no greater love than to hate one's enemies." "We must kill all who threaten our survival. We must crush dissent," Kaldenberg (1998b) insisted. "Mass murder is a sad thing, but Nature dealt the White Race a raw hand. If we do not remove the dark ones from our land, then sooner or later, all White nations will end up as dark as India."

Believing that Jews act as principal agents of the demiurge, Kaldenberg spared no scorn for Holocaust deniers who tried to make Hitler into a Boy Scout who would not hurt his declared racial enemies. Only a mind weakened by reality-distorting Christianity would apologize for killing one's enemy, while a "pagan view of the Holocaust" would be the very opposite. "Human history is a chain of Holocausts. He who kills his opposition wins. Winning is what survival is all about." Accusing the Jews of murdering 300 million European pagans during 2000 years of Jewish Christianity, Kaldenberg felt the proper question Aryans should ask was rather "why we didn't grease the Jews sooner." The revisionist element in the racial movement proved to Kaldenberg that the sons of the sun had yet to awaken to their true mission. "If we were real Aryans, we would not be denying that we defeated the Jews." Places like "Auschwitz and Dachau [should be turned] into religious shrines because evil died there," he asserted, continuing that "Holocaust Remembrance Day must become one of our holy days. We must remember the day when good defeated evil" (Kaldenberg 1996a).

Holocaust deniers are but part of the problem with the racist scene, Kaldenberg (1998) lamented. Most of the activists involved "don't got enough I.Q. to match a lizard." With its Hollywood Nazis and bizarre Christian Identity preachers who teach that Aryans are the true Jews, the racist movement was, as far as Kaldenberg was concerned, a freak show made up of morons who seemed to be engaged in a competition for who was the most retarded rather than in a war for racial survival. Hailing the Nation of Islam as an ideal model of a true racist movement, Kaldenberg called for the establishment of Odinist enterprises to build up an economic foundation that would enable racialists to finance day-care centers, free clinics, schools, and paramilitary defense units patrolling white communities. "The Nation of Islam does everything that is right. They have community outreach programs; they help the poor and provide answers. We just have a bunch of complaints and bitch about the system." Disillusioned with the racist scene, Kaldenberg eventually developed a misanthropic perspective that came to include the majority of the whole white race. "I have just come to realize that most people are scum," he declared. "I used to believe in engaging the white working class in a total warfare . . . but then I realized that that was just bullshit."

If the racial enemies were cast as dehumanized vermin, the white masses were depicted as mindless herds of sheep and cattle. "The Racial Struggle will never become a mass movement, because most Whites are cattle, waiting to he herded" (Kaldenberg 1998b). Life in affluent America was the primary cause of this collective degradation. "The hardship of the Ice Age made Aryans into a super race. The tremendous prosperity of the Industrial Age is making the White man too weak and inferior to survive" (Kaldenberg 1996b). The only solution feasible to Kaldenberg was to forge a stern Odinist leadership that would refuse to compromise its racism and brutal force. "We come not to liberate the worthless White sheep, but to conquer them" (Kaldenberg 1995b, 5). What was needed, then, was a "White racist dictatorship to force the cattle to want survival" (Kaldenberg 1998b), because "weak people need a strong leadership. The [white] masses need a Herculean domination" (Kaldenberg 1996c). Only by building a war chest through expropriating the riches from the decadent white upper and middle classes and forcing the masses to obey orders could the true Aryans — that is, the enlightened Odinist elite — get the race behind the total war deemed necessary (Kaldenberg 1995c; Kaldenberg 1995a). Reforming the system was a futile pipe dream, Kaldenberg claimed. "We are not fighting some unfair tax. We are fighting how many Kikes can fit in an oven" (Kaldenberg 1998b). The "only earth the meek shall inherit is a six foot deep grave. People who try to reform the System only make it stronger. The only chance the White Race has of surviving is through violence and terrorism. The Mud Races will never leave peacefully" (ibid.).

Primarily politically oriented, Kaldenberg was hardly more interested in rituals, rune magic, and heathen techniques of spiritual development than Else Christensen. An increasing misanthropy made him reluctant to organize communal blot ceremonies and other pagan meetings. "All our problems come through gatherings, you know. Police informants would come, and some guy would get drunk and go out and whack somebody. Every problem we've had was around these stupid pagan meetings" (*Kaldenberg 1998*). Favoring the lone-wolf strategy of leaderless resistance, it was hardly surprising that Kaldenberg would dismiss Christensen's call for establishing pagan communities. "That's been tried and it'll never work. The more you try to bring people together, the more you end up hating each other. Every time you try something like that, it'll always end up in infighting. Togetherness won't work. It's hard enough in a marriage, and with 'movement people' it'll never work." In this respect, Kaldenberg took the opposite route of Jost, with his efforts to establish a pagan communal settlement and to develop consciousness-raising techniques for becoming a Nietzschean superman.

The National Socialist Kindred and the Norse-Hindu Connection

After two years of combat in Vietnam with a reconnaissance platoon of the 101st Airborne, Jost (1946–96) returned to his native California embittered, confused, and haunted by traumatic war memories. Finding himself alienated at the height of the flower-power era, Jost began searching for the truth he said he knew had to be out there somewhere. Exploring the occult and the emerging New Age scene, he came across the *Autobiography of a Yogi* by Swami Paramahansa Yogananda, an Indian missionary who had been instrumental in introducing Hinduism in the United States in the 1920s. Jost received training in Kriya Yoga from Yogananda's Self-Realization Fellowship and for two years lived in an American ashram, or intentional community, in northern California (Jost 1995a). In the mid-1970s, Jost became attracted to occult national socialism and the Norse pagan revival, developing contacts with the Los Angeles and northern Californian chapters of Odinist Fellowship, as well as with the Asatrú Free Assembly in its first incarnation. Eventually the three spiritual streams of tantric Hinduism, occult national socialism, and esoteric Odinism would contribute to the well of Arya Kriya.

Jost married Stephanie Hutter, sister of Stephen McNallen's first wife, Maddy Hutter, and the families remained in close rapport, despite the fact that Jost allegedly left the AFA because McNallen had turned explicitly against national socialism (Kaldenberg 1998a; McNallen 1996). Dissatisfied with American society, Jost called for an Aryan back-to-the-land movement ("Aryan Destiny" n.d.) and founded the National Socialist Kindred and the Volksberg community on a symbolic eighty-eight acres in the mountainous woodlands of northern California

in the mid-1980s. "We must form new Folk-communities," the National Socialist Kindred declared, "from which we must make every effort to bring forth
a more highly-evolved species, Übermenschen, who will one day lead the world
back into harmony with Nature and toward that golden age envisioned by Adolf
Hitler" ("Folk and Fatherland" n.d.). Inspired by Nietzsche, Jung, and the esoteric Hitlerite Miguel Serrano, Jost viewed Wotan as a personification of man's
highest evolutionary level. To Jost, Odinism shared with national socialism the
aim of bringing forth a race of supermen ("Incarnation of Wotan" n.d.). Much
like Else Christensen, he interpreted "true" national socialism as essentially a
decentralized communal vision: "National Socialism is simply a modern-day
revival of Aryan tribalism" ("Folk and Fatherland" n.d.). Aiming to become self-
sufficient economically by farming, weaving, and other handicrafts, Volksberg
also established a small Wotan school for providing primary education for the
commune's children.[10] Searching for the roots of ancient Norse Ariosophic wisdom, Jost in the 1990s returned to his earlier exploration of tantric Hinduism, inspired in part by the seminal national socialist esoterics Savitri Devi and Miguel
Serrano, and added his findings to an evolving Norse-Hindu synthesis.

Based on earlier theories of the Aryan origins of ancient civilizations, there
has long been a fascination with Vedic India among an undercurrent of national
socialists of both secular and occult bent. Personifying this interest was Savitri
Devi, whose Hindu-Aryan mystical fascism and esoteric Hitlerism have had an
increasing impact on the worlds of occult national socialism since the 1970s,
not least in the United States.[11] Born Maximiani Portas among Greek expatriates in France 1907, she traveled to India to explore Aryavarta (the Indo-Aryan
territory) and experience firsthand the Hindu caste system she interpreted as
based on racial hierarchy.[12] Concluding that modern Hinduism was the only
living Aryan heritage, Savitri Devi converted, married the pro–national socialist
Brahmin Asit Krishna Mukherji, and became instrumental in the construction
of a pro-German Hindu nationalism. Following the war, Savitri Devi proceeded
with an international national socialist career, cofounding the World Union of
National Socialism in 1962 and becoming a widely read spokeswoman for esoteric Hitlerism. On her death in 1984, Devi's portrait was adorned with Hitler's
funeral sash and her ashes placed beside George Lincoln Rockwell's and the
eternal flame of national socialism in the Arlington, Virginia, sanctuary housed
by the American religious national socialist group, New Order.

Based in part on Hindu cosmology and concepts, Devi's occult national socialism is outlined in a series of books, chief of which is the Lightning and the
Sun (1958). Hindu cosmology conceptualizes time as moving in eternal cycles

of birth, death, and renewal. Puranic Hinduism divides cosmic time into four *yugas* (eras). Life commences in a stage of perfection in the Satya or Krita yuga, progresses through the Treta and Dvapara yugas, eras of diminishing enlightenment and duration, and ends in Kali yuga, a miserable era of negated enlightenment that ends with a cleansing apocalypse and the birth of a new golden age. During the turning wheels of cosmic history, the divine descends to the world as various avatars or incarnations, in superhuman, human, or animal form. In Vaisnava Hindu literature (the *Mahabharata*, the *Ramayana*, and the *Vishnu Puranas*) the transcendent Lord Vishnu descends ten times as an avatar in the successive forms of a fish, tortoise, boar, man-lion, dwarf, Rama-with-an-axe, Rama, Krsna, Buddha, and Kalki.[13] Vishnu enters Kali yuga twice, at its beginning as the redeeming Lord Krsna and at its end as Kalki, the fiery sword-wielding destroyer who cleanses the world to usher in Satya yuga.

To Savitri Devi, this provided the proper context for fully appreciating the nature of national socialism and Adolf Hitler. Devi proceeded by developing a distinction between three types of uniquely gifted historical actors: Men in Time, Men above Time, and Men against Time, each representing one of three different responses to the bondage of time most of mankind might dimly feel but unconditionally submits to. Men in Time embody the characteristics of their age. In the dark age of Kali yuga, Men in Time (exemplified by Gengis Khan and Stalin) are possessed by the destructive forces of nature, remorselessly used to further goals of self-gratification and self-enrichment. Such men represent the "lightning" in her title work. The enlightened Men above Time sense the reality beyond time and embody ideals of the golden age, but their message can only be received according to the imperfections of the time in which they are presented. Representing the "sun" of her theory, such men are exemplified by Buddha, Akhnaton, and Jesus Christ. Men against Time partake in both the lightning and the sun by ruthlessly employing all the destructive forces of Kali yuga to promote the realization of the golden-age ideals by which they are animated. To Savitri Devi (1958, 39), "Adolf Hitler is a typical Man against Time." He was possessed by cosmic truth, the national socialist ideal of the golden age, and was prepared to use brutal force to forward the reestablishment of society in harmony with cosmic order. Hitler was to Savitri Devi an avatar of Vishnu, coming like Krsna in Kali yuga to pave the way for the last incarnation, Kalki the Destroyer. She believed that Hitler probably was aware of his incarnate divinity but claimed that he was too benign a character, had too many sun qualities, to make use of all the destructive dark age forces. Referring to Hitler's 1928 statement "I am not he, but while nobody comes forward to prepare for him, I do so," Savitri Devi comforts her fellow believers that the last avatar of Vishnu is bound to come. He will incarnate as Kalki and completely destroy the Jewish dark-age regime to restore the golden age of true cosmic national socialism (Devi 1958, 417).

Among those inspired by her view of Hitler as an avatar of Vishnu was the Chilean mystic Miguel Serrano. Born in 1917, Miguel Serrano joined the Chilean Movimiento Nacional Socialista in his early twenties and edited the pro-Axis *La Nueva Edad* during World War II. Serving as Chilean ambassador to India (1953–62), Yugoslavia (1962–64), and Austria (1964–70), he was dismissed by the socialist administration of Salvador Allende and stayed in Swiss exile before returning during the regime of Augusto Pinochet. While in India, Serrano explored Hinduism and the Sanskrit Vedas, developed long-lasting friendships with Herman Hesse and Carl Jung, and became a respected poet and mystical writer. Blending Gnosticism, tantric Hinduism, Teutonic mysteries, Nietzschean philosophy, and Jungian psychology, Serrano constructed an occult Ariosophy, outlined in several works, including a trilogy on esoteric Hitlerism — *El Cordón Dorado: Hitlerismo Esotérico* (1978), *Adolf Hitler, el Último Avatára* (1984), and *Manú: "Por el hombre que vendra"* (1991) — and the hermetic *NOS: Book of the Resurrection* (1984).

As one of the most important occult fascist ideologues in the Spanish-speaking world, Serrano outlined, on a scale comparable to Blavatsky or Tolkien (Godwin 1996, 72), an epic hierohistory that has made an inroad among esoterics and fantasy lovers even outside the world of Ariosophic national socialism. In his contribution to the polar myth of Aryan origin, Serrano gave divine Aryan man, the Aesir and Vanir, sons of the black sun, an extraterrestrial origin in the first world and spiritual Hyperborea. Entering a holy war against Yahweh, the evil demiurge that rules this material planet, the divine Aryans created a second hyperborean civilization, Asgård or Ultima Thule, at the North Pole. During the golden age, Satya yuga, the ancestral Aesir began to spiritualize earth and developed consciousness-raising techniques by which man could ascend into divinity. Descending cosmic time-cycles, the fall of a giant comet, and mongrelization between the divine Aryans and the carnal races of the demiurge caused the downfall of hyperborean civilization. Some immortal Ariosophic masters relocated to Agartha, the legendary subterranean city somewhere in the Himalayas, while others eventually found the north and south polar entrances to the inner Earth. According to this cosmology, Adolf Hitler was simultaneously a personification of the Wotan archetype in the Aryan racial unconscious and an avatar of Vishnu (also identified as Wotan) who came at the end of the present Kali yuga to usher in a new golden age. A believer in the Hitler escape legend,

Serrano claims that Hitler left Berlin in a German flying saucer and traveled to a secret national socialist base in Antarctica. Eventually, Hitler transferred to the super-Aryan civilization inside the hollow Earth, from where he leads the esoteric war that has followed the end of the exoteric war.

Intentionally ambiguous concerning the nature of the inner Earth, which need not necessarily be a physical location, Serrano described it as simultaneously a subterranean and extraterrestrial realm, a paradise land that is no longer and yet does exist, "the inner earth, the Other Earth, the counter-earth, the astral earth, to which one passes as it were with a 'click,' a bilocation, or trilocation of space" (Serrano 1984a; quoted in Godwin 1996, 73). Due to a complex series of microcosmic-macrocosmic correspondences, Aryan man can make his contribution to the esoteric war by adding the strength of a self-realized Nietzschean übermensch in the cosmic will-to-power. By using ancient Aryan yoga techniques, he might reawaken *kundalini*, the astral fire sleeping at the base of the spinal chain of runic charkas, and progressively raise his consciousness, ascending into divinity. This path is exclusive to Aryans of unmixed lineage, since undefiled blood is a condensation of the green ray, the light of the black sun, and carries memories of the hyperborean race. The advanced Aryan yogi might thus reach a point at which he goes through a mystical death and "clicks" into the hyperborean dimension parallel to ours (Godwin 1996, 71). The occult national socialist quest of Miguel Serrano and Savitri Devi, with its reference to Arthurian mysteries, lost worlds, tantric techniques, and esoteric lore attracted a growing audience among Ariosophic heathens in the 1990s, not least among Odinists and darkside Asatrúers. Katja Lane of Wotansvolk has secured the rights to Serrano's writings and is currently translating his trilogy on esoteric Hitlerism, and Zündel issues reprints of *The Lightning and the Sun* by Devi.

In his Arya Kriya teaching, Jost merged the Hindu-Aryan myths of Devi and Serrano with Norse mythology, racial New Age elements, and the tantric Hindu ideas and practices of Swami Yogananda. Introducing Yogananda to a national socialist audience, Jost claimed that Yogananda had "realized that anything at odds with the coming political correctness would restrict the spread of his Kriya Yuga," which was why he had instructed his disciples to edit his autobiography and other writings to make them acceptable to prevailing attitudes. That was why, Jost asserted, the public was fed an incorrect presentation of Yogananda as an effeminate New Ager with a love for all of mankind. Against that prevailing image, Jost held that Yogananda "did not see Adolf Hitler as an incarnation of evil" (Jost 1995b, 17). He "admired and supported Charles Lindbergh and Senator Taft" and supported the noninterventionist cause of the America First

Movement during World War II. Moreover, Yogananda hailed the war effort in Korea "as a holy war against the forces of evil" and "foresaw the massive problems" of multicultural America (ibid.). Yogananda, Jost claimed, had insisted that he had not come to convert Americans to Hinduism but that his Kriya yuga would empower everyone to spiritual realization according to their own native religion. Reading Devi and others, Jost soon concluded that the "originators of Kriya was of the same blood as myself" and that the teaching was perfectly compatible with Odinism, as its "path of accelerated evolution was what was symbolized by the allegories of Wotan, Thor, Yggdrasil, etc." (ibid., 27).

This discovery led Jost directly to Yogananda's own guru, Babaji Nagaraj, allegedly an immortal Aryan *siddha* (self-realized divine being). According to legend, Nagaraj (literally "king of the serpents," referring to control of kundalini) was born to a brahmanic Shiva priest in the year A.D. 230. As a youngster, Nagaraj joined a group of wandering sannyasins in search of spiritual truth and was initiated in the yogic technique of *kundalini pranayama*. Instructed by his guru to practice in solitude at an isolated place at the heart of Himalayan Aryavarta, Nagaraj achieved the highest state of human evolution, manifesting complete physical immortality and divine enlightenment by the age of sixteen. Nagaraj purportedly became the greatest siddha in the world and remains alive to this day, heading a small ashram of immortal beings, the ashram being identical, Jost claimed, to the "immortal ashram" at Agartha that Miguel Serrano searched for throughout the Himalayas during his Indian years (Jost 1995b, 13). Besides Yogananda, a series of gurus claim to have been sent by Babaji Nagaraj to teach the consciousness-raising techniques. Jost alleged that as he evolved mentally through the practice of Kriya yoga, Nagaraj drew him into his circle, guiding him to partake in the cosmic struggle against the dark-age forces. After Jost had been initiated in the "original 144 Kriyas" by Marshal Govindan (another American Nagaraj disciple) in the early 1990s, Nagaraj instructed Jost to open a Kriya path from an "original Aryan perspective," Arya Kriya. This new school was to be open "especially for Aryanists, Odinists, National Socialists, and other true heirs to the ancient Aryan science of accelerated evolution" (ibid., 28).

Jost (n.d.) insisted on the cosmic significance of Arya Kriya, or "the Path of Wotan," in this particular age. Using a more complex Hindu cosmology than Savitri Devi, Jost presents two stellar time-cycles, the equinoctial and the galactic. The former cycle lasts 24,000 years and is divided into two sets of four yugas of decreasing length. In Jost's cosmology, the golden age of Satya yuga corresponds to the Norse axe age, Treta yuga to the sword age, Dvapara yuga to the wind age; and Kali yuga to the wolf age. These two 12,000-year cycles of descent and ascent then move within a giant galactic cycle that takes more than four million years to complete and that also is divided into four giant yugas of decreasing enlightenment and duration. The impact of the galactic cycle is more subtle and indirect, as it affects the revolving equinoctial yugas. The last equinoctial Satya yuga, according to Jost, reached its zenith around 11,500 B.C., when enlightened Aryan supermen created magnificent civilizations in Egypt, Europe, and South America, to which the pyramids, Stonehenge, and other megalithic structures bear witness. Interestingly, Jost then departs from most Hindu-Aryan theologians by claiming that the world has already passed through the last Kali yuga, said to have been between the years A.D. 500 to 1600, "indeed a dark age and woesome period on earth." With the Renaissance began the ascending Dvapara yuga, and man's consciousness was again on the rise, as evidenced by the age of discovery and science.

Jost then reintroduced a dramatic element by stating that the world's ascent was being adversely affected by the opposite, downward movement of the galactic cycle. Thus, the world is now entering the *galactic* Kali yuga (the duration of which is 400,000 years), which slows down the planetary evolution by 400 years, making selfishness and materialism much more intense than it normally would have been in the beginning of equinoctial Dvapara yuga. Facing dire prospects in the prolonged galactic dark age, Aryan man should not despair but rather sharpen his mental sword to fight his way out of the wolf age. "Fortunately, human evolution does not need to be dependent on either the genetic process or the stellar cycles," Jost announced. "Thousands of years ago, during the golden ages, when humankind was highly evolved, a science was developed which could rapidly accelerate human evolution, so that even during the dark ages of this earth men and women of sufficient physical development could, by self-effort, attain super-consciousness in their life time" (Jost 1995b, 8). This refers to the "ancient science" of Arya Kriya, originated by Babaji Nagaraj in the flourishing Aryavartan culture during the last Satya yuga. Realizing that the galactic wolf age would descend on Aryan man, Nagaraj and his brotherhood of immortal siddhas had decided to remain on earth "to maintain some sort of order" and to "preserve the ancient Aryan science" (ibid., 10–11), made available to Aryans of worth through Jost.

Arya Kriya follows the general pattern laid out by most yoga schools but differs in interpretation of certain key concepts. A set of moral prescriptions for purifying body and mind (*yama* and *niyama*) set the stage of consciousness-raising yoga, which then progresses through correct body posture (*asana*) and meditation (*dhyana*) to achieve enlightenment (however this may be described).

In classical Hinduism, this process is succinctly presented in the famous *Patañ-jali Yoga Sūtra* as the eight limbs of yoga: (1) ethics or restraints, comprising non-violence (*ahimsa*), honesty, nonstealing, celibacy, and nongreed; (2) personal discipline, comprising cleanliness, serenity, asceticism, self-study, and devotion to the Lord; (3) physical postures; (4) breath control; (5) withdrawal of the senses; (6) concentration; (7) meditation; and (8) absorbed concentration or oneness with the absolute (*samadhi*).[14] Concerning the first set of moral obligations, Jost departed from Patañjali and most yogi teachers on two issues, arguing that sexual abstinence and celibacy as a prerequisite for spiritual advancement was a Christianized dark-age distortion of true Arya Kriya, as was the interpretation of *ahimsa* as "nonviolence." Jost claimed that ahimsa was an ancient Aryan virtue that had been misrepresented as a "dogmatic injunction to do no harm to any living creature," which is "far from [its] original Aryan meaning" (Jost 1995d, 12). It is certainly potentially necessary to "take up arms" in a revolutionary war "against the oppressors," but "while we may be compelled by duty to harm or kill . . . it is important that our mind be kept clear of hatred, animosity and any desire for revenge or harm" (ibid.). Contrary to signifying nonviolence, "Aryan ahimsa" to Jost means that one should apply whatever amount of violence deemed necessary to accomplish one's higher racial goal provided that one is not mentally distracted by the act of killing through feelings of pleasure or guilt. Jost, who emphasized the necessity of honesty, truthfulness, and devotion (to race and cause), accepted the other ethical precepts as ancient Aryan virtues.

To further purify body and mind, Jost argued, Aryan man should keep a vegetarian macrobiotic diet, preferably organically grown, and abstain from all processed and chemically produced food. Daily baths, using only soap made by all-natural ingredients, would keep the trained body clean. As hair is energy, hair and beard should be kept long like the Berserks did in the days of the Vikings, to increase the energy surrounding the brain. In line with the tribal ideals of his National Socialist Kindred and the Volksberg project, Jost in addition argued for the necessity of escaping multicultural and metropolitan settings in favor of a monoracial rural life in harmony with nature. "Cities and empires are dark age creations. During the golden ages the planetary population is small and mankind lives close to Nature with those of common spiritual values" (Jost 1995d, 13). Purified in body and mind, the Arya Kriya disciple could then advance on the path of self-deification through several yoga techniques. Sitting in the favored body posture, the "swastika position" (*swastikasana*), several methods could be used to awaken kundalini at the base of the spine and circulate it up and down the central energy channel through the chakras (energy centers). Depending on the method used, an Aryan yogi might concentrate mentally on images such as runes, the swastika, or oneness with Wotan. He might also chant mantras appropriate to the respective chakra centers (like *aum* for the sixth chakra center, the eye of Wotan) or to the greater work of becoming an immortal siddha (like "I am Wotan"). Daily practice along with natural diet would, Jost assured, eliminate every disease (including cancer and other incurable conditions), rejuvenate life, prevent aging, and raise consciousness dramatically (Jost 1995c).

Aside from these obvious advantages, Arya Kriya also leads to "the highest state of human evolution—the Übermensch—[who] lives without limitations in Superconsciousness" (Jost 1995d) as a self-realized Aryan man-god, at "One with Wotan" (Jost 1995f, 17). Much like Serrano, Jost ascribed a cosmic significance to this becoming. Aryan man is a microcosmic body; his inner energy system is interrelated to the physical cosmos, the chakras corresponding with the sun and the twelve constellations of the zodiac. Rejuvenating the microcosmic organism would therefore have a bearing on the macrocosmic, including the racial organism and the outer world. The siddhas of Aryavarta "recognized that humans of high evolution were absolutely indispensable to keep the planet from degenerating into chaos and complete destruction during the dark ages," Jost declared (1995e, 4). Living in the golden age, the siddhas were unrestricted by the political taboos of wolf-age distortion and could establish their science on the cosmic truth that individuals and races are unequal, differentiated along lower and higher levels in the evolutionary hierarchy and peaking with the immortal Aryan masters. With the reintroduction of Arya Kriya, that "precious gift from our cherished ancestral heritage" (ibid., 10). Aryan man must live up to the obligations that come with the higher evolutionary stage of his race. "The siddhas are counting on all of us [Aryans] to use this technique to advance our own evolution so that we can advance the evolution of the world and pull it up from its tailspin into degeneracy. This is a sacred Aryan duty, and one in which we dare not fail" (ibid.). In 1996 Jost died of a heart attack while meditating at the age of fifty. However, his legacy, Arya Kriya, lives on and is practiced by small number of devotees in Canada, the United States, continental Europe, and Scandinavia.

CHAPTER FIVE

By the Spear of Odin: The Rise of Wotansvolk

The most prominent voice of racially based Odinism is Wotansvolk, established in early 1995 by a creative troika, David and Katja Lane and Ron McVan. With headquarters on a mountain outside St. Maries, a small lumber town southeast of Coeur d'Alene in northern Idaho, Wotansvolk evolved into a dynamic propaganda center, spreading its message throughout the United States as well as among Aryan racial activists in Europe, Russia, Australia, South Africa, and Latin America. Order member David Lane emerged as one of the more important Aryan "prisoners of war," coining the "14 Words," one of the very few concepts that has won almost universal acceptance in the notoriously factious milieu of white-racist revolutionaries. The artwork, religious philosophy, and poems produced by Ron McVan are frequently recycled in counterculture magazines, and a number of pagan white-power bands have put his lyrics into music, such as Darken's *Creed of Iron* album or Dissident's song "Roots of Being" on the album *A Cog in the Wheel*.[1] Katja Lane was the power behind the scene, the machinery that kept the Wotansvolk vehicle running by operating their Web page, communicating electronically with the outside world, and running a quite successful prison-outreach program that catered to several thousand heathen prisoners in U.S. penitentiaries. In the spring of 2002, administration was transferred to John Post in Napa, California.[2]

David Lane and the Silent Brotherhood

David Lane is an veteran Aryan revolutionary who began as an Identity Christian Klan activist in Colorado, although he now downplays his former affiliation with racist Christianity. Born in 1938 as one of four children of an alcoholic itinerant farmer in rural Iowa, Lane was at the age of five adopted by a fundamentalist

Lutheran family. His new father was serving as pastor at various churches in Texas, Colorado, and the Midwest, and Lane recalls being subjected to endless hours of preaching and Bible studies, which made Jesus a personification of pure boredom (David Lane 1994a, 1; David Lane 1996).[3] In reaction to the federal administration's concession to the civil-rights movement to end segregation, the John F. Kennedy assassination, and the Vietnam War, Lane gradually adopted a conspiracy theory of history. "I spent at least half a dozen years trying to find out who was behind it and what their motivations were . . . and why America is in these constant wars from one end of the globe to the other, murdering and maiming. I mean, it's a red-white-and-blue nasty murder machine," Lane explained (1996). A brief involvement with the John Birch Society introduced Lane to anti-Semitic writings that purported to expose Jewish control of mass media, until finally, he says, the truth dawned on him: "The United States is ruled by a Zionist conspiracy" (ibid.) that tries to establish a global dictatorship. In order to secure its evil scheme, the Zionists seek to exterminate the freedom-loving Aryan race. That is why they engaged the United States in the "War to destroy the White race" (WWII) (David Lane 1994a, 7). That is why they came up with the Cold War hoax, which served as an excuse for using "America's racially mixed military to mix races in America and Europe" (ibid., 9).

This conviction later moved Lane to distance himself from the "reality denying" conservative spectrum of the far right with its "100 percent Americanism," known in Lane's writing under the telling acronym CRAP: "Conservative Rightwing American Patriots."[4] Whereas the constitutionalists, militias, and John Birchers of the scene tend to believe that a second American revolution is needed to return the state of society to the original vision of the Founding Fathers, Lane reinterpreted the whole of American history in the context of a Zionist conspiracy. "They may say that America was born to be a sovereign nation," Lane (1996) explained, but "look at the great seal of the United States and see the symbolism with the thirteen stars representing the thirteen original states and the Star of David over the eagle, and the symbolism is plain: the United States would be used to build a world Zionist empire!"[5] He emphasized that the men who designed the seal were Masons, then added his own twist to the popular underground theory of a Masonic-Zionist conspiracy: "America was formed with a 222 year Jewish Cabalistic timetable to destroy every Race, Nation and Culture on earth in pursuit of the Jew World Order" (1995e). For example, the motto of the United States—E Pluribus Unum (out of many, one)—to Lane "equals genocide by race mixing" (1996e). Some of the Founding Fathers might have been unaware of being used by the cabal, Lane admits. "The original concept, when we were governed by the articles of the confederation, shows that at least some members of the Founding Fathers had ideas of freedom" (*David Lane* 1996). But, he continues, if you look at the result, the underlying truth of the American project indisputably stands forth: "America immediately traveled to Dixie, Cuba, Panama, Grenada, Libya, Germany twice, Japan, Korea, Vietnam, Iraq, Waco, Ruby Ridge, Whidbey Island, and a hundred other wars, occupations, and assassinations, murdering tens upon tens of tens of millions in the pursuit of this Zionist new world order" (ibid.). In fact, Lane distances himself so far from the Patriot right wing that he states, "You can no more be both White and American than you can stop the motion of the planets. The singular intent of America in all its facets is to mix, overrun and exterminate the White race. How can you *be* what destroys you?" (1994d, 14).

In the late 1970s, Lane stepped up his political involvement, producing his first racial pamphlet, *Death of the White Race*, and getting involved with the Church of Jesus Christ, Christian/Aryan Nations as minister of information. In 1982 his sister Jane, who worked as a secretary at the Aryan Nations, was married to Carl Franklin of Easton, leader of the Pennsylvania state chapter of the church. Pastor Richard G. Butler of the Aryan Nations led the ceremony, accompanied by the Aryan Victory Singers. After exchanging vows, the newlyweds moved in procession between rows of uniformed men with their hands raised in the national socialist salute. At the Aryan Nations and its 1982 and 1983 Aryan World Congresses, Lane came to know Robert J. Mathews, founder of the legendary Aryan revolutionary underground Brüders Schweigen, popularly known as the Order (*David Lane* 1996; *David Lane* 1994a; *David Lane* 1994d; *David Lane* 1998a, 16; Flynn and Gerhardt 1989, 70, 90, 177, 213–15).[6]

Frustrated with white radical racist lack of action, Mathews in September 1983 gathered a group of nine militant young men, including Lane, for a "pagan" initiation ritual at his Metaline Falls, Washington, homestead (*Kemp* 1997). Standing within a circle of lighted candles watched over by a portrait of Adolf Hitler and with a six-week-old female baby placed on a blanket at the center, the men clasped hands repeating the high-flown words recited by Mathews. As "free Aryan warriors," they swore an "unrelenting oath upon the green graves of our sires" and "upon the children in the wombs of our wives" to "do whatever is necessary to deliver our people from the Jew and bring total victory to the Aryan race" (Flynn and Gerhardt 1989, 98). Involved with radical politics since his Phoenix, Arizona, high school days, National Alliance member and Odinist Mathews propelled a disparately composed group of Identity Christians, Odinists, longtime activists, and inexperienced men into an accelerating campaign of guerilla warfare.[7] Mathews took the group's nickname, the Order, from the name of the clandestine elite that overthrew the American administration and reinstated white supremacy in Pierce's fictional race-war novel *Turner Diaries*. Pierce (1997) prided himself with having authored the book for "educational purposes" and hailed Mathews for courageously acting on what he had learned.

The extent to which Mathews and the Brüders identified with the Order of the *Turner Diaries* in an ultimate goal to overthrow the U.S. government is uncertain. Retrospectively, imprisoned Order members differed widely in their assessments of what they had intended, ranging from modest hopes of contributing financially to racist organizations to optimistic expectations of igniting an armed Aryan revolution. David Tate and Gary Yarbrough insisted that *Turner Diaries* was only an entertaining pulp fiction that "in no way" functioned "as a blue print for the Order" (Yarbrough 1997). "We had all discussed these things for years," Tate (1997) insisted. "All we wanted was money to finance the organizations so that they could get the work done. That was the main drive, the whole thing. As far as assassinations and all that stuff, that was all secondary."[8] Randy Duey (1997) took the opposite view: "We wanted to destroy the authorities and the powers that be." It was a Holy War, he continued, "and we wanted to eliminate the immoral lifestyle, although we didn't know exactly what morals we wanted to replace it with. We wanted to overthrow the government, although we didn't know exactly what government we wanted to replace [it] with. But we knew that something had to be done." To Duey, *Turner Diaries* was "a blueprint of activity" and something of a "Bible" to "Bob and the non-Christians" in the Order, "because it gave us a schedule and an organizational framework." Combining those views was Richard Kemp (1997), who believed Mathews wanted to give the movement teeth and inspire others by propaganda and by deed to engage in an Aryan uprising. He recalled how a conspiracy mindset had left the impression among members of the Order that they belonged to the remnants of a once-glorious race now besieged by an omnipotent enemy that ceaselessly worked to exterminate what resistance remained. "We felt like being under attack, and it was like, you could either hide in a hole like a mouse or you could come out roaring like lion." Kemp also acknowledged the impact made by *Turner Diaries*. "Not so much the science-fiction part, but the underlying message of how to set up an organization and what to do with it, how to assassinate, and things like that. Although I am embarrassed to say that that was what we patterned ourselves after . . . I think that as far as *Turner Diaries* being a guide, I think it was more than a guide, all our criminal activities were patterned after that."

By trial and error, making new plans as they went along, the Order became successful armored-car robbers and counterfeiters. Among the crimes committed were bank robberies ($25,000 in Seattle, Washington; $3,600 in Spokane, Washington); armored-car robberies ($40,000 against the Continental Armored Transport Company; $500,000 at a robbery in Seattle; $3,6000,000 against Brinks in Ukiah, California); the bombing of a synagogue in Boise, Idaho; the murder of Aryan Nations member Walter West; the killing of Alan Berg; and counterfeiting. A multimillion-dollar war chest helped escalate the wheel of events. Besides enabling the Order to contribute to racist organizations and churches, the money allowed the acquisition of arms, cars, and motorcycles; the purchase of military and technical equipment; the rental of safe houses; and the setting up of an "Aryan academy" training camp. In lieu of consolidation, the Order rapidly ventured into new areas of activity, involving more and more people, who were sworn in and assigned a code name after passing a lie-detector test—the Order's rudimentary and insufficient security device. The group had already killed one suspected informer, Walter West of the Aryan Nations; he was declared a security risk after reportedly discussing Order activities while on drinking rounds at local bars. Following the July 1984 robbery of a Brinks armored car, which landed the Order $3.6 million, and the June 1984 assassination of racist-baiting talk-radio host Alan Berg, the FBI began closing in on the group. Engaging its Aryan Nations informants and recruiting collaborators from within the Order, the FBI soon gained a fairly good picture of what was going on.

Acting on inside information, the federal agents eventually surrounded Mathews's remote hideout on Whidbey Island, outside Seattle, Washington. Negotiations stalled as Mathews declined to lay down his arms unless the U.S. administration allowed the establishment of a secessionist Aryan republic in the northwestern states (Scutari 2000; Flynn and Gerhardt 1989, 378). Refusing to surrender even when the agents set the house on fire with pyrotechnic devices, Mathews died the ideal death of a warrior, his boots on and machinegun in hand, on 8 December 1984, now hailed as the Day of Martyrs in Aryan revolutionary circles. "December 8, 1984, will forever be a holy day for Aryans," a Wotansvolk commemorative statement reads. "Lifting the sword of the long overdue revolution," Mathews led a "brave group of men into battle against the ZOG" but was "ruthlessly exterminated" on "that fateful day" in the "massacre on Whidbey Island" ("Brüders Schweigen Remember" 1996). The wording is significant, as it demonstrates that Mathews grew larger-than-life after his death. After all, the death of one man can hardly be called a "massacre." Such concepts suggest the construction of Mathews as a legendary Aryan warrior-martyr. "It is the blood of our martyrs that baptize our banners," George Hawthorne (1995ab) wrote, hailing Mathews, the godlike warrior who was called by destiny to rise above men as a bringer of storm. "Mathews chose martyrdom over slavery," Mike Raven wrote in a WAR article. "Like his Viking ancestors," he "died in a blaze of glory in a raging pyre" (Raven 1993).[9] David Lane (1996g) wrote in the bombastic style characteristic to the scene about the compelling call of Mathews the martyr.

> As you march through Valhalla
> Asgard's mighty hall
> number one among the Vikings
> I can hear you call:
> "Arise, you Aryan Warriors
> I've shown you how to fight!
> You owe it to my children
> To battle for the right"

White-power bands from all over the world hail his heroism and death as ideal, as exemplified by the song "RJM" (Robert Jay Mathews) by Max Resist. The Day of Martyrs is commemorated with ceremonies or concerts in the United States and abroad, and is considered an appropriate date for a pilgrimage to Whidbey Island. Much to the consternation of its new owners, the site of Mathews death has become something of a must-see for racist tourists paying homage to their martyred icon. Nathan Zorn Pett of the White Order of Thule has organized ritual blots and swastika-burning ceremonies outside the gate of the property, as have other groups of Aryan radicals. Although still largely uninformed about Odinism in general, it is this martyrology that has caught the interest of the FBI. In *Project Megiddo* (1999, 20), an FBI intelligence report on the potential for domestic terrorism to occur with the arrival of the new millennium, the bureau makes note of Odinism as a "white supremacist ideology that lends itself to violence." The report concludes, "What makes the Odinists dangerous is the fact that many believe in the necessity of becoming martyrs for their cause" (ibid., 19).

Observers of the racist scene have frequently labeled the Order "Christian Identity" and linked its underground activism with the Aryan Nations. While Mathews provided Butler with security and used the AN printing press for his counterfeit operation, the Brüders operated independently of Butler and were only partially Christian. About half of the inner circle—Randy Duey, David Tate, Bruce Pierce, Gary Yarbrough, and Randy Evans—were hardcore Identity Christians at the time of the Order activities, so statements by Mathews cited to prove his affiliation with Christian Identity are probably better attributed to his diplomatic wish to appease this Identity element of the circle, rather than taken as indicator of his personal beliefs. When talking with Randy Duey or Bruce Pierce, Mathews would refer to Yahweh or Yahshua to get them behind the idea of a holy war, but he could as easily quote Hávamál of the poetic Edda when recruiting Richard Scutari: "Cattle die, kinsmen die, and I too shall die. The only thing I know that does not die is the fame of dead man's deeds" (stanza 77). Mathews himself was an Odinist and is known to have performed Odinist offering rituals and blots at his homestead. The pagan element within the Order was to grow with time. Of the inner circle, five members—Robert Mathews, David Lane, Frank Silva, Richard Kemp, and Richard Scutari—either were or would become Odinists or Asatrúers.

An analysis of the initiation ceremony Mathews designed reveals the heathen perspective of its founder. Every initiation followed the same pattern: nine men formed a circle with a newborn baby at its center, swearing an oath on the graves of their sires and on the unborn children in the wombs of their wives. Agreements, affiliations, initiations, and bonding are in Norse paganism always sanctified by an oath rather than by signing a contract. Most pagan ceremonies begin with consecrating a holy space by the ritual casting of a circle. The number nine is of especial significance in Norse paganism, representing potency, completion, and fulfillment. The ninth rune of the futhark, "H" (Hagalaz, English Hail), "involves the projection (from the 'above' or 'beyond') of a hard and dangerous substance which is also the 'seed of becoming,' new creation and transformation—sometimes through crisis," rune magician Edred Thorsson explains (1993 [1988], 35). "This is transformation within the framework of cosmos, and the re-unification of polar opposites in a productive way. Like the number nine it represents completion" (ibid.). Reconciling racist pagans and Christians, and uniting polar opposites such as love/hate and life/death, the initiation ritual sought to call down the terrible forces of war craft embodied in the Norse gods and goddesses, thus empowering the initiates to become the seeds of transformation. Mathews wanted the Order to hasten the racial crisis in America and cast society into a chaos out of which a new Aryan golden age would be born (symbolized by the infant at the center of the circle). The pagan dimension is also present in the oath's reference to ancestors and unborn children. This points to the Odinist view of man as linked by blood with his past, present, and future kin, his identity derived from belonging to a clan, tribe, and folk that transcends the borders of birth and death.

After Mathews's death, the FBI continued to hunt down the remaining inner circle with the help of less-than-silent members of the brotherhood. By the spring of 1986, the whole Brüders Schweigen were either behind bars or had turned collaborators. Having received a total of more than 900 years in prison, Order activists Frank Silva, Randy Evans, Richard Scutari, Richard Kemp, Gary Yarbrough, David Tate, Randy Duey, David Lane, and Bruce Pierce are now hailed as heroic Aryan prisoners of war in numerous poems and white-power lyrics. The Order has grown in significance over the years, assuming a legendary status as an ideal model for Aryan revolutionary warriors. "The Brüders Schweigen, its achievement in battle, the heroic death of its leader . . . and the sacrificial steadfastness of his imprisoned comrades . . . has been the most outstanding instance of revolt of our race since the World War II," wrote Colin Jordan (1999, xviii), British national socialist veteran and co-founder of World Union of National Socialists. "Amid all the gloom and defeat and despondency since then, the determined emergence and daring deeds of the Brüders Schweigen have been as a unique lantern of luminosity for all who remain wholeheartedly loyal to our race" (ibid.). A growing segment of the Aryan counterculture has abandoned as unrealistic conventional politics in favor of a revolutionary stand against the system, a shift in perspective for which the Order acted as a catalyst. "The killing of Alan Berg was about as meaningless as assassinating the White House gardener," wrote George Hawthorne, then editor of *Resistance* (1996b, 4). "But historically speaking, in the wider context, it was of unfathomable significance. It marked the transition from conservatism to radicalism" and was thus "a watershed moment in the movement" (ibid.). In both Europe and United States, small bands of Aryan militants have occasionally engaged in violent direct action against system representatives and financed their underground activities by robbing banks and value transports. Although some Order members today seem disappointed with the fact that their call to arms practically went unheard, the Order did provide the Aryan resistance with a model to emulate, thereby contributing to further disconnecting the milieu from mainstream politics.

Revolution by Number 14

David Lane's initial claim to fame came through his involvement with the Order. As a member of its inner circle, Lane was, among other things, instrumental in its counterfeiting scheme. Following Mathews's death at Whidbey Island, Lane was captured in March 1985 after Ken Loff, another Order-member-turned-FBI-informant, gave him up to the agents in exchange for a five-year sentence reduction (Flynn and Gerhardt 1989, 395). Lane was convicted for racketeering, conspiracy, and violating the civil rights of Alan Berg (by killing him), receiving a total of 190 years. After several years at the notorious federal penitentiaries at Marion and Leavenworth, Lane was moved to a federal maximum-security prison complex deep underground in mountainous Florence, Colorado.

In prison, Lane dedicated his time to studies in history, philosophy, mystery religions, and Odinism, gradually developing an Aryan interpretation of paganism. During the 1990s, Lane evolved to becoming one of the more important prisoners of war on the scene, sometimes ironically referred to as the "Mandela of the White Revolution," held to be unjustly incarcerated "for resisting the genocide of the white race" (McVan 1999). He is presented as "truly a hero," who amid "the torture of tremendous imprisonment" continues to "fight the good fight with unbowed head and a song in his heart, a Viking song of satisfaction in waging war on the enemies of our race" (Jordan 1999, xxii). His record of unyielding racist commitment should, Colin Jordan argues (ibid., xvii), therefore "win respectful attention to what he has to say." Lane's call to arms and mystical teachings are spread throughout much of the white-racist world, and he is frequently featured in the white-power/Aryan revolutionary press on all continents. Reflecting on the paradox of having attained global influence only after having been restricted to live within the confines of a few square feet deep beneath the ground, Lane sees the wisdom of the ancient Gods who guided him to this position to fulfill his mission. "I came to this realm specifically for the purpose of stopping the Zionist murder of the White Aryan race and to reinstitute the rule of the Philosopher-Elect" (David Lane 1996). Convinced that Aryan man is at the brink of extermination, Lane coined the "14 words" as a rallying point for a pan-Aryan militant uprising: "We must secure the existence of our people and a future for White children." This motto has taken hold all over the white-racist world, as evidenced by the almost universal reference to the 14 words in poems, lyrics, articles, and books and by the common racist habit of signing a letter "14/88" (code for the 14 words and Heil Hitler).

Lane repeatedly emphasizes that nothing less than a total, uncompromising war must be waged if the 14 words are to be implemented. Strategically, he embraces the "leaderless resistance" concept suggested by Klan veteran Louis Beam in 1992. Beam argued that the traditional pyramid organizational structure is "not only useless, but extremely dangerous for the participants when it is utilized in a resistance movement against state tyranny" (1992, 3). He elucidated, "Experience has revealed over and over again that anti-state political organizations utilizing this method of command and control are easy prey for government infiltration, entrapment and destruction" (ibid.). Inspired in part by the cell system of communist revolutionaries and the minutemen of the American Revolution, Beam designed a "phantom cell" mode of organization. Leaderless resistance means that "all individuals and groups operate independently of each other, and never report to a central headquarters or a single leader for direction and instruction" (ibid., 4). Substituting unity of organization with unity of purpose, participant revolutionaries should acquire appropriate military skills and take action when needed. Overt organs of information should keep participants informed of events, enabling them to act when time is ripe without anyone having to issue an order. "The last thing federal snoops want . . . is a thousand different small phantom cells opposing them," Beam nails down. "Such a situation is an intelligence nightmare" (ibid., 5). By 1999, the FBI had reached the same conclusion. "The overwhelming majority of extremist groups in the United States have adopted a fragmented, leaderless structure where individuals or small groups act with autonomy. Clearly, the worst act of domestic terrorism in the United States historically was perpetrated by merely two individuals: Timothy McVeigh and Terry Nichols. In many cases, extremists of this sort are extremely difficult to identify until after the incident has occurred" (FBI 1999, 4).[10]

Endorsing Beam's leaderless resistance strategy, Lane argued for tactical separation between an open propaganda arm and an underground paramilitary arm termed WOTAN (Will of the Aryan Nation). The function of the overt wing is to "counter system sponsored propaganda, to educate the Folk, to provide a man pool from which the covert or military arm can be [recruited] . . . and build a revolutionary mentality" (David Lane 1994a, 26). Since the open racial propagandist "will be under scrutiny," Lane emphasized that the cadres involved need to "operate within the [legal] parameters" and keep "rigidly separated" from the military underground. The WOTAN paramilitary "must operate in small, autonomous cells, the smaller the better, even one man alone," and it was "incumbent" that no "system attention" was to be drawn "to the overt cadres" (ibid., 27). The aim of the military underground was, Lane hammered down, to "hasten the demise of the system before it totally destroys our gene pool" (26). Revolutionary activity meant utilizing "fire, bombs, guns, terror, disruption and destruction. Weak points in the infrastructure of an industrialized society are primary targets. Whatever and whoever perform valuable service for the system is targets, human or otherwise. Special attention and merciless terror are visited upon those White men who commit race treason" (27).[11]

Lane was aware of but indifferent to the possibility that his message might contribute to inspiring a lone wolf with a warrior complex to commit an act of blind terror along the lines of the Oklahoma City bombing, which counted fifteen children among the victims killed. "In the coming revolution there will be no innocents," Lane (1996) states uncompromisingly. "There are only those who are for our cause and those who are our enemies . . . the masses are selfish, greedy asses. They have always been and they always will be. They will either follow us or follow them. They are now following their terrorism. When the time comes that our terrorism is superior to theirs, they will follow us. They will worship and adore whoever is the greater tyrant. That's the nature of the masses."

For the postrevolutionary era, Lane envisioned an all-Aryan Odinist federation inspired in part by the tribal socialism advocated by Else Christensen, the Armanen ideal of Guido von List, and the undemocratic ideal republic of Plato. Much like national syndicalists and radical localists, Lane argued that power should be invested in the smallest unit of government, the local community. Autonomous tribes may cooperate voluntarily with other independent tribes in matters of mutual concern, but there should be no central government, lest tyranny again grow. Thus far in agreement with many other pagans, Lane then departs by substituting the tribal Althing democracy with a confederacy of Armanen dictatorships run by Plato's philosopher-elect. The Aryan republics should reinstitute the mystery schools, Lane asserted, and be governed by a succession of hermetic sages guided by altruistic instincts. Adding yet another contradictory element, Lane believed that the future libertarian-organic golden age of maximum freedom would only become reality by passing through a transitory phase of strong dictatorship, during which all individual rights of necessity must be sacrificed. Considering the corrupting nature of absolute power, Lane (1996) suggests himself as "the leader of this particular phase in the history of our people. Because I know in my own heart that while I would need [absolute] power, cleansing power, war power and so on, if we are to survive [as a race], I also know from deep in my heart that my ultimate purpose is to destroy power. Once the people are safe and secure in their existence it is my hope that they then will be ruled by the philosopher-elect."

Lane's religious philosophy is a dual construct of a straightforward exoteric message and an undercurrent of esoteric mysticism. While the former is for consumption by his "warrior cast" of followers, the latter is intended for a philosophically advanced elite. Lane singles out Christianity as a main reason for the decay of Aryan culture and the rise of a globalist society. Christianity, Lane (1996) says, is "diametrically opposed to the natural order" that the Gods have created.

It teaches that everyone primarily belongs to a universal humanity, and it wants each man to love the alien as much as he loves himself and to turn the other cheek when he is being treated unjustly. "God is not love," Lane emphasizes. "God the Creator made lions to eat lambs, he made hawks to eat sparrows. Compassion between species is against the law of nature. Life is struggle, and the absence of struggle is death."[12] Aiming to liberate Aryan man from the Jewish spell of religious insanity, Lane contrasts the "Ten Commandments for racial suicide" he finds in the New Testament with "Wotansvolk wisdom for Aryan man." In Luke 6:27, for instance, Christians are advised, "Love your enemies." In contrast, Lane's Wotanism says, "Smite your enemies and the enemies of your people with the hammer of Thor. Feed their bodies to the vultures in the market place, that your next enemy will depart in fear" (David Lane 1999, 82). Lane also claims that the Bible wants man to submit to corrupt politicians as is evidenced by Mark 12:17: "Render unto Caesar the things that are Caesar's." Wotanism wants man to stand up to the system: "Cut off Caesar's head and feed it to the dogs" (ibid.).

Lane regards Christianity as an integral part of the grand Jewish conspiracy to establish global tyranny. The "world rulers got their position by following the philosophy of the Old Testament," which teaches "ruthless removal or extermination of others" to further their own race, Lane asserts. Those "to be conquered and enslaved are taught the opposite, the New Testament, with its unnatural idealization of the meek and the weak." Only a "shallow thinker" who seeks protection from the wolves of the world embraces the "suicidal doctrine" of relying on Jesus or the pastor as the "good shepherd," Lane argues. "The deeper thinker knows that the shepherd only protects the sheep until they are ready to be sheared and led to the slaughterhouse. In actuality, the shepherd is far more dangerous to the flock than wolves" (David Lane 1996f; David Lane 1998a). If Aryans are to survive as a race, the otherworldly and self-denying Christianity must be abandoned in favor of Odinism, a religion based on nature's order, "a natural religion" that "preaches war, plunder, and sex" (David Lane 1996).

Considerably more complex, Lane's esoteric teaching is an Ariosophic blend of numerology, Theosophy, Gnosticism, hermetic philosophy, and ancient mystery religions. Lane casts himself as being guided by a secret brotherhood of Aryan masters, "the Watchers," an idea borrowed from Theosophy. In Wotansvolk philosophy, these are noncorporeal, immortal Aryan supermen who guide the elect to influence world history and ensure racial survival.[13] Lane (1996) recalls that when he received news about Mathews having been killed, he spent he "spent forty days and forty nights" meditating "on a mountain top," communing with "whatever powers there might be, if they would use me to stop this murder of my race. And the ideals of the eighty-eights precepts and 14 words and what they should be and the sacrifices that would have to be made . . . just came to me somehow." Emphasizing that it ha been "nothing but misery" for him since he received his Calling, Lane also states that he is "predestined" to fulfill his mission and will stand firm until completed.[14] The Watchers later provided him with the "Key of David," a mathematical code that unlocks the secrets of the Bible. Despite his contempt for the corrupt teachings of the holy writ, Lane thus bases his esoteric teaching on a numerological analysis of the Bible. This is motivated by the theory that the original (pre-Christian and non-Jewish) Bible was designed by Aryan hermetic masters to secure ancient Gnostic wisdom for coming generations by encoding therein a hidden truth. "The hermetic philosophers had seen their race die by mixing and blending with the cultures of Persia and Egypt and elsewhere, and they undoubtedly created the [original] Old Testament religion" (David Lane 1996).[15]

It was, in fact, Lane (1999, 59) asserts, from learning the hermetic mysteries that the sinister Jews originally gained power enough to mastermind their plan for world control. In 325 C.E. they "hired" the "corrupt" Roman Emperor Constantine "to murder anyone in Europe who would not accept a new universal religion in which the Jews are the Chosen People and destined to own the Gentiles as slaves" (ibid., 53). Although the conspirators corrupted the Bible by subtractions and additions, Lane insists that the encoded Aryan teaching remains embedded therein, the hidden wisdom having survived the translation into English, as Sir Francis Bacon (whom Lane credits for the King James Bible) was guided by the Watchers to ensure that the writ would remain a coding device (ibid., 65).[16] Decoding the scripture with the numerical Key of David, Lane learned that the world has moved into the era known in Christian apocalyptic doctrine as the reign of the Antichrist. This means in effect the completion of global ZOG rule "exactly as planned by their Kabalistic target date of July 4 (74) 1998 (666+666+666)" (David Lane 1998b). The timetable has been largely met, Lane adds gravely, even if "pockets of resistance are still extant" (1999, 56). Though these are desperate times, Aryan man should still not despair, Lane (1996) states consolingly. The number 666 is not only the Number of the Beast but also the Number of a Man. This man would embody the warring spirit of Mars, Thor, and King David, and he would, according to the hermetic prophecy now decoded, be born on 2 November 1938, which happens to be the birth date of David Lane. Furthermore, using the same numerological key, the veil of mystery concealing the inner meaning of the holy scripture was lifted, and it all revolves around a name, a name of innate cosmic significance, of a man born to defeat the evil empire: David Lane.[17]

Temple of Wotan

Instrumental in spreading the teachings of David Lane and the wider Wotans-volk message is David Lane's wife Katja (née Maddox). Born in 1951 as the daughter of an intelligence officer for the air force, Katja was given a conservative upbringing and traveled extensively outside the United States. In 1967 her father was shot down in Vietnam and has been missing ever since, an event that propelled Katja into antiwar activism with Vietnam Veterans Against the War. Cross-culturally competent due to her travels and her university studies, which earned her a bachelor's degree in Spanish and Portuguese literature and a master's in economics, Katja gradually came to the conclusion that international capitalism not only threatened indigenous cultures abroad but was also destroying the Aryan civilization. Adopting an increasingly radical position racially and politically, she moved through Christian Identity, "which at that time was the only racial religion out there" (*Katja Lane* 1997), into Odinism in the late 1980s. In the meantime, she married and soon mothered two daughters and three sons.

Explaining that politics at large is male terrain, Katja (1997) emphasizes what she sees as the principal female responsibility in the greater Aryan cause: "I felt my role toward our struggle was to build up our race as a mother. . . . My role was at home, to make a refuge for my husband who was out there in the big battle of the world, and to breed and nurture our children." Like many parents involved with the racist scene, Katja believes that public schools are detrimental instruments of indoctrination, designed by the enemies of the race to transform strong and healthy Aryan children into mindless and self-hating sheep. "Nature gave me [and not the state] jurisdiction over the fruit of my womb," Katja states emphatically, arguing that home-schooling is the only racially sound alternative. "Nature gave me instincts to do this job, sufficiently and appropriately, and the blood of my ancestors in my veins gives me the wisdom to [teach my children]," and install in them the virtues, values, and knowledge appropriate to Aryan man.

Following her divorce in 1994, Katja took up correspondence with David Lane, whom she knew from racial activism and who previously had eyes for her. The love was rekindled, and they married on 9 October 1994. Skilled in graphic design and layout, Katja immediately became instrumental in propagating the teachings of her husband. By the end of the year, six booklets were published by the newly established 14 Word Press: *White Genocide Manifesto, 88 Precepts, Revolution by Number 14, The Mystery Religions and the Seven Seals, Wodensson in Verse,* and *Auto-Biographical Portrait of the Life of David Lane.* In addition, they began publishing a monthly newsletter, *Focus Fourteen,* the first issue appearing in January 1995. In 1999 Katja Lane edited a compilation of her husband's booklets and *Focus Fourteen* articles as *Deceived, Damned, and Defiant: The Revolutionary Writings of David Lane,* which also featured an introduction by Colin Jordan.

In September 1995 David Lane published an Odinist article, "Wotan's Folk," using the Germanic word for Odin; this article established the Wotansvolk name. By that time, Ron McVan had joined the Lanes to work with the 14 Word Press. Together, they launched Wotansvolk as, in the words of Katja (1997), a "vehicle to unite our race, give us a singular sense of identity as well as destiny." With McVan on the scene, Wotansvolk began to publish monthly Odinist pamphlets of cultural, spiritual, pagan, and esoteric content, and to sell Odinist artifacts such as hammers, rune staffs, cast runes, banners, Odin heads, and Odin eyes of their own production. The reputation of Wotansvolk grew steadily, primarily through cyberspace and an ambitious prison-outreach program. Being in charge of both, Katja Lane's role extended far beyond home-schooling and housekeeping. She spent much of her day by the computer, updating the Wotansvolk Web page, communicating electronically with fellow Odinists and sympathizers in the United States and abroad, and taking care of the needs of the nearly three hundred kindreds established in American prisons.

The third figure in the founding Wotansvolk troika is artist and author Ron McVan. Born in Philadelphia in 1950, McVan moved to Olympia, Washington, in his late teens and got involved in rock music and art. For fifteen years, McVan toured the United States, taking his surrealist and fine-arts paintings to different cities. During these years, McVan developed an increasingly radical anti-government and white-nationalist political position. Being religiously oriented, McVan explored different Eastern creeds in search of a religion close to his perception of nature. Christianity was never an alternative, not even in its Identity recasting. "It was always too Jewish for me," McVan (1996) mused. "I don't understand why they're trying to be Jews—they're white people. They take on Jewish names and name their children Zakariah, Isaiah, and all that stuff. We should be naming our children the great Teutonic names, not taking on the Jewish heritage and Jewish by-laws." Besides this cultural confusion, McVan considered Christianity to be anti-nature. "It takes away the warrior spirit, the survival instincts to fight. The turn-the-other-cheek mentality is not a natural instinct. The animals know better to follow your instincts. If you find a rattlesnake in your baby's crib, your instinct is to get it out of there before it kills your baby. You don't start thinking about that the rattlesnake has a life, that he has a family, and this or that, you kill the rattlesnake. I mean, that's nature's instinct, and Christianity means a reversal of that."

Throughout much of the 1970s, McVan by and large agreed with Nietzsche's view on Buddhism as the religion closest to nature, before he came across the works by Ben Klassen. Reading Klassen's *Nature's Eternal Religion* and the *White Man's Bible* spurred McVan to get active in the cause for racial survival and expansion, and he began contributing articles and artwork, including various logos, to the Church of the Creator. Moving to the Otto, North Carolina, headquarters in 1990, McVan became editor of the COTC paper *Racial Loyalty* and martial-arts instructor of the *White Berets*, the paramilitary wing of the church. Although in agreement with Klassen's iconoclastic anti-Christian fervor, McVan in time found Creativity to be spiritually shallow. Looking for a religious alternative, McVan began searching his ancestral roots and developed an interest in Asatrú. Aiming to "rekindle the spiritual customs and culture of our pre-Christian ancestors," McVan and attorney Reinhold Clinton cofounded the northern Oregon/southern Washington Wotan's Kindred in 1992.[18] Although a cumulation of personal and religious disagreements in time ruined the friendship between McVan and Clinton, the experience of promoting a racially interpreted paganism by organizing blot ceremonies and offering courses in old-world craftsmanship and arts, herbalism, healing, rune lore, and archery was nonetheless a turning point that pointed McVan down a path he would continue to tread.

In 1995 McVan moved on to St. Maries, Idaho, to work with David and Katja Lane. Together, the three established Wotansvolk as a vehicle for disseminating Aryan revolutionary Odinism, "an ancestral faith that puts race first" (*McVan* 1996) In McVan's opinion (1997), whites had to "again learn to think with their blood," and Ariosophic Odinism was perceived as a spiritual path toward racial revival. In 1997 McVan published *Creed of Iron: Wotansvolk Wisdom*, an Odinist manifesto and ritual handbook. In the year 2000 he continued his effort to further an Aryan renaissance by publishing *Temple of Wotan: Holy Book of the Aryan Tribes*, a comprehensive guide to folkish Odinism. Containing explorations of heathen Ariosophy and a translation of *Hávamál*, *Temple of Wotan* includes detailed descriptions of pagan seasonal ceremonies, calendar, rites of passage, invocations, and heathen ethics. McVan wrote most of the Wotansvolk pamphlets (while David Lane wrote most of the articles in *Focus Fourteen*). He also promoted Wotansvolk through his artwork. Besides illustrating Wotansvolk publications, McVan produced Odinist artifacts, such as rune-staffs, jewelry, folk knots, amulets, and ceremonial drinking horns. His artistry added a special aura to the Wotansvolk headquarters and its surroundings. Magnificent wood-sculptured Norse gods and goddesses, wolves, dragons, and ravens were dotted around the headquarters' mountainous woodlands, which also had a hörg and a wooden hof (temple) with elaborate carvings, dedicated to Guido von List. The interior of the main building was filled with shields, swords, sculptures, Viking art, runes, and paintings. Basing his work on historical, mainly pre-Christian Norse proto- types, McVan's artistry added an important cultural dimension to the Wotans- volk effort to recreate a separate Aryan identity by reviving its ancestral faith.

In 2000 Wotansvolk was legally recognized as a church under the name Temple of Wotan, governed by a council of Alsherjargoðar and a board of trustees known as the Guardians of Faith.[19] The meteoric rise of Wotansvolk in the Aryan counterculture increased pressure on the original Wotansvolk staff. In September 2001 the 14 Word Press relocated its headquarters to Maple Shad, New Jersey. In charge of the new distribution center was Steve Wiegand, white- power musician and owner of the music label Micetrap Production.[20] Heat from local press, police, and residents made Wiegand reconsider. In Decem- ber 2001 John Post a construction project manager out of Napa, California, agreed to shoulder responsibility for administering Wotansvolk and the 14 Word Press, building a staff of four to handle the growing propaganda center.[21] Katja Lane retained influence through her position on the Temple of Wotan board of trustees.[22] As of spring 2002 Post reported that the transition was in effect with an additional 1,200 names on the mailing list for Focus Fourteen.[23]

A Creed of Iron: The Pagan Ideology of Wotansvolk

Although Wotansvolk is the product of a team, each individual has a distinct role. The religious philosophy of Wotansvolk discussed hereafter is thus not identical with the heathen ideology of David Lane. Lane's Odinist writings re- volved around its warrior aspect and, though blended with numerology and mys- tery religions, had a distinct political orientation in its call for an armed Aryan revolution. Much like Christensen and Kaldenberg, Lane was largely indifferent to Norse ceremonial practice and left undeveloped most nonwarrior aspects. It was not until the incarcerated Odinist goði Danny Johnson was transferred to the Florence penitentiary in 1998 that Lane and his prison kindred were really introduced to the richness of pagan ceremonies. The evolving Wotansvolk creed and its ceremonies and magic are mainly a product of Ron McVan.

The Wotansvolk creed is essentially a racial mysticism inspired in part by

Aryan pre-Christian pagan traditions, Gnosticism, Theosophy, and Jungian psychology. Dissatisfied with the multiracial reworking of the American nation, Wotansvolk aims at "reaching deep into the ancestral past" to reconnect with the "roots of the Aryan race" in order to redevelop a lost "folk consciousness" (McVan 1996). Asserting that each race has a genetic pool of spiritual identity, McVan (1997, 2) understands Wotanism as "the inner voice of the Aryan soul, which links the infinite past with the infinite future." Accordingly, McVan believes that "all Aryans today retain an element of Wotan consciousness" (ibid., 29), a revival of which would liberate the white man. To Wotansvolk, Wotan symbolizes "the essential soul and spirit of the Aryan folk made manifest" (ibid., 16). As an iron-willed warrior God, Wotan is said to instill in the white race the determination and heroic qualities necessary for them to arise victoriously in the ongoing struggle for Aryan survival and prosperity. Wotansvolk members cast their work as a continuation of the efforts of turn-of-the-century Ariosophist Guido von List, philosopher Friedrich Nietzsche, and psychoanalyst Carl Jung, the goal being to return Aryan man to his perceived true nature. Wotansvolk teaches that each race is by nature unique, given distinct qualities truly its own. To survive and evolve along the desired path of racial greatness, a race must develop a high level of folk consciousness, that is, be in touch with its racial soul. Each race is thus said to possess a spiritual heritage understood as a Jungian collective unconscious. "Every race has its soul and every soul its race."[24]

Engraved in the unconscious of each member of a race, then, are powerful archetypes that can be made conscious by performing the rituals and ceremonies developed by the ancestors in times immemorial. "Our ancient White ancestors understood that in order to ensure our heritage and racial survival, expansion and advancement, we must initiate means to galvanize our Folk Consciousness. Allegories, [rituals,] and myths were developed along with a variety of archetypical gods which best represented Nature's Law and the folk consciousness."[25] These archetypes are the gods of the blood, who will exist as long as there are living members of the race. For the individual Aryan, meeting with those archetypical forces recharges divine energy such that man may evolve into the realization of the Nietzschean superman. Odinism equals the rope over the abyss, connecting man the beast with the superman. "Through Wotanism one may experience the infinitude of life mysteries and the divine completion of [Aryan] man," McVan asserts.[26] No ontological distinction separates Aryan man and Aryan gods; they are conceived of as kin, differing in power rather than in nature. Personifying the divine essence of Aryan man, the significance of Wotan extends beyond his warrior aspect. He is the master of Gnosis who invites man to pursue the upward Ariosophic path of perfection.[27] Following in the occult national socialist tradition of Serrano, Himmler, Wiligut, and Rosenberg, McVan cultivates the theory of the mystery of the blood, believing that unmixed Aryan blood carries genetic memories of the racial lineage with all its gods, demigods, and heroes of the aboriginal golden age. In linking man to his gods, unmixed blood is that mystical essence that enables microcosmic man to reach out to the macrocosm of the universe, to succeed in the great work of individual and racial becoming.[28] In reconnecting with the archetypical gods of the blood and developing his mental powers, "man is able to awaken to a divinity which flows within him."[29] The individual art of becoming corresponds with the great work of the Aryan race organism. For the Aryan race, establishing rapport with its collective unconscious is a necessary prerequisite for maintaining its identity and mission as a unique spiritual being. "A race without its mythos and religion of the blood shifts aimlessly through history" (McVan 1997, 16). Expanding on the meaning of Lane's acronym for the Aryan underground, McVan claims that WOTAN signifies the cosmic will to power, the fulfillment of Aryan collective self-transformation, the becoming of an Aryan super race.[30]

Operating with a less complex concept of cyclical time than Blavatsky, Serrano, and Devi, McVan still reflects in his cosmology the basic structure—an aboriginal golden age, fall, cleansing, and renewal—universal to the world of racist paganism. Although he believes in the prehistoric Aryan civilizations of Hyperborea and Atlantis, McVan focuses his historiography closer to the present age, detailing how the once-glorious Aryan high culture was cast down into the current wolf age following the demise of the Norse gods in the previous Ragnarök.[31] In the tradition of Yockey and Christensen, McVan argues that the primary cause of the fall was spiritual. The advent of Jewish Christianity initiated a dramatic process of degeneration. "If ever there were a birth of tragedy, it was when Aryan man turned his back on the indigenous Gods of his race," McVan writes. "On that day he sacrificed the very roots of his being, ushering in the labyrinth of his own descent."[32] The level of folk consciousness gradually diminished and the metaphysical race lost knowledge of itself as race. As the gods of the blood are transmitted genetically, they remained alive, though mainly dormant, through the centuries of Christian dominion.

Forced underground, the ancient Aryan wisdom (Wotanism and Ariosophy) was cultivated by secret societies, Gnostic orders, and esoteric sects, such as the Knights Templars or the Armanenschaft, the underground Teutonic priesthood figuring in von List's theories. The Aryan sages are assisted, McVan claims, by the Watchers, which he defines as "non-corporal entities which oversee world activities," acting as "Keepers of the Ancient Wisdom" (1996). "Heroic figures" in the history of Aryan man "are constantly surrounded and guided by these astral entities."[33] In addition, McVan asserts, a number of historical or legendary heroes of Western history are manifestations of the archetype Wotan. Among these are Merlin, who allegedly initiated King Arthur into the great Ariosophic mysteries, and Herne the Hunter, said to having been the Gnostic guide of Robin Hood (McVan 1997, 47). With the völkisch revival of the late nineteenth century, the archetypical forces again began to manifest in a resurgent interest in Teutonic folklore and mythology. Acting as virtual magi were Richard Wagner, who "wanted his art to become a revitalized religion of the blood";[34] Friedrich Nietzsche, who illuminated the glorious Aryan past; völkisch mystic Guido von List, hailed as the "undisputed high priest of Wotanism and Ariosophy"; Templar Ariosophist Jörg Lanz van Liebenfels; and Rudolph von Sebottendorff of the Thule Society (McVan 1997, 54).

In their interpretation of racial history, Wotansvolk ideologues rely heavily on a selective reading of Carl Jung, primarily his Gnostic quest into the mysteries and his theories about an Aryan collective subconscious. As suggested by Richard Noll, Jung was both a product and interpreter of his contemporary völkisch culture. Clothing an essentially esoteric pagan worldview in secular scientific prose, Jung was as much a mystic as a scholar. Following Noll's two groundbreaking works on the subject, *Jungkulten* and *Aryan Christ: The Secret Life of Carl Jung*, a heated scholarly debate emerged, in which antiracist Jungians tried to refute Noll's basic arguments. Nonetheless, racial pagans and occult national socialists do see what Noll saw, and the völkisch and mystical aspects of Jung's theories greatly appeal to Wotansvolk.[35]

Experimenting with trance techniques, engaging in spiritual dialogues with the dead, communicating in visions with Gnostic-Mithraic spirit guides, and meeting Wotan in dreams all led Jung to believe in a spiritual heritage, the collective soul of the ancestors, which he later termed the *collective unconscious*. This "ancestral inheritance" was to Jung "the ground of all subjective experience within every individual" (Noll 1997a, 4, 153). Whether suppressed or embraced, the ancient gods were still present in this imaginary land of the dead, or, stated in Jungian terms: in the abyss of the collective unconscious were powerful "dominants" or archetypes, bound to exact an influence on man and culture. Regarding Christianity as a Jewish religion detrimentally imposed on the pagan cultures of Europe, Jung turned to Gnosticism, alchemy, the Mithraic mysteries, and Wotanism in a quest for redeeming deification. Suggesting that the Aryan mystery cults provided the symbols of transformation necessary for initiation into the mysteries of immortality or personal rebirth, these esoteric traditions provided gateways to the murky steps of spiral staircases descending into the deepest levels of the collective unconscious (ibid., 124, 142). The link between the realms of biology and spirituality ensured Aryan man a path to redemption if he was willing to return to the pagan world of his ancestors engraved genetically deep within himself (ibid., 142, 158).

Jung believed that it was of crucial importance for the health of both the individual and the völkisch collective to be conscious of its ancestral inheritance. A long-suppressed archetype, or god, might otherwise suddenly burst forth, forcibly possessing the mind of a person or a whole culture. In his famous essay "Wotan" (1936), Jung applies this theory as an interpretive model in his search for a causal explanation of the national socialist phenomenon. As a personification of a dominant psychic force peculiar to the Germans, Wotan supposedly did not die with the advent of Christianity but disappeared deep into the collective unconscious, where he "remained invisible for more than a thousand years, working anonymously and indirectly" ("Wotan" 1947 [1936], 189). When the "Christian God proved too weak to save Christendom from fratricidal slaughter" in World War I, the one-eyed wanderer "laughed and saddled Sleipner" (ibid.). Bursting forth with the force of a hurricane, Wotan raged through the land, seizing the Germans like a mighty wind that "overthrows everything that is not firmly rooted" (ibid., 188). According to Jung, "the unfathomable depths of Wotan's character" and the "irrational psychic force" of the paramount "German god" explains more about national socialism than would any reference to economic or political processes (Jung 1947).

Jung's initial fascination with the national socialist movement as a natural expression of the German mind was reciprocated by a national socialist interest in Jungian psychology as an Aryan alternative to Freudian "Jewish" psychology (Cocks 1985). While Jung himself was not a national socialist, his theories were in part compatible with parts of national socialist ideology. Defenders of Jung might correctly stress that his more or less implicit anti-Semitism, racialism, and völkisch romanticism were part of the zeitgeist of his time, but evidence indicates that Jung kept his basic perspective intact well beyond the end of World War II.[36] In a letter to racial mystic Miguel Serrano of 14 September 1960, Jung reiterated his basic argument from the 1936 Wotan essay: "When . . . the belief in the god Wotan vanished and nobody thought about him anymore, the phenomenon originally called Wotan remained; nothing changed but its name, as

National Socialism has demonstrated on a large scale. A collective movement consists of millions of individuals, each of who shows the symptoms of Wotanism and proves thereby that Wotan in reality never died, but has retained his original vitality and autonomy. Our consciousness only imagines that it has lost its Gods; in reality they are still there and it only needs a certain general condition to bring them back in full force" (Serrano 1997, 103). Jung continued by issuing a warning that Wotan was bound to return forcibly. "We have largely lost our Gods," Jung lamented. As "the actual condition of our religion" did not offer an "efficacious answer to the world situation in general and to the 'religion' of communism in particular," he believed that "we are very much in the same predicament as the pre-National-Socialistic Germany of the Twenties, i.e., we are apt to undergo the risk of a further, but this time world-wide Wotanistic experiment" (ibid.).

What to Jung was a "risk" is to the Wotansvolk project a comforting forecast of the near future. The turn-of-the-century resurgence of paganism, Wotanism, Ariosophy, and rune magic shows, Wotansvolk argues, that Jung was correct. The racial gods are powerful inborn psychic forces that will never die as long as the white man walks the earth. Wotansvolk publications approvingly recycle Jungian statements.[37] Paraphrasing Jung, Wotansvolk likens Wotan to a long-quiescent volcano that might at any moment forcibly resume its activity (McVan 1997, 36). The suppressed gods of the blood will return with a vengeance and with overwhelming power, Wotansvolk says confidently, pointing to the ascendancy of Hitler as a historical example: "Nowhere since Viking times has the direct, singular effect of Wotan consciousness been more evident than in the folkish unity of National Socialist Germany."[38] By reconnecting with the ancestral roots, Wotansvolk intends to recreate the lost folk consciousness and restore Aryan independence (*David Lane 1996*; *Katja Lane 1997*; *McVan 1996*; McVan 1997). In essence, then, Wotansvolk paganism is at its core an esoteric Aryan nationalist creed whose greater working represents a racist recasting of Jung's mystical quest to "illuminate the obscurity of the Creator" (Serrano 1997, 128), or "to serve the function of making God conscious" of himself as God.[39] By projecting deep into the abyss of the Aryan unconscious, Wotansvolk attempts nothing less than to illuminate the dormant gods of the blood, thus resurrecting the self-consciousness of the race of itself as a race. This will empower Aryan man to emerge victorious in the approaching Ragnarök and usher in a renewed golden age populated by heroic Aryan man-gods.

Wotansvolk Religious Practice

Ceremonies and rituals are to Wotansvolk principal working methods for reconnecting with the archetypical gods of the blood and effective ways of establishing reciprocal relations of power exchange between members of a race and their gods. Wotansvolk thus differs from the Odinist Fellowship in stressing the importance of rituals. A lack of reliable and sufficient sources of knowledge about Norse pre-Christian ceremonies presents a problem in modern efforts to revive Norse paganism, which necessitates experimentation, inspiration, studies, and, to varying degrees, a willingness to incorporate elements from other traditions. With their distinct pan-Aryan orientation, Wotansvolk ideologues take as their point of departure the postulated racial unity of the golden age. Being fully in touch with the racial soul, all golden-age Aryans supposedly shared the same religion. Following the legacy of Gobineau, Wotansvolk argues that the superior Aryans then spilled out over the world, creating every high culture of importance. This means that Wotansvolk need not rely exclusively on historically documented Norse religion but can (and to some extent does) extrapolate from what is known about the pre-Christian "Aryan" traditions of ancient China, India, Persia, West Asia, Egypt, South America, and Europe.[40] During the past two decades, a Norse ceremonial tradition has evolved, enabling new kindreds to learn from pagan elders and previously established ceremonial patterns. The various heathen networks generally share a basic pattern of ceremonial and ritual practice but often differ in emphasis and detail.[41]

Wotansvolk ceremonies can be subdivided into communal rites and private rites. Communal ceremonies include seasonal blots and sumbel, rites of passage (birth, marriage, initiation, death), and magical warfare. As is true for most Norse pagan traditions, the Wotansvolk blot and sumbel ritual complexes, which follow the yearly cycle of nature, stand forth as the most important communal ceremonies. "The practice of Wotanism ritual and ceremony of the annual festivals is recognized as the most effective way of impressing on our Aryan folk the wisdom, ethics and customs of our ancestors. Celebrating our indigenous traditions is as ancient as our race and is essential to our identity, unity, and survival as a people" (McVan 1997, 142). Wotansvolk follows the generic heathen festivity cycle but differs from other Norse pagan organizations in the explicit racial dimension that pervades their ceremonies, as illustrated in a description of a standard blot found in *Creed of Iron*: after sanctifying the ritual circle, the acting Wotansvolk goði, facing the *staller* (altar) and holding high a horn of mead, invites "Wotan, Great God of our Folk," "to bestow upon us here in Midgård your strength, courage and wisdom, that the knowledge of our blood be clearly known." After passing through the ritual stages of sprinkled blessings, readings, anointing, and incantation, the acting goði recites a petition, holding a sword with both hands overhead. "In the mysterious journey through Midgård to our mortal fate we look to you, oh High Gods of the Aesir and the Vanir . . . to be with us in times of struggle and aid us in the battle with our enemy, as we are the blood of thy blood." The participants then join hands, as the Goði raises high his sword or spear, declaring that the kindred is united as one and swearing in the name of Wotan to "remain ever faithful" to "the fourteen words," after which participants shout in chorus, "Hail the Aesir! Hail the Vanir! Hail the Folk!" (143–47).[42]

The racial dimension lends all Wotansvolk blots their special aura. During a 1998 midsummer blot conducted at Wotansvolk headquarters, participants hailed the coming "day of resurrection" of Baldr, which will "usher in the new age of light for Aryan man after Ragnarök." "The wheel of life keeps turning," a participant recited loudly, his voice quavering dramatically. "And in nature's cycle spins creation. Blazing like the sun's great disk, emanations of the high god Balder, a time of sanctification, [highlighting] the mystical nature of race and blood, carriers of primordial substances. The wheel of life keeps turning— the wheel of life keeps turning. I greet the summer solstice, and the promise of a Golden Age."[43] Similarly, a racial focus is key to the Wotansvolk sumbel ceremony. As each participant in turn raises his horn and hails a selected Aryan god, a hero, an ancestor, and a nonpresent kinsmen, many seem eager to demonstrate their racial loyalty. The gods and heroes are frequently hailed for their warrior qualities and honoring racial prisoners of war is standard as is toasting for Aryan victory and the 14 words.

Einherjar is a Norse term for the brave warriors who died in battle and were brought to Valhalla, the abode of Odin. In Wotansvolk terminology, it denotes the community of racial warriors who are willing to die in the revolutionary war to establish an Aryan homeland. The Wotansvolk rite of passage by which a heathen prospect is accepted into the ranks of the elite warrior fraternity is ideally conducted outdoors at a hörg. The participants should preferably dress in Viking-inspired clothing, and all initiates are expected to wear their swords. After setting up the sacred circle, the acting goði invites the gods to "open the mighty gates of Valhalla, Hall of Wotan's chosen warriors, Fearless fighting elite, Pride of the Valkyries," and then to bring before those who have died in battle the name of the initiate who wears a *Valknut*, the "knot of the slain," which looks like three interlinked triangles, symbolizing the power of Odin to bind and unbind the soul. Asking the einherjar to accept the initiate into their ranks, the goði places flat a sword on top of the initiate's head as he kneels down on one knee. The goði turns to the initiate. "Before our gods and chosen warriors, do you pledge by your solemn word that you shall always uphold with honor, dignity and courage the lifelong commitment to Wotan's Einherjar?" Confirming his pledge, the initiate then stands, and the goði places the sword point at the nape of the initiate's neck to symbolize that death is better than dishonoring his commitment. The initiate is then blindfolded, guided to the hörg, and brought before the lords of Valhalla into whose fraternity he now enters. Removing the blindfold, the goði with his thumb presses oil on the initiate's head and gives him the blessings of Odin. Proclaiming that the initiate now is a member of Wotan's einherjar, the goði places a sword in the outstretched arms of the initiate. "Through this sword, ancestors of a thousand ages fill thy being," the goði says. The ritual concludes with all participants repeating in chorus, "Hail Wotan! Victory or Valhalla!" (McVan 2000, 368–70).

The individual Wotansvolk rituals consist of daily invocations and small offering ceremonies, meditation, sejd, rune casting, and magic. The extent to which Wotansvolkers engage in any or all of these practices varies according to the individuals and their life-stages. No Wotansvolk adherent is required to do anything, although McVan recommends that his fellow racial pagans learn by experience the benefits of daily spiritual practice. The single most important of these rites is meditation. "It is through meditation that our most unlimited powers are obtained, marvels and miracles are worked, the highest spiritual knowledge is acquired and union with the great gods of our folk is eventually gained," McVan declares (1997, 108). In this and in other philosophical specifics of Wotansvolk, there are noticeable Hindu and Buddhist influences, although in the watered-down version prolific in the Western milieu of alternative spirituality. Much like Jost and Serrano, McVan envisions Aryan man as a universe with all its worlds, as a microcosmic reflection of Yggdrasil, evolving toward perfection. Along the spine are found seven energy centers, "wheels" or "gateways," each associated with a specific rune. The spiritual ascendancy of individual man begins with meditation, with these chakras of the runic tree of man serving as contemplative focuses (ibid., 74).

An appropriate time for meditation is during the first hour after dawn of each day, when its designated planet (according to the "seven pointed star system" of the week) governs the day. Beginning at dawn on the first day of the week, Sunday, the star system runs clockwise and provides Wotansvolk with a spiritual focus for each day. In addition to its specific planet, each day is associated with a particular god, rune, number, color, tone, sign, (Aryan) wonder, and divine invocation. For example, Wednesday, which is considered the most important day of the week, has its specific god (Wotan), rune (othala), planet (Mercury), number (8), color (yellow), tone (mi), sign (Gemini), Aryan wonder (Great Pyramid of Egypt), and invocation: "Hail Wotan! Giver of victory! Thou who knowest the runes of wisdom and power, I stand before you and welcome you this day. Bring our people to know the strength of your ancient ways. Grant us knowledge of thy wisdom that I may better serve thee and our folk. Great Wotan, it is you who has fired our hearts and our minds in the roaring cauldron of our creative racial instinct. Grant prosperity to us and well-being to our kind as long as we live. We thank thee, Wotan, Allfather and high one of the Aesir and Vanir. May strength and honor be with you and our people always" (McVan 1997, 127). The star system is used in any number of ways among Wotansvolk practitioners; around the breakfast table in the Wotansvolk headquarters, for instance, the children take turns reciting a written text that refers to the god of the day and conduct the appropriate invocation, in this way appropriating the American custom of saying grace before eating.

Individual rites of Norse magic may be performed for attaining practical goals such as increasing the practitioner's strength, steadfastness, safety, or courage; to ensure his or her success in work, social life, or love affairs; to see into the future or other dimensions. Individual rites can also be performed as part of magical warfare, as with the "rite of scorn," a ritual of revenge that can also be conducted as a communal ceremony. Fully in line with the basic Wotansvolk presumption that life is struggle, ideologues assert that it is natural to desire revenge when wronged. To this end man can summon the wrath of the gods of the blood. In the rite of scorn, the practitioner consecrates a sacred space within which a Nidhing ("shameful thug") pole is placed as a symbolically humiliating representation of the target of revenge. After setting the stage in this way, the practitioner then ritually invokes Loki, master of mischief, vengeance, deceit, and dark magic. After ritually opening the gate of the astral gods, the name and deeds of the wrongdoer are presented before the ancient ones. The gods are asked to "weigh these wrongful deeds by the laws of cause and consequences" that they may "cast down darkness and misfortune" on the "malicious perpetrator" (McVan 2000, 395). Inviting Loki's art and guidance, the practitioner then sends an "unceasing curse" through the opened astral gates, intending to hit hard the named offender. "May your bones break painfully! May your mind wander aimlessly! May your skin rot in agony! May your heart die of jealousy. May misery and misfortune be your constant companions" (ibid., 396).

In closing the circle, the practitioner commands the avenging spirits to arise out of the earth to exact the desired revenge and rites of precaution is taken to prevent harm done to anyone but the target.

Pagans in Prison

Wotansvolk/Temple of Wotan runs a prison-outreach ministry recognized as an official vendor to the Federal Bureau of Prisons and by a majority of state-prison authorities; this ministry will remain a top priority for the new Wotansvolk administration of John Post.[44] There are prison kindreds linked with Wotansvolk in every state, including the dozen states where Wotanism/Asatrú/Odinism has not yet been granted full religious recognition. Prisoners incarcerated in those states are encouraged by Wotansvolk to challenge state regulations in court. In Utah, Ohio, and Wisconsin, legal battles are currently being waged for religious rights and for the full recognition of Asatrú as a legitimate religion. As of 30 January 2001, Wotansvolk catered to more than 5,000 prisoners. The states with the strongest presence of Wotansvolk prison kindreds were Arizona, California, Texas, Michigan, Florida, Indiana, Missouri, and Pennsylvania, with three to five hundred Wotansvolk prisoners found in each state.[45] The Wotansvolk prison-outreach ministry has grown with remarkable speed. When I first visited Wotansvolk headquarters in the fall of 1996, there were less than a hundred prison kindreds. By the year 2000 there were more than three hundred.[46] Correspondence between hundreds of individual prisoners and the Wotansvolk headquarters indicates a pagan revival among the white prison population, including the conversion of whole prison gangs to the ancestral religion. To some extent, prison authorities have unwittingly facilitated the Wotansvolk effort by breaking up prison kindreds and transferring leading heathens to other prisons without an organized pagan presence.

Their determined prison-outreach program has earned Wotansvolk a reputation in the world of folkish paganism as being primarily a prison organization. According to Katja Lane, this is far from accurate, as prisoners constitute only an estimated 20 percent of Wotansvolkers in the United States.[47] Yet, the observation has some validity in the sense that Wotansvolk seems more successful in its outreach efforts than other Asatrú/Odinist programs. Partly due to the reputation of David Lane and its association with the legendary Brüders Schweigen, Wotansvolk name-recognition is high among the Aryan prison population. Also, in comparison with most other heathen outreach ministries, Wotansvolk has much to offer incarcerated pagans. For instance, Wotansvolk donates literature, videos, and ceremonial artifacts to assist prison kindreds in holding regular religious service, study circles, and seasonal ceremonies. In addition, Katja Lane corresponds with prison chaplains, sends them complimentary material on request, and assists inmates to legally challenge prison authorities if denied full recognition of Asatrú/Odinism as a legitimate religion. In numerous cases, inmates who have been denied Wotansvolk literature, books on runes, or the wearing heathen symbols have been advised how to proceed legally, as have prisoners whose heathen materials have been confiscated by prison guards. Katja Lane's campaigning has contributed to the fact that all states now permit the wearing of a Thór's hammer as a religious medallion. In March 2002 the new Wotansvolk administrator John Post announced the formation of the National Prison Kindred Alliance, a joint effort of Wotansvolk and a number of independent Asatrú/Odinist tribal networks, the goal being to create a more efficient prison-outreach ministry and to intensify efforts to gain increased religious rights and freedoms for the pagan community behind bars.[48]

Reflecting on the success of the Wotansvolk prison-outreach program, Katja Lane (1997) elaborates.

Most of the males who still have their instinct as warriors, protectors, defenders of their nation, their womenfolk, and their children, these men are the ones who find themselves in prison. They're virtually on the frontline of the battle for the preservation of our race, and they are the first casualties. And there you'll find some of the most fervent interest in Odinism. Men in prison, not having to take time to make a living for their families, take time to love their wives and deal with daily problems, turn inward and look for their spiritual soul, and, so those two factors have created a very strong Wotanist presence in the prisons. Prisons, as you know, are very racially tense . . . and usually violent. The men need a sense of their own identity and having an expression for it. So, nearly every prison now, both state and federal, has a kindred, and in nearly every case . . . Odinism or Wotanism are now officially recognized.

Richard Scutari provides an illustration from the inside, describing the kindred activities at the federal penitentiary in Lompoc, California, after authorities approved Odinism as a legitimate religion in 1997. "What was presented to the men spoke to their soul and we averaged from 50 to 55 prisoners at each weekly meeting. We were not only teaching the religion of our ancestors, but were also teaching White culture and White history. We even did a periodic segment we called 'Heroes of the Ages' in which we told the stories of different White heroes of the past, such as Horatius, Leonidas, Hermann, Vercingetorix, Adolf Hitler [and] Bob Mathews. The men were taking pride in their heritage . . . and we were so successful that we even had the men standing before the gathering and take up the oath ring as they swore to never use drugs again" (Scutari 2000).

In 1998 Scutari was instrumental in organizing the Sons of the Noble Wolf brotherhood of incarcerated heathens, as the prison branch of the tribal Vor Ætt Odinist Organization. Like Wotansvolk, Vor Ætt (our lineage) declares that Odinism springs from the unique collective soul of Aryan man. Developed in a warrior society, Odinism gave Aryan man his "restless and unconquerable spirit" that "broke the fetters made by the Roman Emperors" and "destroyed tyrants and slaves" (Vor Ætt 1998, 25). As it celebrates "warrior knowledge and spirituality," Odinism is considered well suited to "incarcerated members" living "in an extremely dangerous environment where they may be attacked just simply because they are white" (ibid., 54). Vor Ætt seeks to communicate to their "captive Kinsmen" that the opportunities of life have not passed them by because they are in prison. Regardless of how much time an inmate may have to serve, Vor Ætt asserts, he has the ability to improve himself intellectually, spiritually, and morally, and to assume control over his own destiny.

Organized as a hierarchical tribal government, Vor Ætt intends to galvanize Aryan prisoners into a racial advance guard that will stand victorious in the approaching Ragnarök by mastering the way of the teacher and the way of the warrior. Initiates are expected to live by strict codes of conduct and can advance through the nine runic grades by passing tests of learning and physical fitness. Members study runology, mythology, philosophy, psychology, archaeology, and scientific racism; they also exercise daily to meet the mandatory physical standard for the runic rank they aspire to achieve. Emphasizing that Odinism is a martial religion, Vor Ætt expects its members to defend their faith and folk. To explore the way of the Odinic warrior, members may seek initiation into the Úlfhednar (heathen wolfs) Brotherhood modeled on the einherjar elite warriors. "Our world is not a kind and gentle place," the manual reads, and "our Folk need guardians" (Vor Ætt 1998, 13). Like their power animal, the wolf, the úlfhednar will care for their kin and show savagery in their protection. Organized according to a nine-layered hierarchy based on mastery of survival skills, military science, paramilitary tactics, martial arts, communications, intelligence, and physical fitness, the Úlfhednar Brotherhood hopes to "establish a reputation for achievement, dedication and a toughness tampered with bravery, honor, and nobility" (ibid.). While designed to fit the violent culture of U.S. penitentiaries, Vor Ætt hopes also to organize kindreds on the outside so that Aryan convicts will have tribes to link up with on release.

Was Odin an Aryan Israelite or a Viking in the Sky?

The rise of Asatrú/Odinism in the white-racist milieu has come to pose a challenge to Christian Identity. In the 1990s, many American racist youth tended to dismiss Identity as "an old man's religion," and Identity had notable difficulties in recruiting a new generation, at least regionally. While some Identity believers still confused racist Odinism with hedonistic Satanism, it became obvious to many preachers that Norse paganism could no longer be brushed aside as irrelevant to the chosen race.[49] Three distinct responses emerged, two of which sought to appropriate Asatrú/Odinism, either by incorporating its gods and goddesses as "Israelite heroes" or by identifying Odinist elements as basically Christian, while the third sought to call down the wrath of God on the pagan heretics.

The Church of Jesus Christ, Christian/Aryan Nations, took the first approach. Aryan Nation lieutenant Gerald Gruidl (1996) argued emphatically that Odin and Freya in fact were heroic Israelites who had been mistaken for gods by uneducated Norsemen and their American co-religionists. To prove his case, Gruidl enthusiastically presented an Identity genealogical chart tracing the descendants of Jacob (Israel), which neatly positions Odin, Freya, and other Norse divinities as direct descendants of Jacob's fourth son, that is, of the House of Judah. The heathen gods and goddesses are thereby appropriated as historical leaders of the chosen race, related by blood to Adam and Eve, Jesus, and the English Queen.[50] Another effort to appropriate Odinism was led by Mark Thomas, then pastor of the Christian Posse Comitatus of Hereford, Pennsylvania.[51] Instead of claiming that Jesus and Odin were related by blood, he suggested a theological identification, arguing that Odinism began in Ireland with the teachings by Christ Himself when he traveled the British Isles.[52] The Icelandic *Eddas* and the Celtic "interpretation of Odinism" were "allegor[ies] of the Biblical account of Genesis . . . and the Book of Revelations," Thomas declared.[53] Odinism was therefore, he asserted, not demonic heresy but rather "the work of the Holy Spirit without the corruption of judeo-Christianity" (Internet, Thomas 1996a). He identified the image of Odin hanging from the windswept tree with the crucified Jesus, and took Odin's two ravens to symbolize "the union of our spirits with the Holy Spirit."[54] The third Identity response to Odinism was confrontational. Commander Michael L. Hansen of the Identity Christian National Socialist White Revolutionary Party angrily denounced the pagan revival as "a knife in the back of the White revolution!"[55] He described Odinism as a blasphemous, "non-Teutonic [and] non-White" creed that is "contradictory to [Aryan] nature." As neo-paganism had "nothing going for it," Hansen asserted, its adherents had to constantly attack the teachings of the Aryan Christ, which are the solid foundation of national socialism. Odinism was thus denounced as an alien creed that was in effect denying the racial movement its true heritage and ideology.

Wotansvolk, for their part, tend to regard Identity as a "ridiculous" creed, an opinion shared by other racial pagan groups. Wyatt Kaldenberg (1998) recalls how his Odinist articles in WAR used to provoke "hate letters from old Identity believers, saying, 'this Rabbi Kaldenberg is a stinking Jew 'cause he doesn't think that we are the true Jews,' it was so bizarre. It's if you don't believe that Aryans are Jews, you must be a Jew! And to me, that's just the most insane thing." The hostilities between pagans and Christian Identity believers have not, however, prevented Wotansvolk from participating at various Aryan Nation gatherings. Katja Lane spoke on behalf of David at the Aryan Nations Youth Congress in 1995 and at the Aryan Nations World Congress in 1995 and 1996.[56] The fact that Wotansvolk was invited at all, despite article IV of the "Platform for the Aryan National State," which stipulates that paganism will be prohibited in the future Aryan Republic dreamed of, points not only to the fact that both groups might temporarily brush mutual enmity aside when need arises, but also to the tactical desire of Aryan Nations to appropriate Odinism.[57]

Identity's ambition to monopolize the religious dimension of the Aryan revolutionary landscape began to be seriously challenged by Creativity in the early 1980s. Klassen's iconoclastic assaults on Christianity made an inroad into the emerging white-racist youth culture, and quite a number of white-power bands and fanzines adopted the worldview of the Creators. Before long, the Church of the Creator was in turn challenged by the rise of Odinism. Although he regarded Odinists as racial kinsmen, Klassen was contemptuous about the record of accomplishments of Norse paganism both past and present. A firm believer in linear history and of the social Darwinist motto "might is right," Klassen concluded that Odinism had already demonstrated its basic lack of intellectual and spiritual strength, as it could not hold its ground against Jewish Christianity a thousand years ago. "Why would anyone want to resurrect an ancient failure from the scrap heap of history?" Dismissing the Norse gods as yet another set of "spooks in the sky" representing no more than a "silly hangover from our primitive Stone Age ancestors," Klassen was also bewildered as to how any sane white man could be attracted to unrefined Norse culture. Finding Greek religion "rich, colorful and interesting" and Roman mythology "much superior," Klassen asked what could possibly be so special about Viking myths? "The answer is: not much. It is not a great choice" (Klassen 1987, 186–93).

Writing in 1987, at a time when the Odinist Fellowship was the strongest organized racist interpretation of Norse paganism, Klassen felt secure enough to paternalistically dismiss Odinism as a "small and insignificant" religion (1987, 186). With the subsequent Norse revival among white-racist youth, the table turned and racist Odinism dwarfed Creativity. Finding Klassen's summary dismissal of Odinism "arrogant," "uninformed," and "an insult to anyone with intelligence," many racist heathens in the late 1990s wrote off "miniscule" Creativity as "shallow," "rootless," and "culturally deprived."[58] Despite the apparent ideological differences between the two creeds, grassroots Creators and racist pagans often cooperate locally, united in their opposition against the system. Many white-power bands and fanzines have no problem accommodating both creeds as nature-based and militantly racist. The potential tension between these two religious perspectives might temporarily lay dormant but can also easily be reactivated for any number of reasons (not least for personal reasons) in the notoriously conflict-ridden white-racist milieu.

This pattern of cooperation and conflict is reflected in Creator papers and spokesperson statements. Creator reverend Kevin Hansson (1994) bashed Odinism as a "flight into the realms of fantasy" revolving around the superstitious beliefs of the Vikings who were low-life "race traitors" of "limited intelligence and perception." As Odinism had "no set of beliefs, no written guidelines, no program, no plan of action or idea for the future of our race," a Norse revival would only benefit the Jews by diverting whites from the "superior religion" of Creativity. Responding to letters that reported Wotansvolk growth at the expense of Creativity in the United Kingdom, the *Rahowa News* editor comforted the readers by dismissing Odinism as a "dead horse," urging the U.K. pagans to "stop playing silly games with non-existing Viking-spooks [as] only Creativity provides all the answers we need to lead the White Race to a Brighter and Whiter future" (O'Máirtin 1996). Yet, *Rahowa News* began featuring David Lane's *Revolution by Number 14*, and Creator Lisa Turner officially hailed Katja Lane as a white "role model" (Turner 1997).[59]

Ron McVan's prior engagement in the Church of the Creator has earned him continuous respect among Creators who sometimes still invite him to attend their conferences, such as the World Church of the Creator 1999 Labor Day camp in Superior, Montana. Creators sometimes even seek his advice regarding internal matters. In August 1996, for instance, McVan was invited to the meeting of the Keepers of the Faith committee when they elected Matt Hale as new Pontifex Maximus in what would become the World Church of the Creator. In a 1999 interview Hale seemed eager to moderate degrading views on Odinism that had been previously espoused by Creativity, emphasizing that "there are [essential] similarities" between the two creeds: "We are both anti-Christian. We both have a lot of respect and honor of our ancestry. We both believe in nature's laws." Among the minor Creativity organizations established in the wake of founder Ben Klassen's suicide was the Institute of Creativity–14 Words Coalition (IOC), which went yet another step in improving communication with Wotansvolk, establishing actual working relations with that organization. IOC distributed material from the 14 Word Press, hailed David and Katja Lane in unequivocal terms, and published positive articles on Odinist white-power bands such as Bound for Glory and Nordic Thunder.[60]

Creativity and Wotansvolk share a distinctly global perspective and ambitiously seek to transcend current national borders to reunite the scattered white race, a common goal that most likely will make them competitors rather than partners. Both groups boast successful localizations throughout much of the "white world," but Wotansvolk (as of 2000) has the upper hand.

Odinism as a Pan-Aryan National Marker

Wotansvolk ideologues emphasize the need for a territory exclusively their own if the purported ongoing white genocide is to be reversed (McVan 1996; David Lane 1996c). Reluctantly, McVan has come to embrace the thought of establishing a secessionist white homeland in the northwestern corner of the United States, the "white-bastion solution" popularized among Aryan revolutionaries during the 1980s. "I rebelled to the talk about the Northwestern Imperative when I heard that for the first time," McVan (1996) recalls. "Because I don't think that we should give up anything." Being confronted with the increasingly precarious "racial reality" forced him to reconsider the situation, and he now advocates the Northwest homeland solution as the only feasible alternative. Strategically regrouping in a separate, all-Aryan homeland, the white warrior could then "push out again . . . just like we started with the original thirteen colonies and pushed West" paying "in blood" the territory conquered. "We would then try to push back the nonwhite races and we would reclaim our boundaries, most particularly Europe and the United States."

Combined with this territorial imperative is a distinct pan-Aryan ideology that embraces the "world wide White Family from Europe to America to wherever our Folk are scattered" (David Lane 1995a; see also David Lane 1995b; David Lane 1996d). Considering the civil wars in Northern Ireland and the former Yugoslavia to be tragic consequences of artificial barriers imposed by the racial enemies to divide and conquer, Wotansvolk espouses pan-Aryan race nationalism (David Lane 1996a; David Lane 1996b). Regretting that the "leaders of the Third Reich were prisoners of geographical nationalism" (David Lane 1997b), Wotansvolk portrays Odinism as the original Aryan religion,[61] the revival of which will "reunite" all branches of the white race, whether "Slavic, Nordic, Alpine or some other designation" (David Lane 1995g). Here, Wotansvolk makes use of the Indo-European field of research, in particular the work of scholars like Georges Dumézil, who explores linguistic, mythological, and religious similarities between ancient Indian, Persian, and European cultures.

The racial nationalism developed by Wotansvolk is intentionally designed as an alternative to ethnic nationalism and the current multiracial reworking of the American nation. The use of Odinism as a national marker is instrumental in the construction of the Wotansvolk neonationalist project. Common to neonationalist constructs is the nostalgic projection of the imagined nation back into legendary times. To this end, Norse paganism well serves the Wotansvolk ideologues, as the Viking age, the Viking gods, art, and myths are sufficiently well known. While linked with North America through the adventures of Norse seafarers, the geographical center of Viking culture in the remote northern corner of Europe makes it appear "untainted" by nonwhite influences. In projecting the idea of an Aryan racial unity back into legendary Viking age and beyond, the Wotansvolk conjure up an image of a golden era of undefiled heroism, virility, and freedom, a time in which men were men and lived in perfect harmony with nature according to its eternal laws. The subsequent Christianization of the free heathen nation functions as the national trauma. Writes McVan, "American Negroes zealously emphasize the rigors of 200 years of slavery in this country, as if only they alone had ever been enslaved. Jews rant hysterically and endlessly about an alleged holocaust. Yet, if one is to understand horror and suffering in the full sense of the word, then we must comprehend what the free-thinking Aryan pagans, alchemists, and scientists suffered under the Christian pogroms and the Inquisition. This was a deliberate, religious slaughter of the innocents, unparalleled in the Western world, a darkness which reigned for a millennium."[62]

The racial nationalism advocated by Wotansvolk is methodologically constructed in several logical, successive steps. The race is presented as an organic entity bestowed with a soul of its own, transmitted genetically through powerful archetypes in the racial collective unconscious and animated by the blood that flows through the veins of each racial member of unmixed descent. Members of a race are thus united in nature and by nature, making anything less than self-determination in an independent nation a violation of nature. By projecting the imagined racial nation back into legendary times, having it suffer a severe national trauma, and painting a history of repeated threats and transgressions up to the turbulent time of the present, Wotansvolk endows the nation with a sense of eternal belonging. Projecting the image of the corporate national entity further into the promise of a glorious future, assuming the current acute threat of extinction can be overcome, strengthens this notion of eternity.

This Time the World: Wotansvolk Worldwide Mission

Founded at a time when the Internet revolutionized the means by which Aryan racial activists could spread their message, Wotansvolk immediately established itself in cyberspace. The first Web site went up in 1995, followed by an improved, "official" Web site in 1996. In 1997 Wotansvolk got its own domain, "14words.com," and added a number of mirror sites, including one in Spanish. In 2001 a members-only Wotansvolkers chat group, linking heathens throughout the global white-power culture and monitored by Hermann Sitecah, was set up independent of the Temple of Wotan, although with Katja Lane's approval. With the electronic highway, Wotansvolk soon reached far into the global Aryan revolutionary landscape and attracted a growing number of active Wotansvolkers and kindreds abroad.

Wotansvolk, of course, is not a membership organization but rather a propaganda center, providing "a philosophical foundation for independent kindreds and fraternities."[63] In addition to actual kindreds, a large number of active individual supporters help disseminate Wotansvolk material in their local communities. By the spring of 1996, the first European Wotansvolk group was established, with headquarters in London. Since then, the number of associated kindreds has increased rapidly. By January 2000, there was an active Wotansvolk presence in forty-one countries spread over all continents. Germany had the largest number of heathen fraternities with fourteen kindreds, followed by England (eight kindreds), Canada (seven), Australia (six) and Sweden (five). While western and eastern Europe seem to have provided the most fertile ground for Wotansvolk, kindreds have also formed outside the "traditional white heartland," with Wotansvolk associates in Asia (Japan and the Philippines) and Latin America (Argentina, Brazil, Chile, Mexico, and Peru). Around the world, no less than eighty-four different groups have been engaged in translating Wotansvolk material into their native languages, including Polish, Russian, Afrikaans, Serbian, and Finnish.[64] An interesting aspect of this global spread of Norse paganism in its Wotansvolk variation is its localization in northern Europe, historically the home of the pre-Christian heathen traditions that inspired Wotansvolk. Norse gods and customs were thus imported into America for revival, reinterpretation, and modernization according to the Americanized Ariosophy of Wotansvolk, and the resulting creed was then exported back to the areas of origin. Sweden has so far been the Scandinavian country most receptive to Wotansvolk ideas, with five known Wotansvolk kindreds, as compared to Denmark (four), Norway (three), Finland (one), and Iceland (one).

In Swedish society there has long been a tension between pride in the Norse heritage and the ideological sentiments produced by the Lutheran state church, which claims the superiority of Christianity. Students in primary school are introduced to Viking art, customs, and adventures, but also learn how Christianity came to benefit an uncivilized Norse culture lost in pagan superstition. Rock art and rune stones are still found dotted throughout the landscape, but children do not really learn how to read runes. Although enforced by the state, the Christianization of Sweden was at best uneven. In certain local areas, pagan beliefs and customs survived well into the seventeenth century and continued to influence the folklore of popular culture. Among colonized native peoples, such as the northern Saami (derogatorily called Lapps), pagan traditions to some extent have survived up to the present. A process of secularization began in the eighteenth century and escalated in the twentieth. Today, Sweden is one of the least Christian of all nominal Christian countries. In 1999 a survey reported that only one out of ten Swedes believe in Jesus as savior and lord (Österberg 1999). In the year 2000 the church and state finally separated.

Much like the völkisch milieu in Germany, Swedish national romanticism merged with alternative religions, Nordic ideals, nudism, solar worship, and Norse elements into a multifaceted pagan revival in the late nineteenth and early twentieth century, then faded back into obscurity. With the leftist wave of the late 1960s emerged a renewed interest in alternative religions. Among the new religious movements that since then have had an increasing effect on Swedish society are also a number of groups attempting to revive pre-Christian Norse religion. Most heathen networks in Sweden—such as Yggdrasil, Ratatosk, Breidablikk, Sveriges Asatrosamfund (Asatrú Association of Sweden),

Samfälligheten för Nordisk Sed (Norse Tradition Community), Frökulten (Cult of Frey), and Nordiska Ringen (Nordic Ring) — are either antiracist or ethnic in orientation.[65] The 1990s saw a surge of pagan spirituality and a growing popular interest in pre-Christian Norse culture, reflected in numerous well-visited and sometimes publicly sponsored arrangements such as Viking days, Viking weeks, Viking workshops, rune seminars, Viking art exhibitions, Viking villages, and reproductions of Viking long boats. In 2000 Samfälligheten för Nordisk Sed became the first legally recognized Asatrú community in Sweden since Christianization of the country.

Outside the mainstream, Swedish activists involved with the racist scene have long used Norse symbols to further their cause, whether of Swedish ultranationalist or race nationalist orientation. The fact that Swedish ultranationalists appropriate runes and other Norse symbols might appear contradictory and ahistorical, as neither Sweden nor Swedes existed during the Viking Age, but is in fact a good illustration of how mythical dimension inherent in nationalism works to project the imagined "nation" back into legendary times. In the mental universe of an ultranationalist Swede, the Hammer of Thor and the Christian national banner of Sweden melt together in the mythohistory of nationalist production. Primarily, though, it is among activists involved with the pan-Aryan scene that Wotansvolk presence is most strongly felt. During the 1980s and onward, the Swedish racist landscape changed with the entrance of a new and increasingly radical generation of racist activists.[66] This is in part connected to the localization of the global white-power culture and the web of transatlantic links established between white-racist radicals, facilitated not least by the revolution in communication technology. As described by Kaplan and Weinberg (1998), transatlantic ties between fascists in Europe and America were forged by the 1920s and the 1930s through state-sponsored programs of ideological export during the regimes of Mussolini and Hitler. With the 1962 establishment of the World Union of National Socialism under the leadership of American Nazi Party leader George Lincoln Rockwell, the transatlantic flow of ideas began to reverse, and Europe became the recipient of American products, with Ku Klux Klan chapters in Germany, Sweden, the Netherlands, and the British Isles; Swedish White Aryan Resistance and Order copycats; and European chapters of the World Church of Creativity and Christian Identity churches.

The exportation of Wotansvolk is part of this process, its entrance facilitated by the reputation of the Order and its Norse heathen philosophy. Wotansvolk arrived in Sweden primarily through cyberspace and the white-power music scene. Modeled on the American Resistance concept, activists in Sweden founded the glossy white-power music fanzine *Nordland* and the record company 88 Music (later Nordland Records). *Resistance* and *Nordland* activists communicated daily by phone and e-mail, which ensured the flow of transatlantic ideas. At the time, George Burdi Hawthorne was engaged to Katja Lane's oldest daughter, Kacy, and they lived together in his residence in Windsor, Canada. That the Wotansvolk and 14 Word Press projects would be advertised in Sweden through the *Resistance–Nordland* axis was therefore hardly surprising.[67] *Resistance* was "clearly instrumental" in promoting Wotansvolk, running ads, featuring articles on Odinist white-power bands, and inviting as contributing writers Katja and David Lane and Odinist Order members Frank Silva and Richard Scutari.[68] *Nordland* had already published an article by David Lane in August 1995. In issue number 6, *Nordland* sported the headline "88 pages for the 14 words" on the cover and carried a lengthy feature on David Lane and Wotansvolk.[69] Nordland continued to carry articles by David Lane, translations from Wotansvolk publications, Wotansvolk ads, articles on the Order, interviews with Odinist bands, and references to the 14 words.[70]

Another white-power fanzine featuring Wotansvolk was the reorganized *Blod och Ära* (Blood and Honor), which ran Wotansvolk on the cover of their first issue in 1997. Swedish white-power bands soon picked up Wotansvolk themes, hailing Mathews, Lane, berserkr rage, and revolutionary Odinism. Hatecore band Heysel, for instance, put music to David Lane's lyrics in the "Black-Bannered Legion" on their *Motstånd* (Resistance) album.

> Black is the color of midnight
> Which the tyrant shall learn to dread
> As we honor our fallen martyrs
> With steel and fire and lead.

McVan's *Creed of Iron* and *Temple of Wotan* and Lane's *Deceived, Damned, and Defiant* galvanized waves of interest among Swedish race radicals. A number of Swedish racist heathen groups, such as the Svensk Hednisk Front (Swedish Heathen Front) (SHF), began promoting Wotansvolk. The E-zine *Kvasir* of the Allgermanische Heidnische Front, the nationalist international that SHF belonged to, featured a selection of articles by Ron McVan and David Lane on their Web site.[71] In December 1999 Wotansvolk/Sweden was officially established after an agreement between the Wotansvolk headquarters and former Identity pastor Magnus Söderman (Söderman 2000).

Born in 1977 to an ordinary middle-class family in Stockholm, Söderman got involved with the skinhead scene at age fourteen. Attracted to national socialist philosophy as presented to him by older skinheads, Söderman first adopted the Swedish ultranationalist ideology of Sverigedemokraterna (Swedish Democrats). Finding the Swedish Democrats too compromising, Söderman soon graduated to the revolutionary race-nationalist position developed by Vitt Ariskt Motstånd (White Aryan Resistance), among others. Recruited by the national socialist Riksfronten (Reich's Front) as its Stockholm vice commander, Söderman eventually relocated to its headquarters in Fagersta to join its national staff. As in the United States, the Swedish racist landscape is populated by minuscule and self-imploding organizations, and Riksfronten, being no exception, soon died out, leaving Söderman "alone, without any organized structure to lean on" (Söderman 2000). Like many modern seekers, Söderman began browsing the Internet, searching for something to believe in. Having a Nordic heritage, he was initially attracted to Wotansvolk but found their Jungian rationale almost incomprehensible. "I thought that Odinism was simple, like what they taught us in school about Vikings believing in Thor and Odin as physical gods and Valhalla as a physical location, but Wotanism proved too deep for me at that time."

Logging on to the Aryan Nations homepage, Söderman observed the poor quality of its Swedish translations. He contacted Aryan Nations's headquarters, and lieutenant Gruidl responded favorably to his offer to improve the articles in Swedish. While translating AN material, Söderman began to feel that Identity made sense. "I was already convinced that Jews were evil but couldn't figure out why. AN pointed me to John 8:44, and there it was: the Jews were the spawn of Satan." Reading up on Identity theology, Söderman launched a series of dysfunctional Identity forums: Aryan Nations/Sweden, Jesu Kristi Kristna Kyrka (Church of Jesus Christ, Christian), Kristna Nationskyrkan (Christian National Church), and Studiesällskapet Kristen Renässans (Christian Renaissance Study Association), all operating mainly in cyberspace. Disappointed, Söderman eventually concluded that not only were Swedes generally indifferent to Christianity, most racist activists held Christianity in contempt and dismissed Christian Identity as a weird American thing of no relevance to Swedish realities. In the meantime, Söderman plunged deeper into Identity theology, discovering, he says, a multitude of contradictions. Advised by pen pal Bruce Pierce (of the Order) to ignore inconsistencies, Söderman became more deeply dissatisfied. "Too many things in Identity didn't make sense, and I could only store those in a locker for so long." The straw that broke the camel's back came with a visit from members of Aryan Nations/Slovakia. Although they stayed in Söderman's home, the visitors developed contacts with an Identity Christian splinter group in Fagersta and sided against him, reporting him unfavorably to Aryan Nations headquarters in Idaho. Disgusted with such "unchristian ethics," Söderman abandoned Identity, again finding himself alone.

Being a seeker, Söderman was soon on to something new, again finding his mission in the United States through cyberspace. Reading up on the material he ordered from the 14 Word Press and corresponding with Katja Lane by e-mail, Söderman "responded to the calling of the blood" and is now back at his keyboard, posting translated articles by McVan and Lane on-line. Reflecting on his sudden shift from Identity to Odinism, Söderman (2000) borrows an argument from David Lane, saying that there are essential similarities between Aryan Christianity and paganism, both sharing common roots in ancient Aryan mystery religions. Compared with Identity, though, Odinism stands a far better chance of taking hold in the Swedish racist milieu, Söderman believes, and he expresses relief in not having to rely on the Bible as the unaltered word of God. "There is no absolute, dogmatic truth in Odinism. Instead, you need to find out the truth by yourself. It'll grow from within, through your own contact with the gods of the blood." Moreover, the Bible forbade Söderman to have any contact with heathens and atheists, but through the 14 Word Press, he can "get back on the NS scene, cooperating with anybody anywhere who fights for the 14 words."

Söderman hopes that Odinism will be a three-step rocket. First, he will concentrate on translating Wotansvolk material, posting it free on the Web, ready for use by any Odinist kindred out there. In the long run, Söderman hopes to establish an Odinist commune, along the lines drawn by Jost. These preliminary steps are taken in the wider context of an envisioned Aryan revolution.

> Swedish society is becoming more and more materialistic. What we've got is a watered down New Age spirituality and an effeminate Christianity that teaches about this God of Absolute Love who has put us in a world governed by the stern laws of nature. That's a contradiction that will grow increasingly acute, making people wanna return to the laws of nature. It'll be like in Germany. Hitler was a catalyst for an awakening people. . . . The force of redemption will emerge out of the collective unconscious. We, here in the Nordic countries, have this special, pure quality deep down within us. We have a great chance to wake up our dormant warrior spirit. But I think it needs to get worse before it'll happen. A majority of Swedes are confined as it is today. But when it gets worse, then this mysterious thing will reawaken from within. History has proven it. Ordinary housewives will be Valkyries and scholars will be warlords. We will fight again and we will win. (Söderman 2000)

Time will prove to what extent Wotansvolk will succeed in establishing a permanent presence among Swedish race radicals and what role Odinism will play in the militant racist milieu of Scandinavia.

The notion of Odinism as a pan-Aryan religion has moved McVan to embrace all pre-Christian European creeds as genuine expressions of the Aryan folk soul, much to the consternation of Asatrú purists who shun any incorporation of non-Nordic elements.[72] The reluctance of adherents of the ethnic wing of the Asatrú triangle to include elements from pagan traditions outside northern Europe caused an emotional Katja Lane to charge them with "being the evil prejudiced racists they accuse us of being."[73] Most spokespersons of the ethnic position express abhorrence with the racist militancy of Wotansvolk, which they consider negative and too political, charging them with espousing a totalitarian creed fundamentally alien to the libertarian attitude inherent in the Norse psyche.

Robert Ward, Goði of Úlfhethnar Kindred. Sacramento, California. Promotional photo.
Courtesy of C.A.W.

Jack Mohr.

Ernst Zündel. Samisdat/Zündel House. Toronto, Canada. Photo by author.

Goði Max Hyatt of Wodan's Kindred. Qualicum Beach, B.C., Canada. Photo by author.

Michael Moynihan (r.) and Robert N. Taylor, Tribe of the Wulfings. Courtesy of Gerlinda.

Cathy Clinton of Frigg's Web and Wotan's Kindred, and Reinhold Clinton of Wotan's Kindred and Warriors Guild. Camas, Washington. Photo by author.

Goði Robert N. Taylor of Tribe of the Wulfings. Washington Island, Wisconsin. Photo by author.

Else Christensen of the Odinist Fellowship. Vancouver Island, B.C., Canada. Photo by author.

Young Aryan warrior. Photo by author.

World Church of the Creator, Labor Day camp. Superior, Montana. Photo by author.

Katja Lane of Wotansvolk by Wotan Pole. St. Maries, Idaho. Photo by author.

Richard G. Butler, Chuck Tate, and Gerald Gruidl (l. to r.) of the Church of Jesus Christ, Christian/Aryan Nations. Hayden Lake, Idaho. Photo by author.

World Tree Publications tent. Mr. and Mrs. Murray.

Naming ritual by Goði Kirby Wise. Warrior's Grove, Arizona. Courtesy of Berga Figard.

David Lane of Wotansvolk. Florence, Colorado. Photo by author.

William Pierce of National Alliance. Hillsboro, West Virginia. Photo by author.

Goði Valgard Murray of the Asatrú Alliance at a midwinter blot. Roosevelt Lake, Arizona. Photo by author.

Stephen McNallen of the Asatrú Folk Assembly. Grass Valley, California. Photo by author.

Wyatt Kaldenberg of the Pagan Revival/White Aryan Resistance. Fallbrook, California. Photo by author.

Ceremonial offering to Skadi, Úlfhethnar Kindred. Sacramento, California. Courtesy of Robert Ward.

Swastika Lighting Ceremony. Courtesy of Katja Lane.

Richard G. Butler of the Church of Jesus Christ, Christian/Aryan Nations. Hayden Lake, Idaho. Photo by author.

Ron McVan at Wotansvolk headquarters. St. Maries, Idaho. Photo by author.

Kemp's Kindred, FCI prison, Sheridan, Oregon. Courtesy of Richard Kemp.

Edred Thorsson [Stephen Flowers], of the Rune Guild and Order of Trapezoid/Temple of Set. Austin, Texas. Photo by Jim Battles, © 2000.

Christina and Nathan Zorn Pett of Fenris Wolf and the White Order of Thule. Whidbey Island, Washington. Photo by author.

Ethnic Asatrú

Searching for an understanding of Norse paganism that would keep it folkish and "ancestral based" without falling into the trap of negative racism, the cultural underground has evolved a third position between antiracism and militant racism. Attempting to get beyond the race issue, adherents define Asatrú as an ethnic religion, native to northern Europe and therefore natural to Americans of northern European ancestry. The notion of an organic relation between ethnicity and religion obviously implies the assumption that genetics somehow determine mentality, ethos, and ethics. Accordingly, although they take exception to racism, ethnic Asatrúers share fundamental presuppositions with racist paganism. This unresolved element of philosophical ambiguity has left ethnocentric Asatrú open to criticism from both antiracist and racist pagans. Simultaneously being denounced as racists and race traitors, ethnocentric Asatrúers argue that they are neither, insisting that partisans should leave their politics out of pagan activities.

Reflecting efforts to retribalize Americans of northern European ancestry, the world of ethnic Asatrú is organizationally dominated by independent kindreds of Norse pagans. Typically, a kindred is thought of as an extended family and consists of initiated Asatrúers from a given local area that band together for ceremonies, studies, and pagan solidarity. In 1999 there were at least a hundred ethnically oriented kindreds dotted across the United States. Many, but not all, kindreds belong to some network of sovereign tribes, such as the Asatrú Alliance or the Odinic Rite, of which the former is the largest and the oldest.[1] An individual Asatrúer can become a member of a tribal network only through membership in a kindred belonging to an alliance. A number of other pagan associations, such as the Asatrú Folk Assembly, do provide for individual membership. Despite the tribal ideal, however, there seems to be a vast category of Norse heathens who remain unorganized and worship the gods and goddesses alone.

During the past few years, the number of Asatrú forums operating in cyber-space has exploded, presenting an increasingly popular way for individual hea-thens to link up with fellow pagans. Information about Norse history, rituals, mythology, ethos, and magic is readily available at no cost, and there are also quite a few Asatrú chat groups to join for discussions. Individual heathens may accordingly be connected with the larger Asatrú community without actually meeting any fellow pagans other than in cyberspace. While obviously advan-tageous to the growth of Vinland Asatrú, the Internet may also be possibly troublesome to Asatrú as a religion of social practice. Asatrú Alliance chieftain Valgard Murray (1996) expresses concern about the fact that many who "re-turn to their ancestral religion don't wish to join or found kindreds." Murray stresses that Asatrúers need to "rebuild our ancestral tribes" to "regain" native freedom and survive the approaching apocalypse. "The Asatrú Kindred is the foundation for the new Asatrú Nation, and as such is the testing ground for the new tribes of our Folk. In the near future, the Kindred will prove to be the living entity that will survive the onslaught of Raganrok" (ibid.). There are four primary approaches for rebuilding heathen tribes, represented by four seminal Norse American pagans.

Stephen McNallen and the Asatrú Folk Assembly

Stephen McNallen was born in 1948 to a Roman Catholic family in rural Brecken-ridge, Texas. As a college freshman, McNallen came across a book about the Vikings while looking for books on Wicca and the occult. Finding the freedom-loving Vikings morally superior to the Christian monks they fought in the novel, McNallen (1996) read what he could find on Norse paganism and got "hooked by the spirit of the North." In 1969–70 McNallen founded the Viking Brotherhood.[2] Initially, the Brotherhood was not really religious but geared more toward the warrior "ideals of courage, honor, and freedom," McNallen recalls. "Having been raised a Roman Catholic and taught that there is only one God, it was quite a conceptual leap for me to realize that you actually can choose to follow a poly-theist pantheon." Evolving into pagan spirituality, McNallen began publishing the *Runestone* in the winter of 1971–72, which he sent to eleven subscribers he had found through his advertisement in *Fate* magazine. McNallen stresses that his first attraction to Norse paganism had nothing to do with racial politics. "The racial or ethnic end of it was not immediately apparent to me. I think many people first get involved in racial politics, and then later decide that maybe Odin-ism or Asatrú attracts them. With me, it was quite the reverse as I was attracted to the religion first, simply for its own value, and it was only later, that I began to realize that there's an inherent connection between one's ethnicity and the religion that they follow." At the outset, McNallen had no name for his belief, referring in his first texts to the "Norse religion." Influenced by Else Christensen, he then adopted the term *Odinism* before finding a reference to *Asatrú* in a book on pre-Christian Norse culture—he became the first to introduce the concept to the Vinland pagan community.

Shortly after his modest beginning, McNallen enrolled in the army, volunteered for Vietnam, and was sent to Germany where he served for the remainder of his four-year commitment. Although he rebelled against the army's "authoritarian stupidity," the military experience set McNallen on the path of the warrior. Reflecting the sentiments in American mainstream war culture that contributed to the construction of the paramilitary hero, McNallen (1996) stressed the "essence of the warrior" as a "spiritual discipline" beyond mindless military regimentation. The spiritual warrior should not be confused with "your nonviolent warriors, your peaceful warrior, your rainbow warrior, and all that crap." Rather, the way of the warrior is an "art" that "integrates the spiritual aspects with the real-world warrior situations," a way of living and dying with honor. Returning from the army, McNallen in 1976 transformed the Viking Brotherhood into the Asatrú Free Assembly. He began composing seasonal blots and produced a number of booklets that still circulate the pagan scene. Keeping a storefront Norse cultural center, McNallen published *Runestone*, initiated guild formations (such as the Warrior Guild and Mead Brewing Guild), and traveled the country, lecturing at pagan gatherings and conducting public blot ceremonies. Although aiming at organizing kindreds, the AFA remained centered around McNallen and his then partner Maddy Hutter. With the growth in membership came more tasks to attend to and more internal conflicts to handle, not least with an "unwanted fascist element" that "mistook" Asatrú for racial politics.

In 1987 McNallen was burned out, dissolved the AFA, and relocated to northern California. Getting involved in military journalism, McNallen began writing for *Soldier of Fortune*. For several years, McNallen traveled in Asia, South Africa, and eastern Europe, interviewing guerilla groups fighting in Burma, Tibet, Angola, and Bosnia. His experiences reinforced his folkish separatist or ethnonationalist worldview. The military ethos remains a key feature in McNallen's view (1996) on the difference between Asatrú, neopaganism, and the wider New Age scene. "Your typical Wiccan, your typical neopagan, tends to be a person who is more into what I would call the soft virtues, the virtues of cooperation and kindness and being mellow. I find that my kind of Asatrú attracts a different kind of person who is more attracted to what I call the hard virtues—courage, honor, guts, endurance and control." McNallen's fascination with warrior ethics is expressed in *Wolf Age*, a quarterly published by the Warrior's Guild of the AFA and described by McNallen as a "poor man's version of *Soldier of Fortune*," dedicated to the modern warrior who follows the path of the Norsemen.

After extensive traveling, McNallen got back to the pagan scene in the mid-1990s. Appalled by finding it populated with "liberals, affirmative-action Asatrúers, black goðar, and New Agers," McNallen (1996) and his new partner, Sheila Edlund (1996), decided to reestablish the AFA, now renamed the Asatrú Folk Assembly to emphasize the folkish aspect of the northern way. With headquarters in Grass Valley, northern California, the AFA retains much of the old organizational structure, primarily providing for individual members, and, to a lesser extent, kindreds. In 2000, six kindreds were affiliated with the AFA.[3] In 1999 the AFA bought land in the higher Sierras of northern California. Modeled on the Ananda intentional yoga community in northern California, the AFA's intention is to balance private autonomy with community projects. The land provides a place to gather the tribes and has community gardens and places of worship. Plans for building a hof, a conference center, and AFA offices have been made, but residences will be on private land close to the area.[4] In addition to the AFA, Stephen and Sheila also run the local Calasa Kindred, which is affiliated with the Asatrú Alliance, a network of independent tribes.

Valgard Murray and the Asatrú Alliance

Among the kindreds affiliated with AFA in its first incarnation were the Arizona Kindred, headed by Valgard (Michael J.) Murrary, and the Wulfing Kindred, headed by Robert N. Taylor. In the wake of the AFA dissolution, Murray and Taylor launched the Asatrú Alliance as its successor. Born in 1950 in Iowa to a farming family, Murray moved to Arizona and became an electrical engineer. Active in the national socialist wing of the radical right, Murray in the late 1960s learned about Odinism through Elton Hall, then Arizona organizer of the American Nazi Party. Initially studying the works of A. Rud Mills, the Australian Odinist and racial mystic, Murray and Hall formed a kindred and made contact with Else Christensen in the early 1970s. In 1976 Murray's Arizona Kindred became the first kindred certified as such by the Odinist Fellowship, which until then only had had individual members (Murray 1997; Hall 1996). Embracing Odin as a racial archetype, Murray got involved with the Odinist Fellowship and worked his way up the hierarchy, eventually serving as its vice president.

In time Murray (1997) came to see the gods and goddesses as "superhuman deities," existing not only within people of northern European ancestry but also independent of man, in the "astral plane of Asgård," and he left behind the "essentially atheistic or agnostic perspective of the Odinist Fellowship." In 1984 the Arizona Kindred chose to affiliate instead with McNallen and his AFA. When the latter dissolved, Murray and Wulfing Kindred goði Taylor took the lead in forming a new network, the Asatrú Alliance, inviting folkish Asatrú kindreds to a formational Althing in 1988. Some seventy pagans from seven kindreds attended the Althing, ratified a set of bylaws, and elected Murray as its Allsherjargoði, a goði of goðar, or first among equals. The Asatrú magazine Vor Trú, founded in 1977 by pagan veteran Thórsteinn Thórarinsson, became the official publication of the new Alliance with Murray and Taylor as editors.[5] The Asatrú Alliance is not a conventional organization but an association of kindreds that cooperates in fields of mutual interest, primarily to promote folkish Asatrú, but otherwise retaining local autonomy. Reflecting the perception of the ancient "tribal democracy" of pagan Iceland and Scandinavia, the sovereign tribes convene to discuss issues of common concern at the yearly Althing, which is the highest authority of the Asatrú nation.[6]

In 2000 the Asatrú Alliance called itself the "largest Asatrú group in the world," claiming to boost more than fifty affiliated kindreds, in nineteen U.S. states and Canada.[7] The AA differentiates its affiliates according to recognized rank into full (official), prospective (formational), and "hangaround" kindreds.[8] The organizational structure thus resembles outlaw biker gangs, which perhaps is not too coincidental, as Murray has a past as spokesperson of the Arizona-based national socialist outlaw brotherhood Iron Cross MC. Built from the ground up, the AA offers information, advice, and material whenever a group of local pagans declares an interest in forming a kindred. When a formational local tribe coalesces, it might request recognition as a prospective affiliate with the AA, declaring its intent to uphold the AA bylaws. After having proven themselves worthy through consistent pagan practice and by reflecting in their lives the nine noble virtues of Asatrú, a prospective kindred may after a few years of existence send delegates to the Althing and apply for recognition as an official AA kindred (Murray 1996; Murray 1997). While each kindred is urged to incorporate as an official nonprofit church and to seek tax exemption, the AA itself is not incorporated. It does not have a board of directors, does not provide for individual members, and does not charge dues.

Building on international contacts developed as early as the 1970s, Murray expanded the AA effort overseas. Asatrú tribes sprang up in Iceland, Sweden,

Denmark, Belgium, the Netherlands, the United Kingdom, Germany, Australia, and the United States during the early 1970s. Initiated independently, these pioneering tribes quickly became aware of each other and began exchanging information. Especially important to this development was Norse sage Sveinbjörn Beinteinsen, Allsherjargoði of the Icelandic Ásatrúarfélagid (Association of Asatrúers), who came to symbolize the Asatrú revival when Iceland in 1972 became the first modern country to recognize Asatrú as a legitimate religion. When contacts evolved through travels and cyberspace, Murray was favorable to having non-American Asatrú kindreds affiliate with the AA. A brief experience with AA hangaround kindreds in Australia and New Zealand led to a revision of plans, however, in favor of an Asatrú international (Murray 1997). Instrumental to its implementation were Karen and Robert Taylor, who in 1996 traveled to the England to meet with heathens organized in the Odinic Rite (United Kingdom). When the Taylors returned with a favorable report, the AA proposed an alliance with the Odinic Rite (Taylor 1998).

In September 1997 Valgard Murray, Stephen McNallen, and Heimgest, director of the court of goðar of the Odinic Rite, United Kingdom, formally signed a document launching the International Asatrú/Odinist Alliance (IAOA), a "free association of sovereign tribes of Odin's Nation" convening every three years for an international Althing. Later, the Odinic Rite (France) and the Odinic Rite (Deutschland) also ratified the IAOA bylaws. Murray was chosen the first honorary IAOA Allsherjargoði for the three-year period (Ward 1998a; Ward 1998b; Ward 1998c). Collaborations with Beinteinsen's successor, Joermunder Hanson, for a worldwide Asatrúer Althing at the classic Thingvellir in Iceland in 2000 were terminated for unclear reasons, and the second IAOA Althing was again held in Vinland. At that gathering, Eric Hnikar Wood of the Odinic Rite (Vinland) was elected the new Allsherjargoði, and the Australian Assembly of the Elder Troth was accepted as an IAOA prospect tribe.[9] The IAOA project is hailed as the embryo of a postapocalyptic, transatlantic Asatrú national federation. In practice, however, Asatrú international has not meant too much. So far, it has served more as an illustration of the ambition to "think globally, act locally" than as an international actor.

Robert Taylor and Tribe of Wulfings

A third seminal person in the Asatrú revival is poet, artist, musician, and writer Robert N. Taylor, goði of the Washington Island, Wisconsin–based Tribe of the Wulfings. Born in Chicago in 1945 as the only son of a radio and television repairman, Taylor took the far-right views of his father a step further. Involved with white street gang the Tabor Street Dudes in fighting the notorious black gangs, Egyptian Cobras (now El Rukn) and Vice Lords, Taylor in his midteens progressed by forming Sons of Patriotism, a youth group that was involved in racial activities on the West Side of Chicago.[10] Too young to become a member of the American Nazi Party, Taylor joined the Minutemen, a clandestine, anticommunist, "last-line defense" organization founded in 1960 by multimillionaire Robert Bolivar DePugh (Taylor 1998).[11] Taylor in time became head of intelligence, responsible for gathering information about "communists" by having members infiltrating state departments, left-wing movements, and civil-rights organizations.[12] When DePugh was convicted on firearms charges and declared a federal fugitive in 1967, the Minutemen hardcore transformed into an armed underground aiming to overthrow the government. Taylor organized a guerrilla warfare training camp in the Missouri Ozarks and moved between safe houses across the country, but soon grew disenchanted. According to Taylor (1998), DePugh became increasingly paranoid and manipulative, turning the Minutemen into a small microcosm in which he was "a god determining life and death, almost forgetting about the larger world and why they were underground in the first place."

Leaving DePugh, Taylor returned to Chicago to join the dark undercurrent of the otherwise peace-and-love-oriented psychedelic hippie scene as an artist and musician, establishing with Nicholas Tesluk the folk group Changes in 1969.[13] As one of the very few nonleftist folk-music groups of the time, Changes played at a coffeehouse operated by the Process: Church of Final Judgment. An apocalyptic blend of Satanism, Gnostic Christianity, and Scientology, the Process became an urban legend rumored to engage in human sacrifice and cannibalism. Attracted by its gothic aesthetics—Process initiates sported black uniforms, black magician's capes, and swastika-like insignia—Taylor contributed his graphics to its magazine's Death issue and partook in midnight meditations but was never a member (Taylor 1990; Taylor 1996). By that time Taylor had begun to see the problems afflicting American society as mere symptoms of an underlying spiritual crisis in Western culture. Inspired by Spengler and Nietzsche, Taylor concluded that the once-heroic and Faustian Occident had reached exhaustion, as evidenced by debasing modernity, leveling egalitarianism, and otherworldly religion. Searching for a spiritual rectifier to rekindle the grand dreams of Western man, Taylor found the heathen path of his ancestors.

In 1976 Taylor and his wife, Karen, established the Northernway, which partook in the emerging pagan milieu of the Midwest. Following internal disputes, the Northernway split into Wiccan and Asatrú factions. The latter transformed into the Wulfing Kindred, joined the AFA in its first incarnation, and was later instrumental in launching the Asatrú Alliance project (Taylor 1998; "An Interview"; Jolif 1997; Tolmatsky 1997). The Taylors have organized Viking festivals on Washington Island, popular also among nonpagan tourists and local residents, many of whom belong to the island's Icelandic community. On the Taylor estate is a hörg and a wooden hof, decorated with runes and Norse symbols and inaugurated with a nocturnal blood ritual by Wulfing initiates. The Wulfings differ from conventional kindreds in that they disregard locality in favor of seeking "worthwhile people." By 1992–93, Wulfing encompassed initiates living all over the United States and decided to reorganize into a tribe. In the process, Taylor resolutely pushed off nonproductive or less-talented members to further emphasize the group's elitist orientation. By 1998, the Tribe of the Wulfings had forty-eight full members. "Our intellectual level is far higher than any other Asatrú or Odinist group I know of," Taylor (1998) announced proudly. "All of us are essentially mobile people. We can afford to travel, we get around, and the majority of our members are all creative; we've got several sculptors, we have photographers, we have musicians, we have writers, [and we] focus on bringing in such people. The Tribe of the Wulfings has in essence become one of the primary creative focal points of this movement."

Among the talented few is author, publisher, and musician Michael Moynihan, whose "industrial/apocalyptic folk" group Blood Axis has achieved international fame in the globalized, eerie subculture that revolves around art and the dark, occult, mysterious, and gothic in disdain of the modern world. Moynihan and Taylor soon collaborated in a series of joint projects, including releasing old Changes songs on the Fire of Life CD on Moynihan's Storm label and introducing Vor Trú readers to European black metal, ambient electronic, and industrial heathen bands like Enslaved, Unleashed, Burzum, or Sol Invictus. Admitting that some of the Asatrú "old guard" was concerned that too much energy was put into "bad rock music," Taylor pointed out that the tribe of the Wulfings was reaching a much-needed young generation. The first generation Asatrú godar were all in their fifties, and recruiting young, intelligent people to fill the gap between them and their children was necessary in order to build a sustainable movement, Taylor concludes. In 1999 the Tribe of the Wulfings left the Asatrú Alliance, but it remains part of ethnic Asatrú milieu as an independent tribe and cooperates with both the AA and the AFA in fields of mutual interest.[14]

Max Hyatt and Wodan's Kindred

Located on Vancouver Island, B.C., the Asatrú Alliance–affiliated Wodan's Kindred is headed by acting goði Max Hyatt. Born in 1948 to a middle-class family
in suburban Los Angeles, Hyatt joined the Navy in 1966 and was sent to combat in Vietnam. Disillusioned with the U.S. government, Hyatt decided to never
again live under its jurisdiction and migrated to Canada following his release
from service in 1971. Returning from the war on edge, Hyatt initially embraced
Satanism as a method to release his hatred. Finding it too structured and revolving around the "Black Pope," Anton Szandor LaVey, Hyatt construed his own
blend of Satanism and the teachings of Aleister Crowley into the New Order of
Alchemy, but a series of upsetting visions and "strange experiences" made him
abandon the project. Searching in vain for spiritual satisfaction, Hyatt tried Buddhism, yoga, and Baha'i for several years working for the Baha'i International
Center in Toronto.

Nine years into his unruly quest, Hyatt had yet another strange vision: when
he was driving home one day, his Firebird suddenly transformed into the head
of an old man. "I noticed that one of his eyes was missing," Hyatt (1998) recalls.
"This old man had his left eye missing, and I am sitting in the eye-socket looking
out of the eye socket driving down the road." There followed a series of visionary
experiences in which Odin approached Hyatt, convincing him his search was
over. The Allfather had guided him to follow the path of his ancestors. "I've
seen the gods so many times, so I know they exist. Odin has appeared to me
hundreds of times, at one time he spent a month in my house. It was during the
winter. He spent a month in my house, dressed in dark wanderer clothes. The
first time I saw him, I thought it was Death. Then I realized that it was Odin . . .
and I believe that the Allfather has a very special plan for me." That plan became
evident during a rune working. Meditating on the *elhaz* rune, which symbolizes
the connection between the human mind and the divine, Hyatt suddenly felt the
pressure of "two gigantic horns" being placed on his head. "I merely heard the
words, 'Priest of Odin.' And I knew at that moment that Odin had set those
horns on my head, and I felt the pressure, and I knew that Odin had chosen me
to be his priest."

Hyatt founded the Wodan's Kindred in 1991, and soon operated a storefront
Asatrú temple, a prison-outreach ministry, the Wodanesdag Press and an Internet outlet of pagan supplies.[15] Hyatt claims to have received his knowledge of
the old ways directly from the god/desses and ancestors in a series of visionary meetings and soul journeys. Traveling beyond Midgård, Hyatt reached the

abode of the ancestors and was greeted by a circle of armed men with long hair and beards and dressed like Vikings who invited him to stay in their castle.

> The first time it happened, I was standing in the shower and I was taken away and all of a sudden I was standing in the middle of a circle of men, and they were all around me, and it was a natural setting, with lots of trees and stuff, and they were dressed like maybe a thousand years ago, a typical Germanic dress a thousand years ago, and they had long hair and weapons and swords and stuff, and they were standing in a circle, and I was in the middle of the circle, and I wasn't naked, I was fully dressed in a similar clothing to them, and I had weapons and I didn't felt threatened by them, I felt befriended, and they talked to me and they took me to this place, it was like a castle, and I was there for three months and they showed me some amazing tree, an enormous tree, Yggdrasil, and it was a beautiful place, and there was no technology, except for maybe swords more like bronze or iron age, and everybody was friendly and good-looking and basically I was there to be taught how to become a priest of Odin. It was work to be done here, in Midgård. I know that I met with my ancestors, my relatives, and they taught me what to do and loaded me up with information, and I came back to do what I had to do, and I used that information to continue publishing books. (1998)

After months of schooling, Hyatt returned to earth with a revivalist mission to accomplish and has since continued to receive detailed guidance from the worlds beyond. In 1994 Wodan's Kindred joined the Asatrú Alliance, which to Hyatt (1998) is "not so much an alliance as it is a treaty not to make war." Stressing the importance of tribal sovereignty, Hyatt is concerned with the AA effort to forge international links with Norse pagans overseas. "It'll be too much infighting. We're too different. The only way it will work is if we let people be free to do their thing. As soon as we are beginning to make laws and electing people, it will fall apart. Instead of appointing people to be in charge we need to keep it a grassroot movement that grows in different ways."

Asatrú Perspectives on the Nature of Gods and Man

Whereas radically racist interpretations of Norse paganism tend to see the gods and goddesses as racial archetypes, ethnic Asatrúers in general seem to believe that the divine has an existence outside of, but also interdependent with man. "I see the gods and goddesses as superhuman individuals that work together with us [their descendants]," Murray (1997) explains. "I believe that they know about us, I believe they care about us, I believe that they interact with us. I believe that we gain strength and guidance from them, and I believe that they gain strength from us. As we grow stronger on Midgård in our devotion to our ancestors and our devotion to our ancestral gods and goddesses, that power is transmitted to the high ones, makes them stronger, and they transmit that power again back to us."

Typically, Norse pagans combine a pantheistic notion that holds nature to be sacred with a polytheistic view of a plurality of individual gods and goddesses. An underlying, all-pervasive, divine energy animates Mother Earth, the formations and forces of nature, and all living creatures, man included. Pantheistic divinity can be manifest in the condensed form of gods and goddesses, and is as such accessible for direct communication with man. The ancient mythologies depicting the colorful Norse divinities are one of several methods by which the gods and goddesses present themselves. Although such mythological figures are regarded as containing important religious truths, no Asatrúer I have met takes them as literally true. No one believes that Thor is actually a red-bearded, muscular, anthropomorphic entity wielding his hammer to crush giants of flesh and bone. Yet, the condensed manifestations of divine energy imply that each god has limits. There is no notion of an omnipotent and omnipresent god. The gods and goddesses may be present or absent, they have strengths and weaknesses, they have desires for sexual gratification and an appetite for life. They can even die. In short, the conditions of the gods and goddesses are quite similar to man's, which points to the notion of kinship between man and the divine inherent in Norse paganism. Gods and man engage in an interdependent relationship modeled on the family rather than on the paradigm of master and servant. An Asatrúer would never surrender his will to god. Man is neither the property nor the creation of god but his own master and maker. "Odin wants us to grow," McNallen (1996) explains. "He wants us to evolve, to be more like him, to expand awareness, to expand consciousness, to arise to a higher level, just as in our daily lives we want our sons and daughters to grow and to become more capable and to have more ability and more awareness. We don't want them to be our slaves. We don't want to put our sons and daughters in chains, working for us. We want them to rise above, we want them to become free, stronger, and more self-reliant."

McNallen, Murray, Taylor, and Hyatt all stress the perception that the gods and goddesses also exist within man. As McNallen (1996a) put it, "The gods and goddesses manifest in Midgård through our people, the Northfolk." The internal energies of Odin, Thor, Loki, Frey, and Freya are symbolic representations of human potentials or aspects of man's personality that need to be addressed and balanced. Connecting with inherent divine energy sets man on an evolutionary path of self-metamorphosis in an art of becoming-god. God's manlike nature is accordingly paralleled by man's godlike nature. This should not be confused with the quest of the monotheistic mystic to transcend or absolve his individuality to become one with God. "To become one with God is to die," McNallen (1998) states. Rather, the pagan mystic seeks to expand into divine consciousness without absolving his individuality. "I," Hyatt (1998) proclaims, "am a God." While this is similar to sentiments voiced by religious Satanists, the egocentric orientation within ethnic paganism is balanced by a pronounced Asatrú sense of community that places the divine Self within a collective of blood-related kin of the past, present, and future. This may, at least occasionally, imply an extended divinity that includes the whole folk. "Our people are descendants from the gods," Murray (1997) claims. "I believe very strongly that the Northern European people are a divine race."

Northern Europeans are set apart as children of Odin, an exclusive identity not shared with people of other cultures. Compared with other racialized religions, such as Christian Identity, that identify Aryans as the sole children of god, ethnic paganism differs considerably in acknowledging that other people may be divine, too. "Other races were [probably] created by their gods. The races are different and the gods are different" (Murray 1997). Pagan pluralism may be contrasted with the universal ambitions of monotheistic religions. Ethnic pagans may believe that most, if not all, of man's different gods and goddesses have a real existence and may argue that each culture should stick to their organic or native religions. Monotheists typically either reject that any god other than their own is real or define other gods as demons or as satanic, and may engage in missionary activities to "save" humanity by having them abandon their native gods in favor of the one true God. From a pagan perspective, this is commonly perceived as spiritual imperialism on behalf of a megalomaniac demiurge, and they call for defense of their sacred traditions to preserve diversity.

Ethnos Is Ethos, or Gods in the Genes: The Metagenetic Theory

Much like Wotansvolk ideologues, ethnic Asatrúers believe in organic religion as something sprung from the heart of the folk soul of a particular people. "There is a genetic link" between gods and man, Murray (1997) asserts. Engraved "in the very DNA, in every fiber of our bodies," there is a residue of "ancestral memory," a "sacred linkage" that "travels back to distant times for thousands of generations." Asatrú is accordingly not for the whole of humanity but is "the native religion of the Northern European Peoples. . . . Asatrú is our sacred birthright . . . and can only be properly understood and practiced by those who share our tribal ancestry" (Murray n.d.c). To explain the organic relationship between biology and religion, between individuals of a particular people and their gods, McNallen coined the term *metagenetics* in the early 1980s.[16] Presenting metagenetics as "a science for the next century," McNallen (1980) suggests that spirituality is hereditary, resting his case on Jungian psychology, studies suggesting a psychic link between identical twins, and the phenomena of "reincarnation memories," which he interprets as actual recollections of a distant past "carried by the DNA itself." Norse paganism is accordingly not one of several religions people may arbitrarily choose from at the religious market. "Our religion is a function of who we are, not just what we believe," McNallen (1999) emphasizes. "Asatrú is an expression of the soul of our race" (McNallen 1980). Organically linked with northern European ancestry, Asatrú would disappear forever if northern Europeans would cease to exist as a people. "Therefore, the survival and welfare of the Northern European peoples as a cultural and biological group is a religious imperative" (McNallen n.d.a).

The metagenetic theory has been widely accepted by other Asatrú spokespersons, many of whom cite Jung to substantiate their case.[17] Quoting from Jung's "Wotan" essay, the mysterious way the gods and goddesses remain alive but dormant in the ancestral reservoir of engraved spirituality is explained with a metaphor: "Archetypes are like riverbeds which dry up when the water deserts them, but which it can find again at any one time. An archetype is like an old watercourse along which the water of life has flowed for centuries, digging a deep channel for itself. The longer it has flowed in this channel, the more likely it is that sooner or later the water will return to its old bed" (189).[18] To those of Germanic descent, being an Asatrúer is thus following the path of least resistance, Edred Thorsson states in his *Book of Troth*: "These deities are like a secret code present in the very fiber of our being. Other folk carry other codes which are right for them; our code, simply and for no other reason than it is OURS, is right for us" (61). Metagenetics is considered an avenue to overcoming the scarcity of sources about historical Asatrú, as inherited knowledge makes it possible to revive Asatrú "as it is" and "as it was." "We have operated instinctively, on our intuition, our hunches, and then later we read books and we discovered that we did all the right things without knowing that they were the right things," Taylor (1998) asserts. "If all of our heathen past had been absolutely obliterated, if there wasn't a shred of evidence left of it, we would be carrying it within ourselves. And in the proper time, under the proper circumstances and conditions, it will all begin to emerge again. We can recreate everything that has been from the past, right out from within ourselves."

McNallen (1996) emphasizes that he does not consider himself a racist. Metagenetics is to him a theory celebrating human diversity and religious pluralism, purportedly having nothing to do with negative or hostile attitudes toward other races. On the contrary, McNallen reasons, it is only from understanding who you are, only from being fully in touch with the wisdom and knowledge derived from the ancestral base at the root of existence, that one can respect other traditions and relate justly with people of other cultures. With rare exceptions, most pagans involved with ethnic Asatrú repeatedly assert their unequivocal rejection of racism, taking exception to racist paganism of the Wotansvolk variety. Still, the metagenetic theory is at its core racist, if racism is defined as an ideology that asserts that members of a specific race "by nature" share not only racially distinct physical but also mental features. The principal difference in militantly racist paganism is, at the theoretical level, merely conceptual.

When Wotansvolk ideologues talk about Asatrú as an expression of the Aryan soul, they use an inclusive definition of a unified white race in line with the reasoning behind the construction of one monolithic white race. Spokespersons of ethnic Asatrú revert to pre–World War II theories that distinguished between several white races (e.g., the Nordic, Alpine, and Mediterranean races), although ethnicity has come to stand in for race. In the ethnic pagan system of classification, humanity is divided into a multitude of genetically distinct folk groups whose different moral and spiritual characteristics are expressed in a corresponding number of distinct folk-soul religions. To maintain a religion, a culture, and a way of life, one must assure "the preservation of the genetic base" (Murray 1997). Among ethnic Asatrúers, genetic mixing is thought to be an abomination, defiling the purity of the units composing the biospiritual mosaic of mankind. In modern American society, a growing body of individuals with mixed heritage challenges the theory of metagenetics by falling outside of the classificatory system. Had metagenetics been a nonracist theory, a person of mixed ethnic ancestry would have posed no problem. The blood of an individual with a Swedish mother and a Yoruba father would have carried memories both from ancient Scandinavia and western Africa, and it would thus have been appropriate to give homage to both Odin and Ogun.

Asking ethnic pagan ideologues if they thought it appropriate for persons of racially/ethnically-mixed ancestry to join a kindred should they wish to honor their Norse roots proved revealing, as it was perceived as a complicated problem.[19] "There is never any easy answers," said Reinhold Clinton (1997), goði of then AFA-affiliated Wotan's Kindred (not to be confused with Wodan's Kindred). "It's always difficult as to where do you draw the line, is it half, a quarter or what? It's really hard for all people with a mixed heritage" (ibid.). Different folk souls apparently do not blend well. Thórarinsson (1998) suggested that individuals with mixed ancestry would be "torn between the two cultures," struggling with who they really are—one needs to "find one home, spiritually, instead of saying that I am this and I am this one also." In the world of metagenetics, classificatory purity excludes the possibilities of identity-construction from a "queer" perspective.[20] There is no such thing as a white Zulu or an African Viking. Valgard Murray (1997) said that an applicant "needs to look like a white man" and explained that he usually asks forthright questions when confronted with requests from people of mixed heritage: "Do you think like a white man? Do you act like a white man?" How, then, would a man think and act distinctly white? Whiteness here is associated with mental and behavioral qualities such as trustworthiness, honesty, industriousness, nobility, honor, courage, and self-reliance—that is, exactly the virtues believed by white racists to be inherent in whiteness. If this were to think and act white, then to think and act "red," "brown," "black," or "yellow" would, at least implicitly, be characterized by a lack of these same virtues.

Edred Thorsson acknowledged the racist logic implicit in metagenetics in an essay in which he warns against explaining the "phenomenon of Asatrú" with arguments derived from "a rudimentary and primitive 19th century racial ideology" (1996 [1982], 55). While he considers metagenetics a "powerful argument," Thorsson stresses that it has implicit weaknesses in a revivalist scheme. If metagenetics is "carried to its logical conclusion," Thorsson writes, "it ends in an equation of 'racial purity' and 'divine contact.' For if we say that someone is in contact with the Germanic gods because they are mainly of Germanic descent, then we could end arguing that because someone else (anyone else) has more Germanic blood then he is automatically more in contact with these archetypes" (ibid., 57) To get beyond simplistic genetic determinism, Thorsson suggests that the biological metagenetic argument must be complemented with language and culture to form a triangular conceptual model that explains the relationship between man and spirituality. Applying this model, Thorsson (1997) states that it is not impossible for a "black person growing up in this culture to be an Asatrúer," as he "scores two out of three," and pointed out that pagan societies traditionally naturalized aliens through avenues such as blood brotherhood, marriage, and adoption. Still, Thorsson muses, the genetic conditioning of man's spirituality is such a determinant factor that he would look into every individual case very carefully before accepting a person of a non-Germanic background.

To McNallen (1996), persons of mixed or non–northern European ancestry would make a "real mistake" if they chose to follow Norse paganism.

> I think that they are sadly deceived if they try to take on my ancestors. They need to look to their own ancestral line. For me, joining any ancestral religion is not as simple as deciding you're going to join the Elks Lodge or you're going to join the local bridge club. You're not just joining something that exists right there in that moment in time. What you are really joining is something that includes a whole line of ancestors. The "we" that we see now, is just the tiny tip of the iceberg. But to take on our soul, to take on that which is an intimate part of us, is to take on all of those ancestors as well. I don't think that you can just do that arbitrarily. I can never be an American Indian. I can never be a black man. I don't want to be any of those things. I want to follow my ancestors and my way. Likewise, I would strongly encourage them to do the same.

The primacy of genetics over culture and language in the worldview of ethnic Asatrú is further highlighted if one turns it around, asking if a person of northern European descent who grew up in another culture talking that language would qualify for membership. The answer would unanimously be yes. In the words of Valgard Murray (1997): "We're not talking about political or geographical lines, we're talking about bloodlines. If you're a descendant of northern Europeans that happens to grow up in Chile, then you're still a northern European that happens to be a Chilean citizen."

Is Ethnic Asatrú a National Socialist White-Racist Hate Group?

Asatrúers of the antiracist position have condemned ethnic Asatrúers for using Asatrú as a front for racist views while claiming that it is an "exclusive 'Nordic' religion." The antiracist pagan veteran Gamlinginn indignantly argues, "No single group owns the Gods of Asgård." [21] He points out that the nine noble virtues of Asatrú are hardly Eurocentric, but universal. "Every culture that has ever existed in the world has inherently esteemed the virtues esteemed by Asatrú." Stressing that the United States has become a "multi-ethnic nation," Gamlinginn believes that as Asatrú advances, Americans of different ethnic background "inevitably" will embrace it. "Asatrú is a multi-ethnic religion—

not because that might be 'politically correct' at this point in time, but because multi-ethnicity is fundamental to the theology of Asatrú. Asgård, home of the Gods is multi-ethnic. For example, Magni and Modi, the sons of Thor, are also the sons of their mother, Jarnsaxa, who is a Jotunn. Who will tell Thor that his sons should not participate in something because they are not of 'pure' descent?"(Gamlinginn 1993). Murray dismisses the antiracist view as a completely "absurd" "redefinition" of Asatrú: "They call it heresy to state in our bylaws that 'Asatrú is the ethnic religion of the indigenous Northern European Peoples.' Did Asatrú develop from the folk souls of the black Africans, South American Indians? Only a PC type would call the truth heresy" (1993, 37). Pagan veteran and Freya's Folk gyðia Prudence Priest claims to have been "excommunicated" by McNallen when challenging the "racist policies and politics" of the Asatrú Folk Assembly.[22]

While criticized for racializing Asatrú by antiracist pagans, spokespersons of the ethnic position have been condemned as race traitors by militantly racist Asatrú/Odinists. Wotansvolk receives much correspondence from racist pagan prisoners who are disgusted with Murray's and McNallen's "soft stand on race," "cowardly PC politics," and "refusal to work for the survival of the Aryan race."[23] Since the late 1970s, McNallen has made an effort to keep militant fascists and national socialists out of the AFA, a policy adopted also by the Asatrú Alliance. The AA bylaws state that "the Alliance is apolitical; it is not a forum for, nor shall it promote any political views of the 'left' or 'right.' Our sacred temples, groves, things and moots shall remain free of any political manifestations."[24] A number of kindreds have been excluded from the alliance for violating that bylaw by flying national socialist symbols or promoting racism. Among these are Elton Hall's Jomswiking Kindred, which "bolted from the mind control by the PC clerics" in the late 1980s, "because [Murray] doesn't want a political group, and didn't want us to talk about race" and was embarrassingly "scared of the swastika."[25]

That spokespersons of ethnic Asatrú organizations repeatedly have taken exception to racism and national socialism has not prevented them from being branded "hate groups" by media and antiracist civil-rights organizations, such as the Southern Poverty Law Center and the Coalition for Human Dignity. "Asatrú Folk Assembly has at its core a leadership with known and extensive neo-Nazi connections," one article read (Newman 1998). Based on research conducted by Jonathan Mozzochi for the Coalition for Human Dignity, the article typified the AFA program as "blatantly racist." VorTrú was characterized a "white nationalist pagan publication" in an Intelligence Report article on the new generation white supremacists (SPLC 1999e, 19). Other articles call Reinhold Clinton an anti-Semitic for sponsoring a lecture by Holocaust-denier David Irving and associating with American Front skinheads, and name other Asatrúers for past national socialist activities. One article on the threat of racist Asatrú closed by citing University of Denver professor Carl Raschke saying that "a recent biological terrorism threat in New York City may have come from Asatrúers" (SPLC 1998, 16).

Based on fieldwork observations, including interviews and conversations with AA and AFA pagans and an extensive review of their publications and speeches, my conclusion is that neither organization really qualifies as a white-supremacist hate group. Although metagenetics can be analyzed as a racist theory, its adherents do not see themselves as racists. The absence of white-supremacist sentiments is reflected in ethnic pagan fields of activity, and I have found nothing to substantiate the alarmist allegation of Raschke. At pagan gatherings, people generally do not discuss the evils of ZOG or the Jew World Order, much less discuss preparations for an armed underground resistance, for an approaching race war, or for building a war chest through robberies and criminal activities. Activities instead include pagan ceremonies, sejd, drum journeys, útsittning, sauna, rune magic, studies of Norse history and folklore; old handicrafts such as weaving, mead brewing, and smith work; artwork, hunting, folk music, herbalism, healing, and Viking games. Comparisons of ritual contents between racist and ethnic pagans reveal that whereas Wotansvolk blot ceremonies always remain focused on Aryan survival and empowerment, AA or AFA blots are focused on the god/desses in season.[26]

Vor Trú publishes articles about kindred activities, Norse mythology, culture, and history, and reviews music, film, and literature of pagan interest. There are no calls to arms or plans for a secessionist Aryan nation-state. A section highlighting news and events from the universal monotheistic religions that claim they are saving the world does include reports of priests, rabbis, or imams accused of unsavory conduct, such as sexual misconduct or extortion, but is more ironic than hateful in tone.[27] A series of articles by Tribe of the Wulfings member Markus Wolff on the völkisch movement does present völkisch philosophers, heathens, and magicians in a favorable light but also points out that the national socialist regime in Germany generally "was ill-disposed to most völkisch occultism" (Wolff 1996; Wolff 1998; Wolff 1999).

Regarding Wotan's Kindred, while it is true that Reinhold Clinton brought in David Irving—in fact, he did so twice—that does not necessarily imply that Clinton is a fascist. The American Front skinheads he briefly associated with do not consider Clinton to be on their side.[28] Furthermore, nonwhites have been guests at Wotan's Kindred ceremonies, and Clinton claims to have excommunicated Ron McVan for preaching fascism and racial hatred. In an interview, Clinton (1997) said,

> National socialism and Asatrú are diametrically opposed. There are a lot of strange groups out there who would do anything to justify themselves. National socialist groups are using the Asatrú symbols to advance their task, but national socialism is against freedom, Asatrú is freedom, national socialism has a lot of dogma, Asatrú has none. National socialism is centralization and Asatrú is radically decentralized. You couldn't have any more individualistic people than in Asatrú. And if the Nazis ever got into power, the first thing they're going to do is to throw all the Asatrúers in jail. The German Nazis appropriated the Asatrú ancient symbols, like the swastika, so we can't use that now, and as far as Wotansvolk and other fringe groups go, I wish they'd just go away.

Murray, McNallen, and Thorsson all characterize national socialism as an unwanted totalitarian philosophy incompatible with freedom-loving Norse paganism. "The essence of what National Socialism was," Thorsson laid down, "was not anything Nordic or Germanic. It was a Roman Imperial idea" (1997). Murray is a card-carrying member of the Libertarian Party, and both McNallen and Thorsson share his libertarian political outlook. With regard to the political preferences among grassroots members, I have encountered anarchists, libertarians, occult fascists, and members of the National Alliance, as well as many who are politically indifferent. That ethnic paganism attracts national socialists does not make the religion as such inherently fascist, any more than its anarchist members make it an anarchist religion. The libertarian attitudes of the goðar allow members to hold any political view as long as they do not try to force their beliefs on the pagan agenda. Aryan revolutionaries attracted to Norse paganism tend to be impatient with that position and generally prefer to align themselves with the Wotansvolk project and/or to build racist kindreds of their own. This seems true also for international networking. When, for example, the Odinic Rite (United Kingdom) in the late 1990s split into racist and ethnic factions, Wotansvolk linked up with the former and the AA with the latter.[29]

The one possible exception I have found among Asatrú goðar linked with the ethnic position is Max Hyatt of the AA-affiliated Wodan's Kindred. Like Wotansvolkers, Hyatt (1998) sees "each race as an organic entity" and believes that "each race is on this planet for a purpose." He defines Asatrú as a "religion for the white race," as he finds the ethnic definition "too narrow." Yet Hyatt has chosen to align with AA and does refer to Asatrú as a northern European earth religion in his writings. Politically, Hyatt's position rings similar to the strategy endorsed by Christensen. To secure the survival of the white race, Asatrúers should remove overt racism and make sure to "appear normal" and be "beyond reproach." "There are many forces working against us. Let us use AllFather's wisdom to overcome them. Let us speak fair to them . . . laugh with them . . . lure them on" (Hyatt 1997, 17). In fact, "I have no problem with Nazism," Hyatt (1998) declared, "but we should not talk about those things publicly," as it attracts unwanted attention to no avail. "It's obvious that national socialism will never make a comeback. All that energy is being wasted. When I meet [national socialist activists] I used to say, 'Hey, why don't you come to our meeting.' "

He singles out Jewish people as the special enemy to the white race, cleverly enticing unknowing whites to support their scheme of world dominion. Through Christianity, the Jews "have the white race sending energy to Jehovah, to Yahweh. The Jewish God! The ancestral god of the Jewish race! He's not the all-powerful god that Christianity wants to portray him as, he's just a Jewish God," Hyatt (1998) ardently exclaimed. "The Jews are our enemies [but] they don't know when to quit. They won't stop, they just want more and more and more and that's gonna help bring about Ragnarök actually. One of the mechanisms, the catalyst, that will make Ragnarök occur." Hyatt believes in the coming of a "gigantic Ragnarök of biblical proportions" that will "engulf the planet." Odin is gathering his people, and Hyatt is convinced that Asatrúers will affect the way Ragnarök occurs. "Odin has a plan. I am very aware of it. Valgard is aware of it. McNallen is aware of it. Odin has a plan. I've seen it. You can feel it. Sometimes [I get] specific instructions, sometimes it's very obscure." Hyatt was divinely instructed to establish a prison-outreach ministry that by 1998 reportedly catered to one thousand prisoners in the United States.[30]

> [The convicts are] Odin's army, we are Odin's goðar, and I do believe that the goðar have been raised from the dead, you can say, as Christianity killed us, and we've been dead for a thousand years, and now we have awakened and it's many of us, and I felt that these guys in the prisons, they are the army of the goðar, these are the people who will fight to the end. They don't have any qualms of cutting somebody's throats, and at some point it may come to that. I don't know if it's going to be a race war, a religious war, a political war, all of it probably, and we need people in Asatrú who are willing to kill without mercy, and these people have the experience. (1998)

Following the global cleansing, Hyatt believes, man will revert to nature. In the "future society there will be no law, just natural law. If somebody hurts you, you hurt him or her back. . . . Just get rid of all the laws and let people live their lives, and then the strong will survive and the weak will go down and what's wrong with that? That's natural."

Ethnonationalist Tribalism

Despite the official apolitical policies of AA and AFA, there are political implications to ethnic Asatrú, revolving around a call for decentralization in terms of radical localism, tribal communalism, and Jeffersonian republicanism. Ethnic Asatrú is suspicious of state bureaucracies and federal power, and it rejects cities, materialism, and consumerism. A back-to-earth environmentalism emphasizes the need for ecologically sustainable production and small-scale farming and industry, but it is generally not hostile to modern technology. Stressing family values, individual self-reliance, tribal self-sufficiency, and ethnic self-determination, ethnic paganism can be classified as ethnonationalist in orientation. Many ethnic Asatrúers would prefer a redefinition of American federalism in terms of a network of monoethnic sovereign tribes modeled on the "tribal democracy" of ancient Iceland and reflected in the present structure of the Asatrú Alliance.

Projecting the ethnonationalist ideal back into legendary times, Asatrúers portray an original golden age when free Norsemen lived in harmony with self and nature as self-sufficient farmers, hunters, and fishermen. Living on ancestral land, extended families formed tribes that developed their own unique value system and folk-soul religion that reflected the evolutionary history of the group. Authority was based on merit, and there were no states or bureaucracies, no monarchs or politicians, no oligarchs or plutocrats. With the twilight of the gods at the former Ragnarök, all this changed. With Christianity began a process of alienation that would deepen as the wolf age progressed. Tribal self-determination ended as manipulative kings forced the people to submit to the curse of the cross. To further control the people, countries were formed. The number of nonproductive state officials to feed increased. Towns and cities were established to serve the infrastructure of the kingdom. When people left their ancestral land, they lost their organic connection with their souls and the power of state, king, and church became absolute. The alien demiurge would not tolerate other gods. His priests demonized the old god/desses as satanic and enforced baptism to cut off links with the folk soul. Every form of trickery,

lies, military force, economic force, deprivation, kidnapping, coercion, brib-
ery, murder, torture, everything possible was done to smash the ancestral religion. The water in the riverbeds of the collective unconscious of the folk dried
up. The god/desses remained alive but mainly dormant, and their few followers
were forced underground. Alienated man falsely set himself apart and above
nature, exploited Mother Earth, and sought to destroy everything primal, wild,
organic, and mysterious. Body, mind, and spirit were shaped by life in artificial
urban environments. At war with himself, alienated man embraced the universal notions of religion and politics that now threaten to destroy the remnants
of every organic native culture on the face of the earth.

McNallen and Murray both foresee a dramatic change in the near future.
The wolf age is reaching its climax, and humanity is moving into the twilight
of the demiurge. McNallen (1996) emphasizes that Christianity is a relatively
recent phenomenon in the 40,000-year history he claims for the northern Europeans, who only have "been Christians for between 2 and 4 percent of their
existence. . . . There's absolutely nothing at this point to indicate that Christianity is going to be anything of any permanence. . . . There's no guarantee
that this fad out of the Middle East is necessarily going to be able to entrain
the mind and the soul of our people over the millennium." The fact that Asatrú
tribes emerged independently of each other in the United States and northern
Europe in the early 1970s signals a change in the air. "It was as if a wind was
blowing through the branches of the world tree, awakening the collective soul
of the northern peoples" (McNallen n.d.b). As a marker of their separate identity, some ethnic pagans have adopted a Norse calendar. They live in the Runic
Era, dated from the year at which they believe Odin taught his folk the runic wisdom, 250 years before Christ.[31] So, while American nationals lived in the year
2001, Odin nationals lived in the year 2251.

Murray interprets the heathen revival to mean that Odin is "gathering his
warriors" in the build-up to the approaching apocalypse. "It's time for next Ragnarök," Murray (1997) states confidently, when the cycle of the wolf age will close
and the cycle of the reawakening gods will commence. After a time of "total
separation from the God-force" and "the ancestral force," we have now reached
a point at which "those ancient links are once again glowing." By performing
blot ceremonies, heathens retune themselves with the divine realities within and
around them (Murray n.d.b). Since the relation between the realms of man and
divine is reciprocal, the rekindled ancestral spirit in man will reawaken the gods
and goddesses who will return energy that will further empower the divine, enabling us to "break the chains of the oppressors" (1997). "I very much believe in

the old prophecies that when the last day comes, when the battle of Ragnarök begins, we will have the very gods standing on our side. We will work together. We will regain our level as a folk in regards to the relations with our reawakened gods and with the very Earth herself. Once again our people will be free to worship the gods and live in harmony with nature" (ibid.).

Ethnonationalist policies have led to a pagan support of ethnic separatist and national liberation movements around the world, from Tibet and East Timor over to the Karen in Burma, Igbo in Nigeria, and Zapatistas in Chiapas, to the Boer Afrikaner, thought of as the "white tribe," in South Africa. "We are all in this together" Stephen McNallen asserts.[32] "The Saami, the Sioux, the Frisians and the Tibetans are all trying to maintain their identity. When we stand alongside any of these other native/tribal/indigenous groups we stand in opposition to a common foe." The AFA declaration of purpose reads, "The AFA supports the efforts of all cultural and biological groups to maintain their identity. . . . People of all cultures and races must stand united against the forces that would transform us into perfectly interchangeable economic units dominated by a financial or governmental elite" (McNallen n.d.a). McNallen (1996) stresses that he "will gladly stand alongside an Amazonian Indian against a nominally white multinational corporation that wants to level the rain forest. White skin alone is not enough to win my loyalty. There needs to be something a little deeper than that. . . . Now, I realize that we can't always just get along. I'm not naïve in that respect. There may be disputes, and there may be times that we even have to fight. But I think that anytime that we can cooperate, anytime that we can stand together, without sacrificing our independence, without sacrificing our essence, then let's do so." His efforts to reach out to other native cultures stands in contrast with racist pagans, who condemn McNallen for diverting energy from what should be the sole focal point. Have you noticed what he is up to recently? Katja Lane indignantly commented. "He is promoting everything BUT the Aryan cause."[33]

The ethnonationalist perspective is part of the explanation for an emergent pattern of cooperation between Asatrúers and American Indian nationalist spokespersons and religious leaders. The past few decades have witnessed an enormous wave of interest in Native American religion, shamanism, soul journeys, and vision quests. Dotted all over the country are bookstores, centers, and spiritual leaders who cater to an increasing number of urban whites who long for earth religions and alternative religious experiences. Many American Indians consider this a mixed blessing at best, and Native American purists and/or nationalists object strongly to what is perceived to be religious theft. In

1993 a pan-Indian gathering of about 500 representatives from forty different tribes organized by the U.S. and Canadian Sioux Nations issued a Declaration of War against exploitation of American Indian religion. "Whereas for too long we have suffered the unspeakable indignity of having our most precious . . . ceremonies and spiritual practices desecrated, mocked, and abused by non-Indian 'wanna-bees,' hucksters, cultists, commercial profiteers, and self-styled 'New Age shamans' and their followers," read the Declaration, "we hereby and henceforth declare war against all persons who persist in exploiting, abusing and misrepresenting [our] sacred traditions and spiritual practices."[34]

McNallen published the declaration in *Runestone* and gave the American Indians his wholehearted support. The AFA proceeded to contact American Indian groups, asking them to refer the "spiritually adrift" European Americans to them, including in the letters a brochure on Asatrú (McNallen 1995, 15). An AFA flyer distributed at New Age bookstores and centers acknowledges, "The way of the American Indian offers much to those who want to live in harmony with the Earth and their own beings."[35] However, "many Native Americans feel that you should seek out the ways of your people rather than intruding on their ways." Native Americans deserve great respect, and "one way of honoring him is to leave his religion, his spirituality, his ancestors to him . . . and to honor the call of the ancestors to return home." The seeker accustomed to American Indian spirituality would recognize many workings if he could experience indigenous European paganism: vision quests (útsittning), sweat lodges (sauna), great warriors, spirits, guardians of nature, and shamans, the epitome of which is Odin— all are part of Asatrú. "The forefathers and the foremothers . . . beckon you— to heal our people, to heal our world, and to walk again the Way of the Warrior and the Wise One. They call you home."[36] McNallen (1996) claims a positive response, saying that it was the beginning of a series of "diplomatic relations" with American Indian tribal and religious leaders, including *God is Red* author Vine Deloria.

Similarly, Murray (1997) states, "The religion and the cultural sovereignty of the American Indians is on a constant assault. There are so many whites that stick their noses into their culture, debasing their sovereignty, and take on their sacred traditions." Living in the Southwest where Native American and European American cultures coexist, Murray has engaged in discussions with tribal elders among the Sioux, the Apache, the Hopi, and the Navaho Nations. "And I am respected," Murray emphasizes proudly. "I am considered by some of their medicine men to be a holy man, a medicine man, a shaman of my people, just as they are considered to be a holy man, a medicine man, or a shaman among their people." Clearly, Murray states, the American Indian would have been better off if every white man had been a Eurocentric pagan, if more Eurotribes were formed that could develop parallel relationships with the other indigenous tribes that inhabit the Southwest. Asatrúers show that "all white people are not out to steal their culture, rip it off, and subjugate them, that we respect them and that the relationship is one of sovereign peoples, working together to restore the land, live in harmony with each other, and yet still remain [independent] and having separate identities."

The Kennewick Man controversy demonstrated the readiness of the Asatrú tribes not to compromise what they consider to be of vital interest to their ethno-nationalist quest. After three years, in January 2000 the AFA withdrew from the case, citing a lack of finances and a realization that they never could get justice. "In a world where the bones of Leif Erikson's men would be labeled 'Native American' there is no hope for a reasonable, logical, fair solution," McNallen contended.[37] All things considered, McNallen claimed that much had been accomplished. The case gave Asatrú more media coverage than ever before, and the ancestral spirit of the Kennewick Man was hailed with "blessings and horns raised in his memory by Northern folk. Without us, he would have only had the misplaced attentions of a stranger people who were probably his blood enemies." McNallen remained convinced that time would vindicate the Asatrú contention that "Europeans were in North America many thousands of years ago." Ethnic Asatrúers see themselves as the territory's indigenous people, the true "Native" Americans, and urge their kin to learn from history lest it repeats itself. "Kennewick Man is all about extinction," McNallen declared. "His people were bred or wiped out by invaders," and that "can happen to us too."[38]

"We are dying because we have been cut off from our roots," McNallen stated.[39] Reverting to the ancient god/desses and reconnecting with Mother Earth and the spirits of the land is imperative, but not sufficient, to heal the wound and ensure ethnic survival. "We need to be in a position that to where our people will have a refuge" (1999b) McNallen explained. A religious revival is not enough. Time has come for the next step in the Asatrú (r)evolution. Northern-folk need to form tribal communities, to recreate the social context in which Asatrú once existed, "by building the self-help systems that will be the lifeblood of the future tribes" (ibid.). Asatrúers should strive for self-sufficiency by providing medical service, welfare, employment, legal assistance, education, and security to their own (McNallen 1999b). The latter should not be read as if ethnic Asatrúers plan to form their own armies or engage in terrorist activities. Rather, it signals that activists claim the right of self-defense. McNallen invoked the High One to defend the right to bear and keep arms, citing *Hávamál*.

A wayfarer should not walk unarmed
But have his weapons to hand
He never knows when he may need a spear
Or what menace meet on the road (stanza 38)

"I believe that no man or woman who surrenders his or her gun to the government will ever look on the faces of the blessed in Valhalla. Surrender your 'assault rifle,' and be doomed to the cold and murk of Hel's home; you have no place among heroes" (McNallen 1996b).

While McNallen opposes the construction of a global monoculture and the American melting pot by promoting ethnic separatism and cultural diversity, it is also evident that, from his point of view, other ethnics better be separate somewhere else and not claim independence on territory considered entitled to Northernfolk. Alarmed by activities of radical Chicano separatists who want to establish an independent Aztlán Nation out of what is now California and the Southwest, McNallen believes that California soon will be a battleground. "The spiritual descendants of the Aztec are looking northward," and Euro-Americans will either resign to a subordinate position or rise from their slumber to resist the conquest.[40] McNallen suggests that accumulating ethnic tension is a reflection of deeper movements in the collective unconsciousness of Chicanos and northern Europeans. While admitting that the great majority of Mexican descendants are Christian, McNallen uses Jung to explain that the "old Aztec and Mayan deities never really went away, they simply went underground."[41] What if Jung's analysis of the rise of national socialism as a manifestation of the Wotan archetype in the Germanic soul is applied to explain the emergent Hispanic nationalist scene? "Are Tonatzin and Tezcatlipoca moving among their folk, stirring them to conquest?" And who should better lead Euro-American resistance than their own archetypal deities? "Mighty psychic forces, and powerful religious impulses, are on the move. The old Gods of Mexico, and the Gods of ancient Europe, are stirring their respective peoples."[42] The spiritual "awakening" of the northern European folk is vital to accomplish lest they would follow Kennewick Man into obliteration. "Some like the number 88," McNallen wrote. "Some like 14, as in '14 words.' I like it shorter . . . eight words: 'The existence of my people is not negotiable.'"[43]

CHAPTER SEVEN

Hail Loki! Hail Satan! Hail Hitler!

Darkside Asatrú, Satanism, and Occult National Socialism

E dred Thorsson (1997), referring to having been forced out of the Ring
of Troth when his engagement in the Satanic Temple of Set was
"exposed," argues that his heathen detractors acted as crypto-
Christians, fearing the same primal forces that a pastor would be
frightened of. There is, Thorsson reasons, a darker side to Norse paganism that
makes it compatible with elements of Satanism. Thorsson is hardly alone in
merging Norse paganism with religious Satanism. Max Hyatt, Wyatt Kaldenberg, Michael Moynihan, Robert Ward, and Robert Taylor all are or have been
involved with the misty underworld where Asatrú meets Satanism and occult
fascism. Expressed through art, myth, philosophy, and music revolving around
the primal, sinister, and arcane, this emerging scene has its own elitist stars
who, much like the subculture itself, seem intentionally evasive and mysterious. Nurturing an aura of mystique and ambivalence that sets them apart and
above the despised herd mentality of modern man, many seminal leaders of the
Asatrú/Satanic underworld project different faces, mix seriousness with pose,
and use smoke screens and distorting mirrors to enact a Nietzschean masquerade. "One wishes to be understood and one also wishes not to be understood"
(Nietzsche 1974 [1882], sec. 381). During the late 1990s, racist Satanists and
darkside heathens have made a discernible imprint on the Aryan revolutionary counterculture, much to the consternation of national socialist–oriented
pagans and Christians.

Satanism Today

Satanism is not a monolithic worldview but rather a collective term that encom-
passes different outlooks and ideologies with conflicting notions about what
Satan is and Satanism means. A useful distinction to be introduced is the one be-

tween Satanism and devil worship. The religious Satanists to be discussed here have little to nothing to do with worshippers of the Christian devil. Few Satanists would acknowledge as relevant the Christian notion of a conflict between embodiments of metaphysical good and evil. Generally, Satanists set themselves beyond good and evil. No entity, thought, act, or symbol is good or evil as such but becomes one or the other depending on context and perspective. An urge to challenge conventional morality might express itself in imagery or behavior associated with evil, but these are typically employed for their shock value or as antinomian methods to set oneself apart from the "limitations" of prevailing morality and normative mainstream culture. If a Satanist describes someone as "really evil," it is generally a compliment. Obviously, this means that it is "good" to be "evil," which illustrates how the meaning of the concept might be undermined in the satanic discourse. Satanism, moreover, is egocentric, not theocentric. A Satanist is not concerned with the will of god but his own will. The generic Satanist in theory would not acknowledge any power in the universe higher than his or her own ego and accordingly would submit to no entity, neither god nor devil.[1] If there is a god in the satanic universe, this would be the elevated ego, sometimes identified with Satan as an archetypical individuated Self.

Some embrace Satanism as a fashion only, while for others Satanism represents a religious path. This distinction is of special relevance in the subcultures of industrial noise and black metal. With black metal's predominantly "satanic" style, metalheads may, for instance, learn to project all the right trappings without attaching any deeper religious meanings to them. This should not be understood as a difference between "posers," "fakes," or "hobbyists" and those who are "true," "real," or "serious" — in (post)modern American society, religion can be an entertaining hobby, while fashion can be serious indeed. The difference is rather between those who take on the satanic style kit without ever practicing satanic magic or believing its philosophy and those who do, whether or not they also adopt the style kit.

Excluding devil worshippers and fashion Satanists, religious Satanism further divides into a typology of three primary, identifiable subcategories: (1) Satanism as a religion of nature; (2) Satanism as initiatory elitism; and (3) Satanism as Eurocentric heathendom.

Satanism as a Religion of Nature

The Church of Satan was founded on Walpurgisnacht (30 April), 1966, by the "Black Pope," Anton Szandor LaVey at his black-painted, Victorian house in San

Francisco.[2] Photogenic in his black robes, smart suits, shaved head, Mephisto-phelean beard, and with topless witches and a Nubian lion at his feet, the high priest of Satan and Exarch of Hell came to personify Satanism to the American public.[3]

Born Howard Stanton Levey to a predominantly Jewish family, LaVey in-vented himself and his colorful background to an extent that makes it difficult to separate fact from fiction. He claimed a Romanian Gypsy ancestry, recalling how his grandmother enriched his childhood with Transylvanian folklore and tales of Dracula, vampires, witches, and werewolves. Before establishing the Church of Satan, LaVey claimed, he had at age fifteen, played oboe with the San Fran-cisco Ballet Orchestra, then worked as a lion tamer for the Clyde Beatty Circus, a carnival organist, a criminologist, a crime photographer, and a psychic inves-tigator of haunted houses. He talked about his love affair with Marilyn Monroe and his 1945 visit to postwar Germany where he supposedly got access to clas-sified Nazi films portraying ss occult rituals that he later would include in his *Satanic Rituals*. Although these claims were recycled in media reports and the au-thorized LaVey biographies by Burton Wolfe (1974) and Blanche Barton (1992), reporter Lawrence Wright was unable to confirm them when doing research for a 1991 article portraying the life of LaVey.[4] Apparently, no records could document his affiliation with any ballet orchestra, police department, criminology depart-ment, or circus, and there was no evidence to confirm his trip to Germany, his access to classified war archives, or his rendezvous with Monroe (Wright 1991).

Efforts to dismiss LaVey as a fraud by exposing his background as myth over-look a central aspect of his satanic philosophy. According to LaVey, man creates all religions, and the satanic magician may create himself as god in a universe of his own making. As suggested by Thorsson, LaVey's exciting anecdotes may be seen as part of a skillfully employed act of lesser or manipulative magic (Flowers 1997, 175), designed to captivate a willing audience used to empower himself as the ambassador of hell. To further his powers of enchantment, LaVey acted as technical advisor for a number of horror movies and played the devil in *Rose-mary's Baby*. He invited the press to satanic ceremonies featuring naked women at the altar, performed a much-publicized satanic wedding between writer John Raymond and New York socialite Judith Case, staged Topless Witches Reviews, and drove a ghost-white, coffin-nosed 1937 Cord with license plate BOM 666.

A steady stream of young people, occultists, and celebrities, including actress Jayne Mansfield and entertainer Sammy Davis Jr., made their way to LaVey. In 1969 LaVey published the *Satanic Bible*, followed by *The Complete Witch* (1971) and *Satanic Rituals* (1972), all of which remained in print over the decades.[5] While the Church of Satan membership increased, its actual size is hard to determine. LaVey rarely disclosed membership figures, and his church records are an insufficient source anyway, as initiates are bestowed lifelong membership and do not pay annual fees.[6] LaVey developed a degree system of five initiatory levels to reflecting members' successive mastery of satanic philosophy and accomplishment in the outside world.[7] Organizationally, the Church was governed by an inner circle, the Order of the Trapezoid or the Council of Nine, presided over by LaVey, whose position was defined as "monarchical in nature, papal in degree and absolute in power" (LaVey 1970).[8] Local groups, called "grottos," were established at various places in the United States and abroad, until LaVey in 1975 dissolved the grotto system, arguing that it attracted misfits who gained more esteem from belonging to a Satanic grotto than the Church of Satan gained from their affiliation (LaVey cited in Barton 1992, 126). Following a sweeping reorganization, a number of splinter groups spawned the occult scene, and LaVey went into seclusion for many years.[9]

During the late 1980s, a second public phase commenced with LaVey granting media interviews, reinstating the grotto system, and again attracting celebrities to the Church of Satan. In 1992 LaVey published his first book in twenty years, The Devil's Notebook, followed by the posthumously published Satan Speaks (1998), which features a foreword by rock artist Marilyn Manson. Following LaVey's death in 1997, a still-pending legal battle over the LaVey estate ensued between LaVey's oldest daughter Karla (now of the First Church of Satan) and Blanche Barton, the mother of his son, Xerxes. The Council of Nine presently governs an impoverished Church of Satan, and the infamous black Victorian was ultimately demolished. LaVey's brand of Satanism did not, however, die with its founder. His works may today be found at mainstream bookstores. The Satanic Bible has sold nearly a million copies and continues to exact an influence in the States and abroad (Boulware 1999).

Inspired by the anti-egalitarian radical individualism of Nietzsche and Ayn Rand, LaVey proclaimed the death of God and the rise of the age of Satan. Releasing hell on earth returns man to natural law, where the strong will prevail and man will be his own redeemer. LaVey envisioned the divine as an impersonal and indifferent pantheistic force permeating nature. Realizing that there is no caring god to trust, hope, or pray for, the Satanist will take command of his life and make things happen. "Positive thinking and positive action adds up to the results" (LaVey 1969, 41). Satan is not an evil entity to which you may sell your soul, but essentially a personification of the balancing forces of nature. As "god" is nature and nature is "Satan," "Satan" is "god." And as man is part of nature, man is part of Satan, and Satan is part of man. Satan represents creative man's self-awareness, the seed of his true carnal ego or his black flame, the inner individual fire of becoming. If there is a personal god in the satanic universe of LaVey, it is the individual ego. "If you are going to create a god in your own image, why not create that god as yourself. Any man is a god if he chooses to recognize himself as one" (ibid., 96). One's own birthday is consequently the most important satanic holiday, followed by Walpurgisnacht and Halloween (Samhain) (ibid., 94).

Satanism was to LaVey a rational ideology of egoistic hedonism and self-preservation. Man the animal should abide with his true nature and innermost desires to make the most of his life, satisfy his wants, and fulfill his ego. LaVey advocated indulgence into each of the "seven sins" of Christianity as they "all lead to physical, mental, or emotional gratification" (LaVey 1969, 46).[10] A life-affirming religion of "the flesh, the mundane and the carnal," LaVeyan Satanism encourages man to enjoy life. Christianity has always defined as evil anything resulting in physical or mental gratification, "assuring a lifetime of unwanted guilt for everyone." Evil reversed, LaVey pointed out, is live (ibid., 62). LaVey taught that it is only by satisfying his desires that man will be free from frustrations. Satanism, for example, advocates free sexuality, condoning any type of sexual activity as long as it does not infringe on the sexual freedom of others.[11] Rape, child molestation, and mutilation of animals are therefore forbidden, whereas acting out one's innermost sexual fantasies with a willing partner (or two or a dozen) is strongly encouraged.

In his emphasis on sexual energy and the harm that comes from its repression, LaVey is clearly inspired by Freud but inverts Freud's conclusions. Basically, Freud holds neurosis to be the result of a conflict between instinctual demands and opposing official demands. Human beings instinctively seek pleasure through sexuality, but culture and religion represses these natural feelings, resulting in frustration. Religion is to Freud an illusion, the "universal obsessional neurosis of humanity" and largely responsible for the misery of mankind (Freud 1978 [1928], 39).[12] While detrimental to the mental health of man, Freud still holds religion to be necessary, as he defines the nature of man as aggressive, destructive, and hedonistic. Agreeing in part with Freud's misanthropy, LaVey nonetheless fought to free man from his illusions. "Satan represents opposition to all religions which serve to frustrate and condemn man for his natural instincts" (LaVey 1969, 55).

A primary satanic method for achieving self-gratification is magic. Amending Crowley, LaVey defined magic as "the change in situations or events in accordance with one's will, which would, using normally accepted methods, be unchangeable" (1969, 110). Magic is used to reach sexual gratification, material gain, and personal success, or to curse that which deserves destruction. To LaVey, there was no difference between black and white magic. "What is a pleasure to one, is pain to another, and the same applies to 'good' and 'evil'" (ibid.). Manipulative or "lesser" magic utilized sex, sentiment, and wonder in an applied psychology based in part on LaVey's experience from the carnival circuit.[13] Ceremonial or "greater" magic comprised emotional acts of psychodrama designed to rid detrimental attitudes such as guilt or fear, strengthen creative psychological powers, and act out fantasies.[14]

LaVeyan Satanic ethics revolves around putting yourself and your family first, minding your own business, and being a gentleman.[15] Do not give opinions or advice unless you are asked. When in someone's house treat him respectfully, or do not go there. Do not harm children, and do not make unwanted sexual advances. LaVey's ethics differs from conventional morality in its blunt call to restrict love and respect to a select few. Why care for people you do not know? Why be anything but ruthless against enemies? "When walking in open territory, bother no one. If someone bothers you, ask him to stop. If he does not stop, destroy him" (LaVey 1992b, 244). The wisdom of Jesus is thus Satanically reversed. "If a man smite thee on the one cheek, *smash* him on the other" (LaVey 1969, 47; emphasis in original).[16] LaVey accordingly emphasizes limitation, discrimination, and stratification. All men are not equal. Nature is discriminatory, and society should not support the weak at the expense of the strong but should reflect elitist stratification (LaVey 1992c). *Lex Talionis* is the law of nature. "Blessed are the strong, for they shall posses the earth," wrote LaVey. "Cursed are the weak for they shall inherit the yoke" (1969, 34). The latter statement is one of several passages in the *Satanic Bible* that is plagiarized verbatim from *Might Is Right*, an iconoclastic anti-Christian Social Darwinist book published in 1896 by Ragnar Redbeard (pseudonym).[17] The 1996 reissuing of *Might Is Right* provided an instance of resonance between racism, Odinism, Creativity, and Satanism. Sold by Metzger's White Aryan Resistance, it was edited by Katja Lane, had a foreword by LaVey and a postscript by George Burdi Hawthorne. This should not, however, necessarily be interpreted as a racist undercurrent in LaVeyan philosophy. "The true legacy of Satan," LaVey stresses, "transcends ethnic [and] racial differences" (1969, 104).

Satanism as an Elitist, Initiatory Secret Society

Representative of the second satanic model is the Temple of Set, founded in 1975 by former LaVey confidant Michael Aquino and now led by mystery novelist Uncle Setnakt, or Don Webb.[18] Born in 1946, political scientist Aquino is a Vietnam veteran and military intelligence officer who specializes in psychological warfare.[19] This has earned him a special reputation among conspiracy believers. Cathy O'Brien identifies Aquino as a child-molesting mind-controller working for a satanic globalist conspiracy. In the late 1980s, a Salem witch hunt rerun hit the United States, with a "Satanic scare" spreading like wildfire. Hundreds of alleged "survivors" claimed to have been victims of bizarre sexual torture and to have witnessed satanic homicides and cannibalistic rituals, accusing hundreds of named individuals. Aquino was among the accused but was never charged, as the case against him could not be substantiated.[20]

Aquino became a Church of Satan member in 1969 and quickly ascended through its grade system. By 1971 he was Magister Caverni of the IV°; editor of the *Cloven Hoof*, the internal membership organ of the Church of Satan; and appointed to the Council of Nine. In 1973 Aquino rose to the previously unattained level of Magister Templi of IV°. When LaVey in 1975 dissolved the grotto system and decided that degrees now could be earned through financial or other contributions, Aquino felt that the infernal mandate of LaVey had been broken, and he resigned from the Church of Satan (Flowers 1997, 217–21; Aquino 1998).

In a nocturnal midsummer working that year, Aquino invoked the Prince of Darkness, who came forth, dictating the inspired *Book of Coming Forth By Night* (Flowers 1997, 219, 224; Aquino, 1975). Identifying himself as the Egyptian deity Set, the invoked entity declared that he no longer wanted to be called by his Hebrew corruption "Satan." In Egyptian mythology, Set killed his rival Osiris and was the enemy of his brother Horus. When the priests of Osiris came into power in late Egyptian civilization, Set was identified as the originator of evil and eventually, Setians claim, merged with the Israeli Satan.[21] Speaking directly with Aquino, Set transferred the infernal mandate to him and introduced the magic principle of Xeper as the foundation of the Temple of Set. A score of estranged Church of Satan members followed Aquino, and a number of local groups, called "pylons," were established in the United States and abroad.[22]

The meeting with the Prince of Darkness marked a point of departure between LaVey and Aquino. LaVey was basically a materialist to whom Satan was a personification of the forces of nature. Aquino is an idealist, basing his theology on Plato and the Gnostic/Hermetic tradition. Set is "the ageless Intelligence of the Universe," emerging through a process of separation. In a willful act of self-definition, he created himself as Aiwass, the entity who in 1904 gave the *Book of Law* to Aleister Crowley and initiated the age of Horus.[23] This age lasted until 1966, when the age of Satan was proclaimed through LaVey as a prelude to the present Aeon of Set now inaugurated (Aquino 1975).[24] If the age of Satan was an age of indulgence, liberating man the animal to satisfy his carnal needs, the Aeon of Set is held to represent an opening for an elect elite to evolve on the left-hand path to immortality.[25] LaVeyan magic was a path of self-gratification, whereas Setian magic aims at achieving self-theomorphosis.[26]

To Setians, Set represents the first separated and isolated intelligence, the prototypical Self. The mysterious "gift of Set" called the "Black Flame" represents the spark of intelligence or solar energy inherent in man that makes possible the process of self-individuation and self-empowerment. In Setian terminology the key word to individual transformation is the Egyptian *Xeper* (I Have Come into Being). "It is from the moment of perceiving and acting upon Xeper," Webb writes, "that the Setian begins the process of becoming an immortal, independent, powerful and potent Essence which affects the universe" (Webb 1996, 71). The focus here is on separation, and the method by which the initiate first sets himself apart from the surrounding universal order is an antinomian identification with whatever is evil in the moral system of the commoners. Being outside the system is held to provide a uniquely "objective" and liberated perspective, and sets the stage for the willful transformative process of one's own psyche. The goal of the "Setian Hermetica" is self-metamorphosis, to become a god "when still alive" and retain that unique divine individuality in eternity.[27]

A notion of achieving immortality was present in LaVeyan philosophy as well. "The Satanist believes in complete gratification of the ego," LaVey wrote (1969, 94). A strong ego is the foundation for "vital existence" and might, if fully satisfied, "refuse to die, even after the expiration of the flesh" (ibid.). However, LaVey was not particularly interested in the subject, concentrating instead on earthly self-gratification here and now. Aquino believes that man is more than an animal and hence not entirely subject to the laws of nature. The gift of Set constitutes a nonnatural component of man, independent of his physical body, which, Setians assert, "liberates the rational Black Magician to seek immortality according to non-natural technologies" (Flowers 1997, 234). The central Setian objective is hence to transcend nature. Satanism is a path of becoming an elevated god-ego, an immortal Hero, or (disengaged) satanic bodhisattva.[28] Satanists, Aquino explained on a 1988 *Oprah Winfrey Show*, "are not servants of some god; we are our own gods; we are our own decision makers." The Temple of Set is accordingly a collective of radical individualists. "The ultimate purpose of the Temple is to create, by individual work, a psyche that can survive death," Don Webb (1999) explains, admitting that "we are subject to all the inherent paradoxes, in that, as a group, we are looking for something individual."

The Temple of Set presents itself as an initiatory system modeled on the framework Plato envisioned for his utopian philosopher-elect student academy. The neoplatonic influence firmly places the Temple of Set within the Western esoteric tradition, along with occult Masonry and initiatory magical societies such as the Golden Dawn, Ordo Templi Orientis, or A∴A∴. Organizationally, the Temple of Set is divided into several orders to enable the elect to focus on their individual Xeper and to explore the traditions of ancient Egypt or Scandinavia, tantric Hinduism, or vampire mystique according to will.[29]

The Order of the Trapezoid was launched in 1983 following a solitary working Aquino conducted at Walhalla, the subterranean inner sanctum of Wewelsburg, the SS order-castle operated by Heinrich Himmler.[30] Aiming at "retrieving" the "positive aspects" of völkisch romanticism from "the place where the dark arts of the North was last attempted," Aquino then "reestablished" the Order of the Trapezoid as a "chivalric order of Knights sworn to uphold the standards and ethical conduct" (Thorsson 1990). Being darkside Arthurian knights, invited initiates explore Germanic black arts in a quest for their individual grail (i.e., the perfected Self) that will open the gate to immortality (ibid.). This Setian attraction to SS occultism unsurprisingly led observers to identify national socialist sympathies within the Temple.

Satanism as Eurocentric Heathendom

Both Church of Satan and Temple of Set viewed paganism favorably. LaVey taught that the old pagan gods never died when Europe was Christianized. As the heroes of the former culture, they became villains of the new. They were pushed down into hell and turned into devils (LaVey 1969, 56). "Odinism," LaVey (1998, 72) wrote, "is an heroic and admirable form of Satanism." Aquino developed these notions by exploring the pagan paths of Egypt, Greece, and northern Europe as a vital part of his Setian effort. The third, self-proclaimed "traditional" or "pagan" satanic model takes this notion even further, fleshing out a heathen satanic path for its fellow travelers. Among the satanic orders involved are the United Kingdom based Order of the Nine Angles (ONA) and the now-defunct, New Zealand–based Black Order, both of which exacted an influence in the United States and abroad.

Appearing on the scene during the early 1980s, ONA claimed to be the surfacing of an underground "sinister tradition" dating back to the original "solar" paganism practiced in hyperborean civilization some 7,000 years ago. While describing Satanism as "militant paganism" (Beest 1996), ONA does not advocate a return to a heathen past. "All past gods of the various Western Traditions are rendered obsolete by the forces which Satanism alone is unleashing," an ONA tract reads. "Satan is the arrogance within that enables us to leave behind the archaic gods and to find the courage to be the new gods" (Riabhaich 1998).

Led by Anton Long and Christos Beest, ONA numbers remain exceedingly small. Its influence in the milieu depends mainly on the voluminous material it produces.[31] ONA has published philosophical treaties, ritual guidelines, and magic techniques, and produced the *Black Book of Satan*, satanic music, tarot cards, poetry, and fiction.[32] Satanism is to ONA not a religion but a way of life, a "quest for self-excellence involving real danger, real challenges and requiring real courage."[33] ONA guides its adepts along a "sinister seven-fold way." Each stage involves a character-evolving task to accomplish, ranging from living in complete isolation to engaging in terrorist activities. Satan is an inner and outer reality, representing both an archetype in the psyche and the timeless dark force of the "acausal" realm existing beyond man and the causal universe. A genuine satanic order is an invocation of Satan, and a "true" Satanist is a living representation of the Prince of Darkness on earth.

To ONA, this is a far cry from "sham-Satanic groups" like the Church of Satan and the Temple of Set, who like the "glamour associated with Satanism but [are] afraid to experience its realness within and external to them."[34] Whereas LaVey or Aquino issued ethical guidelines, the "genuine" Satanist "actively aids the creative forces of Darkness" by doing "the work of the Prince of Darkness."[35] The subhuman majority needs being reminded of the presence of the dark and sinister. "If this means killing, wars, suffering, sacrifice, terror, disease, tragedy and disruption, then such things must be."[36] Human sacrifice is held to further the work of Satan. As powerful magic, it draws down sinister forces and releases energy that can be stored or redirected. It is said to strengthen the character of the performer and be beneficial to society by removing the worthless. Victims are not chosen randomly, and the manner in which they are dispatched is supposedly achieved either magically or physically. Ideal candidates are journalists or political activists who disrupt the activities of sinister organizations or weak-

HAIL LOKI! HAIL SATAN! HAIL HITLER! 293

lings of low character whose removal will improve the racial stock. The feeble pseudo-Satanists who deny that human sacrifice ever was part of satanic practice also make suitable candidates. "In their last moment of terror, they would at last experience the real, primal, darkness which is Satan."[37]

The individual quest of becoming-god is cast in a wider evolutionary context inspired by Spengler and Yockey. Cosmic evolution is guided by a "sinister dialectics" of alternating Aeonic energies present on earth via organic, racial civilizations that are born, evolve, and die.[38] Each Aeonic civilization has its unique ethos, the present Western civilization being Faustian or Satanic, the essence of which was epitomized by national socialist Germany. Like all civilizations it should end in Imperium, but this outcome is far from certain. Unlike all other civilizations, the present one has suffered an unnatural distortion, infested by the Nazarene, that is, Judeo-Christian, sickness of spirit. Yet, this counter-evolutionary force is seen as part of the Wyrd of Western civilization, presenting a cosmic enemy to be overcome in a triumph of will. If victorious, an Aryan Imperium will be established, from the ashes of which will emerge the sixth, associated Aeon of Fire, during which the Aryan race will fulfill its destiny of exploring and colonizing the galaxy.[39]

In this momentous battle, Satanists must aid the return of fascism. According to ONA, national socialism represents the "light aspect" of the present Aeonic civilization in its capacity to speak to the masses and establish a new golden age for the majority. Satanism is its "dark forces," since it dares to implement what the majority is conditioned by the system to fear.[40] A genuine Satanist should aid the collapse of the present Western regimes by causing explosions of primal terror, engaging in extremist politics, dealing with drugs and pornography, and culling the worthless.[41] Aryans need to regain a sense of "racial superiority" and the "noble ideals of the warrior caste."[42] However, Satanists express and support racism as a "sinister strategy," not because they really believe in it. Similarly, "genuine initiates are pledged to fulfill the aiding of National Socialism" as a "sinister strategy" to achieve a higher Aeonic goal, not because they subscribe to it. An adept should ideally partake in extreme underground fascist operations as a live role-play reenactment, then drift away from political commitments. A true Satanist manipulates everyone else to further both his own and Aeonic evolution.[43]

Aiming to revive the esoteric current of national socialism and to present the dark forces on Earth was the now-defunct New Zealand–based Black Order, cofounded by occult fascist Kerry Bolton. Also cofounder of the New Zealand Fascist Union, Bolton has long explored occult paths. He has been involved with the Thelemic Society, the Temple of Set, the Church of Odin, the Order of the Left Hand Path, and edits the magazine *The Nexus, Metaphysics, and The Third Way*.[44] Bolton concludes with Spengler that Western civilization is dying, and he urges "all Heathen" people to "rejoice" in the coming cataclysm of Ragnarök. In its rituals, the Black Order evokes all the dark gods of the Norse pantheon: Loki, who will lead the dark legion against the god/desses of Asgård during Ragnarök; Jormungandr, the world serpent who will emerge from the bottomless oceans to spit cascades of venom and slay Thor; Fenris, the chaos wolf who, freed from his chains, will devour Odin; Surt, the fire giant of Muspelheim who will engulf the planet; Garm, the hound of Hel; and the frost giants and forces of primal chaos that will end the world as we know it. Out of the ashes arises a new world and a new sun shines over virgin pastures. Baldr returns from the dead to lead a new solar generation of men and gods during the golden age to come. Of all the forces of destruction, Surt survives to be the progenitor of a new generation of dark forces that participates in the eternal cycles of creation and destruction. Borrowing from the ONA, the Black Order calls forth the forces of darkness by extramagical means, "aiding those things that will undermine societies — e.g., drugs, pornography, crime, political unrest, economic misfortune, racial and other social tensions" (Black Order 1993, 36). Only thus will a pagan renaissance be feasible. Western civilization will fulfill its destiny of conquering the galaxy and give birth to a new man-god, Homo galactica (ibid.). The Black Order never lasted more than a few years, but gave rise in the United States to the occult fascist and darkside heathen group White Order of Thule.

Apocalypse Culture

The Church of Satan emerged amid the leftist counterculture of the late 1960s. While in tune with certain themes of the time — free sexuality, a search for alternative religion, a questioning of prevailing norms, insistence on freedom from the authority of church and state — LaVeyan philosophy ran contrary to other main themes. It did not believe in compassion, peace, love, equality, or mind-altering drugs.[45] Against the bright colors of flower-power, the Church of Satan remained a black adversary to the cultural mainstream and the larger part of the hippie-yippie counterculture. With Charles Manson and the Family, the Process: Church of Final Judgement, psychedelic fascists, outlaw bikers, darkside musicians, and dada artists, an eerie minority tendency coalesced, growing in the dark before gaining momentum during what Adam Parfrey (1990 [1987]) termed the "apocalypse culture" of the late 1980s and early 1990s. By then, the leftist counterculture had declined, and ideals of solidarity and egalitarianism were no longer in vogue. The pendulum had swung to the right, as evidenced not least with the Reagan revolution's enforcement of neoliberal economics.

The shift included a new generation Satanists who had been brought up on J. R. R. Tolkien's *Lord of the Rings* trilogy and science-fiction epics such as *Star Wars;* who played *Dungeons and Dragons* or *Vampire: The Masquerade;* and who listened to industrial, goth, noise, dark ambient, or heavy metal musical offshoots, thrash, death, and black metal. These youths saw human stupidity, manifested in consumerism and the entertainment industry, reaching new heights while the world seemed to dance at the brink of an approaching apocalypse. Kali yuga would end in a nuclear or natural cataclysm to purify an overpopulated planet, but the postapocalyptic world was understood more in terms of a *Mad Max* scenario than an immanent return to a golden age. A Satanic ethics based on Nietzschean social Darwinism now seemed in flow with the times and would in its revival embrace concepts of retribalization, Eurocentric paganism, and occult fascism.

Baddeley (1999, 148) considers the 8/8/88 Rally in San Francisco to be the "defining episode of Satanism" of the time. Held at the anniversary of Sharon Tate's murder at the hands of the Manson Family, the evening of "apocalyptic delights" celebrated the death of the sixties, the end of compassion for the weak and of pacifism that breeds stagnation. A "self-conscious cross between an occult ritual, performance art and fascistic political rally," the event was staged by an "unholy alliance" of the Church of Satan, Radio Werewolf, American Front, Adam Parfrey, and industrial avant gardist Boyd Rice of NON. A member of the Church of Satan and American Front and founder of the occult/Gnostic Abraxas Foundation he once described a "fascist think-tank," Rice at that time felt attracted to the national socialist sense of order and saw Hitler as "an occultist trying to bring about a pagan revival" (quoted in Baddeley 1999, 151).

The industrial/noise music scene—pioneered by Throbbing Gristle and followed by the likes of NON, Monte Cazazza, Laibach, and Einstürzende Neubauten—deals with eerie moods, its music seldom danceable and often comprising atonal, atmospheric, deafening, brutal, dissonant, distorted electronic sound experiments.[46] Despite the fact that many of the original bands were anarchist, a definite swing to the right emerged among a segment of the industrial scene in the 1980s. Caricaturing the impersonal technology of modernity, stage acts often draw on totalitarian aesthetics, with uniformed robotic performers against backdrops of fascist, heathen, or occult imagery. It is melodrama performed in the decaying world of the living dead, a postscript to soulless humanity by the artist Übermensch. Drawing on national socialist symbolism to produce an uncanny aura does not necessarily mean that the artists involved espouse fascism as a political ideology. T.R.O.Y. of the anarchist industrial project Kingdom Scum and owner of the Hidden Power Enterprises label comments that such artists may enjoy "the elitist sensation of being above the herd who buy the fascist images as well as the herd who misunderstand/oppose it."[47] While the fascination with fascist aesthetics does not define the industrial-music scene politically, it does reveal a fundamental mood of indifference to what fascism meant to the populations who experienced its dictatorships in real life. A similarly detached attitude is discernible also in the wider apocalypse culture. Exploring the extremes of art, music, sexuality, politics, religion, magic, and the occult, its adherents may revel in anything from pagan Satanism or occult fascism to snuff movies, serial killers, and necrophilia, but from the vantage point of artistic expression rather than of the real—an attitude revealing, perhaps, that most adherents are white, middle class, with the luxury of being bored.

The apocalypse scene has given birth to a number of "extreme culture" magazines including—Propaganda, Esoterra, Cyber-Psycho's AOD, Panik, Ohm Clock, and Fifth Path—in which the artistic advance guard often take turns interviewing each other and contributing essays and artwork. Editor of (now-defunct) Fifth Path was Robert Ward, later editor of Vor Trú and goði of Úlfhethnar Kindred (not to be confused with the Úlfhethnar Brotherhood of Vor Ætt). Following the standard pattern, Fifth Path included interviews and articles on apocalypse culture icons Death in June, Sol Invictus, Fire and Ice, Electric Hellfire Club, Robert Taylor, Michael Moynihan, and Adam Parfrey. It ran an extensive review section on releases of apocalyptic and Eurotribal concern, ranging from music such as industrial, Aryan hatecore, and satanic black metal, to magazines dedicated to paganism, magic, bizarre sexuality, fascism, or extreme art and music. The magazine explored Odinism in heavy-metal music, skinheads in East Germany, black-magic dictators, Hopi prophecies, and it included words of antihumanitarian wisdom by Peter Steele (1994) of Type O Negative. "Pity is weakness. Kindness is stupidity. Take advantage of the errors of others. Believe in yourself. Live to conquer, domination is a right."

Born in 1968 in Sacramento, California, Ward came into the world of tribal paganism and the occult through Dungeons and Dragons and the romantic world of fantasy literature. Initially inspired by LaVeyan Satanism and the gothic milieu, Ward in time developed an interest in Norse paganism. Attracted to rune magic, he became a member of Edred Thorsson's Rune Guild shortly before founding the *Fifth Path* in 1990. Working with the magazine, Ward came in contact with Norse darkside pagans such as Schreck and his project, Radio Werewolf, and Robert Taylor, whose Tribe of the Wulfings he would briefly join in 1995 (Ward 1999). Accumulating personal differences with some of the Wulfings, Ward parted ways with them, cofounding instead the Úlfhethnar Kindred, which held its first blot in 1996. Registering the Úlfhethnar tribe as a formational Asatrú Alliance kindred, Ward invested his energies in *Vor Trú*. Eventually serving as its managing director, Ward would in collaboration with experienced writers/ editors Taylor and Moynihan update its layout and content thereby reportedly increasing *Vor Trú* sales by 500 percent (Murray 1998). In 1999 Ward left his assignment, dissatisfied with the fact that Murray was still running things behind the scene. Consequently, citing the AA leadership's incompetence and lack of vision, Úlfhethnar Kindred left the alliance in the year 2000, claiming that they would continue to promote ethnic Asatrú on a local level.[48]

The gothic and mysterious remains an inspiration to Ward, if the contents of the *Fifth Path* can be held to reflect his obsessions and interests. While the magazine explores the netherworld where occult fascism meets darkside racial paganism, Ward denies being racist or fascist (Ward 1999). "Being white and proud of my ancestors and our culture, I of course cover a lot of Indo-European tribal issues more often than those of other cultures," Ward said, wondering why that "should be so shocking" ("The Fifth Path" 1993). A registered Libertarian more oriented toward primal culture and ethnotribalism than organized politics, Ward seeks to avoid categorization and seems baffled when interpreted as leaning toward national socialism. Yet a 1999 commemorative issue of Aryan revolutionary *Prisoners of War* dedicated to the pagan elements of national socialism includes a lengthy article by Ward discussing the use of runes by the SS. Praising the works by occult runologist Karl Maria Wiligut and the Ahnenerbe SS research department, Ward laments that the research files seized after the Allies' "unfortunate victory" still are classified. Ward suggests that the reason for ignoring or banning the results produced by Ahnenerbe researchers is due to their occult contents. "If they were revealed and understood, an entirely new view of the Third Reich . . . would emerge. The SS activities would not been seen as those of 'Christians' who hated 'Jews,' but Pagans who were taking charge of their ancestral land! . . . If all the forces that were operating in the Third Reich during World War Two were acknowledged it would shake the world," Ward (1999, 37) concludes. "It would mean the end of internationalism based on capital and resurgence of nationalism based on blood." Asked to elaborate on his view of national socialism, paganism, and the SS, Ward in 2001 reiterated his fascination with the occult roots of national socialism and the Ahnenerbe projects. Applauding the ss effort to realize the Nietzschean übermensch, Ward saw as positive the "attempt to apply ethnic and tribal concerns to modern politics," but held as negative "Third Reich policies outside its borders," as it seemed "inspired by the example of Imperial Rome rather than tribal Germany."[49]

By 1992, apocalypse culture heathen artist and author Michael Moynihan of Blood Axis had joined *The Fifth Path* as associate editor. Born 1969 as the only son of an upper-middle-class Boston family, Moynihan developed an early interest in things beyond the ordinary, from extremist politics to occult sciences. Intelligent, energetic, and creative, his inquisitiveness soon began to manifest in music, art, and writings. Having produced his own electronic-noise music under the name Coup de Grâce in his midteens, Moynihan has since the mid-1980s been involved with the industrial projects Sleep Chamber (prior to its S/M-incarnation), fascistic techno band Slave State (of Thomas Thorn of Electric Hellfire Club fame), and NON. He also participated in the Abraxas Foundation and shared a Denver apartment with Rice, before joining Robert Ferbrache to launch Blood Axis in 1989. The band's compositions include musical hymn explorations of the Mithraic mysteries and sound experiments overlaid with a speech by British Union of Fascists leader Oswald Mosley.[50] With Austrian "völkisch anarchist" and industrial artist Kadmon (Gerhard Petak), Moynihan produced a split single on which Kadmon's Allerseelen featured marchlike percussions pounding to German lyrics by national socialist occultist Karl Maria Wiligut.[51]

Released in 1995, Blood Axis's first full-length neoclassical/gothic industrial CD, *Gospel of Inhumanity*, featured spoken extracts by Ezra Pound and Charles Manson set to music by Bach, heroic hymns inspired by Laibach, and operatic tape loops overlaid with readings from Nietzsche. For its European tours of 1997 and 1998, Markus Wolff of Waldteufel and Moynihan's partner, violinist Annabel Lee of Waldteufel/Amber Asylum/Alraune, had joined the group, venturing deeper into the realms of dark ambient/apocalyptic folk, as also can be heard on its 1998 album *Blót: Sacrifice in Sweden*.[52] Contributing to *Germania Occulta*, a compilation of musical explorations of German occultism, Blood Axis produced a track called "Der gefallene Engel" featuring vocals by Edred Thorsson. Besides his own music, Moynihan helped to produce the *Commemoration* CD, with prison recordings by Charles Manson, and he released Robert Taylor's *Changes* on his Storm record label. In 1995 Moynihan relocated to Portland, Oregon, where he worked as managing editor at Adam Parfrey's *Feral House* while Annabel enjoyed the Cascades as ski instructor.

By that time, Moynihan had already inaugurated his own small publishing company, Storm Books. In 1988 he translated Nietzsche's *Antichrist* and in 1992 published *Siege*, the collected writings of Manson devotee and (heretical) national socialist revolutionary James Mason. A prolific author, Moynihan contributed articles on LaVey, Manson, and black-metal bands for such magazines as *Black Flame*, *Esoterra*, *Seconds*, *Vor Trú*, and *Fifth Path*. In collaboration with journalist Didrik Søderlind, Moynihan in 1998 published his first monograph, *Lords of Chaos*, an acclaimed study of the Norwegian black-metal underground, interpreted as an atavistic expression of suppressed archetypes inherent in the Nordic psyche. More recently, he edited the *Secret King*, a compilation of texts by Karl Maria Wiligut (translated by Edred Thorsson), and two translated works by the Italian radical traditionalist/occult fascist Julius Evola, *Introduction to Magic* and *Men among the Ruins*. Written in 1953, the latter work calls for a counterrevolution to return society to ancient traditions based on sacred hierarchy and the noble way of the warrior.

Moynihan first encountered Satanism through the *Satanic Bible*, a work that he initially found hard to take seriously. Having read Nietzsche, Evola, and Spengler, Moynihan considered LaVey theatrical by contrast and felt repelled by the notion that everybody could be a Satanist, which was implicit in the fact that the *Satanic Bible* was a paperback directed toward a mass audience. A few years later, Moynihan revised his opinions after having spent an evening with LaVey in 1989 that ended with him being bestowed membership in the Church of Satan. Officially a priest in the Church of Satan, Moynihan rarely flashes his membership card. While finding satanic aesthetics attractive and agreeing with LaVey's insistence on individual sovereignty and the aspects of satanic philosophy that connect with paganism, Moynihan has long found the heathen path more rewarding. Influenced by völkisch heathen philosophers, Moynihan toured central Europe in the footsteps of Guido von List, made pilgrimages to other sites of ancient pagan presence, and furthered his education through Germanic studies at the University of Colorado and Portland State University. Through his involvement in the apocalypse culture, Moynihan in 1993 came in contact with Robert Taylor and found a kindred spirit. He and (later) Annabel were initiated into the Tribe of Wulfings, and Moynihan has since collaborated with Taylor in several projects of pagan and artistic concern. At the time, Wulfings was still part of the Asatrú Alliance, and Moynihan soon became associate editor of *Vor Trú* and partook in alliance Althings and affairs. Developing a friendship with Stephen McNallen, Moynihan also frequented Asatrú Folk Assembly blots, including the ceremony held in honor of the Kennewick Man.

Nurturing a general interest in Norse pagan culture, Moynihan is especially interested in Asatrú as an Odian, evolutionary ideology with which to transform oneself into a higher state of being, a notion he holds compatible with the Nietzschean quest. "I think people are wrong when they try to fit Satan into Norse mythology . . . and try to find these gods which have some darker or more sinister side to them. The most obvious example of this is when people become unduly obsessed with Loki and Fenris. In reality, if any one deity embodies certain 'satanic' ideas it is Odin, not Loki. I mean, if you consider Loki as an aspect of Odin, as the dark side of Odin, this would fit in with that, but I don't think isolating Loki as 'satanic' is correct." [53] Representing a "principle of evolution," Odin is a self-realized "master of gnosis" who inspires others to embark on the heroic "path of the Übermensch" (Moynihan 1997). Explicitly elitist in orientation, Moynihan dismisses as ludicrous the idea that all men are created equal, arguing that all of history has demonstrated quite the opposite as is manifested in the "eternal stratification" of superior and inferior, genius and ignorant, creative and trivial.[54] The ascending Odinic path toward individual excellence will accordingly not open for the feeble-minded multitude but will remain an exclusive passageway into the mysteries for the daring few.

Featured in the extreme-culture magazines and white-power fanzines, including *Resistance*, Moynihan and Blood Axis came to the attention of antiracist organizations and activists. Interpreting the band's *krückenkreuz* symbol an embodiment of ancient and authoritarian aesthetics, Blood Axis was branded "Nazi rockers," a "Nazi-Satanist band," and "racist metal." [55] Moynihan was labeled "a convinced anti-Semite," a "white supremacist" who "admire[s] 'lone wolves' like the Columbine killers," and a "big player in the effort to bring racism into the metal scene." [56] On tour, Blood Axis began encountering antifascist protesters and had concerts canceled in Seattle, San Francisco, and Norway in 1998. In 1999 the Southern Poverty Law Center published an intelligence report on the generational shift in organized racism, profiling Moynihan as one of the six most influential "new leaders on the radical right." Alleging him to be "deeply involved in race-based Odinism," SPLC (1999e) portrayed Moynihan as a "major purveyor of neo-Nazism, occult fascism and international industrial and black metal music" who champions Manson as an "American Hitler."

Some of these charges are easy to simply dismiss as mistaken and unfounded; others are more complicated. Blood Axis is neither rock nor metal, and Moynihan is hardly anti-Semitic or a white supremacist and is definitely not a radical right "leader" of anything. He has never styled Manson an avatar of Hitler, and there is nothing to substantiate the charge that he fancies lone-wolf assassins or applauds tragedies like the Columbine High School massacre. The anti-Semitic charge followed mainly from a *No Longer a Fanzine* interview with Moynihan in 1994. Responding to a direct question, Moynihan stated that he would have "more lenient entry requirements" than the Nazis had had if he were given the opportunity to start up the next Holocaust; this was interpreted to mean that Moynihan dreams of systematically ridding the Earth of people he judges worthless ("Interview with Michael Moynihan" 1994). Though he certainly does not care about an overwhelming majority of mankind, my impression is that Moynihan cares even less about building gas chambers.

What he presumably does care about is publicity, a craving that has resulted in quite a few oddities that will follow him for some time. When, for instance, in 1988, a researcher placed an ad in the occult section of a Boston paper looking for "genuine vampires" to interview, a black-clad, adolescent Moynihan volunteered as a blood-drinking predator, talking about his contempt for humanity and his admiration for the "feral nature" of Adolf Hitler and Charles Manson (Blood 1994, 195). And instead of ending the *No Longer a Fanzine* session when the questions were silly and irrelevant, Moynihan took the ride. In the same interview he was asked if he denied the existence of the Holocaust, to which Moynihan responded that while he thought "the six million number to be arbitrary" and "probably a gross exaggeration," his "main problem" with revisionism was "the assumption that killing millions of innocent people is inherently 'bad,'" as he felt increasingly inclined "to just the opposite conclusion" ("Interview with Michael Moynihan" 1994). This reasoning was readily interpreted to mean that Moynihan was a revisionist, a charge he has frequently refuted.[57] "I do not believe in moral concepts of 'good' and 'evil,' and thus am not particularly upset about episodes in history where large number of people died," an official rebuttal read. "I am not a Holocaust Revisionist, but I also do not really care about the Holocaust one way or another. I don't feel responsible for it, and while it may mean a lot (understandably) to some people, it has nothing to do with me."[58] In another interview, Moynihan said that he was not "upset" about the Holocaust any more than he was about the Irish Potato Famine, adding "and by any standard the latter should be of more concern," given his part Irish descent (Nelson 1999). This attitude is maybe indicative of the supreme coldness of a Nietzschean lack of empathy but hardly qualifies as anti-Semitic.

Moynihan (1997) takes exception to the ideology of white supremacy and finds no value in "shouting artificial slogans" about white pride.[59] "I certainly don't identify with any vague racial category like being 'white' and have never attempted to project such a notion."[60] Moynihan says that he does not feel particularly connected to most whites around him, supremacists included. "I see many examples in organized racism where they make a lot of excuses for people and are willing to accept a lot of substandard behavior" (*Moynihan* 1997). While not a supremacist, Moynihan does see a connection between genetics and spirituality along the lines of the ethnic Asatrúers. To the extent that metagenetics is a racial philosophy, Moynihan may qualify as a racist, but, again, ethnocentric spirituality should not be confused with Aryan revolutionary activities. There is a world of difference between the Wotansvolk and Blood Axis projects, a lack of correspondence both parties readily acknowledge.[61]

This distinction needs to be emphasized in light of the SPLC *Intelligence Report* article that portrayed Moynihan as one of the top six radical-right leaders, placing him among the likes of cyberwarrior Alex Curtis, who tirelessly sought to promulgate lone-wolfism and violent direct action to his Internet milieu of Aryan activists. To the best of my knowledge, Moynihan does not spend his time pushing frustrated white revolutionaries to engage in an armed underground war against ZOG, nor does he belong to any such organization. He is not a politician but an artist. Conveying a cultural critique of modernity from an elitist perspective that towers above the lack of vision he patronizingly ascribes to mainstream herd-man, Moynihan may perhaps be a "leader" of a self-styled artistic advance guard but more in the sense of a Nietzsche than a Hitler.

In compliance with the ideals of the industrial and occult scenes, Moynihan nurtures an aura of mystique and seeks to evade being labeled according to what he perceives as the simplified binary categories that structure mainstream conceptions of reality. Imagery evoking national socialism and fascism blends in with Satanism, gothic romanticism, Roman totalitarianism, and Norse heathenism. Interviews with fanzines catering to the white-revolutionary counterculture are mixed with interviews for anarchist, pagan, and cultural magazines. Pragmatically oriented, Moynihan has found resonance with selected elements of ideas espoused by fanatics and revolutionaries involved in divergent extreme milieus, as reflected in his attraction to Charles Manson, Mu'ammar al-Qadhdhafi, Michael Bakunin, Julius Evola, James Mason, and Miguel Serrano. Featured in different contexts, Moynihan projects many different faces and has been classified as an "extreme rightist" (Coogan 1999), an "extreme leftist" (Wulfing One 1995), a Nazi, a fascist, and an anarchist. Shrugging at the thought of being "explained" with reference to a "meaningless" label, Moynihan (1997) argues that his beliefs are not that easy to fit into any political category.[62] He feels that to label him a Nazi is to "deliberately misrepresent" his views.[63] "What has fascism to do with anything that's going on?" he told a Portland weekly reporter who asked him about it. "The far right is a bunch of isolated losers. I probably have more in common with anarchists than I would with any right-wing person, and they would probably agree" (Dundas 2000).

It all boils down to a question of semantics and definitions. Fascism and national socialism have always contained elements of both the right and left, a fact obscured by categorizing fascism simply as right-wing extremism. As expressed in the catchy slogan "neither left nor right but forward," fascism seeks a third alternative beyond capitalism and communism, a tendency most strongly voiced by the Third Position. When asked to define fascism, Moynihan (1997) suggested that he would describe it "as a hierarchy and levels of responsibility of different people, everyone has a place in the system according to their ability." Moynihan does not favor fascism in the form of "some kind of totalitarian, all-encompassing government," and his view of fascism differs sharply from its historical manifestations in continental Europe. Contrary to envisioning fascism in terms of collective authoritarianism with soldier-citizens submitting to the will of a dictator, Moynihan talks more in terms of a Jeffersonian-inspired paganism akin to Else Christensen's tribal socialism. "I think that fascism has to function in a much smaller way, on a much more decentralized level." Ideally, there should be no central government but a "tribal society functioning in a fascist manner." Moynihan may then best be described as a heathen anarchofascist, with all the paradoxes and ambiguities that follow with such a categorization.

Metal Rage

A more lowbrow expression of apocalypse culture is another nondanceable but far more adrenaline-laden aggressive music, black metal, a genre many have come to equate with "satanic music" due to the excesses in onstage profanity and occasional outbursts of offstage violence perpetuated by black-metal "legions." With sinister imagery—corpse paint, spiked leather, medieval weaponry, satanic symbols—and stage acts pushing sacrileges to new extremes, the cacophonic growl of black metal grew out from its heavy-metal parentage and once-extreme thrash/gothic/death-metal siblings over the course of the 1980s and 1990s, in a process detailed by Moynihan and Søderlind in Lords of Chaos. Rejecting popular bands of the latter genres as sellouts for signing up with mainstream labels, black metal emerged as an uncompromising underground with small independent record labels and fanzines often run by band members themselves. Today, black metal is a global phenomenon with contributing acts from all continents, although Scandinavia remains an important epicenter as evidenced by the transatlantic influence of Nordic bands such as Mayhem, Dark Throne, Bathory, Burzum, Emperor, Enslaved, and Abruptum. With many black-metal bands now reaching close to worldwide distribution, the under-ground status of black metal is at risk of being undermined by corrupting com-mercialization, which poses a challenge for "true" metalheads to take the scene further to the extreme to regain its aura of pure rage, danger, and furor.

Initially, black metal sounded much like death metal, with unintelligible growling vocals set to down-tuned guitars and manic drums competing in speed with hardcore punk, but it soon came to incorporate influences also from folk, orchestra, opera, and techno. Whereas death metal was an outburst of exces-sive gore, reveling in dismemberment, torture, cannibalism, murder, and rape, black metal is by definition concerned with the occult as seen in its lyrical fixa-tion with Satan or darkside tribal paganism.[64] This orientation is typically re-flected also in band members' stage names, such as Euronymous (allegedly Greek for Prince of Death),[65] Dead, Hellhammer, Occultus, or Fenris, and band names such as Cradle of Filth, Funeral, or Deicide. Black metal as a concept first appeared as the title of a 1982 album by the English heavy-metal act Venom.[66] Pushing Satanism in violent assaults on Christianity, Venom's theater of blas-phemy came to inspire successive acts to endorse the Prince of Darkness. Ac-cording to the black-metal chronicles of Moynihan and Søderlind (1998, 15), King Diamond of Mercyful Fate was one of the only metal bands of the 1980s whose satanic approach went beyond entertainment and mere shock value.

Although most of the early satanic bands seem to have been in the game for fun, their message was taken dead seriously by successive bands in a sec-ond wave of black metal that commenced in the early 1990s. While many of these later bands acknowledge familiarity with the *Satanic Bible*, their satanic philosophy appeared homemade and construed more by elements taken from horror movies, fantasy novels, and the sensationalist tabloid press than from LaVey. Many in the scene emphasized self-mutilation, suicide, self-inflicted pain, misery, hate, suffering, and even torture of animals, all of which stand in sharp contrast to the life-affirming and animal-respecting approach of LaVey.[67] Unsurprisingly, many activists in the 1990 black-metal scene of Scandinavia con-demned LaVey for being a sham satanic humanist, and stickers with crossed-over pictures of the Black Pope circulated as flyers or appeared on album covers.

Bent on serving their cloven-hoofed master, evil seeds coalesced in Norway to form the Black Circle centered at *Helvete* ("hell" in Norwegian), an under-ground black-metal shop at Oslo run by Mayhem's Euronymous (a.k.a. Øystein Aarseth), founder of the seminal label Deathlike Silence.[68] Activists involved with the Black Circle would be linked to a spree of criminal activities, ranging from grave desecrations and church burnings to assault and murder. A series of church arsons began when the Fantoft Stave Church, an amazing twelfth-century wooden church decorated with both heathen and Christian symbols, was burned to the ground at 6:00 A.M. on 6 June 1992 (referring to the satanic number 666). In the years that followed, between forty-five and sixty church fires or attempted arson attacks were recorded in Norway, of which roughly one-third had documented connections to black metal (Moynihan 2000, 29).

To the public, Varg Vikernes of Burzum, currently serving a Norwegian maximum sentence of twenty-one years for stabbing Euronymous to death and for three counts of arson, has come to personify the underground shift toward violent direct action. Entering the scene as Count Grishnackh — a name taken from a warlord in service of Sauron, the lord of evil in Tolkien's Lord of the Rings — Vikernes styled himself a public villain with press statements about spreading fear and devilry and frequently indicating that he knew the identity of the arsonists. While retrospectively claiming to have been misunderstood and downplaying his past involvement with Satanism in favor of emphasizing his dedication to pan-Germanic heathen traditions, Vikernes keeps implying his pivotal role behind the events. "I'm not going to say that I burnt any churches," Vikernes told Moynihan in an interview. "But let's put it this way: there was one person who started it. I was not found guilty of burning the Fantoft Stave Church in Bergen, but anyways that was what triggered the whole thing. That was the 6th of June and everyone linked it to Satanism. . . . What everyone overlooked was that on the 6th of June, year 793, in Lindesfarne in Britain was the site of the first known Viking raid in history, with Vikings from Hordaland, which is my county" (quoted in Moynihan and Søderlind 1998, 88).[69] Vikernes pointed out that Christians had desecrated holy heathen grounds all over Norway, as illustrated by Fantoft being built on top of a heathen hörg. In retribution, he said, the perpetrator built a fire of dried grass and branches as a "psychological picture — an almost dead fire, a symbol of our heathen consciousness" that would "light up and reach toward the sky again, as a growing force. That was the point, and it worked" (ibid., 88, 156). Asked how grave desecrations fit into his ideology, Vikernes responded. "They [the Christians] desecrated our graves, our burial mounds, so it's revenge. The people who lie in the graves are the ones who built this society, which we are against. We show them the respect they deserve" (ibid., 155). In his national socialist/heathen manifesto Vargsmål, Vikernes reiterated his arguments, "For each devastated graveyard, one heathen grave is avenged, for each ten churches burnt to ashes, one heathen hof is avenged, for each ten priests or freemasons assassinated, one heathen is avenged."[70]

Vikernes is part of a general trend within a segment of the black-metal underground that has moved away from Satanism toward a heathen, if still darkside, worldview. In 1988 the Swedish act Bathory (the name is taken from a seventeenth-century Hungarian noblewoman who allegedly murdered hundreds of young girls in whose blood she bathed to maintain her beauty) released its fourth LP, *Blood Fire Death*, which features an evocation of Odin's wild hunt. Other acts, notably Enslaved, Einherjar, Graveland, and Burzum partook in establishing a heathen black-metal outlook that would inspire countless bands in the years that followed. Instrumental to this development was Vikernes, who while incarcerated continued to record music, to write articles and books, and inaugurated the Cymophane Productions network that grew to include a publisher and a record label.[71]

Advocating national socialism, anti-Semitism, eugenics, and racist paganism, Vikernes launched Norsk Hedensk Front in 1993, which soon evolved into a network of independent tribes called the Allgermanische Heidnische Front (AHF). "We seek the elite," Vikernes explained to his American readers of (now-defunct) *Muspellzheimr Journal*, emphasizing the spiritual core of the racial struggle. "Wotan is the meaning. National Socialism is the way" to secure "Aryan supremacy on Mother Earth" and "colonization of the universe" (quoted in Södergren 1998). In 2001 AHF claimed chapters in Norway, Sweden, Denmark, Netherlands, Germany, Vinland (United States and Canada), Russia, and Flanders (Vikernes 1997, 93).[72] Seeing Christianity as incompatible with the Teutonic folk soul, the AHF aims to resurrect a heathen society based on monoethnic tribal democracy and ecologically sustainable production.

Since the AHF talks more about animal rights, environmentalism, and folkish paganism than music, the heathen/fascist wing of the black-metal underground soon found other expressions, notably the Pagan Front and National Socialist Black Metal. The former is a network of bands and record labels that view black metal as an "archetypical and atavistic expression" of the Aryan soul and seek to further the milieu's paganization.[73] The latter sees national socialism as a logical extension of the political and spiritual dissidence inherent in black metal and includes acts such as Burzum, Absurd, and Graveland. Although fascist and heathen sentiments constitute a discernible trend within the black-metal underground, they remain a minor part of black metal and certainly do not define the whole scene.

The Howling Wolf of Darkside Asatrú

Aiming to release the "darkest, most feral and primal side of the Aryan psyche" is Nathan Zorn Pett, editor of the national socialist skinhead/Odinist *Fenris Wolf* fanzine("Fenris Wolf" 1999).[74] In Norse mythology the Fenris wolf is the beastly child of Loki who was finally fettered by a magic chain forged by dwarves. At Ragnarök, the Fenris wolf is prophesied to come loose, engaging on the side of the forces of chaos, killing Odin. In Pett's interpretation, the destructive Fenris wolf turns into a "manifestation of strength unrestrained, unstoppable Aryan power," temporarily contained through the use of "modern day 'Jewish sorcery.' " Eventually, this personification of revenging Aryan rage will break "the zionist chains" and "ravage the earth" ("White Revolution" 1997, 30). In Pett's Yockeyan reading of the Norse sagas, the Aesir represent the Aryan race that has reached the zenith of its civilization. Infested by the culture-distorting influences of capitalism and Judeo-Christianity, Aryan civilization has degenerated to a point at which renewal can only come through cataclysmic destruction. The destructive element embodied in the Fenris wolf archetype has begun to manifest and will consume in flames the present system for Gimle to rise anew. "I see the burning eyes of Fenris in many people around me," Pett (1999) said. "I can see the spirit of Fenris, this dark, Faustian, some would say Satanic presence" in Aryan revolutionary heathen youth all over the world. "What the Jew fears is this Fenris wolf archetype, the destructive Aryan archetype, which the Jew knows is coming, the primal urge combined with diabolical intelligence that the Aryan man is known for. The Aryan man is the world's most efficient, nature's finest killing machine. That is the dark side of Aryan man and that is what the Fenris wolf represents."

Born in 1973 in New Jersey, Pett spent his childhood in San Diego with his born-again Christian father who built radars for the navy. Influenced by the back-to-earth movement, the family moved back east to live off organic farming and hunting in rural southern New Jersey. A few years later, his artist mother came into the picture. A custody battle ended up with Pett living with his mother in the bohemian art community in New York City. In his teens Pett entered the emerging skinhead scene via white-noise music and went on an unruly quest that eventually would land him in a Louisiana prison for a minor weapons violation. By that time, Pett edited a generic national socialist skinzine, *Hail Victory*, and had adopted an Odinist worldview. On his release in 1996, Pett published the first issue of *Fenris Wolf*.[75] A "harbinger of death and destruction to the Jew world," *Fenris Wolf* is a crossbreed of militant darkside heathendom and skinhead culture presented as a zine of "racially pure barbaric hate." Interviews with acts such as No Remorse, Burzum, White Wolf, Swastika, Eric Owens, and Blut Kampf 1488 blend in with articles about Norse cosmology, rituals, and divinities, völkisch philosophers, calls for radical activism, and guides on how-to-beat-up-your-local-SHARP (Skinheads Against Racial Prejudice).

To Pett, white-power music is the most important propaganda tool of revolutionary Aryan paganism and is a manifestation of long suppressed berserkr instincts. "Through the various manifestations of extreme Metal (such as Death and Black Metal) the ancient archetypes of our Germanic ancestors have again begun to whisper the mysteries of immortality and mystical enlightenment," an article on "Asametal" read. The heathen satanic metal acts "*are* possessed by the spirits of Odin's elite," as prophesized in the *Grímnismál* saga, where it says that by the end of this world cycle, five hundred and forty gates of Valhalla will be opened and the souls of the Einherjar recur on earth for the ensuing battle.[76] White racists of the older generation do not understand metal, Pett (1999) contends. They don't appreciate the noise and mistake the aggression for nihilism. "Black metal is a new barbarian music for the youth, and the crashing and the thundering of the music is like the thundering of Mjölnir, Thor's mighty hammer, crushing the skulls of our enemies. The natural chaos, the sheer acoustic assault of the music is like a tornado, it's the natural forces of chaos unleashed."

To Pett (1999), nonracist paganism is an "oxymoron" because "racism is the will of nature" and "paganism represents nature. So, how can you be an antiracist pagan?" True paganism is a reflection of the racial soul, an "organic" worldview based on blood and soil. "We will smash any who try to prevaricate or distort the truth of Asatrú," an article read, warning the "unwarlike Asatrú imposters" for mistaking Odinism for a peaceful "spiritual warrior" type of hippie creed ("What Is Odinism?" 1997). Pett also dismisses most ethnic Asatrúers as "hobbyists" who are "mocking our ancestors by playing Vikings. Our Viking ancestors did not dress up like Stone Age Europeans, trying to pretend that they were stone age Europeans, they were in the here and now, living in the present and that's what we need to do" (Pett 1999; "What Is Odinism?" 1997). In addition to the tendency for historical reenactment Pett sees among ethnic Asatrúers, he also condemns Valgard Murray and the Asatrú Alliance for promoting "sexual promiscuity" and "ethnic favoritism" in a phony creed of "Kosher Asatrú" to "gain favors of the Establishment" (Pett 1999; "From the Wolfs Den" 1998; "What Is Odinism?" 1997).

Far from being "PC," "true" Asatrú appreciates national socialism as the "seedbed of Odinism" in this century. "Heinrich Himmler probably did more to resurrect the spirit of Asatrú than any other man in the twentieth century" ("What Is Odinism?" 1997).[77] Reflecting a racist skinhead recasting of reconstructed Norse paganism, the Fenris Wolf project amends the list of seasonal blots with holidays such as the Day of Remembrance for Ian Stuart (of Skrewdriver), who is hailed as "Bragi incarnate" (24 September); Hitler's birthday (20 April); the Beer House Putsch (8 November); and the Day of the Martyrs, in remembrance of Robert Jay Mathews (8 December) ("Fall Folkish Calendar" 1997; Pett 1999).[78] For the Day of the Martyrs, Pett has organized blot ceremonies at the site of Mathews's death on Whidbey Island complete with swastika lightning and ritual burning of the Star-Spangled Banner.[79]

While hailing Mathews as the "true spiritual leader" and supporting the Wotansvolk effort ("Pagan Liberation League" 1999), Pett also criticizes them and other racist Odinists for trying to revive a religion with inherent weaknesses as proven by history. "The simple fact is that Christianity did prevail over Odinism. To me, that just shows that Odinism was not a strong enough religion" (Pett 1999). Based on sparse archaeological findings and incomplete remnants of Norse traditions recorded by Christians, the modern effort to reconstruct Odinism will be an insufficient tool for realizing Aryan liberation, Pett claims. Suppressed by centuries of bourgeois Christian culture, the darker, primal, primitive, and barbarian aspect of European man is missing. "We need a synthesis of paganism and Satanism," Pett argues, "to combine the dark and the light elements" and make Aryan man whole in a racial individuation process. Inspired primarily by the third "heathen" satanic position, Pett dismisses as "degenerate garbage" the legacy of LaVeyan Satanism as represented by Marilyn Manson or magazines such as Scapegoat. When defining the "true" synthesis of "authentic" paganism and Satanism one needs to be on guard against the "Jewish element, the alien element [that] always will be creeping into [Aryan traditions]; in paganism [you find it] in the form of Wicca and in Satanism in the form of LaVey and the Church of Satan" (1999). Darkside Asatrú will unleash the inherent qualities of Aryan man at levels both esoteric and exoteric in order to realize the quest for individual divinity and racial greatness. "Each European expresses to a degree the divine consciousness which animates the entire culture," a Fenris Wolf article read ("Mystical Asatrú" 1999). Each human has a potential to evolve toward Godhood, but only an elite of individual heroes will succeed at the internal battlefield and reach the gates of Valhalla to join the ranks of the gods. Each mystic victory seeds the new Aeon when divine Aryan man will fulfill his destiny and colonize the universe (Pett 1999).

Concerning the exoteric earthly struggle, Pett argues that American whites need to reclaim their birthright. Aryans thrived on American soil well before the Amerindians came there, Pett argues, and Vikings explored and settled what properly should still be known as Vinland, leaving it to their descendants to uphold their claim. "With the modern day sword, be it AK-47 or AR-15, we will establish here in Vinland a separate Aryan religion, culture and homeland, under the mighty swastika" ("What Is Odinism" 1997). Elaborating on this theme, Pett (1999) is a far cry from the more modest separatist strategy of the northwestern imperative. "The land from Alaska's arctic tundra to the tip of Nova Scotia, from the sunny climate of southern California to the tip of southern Florida . . . is our homeland." Reveling in gory fantasies of racial cleansing, Pett believes that the "manifest destiny" of Aryan man is to follow Odin "to victory over the lower races, utterly destroying them and wiping them out from the face of the earth, not leaving so much as at trace that the untermenschen ever existed" ("Ragnarok in North America" 1998). Meantime, true revolutionary work must be done toward having a "tribal separate culture" with self-sufficient communal settlements living on land of their own, "apart from the consumer, capitalist, destructive effects of society," raising healthy "pagan Aryan children" in "natural environments" free of pollution and public schools.[80]

Inspired by James Mason's *Siege*, hailed by Pett (1999) as "the *Mein Kampf* of the twenty-first century," Pett insists on an uncompromising "war on the establishment" waged from the vantage point of being completely apart from the system.[81] Blasting the traditional right wing for always being on "the wrong side of every issue," Pett advocates a Third Positionist, white-worker militancy in what he sees as a "racially charged class war." The American administration is the main enemy, and it safeguards a capitalist, not a communist global system. To launch war against the One World Government/NATO/America, true white revolutionaries should seek alliances with those forces confused for enemies by the traditional right wing. "We support the communist, the anarchist, the Islamic, and any type of revolutionary against the Judeo-Christian status quo," Pett (1999) emphasizes. "We gain inspiration from Che Guevara as well as from Aryan revolutionaries like Robert Mathews."

Accordingly, the Fenris Wolf project voices support for Slobodan Milosevic and Saddam Hussein, Timothy McVeigh and the Unabomber. Serbian nationalists are depicted as peaceful Aryan separatists who only wish to escape the New World Order, while an enemy-of-my-enemy-is-my-friend logic explains the embrace of Hussein.[82] "Saddam Hussein is an ally of all true Aryan Revolutionaries. As an enemy of our mortal enemy—Imperialist Capitalist Jew America he becomes our 'friend.' As our vile Federal Government sees Saddam and his 'weapons of mass destruction' as a threat to their system, the very system that is responsible for the slavery and murder of the White Race, then we can only view him as an ally" ("Saddam Hussein" 1998). Such rhetorical support for Hussein is quite common throughout the Aryan revolutionary counterculture, from William Pierce of the National Alliance to David Lane of Wotansvolk.[83]

Backing Timothy McVeigh is, however, more controversial. Some claim that there is no honor in killing innocent children, others that it means bad publicity. Some activists suspect that McVeigh was innocent, others that he was a CIA-mind-controlled patsy. Some say that McVeigh never was part of the Aryan struggle to begin with, and some dismiss him as a nonpartisan due to Terry Nichols's Filipino wife. Among those who believe that McVeigh did the right thing, a strong segment voice such opinions in private only, claiming that public endorsement only attracts unwanted attention. Pett belongs to the vociferous hardcore faction that ignores all such precautions. "I'm sick of hearing the jew-federal propaganda about 'all those poor children that died in the blast,' " Pett wrote. "The fact is that a good number of them were nonwhites and also children of the ATF and FBI murderers that would have grown up to hunt us down" (1997, 16). McVeigh is entitled unequivocal support as a "revolutionary freedom fighter" against the ZOG. "His attack on our Federal enemies was totally justified. As we recognize ourselves to be fully in a state of war with the United States government, this clear military target is simply a furtherance of the Second American Revolution, as begun by Bob Mathews and the Order in 1984" (ibid.)

Within the radical environmentalist faction of the racist heathen milieu, there is widespread support for the Unabomber, Theodore Kaczynski, who in 1998 was sentenced to life imprisonment for a bombing campaign that killed three people and injured twenty-three others between 1978 and 1995.[84] Heathens of this category tend to hail Kaczynski as an exemplary ecological warrior whose targets among corporate executives, lobbyists, and medical scientists were all known enemies of Mother Earth. "I support ecoterrorism, ecofascism," Pett (1999) laid down. "If people should have to go to let Mother Nature live, I'm on Mother Nature's side." As do many national socialist activists that adopt a radical environmentalist perspective, Pett claims, "The ecological movement is a white movement, founded by Aryans." Portrayed as founding father of the Green movement is Walther Darré, Reichsbauernführer (peasant leader of the reich) and NSDAP minister of agriculture between 1933 and 1942. Opposed to further urbanization and industrialization, Darré romanticized the peasantry as the "life source" of the Aryan race, coining the "Blut und Boden" concept to connote his belief in an esoteric link between the Nordic race and the soil. As minister of agriculture, Darré sponsored programs for conservation, biodynamic farming, peasant cooperatives, farmers' militias, and favored eastward imperialism to secure what he saw as sufficient geopolitical lebensraum for the toiling race.

Greenpeace, Earth First!, Sea Shepherd, and the Sierra Club are all depicted as continuing the legacy of Darré, being essentially Aryan in membership and values. Lamenting that ecofascism is a minority tendency among American Greens, Pett (1999) points at Dave Foreman, cofounder of Earth First!; Paul Watson, cofounder of Greenpeace and Sea Shepherd Conservation Society; and David Brower, former executive director of the Sierra Club as influential ecologists moving toward a racist position. With more than half a million members, the Sierra Club ranks as one of the more important environmentalist lobby groups. In 1996 a motion stating that environmental concerns called for restricted immigration was barely defeated. Pett believes that this anti-immigration faction of the Sierra Club signifies a growing alliance between radical racism and environmentalism in order to establish a strategy of militant racist biocentrism. Mother Nature demands direct action to halt the threat of population growth, expanding cities, and capitalist exploitation. It will take extreme measures to reverse the extreme environmental situation in North America, Pett claims. When standing against corporate power that seeks to level the redwood forest, only militant action will do. Rejecting tree spiking as ineffective and misguided because it targets working-class white people, Pett states that "you need to start from the top. The big executive owners that are destroying the environment . . . can be assassinated, they can have their cars blown up, and they can be given death threats and warnings. I believe terror works." While styling Kaczynski a Green Aryan warrior and a sign of times to come, Pett emphasizes that the Unabomber in no way came near what needs to be done. "Learn from Pol Pot. He wasted the cities and made people work on farms. His was an agricultural reform movement," Pett says, adding, "An Aryan Pol Pot is needed in the future to clean out these urban cesspools."

In 1998 Pett relocated to idyllic Whidbey Island outside Seattle, Washington, launched the Pagan Liberation League, and aligned with the Richmond, Virginia–based White Order of Thule (wot) as its northwest chapter. Originating in 1994 as the American branch of the racist/heathen satanic Black Order, the wot developed a blend of pan-European paganism, racist Gnosticism, Ariosophic Satanism, and Third Way politics (the wot faction of Third Positionist thought). Drawing on Jungian psychology, Spenglarian history, and

Nietzschean philosophy, the WOT intends to seed the New "Thulean" Aeon by releasing the "Light and Dark Gods and Shadow-Soul of our Folk" ("WOT Articles of Faith" 1998). "Thule" refers to the theory of the Arktos (hyperborean) origin of Aryan man, popular among völkisch Ariosophists and occult national socialists. Founding member of WOT Joseph Kerrick (1996) suggests that Ultima Thule began as an extraterrestrial civilization of white gods from which the present-day Aryans descend. Aryans from the north polar motherland settled Atlantis and Lemuria "before these lands were lost in cataclysmic events," which forced "the surviving Aryans into the highlands of Asia" (Georgacarakos 1997b; Georgacarakos 1998).[85] The migratory pattern of these man-gods then followed a mythical path from north to south and east to west, as can allegedly be detected from the lore of world mythology. The ancient Sumerian, Persian, Chinese, Egyptian, and South American civilizations all originated with the arrival of Aryan man-gods, and Aryan man must now follow his evolutionary destiny to re-ascend into godhood, which is the esoteric aim of the Thulean project (Cox 1998; Adams 1999).

The concept "white" was initially adopted to distinguish WOT from its international Black Order parentage but was soon laden with spiritual and political meaning. Given WOT's larger "black" milieu of operation, with its Goths, vampires, Satanists, metal fans, and occult national socialist enthusiasts, "the only thing white about the Order may be the skin color of its members" (Kalkier 1996, 51), an early article read, arguing for transcending the limits of "low" magic and religion. Inspired by the racial mysticism of Miguel Serrano, the white racial soul is considered to have fallen into the black void, entrapped in the all-darkness of the Abyss, and the task of WOT is to accomplish racial resurrection (ibid.). The Black Order evolved into the White Order and its organ the *Abyss* became *Crossing the Abyss* to signify the need to incorporate and transcend the polarities of the dark and the light, the negative and positive, the malign and benign (*Lujan* 1999). Edited by völkisch anarchist artist Michael L. Lujan, *Crossing the Abyss* became a widely read publication, acclaimed by influential Aryan activists such as Alex Curtis and Richard Scutari.[86] Seeking a crosscurrent of occult fascism and heathen Satanism, *Crossing the Abyss* explored Third Way politics and Aryan esoterica, with articles about Savitri Devi, the meaning of human sacrifice in Norse culture, national socialism as part of the occult cycle of the Aryan race, and the Thulean mysteries.[87]

The intellectual orientation of the WOT project is demonstrated by the theoretical effort to construct a new pan-Aryan synthesis out of the historical pagan traditions of Europe. Representing the creative and destructive forces that permeate the cosmos, all original Aryan pantheons are appreciated as manifestations of Aryan archetypes, held to contain elements of a pagan science and psychology that were valid for their respective times and regions. Every area had its own gods, and all pagan traditions had merit, but all must be considered simple by the standard of modern scientific thought. Accordingly, racial redemption cannot be sought in projects of "morbid revivalism" of now obsolete gods. Rather, living paganism should be consistent with contemporary scientific thought. In the "applied science" of archetypical work, WOT therefore sought to "distill" the underlying essence or esoteric "psychoid" of all Aryan gods and goddesses, aiming to construct a nonredundant pagan pantheon for the new Aeon when Aryan man again will "ascend to the stars" (Lujan 1998; Georgacarakos 1997a; Georgacarakos 1999; Lujan 1999). Arranged in pairs of polar opposites, the distilled god/desses are summed up in Damarasha, the palingenetic child-god psychoid that unites and transcends the essence of the Thulean pantheon and represents the individuated racial soul (Georgacarakos 1999). Seeding the new Aeon, WOT considers it a duty for members to "presence the light and dark gods" with "whatever esoteric and political means are necessary" (WOT 1999b), recognizing Loki as the shadow-self of Odin and catalyst for cleansing of Ragnarök (TBO/WOT 1999).

Translated into politics, this means that WOT seeks to transcend the left and right by arriving at a third-way synthesis (Frith 1998). "That the West is dead is the least grasped, yet most important insight our movement can attain," WOT's pseudonymous Max Frith lays down (Frith 1999, 51).[88] "It is a clinging to the past, that is traditional 'conservative' thought that prevents our further progress" (ibid.). The patriot part of the scene needs still to realize that the U.S. government is the worst enemy of the Aryan race. "We must never turn against any enemy of the United States government, foreign or domestic" (Curtis 1999).[89] Accordingly, WOT pragmatically appreciates not only fascist and national socialist thinkers but also Mao, Stalin, and Che Guevara, Nasser, Khomeini, and bin Laden, not in terms of permanent preferences but as successful revolutionaries to learn from and as tactical allies embraced with the logic of realpolitik. "Revolutionaries must be dogmatic on one count only: the revolution must be won at any cost" (WOT 1999a).

Initially led by Peter Georgacarakos and Joseph Kerrick, the WOT directorship was in 1996–97 transferred to Michael Lujan as Georgacarakos was imprisoned and Kerrick departed due to internal differences.[90] Far more an artist and racial mystic than an administrator, Lujan never felt comfortable as director.[91] In early 2000 Lujan resigned, and WOT headquarters relocated to Pett's residence, first on Whidbey Island and then in Deer Park in the northern Spokane area of Washington state. That move proved bound to fail as it put further stress on Pett who that year fathered his first son, Tyr, and faced accumulating troubles in business and racial politics. A business partnership with Aryan Nations sympathizer Jason Swanson to open up Bullet Proof Valley Tattoo shop in Spokane ended up sour, with the partners turning into heated enemies and Pett losing his investment. Local media gave Pett an unwanted notoriety by blasting the news that "a racist pagan organization that idolizes terrorist members of the Order" had "moved its headquarters to the Spokane area" (Morlin 2000).

In the meantime, Pett's intention to launch a racist heathen black-metal record label turned into a disaster. Pantheon was signed up as the first act released on Fenris Wolf Records, but Pett and Pantheon vocalist and Pagan Front strongman Rubeus soon ended up at each other throats, exchanging gross accusations on the Internet. Even more dramatic was the next falling out. Among the overseas WOT members was Hendrik Möbus of the German black-metal act Absurd and owner of Darker Than Black records. Möbus, who had been in contact with Varg Vikernes since the early 1990s, became head of the German AHF chapter after his 1998 parole from youth detention where he had served time for murder. That same year, he became manager of a branch of the Cymophane Records that he set up. Before long, Möbus found himself in new trouble with the law. With two additional sentences (for giving the banned national socialist salute and demeaning his murder victim in interviews), a revoked parole, and new charges pending for distributing national socialist propaganda through Darker Than Black, Möbus in December 1999 escaped to Seattle.[92] Apparently, Pett paid for Möbus's ticket and housed him at his Deer Park residence, hoping that Möbus would reciprocate by helping him set up the Fenris Wolf label and by letting him in on the American distribution of Cymophane Records.[93]

Again, disaster followed in Pett's footsteps. Möbus registered in Pett's name an e-mail account and a post office box for Cymophane, but soon grew disenchanted with his new partner. He claims that Pett burned his passport and maneuvered to secure full control over Cymophane without investing appropriate funding. Allegedly, Pett got increasingly nervous about housing a fugitive and sent Möbus to live with Lujan in Richmond, Virginia. On arriving, Möbus decided to boot Pett out of the Cymophane business and negotiated instead a deal with Erich Gliebe of Resistance Records to secure funding from its owner, the National Alliance.[94] Pett felt betrayed and accused Möbus of having ripped him and his family off financially.[95] According to Möbus, Pett and Lujan woke him up at gunpoint, handcuffed him, and started systematically beating him bloody with a hammer before dumping him from a car. Badly battered, Möbus managed to contact Gliebe who picked him up and brought him to William Pierce at the National Alliance's Hillsboro, West Virginia, headquarters.[96] Pett says he neither admits nor denies being involved in the incident but indicates that Möbus "deserved his beating fully" and is "very lucky to be alive after this alleged event. (This might have something to do with his robbing of my family and the White Order of Thule, but who knows, right?)."[97]

Pierce, who then controlled the white-power labels Resistance Records (U.S.) and Nordland (Sweden), had eagerly sought to move into black metal. Apparently, Möbus helped Pierce secure a share of Cymophane, and Pierce soon became involved with both the NSBM and Pagan Front outfits. During his ten-week stay with Pierce, Möbus also helped Pierce establish European outlets for his records.[98] When Möbus eventually was arrested in August 2000, Pierce helped him file a petition for political asylum to prevent (or delay) his deportation and organized the Internet-based Free Hendrik Möbus campaign.[99] Pett was widely charged for having provided the police with information about Möbus's whereabouts. This was not the first time Pett had been accused of being a race traitor, and documents supposedly detailing an affidavit in which Pett named a skinhead friend of his as the perpetrator of a highway shooting that paralyzed a black man now showed up at several white-racist Web sites. Pett countered by circulating an alternative affidavit supposedly signed by another skinhead whom Pett claims to be the real traitor. Obviously, one of these documents is false, and both parties soon threw race-traitor charges at each other in an escalating vendetta typical of the white-racist counterculture. With the new WOT director and *Crossing the Abyss* editor immersed in such a mess, the White Order of Thule "went underground," that is, dissolved. Pett, who later that fall was hospitalized after having been severely beaten with a bat in an unrelated nightly brawl, returned to the scene in spring 2001, promising to bring destruction to ZOG and his adversaries in the Aryan heathen milieu.

Satanism, National Socialism, and Norse Paganism

The efforts to fuse Satanism with national socialism and paganism became increasingly apparent in the 1990s, provoking heated internal debates within all three milieus. Satanism and national socialism may on one level be seen as incompatible philosophies, as the former stresses radical individualism and the latter authoritarian collectivism. Heathens engaged in reconstructing Norse traditions may find Satan a Judeo-Christian deity irrelevant to their effort. Yet there is a coalescing netherworld in which all three subcultures meet. Interconnected by flows of ideas and activists, this dark undercurrent is populated by individuals who find resonance with selected elements of Satanism, national socialism, and paganism. Seekers may explore these paths consecutively or simultaneously. They may hold multiple memberships in any given number of groups operating within the three larger milieus or seek to merge the three worldviews into some coherent whole. Their presence may be exploited, encouraged, tolerated, or condemned by satanic, fascist, and heathen ideologues.

Far from all Satanists appreciate the national socialist element in their ranks.[100] Between 1995 and 1997, the Church of Satan's *Black Flame* ran a series of polemic articles disputing whether or not Satanism and fascism were compatible philosophies. Jeffrey Deboo objected to the fact that "modern Satanism" had been "infiltrated" with "the symbols, philosophy and world-view . . . of fascism," as he found fascism "absolutely irreconcilable both with our rational self-interest and with the core principles of our philosophy" (1996, 10). The "only true satanic social order," Deboo argued, was anarchism/libertarianism with its emphasis on individual sovereignty. Lamenting the fact that Satanism had become a safe refuge for weekend führers and racist occultniks, Gavin Baddeley agreed with Deboo. "Those Satanists screaming for a white supremacist state of supermen are yet more Turkeys voting for Christmas. The [fascist] world they want to join has no place for deviance or originality. Satanism is a philosophy of indulgence, of the carnal, not a hate faith for scapegoaters. Democracy fosters the repugnant cancer of conformity, but fascism positively demands it" (Baddeley 1997, 6).

At the other end of the spectrum, Thomas Thorn dismissed as unrealistic any notion of a libertarian satanic world order. He stated that "99% of the people in this world is sheep and cattle, who want to be told what to do," suggesting that Satanism and fascism basically were "inseparable elements" (quoted in Buckley 1997, 18). Michael Moynihan saw the rising fascist attitude within Satanism as a "perfectly natural evolution," a sign indicating that "organized Satanism" had increasingly become "more equipped to deal with the challenges of the future" (Moynihan 1996, 13). Resting his case on Spengler, Moynihan argued that fascism and national socialism at their core were intrinsically Faustian and hence Satanic, and he welcomed a "pure form" of "heroic fascism" as an "antidote" to the "preponderance" of modern "victim culture" (ibid.). *Black Flame* also introduced George Burdi Hawthorne, then lead singer of Rahowa and editor of *Resistance*, to its readers through an interview with Moynihan. "I think that the racialist movement ultimately benefits from having Satanists involved," Hawthorne said. "I know that many Satanists agree with our world-view, so why not work together?" (cited in Moynihan 1997, 42). As a service to the interested reader, the interview concluded with an address at which to contact Hawthorne. *Resistance* followed through by introducing folkish Satanism and the genres of death and black metal to the Aryan revolutionary milieu in a move that provoked negative reactions from segments of its readership.[101]

According to the White Order of Thule, the contemporary national socialist revolutionary would benefit from aligning with the satanic scene. "Within a Judeo-Christian context, Satan is arguably the most potent and negatively-charged archetype," wot writes. "Would it not benefit us to tap into the energy latent in such a . . . destructive symbol in order to aid the natural process that is birthing the New on the ashes of the Old?" (Frith 1997, 8). Most Satanists are pro-fascist to some extent, wot argues.[102] White youth are far more likely to read the *Satanic Bible* than *Mein Kampf*, so the Aryan revolutionary should pragmatically seek to guide the heretics in a racial direction (Frith 1997). Given the emphasis on radical individualism generic to satanic philosophy, not all Satanists seem easily guided into the fold of authoritarian collectivism. WOT's Wulf Grimwald (a.k.a. Kerry Bolton) notes the "considerable number" of Satanists who identify with national socialism, finding it "natural" as "both ultimately spring from pagan origins."[103] However, Grimwald laments, the racial cause will not benefit from everyone combining the pentagram and the swastika. Many of those who embrace a Satanist-fascist synthesis do not comprehend the organic state concept inherent in national socialism and mistake the social Darwinist rationale for nihilistic libertarianism, refusing to submit to the will of the racial/national collective.

Among more conventional or Christian national socialist circles the condemnation of the satanic elements is voiced in more unequivocal terms. While William Pierce of the National Alliance does embrace the heathen fascist segment of the black-metal underground, he dismisses Satanism as "destructive," "hedonistic," and "degenerate," and as such diametrically opposed to the "healthy" moral standards of true national socialism.[104] Unsurprisingly, racists belonging to the milieu of Christian Identity react with abhorrence to the presence of national socialist Satanists. By the turn of the twenty-first century, the British-based propaganda center Final Conflict began a campaign to clear the Aryan scene of satanic persons and influences through their magazine, E-zine, and a book, *Satanism and Its Allies*. "Satanists, Jews and Queers . . . hope to infiltrate [racial] organizations," an E-zine article read. "These creeps are attempting to mess things up, subvert Nationalism and make ties with groups like the

Freemasons, Church of Satan, Bolsheviks and more!"[105] Detailing the history of satanic infiltration from Crowley and LaVey to the likes of Aquino, Mason, Schreck, Rice, Bolton, and Long, *Satanism and Its Allies* devotes a chapter to the satanic use of music to distort the racially oriented Aryan youth. Moynihan is denounced for lack of substance and character, for saying things that "appear 'extreme' or 'alternative' or 'deep,' but when they are looked at closely really tell you little or nothing, other than that the man clearly has no idea of what he believes, or in what direction he is going" (*Satanism and Its Allies* 1998, 65). Clearly alarmed with the rising tide of satanic music, the authors warn, "Behind the intellectualization and the hype, there is an evil influence at work, and it is trying to come to a Movement near you soon" (ibid., 69)

Heathen Aryan racists may also seek to keep the satanic and darkside pagans at arm's length or decry them as Jewish degenerates. Miguel Serrano, the esoteric Hitlerist whose epic works of racial occultism have been met with enthusiasm among satanic and darkside heathens, strongly objected to being appropriated or publicized by darkside ideologues. Discussing the topic in an interview published in *Focus Fourteen*, Serrano stated that esoteric national socialists are engaged in a "glorious War and we have no time for people who will only damage our sacred fight with all the kookiness from California, like Satanism" (Katja Lane 2001). He continues, "I am absolutely against people, or innocents, who on the edge of the abyss are playing like children with the words 'Satanism' and 'diabolical' and even worse, mixing all of this with Nazism and Hitlerism. Many Satanists do not know that they are manipulated, psychotronically, in fact hypnotized, when not infiltrated by the CIA, Mossad and other such secret organizations."

In a similar vein Wotansvolk came out strongly against Satanists corrupting the scene with their egomaniacal dreams, instead of working in concert with the pagan revolutionaries to secure racial victory. Denouncing satanic militants for being notoriously unreliable and amoral, McVan is especially concerned about the effort to fuse the fundamentally incompatible philosophies of Norse paganism and Satanism. "Satanism and Wotanism are almost complete polar opposites," McVan (2001) wrote. "The former is as diametric to the religion of Wotanism as is Christianity. In fact, Satanism is exclusively Judeo-Christian. Primarily and foremost, Satanism is a downward path of the spirit, which works at debasing its adherents through often perverse, if not sadistic, ceremonial practices, which may at times resort to the use of black magic. Wotanism is an upward path, focusing on vibrant, nature-based, folkish values, which aspires to our own indigenous, ancestral tenets such as: honor, courage, heritage and the higher developmental evolution of body, mind and spirit."

Among the heathens supportive of Satanism and national socialism there are basically two different but not exclusive motives for incorporating Satanism. It may be part of an insistence on pragmatic alignment with every force of chaos in order to hasten the downfall of the present era or part of a personal quest of individual becoming. White Order of Thule often argues for the first reason, Satan being conceived of as similar to the dark gods, especially Loki who is thought of as a "revolutionary archetype, challenging the status quo and upsetting the sensibilities of the ruling element, the Aesir" (Frith 1997). In the present day and time, Loki is of greater importance than Odin or the "light gods" of the Aesir and Vanir. "It is Loki who helps to engineer the fateful conclusion to Ragnarök," Frith notes, "aiding Surt and his giants towards the Aesir's downfall, in effect to usher in the New Aeon wherein an even mightier race of gods shall grow and prosper, and thus does the wheel turn again. *That is, Loki is on our side!* . . . Let's give the Devil his due. *Hail Satan! Hail Loki! Hail Surt!*" (ibid.; emphasis in original).

Among pagan ideologues making use of Satanic magic to further individual theomorphosis is Edred Thorsson, whose thoughts on Satanism, Asatrú, and national socialism illustrate the ambitious effort to merge selected aspects of all three worldviews into a coherent whole. Through his books, Thorsson has a discernible influence among Norse pagans and Setian Satanists and his obsession with the magic of the Third Reich has led many observers to classify the Temple of Set a pro–national socialist group. Although he hardly qualifies as an Aryan revolutionary heathen, Thorsson's occult works with pagan, satanic, and national socialist elements are intriguing.

Thorsson began his satanic quest with studying the *Cloven Hoof,* acquiring membership in the Church of Satan in 1972. Twelve years later, Thorsson had completed his Ph.D. and begun exploring the darker aspects of Norse paganism. He founded the Rune Guild in 1980 as an initiatory path of Germanic mysticism, aiming to transform the individual initiate from a mortal enmeshed in the natural world of confusion into an individuated, immortal, godlike master of mysteries.[106] Shortly thereafter, Thorsson was introduced to Aquino and Setian philosophy. He joined the Temple of Set in 1984 and made an unprecedented career, becoming Magister Templi IV° by November of that year and was initiated to the Fifth Degree in 1990. Learning of Aquino's efforts to establish the Order of the Trapezoid to explore the quest for the Holy Grail through Germanic magic, Thorsson embraced the path presented as a possible "Gate to Valhalla" (Chisholm 1996, 86; Hardy 1998). Serving as Grand Master of the Order of the Trapezoid between 1987 and 1995, Thorsson also engaged in Asatrú activities through the Rune Guild and the Ring of Troth.

To Thorsson, the Setian principle of "Isolate Intelligence" as a form of pure self-consciousness, which is a prerequisite for Odin's quest of seeking the hidden, Odin represents "the pure suprarational will to power, knowledge and eternal becoming" and stands out as an archetypical esoteric hero, who through an initiatory ordeal descended into the misty netherworlds in a quest to master the mysteries and obtain immortality (Thorsson 1995c). The significance of Odin accordingly extends well beyond his role as Allfather, and Thorsson is skeptical about much of the pagan landscape, which he considers primarily oriented to the right-hand path. Odin is to Thorsson a Germanic bodhisattva of the left-hand path who shows initiates a way to self-theomorphosis that will allow them entrance in the Hall of Valhalla among the other immortal and individually unique Einherjar heroes of the multiverse (Thorsson 1995b).[107]

Michael Aquino founded the Order of the Trapezoid following a magical working he performed at the Castle of Wewelsburg in 1982. The castle had been the ceremonial headquarters of Heinrich Himmler's SS order, and Aquino's effort to retrieve the "positive elements" of "German romanticism" at a site where it had become the tool of totalitarianism led outsiders to see the Temple of Set as pro-Nazi.[108] That the Temple includes *Mein Kampf* by Adolf Hitler among the hundreds of titles in its recommended reading list added to the argument, which overlooks the fact that the Temple includes members of all races and studies a variety of esoteric traditions including Jewish, Egyptian, and African American. Thorsson shares Aquino's fascination with the occult aspects of national socialism, as is evidenced by his articles addressing the subject and his translations of works by völkisch mystics Rudolf von Sebbottendorf, Guido von List, Siegfried Adolf Kummer, and Karl Maria Wiligut.[109] The energies invested in exploring the occult roots and dynamics of the Third Reich indicate that there is a deeper motive involved, beyond the antinomian identification with whatever is considered evil that makes Nazis perfect villains to the satanic neophyte. Evidently, the attraction is not to national socialism as a political system. Satanism and national socialism are on this exoteric level fundamentally opposites. Whereas Satanism centers on the transformation of the individual self, national socialism centers on the renewal of the racial nation. In Satanism there is nothing higher than the will of the individual self, whereas in national socialism any divergent individual interest must submit to the higher will of the organic racial national body.

However, Thorsson claims that, on an esoteric level, there are lessons to be learned from national socialism for the active student of the occult. Thorsson argues that the rites of the Third Reich can be studied as an exemplary large-scale model of manipulative magic (Thorsson 1995d), and he suggests that the aim of collective (national socialist) and individual (satanic) black magic points to underlying essential similarities. Thorsson contends that both focus on "an internally directed and willed process leading to higher, more powerful or god-like states of being," which, in a sense, qualifies national socialism as a form of black magic, as it seeks to evolve the German nation to a "race of super-men" (Thorsson 1995e).[110] Thorsson (1997) accordingly appreciates the occult workings of esoteric national socialism while dismissing its political manifestation as unwanted authoritarianism, as in essence more Roman Imperial than Germanic.

CHAPTER EIGHT

Globalization, Aryan Paganism, and Romantic Men with Guns

D uring the past few years, the number of racist heathen groups, white-noise bands, homepages, and magazines has risen considerably. These developments have affected the belief systems of white-racist activists organized around older counterculture ideologies. In 1999 for example, a majority of the new recruits to the National Alliance listed Asatrú or Odinism as their religion. The growth of racist paganism is not least noticeable among the U.S. prison population, where the number of openly Asatrú/Odinist prisoners has tripled in the five years between 1996 and 2001. Racist heathenry, with its condemnation of Christianity and American patriotism, represents a further radicalization of the Aryan scene. While this has contributed to the marginalization of the Aryan milieu from mainstream American culture, it has also brought the scene into contact with alternative beliefs and practices circulating in the cultural underground.

In concluding this study, I will discuss five topics: (1) The radicalization of the Aryan revolutionary milieu as highlighted by the reactions to the terrorist attacks of September 11, 2001; (2) where the radical Aryan activist is coming from; (3) national socialism, the "radical right routine," and an alternative approach to contemporary politics; (4) the relationship between white racism, alternative science, and religion; and (5) globalization and racist paganism.

"Victory or Valhalla": Aryan Activist Reactions to September 11

While many mainstream Americans were swept away with patriotic feelings in reaction to the terrorist attack against the World Trade Center and Pentagon on September 11, 2001, Aryan revolutionaries were among the few Americans to openly applaud the event. This should not be understood as if every counterculture activist praised the attack. Given the fundamental disunity of the Aryan revolutionary scene, it is hardly surprising that people disagreed in their assessment of the September 11 attacks. David Duke and Don Black were among those to condemn the attack. Racist electronic discussion forums received opinions from people who declared their feelings of outrage (for example, "I HATE when non-white sand niggers commit a massacre on our soil").[1] However, the more common responses throughout the scene were praise and admiration.

In line with statements by the administration and the intelligence community, white racists in general thought that Islamic radicals were responsible. Prior to the terrorist attack, counterculture groups and ideologues had praised radical Islamic leaders such as Osama bin Laden and Mu'ammar al-Qadhdhafi. The American Front, for example, carried translations of articles and speeches by the Saudi expatriate and the Libyan leader at their Web site.[2] Aryan Nations linked its Web site to Hamas and Islamic revolutionaries. When the U.S. administration publicly named Osama bin Laden as the brain behind the September 11 attack, a significant portion of the Aryan counterculture had nothing but admiration for the Islamic revolutionary and his al-Qa'eda network. White Aryan Resistance leader Tom Metzger wrote, "This operation took some long-term planning, and, throughout the entire time, these soldiers were aware that their lives would be sacrificed for their cause. If an Aryan wants an example of 'Victory or Valhalla,' look no further."[3] The electronic mailing list of the World Church of the Creator was quick to print an interview with bin Laden by John Miller: "So we tell the American people," bin Laden said, "and we tell mothers of soldiers and American mothers in general that if they value their lives and the lives of their children, to find a nationalistic government that will look after their interest and not the interest of the Jews. The continuation of tyranny will bring the fight to America."[4] When asked about civilian casualties, bin Laden said that American outrage at attacks on American civilians was hypocritical. "American [war] history does not distinguish between civilians and military, not even women and children. They are the ones who used bombs against Nagasaki. Can these bombs distinguish between infants and military?"[5] A Creativity adherent approvingly commented, "Osama bin Laden is a fascinating person, and one we Americans would be wise to study. Here is a wealthy man who has no use for wealth, except as it allows him to fight, kill and even die for his sacred beliefs. The only thing most Americans would kill for is their pizza, beer, ball games, shopping malls, and SUV's. We have truly evolved into a degenerate state."[6]

On the day of the terrorist attack, Matt Hale of the WCOTC issued a public statement: "We blame the American government for the tragedy of today," which is the "inevitable and ultimate result of a foreign policy that has been slavishly pro-Israel."[7] While the WCOTC extended their "condolences" to the "families of those killed" and "injured" who "are of our White Race," Creators were quick to point out that "the proportion" of "jews," "muds," and "lackeys of jews" working in the World Trade Center "undoubtedly approached 100 percent."[8] Another Creativity member concluded, "It was NOT primarily an 'attack on America' per se, but rather an attack on the Jews and their gentile lackeys."[9] Reasoning that whites in America probably were more willing than ever to listen to white revolutionaries, the WCOTC decided to seize the opportunity. They printed flyers with Osama bin Laden and the burning Twin Towers captioned with "Let's Stop Being Human Shields for Israel" and organized rallies around demands such as "Close Our Border," "Deport Aliens," and "End Foreign Aid."

Applauding bin Laden internally did not prevent Creators from seeking to take advantage of anti-Muslim sentiments. Attacks on mosques were reported, and racist rallies included signs reading "Arabs and Jews Get Out."[10] In his assessment of the terrorist attack, Michael Hoffman II also pointed at American foreign policy: "The Arabs and Muslims never dreamed of troubling us on our soil until we meddled in their fight for land and religion. The Arabs are a noble, and anti-Communist people. They learned barbarism from us and now the chickens have come home to roost."[11] Aryan Nations praised the Islamic revolutionaries in unequivocal terms as courageous fighters in a justified holy war against the evil of the American administration and the New World Order. Sung to "America the Beautiful" were the new triumphant lyrics to "America the Sinful."

> O' wicked land of sodomites
> Your World Trade Center's gone
> With crashing planes and burning flames
> To hell your souls have gone
> America, America
> God's wrath was shown to thee
> He smote this land
> With His own hand
> And showed His sovereignty.[12]

The AN prayed for an escalating war against ZOG, sporting a running header on its homepage, "Islamic World UNITE against Israeli Terrorism. TERMINATE the Terrorist State of (It-is-a-Lie) Israeli and the last Yehudi-Shataan WORLDWIDE."[13]

Capitalizing on the event was also William Pierce of the National Alliance.

"We were attacked because we have been letting ourselves be used to do all of Israel's dirty work in the Middle East."[14] In a chilling commentary aired on the *American Dissident Voices* broadcast of 15 September, William Pierce said, "This week's attacks are just the beginning of what's in store for America. Of course, I don't exactly know what will be next, but certainly biological terrorism is coming. When it does come the death toll will dwarf anything we've been seen so far."[15] Three weeks later, a photo editor at the Florida tabloid *Sun* died from having been contaminated by anthrax mailed to the journal. The bioterrorist attacks continued with anthrax sent by mail to federal departments, Capitol Hill, Senate Majority Leader Thomas A. Daschle, NBC, the New York Post, Voice of America, and other addresses in Washington, D.C., New York, New Jersey, and Florida. The September 11 attack, which claimed about 2,800 lives, shut down Capitol Hill for one day. The anthrax attack, which had at the time caused only one death, disrupted Capitol Hill for a week and caused a public scare of enormous proportions. Adding to panic, thousands of bogus bioterrorist letters, anthrax hoaxes, and false alarms flooded the nation. After September 11, a cautious individual fearing a terrorist attack could maintain a sense of security by avoiding skyscrapers or traveling by airplane. No such simple measure could restrict the risk of being contaminated by airborne anthrax.

Another factor that probably contributed to the public's fear was the fact that the anthrax targets were chosen for reasons not immediately evident. The hijacking of airplanes for kamikaze attacks against prominent symbols of global economic power and U.S. military might was easily interpreted as an effort to castrate the New World Order—an interpretation supported by the fact that the attack came on the anniversary of the 1990 Congressional speech in which President Bush the elder had coined the term *New World Order* in reference to the Gulf War build-up. Sending anthrax to reporters at tabloids or radio stations communicated a message less self-evident. Perhaps, because journalists in general consider themselves at the center of the world, attacking them would send a message that the world itself is under attack. Another possible rationale might be to cause pure terror. Within the Aryan revolutionary counterculture, this is exactly the rationale behind lone-wolfism, the chaos warriors whose acts of "irrational" violence are hoped to hasten the coming of Ragnarök.

Whether or not the anthrax terrorists prove to be white extremists, the unfolding bioterrorist scenario well matches the wet dreams of Aryan militants, war fantasies in which journalists figure as prominent targets. During the late 1990s, biological terrorism was repeatedly referred to as a viable possibility in parts of the white-racist underground. The 1995 nerve-gas attack on the Tokyo subway system, ordered by Aum Shinri-kyo leader Shoko Asahara, was widely admired in those circles. When discussing bioterrorism, Aryan radicals pointed out several advantages, including the small amount of chemical or biological agents needed, which reduces the number of people that have to get involved; the possibility of huge death toll if toxic agents could be spread through air or water in a big city; the fact that biological agents could easily be carried through security checkpoints with metal detectors, X rays, or trained dogs; and the time delay between the release of an agent and its effect on humans, which increases the possibilities for the lone wolf to avoid apprehension.[16] In 1995 microbiologist Larry W. Harris of Aryan Nations, Ohio, published *Bacteriological Warfare*, with special focus on the cultivation and deployment of five potent biological agents, anthrax included, and on how to produce antibiotics. By the late 1990s, hundreds of threats to release biological or chemical agents were issued each year. An anthrax scare broke out in southern California in December 1998 following a series of threats of anthrax exposure. On an anniversary of Hitler's birthday, 20 April 2000, a director of a Jewish student group at the University of Pennsylvania received a letter with a powder purported to be "anthrax." In June 2000 bogus anthrax was sent to abortion clinics in Syracuse, Utica, and Rochester in central New York, and Aryan militants bragged about lone wolves operating in the area.

Bioterrorist dreams commonly linked anthrax deployment with some other major upheaval. Aryan radicals generally realized that whatever they could accomplish was by itself insufficient to bring down the system. Better, then, to wait for an opportunity to present itself and at that point do what is in your power to add to chaos. If there was any reality to the fantastic bioterrorist plans made for the anticipated Y2K breakdown, these were aborted as the millennium passed without any computer-related havoc. Then came September 11. Not that Aryan revolutionaries were necessarily responsible for the subsequent bioterrorist attack, but a certain element within the milieu has become desperate enough to hail such a scenario as a righteous thing to do. This in itself points at how extreme white racism has become since its right-wing conservative patriot days.

Where Is the Aryan Activist Coming From?

Who is attracted to the Aryan counterculture? The stereotypical image recycled in the media paints a picture of the generic national socialist or Aryan activist as a barely literate young man from a poor working-class family with an absent or alcoholic father and traumatic childhood experiences. As an explanation as to why there are national socialists or racist pagans, this theory is at best incomplete, failing, as it does, to account for all those who fit the stereotype but do not become Aryan activists. Clearly, there are millions of working-class youth, and there are many people with traumatic childhood experiences, but the overwhelming majority seem to find avenues other than national socialism to tread. While people fitting this stereotype certainly do exist on the scene, there were remarkably few of them in the circles of activists I encountered.

To undertake a class analysis of the revolutionary white-racist milieu, it would be beneficial to differentiate between leaders and the rank and file. Leaders here are defined as activists who head or have top positions in racist organizations or who serve as important counterculture ideologues without membership or official rank in any of the existing groups. My material includes verified data on fifty-six individuals who by this standard could be defined as leaders, which, given that the total number of counterculture ideologues active on the scene is relatively limited, is sufficient to present a reasonably accurate picture of where the leadership cadre is coming from. When it comes to the rank and file, the value of my material is less certain. It includes interviews and field notes from conversations with some two hundred activists, mainly among racist heathens, Creators, Identity Christians, and white-power–oriented youth. Only thirty-two of these conversations were tape recorded, and the majority of these followers had only been within the milieu less than five years. How many of these were merely "passing through" the scene, I do not know. Neither am I certain of how representative they are, as their number is insufficient in relation to the estimated total of rank and file populating the counterculture, and as they were not chosen for any other reason than that they happened to be present there and then. The materials presented in this category should therefore be seen as indicators only, pointing in a certain direction, which more research might or might not confirm.

A class background typology for the leaders of Aryan counterculture ideologues presents a picture at odds with the stereotypical white-trash thesis. Most leaders came from unbroken middle-class families. A minority was raised in the upper middle class, all sons of affluent businessmen. A smaller minority came from the educated working class, most of whom were children to families where the father had run his own business as, say, a radio and TV repairman or a mechanic. In the largest category were children whose fathers either served as high-ranking officers in the army, navy, or air force or who worked for the military-industrial complex as engineers or researchers. The second largest category comprised those who had an agrarian background and were brought up on farms, predominantly family farms. Another common background was to have been raised in a family in which the father was a small but independent businessman or manager of a small company. Some leaders came from families where the fathers had been university professors or policemen, and the remainder had fathers who worked as physicians, lawyers, or pastors. All but a small minority came from nonbroken families, and only one had been adopted. Very few of the up-and-coming leaders of the radical white-racist milieu had been raised in a big city. The overwhelming majority had been brought up in small-town or rural surroundings, or, to a lesser extent, in suburbia. White-trash backgrounds were virtually nonexistent.

When it comes to the rank-and-file activists, the picture is slightly different. The majority were raised in families in which the father was a military man, policeman, pastor, farmer, businessman, or middle- to low-white-collar or skilled worker, like an electrician, carpenter, plumber, or mechanic; most of these fathers were either self-employed or worked for a small enterprise. Relative to the leaders, the number coming from skilled working-class backgrounds was higher, and the number coming from families of high-ranking military officers was lower. As with the leaders, few had grown up in a big city. The number raised in smaller cities was higher, and the number coming from suburban, and, by extension, metropolitan backgrounds was considerably higher. The latter data may correlate to age. Most leaders were age thirty to fifty years or older. Only five leaders were between the ages of twenty to twenty-nine, the age group into which a large majority of followers falls. Given the expansion of suburbia in the 1970s and 1980s, it may not be surprising that a relatively high number of Aryan activists born in those decades were raised in the suburbs compared with activists born in the 1930s to 1950s.

Concerning their present occupations: excluded those in prison, the largest category of leaders worked full time as counterculture activists, earning a living from sales of counterculture merchandise, membership dues, and donations. The second largest category had to subsidize what they earned from counterculture activism with other sources of income. Most of these were self-employed. They either had companies selling alternative medicine, stocks, books, or merchandise in areas also outside the counterculture or they operated small enterprises, providing services like graphic design, home-page design, and tattoos. A third category of leaders were both counterculture activists and artists, musician, or authors with audiences also beyond the Aryan revolutionary milieu. A few were farmers or self-employed skilled workers in areas such as television and radio repair or carpeting. Of the remaining Aryan leaders, some were part-time lawyers or teachers, a few were university students or in the military, one was a nurse, and one a politician.

The stereotype of the barely literate Aryan activist was conspicuously hard to find in real life. This does not necessarily mean that they are not there; their absence in my material might indicate that more educated activists were willing to be interviewed than were the uneducated. Throughout the milieu, people are encouraged to study, and since racism and white supremacy were long held to be expressions of scientific truth, there are many books to read. Among scholars popular both inside and outside the counterculture, the three most commonly read and referred to are philosopher Friedrich Nietzsche, psychoanalyst Carl Jung, and historian Oswald Spengler. Counterculture staples include *Imperium* by Francis Parker Yockey, *Siege* by James Mason, *Might Is Right* by the pseudonymous Redbeard, and *Mein Kampf* by Adolf Hitler. Popular novelists include Rudyard Kipling, Herman Hesse, Jack London, and J. R. R. Tolkien. Commonly studied genres include European history, cultural history, archaeology, war and military history, the Third Reich, and alternative science and religion. Works found in New Age bookstores dominate the latter two categories, and include other popular genres such as fringe archaeology, UFO literature, conspiracy theory, numerology, Eastern religion, Euro-paganism, and magic.

Another conventional way of looking at Aryan activism is through the spectacles of metaphysical evil. The white racist has become an American villain, a bad guy, associated with national socialist devilry. In documentaries portraying the Third Reich, Hitler is cast as a master magician; these documentaries typically include scenes in which Hitler is speaking at huge mass meetings. Although Hitler was a renowned rhetorician, the documentary audience is rarely served the real content of his speech. Cuts mix Hitler screaming with regiments marching under the sign of the swastika. Instead of providing a translation of his verbal crescendos, the sequence is overlaid with a speaker talking about something different. All this combines to demonize Hitler as an evil wizard spellbinding an unwitting German people to become his zombified servants until they are liberated from the spell by the Allied victory, after which, suddenly, there were no German Nazis left among the populace. How convenient it would be if this image were correct. National socialism could be defeated with garlic. Watchdog groups could be replaced with a few vampire killers, and resources being directed into antiracist community programs and education could be directed at something else.

The truth, however, is that millions of ordinary German workers, farmers, and businessmen supported the national socialist program. They were ordinary people of flesh and bone, husbands and wives, people who loved their children, had pets, enjoyed nature, danced on Saturdays, liked sports, cars, and arts. They were people who probably considered themselves good citizens, which is far more frightening than had they merely been demons. This is a warning against accepting essentialist notions about the nature of good and evil, as it suggests that there is nothing that "is" good or evil by itself. What to one is good may be evil in another context or to another person. Whoever hijacked the airplanes to fly straight into the twin towers of the World Trade Center probably believed they were doing something good rather than evil. With the possible exception of the vocabulary of a few race-occult Satanists, Aryan activists do not consider themselves as evil. On the contrary, they are convinced that they are engaged in activism for the sake of the greater good. They are heroes in a saga of their own production, playing the role of Robin Hood rather than Prince John or the Sheriff of Nottingham. The overwhelming majority were raised in families in which their parents had had a pro-white racial worldview and were fed certain opinions about blacks, immigration, multiculturalism, affirmative action, American Indians, Asians, or Latin Americans at the breakfast table. Only one person in my material really rebelled against the antiracist sentiments voiced by his parents. Most went a step further than their parents, but in the same, not in the opposite, direction in their formulation of what good society would look like.

While the above characterization of the typical Aryan activist might be surprising to readers accustomed to the white-trash stereotype, it is probably less astonishing to the historian of fascism. The German NSDAP mobilized strong electoral support among small but independent businessmen, artisans, farmers, and military officers—that is, exactly the same classes that the Aryan activists are coming from.[17] Interpretations have suggested that these classes felt "displaced" between big business and the working class of proletarians, and have pointed at agrarian resentment against "degenerate" metropolitan life. A comparable feeling of having been "declassed" nurtures the emotional state of the Aryan activist. Typically, interviewees expressed frustration that their "birthright privileges" were "negated." Claiming to come from those who "built this country," they felt that they were entitled to a certain status and to certain "rights" that had been unjustly bestowed instead on racial, ethnic, religious, or sexual minorities. Being normal was being white, male, and heterosexual, but society mocked those traits and instead praised the "deviant." That made them angry. As self-proclaimed guardians of normalcy, they interpreted multiculturalism and gender equality as a provocation against nature. A society that refused to fully recognize their innately superior qualities was therefore unnatural, infested with the seeds of filth and corruption.

Degenerate society could only be rejuvenated through violence, they felt. Aryan activism was embraced as an avenue of restoring the natural order, in which men are men and women are women and the value of being white would again be fully recognized. The "passionate celebration of violence" that Theweleit found as key to the widely read Freikorps literature that fed the male fantasies of the military corps of the fascist groups in Germany during the 1920s is central to the Aryan worldview as expressed through white-power literature, music, art, and religion. Fed by tales of the paramilitary hero in contemporary American war culture, the legacy of American racism, and patriarchal norms, Aryan male fantasies that revolve around rejuvenation through violence merely accentuate undercurrents in American mainstream culture. While activists populating the Aryan counterculture may feel marginalized and separate from American society, their mental universe is still in part a product of mainstream social processes. The alternative reality of Aryan production is locked in a mirror relationship with surrounding mainstream culture and is defined by mutual rejection. This explains in part the element of obsession characteristic of both sides of the conflict. Mainstream white American apologists may decry Aryan racists as un-American, and Aryan activists may vilify mainstream spokespersons as race traitors, the white majority as soulless lemmings, and the white women who fail to appreciate the Aryan warrior as defilers of their race. Yet, what is to be rejected must first be acknowledged, and the harder the condemnation, the more intense the obsession. Hence the disproportionate mainstream focus on the shattered pockets of Aryan revolutionaries and the Aryan obsession with a few biracial couples or sexual minorities.

In this context, the rise of Odinism in the Aryan counterculture can be partly explained. Odinism provides the Aryan activist who feels declassed with ample material for the production of an alternative reality in which his sense of innate but unrecognized nobility and honor is restored. Mobilizing Norse tales of heroism and adventure sets a stage upon which the falling white male may enact his fantasies. Odinism's tribal mode of social organization bestows the initiated heathen with a local community of bonded males, and the Internet presents an opportunity for linking up with a virtual community of Aryan warriors, thus ensuring mechanisms for having the alternative universe acknowledged as a genuine reality. The few white males who "remain true" to the "calling of the blood" and brave the omnipresent forces of ZOG provide the milieu with significant role models of present-day Viking warrior martyrs. Cast away in the federal dungeons or killed in shoot-outs, they are immortalized by white-power lyrics and electronic channels of information that hail their heroism in bombastic wordings suitable for the romance of violence. The Aryan warrior is a "true man," a *braveheart*, fighting to protect the beauty of the endangered white woman, lifting his sword for the long overdue revolution to restore dignity, purity, and honor to the world.

Instead of the white-trash stereotype, the counterculture is populated by angry white males who feel threatened by the prospect of downward mobility. Born to families of military officers, policemen, farmers, small businessmen, or skilled workers, they feel entitled to a certain social status and interpret the transforming American society to be denying them these birthright privileges. "We felt like being under attack," imprisoned Order member Richard Kemp (1997) said. "And it was like, you could either hide in a hole like a mouse or you could come out roaring like lion."

National Socialism, the Radical-Right Routine,
and an Alternative Approach to Contemporary Politics

National socialism is conventionally understood to be an ideology of the radical right, a concept often extended to include the revolutionary Aryan milieu in the United States as a whole. However, the basis for this categorization is rarely discussed. Instead of exploring or even stating the arguments for analyzing the scene in terms of right-wing extremism, the concept is typically accepted and applied without further ado. The a priori definition of the Aryan counterculture as a far-right phenomenon provides observers with a perspective that does not necessarily facilitate the perception of key elements and concerns characteristic of the milieu. The "radical right" caption obscures the significant differences between the worldviews of an archconservative cleric, an ultralibertarian market fundamentalist, a red-white-and-blue militia patriot, a reactionary aristocrat, and a national socialist. Suddenly, David Lane and Pat Robertson are lumped together as if they were driving in the same direction.

An analytical tool inadequate for understanding the heterogeneity of the right, the radical-right routine also overlooks the common ground found between national socialism and ideologies of the left. Typically, Aryan revolutionaries are not only anticommunist but also anticapitalist.[18] Throughout the counterculture, racist activists frequently address issues conventionally associated with a leftist agenda. Aryan radicals may engage in (white) workers' rights and join organized labor. They might focus on environmental concerns, support

Greenpeace, defend natural forests, and be concerned with global warming. They may be against pornography and engage in campaigns against sexploitation. They may want society to provide for the elderly poor and single mothers and state the need for medical and health-care reform as practical points derived from their ideals of (racial) solidarity. They may want to curtail corporate power and reorganize production to serve the interest of the people (i.e., the Aryan Folk) rather than the plutocratic elite.

This is not said to confuse national socialism with left-wing socialism. Racist anticapitalism obviously differs significantly from the critique of capitalist society elaborated from a socialist, anarchist, or communist perspective. Rather, what is important to recognize is that national socialism embraces elements of both the right and the left. Aryan radicals hail "right-wing" values such as race, nation, family, blood, tradition, hierarchy, order, discipline, heterosexuality, ethnocentrism, conservative morals, and the survival of the fittest. They abhor commercialism, materialism, decadence, multiculturalism, everything queer, and the notion of human equality. At the same time, Aryan revolutionaries include leftist themes, as exemplified above, in their programs of racial, national, tribal, or folkish socialism. Most evident in the worldview of the left-wing fascist Third Position, the combination of right-wing and left-wing themes is typical of the scene as a whole. Generally speaking, national socialists and fascists seek to present their positions as alternative to both capitalism and communism. Claiming a third position is not unique to national socialists but is an ambition of many disparate ideologies. Among others, this marks the efforts of Farrakhan's Nation of Islam, Qadhdhafi's Third Universal Theory, the spectrum of political Islam, the Green Parties, and Lyndon LaRouche. This suggests that the conventional left wing–right wing binary has become increasingly insufficient to map out the scene of contemporary politics.

The three-dimensional model presented below is an attempt to substitute the one-dimensional left-right continuum with a map that allows different views to be positioned more adequately in the world of contemporary politics. The model is construed by three pairs of polar opposites, supplementing the left-right continuum with an axis that operates in terms of centralism/decentralism and a third dimension that operates in terms of monoculturalism/multiculturalism. By placing themselves at a certain position in each of the three continua, political ideologies define their relative position to each other and the political universe as a whole. This model allows for change and the possibility of making sense of the transforming patterns of cooperation and conflict between the evolving political groups as they move through the universe.

Adding to the left-right binary the centralism-decentralism axis, we get a primary set of four ideal types: right-wing centralism, left-wing centralism, right-wing decentralism, and left-wing decentralism. This is more accurately representative of important elements shared by the political philosophies of the right and left that aim at centralizing political authority to the top hierarchy of a totalitarian state administration. Despite the many differences between communism and national socialism, the Soviet Union under Stalin and national socialist Germany after the Night of the Long Knives still shared essential features: party rule, authoritarian collectivism, idolization of the leader, nationalization of natural resources, a state-planned economy, severe restrictions of the rights to exercise freedom of organization and expression, state-run programs of national health, state-controlled education, and state-sponsored efforts to restore infrastructure. The similarities between left-wing and right-wing ideologies close to the pole of centralization explain in part the "Red-Brown" alliance prevalent in post-Soviet Russia, a phenomenon bewildering to observers accustomed to thinking about Stalinism and Hitlerism as incompatible polar opposites.

At the other end of the axis are left- and right-wing ideologies that ultimately aim at abolishing the authority of the state in favor of a decentralized society in which power is invested in small, autonomous local communities. Groups belonging to the family of left-wing anarchism accordingly share fundamental traits with groups coming from the tradition of right-wing radical libertarianism. They are both typically anticommunist and anticapitalist revolutionaries who fight the establishment and idealize individual freedom and local self-determination. Green anarchists and anarcho-syndicalists envision a future confederation of self-sufficient, cooperative communities practicing direct democracy along lines quite close to ethnic and racist heathen visions animated by ideals of tribal socialism in the national syndicalist legacy introduced by Else Christensen. While European fascist and national socialist organizations tend to gravitate toward the pole of centralism, the more successful American fascist groups cluster at the opposite pole of decentralism. U.S. organizations built on the "European" national socialist model rarely manage to attract a substantial following. The largest American organization of the centralized right-wing kind is the National Alliance, which despite its recruitment drives and high media visibility remains modest in numbers, with an estimated nationwide total of less than 3,000. In comparison, right-wing groups closer to the pole of decentralism display patterns of perennial (albeit short-lived) success, as evidenced by many populist groups, the Posse Comitatus, the militia milieu, and racist heathens.

The similarities derived from the decentralist antisystem perspective have frequently misled observers to conclude that radicals to the extreme left and right essentially are identical. As though the left-right continuum formed a circle, a common mainstream argument suggests that the radical left meets with the radical right if one proceeds far enough toward the edge of the wilderness of extremism. To some, this is illustrated with the red-black colors of anarcho-syndicalism, which are mistaken for a symbol of a communist-fascist alliance. This perspective colored quite a few columnist commentaries on the 1999 "Battle in Seattle" and on the street riots that accompanied the "Summit Circus Tour" of European cities such as Cologne, Prague, Barcelona, Gothenburg, and Genoa in the years 2000 and 2001. Militant anarchists and heathen chaos warriors are, however, not birds of a feather. While radicals involved with decentralist left- or right-wing activism oppose the global power structure of the present, they do so for very different reasons. The differences between the worldviews of left- and right-wing decentralism transpire in their respective visions of what the postrevolutionary stateless society would ideally look like. Both milieus believe that such a society would reflect "nature" but differ fundamentally in how this natural society would be characterized. Racist heathens believe that abolishing the authority of the state would lead to a society based on "nature's eternal hierarchy": the strong will survive and the weak will perish in a social system of meritocracy in which the talented few assume a natural authority over the ungifted masses. On the contrary, anarchists believe that stateless society will be egalitarian and based on the "equalizing forces of nature." There are no weak or ungifted people but people with different strengths and talents that complement each other in a society that prospers by mutual aid, respect, and recognition.

Adding to this a third dimension in terms of a continuum between the opposing poles of monoculturalism and multiculturalism completes the model. Monoculturalism foresees an ideal society exclusive to a certain category of people defined either by race, ethnicity, religion, or culture, a position that commonly envisions programs for cleansing present society of those considered to be aliens according to the proposed foundation. Multiculturalism involves no such rules of exclusion as the basis of the ideal society, but embraces as citizens of equal rights all people within the given territory of legislation, irrespective of race, ethnicity, religion, or culture. Thus are formed 8 three-dimensional ideal types of political positions, illustrated as follows by a contemporary political group or tendency: monocultural right-wing centralists (National Alliance); multicultural right-wing centralists (LaRouche); monocultural right-wing decentralists (National Socialist Kindred); multicultural right-wing decentralists (Republic of Texas); monocultural left-wing centralists (Black Panther Party); multicultural left-wing centralists (Revolutionary Communist Party); monocultural left-wing decentralists (American Indian Movement); and multicultural left-wing decentralists (Industrial Workers of the World).

To the extent that organizations and tendencies share one or two of the three components, they will display common features that occasionally cause outsiders to mistakenly identify them with each other. A case in point would be the different political "fronts" of Lyndon LaRouche. Having characteristics common to European fascist organizations but holding recruitment drives that recurrently target the African American and American Muslim communities, LaRouche groups can appear to have a bizarre nature to outsiders. The three-dimensional model, though, suggests that while perhaps unusual, LaRouche may nonetheless be understood as a multicultural right-wing centralist, espousing a European model of fascism with global ambitions but also having an inclusive multicultural orientation and membership.

These examples are obviously based on theoretical abstraction for the sake of clarity. In "real life," few groups are neatly positioned as clear-cut examples of the ideal types presented but are instead positioned at certain points along the continua between the three sets of polar opposites. As was emphasized above, national socialism should generally not be reduced to far-right extremism, as it embraces elements of the left and right. A majority of the national socialist groups on the scene would probably position themselves slightly to the right of the center of the right-left continuum. Most likely, the exceptions would not be dominated by national socialist groups taking a position further to the right, but by national socialists who position themselves to the left of the center as evidenced by the milieu animated by the left-wing Third Position. Similarly, national socialist organizations differ in the extent to which they gravitate toward the poles of centralism or decentralism and to what extent they may pragmatically embrace strategies involving networks of cooperation transcending racial borders.

The three-dimensional model facilitates an understanding of the world of folkish heathenry. All such pagan ideologies are clustered close to the pole of monoculturalism, although they may differ depending on whether they make ethnicity or race the basic unit of classification. With the exception of the transitory centralist phase envisioned by David Lane of Wotansvolk, folkish pagans tend to gravitate toward the pole of decentralism. Animated by ideas of tribal socialism they often talk in terms similar but not identical to anarcho-syndicalism.

While incorporating elements of leftist agendas, racist heathens envision nature as a hierarchy and reject notions of human equality and egalitarianism. Tribal socialism is more a decentralist fascism based on self-sufficient communities governed by corporativist ideals informed by the notion of the ethnic group or race as an organism rather than by anarcho-syndicalist visions of a decentralized tribal society with self-sufficient multicultural communities governed by principles of equality and mutual aid.

White Racism, Stigmatized Knowledge, and Religion

Eurocentric reconstructions of premodern Norse, Celtic, or Mediterranean traditions, racist Satanism, and occult national socialism seem to thrive in the Aryan revolutionary milieu. Why would a white racist eagerly embrace theories about, say, the polar origins of Aryan man, speculations about race-specific divine archetypes engraved at birth in the cerebral cortex in each person of pure Aryan blood, or assertions of a post-1945 esoteric war in which Hitler is still alive as führer of a hidden bastion of supreme Aryan warriors inside the hollow earth? A common denominator between racism, alternative science, and paganism is that adherents accept as truth knowledge that is rejected or ridiculed by the institutions of mainstream culture that claim monopoly in the field of production of knowledge. The three milieus centered around what Michael Barkun terms "stigmatized knowledge" (Barkun 1995; Barkun 1998b), that is, knowledge that claimants regard as empirically verifiable but that has been censored by the universities, academic press, school authorities, and communities of scholars. Barkun subdivides the domain of stigmatized knowledge in five categories: (1) forgotten knowledge, that is, knowledge once known but lost through faulty memories, cataclysm, or some other interrupting factor (e.g., Atlantis, the divine origin of Aryan man); (2) superceded knowledge, that is, knowledge previously recognized but now rejected as false (e.g., astrology and alchemy); (3) ignored knowledge, that is, knowledge claims that persist in low-prestige social status groups but are ridiculed by others (e.g., herbal and folk medicine); (4) rejected knowledge, that is, knowledge that is explicitly rejected as false from the outset (e.g., UFO abductions); and (5) suppressed knowledge, that is, knowledge that authoritative institutions know to be valid but that is suppressed by the powers that be (e.g., alien origins of UFOs, the poisoning effect of fluoride drinking water, the true JFK assassins).

White racists attach importance to superceded knowledge and often claim that ZOG orders authoritative institutions to suppress the scientific truth of racism. Data accumulated during field research suggest that believers in one kind of stigmatized knowledge tend to be receptive or open to other kinds of stigmatized knowledge. The fact that a knowledge claim is not accepted as true by the universities and mainstream media is interpreted to mean that there must be something to it. The ideologues of Wotansvolk, for example, began as firm believers in white supremacy and the scientific validity of racism and were astounded to undergo a process of rejection that culminated in having their racist views be cast by authoritative institutions onto the dump heap of obsolete ideas. Their resulting loss of confidence in mainstream orthodoxy opened their minds to peddlers in other fields of stigmatized knowledge. Searching for hidden truth, the Wotansvolk troika eventually found the pagan traditions of the ancient Norsemen and remained open to other forms of stigmatized knowledge. Adjacent to paganism is the field of ignored knowledge, and practitioners of heathen traditions often aim at reviving or relearning herbal remedies and folk medicine. Wotansvolk leaders are also inclined to accept the claims of the remaining knowledge categories. Katja Lane is deep into astrology and alternative medicine. David Lane explores numerology, alchemy, and the wisdom of ancient mystery religions. McVan is fascinated by the possibility of an Arktos origin of Aryan man, is enthused by theories of sunken continents and hidden cities, believes that the administration suppresses the fact that extraterrestrials frequently visit earth, and suspects that the HIV virus is manmade. In their own terminology, Wotansvolk ideologues are "free thinkers," a euphemism for their readiness to accept as true knowledge rejected as false by a mainstream orthodoxy they identify as ZOG-controlled. In this respect, Wotansvolk is not unique but illustrates well a phenomenon that characterizes the world(s) of folkish paganism.

The flow of stigmatized knowledge circulating the cultural underground is not unidirectional. Activists involved with some other counterculture formation may readily embrace alternative information produced by Aryan ideologues. New Agers may channel fascist or racist messages purportedly from an extraterrestrial intelligence, black separatists may accept anti-Semitic theories produced by white racists, and conspiracy believers may well recognize the claims of Holocaust deniers. A radical Aryan ideologue quick to realize this was Ernst Zündel, the Toronto-based national socialist and Holocaust denier. Writing under the pseudonym Christof Friedrich, Zündel published books detailing claims that UFOs are not manned by extraterrestrials but piloted by the SS, that national socialist German scientists invented the first flying saucers during World War II, that the German military built bases in Antarctica and inside the hollow earth, and that Hitler escaped to this hidden headquarters from where the UFOs still take off to carry out missions on the surface of the earth. Zündel also attempted to organize hollow-earth expeditions in search of secret national socialist UFO bases, and he sold an Official UFO Investigator Pass that included a series of questions in English and German to ask the UFO crew when contact had been established.[19] When asked if he seriously believed in the alternative knowledge he produced, Zündel (1998) burst out laughing, explaining that it was a strategy he tried in the context of expanding Holocaust revisionism. Given the next-to-complete ZOG dominion over media, education, and science, Zündel reasoned that only free thinkers ready to accept knowledge that radically departs from what is presented as truth by mainstream institutions of learning were likely to embrace the thought that the Holocaust was a hoax. When he found an audience willing to accept his UFO theories, he knew that he had found the addressees he had been looking for.

Receptive to flows of alternative knowledge, racist heathenry incorporates also many of the treats offered at the smorgasbord of the revolutionary Aryan counterculture. Animated by white-noise music and fueled by elements of conspiracy theory, anti-Semitism, warrior ideals, populism, and separatism, racist paganism has become a serious challenger to Christian Identity for counting as the religious dimension of Aryan revolutionary ambition. To many of the new generation of Aryan activists that populate the scene, the heathen world, with its ancient mysteries, mythologies, magic, runic script, heroic adventures, and romantic Viking violence, obviously seems sexier than tedious Bible-study courses aiming to prove the somewhat less thrilling "fact" of the Israeli identity of Aryan man. Much like the conflict within NSDAP between those who favored the racialized faith of the Aryan Christ and those who saw national socialism as a pagan project, there is a polarization within the Aryan counterculture between Christian Identity and racist paganism, a tug-of-war that, while far from resolved, presently seems to weigh in on the heathen side.

This is in part related to the meteoric rise of Wotansvolk during the late 1990s. The outcome of the internal rift within the Wotansvolk troika that erupted in the summer of 2001 is still uncertain. The transition of their headquarters to Micetrap Productions in New Jersey was in November 2001 challenged by Ron McVan, who vowed to get Wotansvolk "back on its feet."[20] By December, former Odinic Rite member John Post of Napa, California, shouldered responsibilities of 14 Word Press distributions. Although both Katja Lane and John Post claim the transition to be successful, the outcome is still uncertain, and McVan is openly opposing the new administration. Should Wotansvolk disappear from the scene, this would only be another illustration of the counterculture pattern of organizational formation, ascendancy, and implosion. Irrespective of whether the continuation of the Wotansvolk project fails or succeeds, racist paganism currently is in flow with the times and is therefore likely to remain a primary feature of the Aryan counterculture.

Paganism, Neonationalism, and Romantic Men with Guns

The tide of racist and ethnic paganism in the United States is linked with the processes of globalization and with the mainstream redefinition of the American "nation" to include as co-nationals all people within its territory irrespective or race, ethnicity, or religious preferences. Globalization involves a tension between centripetal and centrifugal forces. The gradual construction of a global culture that increasingly becomes the larger context for all previous cultures of man by necessity involves a relativization of systems of meaning and values. Ill at ease with a process interpreted as a leveling force of cultural homogenization that threatens to exterminate their unique cultural identity, white racists are reluctant to shout "America First," because America today is defined as a multicultural nation.

Globalization and American multiculturalism combine to raise the issue of identity anew, and folkish pagans are not the only Americans looking for an answer by exploring the past. This does not necessarily involve a political dimension or programs of neonationalist separatism, of course. Many Americans answer the question of who they are by embarking on long journeys through a series of forefathers that were Greek, Irish, German, Yoruba, Sioux, or Mandarin in part, quarter, or full, as if this would say something meaningful about who they "are" as particular individuals. Many Americans do this without reflecting on it too much or attaching any value to it beyond the mere personal: it is simply but one of several legitimate ways of being an American. However, as race and ethnicity have long been a primary mode of social classification in American society, this may also constitute a basis for programs of identity politics ranging from all sorts of "quota" demands to formulations of separatist projects. It is here we find the ethnic and racist heathens.

Being an "American" national is among folkish pagans too shallow and all-inclusive to satisfactorily constitute a primary identity. They attach more importance to being white, Aryan, or Northern European, as this sets them apart from other Americans. They mobilize history to further strengthen the separateness of the imagined community, tracing the racial or ethnic nation back to

Europe and beyond Christianity to the perceived point of cultural origin during the golden age of national freedom; this provides folkish pagans with information by which an alternative identity that feels uniquely meaningful can be constructed. Ancient Norse culture seems well suited for this purpose, as it provides ample but incomplete material about an alternative world of old. Paganism therefore allows activists to project their ideals back into legendary times when Aryan society was untainted by the ills of modernity and materialism, when there were no presidents or kings, no federal government or capitalist plutocrats, no junk food, environmental destruction, pornography, or Ricky Lake shows—a wonderful pristine world when not a single Jew wandered through the Nordic woodlands. They imagine a time when Aryan man lived according to his true nature, when men were men and women were women, a glorious time of heroism and adventure, of nobility and honor, a time of campfires and sagas. Practitioners may see the original Aryan society as based on the free yeoman who lived in harmony with nature or focus on the barbarian warrior who bowed to no one. Norse paganism thus appeals to those animated by the mythos of Americanism and moral conservatism as well as to those attracted by the romanticized legacy of American outlaw culture in any of its current manifestations, such as racist skinhead gangs, biker brotherhoods, or satanic metalhead legions. This dual attraction resembles the German national socialist fascination with Norse paganism that appealed to the competing NSDAP factions of Darré and Himmler and their respective romances with the earth-based yeoman and the barbarian warrior-mystic.[21] The national socialist phenomenon stands as a warning against dismissing the milieu of racist paganism as a lunatic fringe of hopeless dreamers: romantic men armed with guns and religious determination have throughout history been a dangerous species.

Introduction

1 Nicholas Goodrick-Clarke (1998) sees the inroad of esoteric themes in today's neo-Nazism as a link between fascism, radical environmentalism, and the New Age, returning to the theme in Goodrick-Clarke (2002), in which he includes a section on racist paganism after having read the manuscript for *Gods of the Blood*. Joscelyn Godwin (1996) discusses occultism and paganism in modern national socialism. Jeffrey Kaplan (1997) includes a full chapter on Asatrú/Odinism and returns briefly to the subject in Kaplan and Weinberg (1998). Some studies of contemporary paganism do mention racist Norse revivalism (Adler 1986) or include American material in studies of racial heathens in Britain (Harvey 1997).

2 For an analysis of globalization and the surge of nationalist activities, see Hettne, Sörlin, and Östergård 1998.

3 Out of which 188 were members of the United Nations ("United Nations Member States" 2000).

4 A good introduction to the cultural impact of the fast food industry is Eric Schlosser's *Fast Food Nation: The Dark Side of the All-American Meal*, 2002.

5 For a brilliant discussion of the global logo web and the transnational corporations' invasion of individual and public space, see Naomi Klein's *No Logo*, 2000.

6 Buchanan, speech 2000a.

7 Buchanan, speech 2000b.

8 Chamberlain belonged to the inner circle at Bayreuth and was married to Wagner's daughter. Continuing the racist revisionism of history in the tradition of Arthur de Gobineau, Chamberlain made his contribution by targeting the Jewish people as the agents of Aryan degeneracy. This suggested a remedy that the Nationalsozialistische Deutsche Arbeiterpartei (NSDAP) would later try in practice.

9 The first German Theosophical Society was founded in 1884. Organizationally fragmented, Theosophy experienced a boom with the first German translation of Helena Blavatsky's *Secret Doctrine* in 1901.

10 Each root race has seven subraces that in turn have seven branch races that may subdivide further into various tribes depending on karma.

11 To a certain extent, research teams sponsored by Rosenberg and Himmler differed in orientation and result. Concerning the tribal society of pre-Christian Germany, two opposing views developed, possibly reflecting, as Stefan Arvidsson (2000) suggests, different notions about the meaning of national socialism. According to one perspective, pagan society was based on the noble virtues of the settled farmer living off land of his own. Pagan religion stressed the sacred link between blood and soil, seasonal rites of fertility, and mythologies in which the cosmos is a law-governed order of culture and nature, created by defeating the forces of chaos. The opposing school of thought considered the *Männerbund*, the band of initiated male warriors, to be the foundation of youthful and freedom-loving pagan society. Warrior ethics stressed the virtues of honor, strength, courage; on the religious front, gods of war, death, and ecstasy dominated, with ceremonies revolving around death and ancestors. Where the former stressed pagan law and order, the latter associated such bourgeois ideas with Roman and other non-German societies that had fallen prey to the vital pagan barbarian Germanic tribes. While a certain overlap existed, Rosenberg's researchers stressed pagan society as a culture of order, while Himmler's Ahnenerbe researchers upheld as ideal the pagan warrior. National socialism was to Rosenberg an ideology of law and order based on conservative morals and the traditional culture of small-town, rural Germany. Celebrating strength, masculinity, war, death, and rejuvenation, Himmler instead portrayed the NS as a revolutionary force that would return society to the pristine glory of the pagan golden age.

12 Das Ahnenerbe, Forschungsintitut für Geistesurgeschicthe. The first head of the Ahnenerbe was Professor Herman Wirth, whose monumental 1928 *Der Aufgang der Menschheit* (Origin of Man) traced the origins of Aryan man to the Arctic polar region. A shift in the poles supposedly had made the originally mild and pleasant Arctic region uninhabitable, and the Arctic race had wandered southward in response to the change in climate.

13 Another important ritual object was the marriage bowl in which bread and salt were presented to the bride and groom with a bind rune for "got," the divine Armanen consciousness on the cover of the vessel.

1. The Transforming Landscapes of American Racism

1 The Cherokee had developed a written language of their own (Hultkrantz 1992).

2 The Constitution of the United States of America, Article 1. For the debate about whether slaves should be considered persons or property and the winning compromise, see Madison 1961.

3 It is erroneous to assume racism was the root cause of slavery. In early colonial America, people of European and Native American descent were enslaved along with those of African descent. Plantation owners came to prefer African slaves mainly for practical reasons: the color of their skin made it easier to identify runaways. When the African slave trade began, antiblackness was not a factor. Instead, antiblack racism emerged with the development of a theological construct based on the fact that most slaves were black; extrapolating from the then conventional Christian argument that certain people were handicapped because God had condemned them, theologians applied the same logic to explain the condition "providence" had given black slaves. Although "white"

people are not actually *white* and "black" people are not *black,* they were seen as such. This perception merged with the Christian dichotomy between the white domain of God and the black domain of the devil. Associated, then, with moral qualities, "blackness" was interpreted biblically as an eternal divine curse for past transgressions in a theology identifying blacks as the descendants of Cain and/or Ham and Canaan. Anglican theologians suggested that blacks would be cured of their "deformity" and rise in perfected white complexion at the glorious day of the Resurrection (Gardell 1996; Gardell 1998).

4 The full title of the novel is *The Awful Disclosure of Maria Monk as Exhibited in a Narrative of Her Suffering during a Residence of Five Years as a Novice and Two Years as a Black Nun in the Hotel Dieu Nunnery at Montreal.*

5 For an excellent introduction to "American" nativism, see Bennet 1995.

6 Italian immigrants in New Orleans frequently associated with African Americans, therefore their status deteriorated into "white niggers" (Jacobson 1998, 57).

7 California and Connecticut passed sterilization laws in 1909; Nevada, Iowa, and New Jersey in 1911; New York in 1912; and Kansas, Michigan, North Dakota, and Oregon in 1913.

8 Advised by the Report of the Eugenics Committee of the United States Committee on Selective Immigration, chaired by Madison Grant, the quota system was based on 2 percent of each group's population according to the 1890 census. As northern and western Europeans were held to be of "higher intelligence," they "provided the best material for American citizenship" (Jacobson 1998, 83).

9 Here and throughout, interview citations will be set in italics.

10 For more on the construction of the black ghetto, see Massey and Denton 1993. An excellent study of the Great Migration is Lemann 1992.

11 Pan-African populist Marcus Garvey remarked, "For the Anglo-Saxon to say that he is superior because he introduced submarines to destroy life, or the Teuton because he compounded liquid gas to outdo in the art of killing and that the Negro is inferior because he is backward in that direction is to leave oneself open to the retort 'Thou shalt not kill,' as being the divine law that sets the moral standard of real men" (Garvey 1986b [1925], 120).

12 Franz Boas first articulated his view on the equality of the human races in 1894 but long remained an isolated voice of dissent in a science dominated by eugenic proponents. A paramount antiracist thinker, Boas's work has greatly influenced American cultural anthropology.

13 For an alarmist opinion concerning the shift in immigration policy, see Brimlow 1996.

14 For these statistics, see the "State of Black America," published yearly by the National Urban League.

15 For more on coded racism in presidential campaigns, see, for instance, Ansell 1997, Feagan and Vera 1995.

16 Italy's Bureau of Fascism Abroad supported the Fascist League of North America with an estimated 12,000 members, mainly Italian Americans. The German NSDAP had an American branch of some 1,500 members, while the more loosely connected German American Bund claimed a membership of 8,500. Headed by German expatriate Fritz

Kuhn, the Bund attempted to Americanize national socialism and structured paramilitary units and youth corps on the basis of German models. In 1939, 22,000 people jammed into Madison Square Garden for George Washington's birthday, singing "Horst Wessel" and flying swastika banners, an event that provoked a backlash against what appeared to be un-American activity (Kaplan and Weinberg 1999, 26–31).

17   Pelley launched his Silver Shirt Legion on 31 January 1933, the date Hitler swore his oath as Reich Canceller in Berlin, after which Pelley would soon organize the Christian Party as an Americanized NS third-party alternative. Prefiguring later developments, Pelley merged national socialism with mystic Christianity in a Manichean vision of a global conflict between the "real Chosen People" (i.e., the Christian-Nordic-Gentiles) and the Jewish-Russocrat-Communist enemies of God. He saw himself guided by "Cosmic Intelligence" to lead Nordic Americans through the cataclysmic times to come, when the "Protocolian State" of the anti-Christ would fall. A firm believer in "pyramid prophecy," Pelley decoded a message from God set in the stones of the Great Pyramid to mean that the age of bondage would end 16 September 1936 ("Bright Change with Autumn"). The Silver Shirts would do what the Black Shirts had done in Italy and the Brown Shirts in Germany: train a community of future leaders. "Ye are races of gods in your earthly classrooms learning the skills of your own divinities" ("I See Six Legions"). After the "mystical Exodus commencing this September," Pelley wrote, "The New Israelites will pass into the splendid national isolation of the mystical Sinai Desert and learn how to become citizens of the Christ State," and then conquer the "World Canaan" ("Judgement of Nations. . ."). Combining an esoteric NS Christianity with populist slogans like "Abolish Taxation" and "No More Hunger," Pelley envisioned an America transformed into a nationwide corporation, run by Christlike legionaries. Pelley apparently calculated on winning the 1936 election, but voters largely ignored his Christian Party, which appeared on the ballots only in Washington State, where it received a mere 1,598 votes, 300 fewer than the Communist Party. After his 1936 failure, Pelley's support dwindled. In 1942, his mission ended behind bars, as he was convicted of sedition. Organizing mainly in the West Coast and Great Lakes regions, Pelley's Silver Shirts never had more than 15,000 members, a seemingly insignificant number, yet remarkably high by American NS standards. (Barkun 1997, 53, 91–96; Bennet 1995, 246; "Bright Change" 1936; "I See Six Legions" 1936; "Judgment of Nations" 1936. See also, "At Last" 1936; "You Are Part of a Program" 1936; "Escape Is Prohibited" 1936; "Once More, 'Liberty or Death' " 1936)

18   The American Jewish Committee advocated a quarantine strategy that would meet Rockwell with silent treatment. Yet, Rockwell's skillfully designed inflammatory acts made him the most publicized "hatemonger" by the mid-1960s. Largely met by silence in the Jewish press, Rockwell would only occasionally succeed in provoking Jewish violence or press coverage.

19   Rockwell's slogan "White Power" was coined in 1967, one year after H. Rap Brown stunned the American public with his "Black Power."

20   This phenomenon, of course, had historical precedence also in Hitler's cooperation with Japan and other non-Aryan forces such as anti-British Hindu nationalists.

21   Conspiracy stories naming his rival Robert Boliver DePugh, leader of the Minutemen guerillas, and/or his successor Matt Koehl and/or ANP officer William Pierce and/or the

ADL and/or the FBI as the real instigators still circulate widely through the Aryan landscape.

22 Traditional Klan titles for office were replaced with more mainstream, less archaic titles; Imperial Wizard, for instance, became National Director, and Kludd became Chaplain.

23 Robertson blamed the liberal policies of egalitarianism, which he felt had furthered the erosion of white racial awareness and increasingly rampant minority racism that had eventually degraded the majority to second-rate citizens, a process of decline he felt had begun with the Civil War.

24 Bridges (1994, 67) claims there were only seven and that it "was a comical evening," with reporters far outnumbering the Klansmen and trying not to crash into each other as they followed the Klansmen's three old cars.

25 Duke (1997) claims that ordinary patrolmen "loved" the Klan initiative, and Zatarain (1990, 245) reports that local officials of U.S. Immigration and Naturalization Service have said that they "would welcome help from anyone, including the Klan."

26 Duke resignation letter. Quoted in Bridges 1994, 88; see also Rich 1988, 2:281.

27 Four died on the spot and one died after two days in intensive care.

28 The jurors included an anticommunist Cuban expatriate who called the Klan "patriotic" and national socialism "more patriotic"; a friendly former next-door neighbor of one of the Klan members who said the defendant was "a good guy"; and a person who stated under oath that he thought it was less of a crime to kill a communist than to kill a regular person (Rich 1988, 2:249).

29 CWP won in a third trial.

30 Former UKA Indiana Grand Dragon Bill Chaney established the (now defunct) Confederation of Independent Orders of the Invisible Empire, Knights of the Ku Klux Klan following a Klan Unity Conference in 1977 as a network of former unaffiliated local Klans. Chaney has long since abandoned Klandom (Sims 1996, 282–91).

31 Unsurprisingly, Duke denies having made any such offer. He recalls that he made an effort to bring about Klan unity, as he was to abandon his leadership in favor of the soon-to-be established NAAWP project. According to Duke, the intent was not personal profit but to allow Wilkinson to recruit from Duke's Knights; in return, he wanted an allowance for the NAAWP to be able to contact members of the Invisible Empire. The $35,000 was supposedly not for Duke personally but to fund the new organization. Irrespective of whose story is closest to the truth, it was Wilkinson's version that hit the press, forcing Duke to resign from Klandom in a flurry of media reports about his corrupted sellout (Rich 1988, 2:279–81).

32 During his few remaining years as Imperial Wizard, Wilkinson implemented some dramatic turnarounds of Klan policies. Wilkinson banned the use of wearing masks at public gatherings and declared that the ceremonies and constitution of the secret society should be available to anyone who might want it. The no-longer-invisible Invisible Empire even aborted its mission to reinstitute racial segregation. The effort to halt integration had failed, Wilkinson wrote in a *Klansmen* article: "Frankly the country was ready to give 'equal rights' to all people and it was done." With dwindling membership of his crumbling Empire, Wilkinson's fate was sealed by Morris Dees of the Southern Poverty Law Center, which sued him and twenty other Klan members for a 1979 club-wielding

attack at an antiracist rally in Decatur, Alabama, seeking one million dollars in damages. In 1983, Wilkinson declared the Invisible Empire of the Ku Klux Klan bankrupt and filed for protection under federal bankruptcy laws. By the following year, he resigned as Imperial Wizard. To complete the circle, Wilkinson again mimicked Duke, claiming to be disillusioned with the Klan and opting instead for a role in mainstream politics; blaming the media's misrepresentations of the Knightly order, he had finally concluded that he had to abandon Klandom to achieve his higher aspirations.

33   In Wilkinson's case, the exposure was most probably true, however, judging by his own efforts to explain his double role in terms of the duty of American patriots to cooperate with law enforcement agencies.

34   This was the "secret" Klan intelligence organization, the National Intelligence Committee (NIC). See Sims 1996, 108.

35   World War II navy veteran, radio operator, and insurance businessman Robert Miles gravitated to the radical right via the Republican Party, the Wallace campaign, and the anti-desegregation struggle of the 1950s. In 1969, Miles became UKA Grand Dragon of Michigan and was in 1970 promoted to the position of Imperial Kludd (National Chaplain). In 1971 Miles founded the Dualist Mountain Church, with headquarters at his farm outside Cohoctah, north of Flint, Michigan, and his evolving teachings became part of the process of radicalization. Described by Miles as a "cousin" of Christian Identity, Dualism is a racist interpretation of Christianity that claims an extraterrestrial angelic identity of the white race, presently fighting the spawn of the devil in the apocalyptic race war called world history. The war on earth is but part of a larger stellar war, an idea that for all its seeming oddity is far from unique in Identity circles. In 1973, Miles received a nine year prison sentence for bombing buses used in busing programs in Pontiac, Michigan, and tarring and feathering a pro-integration school principal in Willow Run, Michigan (he pleaded not guilty on both charges). Released after six years, Miles began organizing yearly trans-organizational racist conferences on his farm grounds. Miles 1988 and many other Klan related articles are posted on the Klan Web site k-k-k.com, an "ecumenical" Klan "museum of Ku Klux Klan history and artifacts" (http://www.k-k-k.com/miles.htm).

36   Long time Klan activist and Identity Christian Louis Beam, a highly decorated helicopter gunman and Vietnam veteran, published his compilation shortly after Houston federal judge Gabriella McDonald had ordered his 2,500-men-strong paramilitary Klan militia, the Texas Emergency Reserve, to disband following a conflict with Vietnamese fishermen at Galveston Bay, Texas. Beam, who served as Texas Grand Dragon of Duke's Knights of the Ku Klux Klan, had in 1981 accepted a request from a group of white American fishermen to help them drive some seventy Vietnamese shrimp fishermen from the area. Following a Klan campaign of terror and intimidation, the Vietnamese were on the verge of selling their boats and moving somewhere else when Morris Dees of the Southern Poverty Law Center intervened in their interest and defeated Beam in court. To Beam, the "anti-white" verdict confirmed his identification of the federal authorities with the forces of evil.

37   Fadeley would later testify that Randy Weaver had been reluctant to break the law (Bock 1996, 52).

38 For a discussion about the role of post-Vietnam paramilitarism in the Ruby Ridge stand-off, see Aho 1994.

39 Freeh speech 1995. Twelve FBI employees had been disciplined, Freeh stated, and he informed the Senate that the bureau had "changed policies and procedures to prevent similar, tragic mistakes in the future." Freeh also announced that it was proper for the FBI to investigate itself, even regarding the case against Horiuchi. When the federal self-investigation after two years concluded that no charge should be brought either against the sniper or any high-ranking FBI official, Boundary County Prosecutor Denise Wood-bury filed a state charge for manslaughter against Horiuchi. Supported by the bureau, Horiuchi won a petition for the federal court to take over the case, and U.S. District Judge Edward Lodge in May 1998 dismissed the charge on the ground that Horiuchi was acting in the line of duty (Wiley 1997; Gallhager 1998; "Judge Dismisses Case" 1998).

40 Interview with Eva Vail, Coeur-d'Alene, Idaho, 26 September 1996.

41 There were Pastor Richard G. Butler of the Church of Jesus Christ, Christian/Aryan Nations; Tom Stetson of Concerned Citizens of Idaho; Chris Temple and Paul Hall from Identity Christian paper *Jubilee*; Klan veteran Louis Beam; Randy and John Trochman from Montana; Kirk Lyons from far right judicial group, the CAUSE foundation (Canada, Australia, United States, Europe); Earl Johns from the New Mexico–based conspiracy-peddling Christian Crusade for Truth; Larry Pratt, founder of Gun Owners of America; and a number of conspiracy believers, Klan activists, Identity ministers, Constitution-alists, and patriots of different far-right persuasions.

42 Founded by visionary Ellen White (d. 1915) as one of several Christian branches that evolved out of the great disappointment that followed William Miller's failed prophecy that Christ's Second Coming was to occur on 23 October 1844, SDA has today about three million members in the United States. Speaking for the Third Angel (Miller spoke for the First and Second Angels) of Revelations 14, White taught her followers to stay separate from the worldly powers of Babylon, to celebrate Sabbath rather than Sunday service, and to keep a healthy vegetarian diet based on Old Testament precepts. The SDA wellness centers soon became famous, and SDA pioneer John Harvey Kellogg helped one of its health food products, corn flakes, to become an American breakfast favorite. Un-able to find a worthy successor to White, the SDA has since her death been an umbrella body of numerous branches headed by more or less visionary leaders, one of whom was Bulgarian immigrant Victor Houteff, who founded the Mt. Carmel commune northwest of Waco in 1934.

The commune's name reveals the millenarian strain that is the trademark of Seventh-Day Adventism. In biblical terms, Mt. Carmel was where Elijah fought the disciples of Baal, which indicates that Fourth-Angel messenger Houteff saw himself as the "antitypi-cal" Elijah, that is, the fulfillment of the role toward which the prophet Elijah pointed. As Elijah is expected to return before the coming of the Day of the Lord, Houteff's fol-lowers, who anticipated the imminent announcement of the Second Coming, were cast into confusion when the modern Elijah died suddenly in 1955. Among the competing groups that arose in the wake of frustrated expectations was "The Branch," headed by Ben Roden, messenger of the Fifth Angel. Intending to restore the throne of David, Roden taught a strict return to the ways of the Old Testament, instructing his flock to celebrate Hebrew holidays only and to follow in detail the dietary Mosaic laws. On his death in 1978, Roden's wife, Lois, assumed the role of the messenger of the Sixth Angel, renamed her group the Living Water Branch Davidian SDA, and developed a feminist theology according to which the Holy Spirit is the female partner to the male God—together they made man, male and female, in their image. In 1980, having accused not only the papacy but also Protestant denominations of engaging in a Satanist conspiracy to keep man uninformed of the Spirit's femininity, Lois Roden was ousted from the SDA General Conference as a heretic.

A year later, Vernon Howell joined her at Mt. Carmel, gaining her trust in bed and pulpit to the great consternation of her son George Roden. Claiming that he himself was the antitypical Immanuel, Roden identified Howell as an antitypical Lucifer, underscoring his opinion with the power of an Uzi. Howell moved to a second Branch camp, Palestine, Texas. When Lois died in 1986, Howell led a failed paramilitary operation to oust Roden from Mt. Carmel, which might have landed him in prison had it not been for Roden's counterproductive testimony at the trial. Roden told the jurors of his habit of closing prayers at Mt. Carmel with the words "in the name of George B. Roden, amen" and admitted to having dug up a decade-old corpse in an attempt to prove his divinity by resurrecting the person. Howell and his commandos were acquitted, ordered to pay Roden's back taxes, and authorized to return to Mt. Carmel.

As messenger of the Seventh Angel, Howell added to the teachings of Ellen White and Lois Rodin a messiology centered on the Seven Seals of Revelations. White had believed that innumerable worlds were inhabited, some of which she claimed to have visited herself, accompanied by angelic hosts piloting what SDA visionaries like Houteff and Roden later identified as celestial flying saucers. Howell claimed a similar experience, saying that he was taken up to the City of God, located beyond Orion, to confer with God Himself, who armed him with a perfect understanding of the Bible and a divine mission. God informed Howell that he was the antitypical Cyrus (Hebrew: *Koresh*) of the Bible. According to Isaiah 40–66, God had anointed Cyrus to subdue the nations before him in order to free the chosen people from the grips of Babylon and restore Israel to its predestined glory. Renaming himself David Koresh in honor of his mission, Howell was thus anointed to fulfill the role as the antitypical Christ of our age.

43 Livinstone Fagan is one of the more important Davidian post-Waco theologians. His voluminous writings include "Mt. Carmel: The Unseen Reality" and "David Koresh as a Messiah," which may be found online at http://home.maine.rr.com/waco/lf.html.

44 Koresh had learned the (fully legal) gun trade in 1990, marketing weapons and paramilitary gear, including David Koresh Survival Wear, at various gun shows. Alerted by a local sheriff, the ATF opened an investigation to look into suspicions that Koresh was at that time converting nonrestricted semiautomatic AR-15s to automatic M-16s, suspicions that later proved unfounded. Another set of unsupported charges came from Marc Breault, a young theology student who had joined Koresh in 1986. When Koresh in 1990 claimed Breault's newly wedded wife, Breault turned against his teacher. A longtime visionary himself, Breault asserted that he had received divine messages ordering him to oust Koresh as a fraud and adversary to God. Breault and his dissident flock began informing American authorities about alleged child abuse and stockpiling of ille-

gal weapons, charges that early in 1993 found their way to the ATF via reporters at the *Waco Tribune-Herald*.

45   Koresh had been alerted by the strange behavior of eight undercover agents posing as overaged students at a "technical college" that they could not answer questions about. The agents rented the neighboring house but refused to let their cultist neighbors enter. In addition, the Davidians detected surveillance cameras and low-flying helicopters. The bureau knew that Koresh suspected that something was coming down. Special agent Robert Rodriguez, one of the undercover neighbors, visited Koresh on the morning of 28 February to make sure that everything was normal, when their chat was interrupted; David Jones, longtime friend of Koresh and former resident at Mt. Carmel, rushed in and took Koresh aside to inform him that he had seen a carload of armed snipers moving toward the ranch. Koresh returned to the room, looked out the window, then turned an eye on Rodriguez, saying, "Robert, we know that they are coming." Making his excuses, Robert left the house, knees shaking, walked to his car fearing a shot in the back, then drove off to warn his superiors. Still, the raid was not called off.

46   The bureau was fully aware of the dangers of using CS and methylene chloride in larger quantities inside a building. They had also been told that the residents had stacked bales of hay against the wall as protection from more gunfire, and they knew that the besieged were using lanterns. Who started the fire that consumed Mt. Carmel is controversial. Government spokespersons claim that the cultists ignited the fire themselves, while survivors and critics of the FBI assert that it started when tanks ran over a gasoline lantern.

47   The pro-Koresh Davidians split again after what they termed the Waco Holocaust. The majority now rallies around Clive Doyle and imprisoned black SDA theologian and Waco survivor Livingstone Fagan, and they await the Second Coming of Christ, that is, David Koresh. Another prisoner, Renos Avraam, heads the Hidden Manna faction. Avraam claims to be the Chosen Vessel of the Remaining Bride destined to lead the Students of the Seven Seals prior to Koresh's return. A third group, headed by Ron Cole, teaches that David never did complete his mission as the messenger of the Seventh Angel, a task that has now fallen to Cole. Supported by far rightist Gary Hunt, Cole also founded the First Colorado Light Infantry Militia and the North American Liberation Army and subsequently landed in prison for illegal weapon possession.

48   Calls of support from patriot and Aryan corners began pouring in as the siege dragged on. Among the disgusted was Ron Engelman, a veteran patriot and constitutional fundamentalist talk-show host at KGBS radio, broadcasting from Dallas. A communications technician called in to report discrepancies between what he had seen on raw television feeds from the siege and the edited versions aired on TV. He also suggested that the satellite dish at Mt. Carmel could be used as a signal device to communicate with the besieged. The besieged were told to move the dish if they could hear Engelman's radio communications; when the dish moved, Engelman knew communication was established. He engaged members of the Constitution Foundation Association (CFA), a small, Dallas-based patriot group, to try to get medics into the Branch Davidian compound, but they were rebuffed by the FBI. The Davidians reciprocated by flying a banner reading, "Send in the CFA." The KGBS show, with its alternative direct-communication link with Mt. Carmel, attracted the interest of other radical activists, such as Gary Hunt, editor of

Outpost of Freedom, and Kirk Lyons, an Identity Christian attorney, who both established contact with the besieged.

49 Carol A. Valentine, *Waco Holocaust Electronic Museum*, 19 April 1996, http://www.Public-Action.com/SkyWriter/WacoMuseum or http://206.55.8.10/SkyWriter/WacoMuseum; Mark Swett, *Waco Never Again*, http://home.maine.rr.com/waco/.

50 Conversation with Eva Vail, 26 September 1996. See also Keith 1994, 93; Barkun 1997, 260.

51 The results are discussed in Dahl 1997, 11.

52 See also Loman 1994; Lyons and Payne n. d.

2. The Smorgasbord of the Revolutionary White-Racist Counterculture

1 See, for example, the subsection on "homosexual infiltration in the U.S. nationalist movement" in "Deguello Report" 2000, 401.

2 Louis Beam, conversation with author, Coeur d'Alene, Idaho, 26 September 1996; Beam 1996, Internet.

3 "Ku Klux" is probably derived from the Greek word *kuklos*, meaning circle or wheel. The founders changed the spelling to Ku Klux, then added "clan" spelled with a "k" to match the first part. At the first Klan "konvention" in Nashville, Tennessee, 1867, General Nathan B. Forrest was elected its first Imperial Wizard. The "invisible empire" of the Klan was divided into realms, dominions, provinces, and dens, headed by Grand Dragons, Titans, Giants, and Cyclops, respectively. In 1869 Forrest dissolved the Klan after finding that the aims and methods of the secret society had been perverted. Although most Klan chapters followed his instructions and did close up shop, Klan activities continued in several areas until martial law, mass arrests, and many convictions effectively shut down the Klan in 1871–72. By that time, "law and order" (i.e., white power) had largely been restored.

4 Born in 1880 to an Alabama medical doctor who had been an officer of the first Klan, Simmons fought as a volunteer in the Spanish–American War of 1898. Returning from service, Simmons opted for a career as a Methodist minister but was after twelve years denied a pulpit due to his moral impairment. He found his "true" calling as an organizer of fraternities, rising to the rank of colonel in the Woodmen of the World. In addition, Simmons belonged to the Knights Templar and a number of Masonic fraternities. His long dream of establishing a fraternity of his own came to fruition after a car accident that laid him up for three months, which he used for planning. Basing his fraternity on the old Ku Klux Klan, he timed its inauguration with the opening of the *Birth of a Nation*. Gathering some twenty men from various fraternal organizations, including two members of the original Klan, Simmons took his crowd to the top of the Stone Mountain near Atlanta. Simmons lit a kerosene-drenched cross, calling forth the invisible empire "from its slumber of a half century to take up a new task and fulfill a new mission for humanity's good." Initially being only a fraternity that celebrated 100 percent Americanism and the supremacy of the white race, the Klan found a new purpose after World War I. Fighting the emergent labor movement, new immigrants, and northbound blacks, the Klan added political ambitions to its fraternal agenda. Being more a mys-

tic than an effective administrator, Simmons in 1920 delegated most practical tasks to successful salespersons Edward Young Clarke and Elizabeth Tyler, whose organizational skills contributed to making the Klan a forum for Anglo-Saxon Protestant "Americanism."

5   By 1927, when the talk movies came, *Birth of a Nation* had sold 50 million tickets. Dixon published *The Clansman* in 1905.

6   "The Kloran of the 1920s Klan," reprinted in Wade 1987, appendix B.

7   In addition, Klan-supported candidates won the Senate race in Texas and the governorship in Kansas.

8   For Morris Dees's own descriptions of these events, see Dees and Fiffer 1991; Dees 1993; Dees and Corcoran 1996.

9   See also "Dees a 'Bi-Sexual' " flyer; "Dees the Great Satan" flyer; "Morris Dees: A Fact Finding Report" 1995; Kaldenberg n.d.

10 Thus, for instance, Harold Covington, writing under his favorite alias, "Winston Smith," accuses Tom Metzger of being "a traitor who sells names and addresses to Morris Dees on a daily basis" (Smith 1994).

11 The known Klan groups operating in 1999 were as follows (number of affiliated chapters in parentheses): Alabama White Knights of the Ku Klux Klan (13); Alabama's White Pride (1); America's Invisible Empire Knights of the Ku Klux Klan (6); American Knights of the Ku Klux Klan (20); Christian Knights of the Ku Klux Klan (1); Confederate Knights of the Ku Klux Klan (3); Ghost Riders of the Ku Klux Klan (1); Imperial Empire Knights of the Ku Klux Klan (1); Imperial Klans of America (14); International Keystone Knights of the Ku Klux Klan (3); Invincible Empire Knights of the Ku Klux Klan (11); Invisible Empire, Indiana Ku Klux Klan (1); Invisible Empire, Pennsylvania Ku Klux Klan (1); Kalifornia Knights of the Ku Klux Klan (1); Knights of the Ku Klux Klan (Arkansas faction) (1); Knights of the Ku Klux Klan (Missouri faction) (1); Knights of the Ku Klux Klan (Pennsylvania faction) (1); Knights of the White Kamellia (21); Liberty Knights (4); Missouri Federation of Klans, Inc. (1); Mystic Knights of the Ku Klux Klan (1); National Knights of the Ku Klux Klan (2); New Knights of the Ku Klux Klan (Florida faction) (1); New Knights of the Ku Klux Klan (1); New Order Knights of the Ku Klux Klan (5); North Georgia White Knights of the Ku Klux Klan (1); Northwest Knights of the Ku Klux Klan (2); Rangers of the Cross Knights of the Ku Klux Klan (1); Rebel Knights of the Ku Klux Klan (1); Southern Cross Militant Knights (1); Southern Mississippi Knights of the Ku Klux Klan (1); United Confederate Knights of the Ku Klux Klan (2); White Camellia Knights of the Ku Klux Klan (2); White Christian Knights of the Ku Klux Klan (1); White Knights of the Ku Klux Klan (1); and White Shield Knights of the Ku Klux Klan (8) (SPLC 1999a).

12 The more noteworthy include (number of known local chapters in parentheses): National Alliance (45), American Nationalist Party (1), American Nazi Party (1), Central New York White Pride (2), Christian Defense League (1), Euro-American Alliance (1), German American Nationalist PAC (1), National Socialist German Workers Party (1), National Socialist Irish Workers Party (1), National Socialist Movement (4), National Socialist White People's Party (1), National Socialist Vanguard (1), Nazi Party U.S.A. (1), Volksfront (1), NSDAP/AO (?), and American Front (?).

13 The note continued, "Although the author states that his article contains his own conclusions, his knowledge and understanding are noteworthy." Continuing to write about himself in third person, Cooper included in the issue an account of NSV "operations." Cooper described how he drove to Seattle to listen to Morris Dees and talked to a reporter, offering the latter documents from a Dees court case to prove why Dees is called the Sleaze. "Unfortunately, the article was to be completed that day, so Dir. Cooper never sent a copy of the court case. A couple of days later, Dir. Cooper remembered that Tom Metzger's WAR has this case on the Internet." The only other NSV operation consisted of a thirty-minute lecture Cooper had given before a University of Portland class of seventeen students, of whom "most listened and took notes."

14 NSLF flyer by Joseph Tommasi, reprinted in Mason 1992, 24.

15 Mason saw Manson as "GREATER than all the leaders/fakers in the Movement combined," destined to be "The Leader as long as he is alive" (1992, 311). Manson advised Mason to drop the NSLF and start the Universal Order. NSLF leadership was given over to Karl Hands.

16 Rockwell recounts a series of dreams he had while living in Atlanta in 1957, each dream a variation of the same theme. A man would approach Rockwell, saying, "Someone wants to see you." The man would take Rockwell into a room, where he would find Adolf Hitler waiting for him (Schmaltz 1999, 29, 41). Rockwell in *This Time the World* describes the building of a Hitler shrine. "I hung the [swastika] banner completely across the living room wall. In the center I mounted a plaque of Adolf Hitler. Then I placed a small bookcase under it, and set three candles to burning in front, to make a holy altar to Adolf Hitler. I closed the blinds, lit the candles, and stood before my new altar. For the first time since I lost my Christian religion, I experienced the soul-thrilling emotion of a . . . religious experience." Matt Koehl uses this episode to legitimize his own religious recasting of Rockwell's party, including it in his *Religion of Lincoln Rockwell*.

17 Koehl letter 1982; "History and Organization" flyer n.d.

18 *Resistance* magazine was started by Hawthorne and his associates Jason Snow and Joseph Talic, with Hawthorne serving as editor-in-chief.

19 In 1997 a bloody rift erupted between Resistance/Nordland and a rival music empire run by the British Combat 18 (C18). C18 began with a campaign of threat and intimidation, attempting to force bands to leave Resistance or Nordland and reassign with C18-controlled labels. The civil war escalated with letter bombs and a few deaths before the C18 cadre were imprisoned for murder (Lööw 2000, 345; Lööw 1998, 180).

20 For studies of skinheads in America, see Jack B. Moore 1993 and Hamm 1995.

21 Hawthorne e-mail 2001. He also explained, "I cannot allow the irresponsible and inflammatory rhetoric of my younger years to stand as my legacy. The people of the world suffer from a lack of respect and understanding for one another. As a white racialist, I positioned myself as 'against' so many things that I lost sight of what I was supposed to be for. I was ignorant and uneducated, while ironically deluding myself that I was fighting against ignorance. I have not betrayed the cause of my youth; I have elevated my perspective above it."

22 Persistent counterculture gossip suggests that the initial legal difficulties with American tax authorities began with a tip from one of these two contenders. What is known is that

Willis Carto first secured controlling power through a shell company run by Todd Blodgett, a former Republican strategist who had been a member of Ronald Reagan's White House staff. Resistance headquarters relocated to California, and subscribers were sent Carto's *Spotlight* weekly as compensation for having to wait for *Resistance* magazine. Carto then lost a court case against former associates for control of the Holocaust-denier flagship, Institute for Historical Review. When Carto was forced to declare bankruptcy, Blodgett seized his opportunity. Apparently reasoning that Carto would not publicly announce his own part ownership, wrote an *Intelligence Report* researcher investigating the case, Blodgett offered Pierce the opportunity to buy *Resistance*. In April 1999 Resistance Records was incorporated in the District of Columbia by Pierce and Blodgett. Pierce invested more money to reissue *Resistance* magazine, with Blodgett as manager. When Blodgett failed to get *Resistance* out on time, despite the fact that its schedule had been widely announced, he aroused the anger of militant skinheads. Pierce finally had to assume full control, and the first issue of National Alliance–controlled *Resistance* magazine was out by the end of 1999. Blodgett wound up reviled all around. After being exposed for his counterculture involvement by SPLC's *Intelligence Report* (SPLC 1999f) and the *Washington Post*, then threatened by angry skins who charged him with milking skinheads for profit, he publicly renounced his past: "I've been threatened with beheading, and had the office next to mine torn up by a Skinhead — the same Skinhead I ended up paying off with $2,000 in the company of armed guards. I didn't want to come home some night and find my house burning down. . . . Today, I am sorry I ever got wrapped up in this kind of environment" (SPLC 2000b).

23 Pierce speech 2000b.

24 Pierce speech 2000a.

25 Celebrated heroes like William F. Cody ("Buffalo Bill") and his Rough Riders enlisted in the First Cavalry and joined the invasion of Cuba 1898. The emerging film industry from the outset contributed to the construction of the good soldier as a cultural icon. To encourage U.S. intervention in World War I, President Theodore Roosevelt and Vitagraph (the company behind *Birth of a Nation*) in 1915 together promoted the first full-length war movie *Battle Cry for Peace*, a story about a German invasion of America. Roosevelt, who had served as second-in-command of the First Cavalry in the Spanish-American War, had brought two cameramen from Vitagraph to Cuba. After Roosevelt's victory at San Juan Hill, Vitagraph staged a mock battle in which captured Spanish soldiers (whose cartridges had gunpowder but no bullets) repeated their defeat at the hands of daring Rough Riders commanded by Theodore Roosevelt. Vitagraph in this way built Roosevelt's reputation as a national war hero, which helped him get elected as vice president under McKinley in 1900. After the 1901 assassination of McKinley, Roosevelt became president. Thus commenced a long history of Hollywood–Pentagon cooperation. More than 1,800 war movies were produced between 1941 and 1968, hundreds of which were assisted by the Hollywood branch of the Defense Department. These movies had an effect on the majority of the 3.5 million soldiers America sent to Vietnam. James Gibson shows how idealized war movies influenced the war itself. Some soldiers sought to reenact movie scenes while others grew disenchanted when fantasy met reality: "Only political and military leaders far removed from the battlefield were able to go through the

Vietnam War without having their movie-informed fantasies of 'regeneration through violence' severely shaken" (1994, 25). President Nixon was reportedly influenced by the war movie *Patton* when he decided to invade Cambodia—he even ordered American chaplains to pray for a change in the weather, just as Patton had in the film. But neither heroic war movies nor massive use of superior weaponry could sustain the mythology, as reality did not comply in producing a happy end.

26   By 1988 more than a thousand paintball war-playing fields had been established. At War Zone in Fountain Valley, California, masked players dressed up in camouflage were given the opportunity to play at stations such as Hanoi Hilton, Temple of Doom, and Rambo Hotel. Mock tanks, helicopters, and loudspeakers blasting battle sounds provided a fitting atmosphere. The war-game industry offered "authentic missions" to teams of players sent to "Vietnam" (i.e., Sat Cong Village in Los Angeles, of *Platoon* fame) or "Nicaragua" or "Urban Ghettos," providing them with walkie-talkies and paintball machine guns.

27   To mention a brief selection: On 19 July 1984, forty-one-year old James Oliver Huberty, dressed in black T-shirt, camouflage pants, and dark glasses, brought his Uzi, a 12-gauge shotgun, and 9 mm pistol to a McDonalds restaurant in his hometown of San Ysidro, California, killing twenty-one and wounding nineteen persons before a policeman shot him. In August 1986, an Edmonton, Oklahoma, postal worker killed fourteen of his co-workers. Later the same year, a fired University at Kentucky utility serviceperson returned to campus dressed in a ninja suit, carrying a rifle and samurai sword, with ammo belts across his chest, but he managed only to wound one man before he was disarmed. In 1987, a Florida man killed six persons with a Ruger Mini-14; a camouflaged Texan (nicknamed Rambo) also killed six persons. In 1989, the first of a series of school mass murders came when army-dressed Patrick Purdy brought his AK-47 to a Stockton, California, school, killing five children and wounding twenty-nine before killing himself. Ten years later, it was time to take paramilitary reenactment to church. On 15 September 1999, Larry Ashbrook went into Wedgwood Baptist Church in Forth Worth, Texas, and killed seven people with his semiautomatic Ruger 9 mm before committing suicide.

28   The choice of the date for this episode—known as the "Littleton massacre"—seems unrelated to its counterculture importance. The masked perpetrators threw bombs and shot at students while making their way into the school, laughing and tossing out action-movie lines, such as, "It's a good day to die." Walking around in the library, asking people why they should let them live, these New Warriors treated their act like a video game, survivors said. Finding a girl under a table, one perpetrator yelled, "peekaboo," then shot her in the neck. Wounded children were told to quit crying. "It'll be over soon, you'll all be dead."

29   Hillary Clinton speech 1999; see also Bill Clinton speech 1999a.

30   Clinton had two campaigns to handle simultaneously—one against the culture of violence, the other a bombing campaign—pressing Congress and Senate to support both gun restrictions and supplemental funding for the ongoing military effort. On 20 May 1999, for instance, President Clinton issued a press release on his departure to Littleton, Colorado, dealing with both issues: how to alter the American war culture and get the Senate behind the campaign against violence on the one hand, and the campaign

of violence in Serbia on the other. "It is absolutely imperative that the Senate" approve more funding, in order to give "our military what it needs to see its mission through" (Bill Clinton speech 1999b).

31   In 1978 National Alliance leader William Pierce published the race-war novel *Turner Diaries*, which had first appeared as a series in NA's *National Vanguard*. With hundreds of thousands of copies sold, *Turner Diaries* is a counterculture best-seller read throughout the global Aryan landscape. Purported to have been published at the centennial celebration of the Great Aryan Revolution, the novel is written in the form of a rank-and-file warrior's diary found at the excavations in the ruins of the old-era capitol, Washington, D.C. When the system outlaws all private ownership of firearms through the Cohen Act, Earl Turner and his fellow white patriots join the underground. The "Organization" and its inner circle, the "Order," lead Aryan resistance. "The 'Order' is not like any other army. We have claimed for ourselves the right to decide the fate of all our people and, eventually, to rule the world in accord with our principles" (Macdonald 1989, 98). The elite cadre forms the nucleus of a new civilization that will rise from the ashes of the old following the cleansing revolution. "There is no way a society based on Aryan values and an Aryan outlook can evolve peacefully from a society that has succumbed to Jewish spiritual corruption" (ibid., 111). The Aryan resistance initiates the struggle with robberies to build a war chest and assassinations of targeted system representatives. Earl Turner is given the task of blowing up the FBI headquarters, and readers are instructed how to build a truck bomb with ammonium nitrate fertilizer (a blueprint that helped inform Oklahoma City bombers Timothy McVeigh and Terry Nichols). About 700 people die in the blast, and while Turner finds it hard to see so many of his own people suffering, he realizes that "there is no way we can destroy the System without hurting many thousands of innocent people" (ibid, 42). As the Organization grows, it decides to treat the white masses "realistically—like a herd of cattle." "We will take the food out of their tables . . . and when they begin getting hungry, we will make them fear us more than they fear the system" (ibid., 101). As they distribute counterfeit money and launch large-scale attacks on selected economic targets, power stations, fuel depots, key industrial plants, food sources, and transportation facilities, terror and hunger spread across the land. Eventually, the Organization takes control of California and begins a massive campaign of ethnic and enemy cleansing, using preprepared dossiers of "race traitors" and nonwhite residents. Tens of thousands politicians, lawyers, reporters, judges, actors, teachers, and priests are hanged from lampposts and trees all over Los Angeles. Thousands of white women known for having lived in biracial relations are hanged on "the Day of the Rope," all carrying placards reading, "I defiled my race" (ibid., 160). Nonwhites are simply killed or forced out of Aryan territory, evacuated at a rate of a million a day. The Order then unleashes a nuclear war, bombing New York, Miami, Charleston, Toronto, and Tel Aviv. When North America has been liberated, the Order expands the revolution globally and, through nuclear, chemical, and biological warfare, makes "the dream of a White world . . . a certainty" (ibid., 210).

When *Turner Diaries* became a counterculture best-seller, Pierce (1997) realized, "This is the way to teach people. Write novels, write plays, write film scripts, because a person not only experiences the actions of the protagonist, but if you have the protagonist

in decision-making situations, when he has some sort of a conflict that he has to resolve, the reader, or the viewer, undergoes the same thought processes, and then you
can carry the audience along, to educate them, to get them to change their minds, to
get them to see things the way the protagonist learns to see things." *Turner Diaries* being
primarily a counterculture wet dream, Pierce decided to write a "more realistic novel,
Hunter, which shifted away from the idea of an organized group to what an exceptional
individual can do. *Hunter* serves a real educational process" (Pierce 1997). A former combat
pilot in Vietnam, the lead character, Oscar Yeager, returns disillusioned with the government. Disgusted with multicultural America, Yeager develops his skills as a terrorist
and assassinations expert, killing biracial couples, homosexuals, race traitors, and Jews
as a sort of personal therapy. Initially ignorant of the "Jewish question," Yeager is illuminated by a couple of "National League" (read National Alliance) instructors who also
educate him in the basics of true national socialist philosophy, the grandeur of Aryan
civilization, the errors of counterculture rivals (such as Christian Identity), and the faults
of the conservative vision of "law and order." Law and order does not mean a thing if
the racial and Jewish questions are not first resolved, they tell him. "Government is not
an end in itself. It's the race that's important. It's the race's mission of improving itself,
of bringing forth a higher type of human [Aryan] being that's important. The government should only exist to serve that purpose. Stability is only desirable when it serves
that purpose" (Macdonald 1993, 246).

32   A small Caribbean island 2,000 miles southeast of New Orleans, with 80,000 inhabitants, Dominica gained independence from Great Britain in 1979. The autocratic ways
of its first prime minister, Patrick John, his links to South Africa, and his union-busting
policies provoked popular resentment, and he lost the general election of 1980 to Euge-
nia Charles. John decided to hire mercenaries and signed a contract with Klan member
Michael Perdue to oust his rival in return for advance money and tax-exempt opportunities to develop the country's resources. Perdue gathered about a dozen mercenaries from
the National Socialist Party and from Canadian and American Klan groups, including
Don Black of the Knights of the Ku Klux Klan. Had Perdue not happened to discuss his
plans with an F B I informant, the coup might have succeeded. Charged with violation of
the Neutrality Act, which prohibits preparing or providing money for a military or naval
expedition or enterprise against a nation with which the U.S. is at peace, Black argued in
his defense that the N S-Klan operation was fully in line with an established tradition of
American foreign policy as evidenced by the Reagan administration's Central American
policies, not least in Nicaragua. Black triumphantly declared from his cell that he had
been vindicated when the United States invaded Grenada in October 1983.

33   Trochman speech 1997; *Trochman* 1996. Trochman insists that the W H O, pretending to
vaccinate Africans against smallpox, caused an A I D S epidemic on that continent, then
gave it to American homosexuals on the East and West Coasts.

34   Many militias and paramilitary groups existed on paper or in cyberspace only; others
were the projects of single individuals or, perhaps, a party of two. If a "militia" were to
be defined as a paramilitary group consisting of more than a handful of participants that
carried out at least some kind of organized activity, a count of militias at any given date
in 1996 would have turned up no more than a hundred. Most of these "real life" militias

were not organized on Aryan revolutionary ground, a fact confirmed by Dees who out of his 441 militias and 368 patriot groups found only 137 with "ties to the racist right" (Dees 1996, 200.) The Militia Tax Force of the SPLC identified 858 groups active in 1996. (SPLC 1997). Carl Rowan (1996, vii) estimated the number of militias and paramilitary groups to more than 800.

35 Trochman acknowledged having been to the Aryan Nations five or six times. He spoke at the Aryan World Congress in July 1990 and had his sons participate at the AN Youth Congress the same year.

36 FBI statement 1999.

37 Posted on AxCurtis@aol.com, 4 September 1999.

38 Franklin is currently accused of killing twenty-seven people and is currently on trial for murdering a black man and paralyzing his white wife.

39 Word in the counterculture setting in Northwest tells about Furrow being troubled by being in the shadow of martyred Bob Mathews. Living with Mathews's widow, Deborah, Furrow allegedly felt that others in the milieu compared him unfavorably to the Aryan Hero. Intent on proving to everybody that he, too, was a Warrior, he reportedly set aims at the Simon Wiesenthal Center in Los Angeles. Finding the security too tight he gave up on that plan but knew that he would lose face if he returned without committing an act that would match his bravery. Driving at random in LA, Furrow then stopped at a gas station from which he saw the Jewish Community Center.

40 Blueyedevil Internet 1999; Alex Curtis (AxCurtis@aol.com) bestowed the kamikaze label; "RIP Smith" Internet 1999.

41 "Criticizing Racist Action" Internet 1999.

42 Butler speech 1999.

43 Gruber Internet 1999.

44 Commentaries posted at AxCurtis, *Nationalist Observer Racial Reader's Forum*, 19 October 1999.

45 "Furrow Aryan of the Month" Internet 1999. Ben Smith had been given the same counterculture honor the month before ("Aryan of the Month Benjamin Smith" Internet 1999).

46 Curtis Internet 1999a.

47 Curtis Internet 1999b.

48 The Illuminati were a secret society founded by the Bavarian judicial scholar and Enlightenment champion Adam Weishaupt in 1776 to liberate mankind from all religious and political authority. Although the Illuminati most likely were dissolved in 1787, their aims, clandestine tactics, and Masonic mode of organization influenced subsequent revolutionary organizations. Conspiracy theories claim that the Illuminati never died but perfected their clandestine strategy, secretly orchestrating human history. Most Illuminati conspiracy theorists moreover date its origin far earlier than 1776, linking it to the Knights Templars, Cabalists, the Babylonian empire, or further back into the prehistory of man or even to some far away galaxy.

49 Bush first referred to the New World Order in an 11 September 1990 televised speech before the Congress: "A new partnership of nations has begun. We stand today at a unique and extraordinary moment. The crisis in the Persian Gulf . . . offers a rare opportunity to move toward an historic period of cooperation. Out of these troubled times . . . a

new world order can emerge; a new era—freer from the threat of terror, stronger in the pursuit of justice, and more secure in the quest for peace. An era in which nations of the world, East, West, North and South, can prosper and live in harmony. . . . A world in which nations recognize the shared responsibility for freedom and justice" (Bush speech 1990). Bush kept coming back to the New World Order theme, making at least twenty references to it during the Gulf War. Eleven years to the day after his speech— 11 September 2001—terrorists attempted to castrate the New World Order by hijacking airplanes and crashing into the World Trade Center and the Pentagon (see chapter 8).

50 Not all conspiracy believers thought that Bush was necessarily aware of the supposedly true, inner meaning of the New World Order. Televangelist Pat Robertson, whose 1991 best-seller *The New World Order* quickly became one of the most influential works "exposing" a sinister Illuminati conspiracy, argued, "Indeed, it may well be that men of goodwill, like Woodrow Wilson, Jimmy Carter, and George Bush, who sincerely want a larger community of nations living in peace in our world, are in reality unknowingly and unwittingly carrying out the mission and mouthing the phrases of a tightly knit cabal whose goal is nothing less than a new order for the human race under the domination of Lucifer and his followers" (Pat Robertson 1991, 37). The NWO conspiracy theory exists in many different versions, colored not least by the campaigner's personality, religious conviction, political persuasion, and standpoint on the "racial issue." Circulating the cultural underground, NWO conspiracy theory is not inherently racist. Yet information revealed by conspiracy researchers is recycled throughout the Aryan revolutionary milieu. Space considerations unfortunately exclude a review here of the enormous and ever-growing body of NWO literature and its main influences and producers, but an outline of the generic NWO conspiracy theory runs as follows: an omnipotent cabal is about to complete the takeover of the United States and the world, terminating the American way of life in the process. The plotters may either be Masons, Illuminati, aliens, satanists, Jews, plutocrats, or any combination of these. They belong to a secret ring that stretches far back in history, a history it has directed toward the sole aim of global hegemony. The cabal is held responsible for significant events, such as the French Revolution and the World Wars; "detrimental" ideologies, such as communism and humanism; "false" religions and utopian dreams, such as equality and world peace. It was behind the Russian Revolution and the phony Cold War only in order to dismantle the Soviet Union, from whence it had served its distracting purpose of allowing the globalists to secretly secure worldwide control. Under the pretext of global transnational cooperation against famine, environmental destruction, ethnic conflicts, and mad dictators—all creations of the sinister cabal—it manipulated the opinion to support United Nations empowerment, with the covert aim of undermining national self-determination and establishing a totalitarian global dictatorship through a process of globalization/homogenization that will reduce mankind to mind-controlled producer robots. Orchestrating American history, the cabal has gradually undermined local and individual liberties and built an increasingly autocratic federal administration through creations such as the Federal Reserve, the New Deal, IRS, FBI, CIA, the Bureau of Alcohol, Tobacco, and Firearms (BATF), the Drug Enforcement Agency (DEA), and the Federal Emergency Management

Agency (FEMA). Secretly having completed its preparations, the cabal is now ready to enter the final phase. In a nationwide clean-sweep operation, UN soldiers and federal agents will seize all privately owned guns, crush any pocket of resistance, round up all freedom-loving Americans, and incarcerate them in concentration camps already constructed by FEMA.

51 The "King" corresponds to the Sun God and the "Queen" to the Moon Goddess (Diana), and their ritual murders supposedly recapitulated ancient diabolic fertility rites.

52 Hoffman's German-American father was chief of physical therapy at Clifton Springs Hospital, and the father of his Italian-American mother owned a hotel chain. The Anti-Masonic Party that arose in the wake of Morgan's disappearance became a short-lived populist mass movement of some signficance in upstate New York, Massachusetts, and Rhode Island; it also elected a governor in Pennsylvania and dominated political life in Vermont through 1932 when leaders and members began drifting away to the new Whig Party (Bennet 1995, 49; Hofstadter 1996, 15.)

53 Hoffman covered the Zündel trial, making a series of video interviews with leading Holocaust deniers who attended, which he aired on cable TV from Ithaca, New York, in 1985. Hoffman also wrote a book (1995 [1985]) on the subject of the trial, but his relationship with Zündel eventually soured. Writing for the weekly *Spotlight*, Hoffman then worked for a year (1986) with the Institute of Historical Review in Los Angeles, the institute being at the time under the auspices of Carto—again, accumulating conflicts and internal intrigues resulted. After the IHR episode, Hoffman worked with the American headquarters of the Australian Veritas Press, attempting in vain to make it the leading "revisionist" publishing company in the world, until, once again, internal intrigues developed. So, Hoffman explains, "we ended up busting up about two years later, and there were lawsuits and everything else and it turned out to be a mess, and I was attacked by some of my own friends, and David Irving and I had a falling out because of that, but we patched it up, but it was really a mess" (1998). His next project was with Tom Metzger of White Aryan Resistance, but according to Hoffman, Metzger unfortunately "became more and more difficult to work with," demanding "fidelity" and "began to see himself as the One Way," so they, too, parted ways (ibid.). In the end, disillusioned also with the skinhead scene that he had originally been drawn to, Hoffman eventually came to question the whole NS scene.

54 Hoffman Internet 1999a; *Hoffman* 1998; Hoffman Internet 1999d.

55 On 11 January 2000, Hoffman stated, "Since I wrote last December concerning financial support for THE Hoffman WIRE I have heard from a little more than a half-dozen contributors out of nearly 2,000 recipients of THE HOFFMAN WIRE. I cannot write this online bulletin for seven people. . . . If memory serves me I am the only former establishment journalist working in hard-core World War Two revisionism and conspiracy research. . . . Had enough of you shown with your wallets, and not just with the kind of empty, laudatory rhetoric I get in e-mail, that you cared for my work, then I would be reporting and digesting these and other subjects now. . . . From henceforth I'll restrict my e-mailings to emergencies, notifications of my picketing and protest activism, time and location of my speeches, ads for my books and other brief bulletins. I do not do this in a penal spirit. I am not seeking to punish my parsimonious e-mail

audience. I simply cannot afford to spend my time in this forum any longer; minimum remuneration is required and is not forthcoming. Therefore I must of necessity discontinue these HOFFMAN WIRES" (Hoffman Internet 2000). The counterculture reaction to Hoffman's complaints was characteristically negative. Counterculture writer, Harold Covington, wrote that all these " 'Great White Leaders' start out the same way—in first getting a check or so, and then thinking that they have 'A RIGHT' to continued support so they no longer have to earn a real living. In effect, these people are more like merchants and tradesmen putting a value on their wares that most other people do not—hence Hoffman's snit about only a half-dozen or so 'paying their fair share.' "

56 Satan means "adversary to God," and the thought of trying to perfect what God has created is to Hoffman satanic.

57 Hoffman Internet 1999b; Hoffman Internet 1999c.

58 Conversation with anonymous Aryan activist, May 1997.

59 Riley speech 1996.

60 For a discussion about anti-Semitism in the United States, see Wistrich 1991, Jack Nelson 1993, Langmuir 1990, Quinley and Glock 1979, and Higham 1975.

61 The *Protocols of the Learned Elders of Zion* is an infamous forgery made in 1897 by the Tsarist intelligence in Russia and published in 1905. It has the form of a protocol detailing the decisions made at a secret meeting of the elite of world Jewry at which they plan to conquer the world and establish a global Jewish dictatorship. The *Protocols* is the most notorious and successful piece of modern anti-Semitism, used as an actual document by men such as Henry Ford and Adolf Hitler. On 17 February 1921 Henry Ford said, "The only statement I care to make about the *Protocols* is that they fit in with what is going on. They are sixteen years old, and they have fit the world situation up to this time. They fit it now." The *Protocols* was printed in Ford's newspaper, the *Dearborn Independent* and cited as evidence of an alleged Jewish threat until at least 1927. In *Mein Kampf*, Adolf Hitler wrote, "To what extent the whole existence of this people is based on a continuous lie is shown incomparably by the *Protocols*."

62 Gerald K. Smith later abridged the original four-volume edition into a single volume (Smith 1995 [1948]).

63 During the trial, *Independent* editor and British-Israelite William J. Cameron absolved Ford from all responsibility for the paper's content, testimony questioned by Ford intimate Stanley Ruddiman. "I don't think Mr. Cameron ever wrote anything for publication without Mr. Ford's approval" (cited in Barkun 1997, 35).

64 Some analysts estimated an audience of thirty million by the mid-1930s. Even if reduced by two-thirds, it would have been "the largest radio audience of the world" (Bennet 1995, 254).

65 Estimations of the NUSJ membership vary considerably. In 1936 Coughlin claimed a membership of more than five million with an additional eight million supporters. On another occasion he referred to an active membership of 1.6 million, with six million passive members.

66 Informed by history that wealth and power are no guarantee against pogroms, Jewish American organizations stand on guard against anti-Semitism. However, the close monitoring of the activities of miniscule white-racist groups and marginalized anti-

Semites may create an optical illusion of rampant anti-Semitism despite the fact that social scientists find hostility toward Jews, as measured in opinion polls, at virtually zero. Contributing to the fear of increasing anti-Semitism were probably also the fierce sermons preached by black Islamic nationalist minister Louis Farrakhan (Gardell 1996; Gardell 1998)

67   "Who Rules America?" Internet 2000.

68   Mohr fought in World War II and the Korean War.

69   Mohr converted to Identity after meeting with Sheldon Emry, then of the Lord's Covenant Church in Phoenix, Arizona, at the annual festival of the Christian Patriot's Defense League in Louisville, Illinois. Emry gave Mohr the classic *Judah's Sceptre and Joseph's Birthright* to study. In the fragmented world of Identity, Mohr cooperates with Pete Peters of Scriptures for America, Earl Jones of New Mexico, and David Marilee of America's Promise in Idaho, Louis Beam and the Jubilee crowd, but he takes exception to Butler's Church of Jesus Christ, Christian and other hardcore two-seedliners.

70   Among his works are Mohr n.d., Mohr 1992, Mohr 1993a, Mohr 1993b.

71   Lending credence to official suspicions regarding the anti-Semitic production of fake works, in the 1970s Walter White and Richard Butler crafted *The Rosenthal Document* in an effort to forge a Jewish confirmation of the Jewish conspiracy as detailed in *Protocols*. Presented as a highly confidential interview with top political aide "Harold Wallace Rosenthal," the document purports to reveal the operations of the Jewish cabal. "We Jews continue to be amazed with the ease by which Christian Americans have fallen into our hands" (1), Rosenthal supposedly says. "This country could never be the land of the free as long as it is the land of the Jews" (23). Detailing the Jewish stranglehold on American politics, economy, education, and media, Rosenthal brags that nothing can undo the Jewish plan for world power but admits that Jews fear the "light" that is coming forth in this country, "especially" Identity.

72   Blacks are to Mohr an uncultured "servant race" without ingenuity, as "proved" by "savage life in Africa" where people live exactly as "they did 5,000 years ago and [do] not even know how to start a fire." Controlled by Jews, black Americans are employed to destroy the American social fabric and to further cultural degeneracy with that beat of "satanic African savagery" known as rock and roll.

73   This supposedly fulfilled Deuteronomy 28:33 and 43–44. "The fruit of thy land, and all thy labors, shall a nation which thou knowest not eat up, and thou shalt be oppressed and crushed away. . . . The stranger that is within thee shall get up very high; and thou shalt come down very low. He shall lend to thee and thou shalt not lend to him; he shalt be the head and thou shalt be the tail."

74   Armageddon is supposedly approaching, and, as Mohr informs his audience, "It is your glorious duty to be in the forefront of the army of God." Besides using biblical arguments, Mohr construct his anti-Jewish worldview with a technique common to the counterculture: he bases his books and lectures on a selective reading of Jewish authors, scholars, philosophers, and rabbis, a methodology he feels enhances the credibility of his work, since the "information" presented to his audience is not from his own theories but from "facts" compiled from "official Jewish sources." As all Jews are held to organically belong to one single body, any statement by any Jew is believed to be repre-

sentative of the thoughts of every Jew everywhere. This method is convenient as it easily "proves" whatever one wishes to prove. For instance, if Mohr wants to prove that Jews have masterminded secularism to turn Aryan man from his savior, he cites the Jewish materialist philosopher Ludwig Feuerbach: "Man will be truly free when he realizes that there is no god of man, but man himself." If Mohr wants to prove that communism is Jewish, he may turn to an article in the *Jewish Chronicle* from 1918, where the author claims, "The ideals of Bolshevism are consonant with the finest ideals of Judaism," or to a 1935 statement by red Rabbi Stephen Wise, "Some call it Communism, I call it Judaism." By citing selective quotations like these and through extensive use of the Talmud and the Bible, Mohr constructs an image of the "eternal Jew" as a satanic adversary of God. He complains that Christians are blinded to his message by two key hoaxes: the false claim that Jews (and not Aryans) are the chosen people and the fabricated story of the Holocaust. (Mohr 1997; Mohr 1993a, 116; Mohr 1992, 63; Mohr n.d., 68; Mohr 1993b, 118)

75 Officially, the founder was Lewis Brandon (alias for William David McCalden), who served as its first director until 1981 when he was ousted in a conflict with Carto, who remained the controlling power of the IHR until 1993, when he was ousted by the new IHR leadership. McCalden, who died in 1991, spent the remainder of his life attacking Carto and the IHR.

76 Zündel was tried twice, in 1984 and 1988, for distributing revisionist material, such as Richard Harwood's *Did Six Million Really Die? The Truth at Last.* In his own defense, Zündel summoned revisionists such as David Irving and Robert Faurisson, attempting to turn the trial into a debate about whether the Holocaust actually had happened or not.

77 Tom Marcellus was director from 1981 until 1995. His membership in the Church of Scientology is part of the conspiracy theory presented by Carto.

78 Smith E-zine 1996.

79 Ibid.

80 Anonymous e-mail 2000.

81 Limited space prevents the possibility of presenting or even mentioning here all populist movements and ideologies that have made an imprint on American society. More comprehensive introductions to populism can be found in Taggart 2000, Berlet and Lyons 2000, Westlind 1998, Bennet 1995, and Åsard 1994.

82 For a discussion about populism as a concept, see Taggart 2000, Canovan 1981.

83 "We have witnessed for more than a quarter of a century the struggles of the two great political parties for power and plunder, while grievous wrong have been inflicted upon the suffering people," the People's Party platform read. "The fruits of the toil of millions are boldly stolen to build up colossal fortunes for a few. . . . [A] vast conspiracy against mankind have been organized on two continents, and is rapidly taking possession of the world. . . . [W]e seek to restore the government of the Republic to the hands of the 'plain people,' with which class it originated" (from the preamble to the platform established at the national convention in Omaha, 1892; quoted in Taggart 2000, 28).

84 Reaching out to industrial workers, the People's Party proposed a coalition between the Farmers' Alliance and the Knights of Labor.

85 He received some 10 percent in the opinion polls and had plans for building alliances

with other populist leaders such as Francis E. Townsend, whose Old Age Revolving Pension Plan movement had an estimated 3.5 million members.

86 The first two Posse Comitatus groups were founded in 1969 by former Silver Shirt member Henry L. Beach and Identity Christian William Potter Gale and grew particularly strong in Kansas, Nebraska, North Dakota, Montana, Colorado, Texas, California, Wisconsin, Illinois, Michigan, and Delaware.

87 Rejecting the federal administration as unconstitutional, Posse espouses a radical localism. "A county government is the highest authority of the government in our Republic as it is closest to the people, who are in fact, the government. The County Sheriff is the only legal law enforcement officer in the United States. . . . He is responsible to protect the citizens, even from unlawful acts of officials of government. If he refuses to do so, he should be removed" (Posse Comitatus n.d.).

88 Several key Identity Christian pastors were involved with the Posse, notably Richard G. Butler, William Potter Gale, and James Wickstrom.

89 For the story of Kahl, see Corcoran 1990.

90 The Populist Party of America was founded in 1987 and fared poorly. Receiving negative press coverage in Carto's *Spotlight* weekly, the party filed a libel suit, which in 1997 was ruled in their favor. On 30 October of that year, a federal jury in Pittsburgh held that the Populist Party and its national chairman, Don Wassal, had been libeled by the Liberty Lobby and *Spotlight*, awarding Wassal $100,000 and the party $2 million in damages.

91 Garvey argued that *all* whites shared the perspective of white supremacy but differed in the methods they used to perpetuate its hegemony. White liberals, unionists, or communists pretended to be friends of the black man to divert their attention from the race struggle to "the impossible dream of equality that shall never materialize." The greatest enemies of the African American are those whites who "hypocritically profess love" for the black man while "in reality they despise and hate him." Garvey regarded the Klansman a far better friend of the black man than any pseudo-philanthropist, because "potentially, every white man is a Klansman as far as the Negro in competition with whites socially, economically, and politically is concerned, and there is no use lying about it" (Garvey 1989a, 37; Garvey 1989b, 70).

Garvey's logic was accentuated by the Nation of Islam, which advanced a theory of the genetic evilness of all whites, reducing the difference between white racists and professed antiracists to a distinction between the devil's strategies to get their prey: the people of color. In NOI terminology, there are two categories of devil: "wolves" and "foxes." Like Garvey, leading NOI spokesperson Malcolm X undoubtedly preferred the former. He stated that while white conservatives may not be the black man's friends, they "at least don't try to hide it." Like wolves they show their teeth in a snarl that keeps the black man aware of where he stands with them. "White liberals are foxes who also show their teeth but pretend that they are smiling. White liberals are more dangerous . . . and as the black man runs from the growling wolf he flees into the open jaws of the smiling fox" (Malcolm X 1971, 137). A series of open and covert relations developed between the Nation of Islam and various leagues of wolves. NOI spokespersons like Jeremiah X participated in Klan rallies and Imperial Wizard Robert Shelton publicly praised the Nation. In 1962 American Nazi Party leader George Lincoln Rockwell was invited to address the

NOI convention. Flanked by ten stormtroopers, he praised then leader Elijah Muhammad for being to his people what Hitler was to white people. Led by Malcolm X, an NOI delegation conducted a series of secret meetings with the Klan for the purpose of developing a joint action program for racial separation. The two once-leading Klans, the Invisible Empire and the Knights of the KKK, routinely informed the Nation of their public rallies so it could keep its members from participating in potential antidemonstrations. The Nation sought and found Klan support when it bought farmland in the Deep South, keeping white-racist resistance to black-owned farmland to a minimum (Gardell 1996, 273; Gardell 1998, 318; Black 1996; Baumgardner 1996).

92 From start, WAR declared that it would ally itself with "any individual or group that makes a positive contribution toward racial separatism," including black nationalists. Even as a Klan leader, Metzger occasionally contacted the black Muslims. These contacts were primarily to avoid confrontations like an incident in the 1970s when a black worker was shot; word in the black community blamed Metzger's Klan and, knowing that his Klan was not involved, he phoned the Muslims, who were preparing for action, asking them to call off the heat until the murderer's identity was known. A more intimate relationship developed following the establishment of WAR and peaked in 1985. In that year Metzger was invited to an NOI rally for black economic empowerment, at the Forum in Los Angeles. Donating one hundred dollars as a symbol of support, Metzger was quite impressed with what he saw. The same year, he flew to Virginia for a meeting with Alim Muhammad, minister of the NOI mosque in Washington, D.C., to discuss the possibilities for closer cooperation. They agreed to meet again in Chicago, and Alim indicated the possibility of Metzger's addressing the NOI convention of that year.

While discussing what common ground they might work out, Metzger (allegedly) offered the Muslims a business deal. Metzger had a friend who was (allegedly) very close to a Liberian politician in the former President Taylor's government, who aimed at wresting power from Samuel K. Doe in a coup d'etat. If the coup succeeded, there was a chance for taking over an oil-producing company, and Metzger suggested a joint WAR–NOI venture. While the American racialists were working out the details, Farrakhan was touring West Africa when a coup attempt against the Liberian regime was exposed. Apparently, Metzger says, the former president had involved South Africans and four white American Nazis in the conspiracy. Farrakhan got cold feet, maybe suspecting that Metzger had more than oil on his agenda. The deal never materialized, and Metzger says that their relationship never really got serious after this incident. Resembling more the relationship of the 1970s, it is confined to information exchange and occasional articles of support in Metzger's paper.

Metzger continued to work with other black separatist groups, such as the Black Panthers and the Pan-Afrikan Internationalist Movement. In the early 1990s, he was invited as guest speaker to the Black Panther convention in Austin, Texas, where he claims to have received a standing ovation. Asked what common ground he finds with black nationalists, Metzger said, "We're separatists and we're straight out with it, and we simply say, 'Let's make a deal. There's gonna be a fight in this country and that's either gonna be a winner-takes-all situation, which gonna be really bloody, or there may be that we could make a deal on territory." Metzger thus advocated a division of the country into monoracial states but abstained from explaining how it could become a reality. Until that time should come, black and white separatists in southern California have allegedly "decided on separate spheres of influence," a treaty of noninterference in each other's communities, wherein black nationalists have agreed to stay out of white, working-class areas and Metzger has agreed to keep his men out of black neighborhoods. After the Los Angeles uprising of 1992, Metzger again reached out for an agreement, saying that his men would support a black uprising "as long as you wanna attack the government buildings, you wanna attack the Beverly Hills or rich areas. . . . Just don't come in to the white working class community, because then we would have a problem." Metzger claimed that they made an agreement, "but the question is how much control they really have when things start" (Metzger n.d.; *Metzger 1996; Metzger 1998; Farrakhan 1989a; Farrakhan 1989b;* Gardell 1996).

Willis Carto had nothing but praise for Minister Farrakhan. In 1990 Farrakhan granted *Spotlight* an exclusive interview, in which he confirmed the white-racist position that the United States was "founded by white people for white people," and elaborated on the theme of racial separation. "You're not going to integrate with the blacks in the ghettos of Washington," Farrakhan stated. "But when we [the NOI] get finished with these people, we produce dignified, intelligent people. The American system can't produce that. We can. Give us a chance to make our people worth something" (*Carto 1996;* "Islam Nation Leader Says" 1990).

Louis Beam claimed to have developed covert links with black separatists in general and Farrakhan in particular, and he told me of his and his associates' exchange of information with the Nation. Supporters in the intelligence communities could, for example, leak information about CIA cocaine-trading operations to Beam who would pass it on to the Nation for public use (Conversation with Louis Beam, Coeur d'Alene, Idaho, 26 September 1996).

Jack Mohr boasted that information he passed on to the NOI research department about Jewish involvement in the slave trade became standard in NOI teachings and literature during the late 1980s and early 1990s.

Cultivating black separatists as potential allies was a recurrent theme in British National Front publications during the 1980s, primarily due to a skillfully planned coup that brought a group of Strasserite theoreticians to power in John Tyndall's previously more conventional nationalist socialist organization. With the neo-Strasserites espousing anticapitalism, anticommunism, environmentalism, and class-based racism, an interest in black nationalist and Third World ideologies followed. The two NF publications, *Nationalism Today* and *National Front News,* ran a series of articles about African revolutionaries such as Burkina Faso's Thomas Sankara, Ghana's Jerry Rawlins, and Libya's Mu'ammar al-Qadhdhafi, and flirted with Islamist movements, praising Ayatollah Khomeini. American black nationalists Marcus Garvey, Malcolm X, and Elijah Muhammad got recurrent praise. Garvey was considered an important predecessor to the new NF project, having been the first to establish a "broad front of racialists of all colors." Through its support for Jesse Jackson during the 1984 presidential primary, the NF discovered Louis Farrakhan, whom they lyrically hailed as "God-send to all races and colors," and invited *Final Call* editor Abdul Alim Muhammad to contribute with a five-page article, including photoessay, on the NOI program. Logically, the next step was to establish direct contact with the Nation as the "common cause must be turned into practical cooperation." In May 1988 a senior NF official traveled to the United States and was met by American Strasserites Mat Malone and Robert Hoy, who had developed contacts with black separatist organizations. During his U.S. tour, the NF official was invited to Washington, D.C., and, by Minister Alim Muhammad, to study the much publicized NOI drug-busting program.

Back in Britain, the NF leadership began to distribute leaflets in support of the NOI and declared in its papers, "Black and White power are . . . allies. Unity in diversity is not a slogan. It is a Way of Life." The NF rank and file, however, did not unanimously acknowledge the strategy of creating a closer working relationship with black nationalists. The Manchester chapter notified the leadership that it refused to distribute issue 99 of *National Front News* because of its front-page slogan "Fight Racism" encircling a clenched black fist. Under the caption "Rantings from the Bunker" the editorial board published correspondence from dissident members charging the leadership for "Bolshevik jargon." "I prefer Hitler as 'comrade' to any black power hottentot who wants to shake my hand," one letter stated, "because Hitler is of my people, my culture, and my ideological kindred," its author going on to wonder what weird kind of national socialism the leaders had developed that would let them call Farrakhan a comrade. The Strasserite theoreticians continued espousing their ideas, though, declaring that they had "little or nothing" in common with their Nazi predecessors. They viewed "negative racism" as a product of Britain's imperial past, arguing that true racialism was an anti-racist ideology, dedicated to the preservation of all races and cultures. Mindless thoughts of white supremacy had to go, and the membership was advised not tell racist jokes, as that would cause division among allies. ("Garvey's Vision" n.d.; Muhammad n.d.; "A Common Cause" n.d.; "Rantings from the Bunker" n.d.; "Race: The New Reality" n.d.)

93 Grand Dragon is the highest Klan rank in a state; "Imperial Klaliff" is national vice-president, second in command to Imperial Wizard.

94 Theologically, Pastor Pete Peters and James Wickstrom are primary influences for Baumgardner. Other influential figures are Pastor Richard G. Butler and the first generation Identity preachers, chiefly Bertrand Comparet and Wesley Swift.

95 Khallid Abdul Muhammad was silenced by Minister Farrakhan after a series of overtly anti-Semitic remarks.

96 Akkebala asked Trochman if his militia would be willing to train a black separatist militia, which would be organized for three purposes: first, to deal with injustices in the black community; second, to deal with black-on-black crime; and third, to organize a black counterpart to the South African–based mercenary army called the Executive Outcome. Negotiations began between PAIN and MOM began in July 1996, which was confirmed by John Trochman in an informal conversation I had with him on 9 November 1996 in Denver, Colorado. A public announcement was originally scheduled for January 1997, but the outcome is still pending. (Akkebala 1996; Trochman 1996).

97 The notion that Jesus was Aryan and not a Jew circulated widely in European thought a hundred years ago. In the völkisch milieu, legends identified Jesus as descending from the Aryan tribes that originally settled the Holy Land. Another völkisch fable, introduced

a Roman centurion named Pandera as the true biological father of Jesus to explain his noble Aryan features. Ariosophist Jörg Lanz van Liebenfels saw Jesus as an Aryan master of divine gnosis. Jesus was an Aryan Christ and the Holy Grail—seen as a sacred container of divine Aryan blood—became a powerful völkisch symbol for rejuvenation, explored by Wagner in his *Parsifal*. In the United Kingdom legends linked the holy history of the Bible with the British Isles. The coronation stone at Westminster Abbey had supposedly been used by Jacob, father of the ten tribes of Israel, and brought to the British Isles by Jeremiah the Prophet. Local tradition held that Jesus visited the British Isles during the "missing years" of his biography. According to legend, Joseph of Arimathea founded the Abbey in Glastonbury. As early as 1563, historian John Fox stressed the "uniqueness of the English as 'a chosen people' with a Church lineage stretching back to Joseph of Arimathea." Pioneering British-Israelites took the notion further by claiming that Britons in fact were Hebrews.

A predecessor to British-Israelism was the retired naval officer Richard Brothers who in a series of visions in 1791–93 was informed that he was a direct descendant of the House of David and that the British people were in fact the children of Israel who had forgotten their true identity. Presenting himself as "Prince of the Hebrews and Nephew of the Almighty," Brothers promised to lead the lost tribes of Israel back to Jerusalem and predicted the millennium to begin on 19 November 1795. His mission to return the "hidden Israel" to the Holy Land was aborted when he was declared insane and institutionalized from 1794 to 1806, and his idea lay dormant until it was revived by John Wilson and his self-proclaimed disciple Edward Hine. Wilson's *Our Israelitish Origins* (1840) and Hine's *Identity of the Ten Lost Tribes of Israel with the Anglo-Celtic-Saxons* (1874) eventually formed the base for an interdenominational British-Israelite vogue among upper- and middle-class Britons, including military officers and aristocrats. Both Wilson and Hine claimed that the legendary ten tribes of Israel that had disappeared from history with their Assyrian captivity around 721 B.C. had migrated to northwestern Europe and North America and in time forgot their Hebrew origins. Building their case on innovative interpretations of the Holy Writ, historical records, and homemade philology (Saxon meaning "Isaac's son," and Denmark meaning "the land of Dan"), Wilson and Hine differed mainly in their views on non-Anglo-Saxon northern Europeans and Jews.

Wilson dispersed the ten lost tribes among the Anglo-Saxon–Teutonic–Scandinavian peoples, which reflected a then current romantic idealization of ancient Norse and Teutonic cultures. Anglo-Saxon ideologues of that time linked the notion of a distinct Anglo-Saxon superior race uniquely qualified for self-government and world dominion to its origin among the noble, heroic, and freedom-loving Germanic tribes practicing natural democracy in the forests. Hine, on the other hand, wrote at a time when pro-Germanic sentiment had begun to falter, as Germany had been reunited under Emperor Wilhelm I after Bismarck's victory in the war against France, 1870–71, and had begun to challenge Britain's place as the leading power of Europe. Hine courted his audience by assuring them that all of the ten tribes of Israel had been reunited on the British Isles when the kingdoms of England and Scotland united under James I and that only Britain fit the scripture's description of Israel. Israel, Hine said, must be on islands northwest of Palestine, be a monarchy, possess colonies, have Jacob's stone, and be ruled by a descendant of the House of David. Not only was Germany not of Israel, Hine stated, but it was in fact identified with another "lost" people, the Assyrians. The British–German conflict of his day was thus but a continuation of the ancient battle between historical archenemies.

Using the same logic, Hine claimed that the conflict between Israel and Canaan was being replayed in the British Isles in occupied Ireland. In Numbers 33:53–55, God orders Israel to "dispossess the dwellers of the land and dwell therein: for I have given you the land to possess it." He also warns, "If ye not drive out the inhabitants," then "those which ye let remain" will be "pricks in the eyes and thorns in your side." Hine identified the "people of the South of Ireland to be descendants of the Canaanites," as "they, and they only" have been "thorns in our sides" as their struggle for independence and home-rule demonstrates (1874, 36). Clearly then, British-Israelism fit the imperial ambitions of the British Empire quite nicely, and Hine emphasized that the most important evidence that proves the British-Israelite identity comes from its undefeated imperial army. God had promised Israel that He would "strengthen thee" to defeat all their enemies that will "come to nothing" (Isaiah 41:9–12). "All who have warred against us have been as nothing, and no other nation can say this," Hine wrote triumphantly. "It can only be verified in Israel; it is only verified in us, ergo, we must be Israel. The French— the Russians—the Spanish—the Dutch—the Chinese—the Indians—the Germans— the Austrians—and the Italians, cannot, any of them, be Israel, because they have been defeated. The British stand out alone as a nation never defeated, a fact, in itself which establishes our Identity" (50).

Barkun notes that Hine's version prevailed over Wilson's Israelite identification with the Anglo-Saxon–Teutonic–Scandinavian people. When Christian Identity emerged out of British-Israelism in the United States, it would tip back to Wilson's more inclusive theory, not least because of the pro-Nordic and pro-German sentiments integral to American national socialism. The same might be said about Hine's and Wilson's conflicting views on the Jewish people. Both agreed that the present-day Jews were descendants from the two tribes of the Southern Kingdom of Judah, but whereas Wilson introduced the first steps of their coming degradation (as the spawn of Satan, the false-Israel) by stressing their pattern of interbreeding with spiritually inferior people, Hine looked on Jews as kindred people. According to Hine, Jews were part of "All-Israel," which would soon be reunited in Palestine, at that time a British protectorate. Compared to the extreme anti-Jewish sentiments of American Christian Identity, though, even Wilson appears rather philo-Semitic, although not on par with Hine's support of his southern brethren. Hine's philo-Semitic views made British-Israelites enthusiastically throw their support behind Herzl and the early Zionist movement, as it seemed to bring about the reunification of the southern and northern kingdom and thus set the stage for the Second Coming. When the Zionists raised demands for British withdrawal and an independent Jewish national state, however, British-Israelites began to wonder just who these people really were, working against their Israelite brethren and a reunified kingdom, suspicions that fed emergent anti-Semitism (Barkun 1997; Kaplan 1997; Noll 1997b, 101; Noll 1997a, 144; Goodrick-Clarke 1992, 94; Horsman 1981; Hine 1874).

98 Both Wilson and Hine looked on the United States as an extension of Israel. Britain

was identified as Ephraim, son of Joseph, (to Wilson as a tribe only and to Hine as synonymous with the consolidated "Island" Israel), while the United States was identified as Ephraim's brother, Manasseh. God blessed both and Jacob (Gen. 48) transferred to them his birthright privileges, promising that Manasseh would be "great" but Ephraim "greater" as "his seed shall become a multitude of nations" (interpreted as a reference to the British Commonwealth). British-Israelism had found its way to North America during the first half of the nineteenth century and had established local centers in Northeast, the Midwest, and the far West by the time Hine toured the country (1884 to 1888). Prominent among first generation British-Israeli theologians in the United States include M. M. Eshelman (*Two Sticks: Or, the Lost Tribes of Israel Rediscovered* [1887]), J. H. Allen (*Judah's Sceptre and Joseph's Birthright* [1902]), and C. A. L. Totten (*Our Race: Its Origin and Destiny* [1891]; *The Order of History* [1897]), as well as by evangelists John Fox Parham, father of Pentecostalism; Frank Sandford, founder of the Shiloh Bible school; and (again) J. H. Allen, cofounder of Church of God (Holiness). British-Israelism had several influential periodicals, such as *Our Race*, edited by Totten, and *Watchman of Israel*, edited by A. A. Beauchamp, and a number of organizational vehicles, such as Lost Israel Identification Society, the Anglo-Israel Association, the Anglo-Israel Research Society, the Anglo-Saxon Federation of America, and the (London-based) British Israel World Federation.

The theory that the lost ten tribes were to be found in North America was not unique to British-Israelism, nor was the idea that the United States somehow was the modern equivalent of Israel. The Mormons had for decades linked themselves and America to the lost tribes and Israel. Beginning in 1820, Jesus allegedly visited Mormon founder Joseph Smith in a series of visions to correct the prevailing corruption of true Christianity. In 1827 the angel Moroni is said to have informed Smith where to find buried plates that recorded the history of the ancient inhabitants of America—the Book of Mormon, which told the story of three Hebrew tribes that had crossed the ocean hundreds of years before and had built an ancient American civilization. Jesus Christ had appeared in person following his crucifixion and had taught these ancient Americans an advanced Christianity that ushered in a golden era. Parts of the Lamanite tribe then defected and were cursed by God with dark skin and turned into wild, red Indians. The Native American is thus of Israel, and the Mormons believe that many of the Latter-Day Saints in fact were descended from Ephraim and Manasseh and thus kin to the apostate Jews called Indians. When the lost tribes reunite under Christ in North America to build there the new Zion, the American Indians will revert to the true faith again. The curse will then be lifted, and they will partake in Israel in perfected white (Book of Mormon). For a discussion about Mormonism, see Arrington and Bitton 1992. On possible Mormon influence on Christian Identity, see Barkun 1997, 185.

99 *Jubilee* newspaper is a northern California tabloid and has probably the largest circulation of Identity papers. It features Louis Beam as one of its correspondents and lists Yahweh as its Supreme-Editor-in-Chief.

100 Tate said, "In a person we have a lot of white and red blood cells, right, and its gotta be many more red blood cells than white, but there is a select group of white blood cells that go through that refinement, that go to war to preserve the body. This is part of our trial and the trying part is a refining process for us in this state of being" (1997).

101   The primary non-Identity source frequently referred to is Sydney Bristowe's *Sargon the Magnificent*, published in 1927 and still widely circulated among Identity Christians. Bristowe argues that Cain's story shows that although "Adam was the first man into whom God breathed a 'living soul,' he was not the first human being upon the earth" (15). Partly building her case on archeological finds that date man's presence on earth earlier than the 6,000 years claimed by fundamentalist Christians, Bristowe concludes that figurines, monuments, and sculptures show that those pre-Adamic humans were nonwhites. This solves the riddle, Bristowe proposes. "It is easy to imagine Cain, a white man endowed with superhuman knowledge and physique . . . taking command over those pre-Adamites; and that he did so seems proved by the fact that he built a city and called it after his son Enoch. We see, therefore, that the Bible sanctions the beliefs in pre-Adamites" (15). Concluding that these pre-Adamic people were nonwhites, Bristowe aims at finding biblical support for the nineteenth-century scientific theory of polygenesis, a thesis widely supported by Identity theologians.

102   In defining the racial identity of the pre-Adamites, current Identity thinkers generally differentiate between the "black" and "yellow" races. Both are seen as bereft of the "spirit of God" and have never been "living souls," although not all Identity Christians dismiss the thought that they can be saved. The pre-Adamic (black) races are believed to be deprived also of ingenuity, the power of reason, and the capacity to build civilizations, while the yellow race is thought capable of having a "much higher civilized standards than the blacks do" (Butler 1996). This does not necessarily mean that Identity ideologues acknowledge ancient Chinese, Japanese, or Indian civilization as Asian. On the contrary, these ancient high cultures are often thought to be Aryan in origin, as are the Egyptian, Mayan, and Incan civilizations. Gobineau's ancient super-Aryan world civilizers thus returned with a vengeance in twentieth-century theological speculation. Pastor Butler, representative of hardcore Identity, argued that God "told the Aryan race through Adam to replenish and subdue the earth. And we did. There was no civilization before us, no culture. All civilization on earth is the creation of the white Adamic man. . . . Ancient China was a white civilization. . . . The pyramids were built by whites and their designs were made by whites. . . . China, India, Egypt, Persia all originated as Aryan civilizations but then degenerated through race mixing" (1996). Still, Identity Christians maintain, there is a world of difference between the Asian and African pre-Adamites. While Asians belong to "culture," Africans are associated with "nature" and are generally held to have lived uncultured lives as animals before Aryan man conquered them.

103   "In no place in Africa has there ever been what we could call a civilization that has been developed by the native people," Mohr (1997) claimed. He believed that prior to colonization, Africans could not make fire, had never seen a wheel, could not fish or till the soil, had never developed a sophisticated language, a refined religion, made any meaningful invention or any progress above savage, animal, beastly life. When asked about the ancient civilizations of present-day Zimbabwe and Mali, Mohr and other Identity believers only shook their heads in disbelief, suggesting that if such tales were true, these civilizations simply could not have been native African in origin.

104   According to Ted R. Weiland (1999), this is a subject on which there is much crossover between hardcore and soft Identity.

105   For a non-Identity reader, this may seem of secondary importance as both the hardcore
       and soft schools of Identity agree that Jews are the agents of Satan. From the Identity
       perspective, however, there is a world of difference.

106   It was taken over by such influential hardcore Identity teachers as Richard G. Butler,
       Harold X of Tennessee, Mark Thomas of Pennsylvania, James Wickstrom of Wiscon-
       sin, and X of Eleventh Hour Ministries of Idaho, with only minor revisions in terms of
       emphasis and updating.

107   Thomas Internet 1996e.

108   Ibid.

109   Thomas Internet 1996d.

110   Thomas Internet 1996a.

111   Thomas Internet 1996f.

112   Thomas Internet 1996c.

113   Thomas Internet 1993.

114   Thomas Internet 1996d.

115   Redfeairn Internet 2001. However, as of October 2002, the leadership has passed on
       to Charles John Juba (national director), and the headquarters has relocated to "God's
       Country" in Potter's County, Pennsylvania.

116   Klassen rejects the term as derogatory and, as will be noted later, although admitting
       the common ground between Creativity and atheism, claims that atheism differs by not
       presenting a positive alternative to religion.

117   This stand is contradicted by other statements in which Klassen claimed that he would
       defend anyone's right to espouse any religious belief, no matter how silly (1987, 166).

118   The sixteen COTC commandments being: "1) It is the avowed duty and holy responsi-
       bility of each generation to assure and secure for all time the existence of the White Race
       on the face of this planet. 2) Be fruitful and multiply. Do your part in helping to popu-
       late the world with your own kind. It is our sacred duty to populate the lands of this
       earth with White people exclusively. 3) Remember that the inferior colored races are our
       deadly enemies, and the most dangerous of all is the Jewish race. It is our immediate
       objective to relentlessly expand the White Race, and keep shrinking our enemies. 4) The
       guiding principle of all your actions shall be: What is the best for the White Race? 5) You
       shall keep your race pure. Pollution of the White Race is a heinous crime against Nature
       and against your own race. 6) Your first loyalty belongs to the White Race. 7) Show pref-
       erential treatment in business dealings with members of your own race. Phase out all
       dealings with Jews as soon as possible. Do not employ niggers or other coloreds. Have
       social contacts only with members of your own racial family. 8) Destroy and banish all
       Jewish thoughts and influence from our society. Work hard to bring about a white world
       as soon as possible. 9) Work and creativity are our genius. We regard work as a noble
       pursuit and our willingness to work a blessing to our race. 10) Decide in early youth that
       during your lifetime you will make at least one major lasting contribution to the White
       Race. 11) Uphold and honor your race at all times. 12) It is our duty and our privilege
       to further Nature's plan by striving towards the advancement and improvement of our
       future generations. 13) You shall honor, protect and venerate the sanctity of the family
       unit, and hold it sacred. It is the present link in the long golden chain of our White Race.

14) Throughout your life you shall faithfully uphold our pivotal creed of Blood, Soil and Honor. Practice it diligently, for it is the heart of our faith. 15) As a proud member of the White Race, think and act positively. Be courageous, confident and aggressive. Utilize constructively your creative ability. We, the Racial Comrades of the White Race, are determined to regain complete and unconditional control of our own destiny" (Klassen 1992, 256.)

119 COTC veteran McVan, who by then had converted to Odinism, was invited to participate in the meeting held at "two-gun Slim's" property in Superior, Montana, 27 July 1996.

120 WCOTC had in 2000 seventy local chapters affiliated with the East Peoria, Illinois, world headquarters: Cabot, Arizona; Pine Bluff, Arizona; Florence, Arizona; Mesa, Arizona; Tucson, Arizona; Manhattan Beach, California; Seal Beach, California; Sierra Madre, California; Tehachapi, California; Fairfield, Connecticut; Hawleyville, Connecticut; Wallingford, Connecticut; Chipley, Florida; Davie, Florida; Defuniak Springs, Florida; Milton, Florida; Monticello, Florida; Okeechobee, Florida; Carrollton, Georgia; Columbus, Georgia; Davenport, Iowa; Chicago, Illinois; Dixon, Illinois; Ina, Illinois; Mattoon, Illinois; Pontiac, Illinois; Sheridan, Illinois; Wilmette, Illinois; Springfield, Illinois; Boston, Massachusetts; Peabody, Massachusetts; Finksburg, Maryland; Towson, Maryland; Ionia, Michigan; North Bayport, Minnesota; Clarkston, Missouri; Raymond, Mississippi; Missoula, Montana; Superior, Montana; Cullowhee, North Carolina; Huntersville, North Carolina; Bridgeton, New Jersey; Island Heights, New Jersey; Jersey City, New Jersey; Trenton, New Jersey; Albuquerque, New Mexico; Rio Rancho, New Mexico; Carson City, Nevada; Alden, New York; Marcy, New York; New York, New York; Sleepy Hollow, New York; Akron, Ohio; Cincinnati, Ohio; Columbus, Ohio; Youngstown, Ohio; Altona, Pennsylvania; Wrightsville, Pennsylvania; Edgefield, South Carolina; Ramer, Tennessee; Somerville, Tennessee; Austin, Texas; Groveton, Texas; Midway, Texas; Tennessee Colony, Texas; Vidor, Texas; Salt Lake City, Utah; Jarratt, Virginia; New Berlin, Wisconsin; Milwaukee, Wisconsin. In addition, the Sisterhood of the WCOTC had by then established ten local chapters: Carmichael, California; Bourdonnais, Illinois; Bristol, Indiana; Butler, Indiana; Fort Wayne, Indiana; Westland, Michigan; Hamilton, New Jersey; Austin, Texas; Salt Lake City, Utah; Lynnwood, Washington.

121 Turner Internet n.d.c.

122 Turner Internet n.d.b.

123 Turner Internet n.d.a.

124 Turner Internet n.d.d.

125 Turner Internet 1999.

126 Katz Internet [n.d.]; Turner Internet n.d.d; "Kathy Ainsworth" Internet n.d.

127 "Building a New White World," flyer.

3. The Pagan Revival

1 See, for example, Adler 1986, 11; Berger 1999, 11.

2 Having spent much of his life in the Asian colonies of the British Empire, Gardner developed an interest in anthropology, folklore, and Eastern religion.

3   For a study of British Wicca, see Hutter 1999.

4   Gerald B. Gardner founded Gardnerian Wicca. Alex Sanders, who claimed to have been initiated into the Craft by his grandmother in 1933, founded Alexandrian Wicca. George Patterson founded Georgian Wicca. Dianic Wicca takes its name from Margaret Murray's book *Witch-Cult in Western Europe* (1921) in which she claims that witchcraft could be traced to the pre-Christian old religion centered on the horned god Dianus and the goddess Diana.

5   That is, 52,800 of 150,000 and 76,000 of 200,000.

6   An interesting discussion about the Wiccan religious experience can be found in diZerega 2001.

7   Introductions to Wicca ceremonies include Harvey 1997; Adler 1986; Vivianne Crowley 1996a; Starhawk 1979; Starhawk et al. 1997.

8   Crowley's parents belonged to the Plymouth Brethren and went to the Brethren school in Cambridge.

9   *Thelema* is Greek for "will." Crowley borrowed the maxim from the Abbey of Thélème described in the famous Gargantua novels by Renaissance author François Rabelais.

10 See, for instance, Vivianne Crowley 1996a.

11 Berger (1999, 51) reports that 50 percent of the respondents to her pagan census were solo practitioners.

12 Bachofen suggested in *Das Mutterrecht* (1861) that aboriginal society was ruled by women and held that the subsequent establishment of patriarchy represented a higher level of human evolution. A reversal of this pro-patriarchal evaluation began with Friedrich Engels and continued with modern feminist-oriented research, notably Gimbutas 1990 and Gimbutas and Dexter 1999.

13 Referring to Gimbutas, Carol Christ (1997, 60) writes,

> The peaceful and egalitarian matrifocal societies of the Neolithic period came to an end as agricultural began to be transformed through the invention of technologies such as the iron plow and centrally organized techniques, that over time allowed some individuals to control large plots of land that were worked by others. This process was hastened by the invention of more deadly (bronze and iron) weapons and by the establishment of marauding and warfare as a way of life. It is likely that in some areas, internal developments prepared the way for the dominance of warriors, while in others, relatively peaceful agricultural societies were attacked by warlike pastoral nomadic groups, such as the Indo-Europeans who invaded southern and eastern Europe and progressed as far into Asia as the Indus valley.

14 This aspect of goddess paganism has been criticized by black womanist thealogians for reflecting a white middle-class feminist position of "seeking 'freedom' at the expense of relationships and responsibilities to family and community." Adopting black feminist Dolores Williams's model of "relational independence," Christ argues that personal freedom must be found in the context of ties and obligations to others. "Selfhood is not gained by becoming independent of relationships, but by learning to live independently and interdependently within them."

15 The two most important of these sagas are *Grönländigasagan*, or *Graenlendiga Saga*, included

in the saga collection *Flateyarbók* (Erik's [the Red] Saga), found in two vellum manuscripts, *Hauksbók* and *Skálholtsbók*. There has been a long scholarly discussion about which saga is to be considered the oldest and the most reliable. Most researchers today date both sagas to between 1230 and 1270 (Larsson 1999, 18)

16   *Scraeling* was a derogative, Old Norse term used to designate the inhabitants of Greenland and North America. The scraelings of Vinland might have been either Micmac or Beothuk (See Magnusson and Pålsson 1976, 61 n1).

17   Compare with Ingstad 1985.

18   Söderberg argues that the name Vinland is derived from the Old Norse syllable *vin* (with a short "i"), a term for pastures, meadows (Ingstad 1985, 307, 437). This etymological theory contradicts the sagas' description of abundant wild grapes and still represents a minority faction in the scholarly debate as to the location of Vinland. In Icelandic— and Swedish—*vín* (with a long "i") means "wine." *Vin* and *vín* are not to be confused, and Magnusson and Pålsson (1976, 58) dismiss Söderberg's theory as "nonsensical" on phonological grounds. Larsson (1999, 43) agrees, adding that *vin* for "meadows" is not found in Icelandic literature and that had the land been known as "the land of meadows," it would have been designated *Vinjaland*, not *Vinland*, as is evidenced by every other known example.

19   See also Larsson 1999. Pondering why Norsemen would settle at windy and barren L'Anse aux Meadows, Larsson suggest that it might not necessarily have been a voluntary choice but a temporary settlement following a shipwreck. Larsson argues that the sagas' Vinland most probably was located in Nova Scotia.

20   Statement issued by the Royal Ontario Museum in 1961, quoted in Fell 1980, 341. The Ingstads are among those who conclude that the find is too suspect to be acceptable (Ingstad 1985, 432).

21   Storm, like Deer Tribe founder Swiftdeer, is of mixed Native American and European descent and has also chosen to transmit Native American sacred traditions to Euro-Americans and Europeans of serious intent, for which both have been bitterly criticized by spokespersons from the American Indian Movement and by other Indian nationalist activists. Storm's popular books include the best-seller *Seven Arrows* (1972), *Song of Heyoehkah* (1981), and *Lightning Bolt* (1994).

22   Storm also discusses a connection between the sauna of the Iron Shirts and Native American sweat lodges (1994, 508).

23   According to historian of religion Carl Johan Gurt (conversation with author, 14 April 1999), a fascinating conspiracy theory has begun circulating among the Native Americans, purporting that white racists had buried a skeleton they got in Europe to be able to argue as McNallen did. A detailed account of the controversy can be found in Downey 2000.

24   McManamon Internet 1997.

25   See also Lee 2000c.

26   For more information about the festivities, see Project Leif Internet 2000.

27   Hyatt (1998) says that Odin has frequently visited: "At one time he spent a month in my house. It was during the winter. He was dressed in dark wanderer clothes. The first time I saw him, I thought it was Death, and then I realized that it was Odin. I've seen the

gods so many times, so I know they exist." Hyatt also tells about visits by Frigg. "Every now and then, we have Frigg visiting our house. She is always dressed in white flying garments, and she always stays in the kitchen."

28 Should reliable statistics be developed, it would hardly come as a surprise if the number of nonaffiliated Asatrúers were to match the Wiccan census estimation of 50 percent.

29 Not all kindreds have developed a cadre of goðar, and some kindreds would hesitate to make permanent any seat of authority, opting instead to chose a competent member as acting goði or gyðia for the particular ceremony at hand.

30 In the Asatrú calendar each month has a Norse name. January is Snowmoon, February is Horning, March is Lenting, April is Ostara, May is Merrymoon, June is Midyear, July is Haymoon, August is Harvest, September is Shedding, October is Hunting, November is Fogmoon, and December is Yule.

31 As of 1999, there were hofs established in at least six states: Idaho, Washington, California, Arizona, Texas, and Wisconsin.

32 Rún means "mystery" in Icelandic. The myth is recorded in *Hávamál* in the Poetic Edda.

33 The reader who is eager to explore more about rune magic in living Asatrú will find useful information in the works of Edred Thorsson (1984; 1993; 1994; 1998).

34 McVan folder n.d.b.

35 Ellis e-mail 1999; "The Raven Kindred Principles" Internet 1999.

36 "Our Vision" Internet 1999; "Race and Asatrú" Internet 1999; Gillette and Stead Internet 1994.

37 Ellis e-mail 1999. The second Raven Kindred (South) was formed when two members moved down to Maryland.

38 Among his books are *Futhark: A Handbook of Rune Magic* (1984), *At the Well of Wyrd: A Handbook of Runic Divination* (1988), *Fire and Ice: Magical Teachings of Germany's Greatest Secret Occult Order* (1990), *A Book of Troth* (1992), *Rune Might: Secret Practices of the German Rune Magicians* (1994), *Black Rúna* (1995), *Green Rúna* (1996), and *The Lords of the Left-Hand Path: A History of Spiritual Dissent* (1997). Guido von List's *The Secrets of the Runes* (1908) was translated by S. E. Flowers in 1998.

39 Gundarsson Internet n.d.; see also Gundarsson 1993 and 1994.

40 Here, spokespersons from the ethnic and racist camps unite in condemnation (*McNallen* 1996; *Murray* 1997; *Taylor* 1998; *McVan* 1996; *Katja Lane* 1997).

41 For a review of the internal schisms within the Ring of Troth, see Kaplan 1997, 21–30.

42 The American Vinland Association seems broader than the Ring, including Asatrú, Vanatrú, Finnish, Polish, and indigenous Siberian paganism ("American Vinland Association" Internet 1999).

4. Wolf-Age Pagans

1 This biographical sketch is based on a 1998 interview with Else Christensen.

2 The Danish NSWP never gained more than 2.1 percent of the vote, and Clausen was kept at arms length by his German co-ideologues, shattering his dreams of becoming a Danish Quisling. After the war, Clausen received the death penalty for treason but died before his execution.

3   On Jews as alleged instigators of World War II, see Yockey 1991 [1962], 571–77. On Yockey's background see Carto 1991, xi, and Coogan 1999.

4   See also "The Power of Wotan" 1982.

5   Part of Thor Sannett's interview (see Christensen, "Speeches and Statements" section in Works Cited) was published in Var Trú, no. 49.

6   For an introduction to the leftist wing of early national socialism and fascism, see Griffin 1991.

7   The Odinist Fellowship code of conduct reads, "1) Every Odinist is a member of a kinship bound by heritage recovered from pre-christian times. 2) Be true to kith and kin; help and support kinsfolk when you can. 3) Stand by promises made—your word is your bond. 4) Live in harmony with Nature and obey her laws. 5) Improve your powers of body, mind and spirit. 6) Promote and protect our spiritual heritage. 7) Strengthen the bonds of your cultural heritage and teach your children its value. 8) Stay within the legal laws of the country in which you live. 9) Combat the distortions of our ancient history, both in the subtle and more obvious forms."

8   Christensen (1998) emphasized, "I do not use the word 'Aryan' [any longer], that's a no-no."

9   Pagan Revival has been issued in the forms of open letter, E-zine, and tabloid.

10 For a description of the Volksberg project, see Kaplan and Weinberg 1998, 152–58.

11 A great introduction to the life and thoughts of Savitri Devi is Goodrick-Clarke 1998.

12 She was born to an English mother and a father of Italian-Greek ancestry. He was a French citizen and an active member in the Greek community of Lyons, France.

13 Hinduism is a collective term for a series of traditions, one of which is devoted to Vishnu and known as the Vaisnava tradition(s). Among the more important Vaisnava texts are the renowned epics Mahabharata and Ramayana and the Vishnu Puranas ("stories of the ancient past"). By the eighth century the number of Vishnu avatars was generally standardized to ten, although the Vaisnava theology is complicated by the existence of several other traditions with conflicting information about his successive incarnations (see Flood 1996, chap. 5; Glasenapp 1967; Gonda 1970).

14 See, for instance, Flood 1996, 96.

5. By the Spear of Odin

1   Dissident music 2000; Graveland music 2000.

2   The transition of Wotansvolk headquarters was still in progress during the completion of this study. This chapter mainly covers Wotansvolk as it was during 1995–2002, when headquarters were still based in St. Maries.

3   Whereas Lane tends to emphasize the uselessness of his adopted father, authors Flynn and Gerhardt (1989, 215) found him to be an amiable and successful Colorado businessman.

4   See, for instance, Lane 1996e.

5   See also Lane 1998a.

6   The Brüders Schweigen was originally called the Aryan Resistance Movement, a name now largely forgotten.

7   Born in Texas in 1953, Mathews was raised in a lower-middle-class family and grew up
    in Phoenix, Arizona. Early in life Mathews developed an interest in conservative poli-
    tics, joining the John Birch Society at age eleven. Attracted to Mormonism due to its
    discipline and conservative morals, Mathews then graduated to a more radical and mili-
    tant position. In his late teens Mathews cofounded the Sons of Liberty, a paramilitary
    underground of constitutionalist fundamentalists composed of far-right Mormons and
    survivalists, dedicated to countering what they perceived as the corruption of true Ameri-
    canism. A publicity stunt brought the attention of the FBI, which began surveillance,
    but it was Mathews's refusal to pay income tax that first got him into trouble with the
    law, earning him a six-month probation sentence. Disappointed on a personal level with
    the Sons of Liberty, Mathews in 1974 decided to move up to Metaline Falls, Washing-
    ton, to start anew. Building a homestead, marrying Debbie, and having his family join
    him up north did not long prevent Mathews from gravitating again toward radical poli-
    tics. Joining the National Alliance and getting acquainted with the circle around Church
    of Jesus Christ, Christian/Aryan Nations in nearby Hayden Lake, Idaho, Mathews grew
    increasingly frustrated with the impotency of the Aryan revolutionary organizations.
    Delivering the much-publicized "A Call to Arms" speech at the 1983 National Alliance
    convention, Mathews that year graduated from words to deeds, establishing the Brüders
    Schweigen.

8   Gary Yarbrough (1997) supports Tate's view: "We tried to obtain means to educate people
    to press for fundamental change, and you know, we've been living in the age of darkness
    for too long, so its gonna take violence to change it."

9   "Mike Raven" is clearly an pseudonym and might be an alias for David Lane.

10 For McVeigh's story, see Michel and Herbeck 2001.

11 Interestingly, when *Revolution by the Number 14* was reissued in *Deceived, Damned, and De-
    fiant: The Revolutionary Writings of David Lane*, the list of targets were substituted with an
    "of course, in occupied countries, the overt arm of the revolution must not detail spe-
    cifics" (47).

12 See also Lane 1995c.

13 McVan folder 1998.

14 David Lane 1996; Katja Lane e-mail 1999.

15 As do many other Aryan revolutionaries, Lane believes that the ancient Egyptian civili-
    zation was Aryan and that the pyramids were built by Aryan architects.

16 Here Lane follows a long tradition that identifies Sir Francis Bacon with Shakespeare
    and as an adept in the ancient divine wisdom.

17 See also David Lane 1994c; Lane flyer n.d.a. "The King James Bible (KJB) is in actu-
    ality a Hermetic coding device, at least as old as the pyramids," Lane explains in *Pyramid
    Prophecy 666*. "The prophecy is about a man named David, to be born at the eleventh day
    of Scorpio, which is November 2, in the year 1938. He will show the origin of the mys-
    tery religions including Christianity, and teach that nature's laws are the work of the
    Creator, and are therefore God's laws. His teachings on nature's laws will be codified
    in a 'Little Book' (Revelations chapter 10) titled 88 Precepts." Decoded, the Bible also
    purportedly links the beginning of the reign of the Antichrist with the appearance of
    the man who will challenge its global power. The target date of the Antichrist's (a global

Zionist dictatorship) ascension was 1998, which equals 3 x 666 and is also the sum of 1776 + 222. The number 1776 appears in the numeric square of Mars in which is found the Star of David and its 741 formula, 741 also being the numerical value of "Vernon David Eden" and the numerical value of the 14 words. Thus, Lane concludes, "Vernon David Eden is the birth name of a man now known as David Lane. He was born November 2, 1938 in Woden, Iowa. He uses the pen-name Wodensson and is imprisoned for fighting against the judeo-american/judeo-christian murder of the white race. Thus fulfilling the prophecies of Revelation 3 verse 12 and Revelation 2 verse 17 that 'God will take a new name, written in a MAN, and in a CITY, and in a WHITE STONE. David Lane is the author of a LITTLE BOOK which is called 88 PRECEPTS" (David Lane n.d.). During the past few years, the messianic ambitions of David Lane have been censored by Wotanvolk strategists. Significantly, *Pyramid Prophecy 666* is not included in the collected works of David Lane, which confines the numerological work to *Mystery Religions*. The most likely reason being that a messianic claim might be considered counterproductive by turning off potential followers. That I chose to discuss the *Pyramid* text in the endnotes and not in the main text reflects its secondary status in the official Wotansvolk message.

18 "Wotan's Kindred" flyer n.d.

19 The individuals in these positions wished not to be identified by name.

20 Wiegand e-mail 2001; Katja Lane e-mail 2001c; Katja Lane e-mail 2001d; Katja Lane e-mail 2001e; Katja Lane e-mail 2001f; Katja Lane e-mail 2001g.

21 Born in Tucson, Arizona, on 3 February 1959, Post was raised all over the world, his father being an officer in the U.S. Air Force. Gradually adopting a heathen perspective, Post became a practicing pagan in the early 1990s. By 2000 he was admitted as an apprentice in the Odinic Rite, Vinland, and began proceeding through the OR goði program. Post first heard about Wotansvolk through a fellow heathen who shared some of their literature. Initially finding the Wotansvolk message too "strong," Post eventually came to accept its heathen program as a path to revealing the truth and bringing about social change. "American society is manipulated," Post says (e-mail correspondence). Reconnecting with the ancestral wisdom at the root of existence is imperative, he feels, for break the mind-distorting spell of the media and developing the spiritual perspective necessary to secure racial survival. As the transition of the Wotansvolk and 14 Word Press administration concurred with the completion of this manuscript, Post was only able to share his preliminary agenda for developing the press, including plans of publishing a body of texts produced by heathen prisoners and free folks. As the Odinic Rite belongs to the "ethnic" wing of the Norse heathen scene, Post's acceptance of Wotansvolk responsibilities will likely be considered problematic by the OR leadership.

22 Katja Lane e-mail 2001h. Katja Lane and Ron McVan are currently at odds over this transition. As the reasons are personal, I will not comment on this development.

23 Post e-mail 2002.

24 McVan folder n.d.d.

25 McVan folder n.d.h.

26 McVan folder 1998.

27 McVan folder n.d.c.

28 McVan folder n.d.g.

29 McVan folder n.d.f.

30 "W.O.T.A.N." folder n.d.

31 In private McVan elaborates at length about the aboriginal hyperborean Aryan civiliza-
    tion, the lost worlds of Atlantis and Lemuria, and the subsequent Aryan foundations of
    now-lost high cultures in the Americas, Egypt, and Asia. Convinced by his numerous
    personal sightings of UFOs over the mountains close to his Idaho residence, McVan also
    suggests the probability of an extraterrestrial connection but has not yet reached any
    conclusions about how exactly this would fit in.

32 McVan folder 1999.

33 McVan folder 1998.

34 McVan folder n.d.g.

35 It is Jung's mystical, völkisch practices that I describe here. I make no claim to offering
    a comprehensive portrait of Jung, his overall mystical quest, or his work in its totality.

36 For a discussion about this topic, see "Jung och Nazismen" 1992.

37 See, for instance, McVan folder n.d.a.

38 "W.O.T.A.N." folder n.d.

39 Eugen Bohler, a Swiss scholar and longtime friend of Jung (quoted in Noll 1997a, xiv).
    According to Bohler, "Jung regarded his life as a mission: to serve the function of making
    God conscious. He had to help God to make himself conscious, and not for his own
    sake, but for the sake of God."

40 A compulsive reader, McVan continuously digests new information but does not always
    applies the strict criteria established in the world of academia, although he does tend
    to credit equally works by respected scholars and works by laymen unknown outside a
    New Age bookstore. This tendency is strengthened by his belief, common among racist
    Aryans, of a grand conspiracy to suppress truths about significant racial matters such as
    ancient Aryan wisdom, lost worlds, and UFOs. As he feels that most modern scholars are
    either part of the conspiracy or restricted by its power over academia, he places little value
    on modern academic credentials. McVan argues for the need to read between the lines
    of works produced by system publishers and to use alternative sources of information,
    including New Age bookstores and researchers of academic dispute.

41 Although I herein describe the ritual practices and content peculiar to Wotansvolk,
    Wotansvolkers (like most pagans) emphasize the need for continuing studies and ex-
    periments, so new rituals and details are likely to emerge. While some aspects of these
    rituals may be abandoned, the basic direction will most likely remain the same.

42 The exact wording may differ according to kindred, occasion, and the personality of the
    acting goði, although all should be true to the racial content.

43 From author's field notes.

44 Post e-mail 2001.

45 Records provided by Katja Lane (e-mail 2001a; e-mail 2001b).

46 Records provided by Katja Lane (e-mail 2000d).

47 This percentage has remained relatively stable over the years. Records exclude Wotans-
    volk international. Katja Lane e-mail 2001a.

48 Post e-mail 2002.

49 From conversations with Identity believers in congregations in Washington (August 1998), Idaho (September 1996), and Pennsylvania (June 1997).

50 "Aryan Genealogy of the Forth Son of Jacob" chart.

51 Mark Thomas later inspired the Aryan Revolutionary Army but turned against his protégés when they got caught and is today out of touch in the federal Protected Witness Program.

52 Thomas Internet 1996b.

53 Thomas Internet 1993.

54 Thomas Internet.

55 Hansen flyer n.d.

56 The speeches are published in *Focus Fourteen*, nos. 505, 507, and 605.

57 "Platform for the Aryan National State" folder 1996.

58 These views were repeated in several discussions with active Odinist youth in Washington, Idaho, California, Arizona, and Texas, 1996–99.

59 Correspondence between Reverend F. Martin and Katja Lane, *Rahowa News* 1995.

60 See for instance issue 3 of the IOC periodical, *The Creator*.

61 Ron McVan, specifically, characterized Odinism as the original Aryan religion in a conversation with the author in St. Maries, Idaho, 8 December 1998.

62 McVan folder 1999.

63 Katja Lane e-mail 2000a.

64 Official Wotansvolk worldwide numbers provided by Katja Lane (e-mail 2000b): eighty-four different kindreds that also translated and published Wotansvolk material composed the full number of Wotansvolk groups around the world as of January 2000. In addition, 555 individual Wotansvolk activists disseminated Wotansvolk material. All together, Wotansvolk was present in the following forty-one countries (the first figure represents individual activists and/or translators, the second kindreds): Argentina (3–1); Australia (23–6); Austria (15–2); Belarus (1–0); Belgium (10–4); Brazil (5–2); Canada (40–7); Chile (4–1); Czech Republic (10–3); Denmark (4–0); England (62–8); Estonia (1–0); Finland (11–1); France (39–3); Germany (102–14); Greece (5–1); Holland (16–1); Hungary (2–0); Iceland (5–1); Ireland (7–1); Italy (21–2); Japan (3–0); Latvia (1–0); Lithuania (1– 0); Mexico (2–0); New Zealand (9–2); Norway (23–3); Peru (1–0); Philippines (1–0); Poland (15–2); Portugal (7–1); Russia (5–1); Scotland (3–1); Serbia (6–2); Slovakia (3–1); South Africa (14–2); Spain (23–3); Sweden (37–5); Switzerland (5–1); Uruguay (5–1); Yugoslavia (5–1).

65 Oldest among the current Asatrú groups in Sweden is Breidablikk-gildet, founded in 1975 by Arne Sjöberg. Yggdrasil was established in 1982 and later merged with Merlinordern (Order of Merlin, an initiatory order following the Western esoteric tradition) as a suborder oriented toward Norse shamanism. Ratatosk was launched in 1996 as an eclectic network of Asatrúers, Wiccans, shamans, and esoterics. Sveriges Asatrosamfund was established in 1994 and has a more traditional organizational structure with formal members. Samfälligheten för Nordisk Sed was launched in 1996 as a network of independent kindreds but, in an effort to facilitate state acceptance as a legitimate religion, has reorganized according to judicial state demands and is now modeled on the former state church. Frökulten has existed since 1985 and is Vanir-oriented (as opposed to Aesir-

oriented); its leader, Frömund Refglenssen Fröjsgode, claims to have surfaced as a successor of a 7,259 year unbroken line of Frey goðar that was forced underground first by the Asatrúers, then by the Christians. (Yggdrasil veteran Hedlund [1999]; Ratatosk founder Rehbinder [1998]; conversation with goði Keeron Ögren, co-founder of Samfälligheten för Nordisk Sed at the 1997 Althing in Torsåker; conversation with former Samfällighet member Aldo Gratz following the 1998 reorganization, Stockholm, 5 August 1998; Gunnarson 1997)

66 This process is best described in Lööw 1998.

67 *Hawthorne 1996*; multiple conversations with Katja Lane.

68 Assessment by Katja Lane (e-mail 2000c). See *Resistance* issues 7 and 8.

69 "Möte med David Lane" 1996.

70 See, for example, David Lane 1997a; "Focus Fourteen" 1997; Hawthorne 1997; "Robert J. Mathews" 1997. Wotansvolk is not the only American racist organization that has been featured in *Nordland*. Aiming for "global Aryan" victory, *Nordland* publishes information about the worldwide white-power scene but is in terms of influences mainly open to American exports, such as Church of the Creator (Anderson, Grenbäck, and Sundquist 1997), Pierce's National Alliance (Nilsson 1997), George Lincoln Rockwell and the American Nazi Party (Berner 1998), and the Aryan Nations (Owens and Dobbs 1998). Pierce eventually bought *Nordland*.

71 http://www.heathenfront.org/kvasir/.

72 Conversation with Ron McVan, St. Maries, Idaho, 2 August 1998.

73 Conversation with Katja Lane, St. Maries, Idaho, 4 August 1998.

6. Ethnic Asatrú

1 The Odinic Rite was established in Britain 1977 and is open for individuals and local groups, called hearts. In the 1990s, the OR branched out to France, Germany, the United States, and Canada. As of the year 2000 the Odinic Rite had three hearts in Vinland.

2 The starting year is sometimes said to be 1971, which refers to the time when the Viking Brotherhood became explicitly religious.

3 Official AFA kindreds were Hammerstede Kindred (New Jersey), Vor Stead Kindred (Virginia), Gungnir Kindred (Colorado), Gullinbursti Kindred (California), Teutoberg Kindred (Texas), Cow Creek Kindred (Oregon), Wolfbinder Kindred (Delaware), and Calasa Kindred (California).

4 See, for instance, McNallen Internet 2000c; McNallen Internet 2000d; McNallen Internet 2000e.

5 Born to a civil servant in 1953 in Atlanta, Georgia, Thórarinsson at an early age developed an interest in magic and the occult. Setting himself on a spiritual quest, Thórarinsson was during his youth attracted to Jewish kabbalah, for several years studying Judaism and attending a synagogue. After moving to Arizona, he came across Celtic Wicca and eventually got initiated in the Craft in a Gardnerian, Kentucky-based coven. During the 1970s, Thórarinsson found Norse Wicca and through that came to learn about Asatrú, developing contacts with Christensen, Murray, and McNallen. In 1977 he founded *Vor Trú* and joined the Arizona Kindred (*Thórarinsson 1998*).

6 Murray 1997; Thórarinsson 1998; conversation with Murray, Roosevelt Lake, Arizona, Yule, 1999; Murray Internet 2000.

7 Murray Internet 2000.

8 In 2000 there were twenty official kindreds and twenty formational kindreds aligned with the AA. If Murray's estimate of "over 50" is correct it means that AA had at least an additional ten hangaround or wannabe kindreds. The official kindreds were Sachrimer Kindred (Alabama); Arizona Kindred (Arizona); Calsa Kindred, Gjallarhorn Kindred, Raven Kindred Inc., Raven's Troth Kindred, Thorr's Hammer Kindred, Ulfheim Kindred, and Úlfhethnar Kindred (California); Gungnir Kindred (Colorado); Eagle Kindred (Idaho); Hofbrau Kindred (Indiana); Hammerstede Kindred (New Jersey); Skidbladner Kindred (North Carolina); Markland Kindred of Folkish Asatrú and Oregon Kindred of Asatrú (Oregon); Eagle Kindred of Utah (Utah); Mountain Kindred (Wyoming); Vinland Kindred (Alberta, Canada); and Wodan's Kindred (B.C., Canada). The formational kindreds were Falcon Kindred (Arizona); High Reaches Kindred (Colorado); Fjolskyldann Kindred and Othalar Kindred (Florida); Catamount Kindred (Illinois); Wolfhammer Kindred (Kansas); Kindred of the Great Bear (Massachusetts); Thorncrest Kindred and Wings of Asatrú Kindred (Nebraska); Har Steggi Kindred and Midgard Kindred (Ohio); Cow Creek Kindred (Oregon); Central Texas Asatrú Kindred (Texas); Aesir Kindred, Boar's Kindred, Silent Tower Kindred, and Yggdrasil Kindred (Utah); Asatrú Wizard's Kindred (Wisconsin); and Heritage and Tradition Kindred (Quebec, Canada).

9 Eric Wood in 1986 joined the AFA in its first incarnation. Besides being a member of the Odinic Rite (Vinland), Wood is also a member of the current AFA as well of as Asatrú Alliance affiliate Raven Kindred. Citing disillusionment with the intrigues perpetuated by a few "dishonest, grotesque and self-promoting" individuals involved with organized Asatrú, Hnikar in 2001 resigned from his position (Wood Internet 2001).

10 The Egyptian Cobras transformed into the Black (P) Stone Nation. When strongman Jeff Fort (now Imam Malik) became a black nationalist Moorish American, the gang was renamed El Rukn.

11 For a description of the Minutemen, see Wilcox and George 1992, 274–98, and Jones 1968.

12 Information was also collected by breaking into the offices of targeted groups or by installing electronic surveillance devices. Taylor estimates that the Minutemen had an archive of around 100,000 names.

13 Leaving was not unproblematic, Taylor (1998) recalls, and he believes that DePugh at one time was out to assassinate him. Relations improved when DePugh was caught in July 1969 and Taylor appeared as a defense witness. The Minutemen had by then split into several competing groups. In charge of one of these, Taylor in vain tried to revive the dormant resistance but ended up dissolving the Minutemen in 1971.

14 By 1999, Moynihan and Taylor had left the editorial board of Vor Trú. Shortly thereafter, the Tribe of Wulfings decided to leave the alliance. However, the Wulfing decision seems to be based less on ideological differences than on the conclusion that the time and energy that went into AA business could be better spent on more rewarding tasks (Conversation with Michael Moynihan, Portland, Oregon, September 1999; Ward 1999; conversation with Valgard Murray, Arizona, September, 1999).

15 Wodan's Kindred was originally named Kindred of Dashwood Mews.

16 McNallen first presented the concept in an article in 1980. The seminal essay was also included in the AFA volume *An Odinist Anthology* (1983).

17 This suggestion contradicts Kaplan's conclusion. In his study of radical religions, Kaplan (1997, 80) found that the metagenetic theory had "remarkably few adherents in either Asatrú or Odinism." Almost all Asatrúers I have interviewed or spoken with at pagan gatherings suggested metagenetics as an explanation of the link between a particular folk and their gods. However, few could elaborate on the subject beyond referring to Jung.

18 McNallen, Murray, Thorsson, Moynihan, Thórarinsson, Ward, Taylor, and Clinton all referred to this quote and most had memorized it verbatim.

19 When in Austin to interview Edred Thorsson, I met a half-Celt, half-Blackfoot who expressed an interest in both Asatrú and Native American spirituality. I used him as an example in the subsequent interviews, asking if he would be welcome. Those asked on tape were Edred Thorsson, Reinhold Clinton, Cathy Clinton, Max Hyatt, Stephen McNallen, Sheila McNallen, Valgard Murray, Robert Taylor, and Thórsteinn Thórarinsson.

20 I use "queer" to refer to a hybridization transcending limiting constructs of "folk" or "ethnicity" into one self-made identity.

21 Gamlinginn Internet 1997.

22 Priest worked with the AFA in the early 1980s. Her Camptonville, California–based Wotanwald Kindred hosted some AFA Althings until a "falling out over Steve's racist policies and politics" in 1984 (SilverWitch 1997).

23 Correspondence shared by Wotansvolk.

24 Bylaw number four. *Bylaws of the Asatrú Alliance.* Approved at Althing, 11 June 2243 Runic Era.

25 Hall e-mail 2000; *Hall* 1996.

26 The interested reader may compare the rituals described in McVan 2000 with the ritual textbooks produced by McNallen 1992a, McNallen 1992b, and McNallen 1992c.

27 "Star Crossed & Moonstruck" appears irregularly.

28 Interviewees prefer to stay anonymous.

29 Taylor (1998) understood the Odinic Rite split as a schism between a more "extreme group" that "wanted to indulge more in politics than the one we are connected with, the one that is more spiritual."

30 This number has not been confirmed by independent sources.

31 Michael Moynihan suggests that the dating comes from the earliest archaeological finding of the runic script (Moynihan e-mail 2002).

32 McNallen Internet 2000b.

33 Katja Lane, personal correspondence with author, 18 February 2000.

34 "Declaration of War" statement 1993.

35 "So You're a European-American" flyer n.d.

36 Ibid.

37 McNallen Internet 2000a.

38 Ibid.

39 McNallen e-mail 2000.

40 McNallen Internet 2000a.

41 Ibid.

42 Ibid.

43 McNallen e-mail 2000.

7. Hail Loki! Hail Satan! Hail Hitler!

1 In practice, however, quite a few Satanists seem to submit their will to a strong leader.

2 The Church of Satan began as an outgrowth of LaVey's Magic Circle, which had included among its ranks people like underground filmmaker Kenneth Anger and anthropologist and neoshaman Michael Harner.

3 He was consulted as technical advisor in a number of horror movies, including *Rosemary's Baby*, *Devil's Rain*, and *Dracula*.

4 Wolfe was a member of the Church of Satan, and Barton was LaVey's partner and mother of his son, Xerxes.

5 *The Satanic Witch* (1989) was originally published as *The Complete Witch* (1971).

6 In the early days, LaVey was fond of inflating its numbers, claiming a membership of 25,000 and suggesting that it would soon grow to encompass millions (Flowers 1997, 179). Later, he refused to disclose membership figures. "If it's too low, we would be perceived as insignificant, and was it too high, we'd be considered too much of a threat and there would be reason to destroy us" (LaVey, cited in Barton 1992, 202).

7 The initiatory levels were: °I. apprentice; °II. warlock/witch, which consisted of members who passed a formal examination and could be leaders of a local grotto; °III. priest/priestess, which consisted of people who had successfully maintained a grotto and been deemed worthy by LaVey (LaVey thought it important that high-degree representatives of the Church of Satan uphold a dignified image of Satanism by being successful and recognized in society as writers, inventors, actors, musicians, doctors, and so on. The Church of Satan should not be a substitute career for people who could not make it in mainstream society.); °IV. magister or master, which had successfully run and expanded a grotto to the degree that it would subdivide; °V. magus, a degree held exclusively by LaVey (Flowers 1997, 182).

8 The Order of the Trapezoid was an outgrowth of the Magic Circle, a LaVeyan group preceding the Church of Satan.

9 Among these were Temple of Set, the Satanic Church, First Church of Satan, Church of S.A.T.A.N., the Orthodox Satanic Church, Order of the Black Ram, and the Order of Baal.

10 The seven sins are greed, pride, envy, anger, gluttony, lust, and sloth.

11 It is imperative to focus on one's individual desires and abstain from infringing on others or feeling compelled to engage in something only because it is forbidden. Should one's fantasies be conventional or asexual one should stay true to these desires.

12 In this late work, *The Future of an Illusion*, Freud had grown increasingly pessimistic. For his earlier theory of religion see Freud 1938 [1913].

13 *The Satanic Witch* (1989), which teaches a woman how to enchant men sexually, is basically a textbook of LaVeyan lesser magic.

14 LaVey detailed a collection of psychodramatic ceremonies in *Satanic Rituals* (1972). Care-

ful with details, LaVey specified the decoration of the ritual chamber, the use of Baphomet (a sinister god or demon) to represent the Prince of Darkness, Luciferian candles, conjuring of demons, and the use of classical music, gongs, bells, swords, and phalluses. Men should wear black-hooded robes and women should dress in a sexually appealing manner—if they were not too unattractive or old, in which case they had to be fully dressed. A nude woman should be used as an altar, as Satanism is a religion of the flesh. That men's magazines found the misogynistic rituals fit to print is hardly surprising.

15 Ethics pervades much of LaVey's writing and is condensed in the "Nine Satanic Statements," "Nine Satanic Sins," and "Eleven Satanic Rules of the Earth."

16 By releasing hatred against those who deserve it, LaVey reasons, negative emotions are cleansed and therefore not taken out on those you love.

17 The "Book of Satan" section of the *Satanic Bible* is plagiarized verbatim from the "Introduction" and "Iconoclastic" chapters of *Might Is Right*. Later, LaVey would acknowledge this, saying that "nobody's even heard of the damned book. . . . The copyright, even with renewal; would have recently expired so it suddenly became part of The Satanic Bible" (1996, 4). Redbeard's identity is not known; Jack London and Arthur Desmond have been suggested.

18 Born in 1960 in Amarillo, Texas, to a private detective mother and a warehouse-managing father, Webb became involved with the Temple through Stephen and Nancy Flowers after having been impressed by Michael Aquino on a Geraldo show in 1989. Webb made an almost unprecedented career in the Temple and assumed the responsibilities as high priest in 1996.

19 Aquino holds a Ph.D. in political science and was professor at Golden Gate University between 1980 and 1986. His military career began with the Eighty-Second Airborne at Fort Bragg. He then was a Psychological Operations/Special Forces officer at JFK Special Warfare Center. Between 1969 and 1970, Aquino served in Vietnam at the Sixth PSYOP Battalion, engaging in psychological warfare against the Vietnamese. Returning home, Aquino served at Fort Knox, then, after a few years of civilian life, he returned to the army in the 1980s. He was first stationed at Presidio, California, and then in Washington, D.C.

20 The satanic panic began in 1983 with a series of allegations against sixty-two-year-old Peggy McMartin Buckey, her son, and five child-care workers at McMartin Preschool who were accused of leading a satanic cult that victimized 360 children with bizarre sexual acts over a five-year period. In 1985, Geraldo and 20/20 aired programs about devil worshippers engaged in cannibalism, sexual torture, and ritual sacrifice. Police, "Satanist hunters," the Christian Right, therapists, and "survivors" propelled a scare that in waves made an imprint on America and abroad. In Kern County, California, a local satanic panic resulted in investigations of seventy-seven people. Scores of people were convicted on scarce evidence. For example, seven people were imprisoned for allegedly having been engaged in bizarre urine sadomasochistic sexual acts with children. The only direct evidence was the children's testimony. In 1990 some of the children recanted the stories, and the convictions were successfully appealed. Another 1985 case was at Holland, Ohio, where a local police officer was told about a secret satanic cult involving two hundred locals who supposedly had been murdering children ritually since 1969. An extensive excavation failed to produce any substantial evidence. Survivor books swept

the nation. After a peak in 1988–89, the satanic scare declined in intensity, although it did erupt occasionally, as in the 1991 allegations that the Mormon Church hierarchy had been infiltrated by secret Satanists who sexually molest children, or in the 1992 San Diego craze.

In 1987 the three-year-old daughter of a Christian clergyman pointed out Michael Aquino and his wife, Lilith, as having ritually molested her in a black-painted satanic ceremonial chamber in their private home in Presidio. According to the child, her army day-care teacher (who was later charged with several cases of sexually assaulting children) had brought her to the Aquino home. Police investigators searched the Aquino house, seizing videotapes, notebooks, and photo albums without finding any evidence. No charges were brought against the Aquinos, who lived in Washington, D.C., during the time the alleged ritual rape would have occurred. The day-care teacher was charged for sexually molesting ten children (out of sixty claimed victims), but the case was dismissed by the judge. (For an article critical of how the prosecution handled the case, see Goldston 1998. On the satanic scare, see Victor 1993. For an opposing view, see Raschke 1990.)

21 Although "Set" etymologically seems unrelated to the Hebrew "Satan," Setians claim that Satan is a corruption of Set and that his identification with evil was a late Egyptian development eventually taken over by the Israelites. According to Egyptologist Budge (1969; 1988), Set was originally a beneficial god and it was not until the cult of Osiris had been firmly established that he came to be identified with the originator of evil in the world. The book of the afterlife produced by the Osiris cult was the Book of Coming Forth By Day. Evidently, it was time for Set to tell his story.

22 As of 2000, the Temple of Set had thirteen pylons in the United States, Germany, Australia, and Sweden/Finland. Since 1975 Aquino has nurtured an obsession with LaVey, whom, he said, he had regarded as a "friend, mentor, and ultimately Devil-father." His own biographical history of LaVey and the Church of Satan expands continuously (it now runs to more than 800 pages). As noted by Jack Boulware, Aquino "has gone out of his way to make public court documents that reflect negatively on LaVey's personal life, including restraining orders, divorce proceedings and LaVey's bankruptcy filing." To this end, Aquino welcomed LaVey's daughter Zeena and her husband, Nicholas Schreck who also direct much energy to discredit LaVey as a charlatan (Boulware 1999, 28).

23 In Egyptian theology, Set and Horus were initially the same entity, an idea seized on by Aquino who identifies the separation process with Lucifer's or Satan's rebellion against God in the Judeo-Christian system.

24 Set "proves" his identity by "solving" the numerological riddle included in the Book of Law 3:76: "Aye! Listen to the numbers and the words—4 6 3 8 A B K 2 4 A L G M O R 3 Y X 24 89 R P S T O V A L—What meaneth this, o prophet? Thou knowest not; nor shalt thou ever. There cometh one to follow thee he shall expound it." Aquino here joins the ranks of competing successors to Aleister Crowley, by claiming that the mysterious passage means, "Destined First Century heir—Aquino—breaking Keys by doctrines Anton LaVey—great Magus of reconsecration coming Year Xeper—founding his rightful priesthood—Set—true origin Volume AL."

25 Flowers (1997, 233) gives two levels of meaning to the elitist concept of the elect. On

the one hand, it refers all Temple of Set initiates of the second degree and above, and on the other hand, it is a general reference to all those who have "realized their sepa-rateness from the Universal order—and who have thus been selected out by the Prince of Darkness."

26   In Setian magic there are no nude altars or phalluses, and the press is not invited. Setian lesser magic applies "obscure" mental or physical laws of the "objective" uni-verse, whereas greater magic aims at changing the subjective universe in accordance with will—a task that is believed to cause a proportionate change in the objective universe (Flowers 1997, 235–39).

27   See, for example, Webb 1996a, 5.

28   In Mahayana and Virayana Buddhism, a bodhisattva is an individual who has achieved true enlightenment in his lifetime. Instead of dissolving into nirvana, the bodhisattva extends his individual life to assist man. While this would be far too altruistic for a Satan-ist who remains indifferent to the plight of humanity even after death, it does serve as an example.

29   Most orders are then subdivided into "lodges" and "houses." By the year 2000, Temple of Set orders included the Order of Amon, the Order of the Black Tower, the Order of the Claw of the Bear, the Order of Horus, the Order of Leviathan, the Order of Merlin, the Order of Sethne Khaumuast, the Order of Shuti, the Order of the Trapezoid, the Order of Uart, the Order of the Vampire, and the Order of Xnum.

30   Another order of interest is the Order of the Claw of the Bear, founded in 1999 by Finnish and Swedish initiates and oriented toward the exploration of northern European magic.

31   Word in the satanic communities says that ONA most likely consists only of Long and Beest. In a 1994 interview Beest said that the order had ten members and a few hangers-on (Baddeley 1999, 164). Anton Long claims to have been initiated by a mistress who recruited suitable candidates from existing groups such as the Temple of the Sun or the Black Order in the late 1960s (Kaplan 2000b, 236). In an e-mail in 2001, Michael Moynihan said, "At one point an American individual using the name Eric Thompson at-tempted to start up a USA distribution point for ONA materials, but this was short-lived and Thompson allegedly converted to Christianity when he dissolved the operation."

32   Most of which is available for free on the Internet. See http://www.nasz-dom.net. See also ONA journal Fenrir.

33   ONA Internet 1991a.

34   ONA Internet 1994c.

35   ONA Internet 1991b.

36   Long Internet 107yf [1996].

37   ONA Internet 1994a; ONA Internet n.d.b; ONA Internet 1990; ONA Internet 1994b.

38   According to ONA, humanity has seen five Aeons and associated civilizations: the Primal, Hyperborean, Sumerian, Hellenic and Western. In a few hundred years, the dark forces will return to cast the Western civilization back into chaos to birth the sixth "galactic" civilization (Long Internet 1994).

39   Riabhaich Internet 1998; ONA Internet 1991c; Temple 88 Internet n.d.

40   ONA Internet n.d.c.

41   See, for instance, ONA Internet 1991b; ONA Internet 1996.

42 Ultima Thule 88 Internet n.d.

43 ONA Internet n.d.a; Riabhaich Internet n.d.; ONA Internet 1991c. "An ONA member doesn't 'become' a Nazi or a communist," Christos Beest explained. "He just uses those movements. Obviously, in order to use them you have to enter into a role in a very de-monic sense, you also have to know where it ends" (Baddeley 1999, 165).

44 Not to be confused with the Australian-based *Nexus* that mixes all forms of stigma-tized knowledge, from New Age to conspiracy theory. Furthermore, this Church of Odin should not be confused with the Australian group by that name that was established by A. Rud Mills, but refers to the Paraparaumu, New Zealand–based Church of Odin co-founded by Bolton. According to a letter of 1999, the group was "no longer operative" due to "a lack of interest" (Bolton letter 1999).

45 That said, it should perhaps be added that not all Church of Satan members abstained from mind-altering substances.

46 *Industrial music* was a term first used by Throbbing Gristle (U.K.) and Monte Cazzaza (U.S.) in the mid-1970s, later picked up by Laibach (Slovenia). Part of the idea was draw-ing a parallel between music productions and assembly-line manufacture, such as the car industry. Early industrial music ranged from the acoustic clash of metal such as Test Dept. (U.K.) and Einstürzende Neubauten (Germany) to the production of noise/rhythm on electronic equipment, like that of Throbbing Gristle. There has never been any single industrial-music sound but a wide variety of styles, which have grown to encompass ambient soundscapes, ethnic-folk, apocalyptic folk, dub, goth, classical, moody rock, spoken word, metal, synthesizer-based rock, and even hip-hop. An attraction to black humor, shock value, and taking things to the extreme have been prevailing themes for many of the artists regardless of which particular brand of industrial they adhere to. For an introduction to industrial culture, see Re/Search 1994 [1983]. See also Dwyer 1995.

47 T.R.O.Y letter 2001.

48 Úlfhethnar Kindred statement 2000; Ward e-mail 2001a.

49 Ward e-mail 2001b.

50 Blood Axis song "Lord Of Ages." Appeared originally on the *Lamp of the Invisible Light* compilation. Remixed on the *Blót* album.

51 "Blood Axis/Allerseelen–split 7," music, (n.d.).

52 Listen, for example to the songs "Seeker" and "March of Brian Boru." *Blót* also includes the bombastically set "Herjafather," with lyrics by Jost (Blood Axis music 1998).

53 *Moynihan* 1997; slightly adjusted by e-mail 2001a.

54 See introduction to his interview with Anton LaVey in Moynihan 1995.

55 The krükenkreuz is an old pagan symbol that also was used by the crusading Templars. Adopted by Austrian nationalists in the early twentieth century, it was eventually banned by the NSDAP. Quotes from Hoddersen Internet 1999 and Conason Internet 1999. The frequent categorization of the band as "metal" shows that the labelers did not bother to listen to the music.

56 *Anti-Semitism Worldwide 1998/9* 1999; Conason Internet 1999; Robert Crawford of the Northwestern Coalition for Human Dignity wrote in an *Oregonian* guest editorial on 13 May 1999, "The Portland leader of a metal band, Blood Axis . . . is a big player in the effort to bring racism into the metal scene" (quoted in Dundas 2000).

57 For Moynihan's discussion about the particular *No Longer a Fanzine* interview, see Cletus Nelson 1999.

58 Moynihan statement 1998.

59 See also Dundas 2000.

60 Michael Moynihan, quoted in White Internet 2001.

61 Repeated conversations with Katja Lane, Ron McVan, and Michael Moynihan, 1996–2001.

62 Conversations in 1998 and 1999.

63 Quoted in White Internet 2001.

64 Obviously, this is not unique to extreme metal. The fascination with the occult and the Prince of Darkness runs like an undercurrent in Western music and has manifested in folk music, classic compositions, jazz, blues, soul, and rock, and had been spread for mass consumption by modern classics such as Rolling Stones, Led Zeppelin, and Black Sabbath.

65 According to historian of religions Erik af Edholm (e-mail, 11 September 2002) *Eurynymous* seems to be a corruption of *Eurynomos* (Greek; Latin, *Eurynomus*) and does not mean the prince of darkness. The source of the misunderstanding is probably the one ancient Greek text that mentions a daemon by this name: the tenth book of the *Pausanias* mytho-history:

> Higher up than the figures I have enumerated comes *Eurynomos*, said by the Delphian guides to be one of the demons in Hades, who eats off all the flesh of the corpses, leaving only their bones. But Homer's *Odyssey*, the poem called the *Minyad*, and the *Returns*, although they tell of Hades and its horrors, know of no demon called *Eurynomus*. However, I will describe what he is like and his attitude in the painting. He is of a color between blue and black, like that of meat flies; he is showing his teeth and is seated, and under him is spread a vulture's skin.

66 Musically, Venom comes across as a speeded-up version of classic heavy-metal acts such as Deep Purple, Black Sabbath, or Judas Priest.

67 This was evident not least in Scandinavian black-metal circles (Moynihan 2000; Moynihan and Søderlind 1998). Glenn Benton of Deicide even acknowledged having tortured animals at his Florida home (Baddeley 1999, 171).

68 Formed in 1984, Mayhem released its classic debut demo, *Pure Fucking Armageddon*, in 1986. Following the release of *Deathcrush* in 1986, Mayhem found a new drummer in Hellhammer and recruited as vocalist Dead from the Swedish band Morbid. In April 1991 Dead shot himself in the head with a shotgun. His fellow band members reacted by taking pictures of the scene for future CD covers, collecting pieces of the brain for talismans, and, allegedly, Euronymous even used parts of Dead's brain substance in a stew to be able to claim himself a cannibal (Moynihan and Søderlind 1998, 59).

69 Moynihan (e-mail 2001a) points out that Vikernes's claim is incorrect, citing that the Anglo-Saxon chronicle dates the raid to 8 June.

70 "For hver kirkegård som totalødelegges, er én hedenesk grav hevnet, for hver ti kirker som legges i aske er ett hedensk hof hevnet, for hver ti prester eller frimurere som likvideres, er én hedning hevnet!" (Vikernes 1997, 33; translation mine).

71 In addition to *Vargsmål*, Vikernes in 2001 published *Germansk mytologi og verdensanskuelse*. Cymophane Productions was initially based in Bergen, Norway. Within a few years it had grown to include Cymophane Publications, based in Stockholm, Sweden, and Cymophane Records, initially based in Germany. The strong man in the latter was Hendrik Möbus, a German black-metal musician who had been in contact with Vikernes since the early 1990s. When Möbus was released from jail in 1998, he set up Cymophane Records, which he took to the United States and eventually to Pierce's National Alliance. About Vikernes and Cymophane, see Vikernes 2001a.

72 For the AHF chapters see http://www.heathenfront.org/chap.htm. Moynihan (e-mail 2001b) comments that most of these AHF chapters "revolves around a few websites, which are mainly propaganda platform or merchandise sellers."

73 In 2001 the Pagan Front included a dozen labels: Ancient Blood Productions, Ancestral Research Records, Old Legend Production, Combat Productions, Darker Than Black Records, Dark Blaze Stronghold, Eastclan Productions, Stellar Winter Productions, Dead Christ Commune, Eastern Hate, Frontier Productions, and Hakenkruez. Among the bands were Gontyna Kry, Abyssic Hate, Swastyka, Thunderebolt and Thor's Hammer (see http://www.paganfront.com/index2.html).

74 Pett is his father's family name, Zorn is his mother's, and Nathan alternates between using Pett and Zorn. In the following text I will use Pett also when quoting him under his Zorn alias.

75 After an accident working on a boat in Louisiana, Pett received some money and relocated to Wright City, Missouri (Pett 1999).

76 Specifcally,

> Five hundred doors down and forty more
> I know that there are to Valhalla;
> Eight hundred Einherjar emerge at once
> From each, when they go to fight the Wolf. (*Grímnismál* 24)

Pett's enthusiastic celebration of the Fenris wolf, of course, fits uneasily with the more common interpretation of Asatrú ("ASAMETAL" 1999).

77 See also "The Enigma of the Swastika" 1998.

78 "Ian Stuart was a God," a *Fenris Wolf* article read. "He should always be remembered as the Godfather of our movement and as the Bragi spirit sent down by the Gods and manifested in the divine music of Screwdriver" ("Ian Stuart Donaldson" 1997, 20).

79 Described by Pett during a pilgrimage to the site, 10 September 1999.

80 See also "New Barbarians" 1998.

81 For a comprehensive outline of this approach, see Mason 1992.

82 An official PLL statement read "We of the Pagan Liberation League–WOT Northwest, denounce the attack on our Aryan brothers in Serbia, whom only wish to have a separate homeland and culture for their peoples self-determination, free from the shackles of Zionist slavery, capitalist exploitation and marxist-democratic servitude forced on free and independent peoples by the Imperialist Jew World Order" (PLL 1999).

83 See, for instance, Pierce's radio broadcasts in November 1998 and David Lane's correspondence with Nathan Zorn Pett, published in *Fenris Wolf*, no. 4 (1998).

84 The FBI dubbed him the Unabomber because his first targets were Universities and airline companies.

85 See also Godwin 1996.

86 Alex Curtis hailed the *Crossing the Abyss* as "easily the best publication in the movement in terms of contents and presentation" (SPLC 2000c, 28). Scutari praised the paper as "one of the main voices of our folk" (ibid.). Curtis would later receive an unfavorable review of his *Nationalist Observer* by WOT founder Peter Georgacarakos and had a falling out with Pett.

87 Bolton 1999; Devi 1999; "Hail Odin" 1999; Cox 1996; Georgacarakos 1997b. Kerry Bolton is the cofounder of the Black Order, and Stephen Cox is the cofounder of the British Order of the Jarls of Baldr.

88 Max Frith is not a person but a name under which several different WOT members write when expressing opinions deemed controversial.

89 Alex Curtis is not a member of WOT.

90 Born in Chile to an American diplomatic couple, Lujan was mainly raised overseas. Initially developing a far-left perspective, Lujan began gravitating toward the realm of the occult. Working with "chaos magic" and eventually moving into Satanism made Lujan abandon the egalitarian ethic. Reading Mason's *Siege*, Lujan was impressed with Mason's uncompromisingly radical onslaught of the system. Lujan developed an Aryan revolutionary worldview that would incorporate elements from both the radical left and right into what he terms a "folkish anarchist" perspective. Finding an ad for Kerry Bolton's Black Order in *Ohm Clock*, Lujan in 1995 sent in his 500-word biographical essay and was accepted as member. A graphic designer and artist, Lujan works at a bookstore and continues to run Web sites for Third Way and occult Aryan outfits, including the Fenris Wolf press (Lujan 1999; Lujan e-mail 2001).

91 Lujan 1999; Lujan e-mail 2001.

92 One of the interviews was with Michael Moynihan for his *Lords of Chaos* book on the black-metal underground. In 1993 Möbus and his accomplice murdered a fifteen-year-old schoolmate. "Unconsciously, we imitated an archaic sacrificial rite: first Sandro was hit with a knife, then strangled and then buried in the earth—a sacrifice to the Chthonic forces." Dismissing his victim as a "leftist faggot," Möbus said, "Every passing second, a human dies, so there's no need to make a big fuss over this one kill" (Moynihan and Søderlind 1998, 256).

93 Möbus (letter 2001) says that Pett paid for his ticket and housed him at his residence. Pett denies this, saying that "there is no proof at all that I ever had Mobus staying with me . . . no one ever saw him with me" (Pett e-mail 2001a).

94 Möbus letter 2001.

95 Pett e-mail 2001a; Pett e-mail 2001b.

96 Möbus letter 2001.

97 Pett e-mail 2001a. Pett writes, "I will not argue nor disargue or even make any comment on the alleged beating that I supposedly gave to Hendrik Mobus—I will only say, that if he was truly beaten nearly to his death, and barely escaped with his life (to go stay with W. Pierce and the National Alliance), then not only do I believe that he deserved his beating fully, but that he is only, also very lucky to be alive after this alleged event."

98 Pierce speech 2000c.

99 Pierce speech 2000d. For media reports about Möbus and Pierce, see "INS Gets Hand" 2000; Worden 2000; Vise 2000; Braun 2000.

100 While LaVeyan radical individualism was antithetical to totalitarian collectivism, LaVey was also notably attracted to national socialist aesthetics. He developed contacts with occult fascist James Madole of the National Renaissance Party, and his church did include members of national socialist orientation. Among them was LaVey's son-in-law, Nicholas Schreck, whose Werewolf Order Baddeley characterizes as "a gothic extreme of modern fascism" (1999, 150). Influenced by Guido von List and the Thule Society, Schreck aligned Satanism with occult national socialism and Teutonic paganism in a call for a "daemonic revolution." Led by Schreck and his partner Zeena LaVey, the lycanthropic order affiliated with the Church of Satan in 1988. According to Baddeley (ibid., 213), internal church debate was at the time "polarized into those who embraced sinister Nazi-chic as a confrontational individualism, and those who regarded Nazism as the repellent epitome of conformity." When Schreck and Zeena in 1990 publicly branded LaVey a charlatan, some of the "more grimly" fascist elements were supposedly taken back into the periphery. In his *Satan Speaks*, LaVey distanced himself from racial fascism by aligning Satanism with national socialit aesthetics and the Jewish people. "The Jews have always had the Devil's name. They just haven't owned up or taken pride in it" (21). He predicted that Gentiles without a drop of Jewish blood would concoct a Jewish great-great-grandfather in order to present themselves as hereditary Satanists, just as modern Wiccans invent lineages to claim a great-great-grandmother burned at the stake as a witch. In fact, LaVey held a faked Jewish lineage to be superior to a faked witch lineage. "Grandpa was a winner, Grandma was a loser. Grandpa may have been a Jew, but he was a survivor and maybe even made something special of himself, despite his devil's name. The burned grandmas, very few of whom were actually Jews, were 'witches' for reasons other than their religious affiliation. If Jews were destroyed in wholesale lots, it wasn't because they were witches, but because they were Jews, whose only purpose in life was to kill Christians and propagate evil" (22). LaVey foresaw the rise of a "new Jew" who would not be as desperate for acceptance as the "old Jew" traditionally had been. A vast number of young people with mixed Jewish/Gentile ancestry would, he predicted "need a tough identity. They won't find it in the Church, nor will they find it in the synagogue. They certainly won't find acceptance among identity anti-Christian anti-Semites who use noble, rich, and inspirational Norse mythology as an excuse and vehicle to rant about the 'ZOG.' The only place a rational amalgam of proud, admitted, Zionist Odinist Bolshevik Nazi Imperialist Socialist Fascism will be found—and championed—will be in the Church of Satan" (22). LaVey lamented that the Jewish people have "attempted to defend themselves . . . instead of declaring that Jesus was a nut and a shit disturber and he got what he deserved and we'd do it all over again" (21). (LaVey 1998, 21; Baddeley 1999, 150, 213, 159)

101 See, for instance, O'Malley 1995; "Sweden's Death Metal Odinists" 1996; "The Thousand Swords of Graveland" 1996.

102 WOT folder 1997.

103 Grimwald folder 1997.

104　See, for instance, Pierce speech 2000b.

105　"More on Colorado Jewish Killer" Internet 1999.

106　The Rune Guild was founded in 1980 and has three levels of initiation: Learner, Fellow, and Runemaster. The first level is conceptualized as the Outer Hall, and its work is to master the lessons contained in the "Nine Doors of Midgård." The second two levels compose the Inner Hall, and the curriculum is adapted to the need of each individual to suit his own esoteric path toward divinity. In 1999 the Rune Guild had six Halls outside Texas, in Australia, London, the Northeast, southern California, and northern Michigan. Besides these Halls, which operate ceremonies, there are individual members in the United States, Scandinavia, Continental Europe and Australia (Thorsson 1999; Thorsson 1996b; Thorsson 1996c).

107　See also Flowers 1997, 43.

108　"Order of the Trapezoid Mission Statement." Among those who classify the Setian effort as occult national socialism are Raschke 1990 and Levenda 1995.

109　He translated Sebbottendorf's *The Practice of the Ancient Turkish Freemansons*, von List's *The Invincible* (1898) and *The Secret of the Runes* (1908), Kummer's *Rune Magic* (1933), and a compilation of Wiligut works called *The Secret King* (2001). For Thorsson's view on national socialism and the occult, see Thorsson 1995d; Thorsson 1995e; Thorsson 1997.

110　See also Flowers 1997, chap. 7.

8. Globalization, Aryan Paganism, and Romantic Men with Guns

1　"Aryan Update" Internet 2001.

2　The Web site at www.americanfront.com was "temporarily" taken down immediately following the September 11 attack. It should perhaps be noted that the radical Islamic visions outlined by bin Laden and Qadhdhafi differ greatly from each other, a distinction unacknowledged by the American Front.

3　Metzger Internet 2001.

4　Miller Internet 1999. The full text of Miller's bin Laden interview was also published by wcotc at PMHale1@aol.com, 12 September 2001. Bin Laden quotes also quickly appeared at "Why did this happen?" Internet 2001 and "The Message Was Very Clear" Internet 2001.

5　Miller Internet 1999.

6　"The Meaning of Life" Internet 2001.

7　Hale Internet 2001a.

8　Ibid.; "Explosives?" Internet 2001; "Attack on America" Internet 2001. Similar sentiments were posted at the Wotansvolk mailing list. "It makes no difference who did the hit. . . . It hit the trade center which is controlled and owned by the jews, and the last report I saw on TV stated 4,000 jews were killed in the trade center, and I read another report that said 1,500 arabs worked in the trade center. . . . that's 5,500 jews and arabs that went up in smoke to their fat jewish god. There were 6,000 body bags ordered . . . we won that deal" ("Islam Zion and Ragnarok" Internet 2001).

9　"Attack on America" Internet 2001.

10　Hale Internet 2001b; "Lets Stop Being Human Shields" flyer 2001.

11 Hoffman Internet 2001.

12 "America the Sinful" Internet 2001.

13 "Islamic World Unite" Internet 2001.

14 Pierce speech 2001b.

15 Pierce speech 2001a.

16 All these "advantages" of biological and chemical warfare were also discussed at electronic forums. See, for instance, "Biological Terrorism" Internet 2000.

17 Passchier 1980. See also Merkl 1980; Felice 1980; Zipfel 1980; Griffin 1998.

18 This fact is frequently provoking to activists of the radical left who may strongly condemn fascist anticapitalism as phony. Fascists, however, take their anticapitalist position seriously.

19 Friedrich n.d.; Friedrich and Matterns n.d.; 165 *Little Known UFO Sightings* n.d.; "Official UFO Investigator Pass" pamphlet; "Achtung!" Internet 1996.

20 McVan e-mail 2001.

21 For an analysis of German national socialist appropriation of Norse paganism, see Arvidsson 2000.

References are listed in the following sections:

Interviews with Author
E-mail Correspondence and Surface Letters
Internet and E-zines
Speeches and Statements
Music
Flyers, Folders, Posters, and Pamphlets
Papers and Published Sources

Interviews with Author

Akkebala, Osiris. 1996. Interview by author. Tape recording. Orlando, Florida, 2 November.

Baumgardner, John. 1996. Interview by author. Tape recording. MacIntosh, Florida, 1 November.

Black, Don. 1996. Interview by author. Tape recording. West Palm Beach, Florida, 31 October.

Butler, Richard G. 1996. Interview by author. Tape recording. Aryan Nations, Hayden Lake, Idaho, 22 September.

Carto, Willis. 1996. Interview by author. Tape recording. Escondido, California, 12 December.

Christensen, Else. 1998. Interview by author. Tape recording. Parksville, B.C., Canada, 7 August.

Clinton, Cathy. 1997. Interview by author. Tape recording. Camas, Washington, 10 May.

Clinton, Reinhold (Michael). 1997. Interview by author. Tape recording. Camas, Washington, 10 May.

Duey, Randy. 1997. Interview by author. Tape recording. Oxford, Wisconsin, 20 May.

Duke, David. 1997. Interview by author. Tape recording. Mandeville, Louisiana, 3 June.

Edlund, Sheila. 1996. Interview by author. Tape recording. Grass Valley, California, 18 December.

Farrakhan, Louis. 1989a. Interview by author. Tape recording. Chicago, Illinois, 11 May.

————. 1989b. Interview by author. Tape recording. Chicago, Illinois, 18 May.

Gruidl, Gerald. 1996. Interview by author. Hayden Lake, Idaho, 9 September.

Hale, Matt. 1999. Interview by author. Tape recording. Superior, Montana, 4 September.

Hall, Elton. 1996. Interview by author. Tape recording. Cave Creek, Arizona,
23 December.

Hawthorne, George Burdi. 1996. Interview by author. Tape recording. Windsor, Canada,
2 October.

Hedlund, Mickael. 1999. Interview by author. Tape recording. Stockholm, Sweden,
30 November.

Hoffman, Michael. 1998. Interview by author. Tape recording. Post Falls, Idaho,
4 August.

Hyatt, Max 1998. Interview by author. Tape recording. Qualicum Beach, B.C., Canada.
7 August.

Kaldenberg, Wyatt. 1998. Interview by author. Tape recording. Fallbrook, California,
16 December.

Kemp, Richard. 1997. Interview by author. Tape recording. Sheridan, Oregon, 8 May.

Lane, David. 1996. Interview by author. Tape recording. Florence, Colorado,
12 November.

Lane, Katja. 1997. Interview by author. Tape recording. St. Maries, Idaho, 6 May.

Lujan, Michael. 1999. Interview by author. Tape recording. Richmond, Virginia,
4 October.

Lyons, Kirk. 1997. Interview by author. Tape recording. Black Mountain, North Carolina,
20 March.

McNallen, Stephen. 1996. Interview by author. Tape recording. Grass Valley, California,
18 December.

McVan, Ron. 1996. Interview by author. Tape recording. St. Maries, Idaho, 25 September.

Metzger, Tom. 1996. Interview by author. Tape recording. Carlsbad, California,
16 December.

————. 1998. Interview by author. Tape recording. Fallbrook, California, 15 December.

Mohr, Jack. 1997. Interview by author. Tape recording. Little Rock, Arkansas, 13 March.

Murray, Valgard. 1997. Interview by author. Tape recording. Payson, Arizona, 28 April.

Payne, Neal. 1997. Interview by author. Tape recording. Black Mountain, North Carolina,
20 March.

Pett, Nathan Zorn. 1999. Interview by author. Tape recording. Whidbey Island,
Washington, 9 September.

Pierce, William. 1997. Interview by author. Tape recording. Hillsboro, West Virginia,
19 March.

Rehbinder, Calle. 1998. Interview by author. Tape recording. Bagarmossen, Sweden,
5 October.

Söderman, Magnus. 2000. Interview by author. Tape recording. Fagersta, Sweden,
20 January. Translation by author.

Stenzel, Derek. 1997. Interview by author. Tape recording. Portland, Oregon, 10 May.

Tate, David. 1997. Interview by author. Tape recording. Potosi, Mineral Point, Missouri, 22 May.

Taylor, Robert N. 1998. Interview by author. Tape recording. Washington Island, Wisconsin, 21 August.

Thórarinsson, Thórsteinn. 1998. Interview by author. Tape recording. Tucson, Arizona, 21 December.

Thorsson, Edred. 1997. Interview by author. Tape recording. Austin, Texas, 17 April.

———. 1999. Interview by author. Tape recording. Bastrop, Texas, 6 January.

Trochman, John. 1996. Interview by author. Tape recording. Noxon, Montana, 27 September.

Vail, Eva. 1996. Interview by author. Tape recording. Coeur d'Alene, Idaho. 26 September.

Ward, Robert. 1999. Interview by author. Tape recording. Sacramento, California, 11 October.

Webb, Don. 1999. Interview by author. Tape recording. Austin, Texas, 2 January.

Weiland, Ted R. 1999. Interview by author. Tape recording. Scottsbluff, Nebraska, 23 September.

Yarbrough, Gary. 1997. Interview by author. Notes. Leavenworth, Kansas, 15 April.

Zündel, Ernst. 1998. Interview by author. Tape recording. Toronto, Canada, 28 August.

E-mail Correspondence and Surface Letters

Bolton, Kerry. 1999. Surface letter. Correspondence with Wotansvolk. 27 August.

Edholm, Erik af. 2002. E-mail correspondence with author. 11 September.

Ellis, Sandra. 1999. E-mail correspondence with author. 20 April.

Hall, Elton. 2000. E-mail correspondence with author. 22 October.

Hawthorne, George. 2001. E-mail correspondence with author. 2 February.

Koehl, Matt. 1982. "Fresh Start!" Surface letter to members declaring the dissolution of NSWPP, effective 1 January 1983. 9 November.

Lane, Katja. 1999. E-mail correspondence with author. 16 April.

———. 2000a. E-mail correspondence with author. 27 January.

———. 2000b. E-mail correspondence with author. 28 January.

———. 2000c. E-mail correspondence with author. 1 February.

———. 2000d. E-mail correspondence with author. 20 April.

———. 2001a. E-mail correspondence with author. 20 January.

———. 2001b. E-mail correspondence with author. 19 February.

———. 2001c. E-mail correspondence with author. 21 September.

———. 2001d. E-mail correspondence with author. 6 October.

———. 2001e. E-mail correspondence with author. 8 October.

———. 2001f. E-mail correspondence with author. 17 October.

———. 2001g. E-mail correspondence with author. 19 October.

———. 2001h. E-mail correspondence with author. 26 November.

Lujan, Michael. 2001. E-mail correspondence with author. 2 May.

McNallen, Stephen. 2000. "8 Words." E-mail circulation. Forwarded to author. 13 September.

McVan, Ron. 2001. E-mail correspondence with author. 11 November.

Möbus, Hendrik. 2001. Surface letter. Correspondence with author. 16 May.

Moynihan, Michael. 2001a. E-mail correspondence with author. 20 August.

———. 2001b. E-mail correspondence with author. 22 August.

———. 2002. E-mail correspondence with author. 1 March.

Pett, Nathan Zorn. 2001a. E-mail correspondence with author. 13 April.

———. 2001b. E-mail correspondence with author. 29 April.

Post, John. 2001. E-mail correspondence with author. 8 December.

———. 2002. E-mail correspondence with author. 26 March.

T.R.O.Y. 2001. Surface letter to author. 10 January.

Ward, Robert. 2001a. E-mail correspondence with author. 24 January.

———. 2001b. E-mail correspondence with author. 16 March.

Wiegand, Stephen. 2001. E-mail correspondence with author. 24 October.

Internet and E-zines

The first date, when available, reflects the date posted;
the second date (in parentheses) reflects the date downloaded.

ABC News. http://abcnews.go.com/sections/world/dailynews/terror_980609.html.

"Achtung! Samsidat News Bulletin: Samsidat Hollow Earth Expedition $9999.00 in
    Search of Holes of the Pole. Search for Hitler's Antarctic UFO Bases." (n.d.).
    http://bc.ca/hweb/people/zundel-ernst/flying-saucers/expedition.html
    (8 December 1996).

American Front. http://www.americanfront.com.

"American Vinland Association." 1999. http://vinland.org/heathen/ava/ (10 March).

"America the Sinful." 2001. http://Aryan-nations.org/indexpagesnews/America_
    the_Sinful.htm (21 November).

"Aryan of the Month Benjamin Smith." 1999. *Nationalist Observer Racial Reader's Forum,*
    3 August, AxCurtis@aol.com.

"Aryan Update." 2001. *WAR,* http://w.resist.com/updates/2001updates/9.28.01
    aryanupdate.htm (28 September).

"Attack on America." 2001. creativity@yahoogroups.com (12 September).

AxCurtis. 1999a. AxCurtis@aol.com (4 September).

AxCurtis. 1999b. *Nationalist Observer Racial Reader's Forum,* AxCurtis@aol.com
    (19 October 1999).

Beam, Louis. 1996. "The Conspiracy to Erect an Electronic Iron Curtain." *Stormfront,*
    http://204.181.1764/Stormfront/Iron_cur.htm (12 August 1996).

"Biological Terrorism." 2000. *Nationalist Observer,* AxCurtis@aol.com (10 April).

Blueyedevil. 1999. "Negative Impact of Ben Smith." *Nationalist Observer Racial Reader's
    Forum,* posted at AxCurtis@aol.com (17 July).

Conason, Joe. 1999. "Hitler Youth?" *Salon News,* 4 May,
    http://www.salonmag.com/news/col/cona/1999/05/04/nazis/index1.html
    (11 January 2001).

"Criticizing Racist Action." 1999. *Nationalist Observer Racial Reader's Forum*, 17 July, AxCurtis@aol.com.

Curtis, Alex. 1999a. Editor's comment. *Nationalist Observer Racial Reader's Forum*, 9 September, AxCurtis@aol.com.

———. 1999b. Editor's comment. *Nationalist Observer Racial Reader's Forum*, 19 October, AxCurtis@aol.com.

"Explosives?" 2001. creativity-owner@yahoogroups.com (September 13).

Fagan, Livingtone. 2002. "Mt. Carmel: The Unseen Reality, Part I and II." http://maine.rr.com/waco/1f/html (9 September 2002).

———. 2002b "David Koresh as Messiah." http://maine.rr.com/waco/1f/html (9 September 2002).

"Furrow Aryan of the Month." 1999. *Nationalist Observer Racial Reader's Forum*, AxCurtis@aol.com (26 August).

Gamlinginn. 1997. "We Are Not Racists." *Widdershins*, issue 6 (Yule), http://www.widdershins.org/vol3iss6/index.html (18 October 2000).

Gillette, Devyn, and Lewis Stead. 1994. "The Pentagram and the Hammer." *Raven Kindred Online*, http://www.webcom.com/~istead/wicatru.html (22 April 1999).

Gruber, Hans. 1999. "Buford Did a Bad Thing?" Posted on *National Observer Racial Reader's Forum*, AxCurtis@aol.com (9 September).

Gundarsson, KveldúlfR. N.d. "Ancestry and Heritage in the Germanic Tradition." *Ring of Troth*, http://asaru.knotwork.com/troth/kveld/Ancestur.htm.

Hale, Matt. 2001a. "Statement Concerning Today's Attack upon Jew York City." *Creativity Hotline for September 11*, PMHale@aol.com (11 September).

———. 2001b. "Taking It to the Streets." creativity@yahoogroups.com (22 September).

Heathen Front. http://www.heathenfront.org/chap.htm.

Hoddersen, Guerry. 1999. "The High Price of Ignoring Teen-Age Fascists." 30 April, http://www.socialism.com/currents/teenfascism.htm (11 January 2001).

Hoffman, Michael. 1999a. *Hoffman Wire*, 11 January, hoffman@hoffman-info.com.

———. 1999b. "The Mirror World of Columbine." *Hoffman Wire*, 22 April, hoffman@hoffman-info.com.

———. 1999c. "The Matrix." *Hoffman Wire*, 23 April, hoffman@hoffman-info.com.

———. 1999d. "This Is the Hour." *Hoffman Wire*, 15 June, hoffman@hoffman-info.com.

———. 2000. "Advisory from Hoffman." *Hoffman Wire*, 11 January, hoffman@hoffman-info.com.

———. 2001. "Hoffman on September 11." 16 September. Posted on deonmm@earthlink.net (17 September).

"Islamic World Unite." 2001. http://aryan.nations.org, (30 October 2001).

"Islam Zion and Ragnarok." 2001. wotansvolk@yahoogroups.com, Digest 182 (17 September).

"Kathy Ainsworth." N.d. http://www.wcotc.com/wcotcwf/kathy.html (17 August 2001).

Katz, Jesse. N.d. "Hatewatch Interview with Lisa Turner of the World Church of the Creator." http://www.wcotc.com/wcotcwf/hate (17 August 2001).

Kvasir. http://www.heathenfront.org/kvasir/.

Long, Anton. 1994. "Aeonic Magic—A Basic Introduction."
http://www.nasz-dom.net/sol/aeon.html (18 December 2000).

———. 107yf [1996]. "To Presence the Dark." http://www.nasz-dom.net/mars/
presence-dark.html (19 December 2000).

McManamon, Francis P. 1997. "Interior Department answers judges question." *Kennewick Man Virtual Interpretive Center*, 23 December, http://www.kennewick-man.com/
documents/mcnmanomonletter.html.

McNallen, Stephen. 2000a. "AFA Out of Kennewick Man Case." *Asatrú Folk Assembly*,
http://www.runestone.org/kmend.html (24 October).

———. 2000b. "Asatrú and Native Peoples." *Asatrú Folk Assembly*,
http://www.runestone.org/ind4.html (24 October).

———. 2000c. "Gathering of the Tribes." *Asatrú Folk Assembly*, http://www.runestone.org
(23 September).

———. 2000d. "A Little Background on the Asatrú Folk Assembly." *Asatrú Folk Assembly*,
http://www.runestone.org (23 September).

———. 2000e. "Welcome to the Land." *Asatrú Folk Assembly*, http://www.runestone.org
(23 September).

———. 2000f. "Wotan vs. Tezcatlipoca: The Spiritual War for California and the
Southwest." *Asatrú Folk Assembly*, http://www.runestone.org (24 October).

"The Meaning of Life." 2001. 12 September, sent by PMHale1@aol.com via e-mail.

"The Message Was Very Clear." 2001. *Weekly WAR Bulletin*, warmetzger@aol.com
(September 16).

Metzger, Tom. 2001. *Weekly WAR Bulletin*, warmetzger@aol.com (16 September).

Miles, Robert. N.d. "Take Off the Hoods! Scream Our Foes."
http://www.k-k-k.com/miles.htm (10 May 1999).

Miller, John. 1999. "Greetings America, My Name is Osama bin Laden." *Frontline*,
http://pbs.org.frontline, posted at PMHale1@aol.com (12 September 2001).

"More on Colorado Jewish Killer." 1999. *Final Conflict NewsEmail*, issue 833,
finalconflict@dial.pipex.com (26 April).

Murray, Valgard. 2000. "History of the Arizona Kindred."
http://www.anglefire.com/az/odinsfolk/ORIGINS.html (10 September).

ONA. N.d.a. "The Practice of Evil in Context." http://www.nasz-dom.net/mars/evil.html
(18 December 2000).

———. N.d.b. "Sacrifice." http://www.nasz-dom.net/mars/sacrifice.html
(18 December 2000).

———. N.d.c. "Temple 88: Newsletter 1." http://www.nasz-dom.net/saturn/
temple88.html (18 December 2000).

———. 1990. "Victims—A Sinister Exposé." http://www.nasz-dom.net/
mars.victims.html (18 December 2000).

———. 1991a. "The Hard Reality of Satanism." http://www.nasz-dom.net/mars/
hard-reality.html (18 December 2000).

———. 1991b. "Satanism—Or Living On The Edge." http://www.nasz-dom.net/
Saturn/nex-living-edge.html (18 December 2000).

———. 1991c. "Satanism and Race." http://www.nasz-dom.net/saturn/

nex-satanism-race.html (18 December 2000).

———. 1994a. "Culling–A Guide to Sacrifice II." http://www.nasz-dom.net/mars/ culling.html (18 December 2000).

———. 1994b. "A Gift to the Prince—A Guide to Human Sacrifice." http://www.nasz-dom.net/mars/gift-prince.html (18 December 2000).

———. 1994c. "An Introduction to Traditional Satanism." http://home.vest.net/ re-jo/satanism/an.html (18 December 2000).

———. 1996. "Towards Sapanur." http://www.nasz-dom.net/mars/ towards-sapanur.html (18 December 2000).

"Our Vision of an Asatrú Future." 1999. *Raven Kindred Online,* http://www.webcom.com/~istead/Vision.html (6 March 1999).

Project Leif. 2000. *Greenland Guide,* http://www.greenland-guide.gl/leif2000/.

"Race and Asatrú." 1999. *Raven Kindred Online,* http://www.webcom.com/~istead/race.html (21 April 1999).

"The Raven Kindred Principles of Asatrú." 1999. *Raven Kindred Online,* http://www.webcom.com/~istead/RKAPrinciples.html (6 March 1999).

Redfeairn, Ray. 2001. "Greetings from National Director Redfeairn." 27 September, http://Aryan-nations.org/indexpagenews/greetings_from_national_director.html (30 October).

Riabhaich, Coire. N.d. "Nexion: A Guide to Sinister Strategy." http://www.nasz-dom.net/saturn-nex-intro.html (18 December 2000).

———. 1998. Eira: A Satanic Guide to Future Magic." http://www.nasz-dom.net/saturn/eira.html (18 December 2000).

"RIP Smith." 1999. *Nationalist Observer Racial Reader's Forum,* AxCurtis@aol.com (17 July).

Smith, Winston [Harold Covington]. 1996. "The Importance of Holocaust Revisionism." *NSWPP-CSU E Bulletin,* http://members.aol.com/ct8994/private/nswpp/nswpp.html (30 December).

SPLC. 2000. "Active 'Patriot' Groups in the United States in 1999." http://www.splcenter.org/intelligenceproject/patriotlist.html (20 June 2000).

Temple 88. N.d. "The Creative Dialectic, Aeonic Strategy, and National-Socialism." http://www.nasz-dom.net/saturn/creat-di.html (18 December 2000).

Thomas, Mark. 1993. *Watchman,* October. http://www2.stormfront.org/ watchman/oct93.html (12 August 1996).

———. 1996a. "The Bosnian Serbs." *Watchman,* http://www2.stormfront.org/ watchman/jan96.html (9 August).

———. 1996b. "The Hard Men." *Watchman,* http://www2.stormfront.org/ watchman/feb96.html (9 August).

———. 1996c. "Index." *Watchman,* http://www2.stormfront.org/ watchman/index.html#contents (19 August).

———. 1996d. "The Quaternity of God." *Watchman,* http://www2.stormfront.org/watchman/cg.html (12 August).

———. 1996e. "Requiem for a Witch-Doctor." *Watchman,* http://www2.stormfront.org/watchman/oklahoma.html (12 August).

———. 1996f. "White supremacy!" *Watchman,*
http://www2.stormfront.org/watchman/feb96.html (9 August).

Turner, Lisa. N.d.a. "The Co-optation of White Women."
http://www.wcotc.com/wcotcwf/copt.html (17 August 2001).

———. N.d.b. "The Role of Women in the World Church of the Creator."
http://www.wcotc.com/wcotcwf/role.html (17 August 2001).

———. N.d.c. "Welcome to the World Church of the Creator Women's Frontier."
http://www.wcotc.com/wcotcwf/welcome.html (17 August 2001).

———. N.d.d. "Women of the Creativity Revolution."
http://www.wcotc.com/wcotcwf/revol.html (17 August 2001).

———. 1999. "Women's Frontier to the ADL: We Reject Your Feminist Smear!"
http://www.wcotc.com/wcotcwf (17 August 2001).

Ultima Thule 88. N.d. "The Way of the West." http://www.nasz-dom.net/
saturn/nex-way-west.html (18 December 2000).

"United Nations Member States." 2000. http://www.un.org/Overview/unmember.html.

Waco Holocaust Electronic Museum. http://www.Public-Action.com/
SkyWriter/WacoMuseum.

Waco Never Again. http://home.maine.rr.com/waco/.

White, Bill. 2001. "A Dialogue on Race and Hate in Music."
http://www.overthro.com/moynihan.html (11 January 2001).

"Who Rules America?" 2000. *National Alliance,* http://www.natall.com (10 July).

"Why Did This Happen?" 2001. creativity-owner@yahoogroups.com (11 September).

Wood, Eric. 2001. "Going to Sea." 7 April,
http://www.geocities.com/Athens/Forum/5056/goingtosea.html (18 April).

Speeches and Statements

Buchanan, Pat. 2000a. "A Conservative Agenda for a New Century." Speech delivered
before the Conservative Action Committee, Arlington, Virginia.
http://www.buchanan.org/000-p-articles.html. 21 January.

———. 2000b. "The Millennium Conflict: America First or World Government." Speech
delivered before the Boston World Affairs Council, Boston, Massachussetts.
http://www.buchanan.org/000-p-articles.html. 6 January.

Bush, George H. W. 1990. "Address before a Joint Session of the Congress on the Persian
Gulf Crisis and the Federal Budget Deficit." http://www.whitehouse.net.
11 September.

Butler, Richard G. 1999. "Comments on Furrow." *Nationalist Observer Weekly Racist*
broadcast. 17 August.

Christensen, Else. 1992. Interview by Thor Sannhet. Transcript of tape recording. May.

Clinton, Hillary. 1999. "Remarks by the President and the First Lady on Gun Control
Legislation." Washington, D.C., The White House. http://www.whitehouse.net.
27 April.

Clinton, Bill. 1999a. "Radio Address of the President to the Nation." Washington, D.C.,
The White House. http://www.whitehouse.net. 15 May.

———. 1999b. "Remarks by the President upon Departure for Littleton, Colorado." Washington, D.C., The White House. http://www.whitehouse.net. 20 May.

———. 2000. "State of the Union Address." Washington, D.C., Office of the Press Secretary, U.S. Capitol. http://www.whitehouse.net. 27 January.

"Declaration of War against Exploiters of Lakota Spirituality." 1993. Statement. Passed unanimously at the Lakota Summit V. 10 June.

FBI. 1999. "Press Release: FBI Statement to Clarify the USA Today Story Titled 'FBI: Militias as Threat at Millennium,' " Washington, D.C., FBI National Press Office. http://www.fbi.gov/homepage.htm. 20 October.

Freeh, Louis J. 1995. "Opening Statement of Louis J. Freeh, Director of the Federal Bureau of Investigation before the Subcommittee on Terrorism, Technology, and Government Information, Committee on the Judiciary, United States Senate," Washington, D.C. http://www.fbi.gov/homepage.htm. 19 October.

Lane, Katja, and David Lane. 1995. "We Must Secure the Existence of Our People and a Future for White Children." Speech delivered at the Aryan Nations Youth Convention. Written by David Lane and read by Katja Lane. Transcript. April.

Mathews, Robert J. 1987. "A Call to Arms." Speech delivered at National Alliance Convention. Tape recorded.

McNallen, Stephen. N.d.a. "The Declaration of Purpose of the Asatrú Folk Assembly." Grass Valley, Calif.: AFA.

———. N.d.b. "A Little Background on the Asatrú Folk Assembly." Grass Valley, Calif.: AFA.

Moynihan, Michael. 1998. Statement issued following the cancellation of a concert in San Francisco. Transcript. 5 October.

Pierce, William. 1977. "Cosmotheism: The Wave of the Future." Tape recorded speech.

———. 2000a. "Woe to Our People's Enemies." Speech. January.

———. 2000b. "Music of Rebellion." Speech. July.

———. 2000c. "The Case of Hendrik Möbus." American Dissident Voices broadcast: http://www.natall.com/internet-radio/. 9 September.

———. 2000d. "Save Our Freedom." American Dissident Voices broadcast: http://www.natall.com/internet-radio/. 23 September.

———. 2001a. "Provocation and Response." American Dissident Voices broadcast: http://www.natall.com/internet-radio/. 15 September.

———. 2001b. "Who Is Guilty?" American Dissident Voices broadcast: http://www.natall.com/internet-radio/. 22 September.

Riley, Joyce. 1996. "Cover-up of the Gulf War Illness." Lecture delivered at Preparedness Expo, Denver, Colorado. Transcribed. October.

Trochman, John, 1997. "Enemies Domestic and Foreign." Speech delivered at Preparedness Expo, Denver, Colorado. Transcribed. 16 October.

Úlfhethnar Kindred. 2000. "Statement to the Asatrú Alliance of Independent Kindreds." Utah Althing. 9 June.

Music

Bathory. 1998. *Blood Fire Death*. Kraze Records.

Berserkr. *The Voice of Our Ancestors*. Resistance Records.

Blood Axis. N.d. "Lord Of Ages." *Lamp of the Invisible Light*, compilation. Cthulhu.

———. 1995. *Gospel of Inhumanity*. Cthulhu/Storm.

———. 1998. *Blót—Sacrifice in Sweden*. Cold Meat Industries.

"Blood Axis/Allerseelen–split 7." Storm Records.

Centurion. N.d. *Fourteen Words*. Resistance Records.

Dissident. 2000. "Roots of Being." *A Cog in the Wheel*. Nordland Records.

Graveland. 2000. *Creed of Iron*. Isengard/No Colour Records.

Heysel. 1998. "Black-Bannered Legion." *Motstånd*. Nordland Records.

Mayhem. 1986. *Pure Fucking Armageddon*. Posercorps.

Rahowa. 1994. *Declaration of War*. Resistance Records.

Rahowa. 1995. *Cult of the Holy War*. Resistance Records.

Flyers, Folders, Posters, and Pamphlets

"Aryan Genealogy of the Forth Son of Jacob." Chart. Church of Jesus Christ, Christian/Aryan Nations.

"Building a New White World." Flyer from a recruitment folder prepared for the National Alliance by the National Office. Hillsboro, West Virginia: National Alliance.

"Dees a 'Bi-Sexual' Says Ex-Wife." Flyer.

"Dees the Great Satan." Flyer.

Grimwald, Wulf. 1997. "Social Darwinism, National Socialism, and the Folkish Community." Folder. White Order of Thule.

Hansen, Michael L. N.d. "The Pagan Revival." Flyer. National Socialist White Revolutionary Party.

"History and Organization." N.d. *Introducing the New Order*. Folder. Arlington, Va.: New Order.

Lane, David. N.d.a. "Cabala: 882=744." Folder. N.p.

———. N.d.b. *Death of the White Race*. Pamphlet.

"Let's Stop Being Human Shields for Israel." 2001. Flyer. World Church of the Creator.

Lyons, Kirk, and Neil Payne. N.d. "What is CAUSE Foundation." Black Mountain, N.C.: CAUSE Foundation.

McVan, Ron. N.d.a. "Carl Gustav Jung: Understanding Wotan Consciousness." Folder. St. Maries, Idaho: 14 Word Press.

———. N.d.b. "Death." Folder. St. Maries, Idaho: 14 Word Press.

———. N.d.c. "God, Wotan, and Aryan Man." Folder. St. Maries, Idaho: 14 Word Press.

———. N.d.d. "Hieros Logos." Folder. St. Maries, Idaho: 14 Word Press.

———. N.d.e. "The Importance of Richard Wagner." Folder. St. Maries, Idaho: 14 Word Press.

———. N.d.f. "Mind." Folder. St. Maries, Idaho: 14 Word Press.

———. N.d.g. "Mystery of the Blood." Folder. St. Maries, Idaho: 14 Word Press.

————. N.d.h. "Path of Wotan." Folder. St. Maries, Idaho: 14 Word Press.

————. 1998. "Haminga." Folder. St. Maries, Idaho: 14 Word Press.

————. 1999. "Religion: The Good, the Bad, the Ugly." Folder. St. Maries, Idaho: 14 Word Press.

"Official UFO Investigator Pass." Toronto, Canada: Samsidat.

"PAIN Organizational Structure." N.d. Orlando, Fla.: PAIN.

"Platform for the Aryan National State." 1996. Folder. Hayden Lake, Idaho: Aryan Nations.

"So You're a European-American Who's Attracted to Native American Spirituality . . . and Understandably So!" N.d. Flyer. Asatrú Folk Assembly.

"Special Report on Waco." N.d. Black Mountain, N.C.: CAUSE Foundation.

WOT. 1997. "All Hail the Accuser! Satan and the West." Folder. Clinton, Wash.: WOT Northwest.

"W.O.T.A.N.: Will Of The Aryan Nation." N.d. Folder. St. Maries, Idaho: 14 Word Press.

"Wotan's Kindred and the Significance of Asatrú in Today's World." N.d. Wotan's Kindred.

Papers and Published Sources

"A Common Cause." N.d. *National Front News*, no. 93.

Adams, Dean. 1999. "Where Does the Aryan Stand in Ancient Legend?" *Crossing the Abyss*, no. 5.

Adler, Margot. 1986. *Drawing Down the Moon*. New York: Penguin/Arkana.

Aho, James A. 1990. *The Politics of Righteousness: Idaho Christian Patriotism*. Seattle: Washington University Press.

————. 1994. *This Thing of Darkness: A Sociology of the Enemy*. Seattle: Washington University Press.

AIT. "Adam and Eve." 1981a. *Correspondence Bible Course*. American Institute of Theology.

————. "Cain and Abel." 1981b. *Correspondence Bible Course*. American Institute of Theology.

————. "Satan, His True Identity." 1981c. *Correspondence Bible Course*. The American Institute of Theology.

Akkebala, Osiris. N.d.a. *Black Man: Pathway to Freedom: The Real Solution to the African Problem*. Orlando, Fla.: Afrikan Images.

————. N.d.b. "Pan-Afrikan International Movement: Action Plan." Orlando, Fla.: PAIN.

Allen, J. H. 1902. *Judah's Sceptre and Joseph's Birthright*. Merrimac, Mass.: Destiny Publishers.

"All You Ever Wanted to Know about Morris—The Sleaze—Dees. N.d. *Crisis Paper*, no. 40.

"Anarchism." 1989. *Odinist*, no. 125.

Anderson, Benedict. 1991. *Imagined Communities: Reflections on the Origin and Spread of Nationalism*, revised ed. London: Verso.

Anderson, Peter, Joakim Grenbäck, and Matti Sundquist. 1997. "Vår ras är vår religion." *Nordland*, no 10.

Ansell, Amy Elizabeth. 1997. *New Right, New Racism*. Houndmills and London: Macmillan.

Anti-Semitism Worldwide, 1998/9. 1999. Tel Aviv: Stephen Roth Institute, Tel Aviv University.

Appadurai, Arjun. 1990. "Disjuncture and Difference in the Global Cultural Economy." In *Global Culture*, edited by Mike Featherstone. London: Sage Publications.

———. 1996. *Modernity at Large: Cultural Dimensions of Globalization*. Minneapolis: University of Minnesota Press.

Aquino, Michael. 1975. *The Book of Coming Forth by Night*. Ruby Tablet of Set.

———. 1998. "Evolution of the Order of the Trapezoid Insignia." *Runes* 4, no. 2.

Arrington, Leonard J., and Davis Bitton. 1992. *The Mormon Experience: A History of the Latter-Day Saints*. Urbana: University of Illinois Press.

Arvidsson, Stefan. 2000. *Ariska idoler: Den indoeuropeiska mytologin som ideologi och vetenskap*. Stockholm: Symposion.

"Aryan Destiny: Back to the Land." N.d. NSJ, Calif.: National Socialist Kindred.

"Aryan Freedom." 1983. *The Odinist*, no 77.

Aryan Nations. 1996a. "Declaration of Independence, Revised Edition: The Unanimous Declaration of the Aryan Peoples in America." *Calling Our Nation*, no. 77.

———. 1996b. "Platform for the Aryan National State: Articles I–X." *Calling Our Nation*, no. 77.

"ASAMETAL: The Dawn of the True Heathen-Hearts." 1999. *Fenris Wolf*, no. 6.

"Asia and Europe: Friends Apart." 1996. *Economist* (March 9): 65.

Åsard, Erik. 1994. *Janusansiktet: Amerikansk Populism i Historisk Belysning*. Uppsala: Acta Universitatis Upsaliensis.

"Asatrú Calendar." 1996. *Vor Trú*, number 50 (fall 2243/winter 2244 Runic Era).

"At Last, The King's Chamber!" 1936. *Pelley's Weekly* (September 9).

Bachofen, Johann Jakob. 1993. *Das Mutterrecht. Eine Untersuchung über die Gynaikokratie der alten Welt nach ihrer religiösen und rechtlichen Natur*. Frankam Main: Suhrkamp.

Baddeley, Gavin. 1997. "We Are All Individuals (Except for That Guy Sitting on His Own in the Corner)." *Black Flame* 6, nos. 1–2.

———. 1999. *Lucifer Rising: Sin, Devil Worship, and Rock 'n' Roll*. London: Plexus.

Barkan, Elazar. 1996 [1992]. *The Retreat of Scientific Racism: Changing Concepts of Race in Britain and the United States between the World Wars*. Cambridge: Cambridge University Press.

Barker, Eileen. 1989. *New Religious Movements*. London: Her Majesty's Stationery Office.

Barkun, Michael. 1995. "Conspiracy Theories as Stigmatized Knowledge: The Basis for a New Age Racism?" Paper presented at the conference, Brotherhoods of Race and Nation: The Emergence of a Violent Euro-American Racist Subculture, 7–12 December, New Orleans, La.

———. 1997. *Religion and the Racist Right: The Origins of the Christian Identity Movement*. Chapel Hill: University of North Carolina Press.

———. 1998a. "Conspiracy Theories as Stigmatized Knowledge: The Basis for a New Age Racism?" In *Nation and Race: The Developing Euro-American Racist Subculture*, edited by Jeffrey Kaplan and Tore Bjorgo. Boston: Northeastern University Press.

———. 1998b. "Politics and Apocalypticism." In *The Encyclopedia of Apocalypticism*, edited by Stephan Stein. Vol. 3. New York: Continuum.

Barton, Blanche. 1992. *The Secret Life of a Satanist*. Venice, Calif.: Feral House.

Baumgardner, John. 1996. "Who Is that Masked Man? A Short Autobiography by John Baumgardner." *Florida InterKlan Report* (April).

Beam, Louis. 1983. *Essays of a Klansman*. Hayden Lake, Idaho: A.K.I.A. Publications.

———. 1992. "Leaderless Resistance." *The Seditionist*, no. 12.

Beest, Christos. 1996. "Thernn—An Introduction to Natural Septenary Magic." Order of the Nine Angles.

Bennet, David. 1995. *The Party of Fear: The American Far Right from Nativism to the Militia Movement*. New York: Vintage Books.

Berger, Helene A. 1999. *A Community of Witches: Contemporary Neo-Paganism and Witchcraft in the United States*. Columbia: University of South Carolina Press.

Berlet, Chip, and Matthew N. Lyons. 2000. *Right-Wing Populism*. New York: Guilford Press.

Berner, Dan. 1998. "George Lincoln Rockwell." *Nordland*, no 13.

Berry, Mary Frances. 1994. *Black Resistance—White Law: A History of Constitutional Racism in America*. New York: Penguin.

Beyer, Peter. 1994. *Religion and Globalization*. London: Sage.

Black Order. 1993. *Book of Wyrd*. Wellington, New Zealand: Realist Publications.

Blavatsky, Helena P. 1972 [1877]. *Isis Unveiled*. Pasadena, Calif.: Theosophical University Press.

———. 1888. *The Secret Doctrine*. London: The Theosophical Society.

Blood, Linda. 1994. *The New Satanists*. New York: Warner Books.

Bock, Alan W. 1996. *Ambush at Ruby Ridge*. New York: Berkley Books.

Bolton, Kerry. 1999. "Savitri Devi: Priestess of Hitler." *Crossing the Abyss*, no. 5.

Boulware, Jack. 1999. "Has the Church of Satan Gone to Hell?" *Gnosis*, no. 50.

Bowman, Marion. 1996. "Cardiac Celts: Images of Celts in Paganism." In *Paganism Today*, edited by Graham Harvey and Charlotte Hardman. London: Thorsons.

Braun, Stephen. 2000. "Entry of Foreign Extremist into the U.S. Raises Concerns." *Los Angeles Times*, 8 September.

Bridges, Tyler. 1994. *The Rise of David Duke*. Jackson: University Press of Mississippi.

"Bright Change with Autumn." 1936. *Pelley's Weekly* (March 11).

Brimlow, Peter. 1996. *Alien Nation: Common Sense about America's Immigration Disaster*. New York: HarperPerennial.

Bristowe, Sydney. 1927. *Sargon the Magnificent* (reprint). Hayden Lake, Idaho: Church of Jesus Christ, Christian.

"The Brüders Schweigen Remember Robert Jay Mathews, The Martyr." 1996. *Focus Fourteen*, no. 602.

Buckley, Joshua. 1997. "Satan's Little Helper." *Black Flame* 6, nos. 1–2.

Budge, E. A. Wallis. 1969. *The Gods of the Egyptians*. Mineola, Mich.: Dover Books.

———. 1988. *Osiris and the Egyptian Resurrection*. Vols. 1 and 2. Mineola, Mich.: Dover Books.

Campbell, Colin. 1972. "The Cult, the Cultic Milieu, and Secularization." *Sociological Yearbook of Religion in Britain* 5: 119–36.

Canovan, Margaret. 1981. *Populism*. New York: Harcourt Brace Jovanovich.

Carto, Willis. 1991. Introduction to *Imperium* by Francis Parker Yockey. Costa Mesa, Calif.: Noontide Press.

Chalmers, David M. 1987. *Hooded Americanism: The History of the Ku Klux Klan.* 3rd ed. Durham, N.C.: Duke University Press.

Chisholm, James A. 1996. "The Awakening of a Runemaster: The Life of Edred Thorsson." Appendix A in *Green Rûna*, edited by Edred Thorsson. Smithville, Texas: Rûna-Raven Press.

Christ, Carol P. 1997. *Rebirth of the Goddess: Finding Meaning in Feminist Spirituality.* New York: Routledge.

Christensen, Else. 1998a. "Folks of Midgard—Be Greeted." *Midgard Page.* Union Bay, B.C.: Odinist Fellowship.

———. 1998b. "Reorganizing the Odinist Fellowship." *Midgard Page*, April 14.

Christensen, Jim. 1995. "Blind Nationalism: Our Greatest Foe." *Resistance* no. 3, (winter).

Clinton, Bill. 2000. "State of the Union Address." The White House, Office of the Press Secretary, U.S. Capitol, Washington, D.C., 27 January.

Cocks, Geoffrey. 1985. *Psychotherapy in the Third Reich.* New York: Oxford University Press.

Cohen, Sharon. 1997. "Rise and Fall of Robbers with Hate Message." *New Standard*, 5 January.

"The Coming Race of Gods." 1981. *CSA Journal*, no. 3.

"The Communitarian Imperative." 1982. *Odinist*, no. 68.

Coogan, Kevin. 1999. "How Black Is Black Metal?" *Hit List* 1 (February/March): 33–59.

———. 2000. *Dreamer of the Day: Francis Parker Yockey and the Postwar Fascist International.* New York: Autonomedia.

Cook, Terry L. 1996. *The Mark of the New World Order—666: The Cashless Economic System of Global Electronic Enslavement Is Ready Now!* Springdale, Penn.: Whitaker House.

Cooper, Ricky E. 1997. *NSV Report* (January/March).

Corcoran, James. 1990. *Bitter Harvest: Gordon Kahl and the Posse Comitatus: Murder in the Heartland.* New York: Penguin.

Cosmotheism. 1977. Arlington, Va.: The Cosmotheist Community.

Cox, Stephen. 1996. "The Third Reich: Chronicles of the Occult Cycle." *Crossing the Abyss*, no. 2.

———. 1998. "Freyrs Oceanic Western Kingdom, Part 2: Migrations of the Tribes." *Crossing the Abyss*, no. 4.

Crowley, Aleister. 1994a. [1913]. "The Book of the Law: Liber Legis." In *Magick, Book 4: Liber ABA.* York Beach, Maine: Samuel Weiser.

———. 1994b. [1913]. *Magick, Book 4.* York Beach, Maine: Samuel Weiser.

Crowley, Vivianne. 1996a. *Wicca.* London: Thorsons.

———. 1996b. "Wicca as a Modern-Day Mystery Religion." In *Paganism Today*, edited by Graham Harvey and Charlotte Hardman. London: Thorsons.

Curtis, Alex. 1999. "The Enemy." *Crossing the Abyss*, no. 5. Vernal Equinox.

Dahl, Göran, 1997. "God Save the County! Radical Localism in the American Heartland: 'Common Law,' Traditionalist Catholicism, a Pope, Black Indians, and the Republic of Texas." Unpublished manuscript, Lund University, Sweden.

Deboo, Jeffrey. 1996. "Fascism and the Deity of Rebellion." *Black Flame* 5, nos. 1–2.

"Declaration of Purpose." N.d. Grass Valley, Calif.: Asatrú Folk Assembly.

"Deep Calleth Unto Deep." 1982. *CSA Journal*, no. 8.

Dees, Morris. 1993. *Hate on Trial*. New York: Villard Books.

Dees, Morris, and James Corcoran. 1996. *Gathering Storm*. New York: HarperCollins.

Dees, Morris, and Steve Fiffer. 1991. *A Season for Justice*. New York: Charles Scriber's Sons.

"Deguello Report on the American Right Wing." 2000. In *Encyclopedia of White Power*, edited by Jeffrey Kaplan. Walnut Creek, Calif.: AltaMira Press.

Devi, Savitri. 1958. *The Lightning and the Sun*. Niagara Falls, New York: Samsidat.

———. 1999. "The Lightning and the Sun: Part I." *Crossing the Abyss*, no. 5.

diZerega, Gus. 2001. *Pagans and Christians: The Personal Spiritual Experience*. St.Paul, Minn.: Llewellyn Worldwide.

Dobratz, Betty A., and Stephanie L. Shanks-Meile. 1997. *"White Power, White Pride!" The White Separatist Movement in the United States*. New York: Twayne Publishers.

Downey, Roger. 2000. *Riddle of the Bones: Politics, Science, Race, and the Story of the Kennewick Man*. New York: Copernicus.

Dudziak, Mary L. 2000. *Cold War, Civil Rights: Race and the Image of American Democracy*. Princeton, N.J.: Princeton University Press.

Duke, David. 1998. *My Awakening*. Covington, La.: Free Speech Press.

Dundas, Zach. 2000. "Lord of Chaos." *Willamette Week*, August 16.

Dwyer, Simon, ed. 1995. *Rapid Eye*. London: Creation Books.

"Ecology." 1984. *Odinist*, no 82.

Eddan. 1881. Stockholm: Norstedts Och Söner.

"Eirik's Saga." 1976. In *The Vinland Sagas*, edited by Magnus Magnusson and Hermann Pålsson. New York: Penguin Books.

"The Enigma of the Swastika." 1998. *Fenris Wolf*, no. 4.

"Escape Is Prohibited." 1936. *Pelley's Weekly*, (September 2): 3.

Evola, Julius. 2001. *Introduction to Magic*. Rochester, Vt.: Inner Traditions.

———. 2002. *Men Among Ruins*. Rochester, Vt.: Inner Traditions.

"Exploiting the Earth." 1984. *The Odinist*, no. 82.

"Fall Folkish Calendar." 1997. *Fenris Wolf*, no. 3.

FBI. 1999. *Project Megiddo*. Washington, D.C.: U.S. Department of Justice.

Feagan, Joe R., and Hernan Vera. 1995. *White Racism*. New York: Routledge.

Featherstone, Mike, ed. 1990. *Global Culture*. London: Sage Publications.

Fefnir (Robert Miles). N.d. *Voices of the Aryan Separatist*.

Felice, Renzo de. 1980. "Italian Fascism and the Middle Classes." In *Who Were the Fascists? Social Roots of European Fascism*, edited by Stein Ugelvik Larsen, Bernt Hagtvet, and Jan Petter Myklebust. Bergen, Norway: Universitetsforlaget.

Fell, Berry. 1980. *Saga America*. New York: Times Books.

"Fenris Wolf Press Staff Statement." 1999. *Fenris Wolf*, no. 6.

"The Fifth Path—An Interview with Robert Ward." 1993. *Ohm Clock*, no. 1: 9–12.

Flood, Gavin. 1996. *An Introduction to Hinduism*. Cambridge: Cambridge University Press.

Flowers, Stephen [Edred Thorsson]. 1988. "The Life of Guido von List." *The Secrets of the Runes*. Rochester, Vt.: Destiny Books.

———. 1990. *Fire and Ice: Magical Teachings of Germany's Greatest Secret Occult Order.* St. Paul, Minn.: Llewellyn Publications.

———. 1997. *Lords of the Left-Hand Path.* Smithville, Texas: Rûna-Raven Press.

Flynn, Kevin, and Gary Gerhardt. 1989. *The Silent Brotherhood: Inside America's Racist Underground.* New York: Free Press.

"Focus Fourteen—4 Word Press nyhetsbulletin." 1997. *Nordland*, no. 9.

"Folk and Fatherland: The Only Doctrine of National Socialism." N.d. NSJ, Calif.: National Socialist Kindred.

"40 Questions on the Holocaust." 1996. *Resistance*, no. 70 (15 April).

Frenz, Robert. 1994. "Revisionism—Aryan Friend or Foe?" *WAR* (February).

Freud, Sigmund. 1938 [1913]. *Totem and Taboo.* Harmondsworth, U.K.: Penguin Books.

———. 1978 [1928]. *The Future of an Illusion.* London: Hogarth Press.

Friedrich, Christof. N.d. *Secret Nazi Polar Expeditions.* Toronto, Canada: Samsidat Publications.

Friedrich, Christof, and Matterns. N.d. *UFOs: Nazi Secret Weapons?* Toronto, Canada: Samsidat Publications.

Frith, Max. 1997. "Wherefore Satan?" *Crossing the Abyss*, no. 3

———. 1998. "Third Way Political Thought and the Evolution of Ideas." *Crossing the Abyss*, no 4.

———. 1999. "The West Is Dead." *Crossing the Abyss*, no. 5.

"From the Wolfs Den." 1998. *Fenris Wolf*, no. 4

Gallagher, Dan. 1998. "FBI Sharpshooter to Be Tried before Federal Judge." Associated Press, 12 January.

Gamlinginn. 1993. "Race and Religion." *Mountain Thunder*, no. 8 (spring).

Gardell, Mattias. 1996. *In the Name of Elijah Muhammad: Louis Farrakhan and the Nation of Islam.* Durham, N.C.: Duke University Press.

———. 1998. *Rasrisk: Rasister, Separatister och Amerikanska Kulturkonflikter.* Stockholm: Federativs.

Garvey, Marcus. 1986a [1923]. *The Philosophy and Opinions of Marcus Garvey, Vol. I.* Edited by Amy J. Garvey. Dover, Mass.: Majority Press.

———. 1986b [1925]. *The Philosophy and Opinions of Marcus Garvey. Vol. II.* Edited by Amy J. Garvey. Dover, Mass.: Majority Press.

"Garvey's Vision." N.d. *Nationalism Today*, no.42.

Gibson, James W. 1994. *Warrior Dreams: Violence and Manhood in Post-Vietnam America.* New York: Hill and Wang.

Georgacarakos, Peter. 1997a. *Paganism: An Aryan Science.* WOT.

———. 1997b. "What Is Thule?" *Crossing the Abyss*, no. 3.

———. 1998. "What Is Thule? Part 2." *Crossing the Abyss*, no. 4.

———. 1999. "Paganism as an Aryan Science." *Crossing the Abyss*, no. 5.

Giddens, Anthony. 1990. *The Consequences of Modernity.* Stanford, Calif.: Stanford University Press.

Gimbutas, Marija. 1990. *Goddesses and Gods of Old Europe, 6500–3500 B.C: Myths and Cult Images.* Berkeley: University of California Press.

Gimbutas, Marija, and Miriam Robbins Dexter, eds. 1999. *The Living Goddesses*. Berkeley: University of California Press.

Glasenapp, Helmuth von. 1967. *Indiens Religioner*. Lund: Studentlitteratur.

"Glossary of Lies." 1996. *Jubilee* 8, no. 6 (July/August).

Godwin, Joscelyn. 1996. *Arktos: The Polar Myth in Science, Symbolism, and Nazi Survival*. Kempton, Ill.: Adventures Unlimited Press.

Goldberg, Jonathan J. 1996. *Jewish Power: Inside the American Jewish Establishment*. Reading, Mass.: Addison Wesley.

Goldston, Linda. 1998. "Child Abuse at the Presidio: The Parent's Agony, the Army's Coverup, the Prosecution's Failure." *San Jose Mercury News*, 24 July.

Gonda, Jan. 1970. *Visnuism and Sivaism: A Comparison*. London: University of London, Athlone Press.

Goodrick-Clarke, Nicholas. 1992. *The Occult Roots of Nazism: Secret Aryan Cults and Their Influence on Nazi Ideology*. London: I.B. Taurus.

———. 1998. *Hitler's Priestess: Savitri Devi, the Hindu-Aryan Myth, and Neo-Nazism*. New York: New York University Press.

———. 2002. *Black Sun*. Albany: State University of New York Press.

"Graenlendiga Saga." 1976. In *The Vinland Sagas: The Norse Discovery of America*, edited by Magnus Magnusson and Hermann Pålsson. New York: Penguin Books.

Grant, Madison. 1916. *The Passing of the Great Race, or The Racial Basis of European History*. New York: Charles Scribner's Sons.

Griffin, Roger. 1991. *The Nature of Fascism*. London: Routledge.

———, ed. 1998. *International Fascism: Theories, Causes, and the New Consensus*. London: Arnold.

Gundarsson, KveldúlfR. 1993. *Teutonic Religion*. St.Paul, Minn.: Llewellyn Press.

———. 1994. *Our Troth*. Seattle, Wash.: Ring of Troth.

Gunnarson, Katarina. 1997. "Fornnordisk tro idag—skillnader och likheter i utövandet av de årliga ceremonierna—en jämförande analys mellan samfundet Fröjslunda Världshus och Sveriges Asatrosamfund." Unpublished undergraduate thesis, Department of Theology, Uppsala University.

"Hail Odin: God of Death!" 1999. *Crossing the Abyss*, no. 5.

Hair, William Ivy. 1991. *The Kingfish and His Realm: The Life and Times of Huey P. Long*. Baton Rouge: Louisiana State University.

Hall, Paul. 1996. "The Center of Hate." *Jubilee* 8, no. 6 (July/August).

Hamm, Mark S. 1995. *American Skinheads: The Criminology and Control of Hate Crime*. Westport, Conn.: Praeger.

Hannerz, Ulf. 1990. "Cosmopolitans and Locals in World Culture." In *Global Culture*, edited by Mike Featherstone. London: Sage Publications.

———. 1992. *Cultural Complexity*. New York: Columbia University Press.

Hansson, Kevin. 1994. "A Superior Religion for a Superior Race." *RaHoWa News*, no. 9 (December).

Hardy, Pat. 1998. "Order of the Trapezoid." In *The Crystal Tablets of Set*. The Temple of Set.

Harvey, Graham. 1997. *Listening People, Speaking Earth: Contemporary Paganism*. London: Hurst.

Harvey, Graham, and Charlotte Hardman, eds. 1996. *Paganism Today*. London: Thorsons.

Harwood, Richard. N.d. *Did Six Million Really Die? The Truth at Last*. Richmond, U.K.: Historical Review Press.

Hawthorne, George Burdi. 1995a. "The Blood of Our Martyrs." *Resistance*, no. 3.

—. 1995b. "The Brüders Schweigen/Men Against Time." *Focus Fourteen*, issue 512.

—. 1996a. "Debunking the Great Lie." Introduction to the reprint of *Might Is Right*, by Ragnar Redbeard [1896]. Chicago: M.H.P. and Company.

—. 1996b. "History in the Making." *Focus Fourteen*, no. 611.

—. 1997. "Skapandet av historia." *Nordland*, no. 9.

Heinze, Andrew R. 1999. "White Supremacists and Their War against Jews." *The San Francisco Examiner*, 13 August.

Hellberg, Anders. 2000. "Vikingaskepp över Atlanten." *Dagens Nyheter*, 12 February.

Herman, Arthur. 1997. *The Idea of Decline in Western History*. New York: Free Press.

Herrnstein, Richard J., and Charles Murray. 1996 [1994]. *The Bell Curve: Intelligence and Class Structure in American Life*. New York: Free Press Paperbacks.

Hettne, Björn, Sverker Sörlin, and Uffe Östergård. 1998. *Den globala nationalismen*. Stockholm: SNS Förlag.

Higham, John. 1975. *Send These to Me: Jews and Other Immigrants in Urban America*. New York: Atheneum.

Hine, Edward. [1874]. *Identity of the Ten Lost Tribes of Israel with the Anglo-Celtic-Saxons*, abridged ed. N.p.

"Hitler Historian Loses Libel Case." 2000. *BBC News*, 11 April [http://news.bbc.co.uk/].

Hobsbawn, Eric J. 1990. *Nations and Nationalism since 1780*. Cambridge: Cambridge University Press.

Hoffman II, Michael. 1995a [1985]. *The Great Holocaust Trial*. Dresden, N.Y.: Wiswell Ruffin House.

—. 1995b. *Secret Societies and Psychological Warfare*. Coeur d'Alene, Idaho: Independent Research and History.

Hofstadter, Richard. 1996 [1964]. *The Paranoid Style in American Politics and Other Essays*. Cambridge, Mass.: Harvard University Press.

Hollinrake, Roger. 1982. *Nietzsche, Wagner, and the Culture of Pessimism*. London: George Allen and Unwin.

Horsman, Reginald. 1981. *Race and Manifest Destiny: The Origins of American Racial Anglo-Saxonism*. Cambridge, Mass.: Harvard University Press.

Hoskins, Richard Kelly. 1990. *Vigilantes of Christendom*. Lynchburg, Va.: Virginia Publishing.

How You Can Drive a Stake Through the Heart of the New World Order. N.d. Phoenix, Ariz.: Police Against the New World Order.

Hultkrantz, Åke. 1992. *Shamanic Healing and Ritual Drama*. New York: Crossroad.

Huntington, Samuel P. 1996. *The Clash of Civilizations and the Remaking of World Order*. New York: Simon and Schuster.

Hutton, Ronald. 1999. *The Triumph of the Moon: A History of Modern Pagan Witchcraft*. Oxford: Oxford University Press.

Hyatt, Max. 1997. "Asatrú, Society, and the Law." *Wodanesdag*, no. 8.

"Ian Stuart Donaldson. The Earthly Incarnation of Bragi." 1997. *Fenris Wolf*, no. 3.

Icke, David. 1999.*The Biggest Secret: The Book That Will Change the World*. Scottsdale, Ariz.: Bridge of Love Publications.

"The Incarnation of Wotan." N.d. NSJ, Calif.: National Socialist Kindred.

Ingstad, Anne-Stine. 1985. *The Norse Discovery of America: Vol. I*. Oslo: Norwegian University Press.

Ingstad, Helge. 1985. *The Norse Discovery of America, Vol. 2*. Oslo: Norwegian University Press.

"INS Gets Hand on Neo-Nazi Fugitive." 2000. Associated Press, 12 September.

"Interview with Michael Moynihan." 1994. *No Longer a Fanzine*, 1994.

"An Interview with Robert Taylor." *Tribal Resonance*. London: Rising Press, no. 2.

"I See Six Legions ." 1936. *Pelley's Weekly* (1 April): 3.

"Islam Nation Leader Says Blacks Must Gain Equality Separately." 1990. *Spotlight* (23 July).

Jacobson, Matthew Frye. 1998. *Whiteness of a Different Color: European Immigrants and the Alchemy of Race*. Cambridge, Mass.: Harvard University Press.

"James Mason: Illusion vs. Reality." 1995. *Resistance*, no. 5.

Jenkins, Michael M. [Michael Moynihan]. 1992. "Introduction." In *Siege*, edited by Michael M. Jenkins. Denver, Colo.: Storm Books.

Jolif, Thierry. 1997. "An Interview with Robert Taylor." *Ouranus*. France.

Jones, Harry J. 1968. *The Minutemen*. Garden City, New York: Doubleday.

Jordan, Colin. 1999. Introduction to *Deceived, Damned, and Defiant: The Revolutionary Writings of David Lane*. St. Maries, Idaho: 14 Word Press.

Jost. N.d. *Arya Kriya: Guidelines for Arya Kriya Training*. NSJ, Calif.: National Socialist Kindred.

———. 1995a. "About the Author." In *Arya Kriya: The Science of Accelerated Evolution*. NSJ, Calif.: National Socialist Kindred.

———. 1995b. *Arya Kriya: The Science of Accelerated Evolution*. NSJ, Calif.: National Socialist Kindred.

———. 1995c. *Asana Kriya*. NSJ, Calif.: National Socialist Kindred.

———. 1995d. *Dhyana Kriya*. NSJ, Calif.: National Socialist Kindred.

———. 1995e. *Kundalini Pranayama Kriya*. NSJ, Calif.: National Socialist Kindred.

———. 1995f. *Purification of Body and Mind*. NSJ, Calif.: National Socialist Kindred.

"Judge Dismisses Case against FBI Shooter for Ruby Ridge Killing." Associated Press, 14 May 1998.

"Judgment of Nations Starts with September, Says Pyramid." 1936. *Pelley's Weekly* (1 April).

Jung, Carl Gustav. 1936. "Wotan." *Neue Schweizer Rundschau III* (March).

———. 1947. "Wotan." Translated by Barbara Hannah. In *Essays on Contemporary Events*. London.

"Jung och Nazismen." 1992. *Res Publica*, no. 21, Eslöv: Symposion.

Kaldenberg, Wyatt. N.d. "USA's No. 1 White Supremacist: Morris Dees Southern Millionaire Law Center."

———. 1995a. "Aryan Green Man Arise." *WAR* (June).

———. 1995b. "Sitting on the Edge of History." *WAR* (August).

———. 1995c. "The Myth of the Middle Class Revolution." *WAR* (November).

———. 1996a. "Karmic Justice: A Pagan View of the Holocaust." *WAR* (March).

———. 1996b. "Wealth Can Kill a Race." *WAR* (April).

———. 1996c. "White Man's Burden." *WAR* (February).

———. 1998a. "A Short History of Odinism in the English Speaking World." *Pagan Revival*, no. 41.

———. 1998b. "Beyond Love and Hate." *WAR* (December).

Kalkier, Quint. 1996. "What Is a White Order?" *Crossing the Abyss*, no. 2.

Kaplan, Jeffrey. 1997. *Radical Religion in America*. Syracuse, N.Y.: Syracuse University Press.

———. 2000a. "Ku Klux Klan." In *Encyclopedia of White Power: A Sourcebook on the Radical Racist Right*, edited by Jeffrey Kaplan. Walnut Creek, Calif.: AltaMira Press.

———. 2000b. "Order of the Nine Angles." In *Encyclopedia of White Power: A Sourcebook on the Radical Racist Right*, edited by Jeffrey Kaplan. Walnut Creek, Calif.: AltaMira Press.

Kaplan, Jeffrey, and Tore Bjorgo, eds. 1998. *Nation and Race: The Developing Euro-American Racist Subculture*. Boston: Northeastern University Press.

Kaplan, Jeffrey, and Leonard Weinberg. 1998. *The Emergence of a Euro-American Radical Right*. New Brunswick, N.J.: Rutgers University Press.

Kareem, Benjamin, ed. 1971. *The End of White World Supremacy*. New York: Seaver Books.

Keith, Jim. 1994. *Black Helicopters over America: Strikeforce for the New World Order*. Lilburn, Ga.: IllumniNet Press.

Kelland, Kate. 2000. " 'Racist' Historian Irving Has No Regrets." *Reuters* (London), 12 April.

Kerrick, Joseph. 1996. "Close Encounters of the Fifth Kind: Calling the White Gods." *Crossing the Abyss*, no. 2.

Klassen, Ben. 1981. *The White Man's Bible*. Otto, N.C.: Church of the Creator.

———. 1987. *RaHoWa! This Planet Is All Ours*. Otto, N.C.: The Church of the Creator.

———. 1992 [1973]. *Nature's Eternal Religion*. Milwaukee, Wisc.: Milwaukee Church of the Creator.

Klassen, Ben, and Arnold DeVries. 1982. *Salubrious Living*. Otto, N.C.: Church of the Creator.

Klein, Naomi. 2000. *No Logo*. Hammersmith, London: Flamingo.

Knott, Stephen F. 1996. *Secret and Sanctioned: Covert Operations and the American Presidency*. Oxford: Oxford University Press.

Koehl, Matt. N.d.a. *Hitler and We*. Milwaukee, Wisc.: New Order.

———. N.d.b. *The Religion of Lincoln Rockwell*. Milwaukee, Wisc.: New Order.

———. 1985a. "Resurrection." *NS Bulletin* (January–April).

———. 1985b. "Adolf Hitler: Prophet of a New Age." *NS Bulletin* (April).

———. 1985c. "Birth of a Leader." *NS Bulletin* (July–August).

———. 1985d. "A New Religion." *NS Bulletin* 320 (September–December).

———. 1986. "Building a Spiritual Base." *NS Bulletin* (September–December).

Koestler, Arthur. 1976. *The Thirteenth Tribe*. Palmdale, Calif.: Omni Publications.

Kühl, Stefan. 1994. *The Nazi Connection: Eugenics, American Racism, and German National Socialism*. Oxford: Oxford University Press.

Lane, David. N.d. *Pyramid Prophecy 666*. Catoosa, Okla.: Mano in Vinculis.

———. 1994a. *The Auto-Biographical Portrait of the Life of David Lane and the 14 Word Motto*. St. Maries, Idaho: 14 Word Press.

———. 1994b. *88 Precepts*. St. Maries, Idaho: 14 Word Press.

———. 1994c. *The Mystery Religions and the Seven Seals: Introduction to Hermetic Philosophy and the Teachings of David Lane*. St. Maries, Idaho: 14 Word Press.

———. 1994d. *Revolution by the Number 14*. St. Maries, Idaho: 14 Word Press.

———, ed. 1994e. *White Genocide Manifesto*. St. Maries, Idaho: 14 Word Press.

———. 1994f. *Wodensson in Verse*. St. Maries, Idaho: 14 Word Press.

———. 1995a. *Focus Fourteen*, no. 501.

———. 1995b. *Focus Fourteen*, no. 505.

———. 1995c. "We Must Secure the Existence of Our People and a Future for White Children." *Focus Fourteen*, no. 505.

———. 1995d. "Dissension within the Resistance." *Focus Fourteen*, no. 506.

———. 1995e. "The Price of Continued Reality Denial." *Focus Fourteen*, no. 507.

———. 1995f. "Wotan's Volk." *Focus Fourteen*, no. 509.

———. 1995g. "Alfred Rosenberg: The White Soul." *Focus Fourteen*, no. 510.

———. 1995h. "Nedräkning till 1995." *Nordland*, no. 3, August.

———. 1996a. "The Former Yugoslavia and the New World Order." *Focus Fourteen*, no. 603.

———. 1996b. "Ireland—England—Scotland." *Focus Fourteen*, no. 603.

———. 1996c. "Exploding a Buzzword." *Focus Fourteen*, no. 607.

———. 1996d. *Focus Fourteen*, no. 607.

———. 1996e. "Now or Never . . ." *Focus Fourteen*, issue 609.

———. 1996f. "Universalist Imperialism." *Focus Fourteen*, no. 610.

———. 1996g. "Ode to Bob Mathews." *Focus Fourteen*, issue 612.

———. 1997a. "Låt oss vinna." *Nordland*, no. 9.

———. 1997b. "Reality Check." *Focus Fourteen*, no. 710.

———. 1998a. *Focus Fourteen*, no. 803.

———. 1998b. "Money." *Focus Fourteen*, no. 808.

———. 1999. *Deceived, Damned, and Defiant: The Revolutionary Writings of David Lane*. St. Maries, Idaho: 14 Word Press.

Lane, Katja. 1996. Editor's note to reprint of *Might Is Right*, by Ragnar Redbeard [1896]. Chicago: M.H.P and Co.

———. 2001. "Miguel Serrano." *Focus Fourteen*, no 2106.

Langmuir, Gavin I. 1990. *History, Religion, and Anti-Semitism*. Berkeley: University of California Press.

Larsen, Stein Ugelvik, Bernt Hagtvet, and Jan Petter Myklebust, eds. 1980. *Who Were the Fascists? Social Roots of European Fascism*. Bergen, Norway: Universitetsforlaget.

Larsson, Mats G. 1999. *Vinland det goda: Nordbornas färder till Amerika under vikingatiden*. Stockholm: Atlantis.

LaVey, Anton S. 1969. *The Satanic Bible*. New York: Avon Books.

———. 1970. "An Explanation of the Various Degrees in the Church of Satan." *Cloven Hoof* 2:11.

———. 1972. *The Satanic Rituals.* New York: Avon. Books.

———. 1989 [1971]. *The Satanic Witch.* Venice, Calif.: Feral House.

———. 1992a. *The Devil's Notebook.* Venice, Calif.: Feral House.

———. 1992b. "The Eleven Satanic Rules of the Earth." Appendix to *The Secret Life of a Satanist,* by B. Barton. Venice, Calif.: Feral House.

———. 1992c. "Pentagonal Revisionism: A Five Point Program." Appendix to *The Secret Life of a Satanist,* by B. Barton. Venice, Calif.: Feral House.

———. 1996. Foreword to reprint of *Might Is Right,* by Ragnar Redbeard [1896]. Chicago: M.H.P and Co.

———. 1998. *Satan Speaks.* Venice, Calif.: Feral House.

Lee, Mike. 1997a. "Tribes Able to Testify in Kennewick Man Case." *Tri-City Herald,* 3 May.

———. 1997b. "One Year after Kennewick Man Surfaced, Battle over 9,200-year-old Skeleton Rages On." *Tri-City Herald,* 27 July.

———. 1997c. "Corps Allowed Indians Access to the Bones." *Tri-City Herald,* 31 July.

———. 1997d. "Pagan Group Plans Ceremony over Kennewick Man Bones." *Tri-City Herald,* 20 August.

———. 1997e. "Tribes Upset by Rituals for Kennewick Man." *Tri-City Herald,* 27 August.

———. 1999. "Deadline Set for Decision of Bones." *Tri-City Herald,* 22 September.

———. 2000a. "Tribes Disturbed by More Tests on Old Bones." *Tri-City Herald,* 14 January.

———. 2000b. "DNA Testing in Works for Bones." *Tri-City Herald,* 2 February.

———. 2000c. "Scientists Await Answer on Kennewick Man Bones." *Tri-City Herald,* 21 March.

———. 2000d. "Government Releases Plans for More Tests of Old Bones." *Tri-City Herald,* 11 April.

———. 2000e. "Lab Struggles with Kennewick Man's DNA." *Tri-City Herald,* 3 August.

———. 2000f. "Interior Department Rules Bones Belong to Tribes." *Tri-City Herald,* 26 September.

———. 2000g. "Tribes Hail Kennewick Man Decision." *Tri-City Herald,* 27 September.

———. 2000h. "Kennewick Man's Day in Court." *Tri-City Herald,* 23 October.

Lemann, Nicholas. 1992. *The Promised Land: The Great Migration and How It Changed America.* London: Papermac.

Letter to the Editor. 1985. *Odinist,* no. 91.

Leuchter, Fred A. 1988. *The Leuchter Report: An Engineering Report on the Alleged Execution Gas Chambers at Auschwitz, Birkenau, and Majdanek, Poland.* Toronto, Canada: Samisdat Publishers.

Levenda, Peter. 1995. *Unholy Alliance: A History of Nazi Involvement with the Occult.* New York: Avon Books.

Lipstadt, Deborah. 1994. *Denying the Holocaust: The Growing Assault on Truth and Memory.* Harmondsworth, U.K.: Plume/Penguin.

"The Littleton Massacre." 1999. *Time Magazine* (3 May).

Loman, Van. 1994. "ACLU for Patriots: Kirk Lyons of the CAUSE Foundation." *Stormfront.*

Lööw, Heléne. 1998. *Nazismen i Sverige 1980–1997.* Stockholm: Ordfront.

———. 2000. "White Power Music /A.K.A. White Noise Music." In *Encyclopedia of White Power*, edited by Jeffrey Kaplan. Walnut Creek, Calif.: AltaMira.

Lujan, Michael L. 1998. "Toward a New Paganism for a New People." *Crossing the Abyss*, no. 4.

Lyke, M. L. 1997. "Pagans, Tribes, Scientists Battle over Ancient Bones." *Washington Post*, 10 September.

Macdonald, Andrew [William Pierce]. 1989. *Hunter*. Hillsboro, W.Va.: National Vanguard Books.

———. 1993 [1980]. *Turner Diaries*. Hillsboro, W.Va.: Vanguard Books.

Macko, Steve. 1996. "The Aryan Republican Army." *Emergency Net News Service*, 24 April.

Madison, James. 1961. *The Federalist Papers*. Edited by Clinton Rossiter. New York: Mentor Books.

Madole, James H. 1974–1977. "The New Atlantis: A Blueprint for an Aryan 'Garden of Eden' in North America!" Article series, *National Renaissance Bulletin* (May 1973–February 1977).

Magnusson, Magnus, and Hermann Pálsson. 1976. Introduction to *The Vinland Sagas: The Norse Discovery of America*. New York: Penguin Books.

Malcolm X. 1971. "God's Judgment of White America." *The End of White World Supremacy*, edited by Benjamin Kareem. New York: Seaver Books.

"The Manson Debate: Two of Our Readers Take Their Sides." 1995. *Resistance*, no 5.

Marable, Manning. 1984. *Race, Reform, and Rebellion: The Second Reconstruction in Black America, 1945–1982*. Jackson: University of Mississippi Press.

Marrs, Tex. 1993. *Big Sister Is Watching You: Hillary Clinton and the White House Feminists Who Now Control America—And Tell The President What To Do*. Austin, Texas: Living Truth Ministries.

———. 1996. *Circle of Intrigue: The Hidden Inner Circle of the Global Illuminati Conspiracy*. Austin, Texas: Living Truth Publishers.

Mason, James. 1992. *Siege*. Edited by Michael M. Jenkins. Denver, Colo.: Storm Books.

Massey, Douglas S., and Nancy A. Denton. 1993. *American Apartheid: Segregation and the Making of the Underclass*. Cambridge, Mass.: Harvard University Press.

McLamb, Jack. N.d. *How You Can Drive a Stake through the Heart of the New World Order*. Phoenix, Ariz.: Police Against the New World Order.

———. 1996. *Operation Vampire Killer 2000*. Phoenix, Ariz.: Police Against the New World Order.

McNallen, Stephen. 1980. "Metagenetics." *Runestone*, no. 34.

———. 1983. *An Odinist Anthology*. AFA.

———. 1992a. *Rituals of Asatrú: Volume One: Major Blots*. Payson, Ariz.: World Tree Publications.

———. 1992b. *Rituals of Asatrú: Volume Two: Seasonal Festivals*. Payson, Ariz.: World Tree Publications.

———. 1992c. *Rituals of Asatrú: Volume Three: Rites of Passage*. Payson, Ariz.: World Tree Publications.

———. 1995. "Asafolk and American Indians—Solving the 'Wannabe Problem.'" *Runestone*, no. 13.

————. 1996a. "Listen to the Mothers: Wisdom from the Disir." *Runestone*, no. 16/17.

————. 1996b. "What Would Odin Say about Gun Control?" *Wolf Age*, no. 4.

————. 1998. "Fire and the Fog." *Runestone*, no. 21.

————. 1999a. "Genetics and Beyond—The Ultimate Connection." *Runestone*, no. 26.

————. 1999b. "Time for Tribes." *Runestone*, no. 25.

McVan, Ron. 1997. *Creed of Iron: Wotansvolk Wisdom.* St. Maries, Idaho: 14 Word Press.

————. 1999. Foreword to *Deceived, Damned, and Defiant: The Revolutionary Writings of David Lane.* St. Maries, Idaho: 14 Word Press.

————. 2000. *Temple of Wotan: Holy Book of the Aryan Tribes.* St. Maries, Idaho: 14 Word Press.

————. 2001. "Wotanism—Satanism—Not." *Focus Fourteen*, no 2107.

Melton, Gordon. 1992. *Encyclopedic Handbook of Cults in America.* New York: Garland.

Merkl, Peter H. 1980. "The Nazis of the Abel Collection: Why They Joined the NSDAP." In *Who Were the Fascists? Social Roots of European Fascism*, edited by Stein Ugelvik Larsen, Bernt Hagtvet, and Jan Petter Myklebust. Bergen, Norway: Universitetsforlaget.

Metzger, Tom. N.d.a. "White Aryan Resistance Positions." In *WAR Declared.* Fallbrook, Calif.: WAR.

————. N.d.b. "White Aryan Resistance Positions." In *WAR Declared!* Fallbrook, Calif.: WAR.

Michel, Lou, and Dan Herbeck. 2001. *American Terrorist: Timothy McVeigh and the Oklahoma City Bombing.* New York: Regan Books.

Miles, Robert. 1980. *Birth of a Nation: A Declaration of the Existence of a Racial Nation within the Confines of a Hostile Political State.* N.p.

————. 1983. *33/5.* Flint, Mich.: Mountain Church.

————. 1988. "Take Off the Hoods! Scream Our Foes." *The Klansman* (September/October).

Mills, Rud A. 1957. *The Call of Our Ancient Nordic Religion.* Reprint. Union Bay, B.C.: Wodanesdag Press.

Mohr, Jack. N.d. *Christianities Ancient Enemy.* Bay St. Louis, Miss.: n.p.

————. 1992. *The Effects of the Talmud on Judeo-Christianity,* La Porte, Colo.: Scriptures for America.

————. 1993a. *America's Destiny: Christ or Anti-Christ? A Frank Discussion of the Jewish Problem and the Future of this Country as the Zion of Prophecy!* Bay St. Louis, Miss.: n.p.

————. 1993b [1990]. *The Hidden Power behind Freemasonry.* Burnsville, Minn.: Weisman.

Moore, Jack B. 1993. *Skinheads Shaved for Battle: A Cultural History of American Skinheads.* Bowling Green, Ohio: Bowling Green State University Popular Press.

Moore, Leonard J. 1991. *Citizen Klansmen: The Ku Klux Klan in Indiana, 1921–1928.* Chapel Hill: University of North Carolina Press.

Morgan, Lynn. 1996. "Women and the Goddess Today." In *Paganism Today*, edited by Graham Harvey and Charlotte Hardman. London: Thorsons.

Morlin, Bill. 2000. "Racist Pagans Identified." *Spokane Spokesman-Review*, 12 March.

"Morris Dees: A Fact Finding Report." 1995. Militia of Montana, February 15.

Moses, Wilson Jeremiah. 1978. *The Golden Age of Black Nationalism, 1850–1925.* Oxford: Oxford University Press.

"Möte med David Lane." 1996. *Nordland*, no. 6.

Moynihan, Michael. 1995. "Shout at the Devil." *Seconds*, no. 27.

———. 1996. "The Faustian Spirit of Fascism" *Black Flame* 5, nos. 1–2.

———. 1997. "Rahowa." *Black Flame* 6, nos.1–2.

———. 2000. "Black Metal." In *Encyclopedia of White Power*, edited by Jeffrey Kaplan. Walnut Creek, Calif.: AltaMira.

Moynihan, Michael, and Didrik Søderlind. 1998. *Lords of Chaos: The Bloody Rise of the Satanic Metal Underground*. Venice, Calif.: Feral House.

Muhammad, Abdul Wali. N.d. "Nation of Islam." *Nationalism Today*, no. 39.

Murray, Valgard. N.d.a. *Living Asatrú*. Payson, Ariz.: World Tree.

———. N.d.b. *Religious Rites within Asatrú*. Payson, Ariz.: Asatrú Alliance.

———. N.d.c. "What Is Asatrú?" In *The International Asatrú-Odinic Alliance*, by Valgarad Murray. Payson, Ariz.: World Tree Publications.

———. 1993. Editorial comment to a letter by Gárman "Letters to the Editor." *Vor Trú*, no. 50.

———. 1996. "The Asatrú Kindred." *Vor Trú*, no. 55.

———. 1998. "Letters from the Editors—Past and Present." *Vor Trú*, no. 58.

"Mystical Asatrú." 1999. *Fenris Wolf*, no. 6.

National Alliance Membership Handbook. 1993. Hillsboro, W.V.: National Vanguard Books.

Nelson, Cletus. 1999. "Michael Moynihan: From Abraxas to Nietzsche." *Eye* (September/October).

Nelson, Jack. 1993. *Terror in the Night: The Klan's Campaign against the Jews*. New York: Simon and Schuster.

"Neo Tribalism." 1979. *The Odinist*, no. 43.

"New Barbarians." 1998. *Fenris Wolf*, no. 4.

Newman, David. 1998. "Kennewick Man Was a Nazi." *Stranger* (February 26).

Nietzsche, Friedrich. 1974 [1882]. *The Gay Science*. New York: Vintage Books.

Nilsson, Anders. 1997. "Dr. William L. Pierce" *Nordland*, no 11.

Noll, Richard. 1997a. *Aryan Christ: The Secret Life of Carl Jung*. New York: Random Press.

———. 1997b. *Jungkulten*. Stockholm: Ordfront.

O'Brien, Cathy. 1995. "Fervent Wake-Up Call from Mark and Cathy." *Contact: The Phoenix Project*, no. 2. (9 May).

O'Brien, Cathy, and Mark Phillips. 1995a. *Mind Control*. Nashville, Tenn.: Global Trance Formation Info Ltd.

———.1995b. *TRANCE Formation of America*. Las Vegas, Nev.: Reality Marketing Inc.

O'Brien, Thomas E. N.d. *Verboten*. Hayden Lake, Idaho: Church of Jesus Christ, Christian.

"Odinism—Religion of the New Age." 1985. *Odinist*, no. 92.

"Odinism—Religion of Relevance." 1984. *Odinist*, no. 82.

"Odinism and Racial Politics." 1985. *Odinist*, no. 91.

O'Máirtin, P. 1996. "Brickbacks and Bouguets." *Rahowa News*, no. 20 (March/April).

O'Malley, Stephen. 1995. "Nordic Darkness." *Resistance*, no 5.

"Once More, 'Liberty or Death.'" 1936. *Pelley's Weekly* (4 November).

165 Little Known UFO Sightings from around the World. N.d. Toronto, Canada: Samsidat Publications.

Österberg, Thomas. 1999. "Var tionde tror på Jesus som frälsare." *Nya Dagen*, 30 March.

Owens, Eric, and Eric Dobbs. 1998. "Den ariska nationen." *Nordland*, no 14.

"Pagan Liberation League Political and Spiritual Ethos." 1999. *Fenris Wolf*, no. 5.

Parfrey, Adam. 1990 [1987]. *Apocalypse Culture*. Venice, Calif.: Feral House.

Passchier, Nico. 1980. "The Electoral Geography of the Nazi Landslide." In *Who Were the Fascists: Social Roots of European Fascism*, edited by Stein Ugelvik Larsen, Bernt Hagtvet, and Jan Petter Myklebust. Bergen, Norway: Universitetsforlaget.

The Path. 1977. Arlington, Va.: Cosmotheist Community.

Pett, Nathan Zorn. 1997. "Out with the Battle Ax." *Fenris Wolf*, no. 3.

PLL. 1999. "Official Statement of the Pagan Liberation League on the Bombing of Serbia." *Fenris Wolf*, no. 5.

Posse Comitatus. N.d. "Posse Comitatus Handbook." N.p.

"The Power of Wotan." 1982. *The Odinist*, no. 68.

Quinley, Harold E., and Charles Y. Glock. 1979. *Anti-Semitism in America*. New York: Free Press.

"Race: The New Reality." N.d. *National Front News*, no. 84.

"Racial Consciousness." 1984. *Odinist*, no. 83.

"Ragnarok in North America." 1998. *Fenris Wolf*, no 4.

"Rantings from the Bunker." N.d. *Nationalism Today*, no. 39.

Raschke, Carl A. 1990. *Painted Black. The Chilling True Story of the Wave of Violence Sweeping through Our Hometowns*. New York: HarperPaperbacks.

Raven, Mike. 1993. "Viking Glory." *WAR* (February).

Reavis, Dick J. 1995. *The Ashes of Waco*. New York: Simon and Schuster.

Redbeard, Ragnar. 1996 [1896]. *Might Is Right*. Chicago: M.H.P. and Company.

Reid, T. R. 2000. "Historians Fight Battle of the Books." *Washington Post*, 6 April.

Re/Search. 1994 [1983]. *Industrial Culture Handbook*. San Francisco: Re/Search Publications.

Rhodes, Tom. 1999. "Militia Joins Up with FBI to Fight Anarchy." *London Times*, 15 August.

Riabhaich, Coire. 1998. "EIRA: A Satanic Guide to Future Magic." Shropshire, U.K.: ONA Venn Community.

Rich, Evelyn. 1988. *Ku Klux Klan Ideology, 1954–1988*. Ann Arbor, Mich.: UMI Dissertation Services.

Robbins, Thomas, and Roland Robertson, eds. 1987. *Church-State Relations: Tensions and Transitions*. New Brunswick, N.J.: Transaction.

"Robert J. Mathews—en hjälte i vår tid." 1997. *Nordland*, no. 9.

Robertson, Pat. 1991. *The New World Order*. Dallas: Word Publishing.

Robertson, Roland. 1987. "Church-State Relations and the World System." In *Church-State Relations: Tensions and Transitions*, edited by Thomas Robbins and Roland Robertson. New Brunswick, N.J.: Transaction.

Robertson, Wilmot. 1981 [1972]. *The Dispossessed Majority*. Cape Canaveral, Fla.: Howard Allen Enterprises.

Rockwell, G. Lincoln. 1967. *White Power*. Arlington, Va.: ANP.

———. 1979. *This Time the World*. Liverpool, W.Va.: White Power Publications.

Rosenberg, Alfred. 1930. *Der Mythus der 20. Jahrhunderts*. München: Hoheneichen Verlag.

The Rosenthal Document. N.d. N.p.

Rowan, Carl. 1996. *The Coming Race War in America.* Boston: Little, Brown.

Ryker. 1994. "A Note about the Northwest." *Northwestern Imperative*, no. 1 (20 April).

"Saddam Hussein vs. the Jew World Order." 1998. *Fenris Wolf*, no. 4.

Satanism and Its Allies. 1998. London: Final Conflict.

Schlosser, Eric. 2000. *Fast Food Nation: The Dark Side of the All-American Meal.* New York: Perennial.

Schmaltz, William H. 1999. *Hate: George Lincoln Rockwell and the American Nazi Party.* Washington: Brassey's.

Scutari, Richard. 2000. "Unbroken Spirit." *Focus Fourteen* (January).

Serrano, Miguel. 1978. *El Cordón Dorado: Hitlerismo Esotérico.* Bogotá, Colombia: Editorial Solar.

———. 1984a. *Adolf Hitler, el Último Avatára.* Bogotá, Colombia: Editorial Solar.

———. 1984b. *NOS: Book of the Resurrection.* London: Routledge.

———. 1991. *Manú: "Por el hombre que vendra."* Bogotá, Colombia: Editorial Solar.

———. 1997. *C. G. Jung and Hermann Hesse: A Record of Two Friendships.* Einsiedeln: Daimon Verlag.

Shallcrass, Philip. 1996. "Druidry Today." In *Paganism Today*, edited by Graham Harvey and Charlotte Hardman. London: Thorsons.

SilverWitch, Sylvana. 1997. "Just 'Wiccatru' Folk: A Word With Prudence Priest." *Widdershins* (Yule).

Simonelli, Frederick J. 1999. *American Führer: George Lincoln Rockwell and the American Nazi Party.* Urbana: University of Illinois Press.

Sims, Patsy. 1996. *The Klan.* 2d ed. Lexington: University Press of Kentucky.

Smith, Gerald K., ed. 1995 [1948]. *The International Jew.* Boring, Ore.: CPA Book Publisher.

Smith, Winston [Harold Covington]. 1994. "Not These Kids, Metzger." *Resistance* (November).

———. 1995. "Holocaust Revisionism Is Vital." *Resistance*, no. 47 (February).

Södergren, Håkan. 1998. "Burzum: Varg Vikernes Talks of Eugenics, Thule, NHF, Norge, and More." *Muspellzheimr Journal*, no 1.

SPLC. 1997. "Patriot Movement Poses Continued Threat: Groups Are Growing in Number, Hardening in Attitude." *Intelligence Report*, no. 86 (spring).

———. 1998. The New Barbarians. New Brand of Odinist Religion On the March." *Intelligence Report*, no.89 (winter).

———. 1999a. "Active Hate Groups 1999." Southern Poverty Law Center Intelligence Project.

———. 1999b. "Knight of Freedom." *Intelligence Report*, no. 94 (spring).

———. 1999c. "A Mother's Sorrow." *Intelligence Report*, no. 94 (spring).

———. 1999d: "The World of 'Patriots.' " *Intelligence Report*, no. 94 (spring).

———. 1999e. "The Leaders: One Generation Fades . . . And Another Springs Up." *Intelligence Report*, no. 96 (fall).

———. 1999f. "Money, Music, and the Doctor." *Intelligence Report*, no. 96 (fall).

———. 2000a. "Active Hate Groups 2000." Southern Poverty Law Center Intelligence Project.

———. 2000b."Paying the Price." *Intelligence Report*, no. 97 (winter).

———. 2000c. "Pagans and Prisons." 2000. *Intelligence Report*, no. 98 (spring).

———. 2001. "Active Patriot Groups in the United States in 2000." *Intelligence Report*, no. 103 (summer).

Stanton, William. 1960. *The Leopard's Spots: Scientific Attitudes toward Race in America 1815–59.* Chicago: Chicago University Press.

Starhawk. 1979. *The Spiral Dance: A Rebirth of the Ancient Religion of the Great Goddess.* San Francisco: Harper and Rowe.

Starhawk, Macha Nightmare, and the Reclaiming Collective. 1997. *The Pagan Book of Living and Dying.* San Francisco: Harper San Francisco.

Steele, Peter. 1994. "Here Me! Here Me! Here Me!" *Fifth Path*, issue 5.

Stein, Stephan, ed. 1998. *The Encyclopedia of Apocalypticism.* Vol. 3. New York: Continuum.

Stephanson, Anders. 1995. *Manifest Destiny: American Expansion and the Empire of the Right.* New York: Hill and Wang.

Stoddard, Lothrop. 1920. *The Rising Tide of Color against White World Supremacy.* New York: Charles Scribner's Sons.

Stoddard, Lothrop. 1927. *Reforging America.* New York: Charles Scribner's Sons.

Storm, Hyemeyohsts. 1972. *Seven Arrows.* New York: Ballantine Books.

———. 1981. *Song of Heyoehkah.* 1981, New York: Ballantine Books.

———. 1994. *Lightning Bolt.* New York: Ballantine Books.

"Sweden's Death Metal Odinists Unleashed 1995." 1996. *Resistance*, no. 3.

Swift, Wesley A. N.d. *God, Man, Nations, and the Races.* Reprint. Hayden Lake, Idaho: Church of Jesus Christ, Christian/Aryan Nations.

Taggart, Paul. 2000. *Populism.* Philadelphia: Open University Press.

Taylor, Robert N. 1990. "The Process: A Personal Reminiscence." In *Apocalypse Culture*, edited by Adam Parfrey. Second, revised and expanded edition, Los Angeles: Feral House.

———. 1996. "The Process: The Final Judgement, Part One and Two." *Esoterra*, nos. 6 and 7.

TBO/WOT. 1999. "On Polarity." *Crossing the Abyss*, no 5.

Theweleit, Klaus. 1989. *Male Fantasies.* Vol. 2. Cambridge, U.K.: Polity Press.

Thorsson, Edred [Stephen Flowers]. 1984. *Futhark: A Handbook of Rune Magic.* York Beach, Maine: Samuel Weiser.

———. 1990. "Order of the Trapezoid Statement." *The Crystal Tablet of Set*, 1 January.

———. 1992. *A Book of Troth.* St. Paul, Minn.: Llewellyn Publications.

———. 1993 [1988]. *At the Well of Wyrd: A Handbook of Runic Divination.* York Beach, Maine: Samuel Weiser.

———. 1994. *Rune Might: Secret Practices of the German Rune Magicians.* St.Paul, Minn.: Llewellyn Publications.

———. 1995a. *Black Rûna.* Smithville, Texas: Rûna-Raven Press.

———. 1995b [1985]. "On the Way of Wotan and the Left-Hand Path." In *Black Rûna*, Smithville, Texas: Rûna-Raven Press.

———. 1995c [1986]. "Set and Wotan." In *Black Rûna*. Smithville, Texas: Rûna-Raven Press.

———. 1995d [1987]. "Magie und Manipulation." In *Black Rûna*. Smithville, Texas: Rûna-Raven Press.

———. 1995e [1988]. "Nazi Occultism Revisited." In *Black Rûna*. Smithville, Texas: Rûna-Raven Press.

———. 1996a. *Green Rûna*. Smithville, Texas: Rûna-Raven Press.

———. 1996b. "Introductory Information: The Outer Hall of the Rune Guild." In *Green Rûna*. Smithville, Texas: Rûna-Raven Press.

———. 1996c. "On Entry into the Rune Guild." In *Green Rûna*. Smithville, Texas: Rûna-Raven Press.

———. 1996d [1982]. "Rune Wisdom and Race." In *Green Rûna*. Smithsville, Texas: Rûna-Raven Press.

———. 1997. *The Lords of the Left-Hand Path: A History of Spiritual Dissent*. Smithville, Texas: Rûna-Raven Press.

———. 1998. *Northern Magic: Rune Mysteries and Shamanism*. St.Paul, Minn.: Llewellyn Worldwide.

"The Thousand Swords of Graveland." 1996. *Resistance*, no. 7.

Tolmatsky, Dmitry. 1997. "An Interview with R. N. Taylor." *RWCDAX*, July 18.

Tommasi, Joseph. N.d.a. *Building the Revolutionary Party*. Chillicothe, Ohio: NSLF.

———. N.d.b. *Strategy For Revolution*. Chillicothe, Ohio: NSLF.

Turner, Lisa. 1997. "The Woman's Role in the World Church of the Creator." *The Struggle* (January).

"Universalism." 1982. *The Odinist*, no. 65.

Victor, Jeffrey S. 1993. *Satanic Panic: The Creation of a Contemporary Legend*. Chicago: Open Court.

Vikernes, Varg. 1997. *Vargsmål*. E.K.xiv.N.

———. 2001a. "Black Metal—White Warriors." *AHF: News From the Front* (February).

———. 2001b. *Germansk mytologi og verdensanskuelse*. Cymophane Publishing.

Vise, David A. 2000. "Fugitive Neo-Nazi from Germany Is Captured in W.V." *Washington Post*, August 29.

von List, Guido. 1988 [1908]. *The Secrets of the Runes*. Translated by S. E. Flowers. Rochester, Vt.: Destiny Books.

Vor Ætt. 1998. *Mission Manual of the Vor Ætt Odinist Organization*. N.p.

Voyles, Karen. 1993a. "Elderly Suspect Testifies in Pot Trial," *Gainesville Sun*, 19 February.

———. 1993b. "79-Year-Old Gets Prison in Drug Case." *Gainesville Sun*, 17 April.

Wade, Wyn Craig. 1987. *The Fiery Cross: The Ku Klux Klan in America*. Oxford: Oxford University Press.

Ward, Robert. 1999a. "Althing 17 Report." *Vor Trú*, no. 58.

———. 1998b. "The Asatrú Alliance Pre-Thing Gathering." *Vor Trú*, no. 58.

———. 1998c. "The Historic Formation of the International Asatrú/Odinist Alliance." *Vor Trú*, no. 58.

———. 1998d. "Stephen McNallen: A Founding Father of Our Folkish Faith." *Vor Trú*, issue 58.

————. 1999. "The Use of Runes by the SS." *Prisoner of War*, no. 10.

Webb, Don. 1996a. *The Seven Faces of Darkness: Practical Typhonian Magic.* Smithville, Texas: Rûna-Raven Press.

————. 1996b. "Xeper: The Eternal Word of Set." In *Crystal Tablets of Set, 1995–1998.*

Weber, Michael. 1996. "Race Warriors," *Columbus Guardian,* (November).

Weiland, Ted R. 1998. "The Phineas Hoods: A Biblical Examination of Unscriptural Vigilantism." Scottsbluff, Nebr.: Mission to Israel.

Weisman, Charles A. 1991. *Who is Esau-Edom?* Burnsville, Minn.: Weisman Publications.

Westlind, Dennis. 1996. *The Politics of Popular Identity.* Lund: Studentlitteratur.

"What Is Identity Really About?" 1982. *CSA Journal,* no. 9.

"What Is Odinism?" 1987. *The Odinist,* no. 104.

"What Is Odinism?" 1997. *Fenris Wolf,* no. 3.

Whisker, James B. 1990. *The Philosophy of Alfred Rosenberg.* Costa Mesa, Calif.: Noontide Press.

"White Revolution Means a Spiritual Revolution." 1997. *Fenris Wolf,* no. 2.

"Who Is MOM?" 1994. *Taking Aim,* no. 1 (March).

"Who We Are." 1982. *CSA Journal,* no. 7.

"Why Do We Hate the Jews?" 1982. *CSA Journal,* no. 9.

Wilcox, Larry, and John George. 1992. *Nazis, Communists, Klansmen, and Others on the Fringe.* Buffalo, N.Y.: Prometheus Books.

Wiley, John K. 1997. "FBI Sharpshooter Faces State Manslaughter Charge in Ruby Ridge Killing." Associated Press, 21 August.

Wiligut, Karl Maria. 2001. *The Secret King: Karl Maria Wiligut: Himmler's Lord of the Runes.* Translated and introduced by Stephen E. Flowers. Edited by Michael Moynihan. Waterbury Center, Vt.: Dominion Press; Smithville, Texas: Rûna-Raven Press.

Wistrich, Robert S. 1991. *Antisemitism: The Longest Hatred.* New York: Schocken Books.

Wolfe, Burton. 1974. *The Devil's Avenger: A Biography of Anton Szandor LaVey.* New York: Pyramid Books.

Wolff, Markus. 1996. "The Germanic Revival: A Short Overview." *Vor Trú,* no. 56.

————. 1998. "Listomania: The Story of Guido von List and the Armanen Orden." *Vor Trú,* no. 58.

————. 1999. "Fahrenkrog and the GGG: Wotan Triumphant." *Vor Trú,* no. 59.

Worden, Amy. 2000. "German Neo-Nazi Fugitive Caught." *APB News,* 29 August.

WOT. 1999a. Editorial comment to "Stalin Is No Hero." *Crossing the Abyss,* no 5.

————. 1999b. "What Membership in the White Order of Thule Means." *Crossing the Abyss,* no 5.

"WOT Articles of Faith: Constitution." 1998. *Crossing the Abyss,* no 4.

Wright, Lawrence. 1991. "Sympathy for the Devil." *Rolling Stone* (September 5).

Wulfing One [Robert N. Taylor]. 1995. "The Storm before the Calm: An Interview with Blood Axis." *Esoterra,* no 5.

Yockey, Francis Parker [Ulrik Varange]. 1991 [1962]. *Imperium.* Costa Mesa, Calif.: Noontide Press.

"You Are Part of a Program Vaster than Men Have Dreamed." 1936. *Pelley's Weekly* (9 September).

Zacharia, Janine. 2000. "Lipstadt: 'Libel Trial Strengthened Me.' " *Jerusalem Post*, 4 April.

Zatarain, Michael. 1990. *David Duke: Evolution of a Klansman*. Gretna, La.: Pelican Publishing.

Zipfel, Friedrich. 1980. "Gestapo and the SD: A Sociographic Profile of the Organizers of Terror." In *Who Were the Fascists? Social Roots of European Fascism*, edited by Stein Ugelvik Larsen, Bernt Hagtvet, and Jan Petter Myklebust. Bergen, Norway: Universitetsforlaget.

Armanism, 24–25, 27

Arya Kriya, 182, 186–90

Aryan Christ, 20, 22, 64, 117–29, 210, 221, 341

Aryan nationalism, 4, 5, 11, 54, 67–69, 111, 114–17, 123, 165–90, 191–231, 311, 342–43; golden age legends of, 5, 22–28, 213, 224–25; and links with black nationalism, 114–17; and theories of hyberborean origin of Aryan man, 5, 22–28, 81, 185–86, 209. *See also* Race nationalism; White nationalism; White separatism

Aryan Nations, 55–56, 65–66, 94, 112–13, 123, 128–29, 193, 196, 220–21, 229–30, 316, 325–26, 328; Declaration of Independence, 113

Aryan Nations Liberty Net, 76

Aryan Nations/Slovakia, 229

Aryan News Agency, 77

Aryan Revolutionary Army, 123

Aryan Victory Singers, 193

Aryan World Congress, 128, 193, 221

Aryan Youth Congress, 128, 221

Aryavarta, 188, 190

Asahara, Shoko, 327

Asametal, 309

Asatrú, 1, 17, 19, 23–24, 31, 79, 99, 137, 146–64, 166, 197, 206, 217, 220, 225–26, 231, 258–83, 300, 309, 324; American revival of, 152–54; antiracist, 153, 162–64, 273–74; cosmology of, 154–56; darkside/occult, 165, 284, 292–323; ethnic interpretation of, 152–53, 267, 269–74; gods and goddesses of, 154–57; heterogeneity of, 153–64; international revival of, 262–63, 279, 384 n.65; Jungian influence in, 156–57, 270–71, 273, 283; leaders in, 155, 158; and Native American religion, 149; reincarnation theories in, 161–64; rituals and ceremonies, 155, 158–61; and Satanism, 301, 321–23; tribal organization of, 157–58; view of man, 161–62; on the World Wide Web, 259. *See also* Ethnic Asatrú; Norse paganism

Asatrú Alliance (AA), 151, 153, 176, 258–59, 261–63, 265–67, 274–78, 298, 300, 309, 386 n.8; organizational structure of, 262–63, 386 n.8

Ásatrúarfélagid, 263

Asatrú Folk Assembly (AFA), 151–52, 176, 258–61, 265, 274–75, 278, 280–81, 300

Asatrú Free Assembly (AFA), 152, 162, 177–78, 182, 260–62, 265

Aum Shinri-Kyo, 327

Autobiography of a Yogi, 182

Aztlán Nation, 283

Babylonian Brotherhood, 96–97

Bachofen, J. J., 145

Bacon, Francis (Sir), 203

Bacteriological Warfare, 328

Baddeley, Gavin, 296, 318

Baha'i, 16, 266

Bainbridge, William, 164

Bakunin, Michael, 303

Balacius, Robert A., 119

Barbee, Charles, 127

Barkun, Michael, 73–74, 339

Barley, Dave, 58

Barnes, Harry Elmer, 104

Barran, Paula, 150

Barton, Blanche, 286–87

Bathory, 305, 307

Baumgardner, John, 114–17, 126–27

Beam, Louis, 54–55, 59, 65, 76, 81, 83, 114, 199–200, 350 n.36

Beest, Christos, 293

Beinteinsen, Sveinbjörn, 263

Bellah, Robert N., 139

Bennet, David, 36

Berg, Alan, 195, 198–99

Berger, Helen A., 139–40

Berry, Robert, 127

Bertollini, Vincent, 129

Beyer, Peter, 8

Billy the Kid, 89

Bin Laden, Osama, 315, 325–26

Biocentrism, 313

Hitler, Adolf, 6, 19, 25–27, 47, 69, 84–85, 88, 104, 111, 136, 171–72, 176, 183–86, 211–12, 227, 230, 301–3, 331, 339, 341; interpreted religiously, 84–85, 122, 183–86, 211–12, 219, 296, 356 n.166. *See also* Fascism: and occult fascism; National socialism: and occultism

Hobsbawn, Eric, 4

Hoffman II, Michael, 98–100, 326, 365–66 nn.52, 53, 55

Hofstadter, Richard, 95

Holocaust, 5, 103, 124, 180, 302

Holocaust denial, 48, 66, 86, 98, 103–7, 180, 275, 302, 340–41

Holocaust denial fatigue, 103, 106–7

Holstein, Leonard, 71

Home-schooling, 75, 204

Horiuchi, Lon, 57

Hoskins, Richard Kelley, 119, 126–27

Hubard, Sigi, 178

Hunter, 91, 93, 134; reviewed, 360 n.31

Huntington, Samuel P., 46

Hussein, Saddam, 311–12

Hutter, Maddy, 182, 260

Hutter, Stephanie, 182

Hyatt, Max, 157, 168, 176, 266–69, 276–78, 284

Hårdråde, Harald, 148

Icke, David, 96–97

Idunna. See Asatró

Ikhwan al-Muslimun, 4

Illuminati, 95–97, 361 n.48

Imperium, 168–70, 331

Independent History and Research, 98

Industrial noise, 285, 296–97, 392 n.46

Industrial Workers of the World, 338

Ingstad, Anne-Stine, 148

Ingstad, Helge, 148

Institute of Creativity–14 Words Coalition (IOC), 223

Inter-Klan Kartel, 115

International Asatrú/Odinist Alliance (IAOA), 263

Invisible Empire of the Ku Klux Klan, 50–53, 82, 115

Institute of Historical Review (IHR), 48, 98, 104–6

Intelligence Report, 274–75, 303

International Jew, 102

Irminsul Aettir, 162

Iron Cross MC, 262

Irving, David, 98, 105, 275

Islamic nationalism, 4, 5, 6, 8, 13, 14

Ivanhoe, 35, 69

Jackson, Andrew, 35, 107

Jacobson, Matthew Frye, 37

James, Jesse, 89

Jefferson, Thomas, 35, 107, 172, 278; and Anglo-Saxon romanticism, 35; and paganism, 35, 172

Jewish nationalism, 5, 6

John Birch Society, 103, 110, 129, 134, 192

Johnson, Danny, 207

Jomswiking Kindred, 274

Jordan, Colin, 48, 198–99, 205

Jost, 165, 177, 182, 186–90, 215, 230

Journal of Historical Review, 105

Jubilee, 119

Jung, Carl G., 185, 208, 210–12, 270, 283, 313, 331

Kaczynski, Theodore (Unabomber), 312–13

Kadmon, 299

Kahl, Gordon, 55, 108

Kaldenberg, Wyatt, 165, 177–82, 207, 221, 284

Kaplan, Jeffrey, 72–74, 78, 153–54, 227

Karlsefni, Thórfinn, 147

Kemp, Richard, 194, 197–98, 334

Kennedy, John F., 96, 99, 192

Kennewick Man, 149–51, 281, 300

Kerrick, Joseph, 314–15

Khomeini (Ayatollah), 8, 315

King Diamond, 305

King, Martin Luther, Jr., 42–43, 47

King, Rodney, 62

McLamb, Jack, 58, 96, 101

McNallen, Stephen, 150–53, 176–78, 182, 258–63, 268–71, 273–74, 276–77, 279–83, 300

McVan, Ron, 113, 161, 177, 191, 205–16, 222–24, 228, 230–31, 276, 320, 340, 342, 383 nn.31, 40

McVeigh, Timothy, 64, 200, 311–12

Mead Brewing Guild, 260

Mein Kampf, 27, 311, 319, 331

Mercyful Fate, 305

Merlin, 210

Mermelstein, Mel, 105

Merrel, Jay, 127

Metzger, Tom, 66, 87–88, 98, 108, 110–12, 114–15, 129, 131, 172, 177–78, 289, 325

Micetrap Production, 207, 341

Michigan Militia, 64, 93

Midgard Page, 176

Might is Right, 289, 331

Miles, Robert, 54, 79, 81, 112, 114, 350 n.35

Militia of Montana, 58–59, 92–93, 116

Militia movement, 10, 11, 63, 73, 91–93, 336, 360–61 n.34

Millar, Robert, 64

Miller, Glenn, 51–52

Miller, John, 325

Million Man March, 114–15

Mills, Alexander Rud, 167–68, 170–71, 261

Milosevic, Slobodan, 91, 311

Minutemen, 264

Mithraism, 210–11

Möbus, Hendrik, 316–17, 395 nn.90, 92, 93, 97

Mohr, Jack, 98, 103–4, 114, 119, 123, 125, 365–66 nn.69, 74

Molotov-Ribbentrop Pact, 111

Monism, 20, 135–36

Monroe, Marilyn, 286

Morgan, William, 98

Mosley, Oswald, 299

Movimiento National Socialista, 185

Moynihan, Michael, 265, 284, 297–306, 318, 320, 392 nn.55, 56

Mozzochi, Jonathan, 274

Muhammad, Khalid Abdul, 116

Muhammad, Silis X, 116

Mukherji, Asit Krishna, 183

Murray, Charles, 46

Murray, Valgaard, 151, 153, 176, 259, 261–63, 268–69, 272–74, 276–77, 279, 281, 309

Mussolini, Benito, 47, 69, 172, 227

Nagaraj, Babaji, 187–88

Nasser, Gamal, 315

Nation, definition of, 4–5

National Alliance, 55, 82, 91, 103, 134–36, 193, 276, 312, 317, 319, 324–27, 336–37

National Association for the Advancement of Colored People (NAACP), 46

National Association for the Advancement of White People (NAAWP), 50

National bolshevism, 19, 78, 111

National Front, 85, 114

Nationalism, as ideology, 5, 6

Nationalist Observer, 76–77

National Prison Kindred Alliance, 218

National Renaissance Party, 84

National socialism, 5, 19–29, 78–79, 82–85, 106, 110–11, 117–18, 166–67, 178–79, 209, 211–12, 221, 229–30, 261–62, 284, 292, 294, 296–99, 303–4, 306–23, 331–43, 346 n.11, 355 n.12; in America, 47–49, 78–79, 82–85, 106, 355 n.12; and Hinduism, 183–86; and Holocaust denial, 106; and occultism, 19–29, 83–85, 182–87, 209, 298–99, 314–17, 322–23; and Odinism, 166–67, 178–79, 183–90, 308–23; the radical right, 334–39; and Satanism, 292, 294, 296, 306–23, 396 n.100; as a spiritual movement, 84–85, 356 n.16; Strasserite faction of, 110–11, 166, 172; Third Position faction of, 78, 110–12, 178, 304, 311–13, 315, 334–39. *See also* National bolshevism

National Socialist Black Metal (NSBM), 307, 317

National Socialist Kindred, 177–78, 182–83, 189–90, 338

O'Sullivan, John, 37
Owens, Eric, 309

Pagan Front, 307, 316–17, 394 n.73
Paganism, 1–3, 15–20, 30–31, 136–64; in
    Hoffman II's conspiracy theory, 99; and
    völkisch culture, 23–28. *See also* Asatrú;
    Druids; Goddess paganism; Odinism;
    Norse paganism; Racist paganism; Wicca
Pagan Liberation League, 310, 313
Pagan Revival, 177, 179
Paget, Tom, 178
Pan-Afrikan International (PAIN), 114–17
Pantheism, 20, 135, 154, 268, 287
Pantheon, 316
Parfrey, Adam, 295, 296–97, 299
Parks, Rosa, 43
Patañjali Yoga Sūtra, 189
Patler, John, 47, 49
Patriot's Defense Fund, 65
Payne, Neil H., 64–66
Pelley, William Dudley, 47, 348 n.17
People's (Populist) Party, 107, 366 n.83
Pereira, Janna, 162
Perot, Ross, 108
Peters, Pete, 59, 119
Pett, Nathan Zorn, 196, 308–13, 316–17
Phillips, Mark, 97–98
Phineas Priesthood, 118, 126–27
Pierce, Bruce, 196–98, 229
Pierce, William, 55, 82, 89, 91, 98, 134–36,
    194, 312, 317, 319, 326–27
Polanski, Roman, 99
Polanski, Sharon Tate, 83, 99, 296
Pol Pot, 313
Polytheism, 154–57, 268
Populism, 79, 102, 107–12, 341
Populist Party, 104, 108–10, 116
Posse Comitatus, 108, 336, 367 nn.86, 87
Post, John, 207, 217–18, 341, 382 n.21
Pound, Ezra, 299
Preparedness Expo, 101
Priest, Prudence, 164, 274
Prisoners of War, 298

Process: Church of Final Judgement, 264,
    295
Project Megiddo, 196
Protocols of the Elders of Zion, 102–3, 364 n.61
Pålsson, Hermann, 148

Qadhdhafi, Mu'ammar al, 303, 325, 335

Race and Reason, 110
Race nationalism, 4, 5, 48, 54, 224–25, 227,
    229, 342–43
Racial Loyalty, 132, 206
Racial socialism, 132, 170
Racism: introduction to, 29–30, 33–42; in
    American Constitution, 33–35; in Ameri-
    can society, 29, 33–66, 75; antebellum
    Christian theology, 34; dethronement of,
    43–45, 75; as a mode of social classifica-
    tion, 33–42; and slavery, 34, 346–47 n.3;
    and sterilization laws, 38–39
Racist paganism, 1–2, 17–18, 23–29, 66, 78–
    79, 131, 165–90, 191–231, 267, 274, 276–
    78, 292–324, 329, 336–43; and ecological
    issues, 312–13; and ethnic paganism, 267,
    269–74, 309; and globalization, 2, 16–
    18; and occult national socialism, 23–28;
    and radicalization of white racism, 67–
    69, 191–231. *See also* Odinism; Wotanism:
    occult fascism
Racist Satanism, 1, 19, 78, 84, 292–95, 339.
    See also Satanism: and national socialism
Radio Werewolf, 296, 298
Rahowa, 85–86, 318
Rahowa News, 222
Ramayana, 184
Rand, Ayn, 287
Raschke, Carl, 275
Ratatosk, 226
Raven, Greg, 106
Raven Kindred, 162
Raven, Mike, 196
Raymond, John, 286
Reagan, Ronald, 46, 97
Rebelles Européens, 85, 87

White Order of Thule, 113, 295, 313–17, 319, 321
White Patriot Party, 66
White power music, 67, 69–70, 78–79, 85–89, 135, 191, 196, 222–23, 227–28
White racist milieu, 11, 72–74; class-analysis of, 328–34; as a cultic milieu, 73–74; formation of, 46–79; fragmentation and infighting in, 70–72; homoerotic vibes in, 71; homophobic sentiments in, 71; the Internet in, 11, 70, 76–77
White separatism, 79, 112–17; links with black separatism, 367–70 nn.91, 92. See also Aryan nationalism; Race nationalism; White nationalism
Wicca, 17, 31, 99, 137–46, 152–54, 156, 163, 260, 265, 310; compared with Asatrú, 152–54, 156–57; meaning of "Celtic" in, 138, 144; rituals of, 141–46
Wickstrom, James, 66, 119
Wiligut, Karl Maria, 27–28, 209, 298–300, 322
Wilkinson, Bill, 49–53, 81, 349–50 n.32
Wilson, Woodrow, 80
Wodanesdag Press, 168, 176, 266
Wodan's Kindred, 157, 168, 176, 266–67, 272, 276; prison outreach ministry of, 277
Wolf Age, 261
Wolfe, Burton, 286
Wolff, Markus, 275, 299
Women's Frontier, 133
Wood, Eric Hnikar, 263, 386 n.9
World Church of the Creator (WCOTC), 94, 133–34, 222–23, 227, 325–26, 376 n.120
World Union of National Socialists (WUNS), 48, 183, 198, 227
"Wotan," 211–12, 270
Wotanism, 24, 27, 210. See also Odinism

Wotan's Kindred, 206, 272, 275–76
Wotansvolk, 77, 113, 161, 177, 186, 190–231, 269, 270, 274–76, 303, 310, 312, 320, 338, 340–42, 384 n.64; Ariosophical ideas of, 206–13, 215, 225; and Christian Identity, 220–21; and Creativity, 221–23; and ethnic Asatrú, 274–76; Internet usage of, 225, 227–28; numerological speculations of, 203–4; organization of, 204–7; pan-Aryan ideology of, 213–14, 223–25; prison outreach ministry of, 205, 217–20; rituals and ceremonies, 213–17; teachings of, 207–12; worldwide mission of, 225–31, 384 n.64
Wotansvolk/Sweden, 228–30
Wright, Lawrence, 286
Wulfing Kindred, 261–62, 265

X Files, 92, 95

Yarbrough, Gary, 119–20, 194, 196, 198
Yggdrasil, 164
Yggdrasil, 226
Yockey, Francis Parker, 168–70, 209, 294, 308, 331
Yogananda, Swami Paramahansa, 182, 186–87
York, Michael, 154
Young Socialist Alliance, 177
Youth Clan Corps, 51

Zarephath-Horeb, 64, 127–28
Zionist occupational government (ZOG), 12, 54, 57, 68–70, 76, 82–83, 129, 192–93, 195–96, 303, 311–12, 317, 326, 333–34, 339–40. See also Federal administration, as enemy of white race; New World Order
Zündel, Ernst, 66, 86, 98, 105, 186, 340–41

Mattias Gardell is Associate Professor and Senior
Researcher at the Center for Research in Interna-
tional Migration and Ethnic Relations at Stockholm
University. He is the author of *Rasrisk: rasister,
separatister och amerikanska kulturkonflikter* (Federativs
förlag 1998) and *In the Name of Elijah Muhammad:
Louis Farrakhan and the Nation of Islam* (Duke University
Press 1996).

Library of Congress Cataloging-in-Publication Data
Gardell, Mattias.
Gods of the blood : the pagan revival and white
separatism / Mattias Gardell.
p. cm.   Includes bibliographical references and index.
ISBN 0-8223-3059-8 (alk. paper)
ISBN 0-8223-3071-7 (pbk. : alk. paper)
1. White supremacy movements—Religious aspects.
2. Paganism. 3. White supremacy movements—United
States. 4. Paganism—United States. 5. Racism. I. Title.
BL65.W48G37 2003   322.4'2'0973—dc21   2002153598